Automate It with Zapier and Generative AI

Harness the power of no-code workflow automation and AI with Zapier to increase business productivity

Kelly Goss

BIRMINGHAM—MUMBAI

Automate It with Zapier and Generative AI

Copyright © 2023 Packt Publishing

Group Product Manager: Alok Dhuri

Publishing Product Manager: Uzma Sheerin

Book Project Manager: Prajakta Naik

Senior Editor: Rohit Singh

Technical Editor: Maran Fernandes

Copy Editor: Safis Editing

Proofreader: Safis Editing

Indexer: Rekha Nair

Production Designer: Vijay Kamble

DevRel Marketing Coordinator: Deepak Kumar and Mayank Singh

Business Development Executive: Thilakh Rajavel

First published: July 2021

Second edition: August 2023

Production reference: 2250823

Published by Packt Publishing Ltd.

Grosvenor House

11 St Paul's Square

Birmingham

B3 1RB, UK

ISBN 978-1-80323-984-2

www.packtpub.com

In loving memory of my mum, Winnie. No words can express how much I miss you and wish you were still here. I dedicate this book to you.

To my mum, Winnie, and my dad, Eugene, for their love, sacrifice, and wisdom. You taught me to work hard, challenge myself, and follow my dreams.

To my loving partner, Dawn, for always being present and supportive in our journey together. You are my rock. You always believe and trust in my crazy ideas.

To all the members of Team Solvaa, for your hard work and dedication in helping businesses and their teams improve their productivity with no-code tools, automation, and AI. I couldn't do it without you.

To my mentor, Len Blazey, for your unwavering guidance, encouragement, clarity, and insight. Working with you brings incredible value to my life and has significantly impacted my business. Thank you!

To my fellow consultants, contractors, and freelancers, who work tirelessly to help small businesses succeed and drive our economy.

– Kelly Goss

Foreword

In today's rapidly evolving digital landscape, the ability to harness the power of automation and AI is not just a luxury—it's a necessity. As someone who has dedicated his career in tech to the no-code movement, I've had a front-row seat to the transformative potential of tools like Zapier, especially when combined with the capabilities of Generative AI.

I was immediately intrigued when Kelly first told me about the second edition of her book, *Automate It with Zapier and Generative AI*. As a community builder at the forefront of operations and internal system implementation, I've experienced the challenges businesses face in streamlining processes and increasing productivity. The arrival of a guide that combines the building blocks of no-code automation with the extensibility of AI is beyond well-timed, as these domains are elevating each other every day.

Kelly is not just any automation specialist; she is an expert in business process automation. Her credentials speak for themselves. As the founder of Solvaa Automation Academy & Consulting and one of the few Zapier-certified experts globally, Kelly brings a wealth of knowledge and experience to the table. This book is a testament to her expertise and passion for empowering businesses to achieve operational excellence.

The beauty of this book lies in its practicality. Kelly goes beyond explaining concepts – she provides actionable insights and step-by-step guides that businesses can implement immediately. Whether you're a seasoned operations professional or someone just starting in the world of automation, this book offers valuable lessons.

I commend Kelly on her dedication to the field and on crafting a book that is both informative and inspiring. *Automate It with Zapier and Generative AI – Second Edition* is more than just a guide—it's a call to action for businesses to embrace the future of automation and AI.

I'll never forget the feeling of seeing my first Zap in action. It was like magic! Since then, no-code automation has been my not-so-secret superpower at every company I've been a part of, including my own: NoCodeOps. With this book, readers will have the opportunity to hone this magic as they embark on their automation journeys.

Happy Zapping!

Philip Lakin

Co-founder & CEO, NoCodeOps

Contributors

About the author

Kelly Goss is a business process automation specialist and founder of Solvaa Automation Academy & Consulting, an agency that helps businesses systemize using no-code, cloud-based applications and increase productivity with simpler, more efficient automated processes. They provide consulting and implementation services and run courses, webinars, and training sessions to help businesses empower their teams to achieve their operational productivity goals by reducing manual and repetitive tasks with automation. Kelly is one of less than 100 Zapier Certified experts in the world, a Pipedrive CRM Certified Partner, Xero Certified Advisor, SmartSuite Certified Partner, and a keynote speaker. She is a self-taught artist, and a lover of travel, adventure, animals, urban art, and street food.

To the amazing project team at Packt, thank you for your patience and dedication to making this book possible. I would like to personally thank Rohit Singh, Prajakta Naik, Uzma Sheerin, Mayank Singh, and Deepak Kumar.

To Paul Kortman, thank you for your guidance and input while performing the technical review of the book.

To my family and friends, who have shown constant support during this writing process.

About the reviewer

Paul Kortman is the founder of Connex Digital, a company committed to enhancing business efficiency by automating business process workflows. Starting as an IT professional in a marketing agency, Kortman built a digital marketing team that initially focused on social media and SEO. Throughout the years, he has continually reinvented his business, with a recent strict focus on automation with tools such as Zapier and Make.com. Kortman believes in the value of transitioning from menial tasks to high-level thinking tasks, a transition he facilitates through automation. He strongly advocates for constructing **Minimum Viable Products** (**MVPs**) without the use of custom code. Connex Digital builds automations, integrations, and custom apps affordably, thereby fostering the knowledge economy.

Table of Contents

4

Managing Your Zaps   97

5

Troubleshooting and Handling Zap Errors   127

Part 2: Customizing Your Zaps with Built-in Apps by Zapier – Functionality and Practical Uses

6

7

8

Built-In Communication Apps   219

9

Exploring Built-In Apps for Extracting and Compiling Data   239

10

Other Useful Built-In Apps by Zapier   273

11

Advanced Built-In Apps by Zapier   303

12

Managing Your Zapier Account with Built-In Apps   325

13

Newly Released Apps and Features   351

Part 3: Using the Features of the Formatter by Zapier Built-In App

14

15

17

Text Formatting Functions in Zapier – Part 2   443

18

Zapier's Utilities Functions   471

Part 4: Getting the Most Out of Zapier

19

AI and Automation   499

20

Automating Your Marketing Processes   541

23

Automating Your Finance and Reporting Processes   607

24

Tips, Tricks, and Best Practices to Enhance Your Productivity   631

25

Challenging Your Problem-Solving and Zap-Building Skills   639

Assessments   647

Index   655

Other Books You May Enjoy   676

Preface

Organizations experience significant issues with productivity when dealing with manual and repetitive tasks. **Zapier** stands at the forefront of the no-code movement, providing a cutting-edge tool for automating workflows across web and cloud applications to tackle efficiency issues. With its robust capabilities, users can weave together myriad business applications, crafting both straightforward and intricate automations. This tool not only trims down the time spent on recurring chores but also amplifies overall productivity.

Automate It with Zapier and Generative AI – Second Edition, has been extensively revised to help you analyze your processes and identify repetitive tasks that can be automated between 6,000+ cloud-based business applications. This edition is a comprehensive guide to harnessing the power of Zapier for enhancing business operations. Whether you're a business magnate, an enterprising freelancer, or a budding employee, this book is tailored for you. Delve into a hands-on journey, brimming with practical methodologies that ensure you're optimizing Zapier swiftly and elevating your proficiency simultaneously. Packed with clear instructions, invaluable insights, real-world illustrations, and engaging self-tests, we kick off by demystifying the essence of Zapier.

We will guide you through the nuances of crafting impeccable automations. Dive deep into understanding the core features Zapier brings to the table, the myriad applications it syncs with, and the secrets to molding your workflows with finesse. From conceiving advanced automations to nipping troubleshooting issues in the bud, we've got you covered.

It also includes all of the newest features in Zapier such as AI-integrated functionality using the natural language actions and the ChatGPT plugin, the new visual editor, drafts, reordering and duplicating steps and paths, sub-folders and version history, as well as built-in apps such as **Looping**, **Sub-Zap**, **Interfaces**, **Tables**, and **Transfer**.

By the end of this book, you'll be able to automate your manual and repetitive tasks using Zapier depicted through real-life examples.

Who this book is for

This book is for business owners, operations managers, and teams in micro-, small-, or medium-sized businesses looking at automating repetitive tasks and increasing their productivity using Zapier and Generative AI. Service providers offering digital process improvement, systemization, and automation services to their clients such as solutions architects, process consultants, business analysts, virtual assistants, CRM consultants, OBMs, bookkeepers, and accountants will find this book extremely useful. This book is suitable for both, new and experienced Zapier users.

What this book covers

Chapter 1, Introduction to Business Process Automation with Zapier, initially focuses on the basic principles of business process automation with Zapier and then covers features, functionality, and key terminology used to help familiarize you with the Zapier platform.

Chapter 2, Preparing to Automate Your Processes, explores how to brainstorm your processes, simplify them, and assess what can be automated. We cover the process to establish how your apps work with Zapier and explain how to use the Zapier app ecosystem directory.

Chapter 3, Building Your First Automated Workflow (Zap), dives into how best to strategize and plan your workflows ahead of working through a step-by-step process of creating your first Zap. We explore how to connect your apps to Zapier, use the Zap editor, work with different field types, and use pre-built workflows.

Chapter 4, Managing Your Zaps, takes you through the best ways to keep your Zapier account organized. We discuss how to keep your Zaps and folders organized, how to manage your connected apps, and help you to understand Zap statuses. Lastly, we cover some collaboration tips for users working in teams.

Chapter 5, Troubleshooting and Handling Zap Errors, covers typical Zap behavior and the best ways to handle and troubleshoot errors. We discuss how to set up Zaps to report on Zap issues and app status changes and how to use Zap History information effectively, and we explore the various channels of support available.

Chapter 6, Creating Multi-Step Zaps and Using Built-in Apps, teaches you how to set up and customize multi-step Zaps using multiple action and search steps. We also introduce you to all the built-in Apps by Zapier. You will be able to test your knowledge by building your first multi-step Zap.

Chapter 7, Getting Started with Built-in Apps, explores the most commonly used built-in Zapier apps and covers specific functions such as using conditional logic (filtering and paths) and delays in your Zaps, as well as scheduling your Zaps to run as intervals. You will be able to test your knowledge by building a multi-step Zap using some of these built-in apps.

Chapter 8, Built-In Communication Apps, introduces communication-specific built-in Zapier apps such as for sending and receiving emails and sending SMS messages.

Chapter 9, Exploring Built-In Apps for Extracting and Compiling Data, covers how to extract data from emails, use RSS feed readers in your automations, and compile data into digests. You will be able to test your knowledge by building a multi-step Zap using some of these built-in apps.

Chapter 10, Other Useful Built-In Apps by Zapier, describes how to initiate workflows from web pages, shorten URLs, translate text, score lead information, and use weather and astrological predictions in your Zaps.

Chapter 11, Advanced Built-In Apps by Zapier, briefly explores the more advanced functionality in some of the built-in Apps by Zapier, such as using webhooks and code in your Zaps, as well as saving and storing data.

Chapter 12, Managing Your Zapier Account with Built-in Apps, teaches you how to get notifications on integration issues, manage errors with your Zaps, and monitor Zapier account changes.

Chapter 13, Newly Released Apps and Features, covers new Zapier built-in apps and features such as looping through data sets, modular Sub-Zaps, Web Parser data extraction, bulk data transfers, custom Interfaces, and built-in Tables.

Chapter 14, Formatting Date and Time, introduces the versatile Formatter app and covers how to format date and time values and add or subtract time. We provide practical tips on how to use each of the date and time formatter functions.

Chapter 15, Formatting Numbers, dives into the functionality available to format numbers, phone numbers, currencies, and to use spreadsheet-type formulas and math operations.

Chapter 16, Text Formatting Functions in Zapier – Part 1, describes the extensive functionality available to format text. We cover a range of text formatting actions, such as capitalizing and pluralizing text; applying title case, uppercase, and lowercase; finding and replacing text; trimming whitespace; and counting characters and words.

Chapter 17, Text Formatting Functions in Zapier – Part 2, covers more functionality available to format text. We explore how to split and truncate text; remove HTML; assign default values; extract data such as patterns, URLs, and email addresses; and use a superhero name. We also briefly cover more advanced text manipulation features such as how to convert Markdown to HTML, URL Encode and Decode, and converting text to ASCII.

Chapter 18, Zapier's Utilities Functions, explores the Utilities functions within the Formatter app. We cover line-item creation and customization, converting text to line-items and vice versa, using lookup tables and picklists, and importing CSV files.

Chapter 19, AI and Automation, covers how to increase efficiency by merging AI and automation using Zapier's AI-integrated features, AI app integrations, natural language, and AI actions with tools such as the Zapier Chrome extension and ChatGPT plugin, and best practices for GPT prompting.

Chapter 20, Automating Your Marketing Processes, explores some examples of marketing processes that can be automated using Zapier. We will provide practical tips on how to get started with automating these processes. We will also cover how to automate marketing processes with Facebook Pages integration.

Chapter 21, Automating Your Sales Processes, covers some examples of sales processes that can be automated using Zapier. We will provide practical tips on how to get started with automating these processes. We will also cover how to automate sales processes with Pipedrive integration.

Chapter 22, Automating Your Operations Processes, dives into some examples of operations processes that can be automated using Zapier. We provide practical tips on how to address automating these processes. We also cover how to automate operations processes with Google Docs integration.

Chapter 23, Automating Your Finance and Reporting Processes, takes you through some examples of finance and reporting processes that can be automated using Zapier. We provide practical tips on how to tackle automating these processes. We also explore how to automate accounting processes with Xero integration.

Chapter 24, Tips, Tricks, and Best Practices to Enhance Your Productivity, focuses on best practices for utilizing Zapier effectively and builds on the tips and tricks we have presented in each chapter.

Chapter 25, Challenge Your Problem-Solving and Zap-Building Skills, presents you with three scenarios that describe a specific problem that can be solved by using Zapier. We will work through each example practically with tips being given along the way. The scenarios are classified by skill level and you will have the opportunity to test your knowledge while adapting your problem-solving and Zap-building skills.

To get the most out of this book

Each chapter in this book builds on the knowledge and information presented in the previous chapters. If you don't have experience of business process automation with Zapier, we recommend you start with *Chapter 1, Introduction to Business Process Automation with Zapier*, and complete each chapter in the order they are presented. If you have experience with Zapier, feel free to jump to the chapters that cover topics that interest you and will further your knowledge. To get started, we recommend you sign up for a Zapier account. To work through the content and exercises in *Chapter 1, Introduction to Business Process Automation with Zapier*, to *Chapter 5, Troubleshooting and Handling Zap Errors*, the Zapier Free plan will be suitable. From *Chapter 6, Creating Multi-Step Zaps and Using Built-In Apps*, onwards, a Starter plan will be required, and for some topics, higher price plans will be necessary.

Before you start working through the content in this book, we recommend that you get access to all the Zap templates used as examples in this book, as well as the systems and process audit templates, and other supporting materials here: `https://bit.ly/zapier-book`.

Conventions used

There are a number of text conventions used throughout this book.

`Code in text`: Indicates code words in text, database table names, folder names, filenames, file extensions, pathnames, dummy URLs, user input, and Twitter handles. Here is an example: "For example, we could give the digest a title of `New Sales Invoice Summary`."

Bold: Indicates a new term, an important word, or words that you see onscreen. For instance, words in menus or dialog boxes appear in **bold**. Here is an example: "Let's take a look at the different **Frequency** field options."

> Tips or important notes
> Appear like this.

Get in touch

Feedback from our readers is always welcome.

General feedback: If you have questions about any aspect of this book, email us at customercare@packtpub.com and mention the book title in the subject of your message.

Errata: Although we have taken every care to ensure the accuracy of our content, mistakes do happen. If you have found a mistake in this book, we would be grateful if you would report this to us. Please visit www.packtpub.com/support/errata and fill in the form.

Piracy: If you come across any illegal copies of our works in any form on the internet, we would be grateful if you would provide us with the location address or website name. Please contact us at copyright@packtpub.com with a link to the material.

If you are interested in becoming an author: If there is a topic that you have expertise in and you are interested in either writing or contributing to a book, please visit authors.packtpub.com.

Share Your Thoughts

Once you've read *Automate It with Zapier and Generative AI – Second Edition*, we'd love to hear your thoughts! Scan the QR code below to go straight to the Amazon review page for this book and share your feedback.

https://packt.link/r/1-803-23984-0

Your review is important to us and the tech community and will help us make sure we're delivering excellent quality content.

Download a free PDF copy of this book

Thanks for purchasing this book!

Do you like to read on the go but are unable to carry your print books everywhere?

Is your eBook purchase not compatible with the device of your choice?

Don't worry, now with every Packt book you get a DRM-free PDF version of that book at no cost.

Read anywhere, any place, on any device. Search, copy, and paste code from your favorite technical books directly into your application.

The perks don't stop there, you can get exclusive access to discounts, newsletters, and great free content in your inbox daily

Follow these simple steps to get the benefits:

1. Scan the QR code or visit the link below

https://packt.link/free-ebook/9781803239842

2. Submit your proof of purchase
3. That's it! We'll send your free PDF and other benefits to your email directly

Part 1:
Getting Started with Zapier

In this part, you will gain an understanding of the fundamentals of the Zapier platform, how to build and manage workflows, and how to troubleshoot issues.

This part contains the following chapters:

1

Introduction to Business Process Automation with Zapier

Before you start building your first automated workflow, you should understand what **business process automation (BPA)** is and how it can make light work of manual and repetitive processes. We'll cover how applications connect with others to transfer data and how Zapier has impacted the no-code revolution to automate tasks without the need for developers. This background information will put you in a better position to grasp the terms and concepts used by Zapier and will help you understand the features and functionality of Zapier, as well as how the platform works.

If you have only just started using Zapier, you may not know which pricing plan is most suitable for your business and when the right time to upgrade is. We will cover the features available for each pricing plan in this chapter and explain the pros and cons of choosing one over another. Then, we will describe how to set up a Zapier account, and we will provide an overview of how the platform is structured to enable you to find your way around effectively. We will conclude this chapter by working through how to customize your settings and preferences.

We will cover the following key topics in this chapter:

- How process automation helps businesses increase productivity
- The "no-code revolution" and workflow automation with Zapier
- Understanding the key terms used by Zapier
- Choosing the right Zapier plan
- Creating a Zapier account
- Familiarizing yourself with navigation on the Zapier platform
- Changing your settings and preferences

Once you have worked through each of these topics, you will be ready to start building your first workflow automation.

Technical requirements

To get started, we recommend that you sign up for a Zapier account, which will give you access to a 14-day free trial. We will discuss how to set up an account in the *Creating a Zapier account* section. The Zapier Free plan will be adequate to work through the content in this chapter.

How process automation helps businesses increase productivity

Whether you are a solopreneur or your business has a team, every successful business strives to make the most of its resources and improve productivity so that there is more time to increase revenue. Many companies have systems that may not communicate with each other, and as a result will have processes that are manual, time-consuming, and error-prone.

We live in a time where technology is continually evolving to help us make our work easier, and it is now more straightforward and cost-effective than ever to implement and run this technology ourselves. By introducing appropriate business technology tools, connecting those tools, and automating manual and repetitive tasks, businesses can significantly increase productivity. We'll explore this next.

Introducing BPA

According to Zapier, "*Business process automation (BPA) is the practice of using software to automatically execute repetitive tasks related to a company's essential procedures. You can use BPA to streamline and optimize processes for everything from sales and marketing to HR, compliance, training, and beyond.*" BPA is all about using technology to improve the way we work by automatically performing repetitive tasks that would typically require human intervention. It ultimately focuses on the human element in the process rather than the actual applications that are in use. Of course, the tools you use are fundamental and need to be the right ones for their jobs; however, the real goal is to help the people using those systems to be more productive and focus on the tasks that truly matter for the success and growth of an organization.

BPA principles focus on process simplification, optimization and digitization, system integration, and the automation of cloud technologies (or cloud-based applications).

Here are a few examples of when BPA can help you get rid of manual tasks and increase productivity:

- Posting the same information on multiple social media channels
- Inputting new web form leads into your customer database

- Importing sales invoices and payment information from your e-commerce store into your accounting software

- Collating reporting information from numerous sources

- Processing feedback and testimonials from customers

- Adding meeting events to your calendar

- Sending documents for signing

- Following up with leads

It does take time to learn and successfully implement BPA; however, the resulting value far outweighs the time investment. These are just some of the benefits of using BPA:

- Reduced manual data entry and errors

- Reduced operational costs

- More time for growing sales

- Better customer service

- Increased employee engagement and job satisfaction

The most significant benefit of using BPA is the overall time savings. Automation platform users report time savings of a few hours a week by automating certain tasks such as social media posting, to more than 160 hours a month being saved by automating entire sales cycles or operation functions. The value of time savings is relative to the individual case. For example, a time saving of 2 or 3 hours a week may be of significant value to a solopreneur, whereas a 160-hours-per-month saving equates to having a full-time employee working for free. These savings in hours would translate to savings of thousands of dollars in resource time.

Zapier has several case studies and customer success stories on its website: `https://zapier.com/customers`. Here are a few examples of successful use cases of automation that help businesses become more efficient and grow:

- A real estate agent reduces lead management by 40%

- A digital agency saves 30 hours a week with messenger funnel automation

- A coffee shop powers online ordering with automation

- A home entertainment company automates its entire sales cycle

- A freelancer automates client onboarding and grows their business

BPA essentially allows companies of all sizes and in any industry to innovate by using cloud-based technology to work better and more efficiently and stay ahead of the competition. The possible improvements you can make to your business with BPA are endless.

Although automation functions to make processes work better, it is essential to bear in mind that applying automation to an already inefficient operation will increase its inefficiency. As a whole, BPA requires you to take specific steps to look at your processes holistically, understand and simplify them, identify what systems can be connected, and only then decide on which tasks can benefit from automation. In *Chapter 2, Preparing to Automate Your Processes*, we will work through the steps required to map out our business processes and streamline them by identifying what can be simplified, digitized, and automated.

> **Important note**
> In this book, we will use the term **workflow automation** interchangeably with BPA.

Before we can focus on the practical aspects of improving and automating our operations, we need to understand how web applications communicate with each other and what options are available for businesses to connect their tools.

How your business applications communicate with each other

Allowing your business applications to communicate with one another and then automating tasks where possible is key to increasing productivity. Before we can explore how automation with Zapier comes into this picture, we need to understand how business applications can be connected using **API integrations**.

An **application programming interface** (**API**) is a means by which a software program can communicate with another software program. It essentially allows data from different systems to pass between them when they are connected by some form of **middleware**. If you imagine two software programs having their own language in their API – for example, one French and one Spanish – the middleware acts as the translator between the two.

When two software programs are connected in this way through their APIs and middleware, they are said to be "integrated." When an **integration** exists, this allows specific requests to be sent by one application, producing a response by another. The information requests are usually in the form of creating new (**create**), retrieving existing (**read**), editing/updating existing (**update**), or deleting existing (**delete**) resources. This is also referred to as **CRUD**. Upon receipt of a request, the application will try to fulfill the request and send back a response in the form of a three-digit status code, which signifies a possible success or possible issues. If, for example, you type a website URL into your browser and the page is displayed, this would be a success response. If the page does not exist, an error message will be displayed stating `The requested URL was not found on this server`, depicting a 404 error response. How API integration is created and customized defines what range of information can be requested.

As the goal of API integration is to share data efficiently between two connected apps, there must be a way to identify changes in these resources. For example, if you want a new row to be created in your spreadsheet app when a new subscriber is added to your email marketing app, you need to know that the new contact has been created in the first place. At the time of writing, the two most popular methods for identifying changes are **polling endpoints** and **webhooks**.

With the polling method, requests for new events (for example, creating, retrieving, and deleting resources) are repeatedly sent at predefined intervals, waiting for a response. If there is no response, this signifies that there are no new events. So, in the preceding example, the polling method would periodically search for new occurrences of contact records being created, say every 15 minutes.

With webhooks, however, instead of sending requests, you provide a URL that your originating app monitors for new events, thus receiving information in real time. So, in the preceding example, when a new contact record is created, the information would be provided instantly. Webhooks are an instant and much more efficient way of communicating event information. We will discuss webhooks in more detail in *Chapter 11, Advanced Built-In Apps by Zapier*.

The options available for businesses to connect their tools

Building API integrations requires software programming and development skills and can be a lengthy and costly process. Most applications that you are currently using for your business processes are likely to have a section on their website containing a list of the other applications with which they integrate natively. The applications listed in these app marketplaces, or **app ecosystems**, have integrations created using APIs to enable the two apps to communicate with each other. Software providers invest time, money, and technical skills into building and maintaining these **native integrations**. Generally, these providers will create an integration that satisfies the highest priority needs of most users to automate the most frequently used types of activities. They may also prioritize integration development resources on other more commonly used applications rather than smaller, less popular apps.

In some cases, a user of certain software might need to connect another tool that is not listed in the app ecosystem or may need to accomplish a specific task that is not available with the existing native integration. Under these circumstances, a business could employ a programmer to write **code** to create a **custom integration** with the API provided by the software provider. For most companies, the process of developing a custom integration is not a financially viable option. Therefore, there is often a reliance on what integrations are available in these app ecosystems and how flexible they are.

By now, you should have a better understanding of what BPA is and how process automation helps increase productivity. Next, we'll explore how this relates to Zapier.

The "no-code revolution" and workflow automation with Zapier

Thankfully, as technology has developed, it is now possible to create digital processes without the need to write any code. Therefore, anyone can learn how to build a website, create email templates, and connect their systems using, in many cases, visual drag-and-drop editors. These editors give you the ability to add and remove visual blocks in templates rather than writing code in a computer programming language. Instead of needing to use a developer to write this code, the average person with basic IT skills can create these processes themselves. These advances are described as a **no-code revolution**, as software providers have pushed forward to develop solutions that will help the non-IT workforce to execute tasks that could previously only be done by software engineers.

Zapier is one of these technology solutions that allows you to automate and manage your business processes without writing code. Zapier essentially acts as a connector or translator between thousands of cloud-based applications that may not have native integrations with each other or for which the event requests are more limited, allowing them to communicate with each other. The platform enables users to build business-specific workflow automation with a visual editor using pre-built integrations to seamlessly perform manual and repetitive tasks without human intervention.

Zapier is the brainchild of forward-thinking founders Wade Foster, Bryan Helmig, and Mike Knoop. They recognized the productivity struggles that plague small- and medium-sized businesses, where many repetitive tasks are handled manually and with an ever-increasing chance of errors occurring. They developed a powerful solution to help businesses with their efficiency struggles, allowing them to connect their web applications and automate their mundane and repetitive tasks using custom-built workflows. Most importantly, the solution allows the average business owner and their team to use the software without the need for writing code. The first release of the Zapier platform was in 2012, and since then, they have grown their integration marketplace to over 5,000 app connections. Zapier is based in California, USA, and as a company that actively supports an ethos of remote working, they have grown their global team to over 600 people located in the US and over 20 other countries around the world.

As well as allowing the less technical user to build custom workflows, the Zapier platform allows app developers to build integrations with Zapier to connect their apps to the platform. This, in turn, allows their customers to create custom integrations with thousands of other apps, using Zapier as the connector or middleware between thousands of different apps In essence, the Zapier user then becomes the developer without needing to use code. Using no-code technology, we no longer need advanced technical skills to harness the power of **integration automation**.

To help you understand a bit more about BPA and the no-code revolution, you can get access to a free masterclass here: `https://bit.ly/zapier-book`.

You now have a better understanding of how Zapier and BPA work hand in hand to help businesses increase productivity. In the next section, we'll cover the key terms that are used by Zapier, as well as throughout this book.

Understanding the key terms used by Zapier

Zapier uses specific terminology throughout the platform. We will use these terms frequently throughout this book. It is useful to know and understand the most commonly used terms before we discuss the features available in each Zapier pricing plan.

What is an app?

An **application** (**app**) is a technology tool or cloud-based web service. Zapier integrates with thousands of apps to allow you to transfer data between them and automate your manual and repetitive tasks. Most apps are available for use regardless of which Zapier pricing plan you use, except for **premium apps**, such as **Salesforce**, **Facebook lead ads**, and **Xero**, which are only available on paid plans. Zapier has an **app ecosystem** of over 6,000 app integrations listed in a directory. We will cover Zapier's app ecosystem directory in more detail in *Chapter 2, Preparing to Automate Your Processes*.

What is a Zap?

A **Zap** is a step-by-step automated workflow that allows a user to create a flow of data between two or more apps. When an event occurs in one app, this produces an activity such as an action or event in another app. Zaps allow you to connect your different apps and automate repetitive tasks between them. We will cover how to create a Zap in *Chapter 3, Building Your First Automated Workflow (Zap)*.

What is a trigger?

A **trigger** is an originating event that starts an automated workflow. The trigger is always the first step in the workflow, and only one trigger step will ever exist in a Zap.

What is an action?

An **action** is a resulting activity that happens once a trigger starts an automated workflow. Zaps can have one or multiple actions. Actions can also include **searches**.

What is a task?

Once a Zap has been built, tested, and turned on, a trigger in one app will cause an action to happen in another app. A **task** is an activity that the Zap completes. Your Zapier pricing plan defines your monthly task limit. Completed actions, searches, and passed filters all count as a task, which, in turn, count toward your monthly task limit. For example, if you have a single-step Zap with one action and the Zap triggers five times in one day, your task count would be five. If, however, you have a multi-step Zap that has three actions and it triggers five times in one day, your task count would be 15.

> **Tip**
> Use BPA principles to strategize your workflows in advance of actually building your Zaps. Doing this will allow you to reduce the number of steps in your workflows and minimize task usage. Every task counts toward how much you spend on your Zapier pricing plan. Having simple processes from the start will enable you to use Zapier cost-effectively. You can set up a Zap to alert you on task usage related to your monthly allowance. We will discuss this in more detail in *Chapter 12, Managing Your Zapier Account with Built-In Apps*.

What is the Zap editor?

The **Zap editor** is a visual editor that allows you to create and alter your Zaps using simple drop-down lists and a systematic process. The Zap editor enables you to add your trigger app and action app(s) and run conditions in your workflows. We will discuss the Zap editor in more detail in *Chapter 3, Building Your First Automated Workflow (Zap)*.

What is the update time/syncing interval?

The majority of app triggers use the polling method to retrieve new data on events. The **update time** (or **syncing interval**) refers to how quickly your automated workflow triggers and depends on how often the polling runs to check the triggering app for new information. Zapier checks for new activities to trigger an automated workflow every 1 to 15 minutes, and your Zapier pricing plan defines this time interval. Triggers that use the polling method are denoted by the word **scheduled**.

> **Important note**
> Some app triggers use the webhooks (instant) method and allow an automated workflow to run as soon as new event information is available. These triggers are denoted by the word **instant**.

What is a filter?

A **filter** is a condition that you can add to a Zap to prevent the workflow from moving on to the next action step. Filters are only available on paid Zapier pricing plans. We will cover using filters in detail in *Chapter 7, Getting Started with Built-In Apps*.

What is a formatter?

A **formatter** is a function that allows you to alter numbers, text, dates, and times, as well as perform tasks such as looking up data from a list. Formatters are only available on paid Zapier pricing plans. We will comprehensively cover the various formatter apps built by Zapier in *Chapter 14, Formatting Date and Time*, *Chapter 15, Formatting Numbers*, *Chapter 16, Text Formatting Functions in Zapier – Part 1*, *Chapter 17, Text Formatting Functions in Zapier – Part 2*, and *Chapter 18, Zapier's Utilities Functions*.

What are paths?

Paths allow you to create complex Zaps that use "if this, then that" **conditional logic** to perform different actions based on multiple conditions. For instance, if *X* happens in the trigger app, then do *Y* in one or more action steps. Paths are only available with the Professional, Team, and Company plans. We will cover paths comprehensively in *Chapter 7, Getting Started with Built-In Apps*.

What is a multi-step Zap?

A **multi-step Zap** is a workflow that involves one trigger and multiple actions, as opposed to a **single-step Zap**, which contains one trigger and only one action. With multi-step Zaps, you can also add filters, formatter steps, searches, and complex paths to your workflows, which allow you to create flexible automated workflows. Multi-step Zaps are only available on paid Zapier pricing plans. We will cover how to build multi-step Zaps in detail in *Chapter 6, Creating Multi-Step Zaps and Using Built-In Apps*.

What is Zap history?

Zap history shows a detailed log of activity for each of your Zaps. You can view data that has passed through each step of your workflow and use this to troubleshoot errors. We'll cover Zap history in more detail in *Chapter 5, Troubleshooting and Handling Zap Errors*.

What is Autoreplay?

Sometimes, tasks will fail due to app downtime or temporary errors. If this happens, you can enable the **Autoreplay** feature, which allows Zapier to retry running these tasks immediately, and repeat this a few times if the error still exists. The Autoreplay feature is available with Professional, Team, and Company plans, and it can be found in **Task History**. This feature is handy if you use a large number of tasks. We will cover the Autoreplay functionality in more detail in *Chapter 5, Troubleshooting and Handling Zap Errors*.

An example demonstrating the use of these terms

To help you to understand some of these terms, let's look at an example. You can use the Zap editor to build a Zap that involves Google Forms and Google Sheets apps, as follows:

- **Trigger**: Google Form New Submission

- **Search Action (Find)**: Google Sheet Find Row (search by Email Address)

- **Filter**: Continue only if… Row Found

- **Action (Create or Update)**: Google Sheet Update Row (using the Row ID from *Step 2*)

You now have a better understanding of the key terminology that's used on the Zapier platform. Next, we'll discuss the different Zapier pricing plans, what is included in each, and how to choose the right plan for your needs.

Choosing the right Zapier plan

Zapier offers five pricing options to suit your business requirements, as follows:

- **Free plan**

- **Starter plan**

- **Professional plan**

- **Team plan**

- **Company plan**

The following figure summarizes the features available for each Zapier pricing plan:

	Free	Starter	Professional	Team	Company
Monthly price in USD (starting at)	$0	$29.99	$73.50	$103.50	$148.50
Task quota per month (starting at)	100	750	2,000	2,000	2,000
Extra task bolt-on?	No	Yes	Yes	Yes	Yes
Number of Zaps	5	20	Unlimited	Unlimited	Unlimited
Update time (minutes)	15	15	2	1	1
Number of users	1	1	1	Unlimited	Unlimited
Number of Premium Apps	0	3	Unlimited	Unlimited	Unlimited
Drafts	x	x	x	x	x
Copy & paste steps	x	x	x	x	x
Duplicate & reorder steps	x	x	x	x	x
Transfer	x	x	x	x	x
Folders and subfolders	x	x	x	x	x
Multi-step Zaps		x	x	x	x
Filters		x	x	x	x
Formatters		x	x	x	x
Version History		x	x	x	x
Version Rollback		x	x	x	x
Custom integrations (webhooks)		x	x	x	x
Custom logic with Paths			x	x	x
Duplicate Paths			x	x	x
Autoreplay			x	x	x
Custom Error Notifications			x	x	x
Folder permissions				x	x
Shared app connections				x	x
Shared workspace				x	x
Unlimited workspaces					x
Per-Zap Autoreplay					x
Error Ratio Settings					x
Super Admin					x
Advanced admin permissions					
User provisioning (SCIM)					x
Apps access control					x
SAML Single Sign-On (SSO)					x
Account capture					x
Account consolidation					x
Data retention	30 days	30 days	30 days	30 days	Custom
Support	Standard	Standard	Standard	Premier	Premier
Live chat					x

Figure 1.1 – Summary of features available for each Zapier pricing plan

Important note

All prices and plan structures are correct at the time of publishing this book. You may also find that, depending on your region, the pricing and plan structure vary slightly.

Each pricing plan varies in features; however, primarily, the plans are categorized according to the number of tasks you have available monthly, the number of Zaps you can set up, and how short the syncing interval is. On most plans (except for the Free plan), you can retain features and add additional tasks for an extra fee. The availability of Zap history data and access to online customer service and technical support is included in all plans.

The Free plan is free forever, and all paid Zapier plans are available to be paid monthly or annually.

Zapier offers a 14-day trial plan, which gives you access to the majority of features on the Professional plan with 1,000 tasks, except for Autoreplay.

Once you've logged in to your Zapier account, you can view a detailed list of the features and pricing for each plan and change your plan as needed by clicking on the links in the following navigation options:

- **Billing and Usage (Settings)**
- **Wallet** (expandable left sidebar)
- **Pricing** (top menu on information pages)
- **Pricing** (footer menu)

> **Important note**
> Your monthly task allocation does not carry over to the next month. Toward the end of each billing period, if you have unused tasks left over and you are using fewer tasks than you need to, you may be able to downgrade to a lower subscription and still retain your pricing plan features.

Next, let's take a look at different Zapier plans that will be suitable for your business.

Which is the right Zapier plan to use for your business?

Zapier is ideal for any size business that wants to automate its processes. It can be used by solopreneurs or companies with small or large teams. It can also be used by freelancers and consultants to manage their clients' processes.

The needs of your business will determine which price plan is best to use. How many processes you would like to automate and how complex these processes are will impact your decision.

Free plan

For businesses with one user that only have a few simple tasks to automate, this plan is the most appropriate. You will be able to build up to five single-step workflows using the majority of the apps that Zapier integrates with (excluding premium apps). Zapier will search for new data in your trigger apps every 15 minutes and run your Zaps, allowing up to 100 tasks per month to be processed. The Free plan is the best plan to get started with while you get to grips with how Zapier works at a basic level. You will also get access to standard features, such as creating your Zaps in draft, copying and pasting steps, and duplicating and reordering steps. You will also be able to organize your Zaps into folders and subfolders.

Starter plan

If you still only have one user and a relatively small number of processes to automate, but you need to automate multiple activities in one or more apps (including up to three premium apps), try the Starter plan. You can take advantage of additional features, such as using conditions in filters, formatting text, numbers, and dates, accessing version history, as well as creating custom integrations with webhooks. You can build up to 20 Zaps and will have access to 750 tasks per month (1,500 for a higher subscription payment). The update time remains at 15 minutes.

Professional plan

The Professional plan is for single users that want to level up and use Zapier optimally. This plan is best for you if you have a large number of complex, multi-step processes that require conditional logic and you use more than three premium apps in your business. All Starter plan features are included, as well as the ability to create, duplicate, and reorder paths, use Autoreplay, create custom error notifications, and roll back to previous versions of your Zaps. You can take advantage of unlimited premium apps, unlimited Zaps, a quicker update time of two minutes, and access to between 2,000 and 2,000,000 tasks per month (depending on your subscription payment).

Team plan

Businesses with two or more team members that are responsible for automating and managing processes should take advantage of the features available with the Team plan. All the elements of the Professional plan are included, with the added benefits of a faster update time of one minute, and you will be able to export Zaps and access audit logs. The Team plan allows teams to collaborate and automate their processes securely and in an organized way. Team members can securely access multiple apps without the need to share passwords and **API keys** between them, share workspaces, and select who has access to specific folders and apps. An additional bonus of this plan is access to a premier support team with faster, prioritized responses.

Company plan

The Company plan is for organizations that require enterprise-grade security considerations and want to separate their users into teams. You still have access to all the features of the Team plan, plus access to multiple workspaces, per-Zap Autoreplay, and the ability to adjust error ratio settings. Security features include user management, app access control, secure **single sign-on** (**SSO**), and top-level account management.

An additional bonus of this plan is the ability to customize Zap history data retention for shorter periods than the standard 30 days available on other plans to fit with your company's regulatory requirements, as well as real-time support via live chat.

You now have a better understanding of what features and functionality are included in each Zapier plan and which plan would suit your business most. Next, we'll cover how to set up a Zapier account.

Creating a Zapier account

For you to get started with Zapier, the first thing you will need to do is create a Zapier account.

> **Important note**
> The Zapier team is very proactive in trying to create the best experience for the user and often tests different **user interface** (**UI**) changes on user groups. UI updates, new features, and changes to navigation are released regularly, so don't be surprised if, as you work through this book, the screenshots we have used differ slightly from the current, live state.

Work through the following steps to create your new Zapier account:

1. Open your web browser, navigate to the Zapier website home page (`https://zapier.com/`), and click on the **Sign up** button.

2. Create a Zapier account by entering your business email address and your first and last name. Then, click **Get Started Free**, as shown in the following screenshot. Alternatively, you can sign up using your Google, Facebook, or Microsoft credentials:

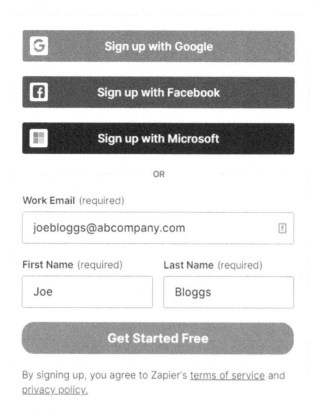

Figure 1.2 – The sign-up area on the Zapier home page

3.   Add a password and click **Get Started Free**, as shown in the following screenshot:

Figure 1.3 – Filling in details on Zapier's home page sign-up area

4. Complete the first step in the onboarding process by identifying your role, adding how many employees your company has, and clicking **Continue**, as shown in the following screenshot:

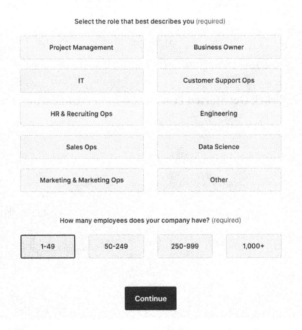

Figure 1.4 – The first step of the Zapier sign-up onboarding process

5.   Complete the second step in the onboarding process by selecting five or more apps that you use in your business so that Zapier can provide you with tailored recommendations. Then, click **Finish setup**, as shown in the following screenshot:

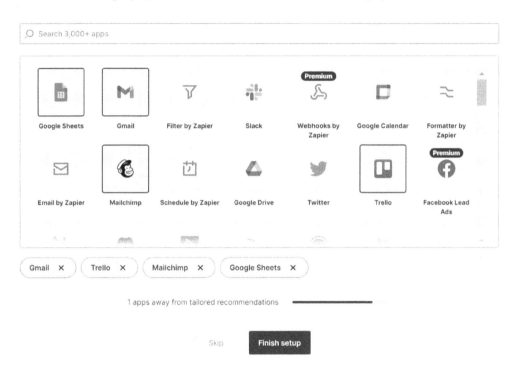

Figure 1.5 – The second step of the Zapier sign-up onboarding process

> **Important note**
>
> By completing this two-step onboarding process accurately, Zapier will be able to customize your user experience and provide you with tailored workflow suggestions. These recommendations will give you ideas of what types of tasks you can automate using your business apps as examples. You can choose to fill this information in as appropriate or skip these steps.

Now that you have set up your Zapier account, you're one step closer to building your first workflow automation. In the next section, we'll cover navigation on the Zapier platform.

Familiarizing yourself with navigation on the Zapier platform

Zapier has made its UI helpful for navigating easily around the platform. When you sign in to Zapier, the first thing you will see is the main **dashboard**. The central dashboard area provides you with useful information to help you get started with tutorials, creating workflows, and using some pre-built workflow examples.

The dashboard's layout is shown in the following screenshot:

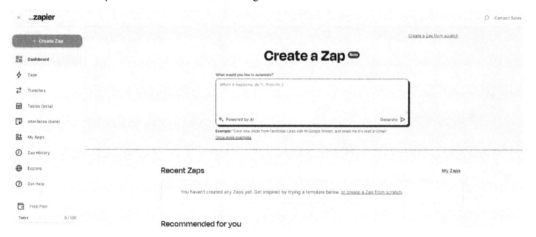

Figure 1.6 – Overview of the Zapier main dashboard layout

On the majority of the pages within the platform, you have multiple navigation options:

- Icons in the left sidebar
- Icons on the top right
- Footer menu

> **Important note**
> These navigation options are available on most Zapier pages except information pages and within the **Settings** area and Zap editor modules.

Icons in the left sidebar

The left sidebar is the most commonly used navigational bar in Zapier. It can be found on every page within the platform (except on information pages and within the **Settings** area and Zap editor modules). The sidebar can be expanded and reduced using the hamburger menu next to the Zapier logo. The following screenshot shows the navigation options in this bar:

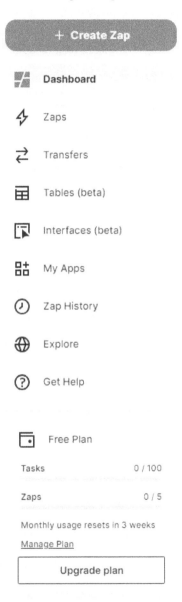

Figure 1.7 – Navigation options in the left sidebar

These navigation options are as follows:

- **+ Create Zap**: This button takes you straight into the Zap editor, where you can start building a Zap. We will cover the Zap editor in more detail in *Chapter 3*, *Building Your First Automated Workflow (Zap)*.

- **Dashboard**: This icon link will take you back to the main dashboard at any time.

- **Zaps**: This icon link will take you into your Zap management area. This area gives you a list of all of your Zaps, where you can organize them into different folders, change team sharing preferences, and enable or disable specific Zaps. We will cover the Zap management area in more detail in *Chapter 4*, *Managing Your Zaps*.

- **Transfers**: This icon link will take you to the **Transfers** area, where you can send data in bulk from one app to another. We will cover the **Transfer** feature in more detail in *Chapter 13*, *Newly Released Apps and Features*.

- **Tables (beta)**: This icon link will take you to the Tables creator. This menu option may not be visible in all accounts while in the Beta phase. We will cover the **Tables** feature in more detail in *Chapter 13*, *Newly Released Apps and Features*.

- **Interfaces (beta)**: This icon link will take you to the **Interfaces** creator. This menu option may not be visible in all accounts while in the alpha phase. We will cover the **Interfaces** feature in more detail in *Chapter 13*, *Newly Released Apps and Features*.

- **My Apps**: The **My Apps** icon link will take you to your list of connected apps. From there, you can connect and authenticate all your relevant business apps. We will cover the **My Apps** module and how to connect your apps in more detail in *Chapter 3*, *Building Your First Automated Workflow (Zap)*, and *Chapter 4*, *Managing Your Zaps*.

- **Zap History**: This icon link will take you into your Zap history, where you can review data that has run in your triggered Zaps. We will cover **Zap History** in more detail in *Chapter 5*, *Troubleshooting and Handling Zap Errors*.

- **Explore**: This icon link will take you into the **Explore** area, where you will find a wide range of information on different ways to use Zapier to automate your business processes.

- **Get Help**: The **Get Help** icon link will take you to the help center, which contains comprehensive how-to articles, FAQs, and support options. We will cover this in more detail in *Chapter 5*, *Troubleshooting and Handling Zap Errors*.

- **Wallet**: This gives you a handy snapshot view of your current plan, task usage relative to your monthly limit, and the number of Zaps relative to your plan limit. From here, you can also manage or upgrade your plan using the links provided.

Icons on the top right

In the top-right corner, you can find the following icons:

- **Magnifying glass**: This icon allows you to search for apps to find out whether Zapier integrates with them. The app ecosystem directory contains a comprehensive list of app integrations and details about them.

- **People icon**: This icon displays a drop-down menu with your account settings and an option to log out of Zapier. This icon might also be displayed as your initials.

Footer menu

In the footer menu, you will find additional navigation options that are available on all pages. The two most useful ones are as follows:

- **Pricing**: This link will take you to the **Plans** page, which will show you the different Zapier plans, features, and associated prices. You can choose to trial, upgrade, or downgrade your plan while reviewing the features and pricing of different plans.

- **Help**: This link will take you to the **Help** area, which we described earlier.

You now have a better understanding of and have become familiarized with navigation in the Zapier platform. Next, we will discuss how to change our settings and preferences.

Changing your settings and preferences

Ensuring that your settings are correct and understanding how specific settings impact other areas of your account is essential for successful account management.

You can access your settings by clicking on the circle icon that contains your initials in the top right of your dashboard and selecting the cogwheel icon/settings option. The settings menu will be shown in the left sidebar, as shown in the following screenshot:

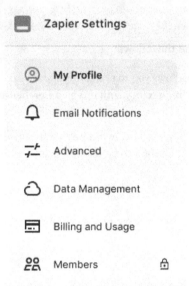

Figure 1.8 – The left sidebar menu in the settings area

> **Important note**
> Team and Company plans have an extra **Organization** menu item, and the Company plan has an **Advanced Security** option. We will cover these settings in *Chapter 5, Troubleshooting and Handling Zap Errors*.

My Profile

This area contains basic data about you and allows you to do the following:

- Authenticate your email address
- Add/change a profile image using Gravatar (an online service that links a picture of you with your email address)
- Change your email address, first and last name, password, and company
- Change your role
- Adjust your time zone

The following screenshot shows the layout of the **My Profile** area:

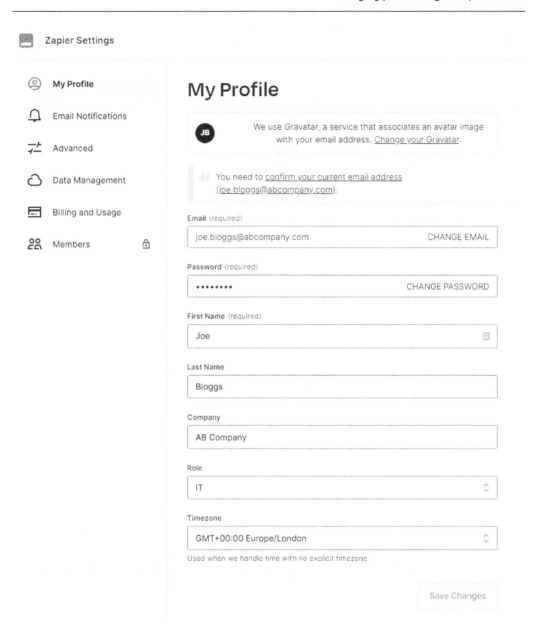

Figure 1.9 – Layout of the My Profile area

Important settings to customize in My Profile

There are a few things that you should do once you have set up your Zapier account:

- Validate your email address
- Add your role
- Add your time zone

Let's go through how to do each of these in Zapier.

Validating your email address

Work through the following steps to adjust these settings:

1. Click on the highlighted text (marked as important) to confirm your email address.
2. Follow the instructions in the email you are sent from Zapier.

This is the first step to protecting your account and allowing Zapier to ensure that it has the right email address to send notifications.

Adding your role

If you did not add your role in the two-step onboarding process when you set up your Zapier account, you can do so here. To do this, scroll to **Role** and choose the closest match to your role from the drop-down list. Completing this step will enable Zapier to make workflow suggestions based on what other users with the same role might be using.

Adding your time zone

To adjust these settings, scroll to **Timezone** and choose your **time zone** from the drop-down list.

Completing this step will enable Zapier to use your time zone when displaying and handling time in your account. The default is **Coordinated Universal Time (UTC)**.

An example of this would be in your Zap history. Times will be displayed in your time zone rather than in UTC. It is much easier to keep track of times when investigating errors if they are in your time zone.

> **Important note**
> Specifying your time zone is crucial for how Zapier defines and uses dates in your Zaps. The importance of adding the time zone to your account should not be overlooked.

Email Notifications

This area will enable you to alter your preferences for how and when you want to receive email communications. The following screenshot shows the layout of the **Email Notifications** area:

Email notifications settings

Activity summary

Schedule email summaries of tasks that Zapier has performed.

Activity Summary

Daily

Error notifications

Customize notification frequency for Zap errors that occur in your account.

Go to error notification settings

Zapier manager

Customize notification frequency for Zaps that use Zapier Manager's new Error trigger.

Send alerts on failed action

Always (recommended)

Email subscriptions

Subscribe to general email communications from Zapier.

Unsubscribe from all

☑ Partner Communications

☑ Zapier Content & Resources

☑ Feedback & Research

☑ Community

☑ Events & Webinars

☑ Zapier Offers & Promos

☑ Product Updates

☑ Zapier Blog & Newsletter

Figure 1.10 – Layout of the Email Notifications area

You can change your preferences for the following:

- **Activity Summary**: Zapier regularly sends you summaries of all the tasks that have been performed over a certain period (within the set frequency). You can choose to receive activity summaries daily or weekly, or if you prefer, never.

- **Error notifications**: In Professional, Team, and Company accounts, you can customize the frequency of Zap error notifications by adjusting your custom error notification. Click the **Go to error notification settings** button. In the **Default Notification Rule** section, choose the frequency of notifications to be applied to all Zaps from **Immediately**, **Hourly Summary**, and **Never**. In the **Custom Notification Rules** section, you can create a customized notification rule for specific Zaps you select. Use the **Select a Zap** drop-down list to choose the Zap and then use the **Select a frequency** drop-down list to choose **Immediately**, **Hourly Summary**, or **Never**. This is shown in the following screenshot:

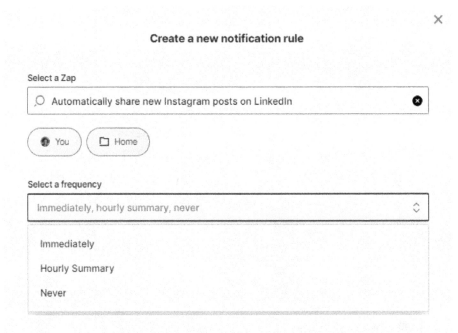

Figure 1.11 – Overview of the custom error notifications

Then, click the **Save Notification Rule** button to save the rule. From the dashboard, you can view the Zap's name, change its **frequency** using the dropdown, or **delete** the Zap from the three-dots icon menu. Error notification settings can also be accessed from the Zap history area, which we will discuss in more detail in *Chapter 5, Troubleshooting and Handling Zap Errors*.

- **Zapier Manager**: In the **Send Alerts on Failed Action** section, you can choose to receive alerts if any of your actions have issues. It is useful to have this information so that you can sort out a problem soon after it happens. You can choose to receive failed action alerts repeatedly, always (this is the recommended setting), or if you prefer, never. You can also pair this notification setting with the Zapier Manager built-in app triggers, which we will discuss in more detail in *Chapter 5, Troubleshooting and Handling Zap Errors*.

- **Email subscriptions**: You can choose what kind of content you want Zapier to send you. You can also unsubscribe from receiving any newsletter content.

Advanced

In the **Advanced** area, you can change your preferences for the following:

- **Two-Factor Authentication**: **Two-factor authentication** (**2FA**) gives you more security by requiring you to enter your standard login details (email address and password), as well as an authentication code that's been generated and sent to a nominated email address or mobile phone number. It is recommended that you set up 2FA on your account.

- **Authorized Applications**: This shows a list of apps that you have granted access to your Zapier account. You can remove apps from this area as needed. This area differs from your connected apps in **My Apps**.

- **SSL Checks**: SSL certificates allow scrambled information to be sent between Zapier and its partners. These settings are turned "on" by default and should only be altered if you have experience with changing them and know the consequences or if you have been advised to do so by the Zapier support team.

- **Sign-in With**: This allows you to change your sign-in settings so that you can use your Google account instead of the standard email and password.

- **Delete My Account**: If you want to close your Zapier account and delete all your account data, you can use this area to proceed. If you wish to delete some data periodically, you can do so through the **Data Management** area.

Data Management

Zapier gives account owners the ability to control their data. In this area, you can export and delete your data periodically and read more about data regulation and GDPR compliance.

Team and Company plans have additional **Data Management** settings that allow you to import and export Zaps in bulk (in a **JSON** file) so that you can make backups or share them with others.

Account

If you have access to your account as well as one or more Team or Company accounts, a drop-down option will be displayed, allowing you to navigate between your different accounts to view the settings for each account.

Billing and Usage

This area is essential for anything related to billing, task, and Zap usage. You will have access to more detailed information about your usage than in the snapshot wallet in the expandable left navigation bar. Here, you can see how many tasks have been used and how many Zaps have been built concerning your limit, as well as what date your usage resets. You will also be able to adjust your price plan, payment method, and billing information and view your invoices.

Members

Unless you are on a Team or Company plan, this area will be locked, denoted with a padlock icon.

The **Members** area gives you an overview of tasks related to Zaps built and owned by this member. You can adjust team member settings as follows:

- Add or remove members

- Change member roles (**Admin** or **Member**)

You now have a better understanding of how to change your settings and preferences.

Summary

In this chapter, we started with an overview of the principles of BPA and how we can use it to increase productivity. We discussed how applications integrate using APIs and transfer data between them. We then introduced Zapier, a no-code tool that integrates with thousands of business apps to help you automate tasks without the need for developers. We presented the key terms used on the Zapier platform and covered how to choose the right pricing plan for your business needs. Then, we discussed how to set up a Zapier account and familiarize yourself with navigating the platform. Lastly, we covered how to customize the various available settings.

You now know how to choose the right Zapier pricing plan for your business, set up your Zapier account, navigate the Zapier platform with ease, and customize your settings.

In the next chapter, we will cover how to use the principles of BPA to improve our processes before we jump into automating them. We'll then discuss how to strategize and plan a workflow in preparation for building a Zap and how to explore Zapier's ecosystem of app integrations and use its features.

Questions

1. What are two benefits of BPA?

2. How do two or more apps have the ability to communicate with each other?

3. How many premium apps can you connect to Zapier on the Free plan?

4. Why is it important to add five or more apps that you use during the onboarding process?

2

Preparing to Automate Your Processes

In this chapter, we will use the principles of business process automation to help you prepare to automate your processes. As we discussed in the previous chapter, it is vital to simplify your processes before attempting to automate them. Therefore, we will start by describing how to improve your business processes and then identify what can be automated. We will then explore how to find information about your business apps and how your apps integrate with Zapier. We will expand on this in the *Getting the most out of the Zapier app ecosystem directory* section of this chapter, where we will cover navigation in the directory of app integrations and how to find new apps to use.

We will cover the following key topics in this chapter:

- Simplifying your processes and assessing what can be automated
- Establishing how your business apps integrate with Zapier
- Getting the most out of the Zapier app ecosystem directory

Once you have worked through each of these topics, you will have successfully improved and simplified your processes, understood how your business apps connect, and learned how to navigate Zapier's directory of app integrations.

Technical requirements

To work through the content and exercises in this chapter, you will need access to a Zapier account. The Zapier Free plan will be adequate to work through the content in this chapter. You can get access to the systems and process audit template used in this chapter at `https://bit.ly/zapier-book`.

Simplifying your processes and assessing what can be automated

Before you look to gain from the benefits of automating your processes, it is essential to analyze, understand, and simplify your existing manual processes. Following this method will ensure that you have more robust processes, as well as help reduce the number of steps you have in your Zaps. This will help lower the number of tasks that will contribute to your monthly Zapier task limit when your workflows run.

When you hear the term **process mapping**, you might immediately think you will need to employ someone with analytical skills to help you detail your processes in flowcharts and documents. You may also believe that it does not apply to you or your business. The fact is that you most likely already map out your processes in one way or another, such as when you create training documents and checklists for new staff. Having documented procedures allows you, the business owner, the manager, and the team members that use the process to have a clear view of how specific tasks are meant to be done consistently. All businesses, small or large, can benefit from documenting the way they do things; we will break this down into an easy-to-follow exercise to help you accomplish this.

To establish how business process automation can best work for your business, we recommend that you take a holistic view of all of your processes and systems, alongside assessing your business goals, then look at each process individually. This exercise involves the following key areas:

- Assessing your top-level management goals
- Involving your team
- Brainstorming your processes and prioritizing them
- Analyzing and simplifying your processes
- Identifying what can be automated
- Documenting the new process

As you're working through each stage, while using an adapted version of a well-known problem-solving technique called the **5W1H method**, you should bear the following questions in mind:

- *Where?*: Where does this task occur? What app(s) is involved in the process? If there is no app, is human intervention required for it to work accurately?
- *How?*: How is the task accomplished? What steps will you need?
- *When?*: When does this step occur in the process?
- *What?*: What do you need to accomplish the task? What data is required?
- *Who?*: Who is involved in the process? This could be members of the team, your leads, or customers.
- *Why?*: Why is this step important and why could it benefit from being automated?

You can read more about the 5W1H method here: `https://en.wikipedia.org/wiki/Five_Ws`.

Let's dive into the details of each of these steps to improve and streamline your business processes.

Assessing your top-level management goals

Firstly, reviewing your top-level business objectives will make the overall intentions clearer and easier to communicate to your team. Document the answers to the following questions:

1. What are your business goals for the next 6 to 12 months?

2. What are the top five most time-consuming manual process problems that you want to solve?

3. What benefit would simplification and automation bring to these processes and the team members involved?

4. How do these benefits align with your business goals?

5. How much time are you willing to allow yourself and your team to spend on improving and automating your processes?

As you work through the next few sections, keep your answers to these questions in mind.

Now that you have a clearer picture of your top-level goals, we will have a look at the importance of involving your team in the exercise.

Involving your team

It is vital to involve the people who use the processes regularly. It is especially important if you have a team (small or large) and tasks that span different departments or roles. Including all relevant team members will ensure engagement and empowerment in the change process and allow teams to take ownership of and manage the processes collaboratively on an ongoing basis. It is also essential to explain the purpose of the exercise (remember your top-level goals) and remind your team that automation will help them do their jobs better and more efficiently. Encouraging your team to learn how to use BPA in their daily roles will boost productivity and job satisfaction.

Next, you need to produce a list of all your processes and prioritize them so that you know what to start working on first.

Brainstorming your processes and prioritizing them

This exercise is best conducted visually. You can add sticky notes to a board or wall and then formalize them in a spreadsheet format to record the various datasets. Take photographs of your brainstorming exercise; this will help you visualize and structure other parts of your process improvement exercise. You can also use digital whiteboard tools such as **Miro** (`https://miro.com/`) or **Mural** (`https://www.mural.co/`) to collaborate with your team online.

To get started with this exercise, nominate a team member to facilitate and own the overall project. Then, work through the following steps with your core team members:

1. Brainstorm a list of all of your processes and what the purpose of each is. Categorize these processes into marketing, sales, operations, finance, or whatever business functions make the most sense to you. You may find that some processes cross over between departments; therefore, make a note of this. An example of this using the Miro app is shown in the following figure:

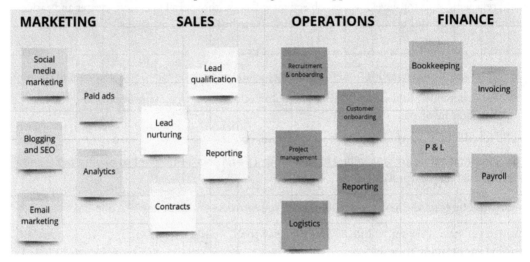

Figure 2.1 – A digital whiteboard brainstorming exercise using Miro

2. Brainstorm a list of all the apps and tools you use in your business, make a note of their specific functions, and do the same with any other apps that you have been considering potentially replacing them with. Again, you can use a whiteboard or add them to a spreadsheet. An example of this using a spreadsheet is shown in the following screenshot:

TYPE	CURRENT SYSTEM (S) e.g. Excel spreadsheet	ANY SYSTEMS YOU ARE CONSIDERING
LEAD GENERATION/ MARKETING		
EMAIL MARKETING	Klaviyo	Mailigen
MARKETING AUTOMATION		
DIRECT MAIL MARKETING		
SOCIAL MEDIA POSTING	Publer	
WEBSITE PLATFORM	Wordpress	
WEBSITE CHAT	Intercom	ManyChat
SALES		
CRM (CUSTOMER DATABASE)	Salesforce	
CONTRACTS/ PROPOSALS/ DIGITAL SIGNATURES	Adobe	
E-COMMERCE PLATFORM	Shopify	Woocommerce
OPERATIONS		
PURCHASING		
STOCK MANAGEMENT	Xero inventory	

Figure 2.2 – A systems audit document

If you would like a copy of a systems and process audit template, you can get access one here: `https://bit.ly/zapier-book`.

3.   Identify and list all the process users.

4.   Nominate one process user to own each ongoing process.

5.   Give each process a score between 1 and 5 (where *1* is low and *5* is high) for each of the following:

   - How time-consuming it is when performing it currently

   - How error-prone it is when performing it currently

6.   Add these scores together to calculate the total, which will give the overall pain-point score for each process.

7.   Add an explanation for each score to elaborate on the pain point and why the problems are necessary to address.

An example showing *Steps 3* to *7* is shown in the following figure:

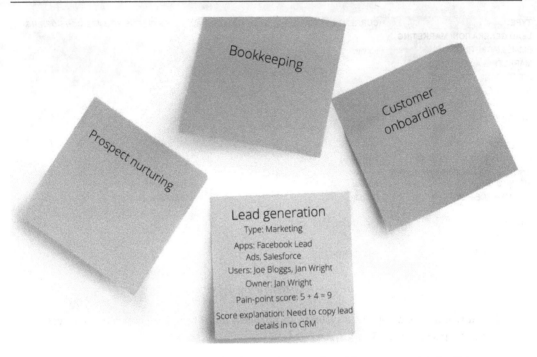

Figure 2.3 – A business process brainstorming exercise with more granular detail

8. Number each process in order of priority of what to work on first.

9. From the priority list, choose the top five processes with the highest pain-point score. Review your top-level goals and ask yourself whether this list aligns with what you noted as your top-level management goals.

Now that you have a list of priority processes to work on, let's take a look at the best way to analyze and simplify each of them.

Analyzing and simplifying your processes

For the top five priority processes that you identified, work through the following steps for each, one by one. Be sure to involve your team of users that are specific to each process. Once again, this exercise is best done visually by using a traditional whiteboard or digital whiteboard for remote collaboration. Let's explore how to do this:

1. Describe the importance of the process and what it achieves.

2. Break the process down into manageable and systematic steps.

3. If the process spans business functions, then categorize each step into marketing, sales, operations, or finance functions, or use other categories that suit your business better.

4. From your list of apps (that you created earlier), identify what business tools you currently use for each step.

5. Review, understand, and describe the importance of each step.

6. Identify steps that can be modified and improved, potentially by introducing other apps.

7. Eliminate irrelevant, ineffective, unnecessary, or wasteful steps.

8. Review the new process for accuracy and assess any change risks.

Repeat this method for each of the remaining top-priority processes.

To help you visualize this process, let's take a look at an example.

The reception team of a small chiropractor practice currently logs all inquiries in **Smartsheet**. The inquiries come from multiple sources, such as a web form on their website, and by email. Any inquiries that are not booked for an appointment at first contact need to be followed up with a second call. These tasks are created in **Trello,** and once the appointment is booked, a patient record and booking are created in the practice management system. All updates to follow-ups and appointment bookings are recorded on the sheet so that there is traceability. This process is very manual and prone to error as tasks are often forgotten. The following figure shows *steps 1 to 4*:

Figure 2.4 – Analyzing the existing process

The team then discusses and records the elements of *step 5* separately.

In this example, the practice staff has established that their practice management system has new functionality that allows them to extract reports and use tasks, so they no longer need to use Smartsheet for reporting or Trello for task management. They can now simplify the process and eliminate unnecessary steps. *Steps 6 and 7* are shown in the following figure:

Figure 2.5 – Simplifying the process

The team agrees that there are no significant risks involved with using this new process, as per *step 8*.

Now that we have streamlined our top-priority processes and broken them down into manageable steps, we can establish whether each one of them can be partially or fully automated. We'll look at this next.

Identifying what can be automated

Work through your priority list and steps from the previous section to identify what can be automated as follows:

1. Ask the following questions:

    A. Is it repeatable?

    B. Can it be done with minimal logical thinking and human intervention?

    C. Is it prone to error when done manually?

    D. Is it consistent across all our business operations?

    If the answer to each of these questions is "yes," then this process is a prime candidate for automation. If you answered "no" to any of those, discuss the options to part-automate the process where possible. If the process is not consistent across all business operations, so long as you answered "yes" to the first three questions, it may be possible to duplicate workflows across business operations to encompass various nuances.

2. If your process can be partially or fully automated, make a note of two or three quick-win solutions and the longer-term solution, with expected timeframes to accomplish each.

Using our example from the previous section, the practice team discusses and records the answers, as shown in the following figure:

Figure 2.6 – Establishing what steps can be automated

Tasks 1, 2, and 3 can be fully automated as follows:

- Task 1, which involves recording the lead in the practice management system, can be automated as the practice management system integrates with Zapier and so does the existing web form app. Emails can be forwarded and parsed to extract information and then added via Zapier.

- Creating the follow-up task, task 2, can be fully automated as workflow automation is available in the software.

- The practice management system allows lead conversion to new patients to be automated and applied to task 3.

All of these automated tasks can be implemented within a week of the decision being made to change the process.

You can now repeat this method for each of the remaining processes. You do not need to do this all at one time; however, this will give you a better picture of how your apps are linked and can work together.

Next, let's discuss how to adequately document your new processes.

Documenting your processes

So far, we've been using a whiteboard tool to illustrate our examples. This method might not work for you; however, whichever method you have used to simplify your processes and establish what can be automated, we suggest that you formally document them once you have completed the exercise. You can document your new process in a spreadsheet, use a digital whiteboard tool such as Miro or Mural, or use a flowchart tool such as **Microsoft Visio** or **Draw.io**. You can also use checklist-style workflow management tools such as **Process Street** or **Process Bliss**, which allow you to create digital **Standard Operating Procedures (SOPs)**.

Important note

When documenting the new process, keep the critical information to a minimum. A simple but effective way of documenting the process involves stating the app it involves, what happens in the task, and whether it requires manual intervention or is automated.

Another example of a visually documented process is shown in the following figure:

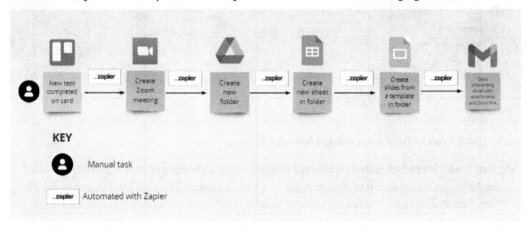

Figure 2.7 – A digitally documented process using Miro

Tip

If you're using whiteboard tools or flowcharts, you can represent your process map vertically or horizontally.

If you want to have a bit more detail in your process maps, you can incorporate the information you pulled together during your problem-solving process using the 5W1H method. This method serves as a reminder to ensure that you should capture all the relevant information as a summary in your process maps:

- *Where?*: Where is the process located? That is, what app(s) is involved in the process?
- *How?*: Identify whether the step is automated or requires human intervention.
- *When?*: When does this step occur in the process?
- *What?*: Make a list of key data values, such as names or email addresses.

- *Who?*: Make a list of any members of the team, or your leads or customers that are involved in the process.

- *Why?*: Make a note of some critical pain points.

We'll show you a visual example of this in *Chapter 3, Building Your First Automated Workflow (Zap)*.

Now that you have simplified your processes and assessed what parts could be automated, let's discuss the best way to establish how Zapier integrates with your apps so that you can begin to automate those processes.

Establishing how your business apps integrate with Zapier

Before you can start automating any tasks, we need to determine which of your business tools integrate with Zapier, as well as what trigger, action, and search functions have been developed into the integration if one is available.

When working through the exercises in the previous section, you created a list of all of your business apps. You also noted which apps were associated with each step in your mapped-out processes. Starting with your five top-priority processes, we can now go through the list of apps related to those processes one by one to establish which of your apps integrate with Zapier.

The steps you should take to establish how your business apps integrate with Zapier are as follows:

1. Search for information about your app.
2. Review the information on the **app profile** page.
3. Assess how to use your app with Zapier.

Let's review each of these.

Searching for information about your app

The easiest way to find out whether your app integrates with Zapier is by clicking on the magnifying glass icon in the top menu bar to search by app, as shown in the following screenshot:

Figure 2.8 – Using the magnifying glass icon to search by app in Zapier

A search bar will appear, where you can type in the name of your app. As you type, any matching name suggestions will be highlighted in a drop-down list, as shown in the following screenshot:

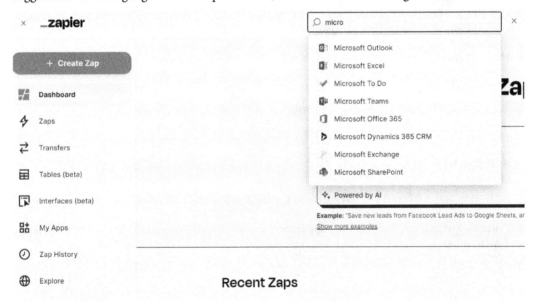

Figure 2.9 – The drop-down list of apps when searching by app in Zapier

From there, you can select your app and will be taken to the app profile page.

> **Important note**
> If you are using a less popular app, you may find that your app does not come up in a search. First, check that the spelling you are using matches the official naming convention of the app. If it still does not appear, this most likely means that integration does not currently exist with Zapier or has not been published in the directory. We will discuss what to do in this scenario in the *Getting the most out of the Zapier app ecosystem directory* section.

Next, let's explore how to review the information about the app.

Reviewing the information on the app profile page

App profile pages show a wealth of information about a specific app and how to use that app with Zapier. We recommend that you review the information on the app profile page thoroughly as it will help you understand the automation capabilities of using Zapier with your app.

Each page is structured with navigation tabs, as follows:

- **Integrations**
- **Help**

We will use **Calendly** to illustrate this, as shown in the following screenshot:

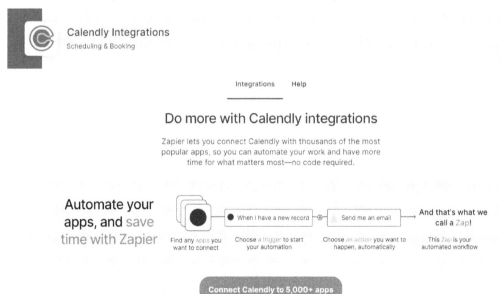

Figure 2.10 – The Calendly app profile page

At the bottom of the page of both the **Integrations** and **Help** tabs, you will find some details about the app. This shows a logo image of the app, a short descriptive summary, and a link to the app website.

> **Tip**
> As you navigate through the information available for your app on the app profile page, keep in mind all your processes that involve this specific app. Refer to the visuals of your brainstorming exercise so that you can see how all your apps fit together. Creating diagrams specific to apps will help. Make notes of any key points that will help you visualize and strategize your workflows.

Let's cover the information shown in each of the different tabs.

Integrations

The **Integrations** tab presents you with detailed information about the app, structured in the following sections:

- **Do more with…integrations**: This section provides a link to the Zap editor when you click the **Connect... to 6,000+ apps** button and a **Search for pairing apps** search bar, allowing you to search for other apps to connect with.

- **Pick an app to pair with**: This section shows a visual representation of several **pairing apps**. Upon clicking on the logo icon, text of each will take you to an **Integrations** page specifically for that app pairing. Scrolling on the arrows under the list will show you additional apps. We will use the **Calendly** and **Slack** integration to highlight this, as shown in the following screenshot:

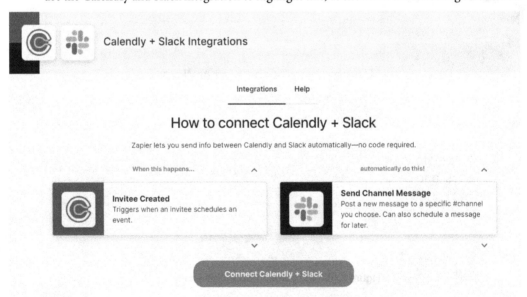

Figure 2.11 – The Calendly and Slack Integrations app pairing page

On that page, you can use the **Connect ... + ...** button to start using the pre-built workflow.

- **Popular ways to use...workflows**: This section lists popular pre-built workflows for your app. You can enter the name of another app from your list of business tools into the search bar and bring up the list of guided workflows to use. We will use **Twitter** to highlight this:

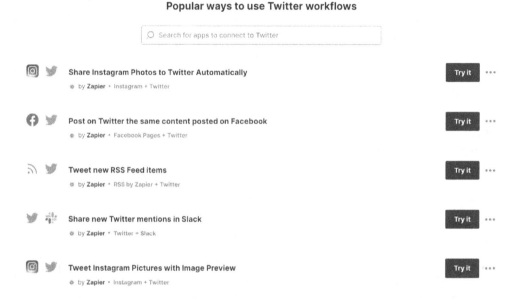

Figure 2.12 – Twitter integrations – connecting to over 6,000 apps

Clicking on the **Load more** button will expand this list. Click on any of the guided workflows, then either the **Try it** button to use the workflow or the **See Zap details** drop-down option, which can be accessed from the three dots icon.

- **Supported triggers and actions**: This section provides information about the available trigger, action, and search functions supported by Zapier, which can be selected from the drop-down menu. Each function has a short descriptive title and a summary of what it does. We will use **Intercom** to highlight this:

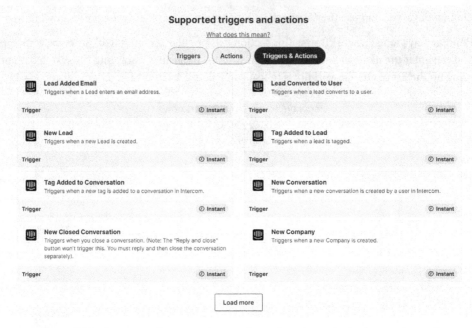

Figure 2.13 – Intercom triggers, actions, and searches shown in the Integrations tab

For some apps, each supported trigger, action, and search has a drop-down menu indicated by a downward pointing arrow icon. Clicking on this icon will expand the box to show the fields and variables that would be shown in the step when building the Zap. This is useful when you're drafting your Zaps ahead of building them so that you are armed with all the information you need, saving you time during Zap building. This is shown in the following screenshot, which uses an example of the Google Drive **Copy File** action event:

Figure 2.14 – The Google Drive Copy File action event expanded to show field information

We will discuss using triggers, actions, and searches in more detail in *Chapter 3, Building Your First Automated Workflow (Zap)*, and *Chapter 6, Creating Multi-Step Zaps and Using Built-In Apps*.

> **Tip**
>
> Use the **Supported triggers and actions** section as a quick reference to find out how your app integrates with Zapier and what triggers, actions, and searches are available to use. These supported triggers, actions, and searches quite often do not encompass all the endpoints available in the app's API. There is often much more you can do on top of the standard Zapier integration by using the API and built-in Zapier features such as Webhooks by Zapier, Code by Zapier, and the API Requests action steps. We will discuss these features in more detail in *Chapter 11, Advanced Built-In Apps by Zapier*.

Next, let's take a look at the **Help** tab.

Help

The **Help** tab is structured as follows:

- **Help & Support**: This section presents you with helpful articles on how to get started and tips on using the app with Zapier, as well as common errors and problems seen with app integrations and how to solve them.

- **Tutorials**: This section displays content created by Zapier to help you get started with using your app in question with Zapier. This includes how to solve common problems, presents examples of popular pre-built Zaps that use your app, and provides other useful content.

Let's explore how to use your chosen apps with Zapier.

How to use your app with Zapier

Now that we have reviewed the information about your app on the app profile page, we should pay particular attention to the **Supported triggers and actions** section, which can be found in the **Integrations** tab.

For each of your apps, make a list of all the function titles and types. For triggers, record whether they are scheduled or instant. For example, for **Google Sheets**, one available trigger is **New Spreadsheet Row**, which is instant. Also, note whether your app is labeled as **Premium** as you will need to ensure you are subscribed to a price plan that supports premium apps, as discussed in *Chapter 1, Introduction to Business Process Automation with Zapier*.

An example is shown in the following figure:

	A	B	C	D	E
1	APP	APP TYPE	FUNCTION	TRIGGER TYPE	WHAT
2	Salesforce	Premium	Trigger	Polling	New Record
3			Trigger	Polling	Updated Record
4			Trigger	Polling	Updated Field on Record
5			Trigger	Instant	New Outbound Message
6					

Figure 2.15 – Recording the Zapier integration options for Salesforce trigger types

You can now repeat this method for each of your associated business apps in the top five priority processes. Once you've done that, you can work through your other business apps. You do not need to do this all at once; however, taking a holistic view of your apps and business processes will position your thoughts better when you create your workflows in Zapier.

> **Important note**
>
> As a bare minimum, it is crucial to work through what we have described for the apps in your first top-priority process. This will give you a clearer picture of how your apps can be connected so that you can start automating your processes.

Now that you understand how to assess how Zapier integrates with each of your apps, we can take a look at the benefits of using the app ecosystem directory.

Getting the most out of the Zapier app ecosystem directory

In the previous part of this chapter, we discussed how to use the magnifying glass icon in the top menu bar to search for your app. Another place to do this is from within the app ecosystem directory. The app ecosystem directory is not only useful for searching for your existing apps but it also serves to direct you if your app does not have an integration with Zapier. Most importantly, the app directory is a comprehensive resource to help you find apps that you may want to start using in your business.

The app directory can be found via the top menu navigation on information pages, as described in *Chapter 1, Introduction to Business Process Automation with Zapier*. It can also be found at https:// zapier.com/apps.

Let's start by familiarizing ourselves with the app directory.

Navigating the app ecosystem directory

The app directory consists of a left navigation sidebar and a central navigation pane, as shown in the following screenshot:

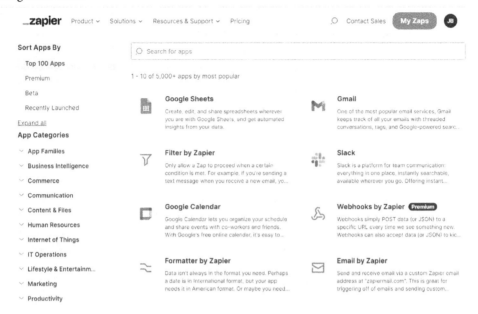

Figure 2.16 – The Zapier app ecosystem directory

We will now look at each of these navigation options.

The app ecosystem directory central navigation pane

The central navigation area displays information that we became familiar with when we discussed app profile pages in the previous part of this chapter and is structured as follows:

- **Search for apps**: The search bar allows you to search the directory by app. It functions similarly to the magnifying glass icon search bar we discussed in the previous part of this chapter.

- **1-10 of 6,000+ apps by most popular**: This section provides a list of the 10 most popular apps out of all the apps listed in the directory with snapshot details.

- **Featured**, **New actions added**, **Coming soon**, and **Recently added**: This section shows four different apps that are either being featured by Zapier; have had new triggers, actions, or searches added; are soon to be integrated with Zapier; or have integrated recently with Zapier.

- **6,000+ apps by most popular**: This section provides a more extensive list of the most popular apps without the snapshot details. If you scroll down to the bottom of the list by clicking on the **Load more** button, the list will expand.

The left navigation sidebar

The left navigation sidebar is useful for displaying apps by group and is shown in the following blocks:

- **Sort Apps By**: You can sort apps by popularity, their **Premium** or **Beta** (an integration undergoing testing that has not officially been released) status, or if they have recently been added. Clicking on each link will change the app lists in the central navigation pane.

- **App Categories**: You can sort apps by their category and subcategory – for example, the **Commerce** category and the **Accounting** subcategory. The central navigation pane view changes slightly to display a useful blog article related to the category/subcategory and lists the top apps, as shown in the following screenshot:

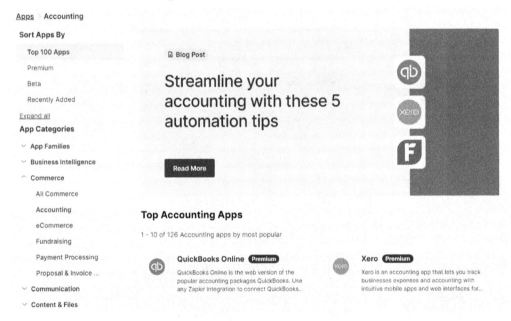

Figure 2.17 – The central navigation pane of the app directory showing Accounting apps

- **Request an app**: If your app does not exist in the app directory, it might mean that integration has not yet been built with Zapier or it is not yet listed in the directory. You can reach out to the customer service team of the app provider to inquire about whether the app integrates with Zapier. Alternatively, the app provider might list details of a Zapier integration on their website, or you might find the information by doing a Google search. From the **Request an app** block, you can click on the **Email us the apps you'd like added today!** link and submit a request to have the app added to Zapier.

- **Add an app**: If you are a software provider or developer, you can access the developer portal to integrate your app and create triggers, actions, and searches by clicking on the **Go to the developer platform** link.

- **Get updates**: Clicking on the **Go to the Updates Blog** link takes you to the updates blog page, where you can sign up for blog updates on new apps and feature releases.

Clicking on any app logo brings up an app profile summary popup, which we'll discuss next.

The app profile summary popup

When you click on any of the app logos in the app directory, you will see a popup for **PandaDoc**, as shown in the following screenshot:

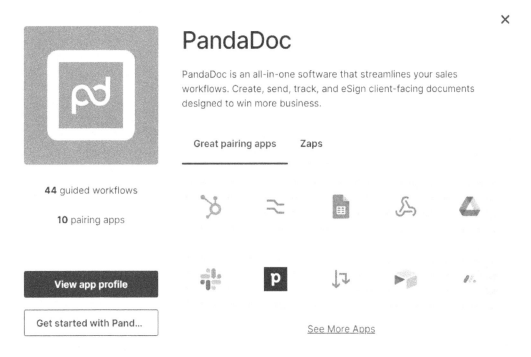

Figure 2.18 – The PandaDoc app profile summary popup

This is a quick-reference summary of the app profile page and is also structured with a left sidebar and a central navigation pane.

Left sidebar

The left sidebar contains the following:

- **App logo**: This shows the logo of the app
- **Guided workflows**: This shows the number of pre-built workflows that have been created for this app
- **Paired apps**: This shows the number of other apps that this app is commonly paired with in workflows
- **View app profile**: Clicking on this button takes you to the app profile page
- **Get started with**: Clicking on this button takes you directly into the Zap editor so that you can start building a Zap with this app as a trigger

Central navigation pane

The central navigation pane contains the following:

- **App name**: The name of the app.
- **Summary**: A few sentences describing what the app is and how it can be used.
- **Great pairing apps**: This tab shows the logos of 10 apps that work well together with this app. Clicking on **See More Apps** will take you to the **Integrations** tab of the app profile page.
- **Zaps**: This tab shows two popular pre-built workflows. Clicking **See More Zaps** will take you to the **Integrations** tab of the app profile page.

Next, let's discuss how to choose new apps for your business.

A brief guide to choosing new apps for your business

The intricate considerations of **digital transformation** could be an entire book on its own. However, it is essential to mention a few points that will help you in your search for new apps that you can add to your business or alternatives to the ones you are currently using. These are listed here:

- Explore your options
- List your key features and requirements
- Define your core app
- Search app ecosystems
- Search the Zapier app ecosystem directory
- Search app comparison directories

- Review feedback
- Arrange product demonstrations and test support resources
- Trial your app shortlist adequately
- Plan to transition to the new app

> **Important note**
> If any of your processes are interconnected and you would benefit from having multiple apps connected to automate tasks, always establish whether your current apps and the apps you are considering integrate with Zapier and in what way. Keep this in mind when you are creating your shortlist.

We will now look at each point in turn.

Exploring your options

Although it may seem logical to settle on an app because it is well-known, it is always wise to explore your options. With **Software-as-a-Service** (**SaaS**) becoming a more popular industry, the release of thousands of new applications to the market has become commonplace over the last few years. There is plenty of competition and there are many different apps available to fit every use case. Therefore, spend more time investigating your options.

Listing your key features and requirements

If you are looking for an alternative to an app you are currently using, make a list of all the features from your existing app that are essential to the way you do business. Also, review what you defined earlier in this chapter in the *Simplifying your processes and assessing what can be automated* section. This information will help you assess what additional functionality you will require. Equally, if you are looking for a new app to digitize your existing processes, this information is vital. Make a note of which features are critical and which are only "nice-to-have" features.

Defining your core app

We previously mentioned that it is important to take a holistic view of your apps and processes so that you know how apps and processes link together. It is also essential to identify the most key application in your business – the app that you consider to be the one source of truth. For example, this might be your **Customer Relationship Management** (**CRM**) tool or your project management tool. If this app is key to your business, knowing what apps it integrates with natively and in what way will allow you to make better decisions about the new apps you intend to introduce. As we discussed in *Chapter 1, Introduction to Business Process Automation with Zapier*, your cloud-based apps are most likely to have a list of other apps that they integrate with natively and can be found in that app's marketplace or ecosystem.

Searching app ecosystems

App ecosystems usually contain a wealth of information about how apps integrate with your core app. You are likely to find user feedback, comprehensive help documents, and videos, as well as pricing and functionality information. These ecosystems are excellent places to start if you are looking for new apps to use with your existing core app and subsidiary apps.

You can now start to create a shortlist with feature comparisons, pricing, and how they integrate with your core app.

Searching the Zapier app ecosystem directory

The Zapier app ecosystem directory is a good starting point to find information about alternative apps that are the closest matches for you in terms of functionality. You can also look for new apps to use by using the left sidebar to sort apps by categories and subcategories.

You can now build on your shortlist regarding how the potential apps integrate with Zapier (triggers, actions, and searches).

Searching app directories

Free directories such as **Get App** (`https://www.getapp.com/`) allow you to search for apps in specific categories, by industry and use case. You will have access to verified user reviews, comparison tables, and articles. You can also use their app finder tool to create a list of recommended apps based on your company size, industry, and the apps you currently use.

Product Hunt (`https://www.producthunt.com/`) is another directory that shows information and up/down votes for products and new features.

You can now compare your apps and add information to your shortlist.

Reviewing feedback

Get App is not the only place to find feedback on apps. You can search social media, forums such as **Reddit** (`https://www.reddit.com/`), and trust sites such as **Trustpilot** (`https://www.trustpilot.com/`). Reaching out to users that have posted comments or asking for feedback on online business groups and communities, such as Facebook or LinkedIn, can be beneficial too. Review feedback carefully and evaluate the pros and cons.

Arranging product demonstrations and testing support resources

Product demonstrations (demos) offer a much better way of initially assessing a tool, more than a free trial will. You might initially think that only larger software providers provide demonstrations of their products. As mentioned earlier, the SaaS industry is becoming more competitive, and even smaller providers offer one-on-one walk-through demos, which then allow you, the potential buyer, to ask questions tailored to your use case. Simply enquire with their customer service team to assess the possibility of a product demo if one is not explicitly offered on the website of the software provider. Providing some flexibility while providing a demo will also give you an indication of what customer support and service levels are likely to be once you have committed to purchasing the product.

> **Tip**
>
> Customer service availability and levels of service are often crucial when you are just starting with a new app. Establishing customer service availability concerning your timezone and query response time will help you make a judgment on whether this fits your needs.

Trialing your shortlist of apps adequately

Once you have made your comparisons, choose two apps to trial alongside each other and the existing app, if appropriate. Using representative data from your existing app or process (if you do not have an app in place currently), run a trial for a few weeks to adequately assess functionality side by side. Free trial periods are often not long enough to properly evaluate the suitability of an app, so enquire before starting your trial about whether trial extensions are available.

> **Tip**
>
> Choosing more than two apps to trial may be time-consuming and overwhelming for your team. It is time well spent to invest in your comparison groundwork to reduce your list to two apps.

Ensure that you have set up the app while following the guidance and best practices provided by the software provider, and make sure that a selection of the key users of the process is involved in the testing. Software providers generally supply comprehensive how-to and training videos and will likely be on hand to address certain issues. You may also find that some providers provide free setup and onboarding services.

Planning for transition to the new app

Once you have decided on the app that you want to implement permanently, ensure that you have created a detailed project plan to manage the transition to using the new app and phase out the old app and process. This plan should include system setup review and customization, data backup, data import, process documentation, and staff training.

You now have a better understanding of how to use Zapier's ecosystem directory of app integrations effectively, can find information about how Zapier integrates with your apps, and can find and assess new apps to use in your business.

Summary

In this chapter, we started by working through how to improve your business processes and then identify what can be automated. We explored how to find information about your business apps and how your apps integrate with Zapier. We discussed navigation in the app ecosystem directory and how to use it effectively to explore new apps to use in your business. We concluded by briefly describing how to find and assess apps to use in your company.

You now know how to simplify your processes, identify what can be automated, navigate the app directory, and find apps to use in your business.

In the next chapter, we will discuss how to strategize and plan individual workflows before automating them. We will cover the steps required to connect your apps to Zapier, discuss navigation in the Zap editor, and work through an example to help you create your first Zap. We will show you how to find and use pre-built workflows, explain field types and data handling, and, lastly, cover continuous improvement.

Questions

1. What does "5W1H" stand for?

2. What are the three critical questions to ask to determine whether you can consider a process for automation?

3. Where can you find information about how your business apps integrate with Zapier?

3

Building Your First Automated Workflow (Zap)

In this chapter, we'll cover all the need-to-know information to enable you to start automating manual and repetitive tasks in your business. We will start by covering how to strategize and plan individual workflows before automating them. We will then dive into working through a step-by-step process of connecting your apps to Zapier, introduce the two versions of the Zap editor, and work through an example to help you create your first Zap from scratch. Then, we will show you how to edit your Zaps and switch between versions, and how you can access a wide range of pre-built or guided workflows created by Zapier to speed up your Zap-building process. We will explain the different field types you may see in your action steps, and how to use the correct data formats for their fields. We will conclude this chapter by delving into the best practices to ensure the continuous improvement of your processes.

We will cover the following key topics in this chapter:

- Strategizing your first workflow

- Connecting your apps to Zapier

- Creating your first Zap in the Zap editor

- Understanding field data types

- Ensuring your processes and automations stay current

Once you have worked through each of these topics, you will have successfully built your first workflow automation using Zapier.

Technical requirements

To work through the content in this chapter, you will need access to a Zapier account. The Zapier Free plan will be adequate to work through the content in this chapter. To use Versions, you must be subscribed to a paid Zapier plan. You can get access to the **Zap templates** used in this chapter here: `https://bit.ly/zapier-book`. Using these templates will help you visualize how the process works.

Strategizing your first workflow

So far in this book, we have worked through how to simplify your processes, establish what can be automated, and assess how your business apps integrate with Zapier. You are now suitably prepared to start planning your first workflow.

The following steps are required to strategize your workflows:

1. Reviewing your process and app information
2. Creating a step-by-step workflow plan

Let's take a look at each of these.

Reviewing your process and app information

From your list of processes, choose one of your five top-priority processes that satisfy the following criteria:

- The process can be automated partly or fully
- One or more apps associated with the process integrate with Zapier
- You have made a list of triggers, actions, and searches for each of your apps

Now, let's explore how to create a workflow plan.

Creating a step-by-step workflow plan

From your chosen process, select one of the most straightforward quick-win solutions that you identified earlier that could be automated. Use this part of your process to work through the following steps to strategize the workflow. We will then create this workflow automation in Zapier in the next part of this chapter.

We will use an example of a sales process to illustrate the steps we need to take to strategize the workflow.

Your company does not have a complex sales process. You have two salespeople who are using **ActiveCampaign** to manage your sales pipeline. New deals are created in the pipeline when marketing leads hit a certain lead score from automated marketing campaign opens and link clicks. There are also members of your admin team that do not need access to ActiveCampaign but need to know a summary of specific details associated with these new deals. This information is manually added to a Google Sheets spreadsheet by the sales team after they have created the deal in ActiveCampaign. The admin team has identified that, on occasion, deals have not been added to the spreadsheet, and there are often transcription errors in the data. The sales team has mentioned that the process is time-consuming and error-prone, which increases with volume. You have already worked through all the steps in the previous sections to simplify this process, establish whether it can be automated, and assess whether ActiveCampaign and Google Sheets integrate with Zapier and in what way.

The following figure shows the preceding example as a mapped-out process with the 5W1H method, which we covered in *Chapter 2, Preparing to Automate Your Processes*:

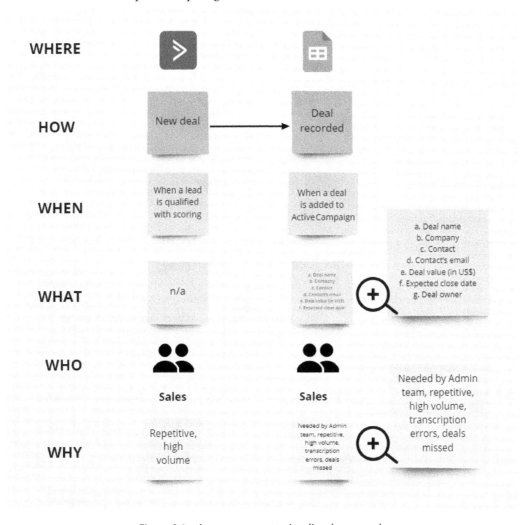

Figure 3.1 – A process map to visualize the example

Let's use this example to work through a step-by-step process to strategize a workflow:

1. **Identify your trigger app**: In our example, the trigger app is **ActiveCampaign**.

2. **Identify your trigger step event**: In our example, the Zapier trigger step is **New Deal Added or Updated**. This event triggers the start of the workflow in Zapier when a new deal is created in ActiveCampaign. This is shown in the following screenshot:

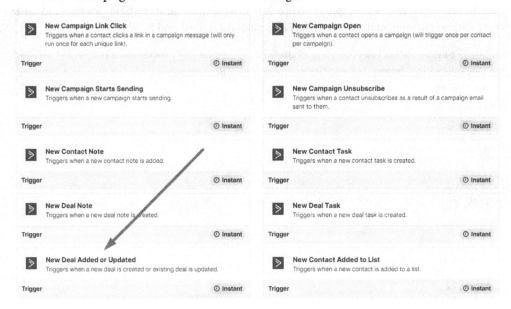

Figure 3.2 – Overview of the ActiveCampaign app profile showing
the New Deal Added or Updated trigger event

3. **Identify whether the trigger is scheduled or instant**: In our example, this trigger is instant, which means that immediately after a deal is created in ActiveCampaign, the workflow in Zapier will be triggered.

> **Tip**
>
> It is handy to know how often your workflows will update. If you have noted that your trigger is scheduled rather than instant, review your Zapier pricing plan to establish how often your workflow is likely to start. For example, if you are using the Free plan, the update time is every 15 minutes, which means that Zapier will look for new data in that trigger app every 15 minutes so that it can start your workflow. This was discussed in *Chapter 1, Introduction to Business Process Automation with Zapier.*

4. **Identify your action app**: In our example, the action app is **Google Sheets**.

5. **Review the data you require for your action step**: In our example, we want to capture the following information from the deal in ActiveCampaign and add it to our Google Sheets spreadsheet:

   - Deal name

   - Company

   - Contact

   - Contact's email

   - Deal value (in US$)

   - Expected close date

   - Deal owner

   Our ActiveCampaign deal is shown in the following screenshot:

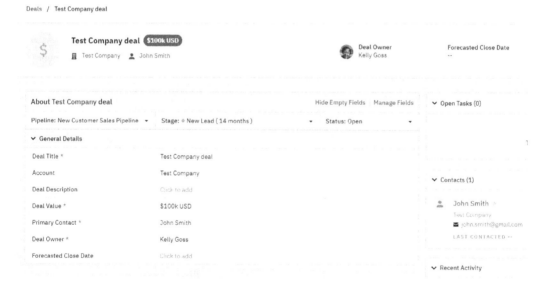

Figure 3.3 – An ActiveCampaign deal to be used as a working example (courtesy of ActiveCampaign)

6. **Identify your action step event**: In our example, the Zapier action step is **Create Spreadsheet Row**. This action will create a new row in a spreadsheet that you will specify. This is shown in the following screenshot:

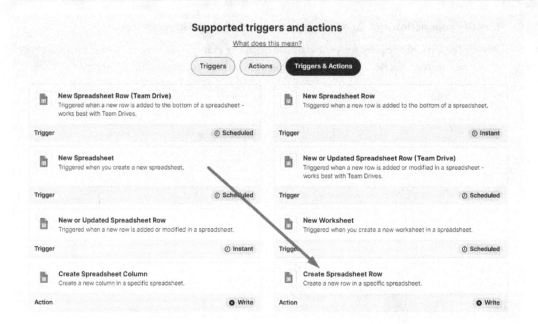

Figure 3.4 – Overview of the Google Sheets app profile showing the Create Spreadsheet Row action event

Next, we need to understand what data we need to capture in our action app. In this case, it is a Google Sheets spreadsheet. Its structure is shown in the following screenshot:

Figure 3.5 – A Google Sheets spreadsheet to be used in our example (courtesy of Google)

It is often the case that your data headings may have slightly different wording in your various apps; thus, it is good practice to make a note of what you may want to map between the two apps. This exercise will make our **data mapping** steps more straightforward to follow when we start building out the workflows in Zapier. Our example is shown in the following figure:

ActiveCampaign	Google Sheets
Deal Title	Deal name
Account	Company
Deal Contact First Name + Deal Contact Last Name	Contact
Deal Contact Email	Contact's email
Deal Value	Deal value (in US$)
Forecasted Close Date	Expected close date
Deal Owner First Name + Deal Owner Last Name	Deal owner

Figure 3.6 – Data mapping between the trigger and action steps

Now that you have strategized your workflow, you can start connecting your apps to Zapier and then create your first workflow automation on the Zapier platform.

Connecting your apps to Zapier

Before we can start building our automations, we need to connect our apps to Zapier to allow Zapier to retrieve and post data in them.

> **Important note**
> Knowing how your data and security are handled by Zapier is an important topic. Allowing Zapier access to your apps using authentication protocols is essential for Zapier to be able to perform task automations on your behalf. The credentials that you use to authenticate your apps so that Zapier can connect with them are stored with bank-level encryption. Zapier has created a comprehensive resource on data privacy and security, which you can read here: `https://zapier.com/help/account/data-management/security-at-zapier`.

App connection can be performed from two places:

- The **My Apps** link in the left sidebar.

- The Zap editor in our trigger, action, or search steps. We will cover this in more detail in the *Creating your first Zap in the Zap editor* section of *Setting up your trigger step*.

Let's look at the **My Apps** method first.

Connecting your apps in My Apps

Follow these steps to connect each of your apps:

1. Start typing in the name of your app in the search bar to reveal a drop-down list. Then, select your app and click the **Connect** button. You can also just click the **Add connection** button to reveal a popup where you can use the search bar to search for an app. This is shown in the following screenshot:

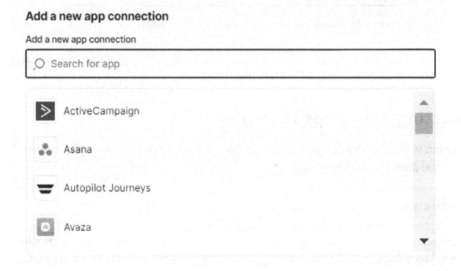

Figure 3.7 – Overview of connecting a new account in My Apps

2. Once you have chosen your app, a new window will open, giving you instructions on how to authorize the app. You may be asked to enter some of the following details:

    *   Google account details (to use **Sign in with Google**)
    *   Username and password
    *   App domain or subdomain URL
    *   API key or token

> **Tip**
> Zapier provides instructions to explain the fields you will need to fill in and how you can find this information if it is not immediately apparent.

The following screenshot shows an example of a subdomain and API key request for **Freshdesk**:

Allow Zapier to access your Freshdesk Account?

Subdomain (required)

This is your registered domain name at freskdesk.com.

https://   .freshdesk.com

API Key (required)

Log in to https://{{your-helpdesk-url}}.freshdesk.com Click on your Profile Picture on the top right and select "Profile Settings" In the sidebar, you will find the API Key Copy-paste this key.

Yes, Continue   Cancel

Figure 3.8 – Authorizing your app with a subdomain and API key in Freshdesk

> **Important note**
> If a new browser tab or window does not appear when you select the app that you want to connect to, try to disable your browser's pop-up blocker.

3. You will then be taken to an approval page, advising you that Zapier wants to access your account and what Zapier will be allowed to do if you approve access. You can read more about privacy and risks, and if you are happy to continue, click on **Allow**. This text may differ between apps. An example of using a Google account is shown in the following screenshot:

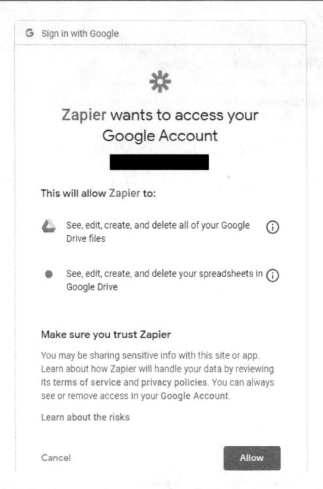

Figure 3.9 – Google approval page to confirm allowing Zapier to access the app

> **Important note**
> You might need to reconnect your app if you have connected the app to Zapier using a username and password and you have changed your password in the app. Here are more details on app authentication and reconnection requirements: `https://zapier.com/help/manage/app-connections/what-should-i-do-in-zapier-if-i-change-an-app-account-password`.

Follow *Steps 1* to *3* for all apps involving a trigger and an action step.

You will now be able to use your connected apps in your workflows, which means you can focus on creating your first Zap. We will discuss how to connect apps from within the Zap editor next.

Creating your first Zap in the Zap editor

There are three ways that you can create a Zap:

- **Create a Zap (beta) feature**: This is an AI Zap builder feature that is currently in beta. It allows you to use a prompt that will use AI functionality to produce a draft Zap for you. We will discuss this feature in more detail in *Chapter 19, AI and Automation*.

- **Suggested workflow templates**: Once you have added the apps you use, in your dashboard, you will be shown some suggestions of workflow templates you can use to quickly get started with Zapier. We will cover this later in this chapter.

- **Build from scratch**: The best way to learn how to use Zapier to automate your processes is to build your Zaps from scratch.

All workflows are created, edited, and maintained in the Zap editor. The Zap editor can be accessed at any time from the expandable left sidebar menu, by clicking on the + **Create Zap** button. First, let's have a look at how to navigate the Zap editor.

Navigating the Zap editor

The Zap editor consists of two views where you can build your Zaps:

- **Classic Editor**: This was the original user interface of the Zap editor for many years and shows steps in static blocks that are vertically stacked. This is shown in the following screenshot:

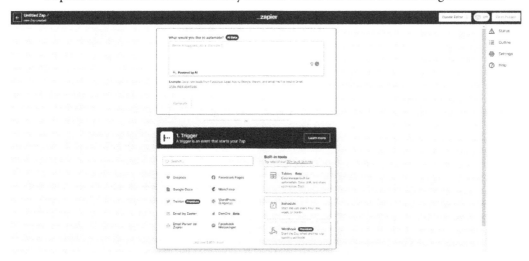

Figure 3.10 – The structure of the Classic Editor view

- **Visual Editor**: This is a newly released feature that allows you to fully visualize your Zap, move and reposition the entire Zap around the screen, zoom in and out to change the view, and export an image of your Zap. Most new user accounts will default to **Visual Editor**. This is shown in the following screenshot:

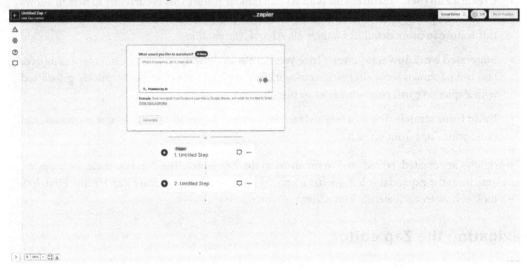

Figure 3.11 – The structure of the Visual Editor view

Both Zap editors are structured with text fields, icons, and buttons along the top bar and either in the right-hand side expandable panel in the case of **Classic Editor** or the left-hand side expandable panel in the case of **Visual Editor**. Let's take a look at this structure in more detail to understand what each section offers us.

The top bar

The top bar contains the following text fields, icons, and buttons, from left to right:

- **Back arrow**: Clicking on this icon takes you to the Zap management area. We will discuss this area in more detail in *Chapter 4, Managing Your Zaps*.

- **Untitled Zap**: This is an editable text field that allows you to give a custom name to your Zap. Adequately naming your Zap is an important part of managing your workflows. We will discuss this in more detail in *Chapter 4, Managing Your Zaps*.

- **Classic Editor/Visual Editor dropdown**: This dropdown allows you to navigate between **Classic Editor** and **Visual Editor**.

- **The "On/Off" button**: This button becomes usable once you have created your Zap, tested it, and eliminated any errors. You must turn your Zap **On** to use it with live data.

- **The Fix to Publish button**: This button allows you to edit your Zap after it has been published. It will only be visible once your Zap has been published for the first time.

- **The three dots menu**: Clicking on this menu item exposes the **Share this Zap** button, which allows you to share the Zap you have created with anyone who has a Zapier account. It will only be visible once you have published your Zap. We will discuss Zap sharing in more detail in *Chapter 4, Managing Your Zaps*.

The left-hand side panel in **Visual Editor** and right-hand side panel in **Classic Editor** contain several icons that, once highlighted with your cursor, show the text that follows, from top to bottom:

- **Status**: This section is represented by an exclamation mark icon in the menu. Any errors related to specific steps in your Zap will be highlighted here. You can get more information on the specifics of the error by clicking on the notification. It is important to address any errors that have been highlighted before you attempt to turn your Zap on.

- **Outline**: This section is represented by a list icon in the menu. It will only be visible in **Visual Editor** once you have published your Zap. It shows a summary of all of your steps in your Zap, as built out in Visual Editor. Selecting any of the steps in this section highlights the step in the editor. Once you start to create complex multi-step Zaps, using this section as a quick-reference tool is handy for identifying where certain steps are in the workflow and for managing steps in your Zaps (renaming, deleting, reordering, and duplicating). The search bar is just as important to use for searching for steps based on their title. We will discuss how to best name your Zaps in *Chapter 4, Managing Your Zaps*. We will apply these naming principles to steps when you start creating multi-step Zaps and also cover how to rename, delete, duplicate, and reorder steps in *Chapter 6, Creating Multi-Step Zaps and Using Built-In Apps*.

- **Settings**: This section is represented by a cog icon in the menu and allows you to manage your Zap from within either editor. You can edit the Zap's name, change the folder it is stored in, add or alter its description (this is useful for making notes), and change the timezone settings of the Zap. We will discuss this in detail in *Chapter 4, Managing Your Zaps*.

- **Versions**: This section is represented by a box and two lines in the menu and will only be visible once you have published your Zap. Users of paid plans will be able to see each saved draft and published version of their Zap. Users on the Professional plan and higher will be able to revert to previous versions as well. We will discuss this in more detail in the *Editing your Zaps – Drafts and Versions* section.

- **History**: This section is represented by a clock icon in the menu and links to the **Zap History** module. It will only be visible once your Zap has been published for the first time. We will cover **Zap History** in detail in *Chapter 5, Troubleshooting and Handling Zap Errors*.

- **Details**: This section is represented by a page and lightning bolt icon and will only be visible once your Zap has been published. Clicking on this icon will take you to the **Zap Details** page for the Zap. We will discuss this in detail in *Chapter 4, Managing Your Zaps*.

- **Help**: This section is represented by a question mark icon in the menu. It is a useful built-in helpdesk that shows "how-to" help articles and videos that can be viewed from within the Zap editor. If you are having a problem with your Zap, at the bottom of the page, you will find a **Get Help** link, which will take you to the Zapier support page where you can submit a support query.

- **Notes**: This section is represented by a comment box icon and can be used to add more information about the steps in your Zap. The following Zapier help article provides further context on how to use this feature: `https://help.zapier.com/hc/en-us/articles/16791272000525`. We will explore how to use AI-powered features to generate Zap notes in *Chapter 19, AI and Automation*.

- **Show**: An arrow icon is shown at the bottom of either panel. In **Classic Editor**, the arrow icon is left-pointing, while in **Visual Editor**, the arrow icon is right-pointing. Clicking on this icon expands the view of the panel to show the other icons and their names.

The bottom-left section in the Visual Editor view

The bottom-left section of **Visual Editor** shows controls that allow you to perform the following actions:

- **Zoom in**: You can increase the screen zoom percentage using the + icon. The zoom percentage is shown between the + and - icons.

- **Zoom out**: You can decrease the screen zoom percentage using the - icon.

- **Fit to view**: This control is represented by an icon of four arrows pointing outward to each corner of a box. Clicking on this control allows you to fit your Zap so that you can view it in full.

- **Export to image**: This control is represented by a downward-facing arrow and line icon. It allows you to download an image of your current view to your device.

  This is shown in the following screenshot:

Figure 3.12 – The Visual Editor controls in the bottom-left section

The editing area

The editing area is where the real magic of Zapier happens. This is where you can create workflow automations step by step. The editing area is structured as follows:

- **Create a Zap AI builder feature (beta)**: New Zapier account users might not see this feature displayed as it is currently still in beta. We will discuss this feature in more detail in *Chapter 19, AI and Automation*.

- **Trigger step box**: This is your trigger step. You can start building your Zap by searching for or selecting an app to add to your trigger step. The trigger step might be shown as a popup when you're creating a new Zap.

- **Plus sign (+) icon**: These icons appear between all steps and after the last step. Clicking on this icon allows you to add action, search, filter, delay, and formatter steps between existing steps, as well as paths after the last step. We will discuss this in more detail from *Chapter 6, Creating Multi-Step Zaps and Using Built-In Apps*, onward.

- **Action step box**: This is your action step. Click on the step to begin setting up your action step.

In **Classic Editor**, Zap customization is made in the main editing area, whereas in **Visual Editor**, the right-hand side panel expands to allow you to make edits to your steps. Once you have added an app to your trigger or action step, an icon will be revealed in the top-right corner of the step box, which is represented by a **three dots icon**. Clicking on this icon will allow you to rename, reorder, copy and paste, and deduplicate steps. For action steps, you also have the option to delete this step. You cannot delete a trigger step but you can edit it. We will discuss this in more detail later in this chapter.

Now that we have a better understanding of how to navigate through both editors, we can start creating our Zap. We previously identified our trigger and action apps, our related steps, and the data we will map between our apps.

> **Important note**
> All screenshots displayed in the rest of the chapters in this book have been taken from the **Classic Editor** view for simplicity. Where relevant, we will discuss the differences between the **Classic Editor** and **Visual Editor** views.

We will now use our working example from earlier in this chapter to illustrate how to create a Zap. You can work through these steps using the workflow you strategized earlier.

Setting up your trigger step

Firstly, we will start with the trigger step. Let's work through a step-by-step guide to set up our trigger step using our example:

1. **Start editing the trigger step**: When you open the **Classic Editor** view, the trigger step will already be open. In the **Visual Editor** view, this will be in the form of a popup.

2. **Choose your trigger app**: From the list of apps presented in the trigger step, choose one to connect as the trigger app. If you don't see it in the list, search for it in the search bar just above. The search bar allows you to search for your chosen app if it is not shown in the list of apps. Selecting any of the apps will allow you to start customizing your trigger and action steps. In our example, we will select **ActiveCampaign**. In the **Classic Editor** view, the changes are made

within the main editing area, whereas in the **Visual Editor** view, the right-hand side panel expands for you to perform the editing.

3. **Choose your trigger event**: Now, select your trigger event. In our example, we will select **New Deal Added or Updated** as our trigger event, as shown in the following screenshot:

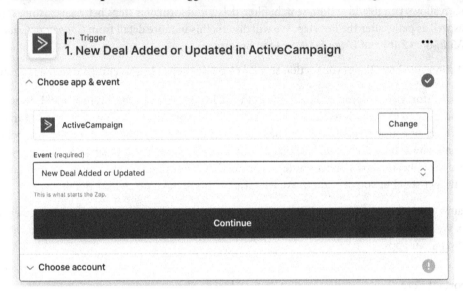

Figure 3.13 – Using the ActiveCampaign app's New Deal Added or Updated trigger event in the Zap editor

Click the **Continue** button.

4. **Choose your trigger app account**: Select your app account from the drop-down list. The list will only show accounts specific to the app you selected in *step 2*, and those you have previously connected to Zapier. You can also click on the **Change** button and then the **Connect a New Account** button to connect and authenticate a new app account. This will take you through the same procedure that we discussed in the *Connecting your apps to Zapier* section of this chapter. Another option is to click on the **Manage all of your connected accounts here** link, which will enable you to edit your connections in the **My Apps** module. This is shown in the following screenshot:

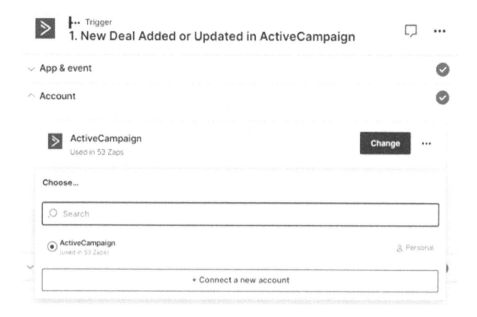

Figure 3.14 – Connecting an ActiveCampaign account to Zapier in the trigger step

Click the **Continue** button.

5. **Choose your sample data and test your trigger**: Next, we need to find sample data from our app (ActiveCampaign, in our example) to test our trigger. This will confirm that we are using the right app account and that the trigger step is working correctly. Click the **Test** button. Zapier will search for data in your app, which, after a few seconds, will be pulled through into the editor, which will show the date the record was pulled in.

> **Tip**
> We recommend creating test data, sample sets of data, or dummy data wherever possible when you are testing your Zaps. This can help you avoid live data corruption in your app accounts.

6. **Review your sample data**: You should review your data to ensure it is what you are expecting. Note that data labels will be highlighted with a lilac background and the data value will be in normal text. In our example, we created a deal called Test Company deal, associated with the deal_title data label. We will use the name of this deal as the **unique identifier** to check that we have the correct sample data to use in the test. You can scroll through the data or use the search bar to find your data. Using the search bar will highlight how many data values contain that text; you can easily find them using the arrow keys and the scroll bar. This is shown in the following screenshot:

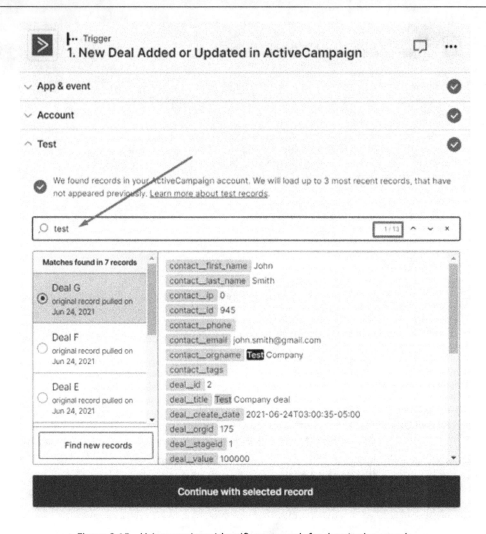

Figure 3.15 – Using a unique identifier to search for data in the sample

7. **Change your sample data**: You can change your sample data by selecting the sample header with the up and down arrows (for our example, *Figure 3.15* shows this labeled as **Deal G**) and selecting another option if available. To retrieve more sample data, select **Find new records**.

8. **Finalize your trigger step**: Select **Continue with selected record** to move on to your action step. If your trigger has been set up correctly, you will see a green check mark next to the app logo, as shown in the following screenshot:

Figure 3.16 – A completed trigger step in the Zap editor

> **Important note**
> Some app integrations only allow a limited number of sample datasets to be brought through. In some cases, only recently created data will be pulled through. You may have to create additional sample sets as you are testing your trigger. Also, some app integrations have issues pulling through any existing sample data from the app and will provide you with dummy sample data to use instead. In these situations, use the dummy sample data to test your trigger step. Your Zap will work correctly with "live" data when the Zap is turned on. Contact Zapier support if this does not work.

Next, we'll set up our action step.

Setting up your action step

In the action steps, you will find two main field types:

- **Choose value…**, from which you can choose set values from a drop-down list brought in from our action app or add **custom values**. We will discuss using custom values in more detail when we explore multi-step Zaps in *Chapter 6, Creating Multi-Step Zaps and Using Built-In Apps*.

- **Enter text or insert data…**, from which you can either manually type in static text if you want that value to always be displayed or insert **dynamic data** that updates every time the Zap runs. You can also add a combination of static and dynamic data. In our example, if we wanted the Deal name cell in the Google Sheets spreadsheet to always display Test Deal when a new row is created, we would enter Test Deal into the field in that step. Using dynamic data, on the other hand, means that the value will represent live data when the Zap runs. This data is retrieved from your trigger app (or previous action steps if you're using multi-step Zaps).

> **Tip**
>
> Mapping out your data in a table helps you identify the dynamic data names in the different apps. Often, the title of the data may be named differently from what you expect. These naming conventions are based on what title the API field is given in the app. Concerning the data table in *Figure 3.6* and trigger data in *Figure 3.15*, in our example, we may expect to see a value for **Deal name** but we see `deal_title` instead, and for **Account**, we see `contact_orgname` or `deal_orgname` instead. As you become more familiar with how field data is named and presented from your trigger and action steps, you can add an additional column to your data mapping table that shows the API field's name.

An example is shown in the following screenshot, where static text and dynamic text are used in the **Deal name** field in two separate action steps:

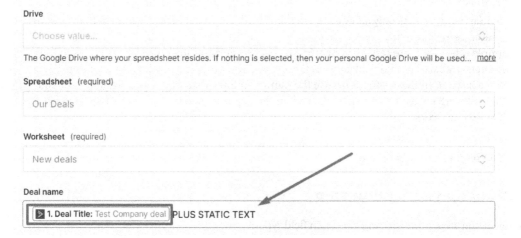

Figure 3.17 – Using dynamic data (in the box) and typing in static text
(indicated by the arrow) to map a Google Sheets action step field

Now, let's work through a step-by-step guide to set up our action step, as follows:

1. **Start a new step**: Click on the second step marked as **2. Action** to reveal the app list.

2. **Choose your action app**: Select your action app from the list of displayed apps. If you don't see it in the list, search for it in the search bar just above. In our example, we will select **Google Sheets**.

3. **Choose your action event**: Now, select your action event. In our example, we will select **Create Spreadsheet Row** as our action event. Click the **Continue** button.

4. **Choose your action app account**: Select your app account from the drop-down list. This step functions in the same way as in the trigger app account step. Click the **Continue** button.

5. **Customize your action step**: Next, we need to customize our action step. In our example, the first thing we need to do is choose which spreadsheet we want Zapier to add data to. Using the **Choose value…** fields, Zapier will bring in a list of fixed values from our action app. In the case of our example, Zapier will bring in a list of spreadsheets, and once a spreadsheet has been selected, a list of worksheets within that sheet. This is shown in the following screenshot:

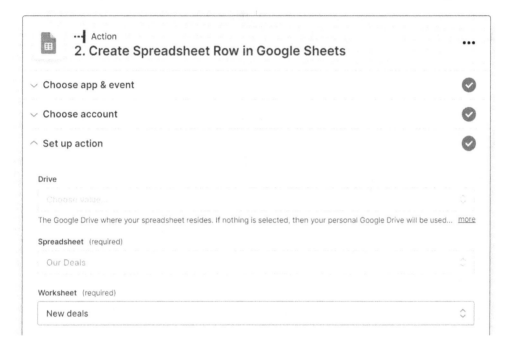

Figure 3.18 – Choosing a Google Sheets spreadsheet and worksheet to use in a Zapier action step

In our example, the rest of the field types are **Enter text or insert data…**; we will use this to describe how to map your fields.

Once you have selected the field you want to map (using an **Enter text or insert data…** field in this case), a drop-down list of dynamic data will be shown. This dynamic data will be presented in the following format:

- **An icon**, which represents the originating app (in our example, ActiveCampaign). It will look similar to the app's logo.

- **A number**, which denotes which step the data has originated from. In single-step Zaps, this will always be 1 . . In multi-step Zaps, this numbering will help you identify which step to map data from.

- **Text styled in bold with a colon**, which represents the name of the field as coded within the app – that is, the **API field name**.

- **Text styled normally**, which represents the dynamic data from the app.

This is shown in the following screenshot:

Deal name

> **1. Deal Title:** Test Company deal

Figure 3.19 – The structure of dynamic data

You can select **Show all options** to show all data, which you can scroll through, or use the search bar to search for specific text.

We can now use the information from *Figure 3.6* to assist us with mapping our field data. Using our example, we can search for the Test Company deal title by typing this in the search bar, as shown in the following screenshot:

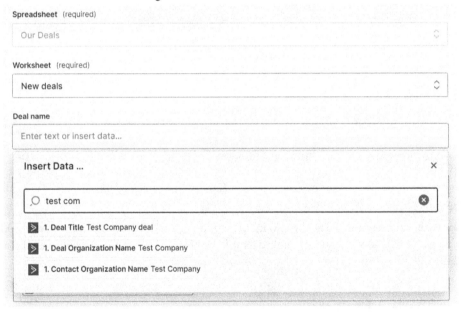

Figure 3.20 – Searching for dynamic data in an action step

Identify the correct dataset to map to that field and select the relevant one. Repeat this for each field.

> **Important note**
> Fill in any fields that are marked as **required**. You will not be able to test your action step without these fields.

Once you have mapped all the fields, the resulting action step form will look similar to what is shown in the following screenshot (using our example):

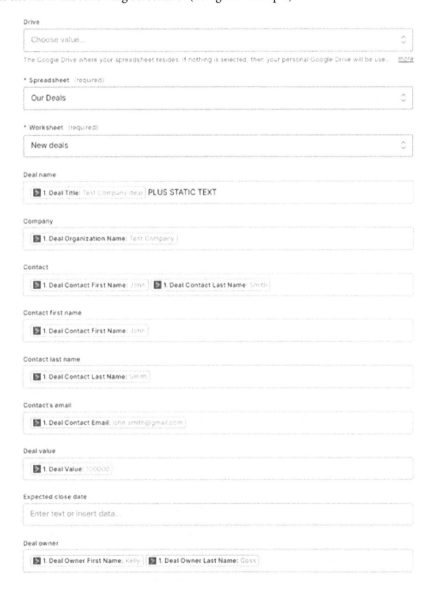

Figure 3.21 – A completed action step form with mapped fields

As you can see from *Figure 3.21*, you can map into the field two or more values dynamically to form a new word. For example, in the **Deal Owner** field, we have added the `Deal Owner First Name` data value and the `Deal Owner Last Name` data value to show the full name.

6. **Test your data**: Once you are satisfied that your **field mappings** are correct, click **Continue**. Next, we need to test our data by sending it to our action app, Google Sheets. You can review the data that we will send and click the **Test action** button. Fields that have not been filled out will be highlighted in the **Empty fields** section. This is shown in the following screenshot:

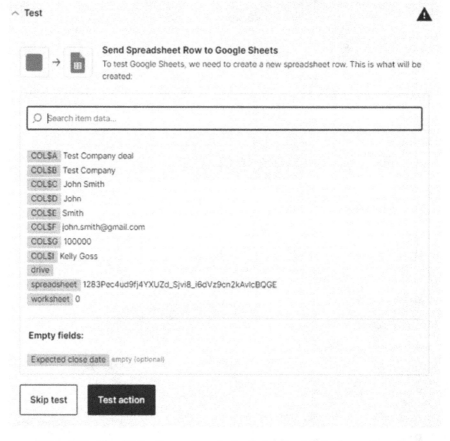

Figure 3.22 – The data testing options in the Test action block of an action step

You can also select **Skip test** if you do not want test data to be sent.

If your request is successful, you will be shown a highlighted success message. You can choose **Retest action** to stay in the **Test** block to see another result or **Publish** to publish your draft and turn your Zap **On**.

A pop-up box will appear stating **Ready to publish your Zap?** and a **Publish** button. Click the **Publish** button to publish and turn on your Zap.

7. **Check your data in your action app**: Always check that your data has been sent correctly to your action. This is shown in the following screenshot, including the expected close date filled in:

Figure 3.23 – Successfully sent test data from the action step shown in Google Sheets (courtesy of Google)

> **Tip**
> Zapier assigns a standard name to trigger and action steps based on what the step does. Get into the habit of changing these standard names and renaming your action steps with keywords applicable to your workflow. You can then search for steps using the **Outline** icon in the right-hand side menu. This is handy when you have complex multi-step Zaps and you're working with a team.

You can get a template of this Zap here and add it to your Zapier account: `https://bit.ly/zapier-book`. Using this Zap template will help you visualize how the process works.

> **Tip**
> With our example, you need to bear in mind that the trigger will run every time a new deal is added or updated in ActiveCampaign. This means that we will also be adding updated deals to the Google Sheets spreadsheet as new rows. You can use a search action step to check the Google Sheets spreadsheet to see whether the deal already exists on the sheet, then a Filter by Zapier step straight after to only allow the Zap to continue if the deal is not on the sheet. We will discuss using search action steps in *Chapter 6, Creating Multi-Step Zaps and Using Built-In Apps*, and using Filter by Zapier in *Chapter 7, Getting Started with Built-In Apps*.

Understanding statuses in steps

While you're building your Zap, be aware of statuses within your steps. This will help you identify whether there are functionality problems in your Zap and ensure that your Zap can be published without errors. Statuses are indicated in two places:

- **Within step blocks**: These are indicated by a **green tick icon** if the section of the step is in working order, or a **yellow exclamation icon** if action is required. This is shown in the following screenshot:

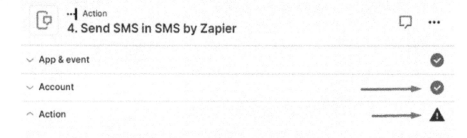

Figure 3.24 – Statuses within step blocks

- **In the Status section in the right-hand side panel**: Issues in your Zaps are highlighted in this section and indicate which step has a problem, a description of what the problem might be, and how it could be solved. This is shown in the following screenshot:

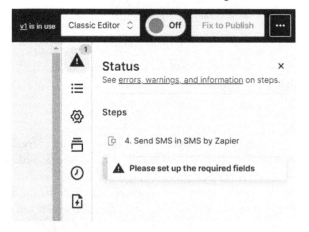

Figure 3.25 – Statuses in the right-hand side panel in the Classic Editor view

> **Important note**
> Address any status issues before attempting to publish your Zap.

Now that you have created your trigger and action steps, addressed any status issues, and tested your Zap, you will need to name it and turn it on so that it can trigger on the selected event in your trigger app and run with live data.

Naming your Zap and turning it "On"

Let's name the Zap so that it can be identified easily. We can do this in the top panel's **Untitled Zap** editable text field or the expandable right-hand side **Settings** panel. Choose a name that represents it well. For our example, we will use Create new Google Sheets row when new deal is added in ActiveCampaign. We will discuss the best way to name Zaps in more detail in *Chapter 4*, *Managing Your Zaps*.

The last thing you need to do is turn your Zap on. This can be done using the **Publish** button in the top menu, or the popup at the bottom of the Zap editor. Once published, your Zap will be in read-only mode, and cannot be adjusted.

Well done, you have just created your first workflow automation from scratch!

Next, let's cover how to edit your Zap and understand the Drafts and Versions features.

Editing your Zap – Drafts and Versions

When you start creating a Zap, Zapier will automatically save any changes as **Drafts**. Once the Zap has been published for the first time, you can make edits to it without turning it **Off**. This means that the Zap will continue to trigger and run while you are making changes to your Zap in the background. Changes to the Zap will not be live until the draft has been published but will be saved even if you exit the Zap editor for the specific Zap.

When editing your Zap, the last time a draft was saved will be indicated by the text below the Zap title, as shown in the following screenshot:

Figure 3.26 – Draft saving timestamp

To make edits to your Zap, click the **Edit** button at the bottom of the Zap editor or the **Edit Zap** button in the top-right panel. This is shown in the following screenshot:

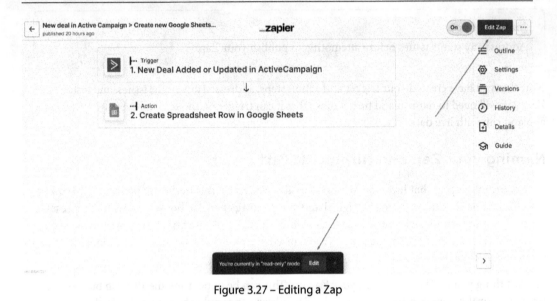

Figure 3.27 – Editing a Zap

If you have previously edited your Zap and have a saved draft, a popup will appear, giving you the option to delete the draft by clicking on the **Discard** button. You can also continue to use and edit your previously created draft by clicking on the **Edit draft** button:

Figure 3.28 – Editing a Zap with an existing saved draft

You can then continue to edit your previously saved draft.

> **Tip**
> It is not possible to save notes on the overall changes that have been made to saved but unpublished drafts, and it is easy to forget the changes that were made if you have not published them. If you plan to work further on a draft in the future before publishing it, make notes of your changes in the **Description** box under **Settings** in the right-hand side panel. This will ensure that you have a record of your unpublished changes.

Publishing a new version of a Zap

When you are ready to publish your changes, click the **Publish** button. You will be presented with a popup so that you can publish your new version by entering a **Version** name. Fill in the **Version name** field with as much descriptive information as possible to help you remember what you changed. Click the **Cancel** button to cancel the publishing operation or **Publish** to proceed to publish the new version of your Zap:

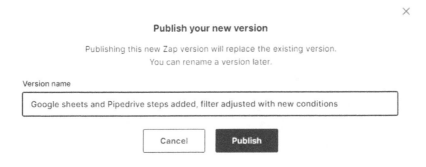

Figure 3.29 – Publishing a new version of a Zap

> **Important note**
> The **Version** feature is not available with the Free plan. Version history is kept for 1 week on the Starter plan, 1 month on the Professional plan, 6 months on the Team plan, and 1 year on the Company plan. Version rollback is only available with Professional plans and higher.

Now that you have published a new version of your Zap, let's explore how to manage the version history of a Zap.

Managing versions of a Zap

You can manage the different published versions of your Zap by clicking the **Versions** button in the right-hand side panel in the **Classic Editor** view or the left-hand side panel in the **Visual Editor** view. This will show you a list of previously published versions of your Zap, with the first version at the bottom and your latest version at the top, normally denoted by the **In use** label. The user that published the version and when it was published will also be displayed. You can then do the following:

- **Rename a version**: Click on the **three dots icon** next to any version to reveal a drop-down menu where you can click on the **Rename version** option to change the name of the version

- **Revert to a previous version**: Click on the version to display that version in the editor, then click on the drop-down menu and choose the **Edit from this version** option to bring that version into the editor to make changes or publish without changes

This is shown in the following screenshot:

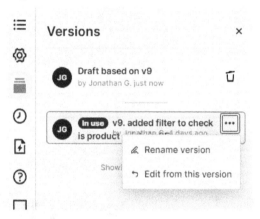

Figure 3.30 – Managing versions of a Zap

Now, let's discuss the benefits of using pre-built workflows.

Using Zapier's guided workflows (Zap templates)

Using either Zap editor to start building out your Zaps is the best way to learn how to use Zapier. You can save time, however, by exploring and using pre-built templates or guided workflows called Zap templates. Zapier has created thousands of single-step Zaps using popular combinations of apps and corresponding trigger or action events. These Zap templates can be accessed from various locations, as we have mentioned throughout this chapter; however, the most practical place to start using guided workflows is from the main dashboard and using the **Make a Zap** interactive tool.

All you need to do is enter the two apps you want to connect, as well as your trigger and action events. Zapier will then present you with a pre-built Zap to use. Select **Try it** to continue, which will take you directly to the Zap editor, or **Cancel** to start again. This is shown in the following screenshot, which is using our working example:

Make a Zap

Connect this app...

ActiveCampaign	

with this one!

Google Sheets	

When this happens...

New Deal Added or Updated	

then do this!

Create Spreadsheet Row	

Create spreadsheet row in Google Sheets when new deal added or updated in ActiveCampaign
ActiveCampaign + Google Sheets

Try it

Figure 3.31 – Using the Make a Zap pre-built workflow tool

Zapier provides variations of the interactive tool, such as with the **Recommended workflows for you** option on the main dashboard. This offers a more specific approach by naming the objective. For example, you could choose a template to post new WordPress posts to your Facebook page, then follow the steps to connect your WordPress and Facebook Pages accounts, customize the Zap, test it, and publish it.

> **Important note**
> Some accounts might show the **Create a Zap (beta)** AI feature in the dashboard, therefore replacing the **Make a Zap** interactive tool. We will explore this feature in more detail in *Chapter 19, AI and Automation*.

You should now have a better understanding of how to create a Zap from scratch, and how to use pre-built workflows created by Zapier. Now, let's take a look at the different field types that may be shown in action steps.

Understanding field data types

Now that we've created our first Zap, we must elaborate on the different types of fields that you may see in Zapier action steps.

In the previous section, we covered the two general types of fields, **Choose value...** and **Enter text or insert data...**, and how to use them to map fields in your Zaps. In addition to these two general field types, five different field data types allow you to add data in specific formats. Each field data type is represented by an icon, as shown in the following table:

Icon	Field Data Type
📅 🕐	Date/time
1 2 3	Number (integer)
●○	Boolean (true/false)
🗋	File
1.0	Decimal

Figure 3.32 – Action step field data types

These field data types are dictated by the data posting format requirements of your action app. For example, if your action app is Xero (an accounting app), and you want to create a new invoice, your invoice date field will only allow you to add date/time data values for the request to be successful.

We will discuss each of these field data types in turn.

Date/time

The **date/time field** type is represented by a calendar and clock icon side by side. This field requires data in the form of a date with or without a time.

An example of a date/time field from an accounting app action step is shown in the following screenshot:

Defaults to creation date if not specified.

Figure 3.33 – A date/time field from an accounting app action step

Supported formats

Zapier recognizes and supports various time/date formats, as follows:

- **Standard international (ISO)** format – for example, 2020-07-15T13:05
- Unix timestamps (the number of seconds since January 1, 1970) – for example, 1591537509
- Today at noon
- Next Monday at 5 P.M.
- 5/15/2020 9 P.M. EST

Timezone settings

In *Chapter 1, Introduction to Business Process Automation with Zapier*, and earlier in this chapter, we discussed altering your account time zone settings and your Zap time zone settings. If you do not specify a time zone in the time/date data, such as today at noon, Zapier will use your account or Zap time zone settings.

The format you should use in the field is needed for the action app. Every app has a different required date/time format and time zone setting. Each app will recognize certain time formats/time zone settings and not others. If you're unsure of the exact format needed for your action app or if the data is not posted as expected, you should contact Zapier support.

We will cover how to format date and time values in *Chapter 14, Formatting Date and Time*.

Number (integer)

The **number (integer)** field type is represented by the numbers **1 2 3**. This field requires data in the form of an integer, which is a positive or negative whole number (which can also be zero). This field is often used for selecting unique identifier records, such as ID numbers for users, companies, and projects, as well as posting strings of numbers in number-specific fields in the action app.

An example of a number (integer) field from an SMS messaging app action step is shown in the following screenshot:

Figure 3.34 – A number (integer) field from a CRM app action step indicating the input for an ID value

Boolean (true/false)

The **Boolean (true/false)** field type is represented by **two dots side by side**, one filled and the other not. This field requires data in the form of a `true` or `false` value and denotes how the field is represented in the action app. These values may be converted as follows:

- `true`, `yes`, `t`, or `1`
- `false`, `no`, `f`, or `0`

In the example shown in the following screenshot, when creating an invoice in the Xero accounting software, you can choose to mark the invoice as **Sent To Contact**. A value of **True** would signify yes, while a value of **False** would signify no:

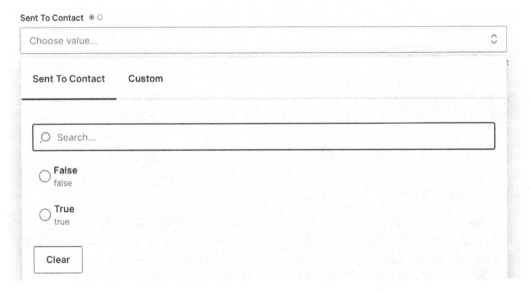

Figure 3.35 – A Boolean (true/false) field from a Xero accounting app action step

File

The **file** field type is represented by a **document icon**. These fields require data in the form of an online accessible document file and not the name of a document. Often, these document files are represented by the text in the dynamic data (labeled (**Exists but not shown**)) and can be in various file formats.

Two examples of a file field from an email app action step mapped with two different formats are shown in the following screenshots:

Figure 3.36 – A file field from an email app action step with two different formats mapped

> **Note**
> It is only possible to add a single file to one field.

You can type text into the field and it will be converted by Zapier into a `.txt` file containing the filled contents. This will then be uploaded to the action app. You can also add a URL and Zapier will inspect the content, attempt to name it accordingly, and upload it to the action app – for example, if you added the URL to an image, rather than the image file itself.

Decimal

A **decimal** field type is represented by **1.0**. These fields require data in the form of a number with a decimal and can be of variable decimal places. The theory is similar to the number (integer) field; however, if the decimal is missing, Zapier will add it before posting the data in the action app.

An example of a decimal field from an accounting app action step is shown in the following screenshot:

Figure 3.37 – A decimal field from an accounting app action step

You should now have a better understanding of the different types of field data that are used in action steps. Now, let's explore how to keep your workflow automations current.

Ensuring your processes and automations stay current

In *Chapter 1*, *Introduction to Business Process Automation with Zapier*, and *Chapter 2*, *Preparing to Automate Your Processes*, we covered using business process automation principles to improve the way you manage your processes and make them more efficient with automation. We now need to discuss the importance of building your workflows with continuous improvement in mind.

Businesses continually change due to economic influences, staff turnover, priorities and goals, and growth. Thus, the way companies work and how tasks are performed is bound to change often. In addition, app integrations are frequently updated and improved. Regularly reviewing your processes will ensure you benefit from these upgrades and align with the way your business functions currently. Business process automation principles take into consideration that businesses and technology evolve constantly, and promote having a plan for continuous improvement.

These are the five key steps for implementing effective workflow automation in your business successfully:

1. **Discover**: Analyze and simplify your processes and plan your workflows step by step.

2. **Create**: Build your workflows and test them. Adjust your workflows as required.

3. **Implement**: Document your workflows, train all users, and make other relevant team members aware of the new process. Set your workflows to live.

4. **Review**: Continually monitor workflow performance. Regularly review your processes to assess whether they can be improved. You can do this by repeating the exercise described in the *Analyzing and simplifying your processes* section of *Chapter 2*, *Preparing to Automate Your Processes*, and checking whether they are still relevant, useful, and not redundant or wasteful.

5. **Improve**: Evaluate what steps can be changed and improved.

Once all five steps have been completed, repeat them from *step 1* at planned, regular intervals.

By reassessing your Zapier workflows regularly, you will be able to remove unnecessary steps, which will ultimately reduce your task usage. Following these principles will ensure that your processes and subsequent automations align with the current situation, and remain lean and error-free.

Summary

In this chapter, we started by discussing how to strategize individual workflows before diving into working through the step-by-step process of connecting your apps to Zapier and creating your first workflow automation (Zap) in Zapier. We explored how to edit your Zaps and utilize the version history to switch between different versions and how you can access and use a wide range of pre-built workflows. We also explored the different types of fields that can be found in action steps and how to use these fields correctly. We concluded this chapter by delving into best practices for ensuring the continuous improvement of your processes.

You now know how to plan your workflows and create them in Zapier from scratch or using Zap templates. You also know how to use different types of field data and perform continuous improvement in your processes. You also created your first automated workflow.

In the next chapter, we will cover the best ways you can organize your Zaps by naming them and using folders. We will discuss how to manage individual Zaps and help you understand Zap statuses. We will also cover how to manage the apps you have connected to your Zapier account before describing how to share copies of individual Zaps with other Zapier users and how to share Zaps and folders with your team.

Questions

1. What three ways can Zapier ask you to connect and authenticate your apps?
2. What are the three options for adding data to your action steps?
3. Other than the two general types of data fields, what are the five specific field data types?

4

Managing Your Zaps

In this chapter, we will discuss the best ways to manage and maintain data in your Zapier account. As you build more Zaps, keeping them all organized will become more of a priority for preserving structure. We will, therefore, start this chapter by explaining how to keep your workflows organized in the Zap management area by using the best naming conventions and by using folders. We will then discuss how to manage individual Zaps and utilize the Zap **Settings** area. Next, we will help you to understand Zap statuses and then cover how best to manage your connected apps. Finally, we will discuss how to share your workflows with other Zapier users.

We will cover the following key topics in this chapter:

- Keeping your Zaps organized
- How to manage your Zaps
- Understanding Zap statuses
- Managing your connected apps
- Sharing your Zaps and folders

Once you have worked through each of these topics, you will know how to keep your workflows organized, how to maintain and share them, and how to manage your connected apps.

Technical requirements

To work through the content and exercises in this chapter, you will need access to a Zapier account. The Zapier Free plan will be adequate to work through most of the content in this chapter. For some of the instructions in the *Sharing your Zaps and folders* section, you will need access to a Zapier account on a Team or Company plan.

Keeping your Zaps organized

In *Chapter 3*, *Building Your First Automated Workflow (Zap)*, we worked through the steps required to create your first workflow automation. As you repeat that process, you will build more Zaps to automate your other business processes. It will eventually become more of a priority to ensure that you have created a system for organizing your workflows. It is, therefore, a good practice to understand how best to keep your Zaps organized and start this process when you only have a few workflows built.

These are a couple of steps you can take to help you to keep your Zaps organized:

- Labeling your Zaps adequately
- Using folders and sub-folders in the Zap management area

Let's discuss each of them.

Labeling your Zaps adequately

From an organizational perspective, you should name your Zaps with sufficient information to ensure a title is descriptive enough to understand what the Zap does. Labeling your Zaps in the right way will allow you to sort them into groups, search for them, and quickly identify them in the **Zap history** and when troubleshooting errors.

There are several ways that you can name your Zaps, and how you choose to do this will come down to what seems most logical for your business and also personal preference. The following are some commonly used methods for Zap naming:

- Using trigger and action descriptions
- Using unique identifiers
- Adding numbers, letters, or Roman numerals

As we review each of these, think of keywords that could help you to identify your Zaps.

Using trigger and action descriptions

The most obvious method is to use a brief description of what happens in action steps when an event is triggered in the trigger app. In *Chapter 3*, *Building Your First Automated Workflow (Zap)*, we used a working example to illustrate the Zap building process. In our example, we built a workflow that triggers when a new deal is created in ActiveCampaign, which then results in a row being added to a Google Sheets spreadsheet. We chose to name that Zap `Create new Google Sheets row when new deal is created in ActiveCampaign`. If your Zap triggered on a new contact being added to **SendinBlue**, which then created an item in **monday.com**, we could name the Zap `Create new item in monday.com when new contact is added to SendinBlue`.

This is the typical arrangement that you will see used in most Zapier pre-built/guided workflows.

Using unique identifiers

You may also choose to specify a unique identifier, such as a user, a file, or an app account that is involved in either your trigger or action step(s) if highlighting this is of particular importance. For example, if you have multiple Zaps that accomplish a similar outcome but trigger based on different conditions, such as something user-specific, you could add the user's name to the title to help you identify the difference between those workflows. In our example, we may choose to highlight the Google Sheets spreadsheet we are using and name the Zap `Create new Google Sheets (Our Deals) row when new deal is created in ActiveCampaign`.

> **Tip**
>
> As you start to build multi-step Zaps, naming your Zaps using this method could get complex. Don't overcomplicate the naming process. Abbreviate where possible, use keywords, and keep your Zap titles short yet descriptive.

Using unique identifiers is especially useful for filtering and searching for Zaps based on keywords.

Adding numbers, letters, or Roman numerals

Another frequently used Zap naming method is to add numbers, letters, Roman numerals, or a suitable combination preceding the short trigger/action description. In our example, we may choose to number and name the Zap `1a. Create new Google Sheets (Our Deals) row when new deal is created in ActiveCampaign`. This method is especially useful if you have split your workflows so that they mirror steps in the actual processes you are automating. As Zaps are listed alphanumerically in the Zap management area, naming your Zaps in this way is also helpful if you want to see your Zaps in a particular order. Numbering your Zaps will also help for quick reference purposes when looking at Zap history information.

Starting to use a suitable naming system soon after you begin using Zapier to automate your processes will save you time and headaches in the future when organizing your Zaps.

> **Tip**
>
> Although Zapier shows a changelog and revision history of a Zap, version history is only available on paid plans. If you are on a free plan or work with a team, you may find it useful to add extra information about changes made to your Zap to the Zap **Settings Description** box, which we will discuss later in this chapter, in the *Utilizing the Zap Settings tab in the Zap editor* section.

Now, let's review how to use folders to bring further organization to your Zapier account.

Using folders and sub-folders in the Zap management area

Adequately naming your Zaps is most certainly a good practice. If we combine that with sorting Zaps into folders and sub-folders (folders within folders), your Zaps will be easy to find and maintain. Folders can be created and managed in the Zap management area, which can be found by clicking on the **Zaps** icon in the left sidebar or by navigating to `https://zapier.com/app/zaps`.

The Zap management area is split into a left-side panel and a central panel, as shown in the following screenshot:

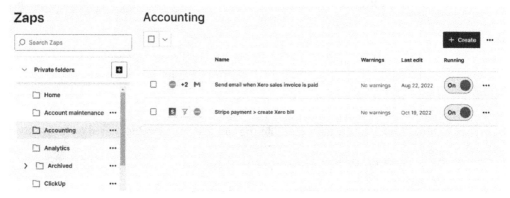

Figure 4.1 – Overview of the Zap management area of Zapier

We will discuss the central panel in the *How to manage your Zaps* section, so let's dive into reviewing how we can use the left-side panel for managing folders.

The left-side panel is used for managing folders and is structured as follows:

- **Search bar**: You can use the search bar to filter your Zaps using keywords. These filtered Zaps will be displayed in the central panel with a header showing the number of results for that keyword search. This is shown in the following screenshot:

Figure 4.2 – Filtering your Zaps using a keyword search

- **Private folders**: This section shows all the folders that you have created with Zaps that are owned by you. If you are using a Team or Company plan, these folders and Zaps within them will only be visible to you.

- **Shared folders**: This section will only be available for use if you subscribe to a Team or Company plan. Folders created here can be shared with individual users or, if you are using a Company plan, specific groups of users that you have set up in teams. We will discuss using shared folders in more detail in the *Sharing your Zaps and folders* section.

- **Held**: This folder contains Zaps that have been paused. We will discuss **Held** Zap runs in more detail in *Chapter 5, Troubleshooting and Handling Zap Errors*.

- **Trash**: This folder holds Zaps that have been deleted. Deleted Zaps are held in this folder for 30 days before being permanently deleted.

> Tip
>
> You can archive your Zaps rather than permanently delete them. Create a folder called `Archived` to store Zaps that you may need to refer to in the future so that they are not permanently deleted if you add them to **Trash**.

From the left-side panel, you can do the following:

- Create and name a folder

- Select a folder to view its contents

- Manage your folders

Let's take a look at each of these.

Creating and naming folders

You can create a new folder by clicking on the + icon next to the sections named **Private folders** and **Shared folders** (if using a Team or Company account). A popup will appear where you can add a title of up to 255 characters that will help you to identify the folder. Then, click on the **Cancel** button if you wish to cancel or the **Done** button if you wish to save your new title.

Naming your folders

As we discussed earlier in this chapter, suitably naming your Zaps is essential for organizing them. The way you choose to group your Zaps into folders is just as important. Once again, this will come down to personal preference and what fits your business needs. However, these are a few examples of ways to sort your folders:

- **By focus app or app category**: You could group your Zaps according to the main app used in trigger and action steps—for example, "Salesforce". Alternatively, you could group them by the app category—for example, "Surveys".

- **By department or business function**: You could separate your Zaps into groups such as "Marketing", "Sales", and "Operations".

- **By client**: If you are a freelancer or contractor and you manage several of your clients' workflows within your own account, you could separate your Zaps accordingly.

As with Zaps, folders are listed in alphanumeric order. Each folder is displayed with the name and number of Zaps stored within it.

Selecting a folder to view its contents

You can select a folder to display and manage the Zaps in the folder in the central panel.

Managing your folders

Click on the **three-dots icon** (not applicable to the **Home** folder) to display a drop-down list allowing you to do the following:

- **Move**: Selecting this option will allow you to move a folder into another folder, therefore creating a **sub-folder**.

- **Rename**: Selecting this option will allow you to edit a folder name.

- **New folder**: Selecting this option will allow you to create a sub-folder in another folder. Using sub-folders is extremely useful for keeping your Zapier account organized.

- **Share**: This option is available for users of Team or Company accounts. You can share a folder along with all the Zaps in that folder. The **Share** option will be available in **Private folders** to the owner of the folder. Once shared, the **Share** option is displayed in **Shared folders** and will be available to admin users only. This option will be displayed if you are using a Team or Company account. We will discuss this in more detail in the *Sharing your Zaps and folders* section.

- **Delete**: Selecting this option will allow you to delete the folder. All Zaps held in this folder will be automatically moved back into the **Home** folder, and will not be deleted. This option will only be available to folder owners for users of Team and Company accounts.

> **Important note**
> The **Home** folder is the default folder, and cannot be renamed, deleted, or shared. Zaps can, however, be added to and removed from this folder.

Now that we have explored how to keep your Zaps organized by using naming techniques and sorting them with folders, let's dive into how to manage your individual Zaps.

How to manage your Zaps

The central panel in the Zap management area shows a list of your Zaps, from either a folder you have selected or as a result of using the search bar. The view defaults to the **Home** folder when you first navigate to the Zap management area. You can manage your Zaps from the central panel, and this displays the folder title as a header, a top navigation bar, and a list of your Zaps.

Each Zap is presented in a clearly defined section, and clicking on the link in the Zap name will take you directly into the Zap editor where you can edit that specific Zap. You will also find a checkbox on the left-hand side of each Zap box. You can use the checkbox to select one or more Zaps to manage using the options in the top navigation bar. Individual Zaps can be managed by doing the following:

- Using the top navigation bar

- Using the options within specific Zap rows

- Removing them from the **Trash** folder

- Utilizing the Zap **Settings** tab from within the Zap editor

We will review each of these in turn.

Managing your Zaps using the top navigation bar

The top navigation bar sits just below the folder header and can be used to manage your Zaps using the following options:

- **The down-arrow icon**: You can use the down-arrow icon to select multiple Zaps depending on whether they are paused (**Off**) or to select all Zaps. Once you have selected your Zaps, you can also use this dropdown for the **Move to folder**, **Export**, **Delete** (to move Zap into the **Trash** folder), **Change owner**, **Select all Zaps**, **Clear selection**, or **Select paused** actions. The **Export** option will be available if you are an admin user of a Team or Company account, where you can export Zaps in a folder as a JSON file. The **Change owner** option will be available if you are the Zap owner or an admin user of a Team or Company account. This is shown in the following screenshot:

Figure 4.3 – Overview of Zap multi-select drop-down arrow in the Zap management area

- **The + Create button**: Although this button does not help to manage the Zaps within the Zap management area, it is a conveniently placed navigational tool to allow you to create a new Zap from this view. By clicking on this button, you will be taken straight into the Zap editor to build a new Zap.

- **The three-dots icon**: You can use this drop-down menu to carry out **Move folder**, **Rename folder**, **Share folder**, or **Delete folder** actions. These options will not be available in the **Home** folder.

Now, let's discuss managing Zaps from within their Zap row.

Managing your Zaps from within their specific Zap rows

Each Zap is displayed within a row that shows the following:

- **App icons**: Single-step Zaps are displayed as a trigger and action app icon side by side. Zaps with two action steps are displayed with the trigger and the two action app icons in sequence. Zaps with multiple action steps are displayed as the trigger, and the action app icons are separated by an icon with a + sign and the number of action steps—for example, **+2**—as shown in the following screenshot:

ClickUp

	Name	Warnings	Last edit	Running
	Copy: New task assigned in ClickUp - Create task in Google Tasks	No warnings	2w ago	On •••
	New task assigned in ClickUp - Create task in Google Tasks	No warnings	2w ago	On •••
+2	Status changed to Done in ClickUp tasks - Update Google Tasks	No warnings	28d ago	On •••

Figure 4.4 – Overview of distinguishing between single- and multi-step Zaps

- **Name**: The full Zap title is displayed in this column.

- **Owner**: The name of the user that created the Zap will be shown in this column if using a Team or Company account.

- **Warnings**: Any issues with the Zap are displayed here. For example, if an app has disconnected, the text **1 connection expired** will be displayed with a link to the **My apps** area to allow you to reconnect the app. The default is the text **No warnings** if there are no issues.

- **Last edit**: The timestamp of the last recorded edit made to the Zap will be displayed here. For example, the text **2w ago** will be displayed if an edit was made in the past 2 weeks.

- **Running (On/Off toggle button)**: The status of the Zap is shown here. You can turn your Zap **On** or **Off** using this toggle button.

- **The three-dots icon**: When this icon is clicked, a drop-down list will be displayed, giving you several options to manage your Zap. This is shown in the following screenshot:

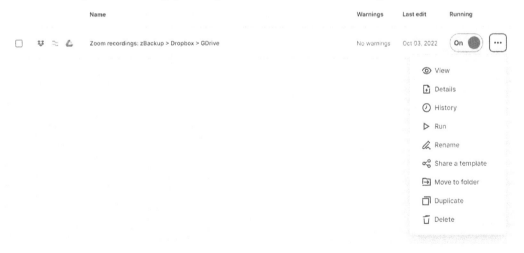

Figure 4.5 – Managing your Zaps using the drop-down options within the Zap box

The drop-down menu gives you the following options:

- **View**: Clicking on this option takes you directly into the Zap editor, where you can view or edit your Zap.

- **Details**: Clicking on this option will take you to the **Zap Details** area. We will discuss this in the next section.

- **History**: Clicking on this option will take you straight to the Zap history of this specific Zap. We will discuss the **Zap history** module in detail in *Chapter 5, Troubleshooting and Handling Zap Errors.*

- **Run**: If the Zap trigger type is **Scheduled**, you can force the Zap to search for trigger data by clicking on the **Run** option. This is useful when testing your Zap when it is **On** so that you do not have to wait for your **update time** to pass. This option will not be available if the trigger is **Instant**.

- **Rename**: You can conveniently rename your Zap directly from the Zap management area without having to navigate to the Zap editor.

- **Share a template**: You can share a copy of your Zap with a link. We will discuss this in more detail in the next section.

- **Change ownership**: You can change ownership to another user, which will grant the new user access to all associated folders and connections. This option is only displayed if you are using a Team or Company account and is only available to the owner of the Zap.

- **Move to folder**: Clicking on this option will allow you to move your Zap to another folder.

- **Duplicate**: You can make a copy of any Zap, which can then be used as a template for creating another Zap.

- **Delete**: You can send your Zap to the **Trash** folder by clicking on this option. Zaps moved to the **Trash** folder will be permanently deleted after 30 days.

> **Tip**
> The **Duplicate** option is handy if you intend to build multiple workflows that have similar steps but may differ with some variations. Using this option allows you to duplicate a Zap and essentially use it as a template. This function is especially useful as a time-saver if you have complex multi-step workflows that you want to use with different triggers and other conditions.

Next, let's explore the **Zap Details** area.

The Zap Details area

The **Zap Details** area is a handy management area for your individual Zaps, allowing you to perform specific functions all from one location, such as adding or changing Zap details such as the Zap title, description, and time zone, viewing and testing the connection for the connected apps, and toggling the Zap **On** or **Off**. You also have **View in Editor**, **Move to folder**, **Run** (if the trigger uses the polling method), **Share a template**, or **Delete** (if it is turned off or a draft) buttons available. This is shown in the following screenshot:

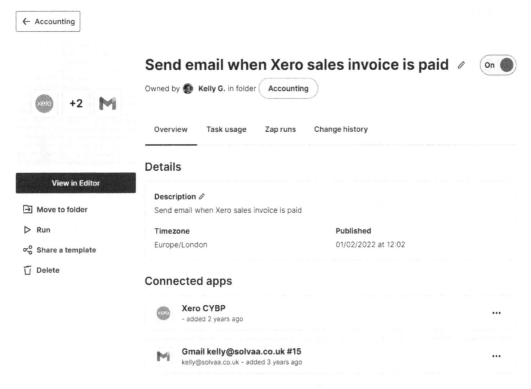

Figure 4.6 – The Zap Details area

If using a Team or Company account, the **Change owner** and **Export** options will be available.

You will also be able to see a bar chart representation of your task usage in the **Task usage** tab, information on Zap runs in the **Zap runs** tab, and some basic Zap changelog history in the **Change history** tab. All of these are very useful for getting insights into how your Zaps are running. An example of data in the **Task usage** tab is shown in the following screenshot:

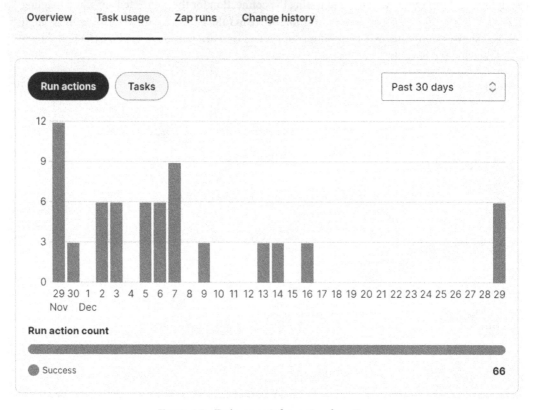

Figure 4.7 – Task usage information for a Zap

The **Change history** tab shows a changelog of activity related to the Zap. You can filter by date range using the **Date** dropdown, and by how the Zap has changed when using the **Change Type** drop-down menu. The types of change you can choose from this menu are **Zap Enabled, Zap Disabled, Zap Created, Zap Discarded, Zap Owner Changed, Zap Restored**, and **Zap Version Published**. The history shown will include the type of change and associated icon, the date- and timestamp of the change, and which user made the change. This is shown in the following screenshot:

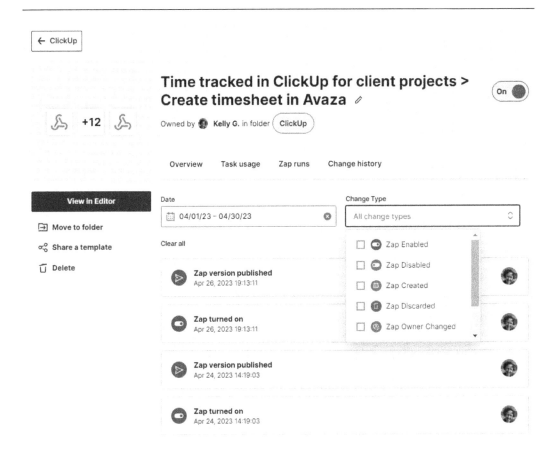

Figure 4.8 – Overview of change history information for a Zap

We will explore the **Zap runs** tab in more detail in *Chapter 5, Troubleshooting and Handling Zap Errors*.

Next, let's review how to restore Zaps that have been moved to the **Trash** folder.

Restoring Zaps from the Trash folder

Zaps that have been sent to the **Trash** folder are held there temporarily for 30 days before being deleted permanently. Once a Zap is in the **Trash** folder, you will not be able to make edits to it until it is restored; however, it can be restored within this time period.

While a Zap is in the **Trash** folder, clicking on the **three-dots icon** will allow you to view the Zap details by clicking on the **Details** option, review the Zap history by clicking on the **History** option, or move it to another folder by clicking on the **Move to folder** option, as shown in the following screenshot:

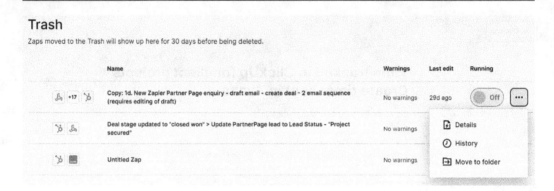

Figure 4.9 – Restoring Zaps from the Trash folder

Select the **Move to folder** option and choose a specific folder to restore the Zap in.

> **Important note**
> Zapier does not show a detailed history of changes to Zaps, so it will not be possible to know how long a Zap has been in the **Trash** folder and when it will be permanently deleted. Remember, you can create another folder to archive Zaps in so that they are not permanently deleted.

Now, let's cover how to best use the Zap **Settings** tab in the Zap editor to manage your Zaps.

Utilizing the Zap Settings tab in the Zap editor

As we discussed in *Chapter 3, Building Your First Automated Workflow (Zap)*, you can manage your Zaps using the **Settings** section from within the Zap editor. When you have a Zap open in the Zap editor, the **Settings** section can be found by clicking on the **Settings** icon in the right-side menu. The options are presented as follows:

- **Name**: The name of your Zap will be displayed here. You can quickly alter it without having to change it in the Zap editor.

- **Add to Folder…**: You can change the folder your Zap is stored in by using this option.

- **Description**: You can add new text or alter any existing notes here. This is useful when you need to add extra details to your Zap where the name might be too long—for example, adding the date it was last edited, the user initials if appropriate, and additional details about what the Zap does and the logic behind it to help other users understand it better.

- **Timezone**: You can alter the **Timezone** settings of the Zap if you want your Zap to run in a different time zone than that specified in your account settings. The **Timezone** settings can only be altered when editing a Zap in draft or the Zap has not yet been published.

This is shown in the following screenshot:

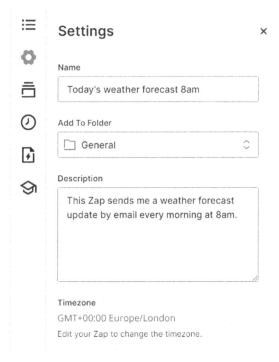

Figure 4.10 – The Zap Settings section in the Zap editor

> **Tip**
> With the exception of customizing a step title, Zapier does not allow you to make notes within individual steps in a Zap. In addition, Zapier also does not show a detailed changelog or revision history of the Zap. The **Description** box is, therefore, handy for adding notes to describe steps in detail and specify changes to the Zap with dates. If you work in a team, you could record the initials of the user that made the revision and record other notes for the benefit of other team members.

You should now have a better understanding of how to manage your Zaps. Let's now take a look at the different statuses that might be assigned to your Zaps. This will help you to manage your individual Zaps better.

Understanding Zap statuses

Understanding what the different statuses are and when you are likely to see your Zaps in those statuses is also a useful tool in the management of your Zaps. When you view your Zaps in the Zap management area, they will be displayed with one of the following statuses:

- **On**: As we discussed in *Chapter 3*, *Building Your First Automated Workflow (Zap)*, once you have built and tested your Zap, you must publish your Zap and turn it **On** for it to work with live data from your trigger app. Once a Zap is turned **On**, Zapier will look for new data in the trigger app to then kick off the workflow and perform the action steps.

- **Off**: If your Zap is turned **Off**, Zapier will not actively look for new data in the trigger app. Zapier may automatically turn a Zap that you have **On** to the **Off** status for the following reasons:

  - Your Zapier pricing plan is downgraded to the Free plan from a paid plan, and therefore you lose access to paid plan features such as multi-step Zaps or Premium apps

  - Your Zap experiences multiple errors when it runs. Zapier will send an email to the account owner to notify you of the Zap being turned **Off**

- **Incomplete**: Incomplete Zaps generally do not have adequate information to be published. They will either be missing a trigger or an action step or both, or steps have not been worked through and tested. Incomplete Zaps are displayed with a status of **Off**, and cannot be turned **On**, as shown in the following screenshot:

		Name	Warnings	Last edit	Running	
☐		ActiveCampaign → Google Sheets	No warnings	Nov 05, 2022	Off	...
☐		New deal in Active Campaign > Create new Google Sheets row	No warnings	Just now	On	...
☐		Untitled Zap	No warnings	1m ago	Off	...

Figure 4.11 – Overview of the Zap management area showing off, on, and incomplete Zaps

On some occasions, your Zaps may be displayed with the following statuses in addition to being **On** or **Off**, which will be displayed in the **Warnings** section:

- **Held**: You may see your Zaps highlighted with the label **Zap runs held**. A link will be shown to the Zap history area where you can run your held Zaps.

  One reason this might happen is when your Zaps are triggered too many times during a short interval. Zapier will then notify you that Zap runs are being held. You can re-enable your Zap and ignore held Zap runs if you wish. We will discuss this in more detail in *Chapter 5*, *Troubleshooting and Handling Zap Errors*.

- **Expired connection**: Sometimes, your connected apps may disconnect. If this happens, your Zap will show an **expired connection** status, indicating one or more apps in your Zap has disconnected. You can reconnect your app by clicking on the link, which will navigate you to the **My Apps** module.

Now that you understand Zap statuses, let's look at how to manage your connected apps.

Managing your connected apps

Once you have connected your apps to Zapier, it's useful to know how to manage the connections. This can all be done from the **Apps** module. You can navigate to this module by clicking on the **My Apps** icon link in the left sidebar or navigating to `https://zapier.com/app/connections`.

From within your personal account in the **Apps** module, you will be able to see a list of your connected apps under the **All apps** tab, how many connections have been added, and how many Zaps they are involved in. You will also see a tab called **Custom integrations** that will list any custom integrations with non-public apps involved in your account.

If you are using a Team or Company plan, your connections will be separated into two sections, as follows:

- **My apps**: Only you can use these accounts. You can, however, choose to share your app connections with your team.

- **Shared with me**: These are accounts that are owned by others in the team but have been made available by other team members for you to use.

- **Custom integrations**: These are private app connections specifically connected to your account.

- **All apps**: If you are an admin user, you will be able to see and manage all apps connected to the account.

This is shown in the following screenshot:

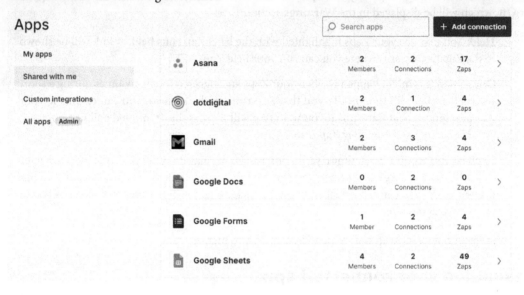

Figure 4.12 – Connected apps in the Apps module

You can manage your connected apps by clicking on the **arrow** button and then selecting the **three-dot** drop-down menu, as shown in the following screenshot:

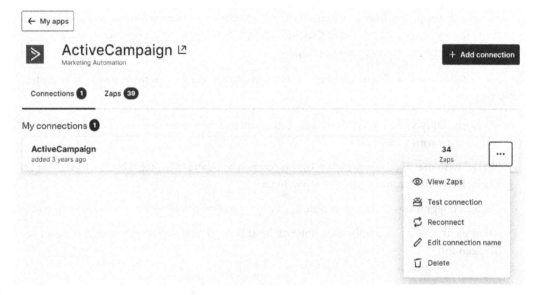

Figure 4.13 – An app connection in My Apps

You can then select one of the following options:

- **View Zaps**: You can view all the Zaps associated with the connection by clicking on the **View Zaps** option in the three-dot drop-down menu. Alternatively, click on the **Zaps** tab to show all Zaps using this connection.

- **Test connection**: It is useful to be able to test whether your app has connection issues. You can do this by clicking on the **Test connection** option in the drop-down menu. A successful connection will be highlighted in green with the word **Success** and, therefore, no further action is required.

- **Reconnect**: When Zapier identifies an app as requiring reconnection, this app is highlighted with a warning triangle. You can reconnect your app by clicking on the **arrow** icon button and following the prompts. This is shown in the following screenshot:

Figure 4.14 – Apps requiring reconnection

- **Edit connection name**: You can edit the name of your connection by clicking on the text next to the pencil icon. Being able to alter the connection name is handy if you want to differentiate between different accounts for the same app; for example, if you are connecting multiple email accounts.

- **Change ownership**: You will be shown this option in Team and Company accounts, which allows you to transfer your connections to other users. This is especially useful if you will no longer have access to the Zapier account—for example, if you will no longer be working with the company and you need to transfer ownership of the app connection to an admin user.

- **Delete**: You may wish to disconnect an app connection entirely from your Zapier account. You can do this by clicking on the **Delete** option. You will be prompted to confirm. Once confirmed, the app connection will no longer be listed in your **My Apps** list.

Lastly, clicking on the **Zaps** tab allows you to see details of the Zaps your app is associated with, including their status, when they were last changed, and how many tasks have run. This is shown in the following screenshot:

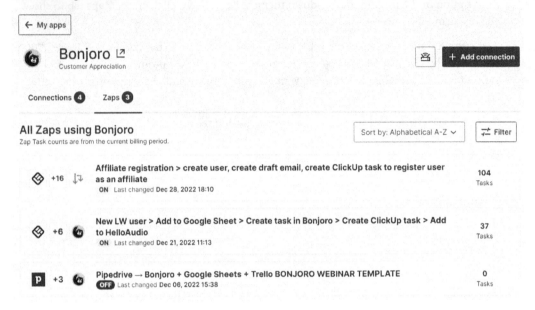

Figure 4.15 – A list of Zaps using Bonjoro as a connected app

Let's discuss how to share your connected apps next.

Sharing your connected apps

When you work with a team, you might want the flexibility for other members of your team to use particular app connections that are owned by you. For example, if your team all have access to a specific app, you could connect that app to Zapier and allow them to use that app connection by sharing it with them.

Sharing connected app accounts

You can share your app connection with others in your team as follows. By clicking on the **Share** button, a popup will appear, as shown in the following screenshot:

Figure 4.16 – Sharing options for private app connections

Add a specific member or team or check the **Share with everyone** box, and then click on the **Done** button to confirm. Some apps will ask you for authorization to give access, and another popup will appear asking you to authorize granting your team access to the app connection. This is shown in the following screenshot using Cognito Forms as an example:

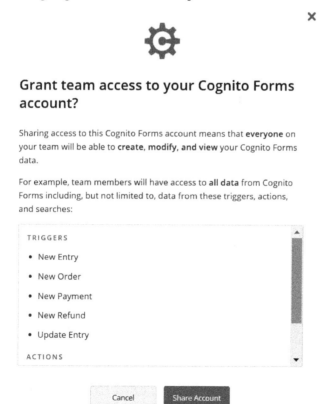

Figure 4.17 – Authorizing a connected app to be shared with your team

Just click on the **Share Account** button to continue. The sharing status button will change to **Everyone**.

> **Important note**
>
> If you are using a Company plan, you will be able to specify which user or team you want to share the connected app with. You can also share the app connection with everyone.

Once an app connection has been shared with your team, all users will be able to do the following:

- View sample data from the app when used as a shared app connection in a trigger step
- View Zap history information from this shared app connection
- Use the shared app connection in private and shared Zaps in triggers and actions to retrieve data from and update the app
- Edit steps in Zaps that use this shared connection

> **Important note**
>
> Only share access to an app connection if you are sure you want other team members to access data in that account. For example, if you share your private email app connection, other team members will be able to access all emails received and will be able to send emails from that account. You could instead create a shared email account for a specific purpose, such as for sending invoices and receiving bills—for example, `accounts@yourcompany.com`.

Stopping sharing a connected app account

You can remove access to a shared connected app, as follows:

1. Click on the **Everyone** button.
2. Uncheck the **Share with everyone** box. Note that if the connected app is only shared with one member, **1 member** will be displayed.
3. Click on **Done** to continue.

> **Important note**
>
> Once you make a shared app connection private again, any Zaps that have been built using that connected app will continue to run and use that account data. Your team members will still be able to see data in any steps using that connected app, although only you will be able to edit these steps. To stop data from being accessed in these steps, you will need to remove the app connection from each step and replace it with another app connection.

You should now have a better understanding of how to manage and share your connected apps on the Zapier platform. Let's now discuss how to share individual Zaps and folders.

Sharing your Zaps and folders

Working through your processes and then creating your Zaps will require some initial time investment. However, once you harness the power of using workflow automation tools such as Zapier, you'll begin to benefit from the time-saving and productivity gains of automating your workflows. You may want others to benefit from the time you have invested in building your workflows and, therefore, Zapier offers you some options to be able to share your workflows with others. This is especially useful if you work with a team of people with whom you can collaborate to automate company processes by building and maintaining your Zaps together.

You can share your Zapier workflows in two ways:

- Sharing copies of your Zaps with other Zapier users outside your company

- Sharing your Zaps and folders with other team members, if you subscribe to a Team or Company plan

First, we will have a look at sharing copies of your Zaps with other Zapier users.

Sharing a copy of your Zap with Zapier users outside your account

If you want to share a copy of your Zap, you can do this without the risk of your connected accounts, data, and Zap history being shared with the recipient. A copy of the Zap will be shared by generating a link that can be disabled if required. You can only share a copy of a Zap that has been completely set up and turned on.

> **Important note**
> Zaps with **Paths by Zapier** and **Looping by Zapier** steps cannot be shared with other users outside of your Zapier account.

Enabling a copy of your Zap to be shared

You can share a copy of your Zap from two locations, as follows:

- **Zap management area**: Click on the **three-dots icon** and select **Share a template**

- **Zap editor**: Click on the **three-dots icon** (**More actions**) dropdown in the top bar and select the **Share this Zap** option

Once you have selected the share option, you can customize your Zap template sharing page by customizing the Zap title (pulled from the name of the Zap) and description to help the recipient identify the Zap and understand what its purpose is. It is also useful if you intend to share the link on social media. In the **Zap description** field, you can enter additional information, such as instructions on what to customize in the Zap; for example, changing the email signature in an email-related action or changing field data mapping that will differ between account connections. This will be very useful for the people you are sharing the Zap with. This is shown in the following screenshot:

Figure 4.18 – Overview of adding a name and description when sharing a copy of a Zap

You can click on the **Preview** link to see what the template will look like to others viewing it. Alternatively, click on the **Share** button to open a popup, as shown in the following screenshot:

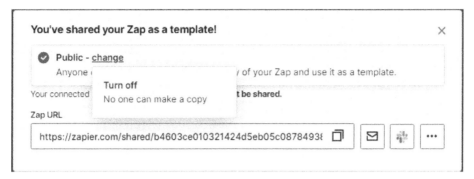

Figure 4.19 – Overview of Zap sharing options

You can then work through the following options:

- **Change**: Click on the **change** link to choose whether you would like the Zap template to be shared with anyone on the internet (**Publicly Shared**), or you can disable the sharing of the link by selecting the **Turn off** option

- **Copy or share**: Copy the link by clicking on the **copy icon** button or share the link by email, Slack, Facebook, Twitter, or LinkedIn using the relevant icons or **three-dots icon**

Once you have worked through the options, click on the **x** icon.

> **Important note**
> Updates to a Zap will not be reflected in the copy shared with a link. To share the updates, you must update the link. You can do this by navigating to the **Sharing Preferences** option in the Zap editor and following the prompts.

You can share copies of Zaps with a link regardless of which pricing plan you subscribe to. If you have a Team or Company plan, however, you have the additional benefit of sharing Zaps and folders with team members in your Zapier account.

Sharing Zaps and folders in your Team or Company account

If you have a Team or Company plan account, you can share individual Zaps and folders that you own with members of your team. You can also transfer ownership of a Zap to another member of your team.

Sharing folders with your team

As we discussed earlier in this chapter, folders are managed from the left-side panel. To share a private folder, hover over a folder to show a clickable **three-dots icon**. Once this icon is clicked on, select **Share**. This will move the folder into the **Shared folders** section, and the folder will, by default, be shared with the team admin and team owner users. All team members will be able to view and edit any Zaps in shared folders.

> **Important note**
>
> You cannot unshare a folder. Once you have shared a private folder, if you want to remove sharing access, you need to move individual Zaps back into a private folder.

Next, let's review how to manage shared folders.

Managing shared folders

Once you have shared a folder, you can change sharing preferences in two places, as follows:

- **Left-side panel**: You can do this by clicking on the **three-dots icon** of any folder and selecting the **Share** option

- **Central panel**: From the **three-dots icon** drop-down menu (next to the + **Create** button), select the **Share folder** option

This is shown in the following screenshot:

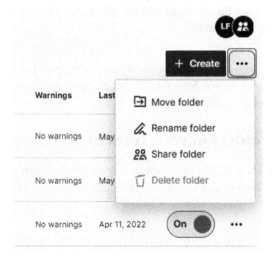

Figure 4.20 – Overview of the Share folder option in the central panel

Once selected, a popup will appear where you can then choose to share the folder with every user by choosing **Share with everyone** or select users by entering their names or email addresses in the search bar. If you have a Company account, you can also select groups of users in teams.

Transferring ownership of a Zap

You can identify the owner of a Zap as their abbreviated name will be displayed to the left of the **On/Off** toggle button in the individual Zap boxes. If you are the owner of the Zap, a team admin, or a team owner, you can transfer ownership of a Zap to another team member. You can do this by selecting a Zap, clicking on the **three-dots icon**, and then selecting the **Change ownership** option from the drop-down menu. You can then enter the name or email address of another member on the account to transfer Zap ownership. This is shown in the following screenshot:

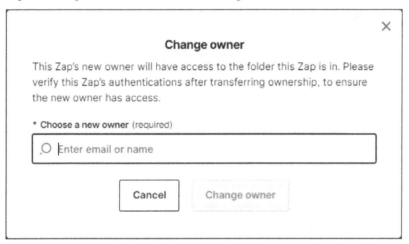

Figure 4.21 – Transferring ownership to another team member

Now, let's cover how to move your Zaps between personal and Team accounts.

Moving Zaps between personal and Team accounts

If you have a personal account and you are a member of a Team account, you can move individual Zaps and folders between accounts. You can do this by navigating to your Gravatar or initials in the top-right menu bar and selecting the **Move Zaps** option in the drop-down menu or by navigating to `https://zapier.com/app/move-zaps/`.

You can then select the personal account you want to transfer the Zap from and the Team account you wish to move it to, as shown in the following screenshot:

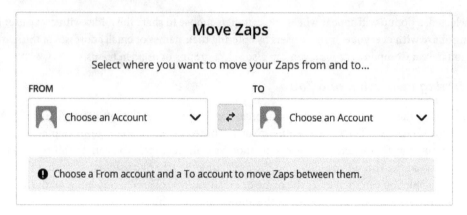

Figure 4.22 – Moving your Zaps from one account to another

You will be shown a list of folders and Zaps. You can then choose which individual Zaps or entire folders you might want to share, and select **Move these Zaps**.

> **Important note**
> Data transfer can take some time, depending on how many Zaps you are transferring. Ensure that you do not navigate away from the page while the transfer is in progress.

You should now have a better understanding of how to share copies of Zaps. In addition, you should know how to share individual Zaps and folders with your team.

Summary

In this chapter, we began by describing how to keep your workflows organized in the Zap management area by adequately naming them and using folders to sort them. We then discussed how to manage individual Zaps and covered the different Zap statuses. We explored managing your connected apps, and lastly, we discussed how to share your Zaps with your team and other Zapier users.

You now know about the best ways to manage and maintain your Zaps and app connections in your Zapier account, how to keep your workflows organized, as well as how to share them with your team or other Zapier users outside of your company.

In the next chapter, we will discuss how to best use Zap history information, and we will cover typical Zap behavior and the best ways to handle and troubleshoot errors. We will help you to manage Zap alerts by adjusting your account settings and by setting up a Zap with the **Zapier Manager** built-in app. We will also discuss the various channels of support available to users.

Questions

1. Name two ways that you can keep your Zaps well organized in your Zapier account.

2. Where can you add further details or notes about a Zap?

3. Which Zaps cannot be shared with external accounts?

5
Troubleshooting and Handling Zap Errors

As you get more familiar with Zapier and start to build complex workflows, you are likely to run into problems occasionally with your workflows. In general, when errors occur, they might originate from the way the Zap was set up, from issues with one of the apps in the workflow, or from general performance problems of the Zapier app itself. The best way to learn how to address these problems is to do some initial investigation work yourself before reaching out for additional help.

In this chapter, we will discuss the critical information that you will need to deal with unexpected errors when using Zapier. We will begin by discussing how to manage Zap error notifications by adjusting your account settings, and by setting up a Zap with the **Zapier Manager** built-in app. Then, we will cover how to manage app status alerts by monitoring the **Zapier Status** page, and by setting up a Zap with the **App Status by Zapier** built-in app. After, we will show you how to best use Zap history information to assess how your Zaps have run and to gather information to help with troubleshooting. Lastly, we will cover the channels available to seek additional support on the Zapier platform.

We will cover the following key topics in this chapter:

- Managing Zap error alerts
- Managing app status alerts
- Utilizing Zap history information for troubleshooting
- Finding help—help center, customer support, communities, experts, and workshops

Once you have worked through each of these topics, you will understand how Zapier processes data, know how to use Zap history for troubleshooting, and be able to adjust your alert notification preferences.

Technical requirements

To work through the content in this chapter, you will need access to a Zapier account. The Zapier **Free** plan will be adequate for most of the content in this chapter. To work through the *Managing Zap history data* section, you will need access to a **Starter** plan or higher for some parts and access to a **Professional** plan or higher for the content on the **Autoreplay** function. You can get access to the Zap templates used in this chapter here: `https://bit.ly/zapier-book`.

Managing Zap error alerts

One of the benefits of using a workflow automation tool such as Zapier is that your processes can run on autopilot while you focus on other things. You will, however, want to know when your workflows run into errors so that you can address any problems promptly, to ensure continuity. Zapier monitors all Zaps for performance when they are running. Whenever a fault is detected with the way any of your Zaps are expected to work, Zapier will highlight that a problem has occurred. The best way to monitor any problems with your workflows and deal with them quickly is to ensure you receive notifications when any issues arise.

You can manage the way you receive your alerts by doing the following:

- Adjusting your email notification settings
- Setting up an error alert workflow with the Zapier Manager built-in app

You will then be able to manage your alerts and take action in a more timely manner.

> **Tip**
> Using alerts with the Zapier Manager built-in app is particularly useful if you are the system administrator for the Zapier account and need to receive alerts because perhaps you don't have access to the Zapier account owner's emails to receive email notifications. It is also handy for Team or Company account users for the same reason.

Now, let's take a look at each method to manage alerts.

Adjusting your email notification settings

As standard, Zapier sends out email notifications for trigger and action error alerts, as well as for issues with connected apps in your Zaps. As discussed in *Chapter 1, Introduction to Business Process Automation with Zapier*, you can adjust the frequency of these alerts in the **Email Notification** area of your account settings. For Professional, Team, and Company accounts, custom error notification settings can be directly accessed via the **Custom error notifications** button in the **Zap history** area.

> **Tip**
> Although Zapier will include alerts relating to the connected apps in your workflows in email notifications, you may want to set up app-specific status alerts. This will give you timely information on incidents occurring with your connected apps. We will discuss this in more detail in the *Managing app status alerts* section.

Now, let's review how to use the Zapier Manager built-in app to trigger an alert workflow.

Setting up an error alert workflow with the Zapier Manager built-in app

You can customize the alerts that you want to receive notifications for by setting up a Zap with the Zapier Manager built-in app as a trigger. I will now explain how to set up a Zap error alert workflow using Zapier Manager as the trigger app and give you a few examples of apps and events that you could use for your action step. You can use the detailed steps we described in *Chapter 3*, *Building Your First Automated Workflow (Zap)*, to set up your Zap effectively.

Selecting your trigger event

Once you have navigated to the Zap editor, select the Zapier Manager built-in app to use in your trigger step. Next, select your chosen trigger event to use. The Zapier Manager built-in app has several trigger events to choose from; however, there are three trigger event options specific to managing errors. These are listed as follows:

- **New Zap Error**: You can select this trigger event if you want this alert workflow to trigger when one of your Zaps encounters an error.

- **New Halted Task**: You can select this trigger event if you want this Zap alert to trigger when one of your tasks in a workflow has the **Stopped Halted** status. We will discuss task statuses in the *Understanding task statuses* section.

- **Zap Turned Off**: You can select this trigger event if you want this alert workflow to trigger when one of your Zaps is turned off or paused by Zapier. This usually happens when a Zap is experiencing several errors repeatedly.

These options are shown in the following screenshot:

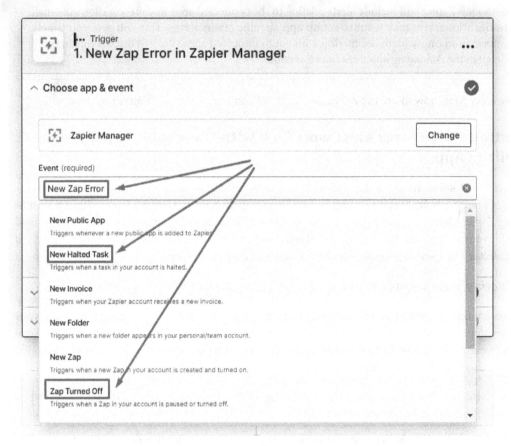

Figure 5.1 – Overview of setting up a Zapier Manager trigger

We will cover the other Zapier Manager trigger events in *Chapter 12, Managing Your Zapier Account with Built-In Apps*.

Customizing your trigger event

Next, customize the trigger event to specify the following:

- **Account**: If you are a member of multiple Team accounts, you can stipulate which account you want to receive alerts for.

- **Folder**: You can stipulate which specific folder you want to receive alerts for. If you specify a folder, this error alert workflow will trigger for all Zaps in that folder unless you specify a Zap in the next field.

- **Zap**: You can stipulate which specific Zap you want to receive alerts for.

None of these fields is required for the trigger to work, so if you want to receive alerts for all Zaps in all accounts, you can leave each of them blank.

Once you've customized your trigger event, you can confirm the sample data you want to use to test the trigger, test it, and move on to setting up your action step.

Now, let's discuss some examples of apps and events that you could use in your action step.

Setting up your error alert action step

After you have set up your trigger step, you can proceed to add one or more action steps and map the sample data to the relevant fields. To complete the workflow, we need to add an action step that will allow Zapier to send a notification to one or more people. Here are a few examples of communication apps and events we could use:

- Send a direct, private, or channel message to your team in **Slack**
- Send an email to you and your team using **Gmail**, **Microsoft Outlook**, or **Email by Zapier**
- Send an SMS to yourself using **SMS by Zapier**

If you're using a Starter plan or higher, you will be able to create multi-step Zaps and add extra steps to your workflow. You could then add further steps to add a log of all your Zap error alerts to a Google Sheets spreadsheet and create a task to review the alert in a task management app, such as Trello.

We've created a template of a Zap error alert with Slack as the notification app, a Google Sheets spreadsheet to record the history of alerts, and a Trello task to check the alert. You can get access to a copy of this Zap template here: `https://bit.ly/zapier-book`.

> **Tip**
> If you only want to receive notifications for error alerts that trigger using the Zapier Manager workflows you have built, remember to change your email notification settings to **Only Zapier Manager Trigger**.

You should now have a better understanding of how to adjust your notification settings and manage Zap error alerts using the Zapier Manager built-in app.

Now, let's take a look at how to manage app status alerts.

Managing app status alerts

In the previous section, we described how to manage Zap status alerts for issues arising with your Zap triggers, actions, and connected apps. When troubleshooting, you will also find it useful to understand how to find information on the overall performance of the Zapier app itself and see updates on any known issues with the connected apps in your workflow. This will help you to exclude these external issues when you begin to investigate problems with specific Zaps.

You can find information on Zapier app performance and manage app status alerts by doing the following:

- Monitoring the **Zapier Status** page
- Setting up an app status alert workflow with the App Status by Zapier built-in app

Let's take a look at each method.

Monitoring the Zapier Status page

When trying to investigate unexpected issues with your workflows, you will find it useful to check for incidents relating to how the Zapier app itself is functioning or any known problems with other connected apps in your workflow. The best place to check for known incidents is the **Zapier Status** page. You can navigate to this page using the following URL: `https://status.zapier.com/`.

The **Zapier Status** page is split into two sections focusing on summary information and then more detailed metrics and statuses.

In the **Summary** section, Zapier reports on known incidents that affect the following:

- **Website**: This relates to the `zapier.com` website where you manage your Zaps and associated tasks resulting from your running workflows
- **Zaps**: This relates to the general working of Zaps, including **Instant Triggers** (powered by Webhooks or other instant methods), **Polling Triggers** (powered by periodic polling), and **Searches & Writes** (actions such as searches, filters, and data writing)
- **Apps**: This relates to all apps that Zapier integrates with and provides general reporting on significant issues
- **Developer platform**: This relates to the Zapier developer platform

If any of those systems are not operational, Zapier will highlight this and specify the issue.

In the next section, Zapier reports in more detail on the following in separate tabs:

- **System Metrics**
- **App Status**
- **Incident History**

This is shown in the following screenshot:

Figure 5.2 – Overview of the Zapier Status page

Let's look at each of these.

The System Metrics tab

The **System Metrics** tab shows details of polling and instant trigger reliability and response times, as follows:

- **Trigger Reliability**: This signifies the success rate of an average Zap shown as a percentage
- **Polling Triggers Response Time**: This signifies the average speed of an average Zap powered by either polling or an instant trigger and is shown in milliseconds

> Important note
> The **Polling Triggers Response Time** value displayed does not include the polling time based on your pricing plan of either 1, 2, or 15 minutes. It purely reflects the response time once a new event is found by Zapier.

The metrics are displayed graphically, and you can select to show them by day, week, or month. You can also move your cursor along the graph to show an exact date and time with the metric, as shown in the following screenshot:

Figure 5.3 – Overview of graph of Polling Triggers Response Time metrics

System metrics are particularly useful when trying to understand whether a Zap error event is associated with the downtime and performance of Zapier and can help to exclude problems with a particular app. This is important to review alongside the information in the **Incident History** tab, as this will give more context to the problem.

The App Status tab

The **App Status** tab shows a list of apps demarcated in boxes displaying the following details for each:

- **App icon**: This shows the image that represents the app.

- **App name**: This shows the name of the app, displayed as a clickable link that will take you to the app profile page.

- **Response time**: This shows the app response time to Zapier queries in milliseconds.

- **Past hour**: This shows a graph of the app response time over the last hour.

- **More Options** menu: This is represented by an icon of three horizontal dots. If you click on this icon, you will be presented with the option to use pre-built workflows to create alerts using the App Status by Zapier built-in app. We will discuss this in more detail later in the *Setting up an app status alert workflow with the App Status by Zapier built-in app* section.

You can search for an app using the search bar just above the list of apps.

It is important to review **App Status** data alongside the information in the **Incident History** tab as this will give more context to the problem.

The Incident History tab

The **Incident History** tab shows a log of recent incidents by day and noted with the time of the last update. This log is especially useful if you are trying to trace back to the source of an issue or if you were experiencing problems with your Zaps on a specific day or period. You can click on the **Incident history** link at the bottom of the page or navigate to `https://status.zapier.com/history` to view historical incident history. You can use the back and forward arrows to scroll by month.

> **Tip**
> You can also subscribe to updates so that you are notified when Zapier creates a new incident and updates or resolves an existing incident. This is handy if you have access to multiple Zapier accounts and need to monitor issues. You can do this by clicking on the **Subscribe to Updates** button at the top of the **Zapier Status** page.

Now, let's review how to use the App Status by Zapier built-in app to trigger an app status alert workflow.

Setting up an app status alert workflow with the App Status by Zapier built-in app

You can set up custom workflows to alert you about issues with app statuses by using the App Status by Zapier built-in app as a trigger. You can build a Zap from scratch from within the Zap editor, or you can choose from three pre-built workflows directly from app boxes within the **App Status** tab on the **Zapier Status** page. We will now explain how to set up an app status alert workflow using App Status by Zapier from pre-built workflows. You can use the detailed steps we described in *Chapter 3, Building Your First Automated Workflow (Zap)*, to set up your Zap effectively.

Choosing which pre-built workflow to use

From the **Zapier Status** page, navigate to the **App Status** tab and search for the app you want to monitor using the search bar. Then, use the **More Options** icon to show the following drop-down menu of pre-built Zaps:

- **Slack Alert**: Choose this option to use a template that sends a Slack message as an action step. You can customize this step to send a direct, private, or channel message to your team in Slack.

- **SMS Alert**: Choose this option to use a template that sends an SMS as an action step. You can customize this step to send an SMS to yourself using SMS by Zapier.

- **Email Alert**: Choose this option to use a template that sends an outbound email as an action step. You can customize this step to send an email to you and your team using the Email by Zapier built-in app.

These options are shown in the following screenshot:

Figure 5.4 – App status for Salesforce displaying options for pre-built Zaps

Select an option, and you will be taken to the Zap editor where you can customize the template.

Next, let's review how to set up the App Status by Zapier built-in app to use in your trigger step.

Customizing your trigger event

App Status by Zapier has only one trigger event option, **New or Updated App Incident**. This event will trigger on new, updated, and resolved app status incidents. We can therefore move on to customizing your trigger event to specify the following:

- **App(s) to Monitor**: If you are using a template and have been directed from the **Zapier Status** page, the app you selected will show here. You can add multiple apps to the list by searching in consecutive fields. You can also reorder the apps by selecting, dragging, and dropping. You can leave this section blank if you want to receive alerts for all apps.

- **Status**: From the drop-down menu, select which statuses you want to receive alerts for. You can choose from **Scheduled**, **Investigating / In-Progress**, **Identified / In-Progress**, **Monitoring / Verifying**, and **Resolved / Completed**. You can add multiple statuses to the list by searching in consecutive fields. You can also reorder the statuses by selecting, dragging, or dropping. You can leave this section blank if you want the Zap to trigger alerts for all statuses.

This is shown in the following screenshot:

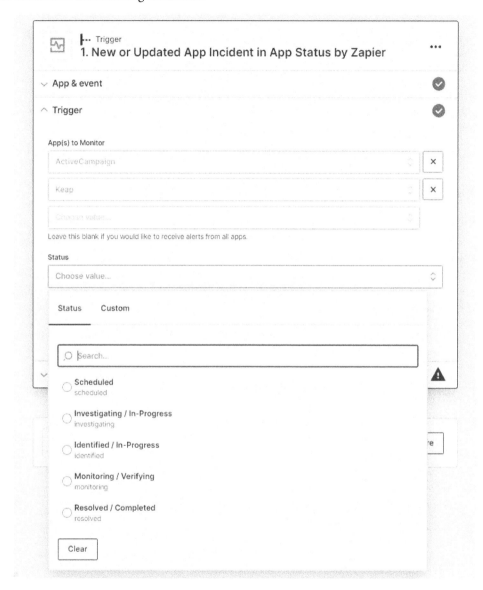

Figure 5.5 – Overview of customizing the App Status by Zapier trigger

Once you've customized your trigger event, you can confirm the sample data you want to use to test the trigger, then test it, and move on to setting up your action step.

Setting up your error alert action step

After you have set up your trigger step, you can proceed to customize your templated action step to your requirements. You can also add extra action steps if required.

We will discuss using SMS by Zapier and Email by Zapier in more detail in *Chapter 8, Built-In Communication Apps.*

You should now have a better understanding of how to review information on the **Zapier Status** page as well as how to manage your app status alerts using the App Status by Zapier built-in app.

Now, let's discuss how to troubleshoot errors by using Zap history information.

Utilizing Zap history information for troubleshooting

So far in this chapter, we have helped you to understand how to manage Zap error and app status alerts so that you can act promptly on any issues that arise. In addition, we've discussed how to assess the information that Zapier provides on the **Zapier Status** page, as having this information to hand will help you to exclude the impact of external issues when investigating problems with individual Zaps. Next, we will discuss how to troubleshoot errors with your individual Zaps by using the information available on the **Zap history** page.

Let's get started with understanding what Zap history is and how you can use it when troubleshooting problems with your workflows.

Understanding the Zap history page

The **Zap history** page provides you with a detailed log of the activities of all of your Zaps. This log shows a list of all Zaps that have triggered successfully when new data has been found in the trigger app. It also shows action steps in a Zap that have been successfully completed and those that have not. The **Zap history** page captures all the data that passes in and out of each of the steps in a Zap when triggered successfully. It also shows task usage. Being able to view this information is extremely useful when troubleshooting unexpected events that have happened with your workflows, as well as when assessing your task usage per Zap.

> **Important note**
> Zapier only guarantees to keep Zap history information for a maximum of one month. It is therefore important to review issues as promptly as possible or download history periodically. We will discuss downloading Zap history data in the *Managing Zap history data* section.

The **Zap history** page can be found by doing the following:

- Clicking on the **Zap History** link in the left navigation sidebar

- Clicking on the **History** link in the three-dots drop-down menu of individual Zap rows within the Zap management area

- Clicking on the **Zap History** clock icon link in the right-side panel in the Zap editor

- Navigating to `https://zapier.com/app/history`

Navigating from the main dashboard or using the URL will take you to the **Zap history** log page showing a list view of workflow events as well as task usage. Navigating from a Zap (either from the Zap title link box in the Zap management area or from within the Zap editor) will take to you the default **Task usage** tab. Clicking on the **Zap runs** tab will show a filtered list of task history for that specific Zap.

The **Zap runs** tab on the **Zap history** page in the list view is shown in the following screenshot:

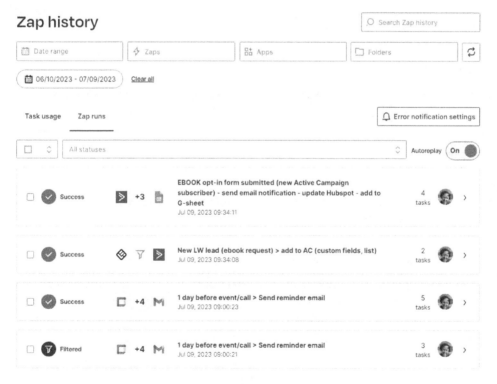

Figure 5.6 – Overview of the Zap history page list view

Let's now discuss the navigation options on the **Zap history** page.

Navigating the Zap history page

The **Zap history** page is split into two tabs, as follows:

- **Task usage**
- **Zap runs**

Let's look at each of these.

The Task usage tab

The **Task usage** tab is the default view when navigating to the **Zap history** page and shows a list of your Zaps with task information related to each of them, as follows:

- **App icons**: This shows you the icons of apps involved in each consecutive step of the workflow. Up to three app icons will be displayed, so if there are more than three steps involved in the Zap, the apps in the first and last steps of the Zap will be shown plus a number depicting the additional app steps in between.

- **Zap details**: This shows you the title of the Zap, whether the Zap is turned **On** or **Off**, and the time and date when it last ran.

- **Tasks used**: This shows you how many tasks have been used in the previous 30 days.

> Tip
> When performing a continuous improvement review of your Zaps, the information you see in the **Task usage** tab is really useful for gaining insight into which of your Zaps have high task usage. This information will help you to prioritize which Zaps to review first to assess whether you can remove steps to reduce task usage. You can gain further insight by navigating to the **View Zap details** screen from the three-dots drop-down menu on the Zap block.

- **Gravatar or initials**: This identifies the owner of the Zap.

- **The three-dots icon**: If you click on this icon, you will be presented with three options. If you click on **Edit**, you will be taken to the Zap editor where you can edit that Zap. If you click on **View Details**, you can see the detailed Zap information page. If you click on **View Runs**, you will be taken to the Zap history filtered specifically for that Zap.

You can sort the list of Zaps by clicking on the arrow icons in the respective headers, where **Zap details** is sorted alphanumerically, and **Tasks used** is sorted numerically.

> Important note
> The **Task usage** tab should only be used as a reference and may not accurately represent actual usage. For accurate information, you should refer to your monthly invoices.

Now, let's have a look at the **Zap runs** tab.

The Zap runs tab

The **Zap runs** tab shows the history of the individual Zap workflow events that have run, with the most recent one at the top. Each workflow event is displayed with the following information in the list view:

- **Checkbox**: This allows you to select a specific workflow event and delete, download, or replay the event. We will discuss how to use the checkbox in the *Managing Zap history data* section.

- **Task status icon**: This shows an icon of the status of the workflow event running. We will look at task statuses in more detail in the *Understanding task statuses* section.

- **App icons**: This shows you the icons of apps involved in each consecutive step of the workflow. This is similar to what is shown in the **Task usage** tab.

- **Zap details**: This shows you the title of the Zap and the time and date when the workflow event ran.

- **Tasks used**: This shows you how many tasks were used when the workflow event ran.

- **Gravatar or initials**: This identifies the owner of the Zap.

- **Forward arrow icon**: If you click on this icon, you will be taken to a detailed view of the workflow event. We will discuss this in the *Viewing detailed Zap run information* section.

An example of a workflow event in the **Zap runs** tab is shown in the following screenshot:

Figure 5.7 – Overview of the Zap runs tab

10 workflow events are shown per page, and you can scroll through the pages by using the arrow buttons at the bottom of the **Zap runs** tab.

You will also find the following options just above the list of workflow events:

- **Checkbox icon**: You can use this dropdown to select or deselect workflow events in bulk. We will discuss using this checkbox for downloading, deleting, and replaying tasks in the *Managing Zap history data* section.

- **Task status**: You can use the drop-down list function to filter your Zap history log by task status. We will look at task statuses in more detail in the *Understanding task statuses* section.

- **Autoreplay On/Off toggle button**: You can turn the **Autoreplay** function **On** or **Off** using this toggle button. We will review using the **Autoreplay** feature in more detail in the *Managing Zap history data* section.

Now, let's discuss how to view workflow events by filtering and searching.

Viewing workflow events as a list, searching, and filtering

The default view is to show all workflow events with the most recent event at the top of the list. You can use the search bar to search for workflow events by keyword. For example, you might want to find all workflow events that occurred that used the name `Joe Bloggs`, the email address `joebloggs@abcompany.com`, or file ID `12345`. If you want to clear the search, hit the **X** icon in the search bar.

You can also filter workflow events using multiple filter options, as follows:

- **Date range**: This filter allows you to select a date range relating to when workflow events ran. For example, you could filter to show workflow events for last week. Bear in mind that workflow events more than one month old will not be shown.

- **Zaps**: This filter allows you to select one or more Zaps from a drop-down list to show only workflow events that originate from that Zap.

- **Apps**: This filter allows you to search for one or more apps and select them to filter workflow events for Zaps using that app.

- **Folders**: This filter allows you to select one or more folders from a drop-down list to show only workflow events for Zaps housed in that folder.

- **Owners**: This filter allows you to select one or more Zap owners when using a Team or Company account.

Another filter highlighted by **All status** can be used to select multiple options to show workflow events with those task statuses. For example, you could filter to show only workflow events that were successful or were filtered and stopped. We will look at task statuses in more detail in the next section, *Understanding task statuses*.

You can use the **Refresh** icon button to refresh the page with new results or the **Clear all filters** button to remove the filters and list all workflow events. You can also clear individual filter fields by hitting the **X** icon in any of the fields.

> **Tip**
>
> As we discussed in *Chapter 4*, *Managing Your Zaps*, if you have a large number of Zaps, ensuring that you label them adequately can help you to quickly identify them and associated workflow events in Zap history. Using numbers, letters, and Roman numerals often helps to break the monotony of word descriptions in Zap names, which can help to easily identify them visually in the **Zap runs** tab and by sorting them in the **Task usage** tab.

Now, let's discuss the different task statuses you are likely to see in Zap history.

Understanding task statuses

When you view your Zap history, you are likely to see workflow events listed with one or more of the following task statuses:

- **Success**: This indicates that the Zap ran, and all tasks in that workflow event were completed successfully.

- **Filtered**: This indicates that the Zap ran but had a filter at some point in the workflow that prevented it from continuing to process later steps in that workflow event.

- **Stopped**: This indicates that the Zap experienced an error while it was running that workflow event. Workflow events can have a task status of **Stopped Errored**, meaning that an issue occurred with the Zap running, or **Stopped Halted**, meaning that Zapier stopped a task from executing. **Errored** statuses one after another will cause Zapier to pause or turn off the Zap, whereas **Halted** statuses do not cause this to happen.

- **Waiting**: This indicates that the workflow event is waiting to be completed because it has a **Delay** action step or is scheduled to replay using the **Autoreplay** function. If the Zap has a **Delay** step, the status will be highlighted as **Waiting Delayed**. If the workflow event is scheduled to be run again using the **Autoreplay** function, the status will be highlighted as **Waiting Scheduled**.

- **Playing**: This indicates that the workflow event is still in progress.

- **Holding**: This indicates that the workflow event is being held for one of several reasons.

Let's review the reasons for **Holding** task statuses.

Reasons for a task status of Holding

Workflow events may show a status of **Holding** for the following reasons:

- **High task use**: Multiple (100 or more) workflow events have triggered at the same time. Zapier uses this mechanism as a preventative measure to stop a high volume of tasks running until you have confirmed that you want to play the tasks. This prevents high task usage. It also prevents the possibility of you having to correct a large number of potentially incorrect records as a result.

- **The app needs to be reconnected**: The named app has disconnected and must be reconnected before you can replay any held tasks. You can reconnect the app from the **My Apps** page.

- **Upgrade needed**: Your account has surpassed its limit for Zaps, tasks, or Premium apps. If the upgrade is related to tasks, you will need to upgrade your plan before you can replay your tasks. Alternatively, you can delete held tasks or assess your number of Zaps and Premium apps instead of upgrading.

- **Payment issue**: Your billing payment method has expired. You will need to update your payment method before you can replay your tasks.

We will discuss how to delete or replay tasks that have been held in the *Managing Zap history data* section.

Now, let's discuss how to view detailed Zap run information related to individual workflow events.

Viewing detailed Zap run information

Being able to view detailed task information is the biggest benefit of the **Zap history** log. Having access to this information allows you to drill down to the specific causes of unexpected events. We'll cover the following key points in this section:

- Navigating detailed **Zap runs** pages
- Assessing step data
- Understanding **Data in** and **Data out** information

Let's review each one.

Navigating detailed Zap runs pages

You can access the detailed task information by clicking on an individual workflow event in the **Zap runs** log. An example of a detailed task information page is shown in the following screenshot:

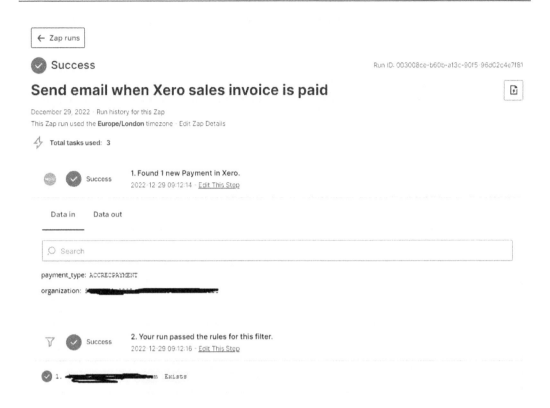

Figure 5.8 – Overview of a detailed Zap information page

Detailed **Zap runs** pages show the following information:

- **Status icon**: The overall task status for that workflow event.

- **Run ID:** This string signifies the ID for the workflow event and is displayed in the URL as well as in the top right-hand corner where it can be copied to your clipboard if you click on it.

> **Important note**
> **Run ID** is an important identifier that allows you to reference specific workflow events when communicating with Zapier customer support.

- **Zap name**: The name of the Zap.

- **Date**: The date the workflow event started to run. You can view the filtered task history log for the Zap by clicking on the link labeled **Run history for this Zap**.

- **Time zone**: The time zone associated with the Zap—for example, America/Denver. You can edit the time zone for the Zap by clicking on the link labeled **Edit Zap Settings**.

- **Total tasks used**: The number of tasks used in the execution of the Zap run.

- **Step data**: The history of all the data flowing in and out of each trigger and action step in the Zap is shown in separate tabs labeled **Data in** and **Data out**.

From within **Stopped** tasks, you will be able to access help documentation about errors by clicking on the **Troubleshoot error** button. This is shown in the following screenshot:

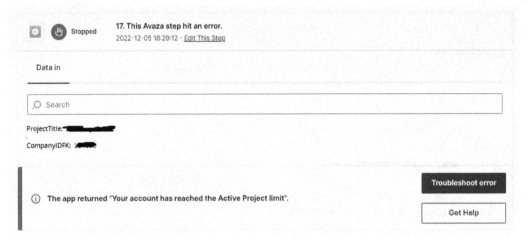

Figure 5.9 – Overview of accessing documentation and help from Stopped tasks

You will also see a **Get Help** button, which can be used to raise a customer support query, which prepopulates with the related Zap and specific task ID information.

You can navigate back to the **Zap runs** log by clicking on the **back arrow** icon at the top of the page.

> **Tip**
> You can use the magic of AI to troubleshoot Zap runs with Stopped Errored statuses in specific steps. We will cover AI-powered troubleshooting in more detail in *Chapter 19, AI and Automation*.

Now, let's review how to assess step data.

Assessing step data

Each step in a Zap will be shown on the detailed task information page and demarcated by a box showing the following information:

- **App icon**: This shows the app icon for the connected app for each step.

- **Task status**: This shows the status icon of each task. The status icon for individual tasks may be different from others in the workflow event.

- **Step number and result**: This shows the step number as configured in the Zap editor as well as the result of the trigger or action running in Zapier. For example, if your Zap triggers on receipt of a new email matching a search in Gmail, your trigger step number and result may show `1. Found 1 new Email Matching Search in Gmail`.

- **Date and time**: This shows the date and time that each step started in the workflow. This information is very useful for identifying when events occurred.

- **Edit this step link**: You can click this link to edit the step in the Zap within the Zap editor.

- **Data in** tab: This displays all the data that was sent to the connected app for any given step. This tab will not be shown in **Filter** and **Path** steps.

- **Data out** tab: This displays all the data received by a connected app for any given step. This tab will not be shown in **Filter** and **Path** steps.

The **Data in** and **Data out** tabs hold crucial information about data that has passed through Zapier. Let's look at this next.

Understanding Data in and Data out information

There are a few things that you may want to make a note of when reviewing **Data in** and **Data out** information, as follows:

- Connected apps generally provide information on data that was added and received by the app, which is posted in the **Data out** tab. However, there are some cases where a connected app does not post any information, and you may not see any data in this tab.

- You may find data posted to your action apps denoted by curly brackets—for example, `{{text}}`. This normally signifies that data for that field from the previous step that you have mapped in the Zap editor is missing. You can find this string in the **Data in** tab of your action step. You can address this by finding the correct field to use in the **Data out** tab of your previous step and remapping the field in the Zap editor with new sample data from the trigger.

- You can enter keywords in the search bar to find specific information. This is useful when you want to find specific data that will identify what may have happened in a step when the Zap ran.

- **Filter** and **Path** steps do not show **Data in** or **Data out** information in tabs; they only display whether the conditions of the filter have been met or not.

> Tip
>
> As we discussed in *Chapter 1, Introduction to Business Process Automation with Zapier*, ensure that your time zone is specified in your account settings so that dates and times are displayed according to that. This will help when you are trying to pinpoint when errors might have occurred on a timeline. You can also specify specific time zones applicable to that Zap within **Settings** in the Zap editor.

Now that you are able to assess Zap history data, let's review how best to manage your Zap history.

Managing Zap history data

Zapier allows you to delete, download, play, or replay tasks in the Zap history log individually or in bulk if you are using a paid Zapier pricing plan. If you want to select or deselect workflow events in bulk, you can use the **checkbox** icon options as follows:

- **Select shown**: This allows you to select only workflow events shown on that specific page (up to 10).

- **Select all (5000 at a time)**: This allows you to select all available workflow events displayed. You can use filters to display events you want to manage.

- **Deselect all**: This allows you to deselect all selected checkboxes in bulk.

> **Important note**
> Use filters to display a list of workflow events that you want to select ahead of using the **checkbox** icon options. This is especially important if you are using the **Delete** function as using **Select all (5000 at a time)** will select the entire history if no filter is applied.

Selected workflow events will display a blue checkbox, and the workflow event box will be highlighted. When any workflow event(s) have been selected, the following options will be highlighted:

- **Play x**: The **Play** button will only be displayed if you are managing workflow events with the **Holding** status as these workflows have not run yet. Clicking this button will allow you to manually run these workflows.

- **Replay x**: Clicking this button will allow you to manually replay any tasks with the **Stopped Errored** or **Stopped Halted** status. The **Replay** button will not be displayed for held tasks. Using the **Replay** function will only replay any steps in the Zap that have failed or have been unsuccessful and not the entire workflow event. For example, you may have two action steps in your Zap—the first to add a new deal to your **customer relationship management (CRM)** system, and the second to send an email. If the first step is successful but the second has failed, the **Replay** function will only attempt to replay the second, so as to send an email.

- **Delete x**: Clicking this button will permanently delete any selected workflow events. Deleting successfully played tasks from the **Zap history** does not reduce your task usage in a billing period. This feature is, however, useful for deleting held tasks that you do not want to play.

- **Download x**: Clicking this button will allow you to generate a detailed .csv file, which will be emailed to the email address associated with your profile and accessible by a link that expires in seven days. You can download up to 5,000 workflow events at one time; however, you can contact Zapier support if you want to download more. It is recommended that you download your **Zap history** regularly as Zapier only keeps 30 days of history.

Each of the buttons will be shown with the number of workflow events selected in place of the **X** icon.

Now, let's look at how to automatically replay your failed tasks using the **Autoreplay** feature.

Using the Autoreplay feature

We have already discussed how to replay tasks manually. If you are using a Professional plan or higher, you will have access to the **Autoreplay** feature, which allows you to automatically replay failed tasks due to temporary errors or downtime. You can switch on this feature by using the **Autoreplay On/Off** toggle button, as shown in the following screenshot:

Figure 5.10 – Overview of locating the Autoreplay On/Off toggle button

Let's explore how the **Autoreplay** function works.

How the Autoreplay function works

Once you have turned the **Autoreplay** function **On**, if a step in a workflow event fails, Zapier will attempt to retry it up to five times using the following schedule: after 5 minutes, after another 30 minutes, after another 1 hour, after another 3 hours, and finally after another 6 hours. Therefore, the last attempt to replay the task would be 10 hours and 35 minutes after the original error occurred. Zapier would not send error emails or trigger Zapier Manager until all replay attempts in the schedule had been completed, and only if the task failed to replay on the final attempt. During this time, you will not be able to manually replay a task, and all tasks that are being replayed or are scheduled to be replayed will display a status of **Waiting Scheduled**. The **Autoreplay** function will only start when the workflow event experiences errors; however, any tasks that have a status of **Halted**, **Errored**, and **Filtered** will be replayed. Triggers will never show as errored and do not replay because of the mechanism used for finding new data.

While the replay schedule is running, you can make small changes to your Zap to attempt to address any errors, and the **Autoreplay** function will incorporate these changes into the next scheduled replay. If, however, your Zap is switched off at the exact time the next replay is due or the **Autoreplay** function is turned off, all further scheduled attempts will be canceled.

Let's now take a look at how to interpret why tasks have not replayed.

Understanding why tasks have not replayed

You may find that after manually replaying tasks or when using the **Autoreplay** function, some of your tasks have still not replayed. This might happen if your Zap has been turned **Off** or is paused, if it has been deleted, or if significant changes have been made to it since the error occurred (as opposed to small adjustments). Zapier will send you notifications to remind you that tasks can be replayed before the replay time expires. Zap runs over 30 days old, those that have already successfully run, and those that are replaying or scheduled to be replayed cannot be replayed.

An example of how to troubleshoot an error can be seen in this *ZapConnect* video recording at `https://community.zapier.com/troubleshooting-99/troubleshooting-your-zaps-session-from-zapconnect-2021-18274`.

In this section, we've reviewed how to use the **Zap history** page when troubleshooting problems. We discussed task statuses, detailed Zap information, and how to manage your Zap history data.

You should now have a better understanding of how to use Zap history information effectively to troubleshoot problems with your workflow events. Now, let's take a look at how to find help on the Zapier platform.

Finding help – help center, customer support, communities, experts, and workshops

Once you have done some initial investigations to troubleshoot errors in your Zaps and workflow events, you will find it useful to know where to look for additional help on the Zapier platform. Zapier provides you with several ways to get assistance, ranging from do-it-yourself information finding to hands-on support. There are a few ways in which you can get help on the Zapier platform, such as the following:

- Finding app-specific help in app profiles
- Utilizing the Zapier help center
- Engaging with the Zapier community
- Reaching out to Zapier customer support
- Hiring a Zapier certified expert
- Courses, workshops, and privately hosted communities

These options are available to all users of Zapier regardless of which pricing plan subscription you use.

Let's explore each of these.

Finding app-specific help in app profiles

As we discussed in *Chapter 2, Preparing to Automate Your Processes*, each app that integrates with Zapier is listed in the Zapier ecosystem directory, and each app has an app profile. Under the **Help** tab of an app's app profile, you will find articles relating to common support issues raised by users. Many popular apps will have three popular articles listed in their app profiles, as follows:

- *How to get started with (app name)*
- *Common problems with (app name)*
- *Tips and tricks with (app name)*

If you're looking to solve a problem related to a specific app, this is an excellent place to start. It's also handy to know in advance the issues you may come across with your apps by researching this information when you first start using the app in your workflows.

Utilizing the Zapier help center

Another place to look when you have a problem with your workflows is to search for related solutions in the Zapier **help center**. The help center provides you with comprehensive articles on all aspects of troubleshooting. You can use the search bar on the main **Help** page to enter your search keywords and terms. Some articles also provide information in the form of videos and tutorials.

The help center is accessible as follows:

- The **Get Help** button in the lower right-hand corner (on some pages)
- The **Get Help** icon in the left sidebar
- The **Help** link in the footer menu
- The **Get Help** button in the **Zap history** area within stopped steps or at the bottom of individual detailed task histories
- The **Help** link in the right-hand panel in the Zap editor
- By navigating to `https://help.zapier.com/`

Some of these are shown in the following screenshot:

Figure 5.11 – Navigation to the help center

There is also a **Get Help** link at the bottom of the section that navigates to the **Zapier Customer Support** page.

For specific information on troubleshooting, you can navigate to `https://help.zapier.com/hc/en-us/sections/14037787600653-Troubleshoot-Zaps`. You will find articles of particular interest that will help you address specific error notifications, such as those involving status codes.

Engaging with the Zapier community

The **Zapier community** forum is a brilliant way to search for particular and niche solutions to problems. You can also post details of your issue, and members of the community will respond with helpful suggestions and comments. It is even a great place to interact with other Zapier users, Zapier customer support staff, developers, and experts.

At the bottom of the main **Help Center** page and on each help article, you will find a link to the Zapier community. You can also click on the **Ask the Community** link at the bottom of the dashboard, as shown in *Figure 5.11*, and navigate there using `https://community.zapier.com`.

Reaching out to Zapier customer support

Sometimes you might need some additional, more personalized help to address issues you might be having with your workflows. The **Zapier customer support** team offers a free email support service to all Zapier users and typically responds within a few hours of you submitting the query, regardless of your time zone, ensuring problems are addressed promptly. They have access to more detailed backend information than what you will be able to see from **Zapier Status** page updates and alerts. If you use a Team and Company plan, you will have access to premier support, meaning that your support queries are likely to be responded to and sorted out quicker than with regular support.

> Tip
>
> When reaching out to Zapier customer support, give as much context as you can. Provide screenshots or video walk-throughs of the issue along with multiple examples from the **Zap history**, if possible. Detail what you have tried to rectify the issue, and be clear and specific. This will reduce the chances of miscommunication.

At the bottom of the main **Help Center** page and on each help article, you will find a link to the Zapier support page. You can also navigate there using `https://zapier.com/app/get-help`.

Users of Company accounts will also be able to reach Zapier customer support using the **Live Chat** option available in their accounts.

Hiring a Zapier Certified Expert

When you need help with troubleshooting really specific issues and have tried all other support avenues, you can hire a **Zapier Certified Expert**. They are individuals or agencies that have gone through Zapier's certification program and are endorsed by Zapier to offer charged support to Zapier users. Zapier Certified Experts are listed on the **Zapier Expert Directory** and are given a badge to display on their websites and social media channels. As they are all independent consultants, there will be nuances in their backgrounds, experience, and service offerings; however, they generally offer training, technical support, and advanced workflow-building services. Most Zapier Certified Experts are likely to offer a one-on-one experience such as phone and video conferencing support.

At the bottom of the main **Help Center** page and on each help article, you will find a link to the Zapier Expert Directory. You can also click on the **Hire an Expert** link at the bottom of the dashboard, as shown in *Figure 5.11*, and navigate there using `https://zapier.com/experts`. These independent consultants that are listed have been given Zapier's official stamp of approval as certified experts. There are currently fewer than 100 certified Zapier experts in the world, specializing in different business areas and applications. For example, Solvaa Automation Academy & Consulting is in the top 15 of listed certified experts, and their listing can be viewed by navigating to `https://zapier.com/experts/solvaa-automation-academy-consulting`.

Courses, workshops, and privately hosted communities

If you need extra help with your learning journey, consider doing a vetted course or workshop or joining a hosted community dedicated to no-code business process automation with Zapier.

Zapier University and YouTube channels

Zapier has created a number of learning options that will help you to achieve your automation learning goals. These are listed as follows:

- **Zapier University**: You can access two streams of learning in *Zapier 101*, which explains some of the fundamentals of using Zapier, and *Zapier 102*, where you can learn some more advanced skills. You can access Zapier University courses by clicking on the **Learning Center** link at the bottom of the dashboard, as shown in *Figure 5.11*, and navigating there using `https://zapier.com/university`.

- **Zapier's YouTube channels**: You can get access to a range of videos on Zapier's main YouTube channel, which can be accessed at `https://www.youtube.com/@Zapier`, and the *Zapier Academy* YouTube channel, which can be accessed at `https://www.youtube.com/@ZapierAcademy`.

Solvaa Automation Academy

Solvaa Automation Academy has a range of courses and live workshops to help you get to grips with business process streamlining, improvement, and automation. You can also learn about best practices for digital transformation, process improvement fundamentals, process mapping, documenting processes in **standard operating procedures** (**SOPs**), and finding the right apps for your business. Learn using pre-recorded videos, audio content in private student-only podcasts, live workshops, and Q&A sessions.

You can also get support from the Solvaa Automation Academy coaches and trainers and other automation enthusiasts in the hosted community to help you along your automation-mastering journey. Navigate there using `https://academy.solvaa.com`. You should now have a better understanding of the different support options available to you as a Zapier user.

Summary

In this chapter, we covered essential information required to troubleshoot errors when using Zapier. We started by covering how to manage error alerts using email notifications and by using the Zapier Manager built-in app. Next, we covered how to manage app status alerts by monitoring the **Zapier Status** page and by using the App Status by Zapier built-in app. We then looked at using Zap history information in detail to help you to troubleshoot problems with Zaps, apps, and individual data issues. Lastly, we reviewed the channels available to get extra support on the Zapier platform.

You now know how to manage your alerts by updating your email notification preferences and how to understand information on the **Zapier Status** page. You also now know how to create alert workflows using the Zapier Manager and App Status by Zapier built-in apps and how to understand Zap history information to help with troubleshooting errors. Lastly, you now know how to find help on the Zapier platform.

In the next chapter, you will learn how to set up and customize multi-step Zaps, how to use the all-important search functionality of Zapier, and how to duplicate and reorder your steps. You will also be introduced to the most commonly used built-in Zapier apps, and you will be able to test your knowledge by building your first multi-step Zap.

Questions

1. Name two Zapier built-in apps that can help you to manage error and maintenance alerts in your Zapier account.

2. Which three native features of Zapier will help you with troubleshooting errors?

3. What are six ways you can find additional help when troubleshooting?

Part 2: Customizing Your Zaps with Built-in Apps by Zapier – Functionality and Practical Uses

When this part is complete, you will understand the functionality of the Zapier platform, how to customize your Zaps using Zapier's built-in apps, and how to create your first multi-step Zap. We will discuss the functionality of built-in apps, teach you practical tips on how to use them, with examples, and you will be able to test your knowledge with a few exercises.

This part contains the following chapters:

- *Chapter 6, Creating Multi-Step Zaps and Using Built-in Apps*
- *Chapter 7, Getting Started with Built-in Apps*
- *Chapter 8, Built-In Communication Apps*
- *Chapter 9, Exploring Built-In Apps for Extracting and Compiling Data*
- *Chapter 10, Other Useful Built-In Apps by Zapier*
- *Chapter 11, Advanced Built-In Apps by Zapier*
- *Chapter 12, Managing Your Zapier Account with Built-in Apps*
- *Chapter 13, Newly Released Apps and Features*

6

Creating Multi-Step Zaps and Using Built-In Apps

As you become more comfortable with using Zapier to automate your business workflows, you will find that in many situations, you may need more flexibility than what single-step workflows can offer. You will start to build more complex workflows, which will allow you to automate multiple action steps in your processes involving tasks in various apps. You may find that often, the data you need to use in subsequent actions is not available in the trigger and existing action steps. In these cases, you will need to know how to use search action events to retrieve data. To complement using triggers and actions, you may also want to customize your Zaps further by using the myriad of built-in tools that Zapier has created to allow you to transform and manipulate data, all from within the Zapier platform.

In *Chapter 3*, *Building Your First Automated Workflow (Zap)*, we covered the basics of how to create a single-step Zap. In this chapter, we will build on the knowledge you have gained and discuss how to develop multi-step Zaps using multiple actions and searches and introduce you to the various built-in apps created by Zapier. We will begin by covering how to create multi-step Zaps by recapping using action steps and adding search steps. Then, we will explore how to delete, duplicate, reorder, and rename steps in Zaps. You will also be able to test your knowledge with an exercise involving a multi-step Zap. Then, we will briefly introduce the functionality of all the built-in apps by Zapier, all of which will be covered in detail in subsequent chapters.

We will cover the following key topics in this chapter:

- Creating multi-step Zaps with multiple action and search steps
- Deleting, duplicating, reordering, and renaming steps
- Introducing apps by Zapier

Once you have worked through each of these topics, you will know how to create a multi-step Zap and use the search functionality in your action steps. You will also have a better understanding of the basic functionality of all of Zapier's built-in apps.

Technical requirements

To work through the content in this chapter, you will need access to a Zapier account. To build multi-step Zaps, you will need to subscribe to the Zapier Starter plan as a minimum. You can get access to the Zap templates used in this chapter here: `https://bit.ly/zapier-book`. Using these templates will help you visualize how the process works.

Creating Zaps with multiple action and search steps

In *Chapter 3, Building Your First Automated Workflow (Zap),* we walked through a step-by-step process to create our first single-step Zap. In *Chapter 5, Troubleshooting and Handling Zap Errors,* we used this knowledge to create alert Zaps using Zapier Manager and App Status by Zapier. Now that you've experienced first-hand what Zapier can offer in just a single-step workflow, it's time to explore the infinite automation possibilities of multi-step workflows to power your productivity.

As we discussed in *Chapter 3, Building Your First Automated Workflow (Zap),* once you have set up your trigger step, you can add actions, searches, filters, and delays after the trigger and between any action step, and add paths at the end, using the + icon.

> **Important note**
>
> You can add up to 99 action steps to a Zap; however, for control purposes, it is better to have shorter workflows and to break your process down into more manageable Zaps where possible.

We will discuss how to add filters, delays, and paths to your workflows later in *Chapter 7, Getting Started with Built-In Apps,* when we will explore some of Zapier's built-in apps. Before we do that, though, we need to understand how to use the search functionality in our action steps. Search functionality allows you to dynamically look up data that may not be present in your trigger and existing action steps. This is possible if the app you intend to use to search for data has search action events available through the integration.

> **Important note**
>
> Many apps offer you the option of searching for data. It's difficult to express in words the usefulness of search action functionality. It gives the user the ability to extract information that you might not have available from the trigger steps or previous action steps. A common example would be when you make a sale in **Shopify** and you're given the product ID of the product associated with the sale. Here, you might want to search for other information associated with the product to then use in other steps.

There are two ways to add **search** action steps to your Zaps:

- Using the + icon

- By going to a **Choose value…** field and using the **Custom** header option

Let's look at each in turn. As we progress through this section, you will see that many of the examples and screenshots refer to **Pipedrive CRM**. We've used this example as it illustrates the search action functionality well. Bear in mind that many apps have search action functionality, which you can utilize as required.

Adding a search step using the + icon

If the app you are using has search action events available through the integration, they will be denoted by **Find…**, plus the item. For example, in Pipedrive, the following search action events are available:

- **Find Person**

- **Find Lead**

- **Find User**

- **Find Organization**

- **Find Deal**

- **Find Activity**

- **Find Product**

- **Find Product(s)**

Searches are most commonly performed using unique identifiers for items, such as names, email addresses, subjects, codes, and record IDs. Most apps with search action event integrations will allow multiple ways to search for items.

> **Important note**
>
> A common mistake that many users make is to search by the "name" associated with a record ID. Record IDs are generally the best way to search for an item as in most cases, record IDs are unique between items in an app. For example, in a CRM, duplicates may exist for a contact that may have variations in data; however, only one record ID will exist to differentiate between those duplicates.

Let's use an example to illustrate implementing a search action event. We will use an altered version of the working example from *Chapter 3*, *Building Your First Automated Workflow (Zap)*, where we will change the trigger app to Pipedrive and the trigger event will be **New Deal**. In this case, we may want to add the contact's full name as well as their first and last name to columns in our Google Sheets spreadsheet. When we try to search for the person's first name, we see that the data that pulls through from the trigger step only presents the contact's full name. This is shown in the following screenshot:

Figure 6.1 – Overview of searching by first name yielding no results

In this case, as the Pipedrive integration has a **Find Person** search action event, we can add a search action step between our trigger and the existing action step to retrieve these details. We can do this by clicking the + icon.

> **Tip**
> Another option would be to add a step using the Zapier built-in app Formatter by Zapier. Here, you can add a **Text** action event with a **Split Text** transform option to split the text in the Person Name data so that you can extract the first and last names. We will cover the Formatter by Zapier text splitting function in *Chapter 17*, *Text Formatting Functions in Zapier – Part 2*.

Next, we can add Pipedrive as our app and **Find Person** as our action event, as shown in the following screenshot:

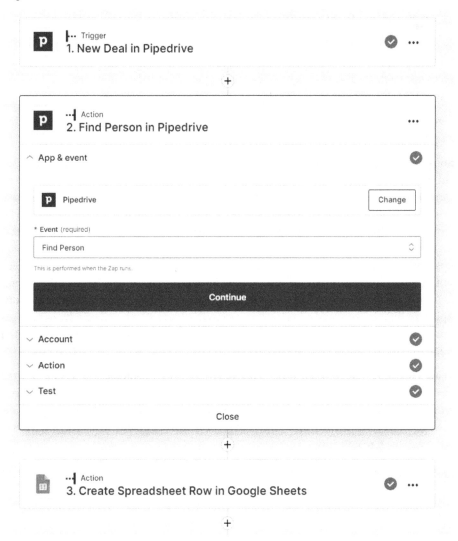

Figure 6.2 – Overview of the Find Person action event

After adding this to our Pipedrive account, we can customize our search – in this example, by adding the following:

- **Field To Search By**: In this case, we can use the person's record ID to search with, so we will choose the **ID** value from the dropdown.

- **ID (Term)**: In this case, we would map the **Person ID** dynamic data value from our trigger step to this field. The ID field is a number (integer) field and the value we enter (whether static or dynamic) should be as such.

- **Search For Exact Match?**: In this case, we will choose the **Yes** option as we want to search for an exact match.

- **Should This Step Be Considered A "success" When Nothing Is Found**: Use this Boolean field to select **Yes (true)** or **No (false)** from the drop-down menu, enter text, or insert data from previous steps for this step to be considered a "success" if nothing is found in the search. The default for this field is **No (false)**, which you should choose if you want the step to "halt" if nothing is found, as this is the most common use case. This means that Zapier will produce a soft error that you will not be notified of; the Zap will not pause. However, all subsequent steps that depend on the data in this step will be skipped. Use the **Yes (true)** option when you want to allow the Zap to continue and subsequent steps to run. If you choose this option, it is best practice to have more control in your workflows by adding **Filter by Zapier** or **Paths by Zapier** conditional logic and allowing those steps to pass or stop based on whether the search returned a result or not. We'll learn how to use conditional workflows with this field option in *Chapter 7, Getting Started with Built-In Apps*.

- **Create Pipedrive Person if it doesn't exist yet?**: Tick this checkbox if you want a new record to be created if the search does not return an existing record. Once ticked, the step will refresh and display the same fields as those for the **Create Person** action event. The entity you want to search for in your specified app – for example, **Pipedrive Person** – will differ between apps, and so will the **Create** entity.

This is shown in the following screenshot:

Field to Search By (required)

ID

ID 1 2 3 (required)

P 1. Person ID Value: 5157

This field requires a minimum of 2 characters unless you have the "Search for an Exact Match?" set to yes.

Search for an Exact Match? ⊙ ○

Yes

If no, a fuzzy match result can be returned. For example, if searching for the name Zap Zaplar when this field is set t... more

Should this step be considered a "success" when nothing is found? ⊙ ○

No

Choose false if you want subsequent steps to always be skipped when nothing is found. This is the most common...   more

☐ Create Pipedrive Person if it doesn't exist yet?

Refresh fields   **Continue**

Figure 6.3 – Overview of customizing the Find Person event in the Pipedrive search action step

We could, however, choose to use any other existing data value, either static or dynamic, to search by. For example, we could use the person's email address or name as the item to search by if we are confident that they are likely to be unique enough to be able to find that specific record.

> **Important note**
> Search action event variables will differ between action events and apps. Therefore, what you see in the **Action** section is likely to be different from our example. The Zap editor shows useful notes as to what you can include in each field.

Finally, if we have mapped our fields correctly, the test using this will retrieve the correct contact, along with all the necessary details. We need to map the contact's first name and last name in our **Create Spreadsheet Row in Google Sheets** action step. This is shown in the following screenshot:

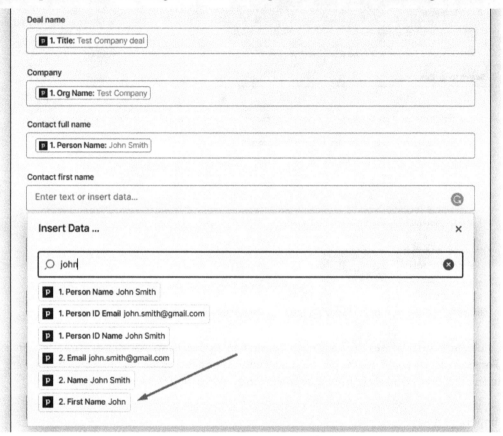

Figure 6.4 – Overview of search for last name yielding a result

Now, we can go ahead and retest our action using the **Retest action** button to see how our data pushes into our Google Sheets spreadsheet. Alternatively, we can **Skip Test**.

As a comparison, the following screenshot shows a search action step using **Mailchimp** as the app:

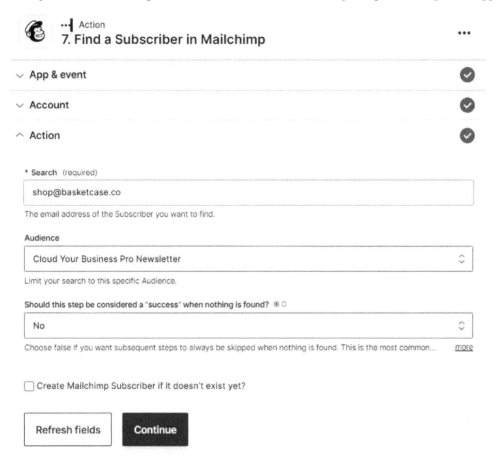

Figure 6.5 – Overview of customizing the Find Subscriber search action step

The following screenshot shows that a large amount of data can be extracted from many search action steps that can be used in your other action steps:

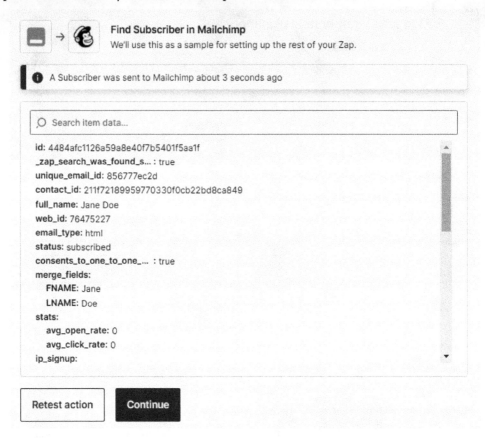

Figure 6.6 – Overview of the results of the Find Subscriber search

Now, let's take a look at how to add a search action step from within a **Choose value…** field.

Adding a search step in a Choose value… field

In *Chapter 3*, *Building Your First Automated Workflow (Zap)*, we introduced the two main field types that you will find in action steps: **Choose value…** and **Enter text or insert data…**. When using the **Choose value…** field type, you can map in either static or dynamic data. Dynamic data retrieved from trigger or previous action steps can be mapped using the **Custom** header option. If the dynamic data that you specifically want to map does not exist in previous steps, you can add a search action if the app you are using allows this through the integration.

Let's illustrate this by adding an extra requirement to the working example. Some CRMs such as Pipedrive have a product module that allows you to store set codes, descriptions, and pricing for products that you might charge your customers for. In our workflow, once we have created a new row in a Google Sheets spreadsheet, we may want to automatically add a product to our deal in Pipedrive. For our specific example, when the deal is created, a "product" is selected from a drop-down menu in Pipedrive. We want to use this to search for the actual product from our Pipedrive product module so that we can add it to the deal. This example may not be that relevant in real life, but it serves to illustrate using the **Choose Value...** field type for searching.

First of all, we will need to add an action step after the **Create Spreadsheet Row in Google Sheets** action step using the + icon. We'll use **Pipedrive** for our app and **Add Product to Deal** for our action event. Under **Action**, for the **Product** field, click on the **Add a search step** button next to the field. This is shown in the following screenshot:

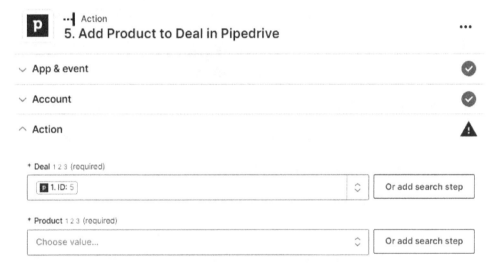

Figure 6.7 – Overview of finding the Add a search step button in the Custom tab

This will produce a popup with instructions, as shown in the following screenshot:

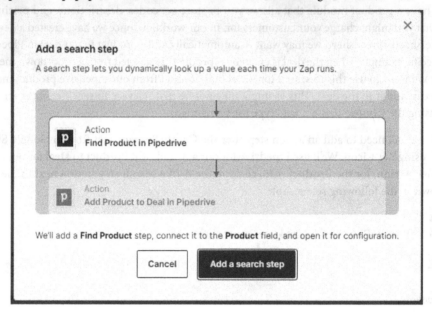

Figure 6.8 – Overview of the Add a search step popup

Once we have clicked on the **Add a search step** button, a Pipedrive **Find Product** search action step will be added automatically before the **Add Product** action step.

Once we have confirmed the Pipedrive account we want to use, we need to map in a value to search with in the **Action** section. In our example, we will use the value we entered from our Pipedrive product field from our trigger step. This is shown in the following screenshot:

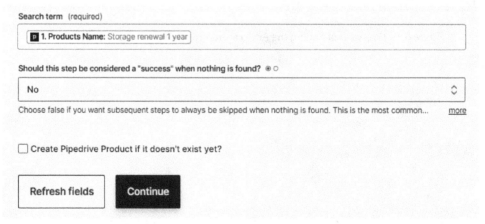

Figure 6.9 – Overview of customizing the Find Product action step

Finally, performing **Test** will retrieve the product information from the products module in Pipedrive; the ID will be automatically mapped to our **Add Product to Deal** action step. This is shown in the following screenshot:

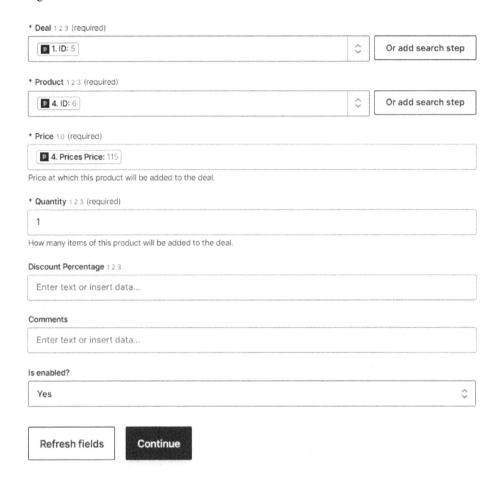

Figure 6.10 – Overview of the search step results are automatically mapped to the originating action step

We can now fill in the other fields by adding static data or mapping dynamic data from previous steps, proceed to **Test**, and complete our workflow.

You can get a template of this Zap and add it to your Zapier account by going to `https://bit.ly/zapier-book`. Using this Zap template will help you visualize how the process works.

Now, you can try this out yourself with the following exercise.

Exercise – creating a multi-step Zap with a search action

Use one of the processes that you defined in *Chapter 2*, *Preparing to Automate Your Processes*, to work through the content in this section to create a multi-step Zap with a search action. Try to incorporate multiple apps in your workflow.

Here is an example that you could use:

1. **Trigger**: A webform is submitted.
2. **Action**: Add a new subscriber to your email marketing app.
3. **Action**: Add a new contact to your invoicing app.
4. **Action**: Search for a user ID on a Google Sheets spreadsheet lookup list.
5. **Action**: Add a new onboarding task to your task management app and assign it to the user from *step 4*.
6. **Action**: Send an email or a message in your messaging app to your team to notify them that new contact and subscriber records have been created.

You can repeat this exercise for any of the processes that you have documented and that would benefit from automation.

You should now have a better understanding of how to create and customize multi-step Zaps with custom values and search functionality. Now, let's cover how to alter steps in your Zaps if you need to delete, duplicate, reorder, or rename them.

Deleting, duplicating, pasting, reordering, and renaming steps in your Zaps

As you become more familiar with building multi-step Zaps, there may be times that you want to delete, duplicate, reorder, or rename the steps in your Zaps. To do this, choose a step that you would like to perform the relevant action on, select the three-dots icon to reveal a drop-down menu, and select the option. This is shown in the following screenshot:

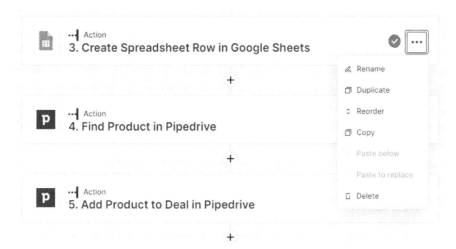

Figure 6.11 – Managing a step in a Zap in the Classic Editor

> **Important note**
>
> In the **Visual Editor**, the **Outline** section does not exist in the left-side panel, therefore, all actions would be performed by clicking on the three-dots drop-down menu in the step. You will also notice that the **Reorder** option is also not available in the drop-down menu as you can drag and drop steps within the main editor section.

Steps can also be managed by selecting the three-dots icon next to the step to reveal a dropdown and searching for them by entering a search variable into the search bar using the **Outline** section in the right-side panel. You can also add a step below a step from the drop-down menu. This is shown in the following screenshot:

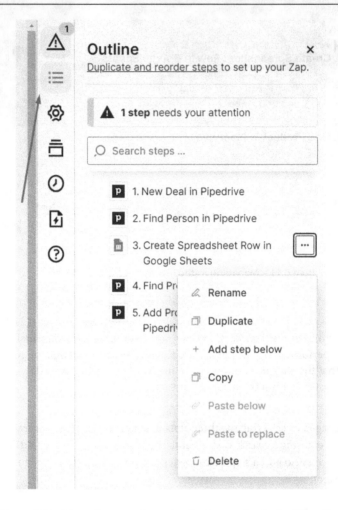

Figure 6.12 – Managing steps from the Outline section in the Zap editor

Let's look at renaming, duplicating, adding, copying, pasting, deleting, and reordering steps in turn.

Renaming a step

In *Chapter 4*, *Managing Your Zaps*, we explored how to name your Zaps adequately. The same logic can be applied to steps in your Zaps. As Zapier will automatically name the step based on the app and the trigger or action event involved, it's useful to be able to change the name to make it more descriptive. This is especially important if you're working with a team, to give more context to the purpose of the step, and if you have many steps in your Zap as you will be able to use keywords to search for steps in the **Outline** section rather than scrolling through your entire Zap.

Clicking on the **Rename** option in the step or from the **Outline** section will allow you to change the text in the step's name. Once you have edited the text, simply click anywhere outside of the text box to save your changes.

Duplicating a step

When you're building multi-step Zaps that have repetitive steps, it is useful to be able to make a copy of a step. These copies might be identical to the original or you might only need to make some minor adjustments. For example, you might need to build a Zap that has multiple steps that happen in a sequence, such as a 7-day sales cadence of activities, where it is useful to be able to duplicate steps. This example is shown in the following screenshot:

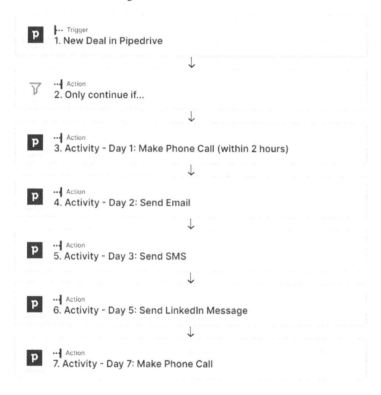

Figure 6.13 – A Zap that created a 7-day sales cadence of activities

Clicking on the **Duplicate** option in the step or from the **Outline** section will allow you to make a copy of a specific step; this will be added directly below the original step. The name of this new step will begin with Copy: and will be followed by the name of the original step. You must proceed by checking the step and remapping the fields accordingly.

Adding steps

You can add steps as a routine by clicking on the + button between steps. You can also add steps below the step you select by clicking on the **Add step below** option from within the **Outline** section.

Copying and pasting steps

The **Duplicate** option will make a copy of a step directly below it. You could, however, choose to make a copy of a specific step and easily paste that copy above or below another step. You can do this by clicking on the **Copy** option in a step or from the **Outline** section. A copy of the step will be added to your clipboard, a notification will be shown at the top of the Zap editor that will dismiss after a few seconds, and a popup will appear in the bottom-left corner of the Zap editor. You can click on the **X** button to hide the popup. This is shown in the following screenshot:

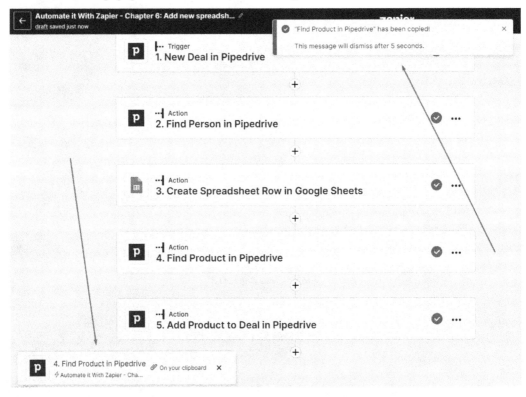

Figure 6.14 – Copying and pasting steps

You can't use your clipboard to view the data and it only contains one Zap copy at any time, which can be overwritten by using the **Copy** option again. Then, in any step in the **Outline** section (in the **Classic Editor**), you can choose to either select the **Paste below** option to paste the copied step below a selected step, or the **Paste to replace** option to completely replace a step. You must then check the step and remap the fields accordingly. This is a time-saving feature that allows you to cut out a few clicks in the process.

Deleting a step

There might also be occasions when you no longer need a step in your workflow and you need to delete it. Clicking on the **Delete** option in the step or from the **Outline** section will allow you to remove the step entirely from your Zap. A prompt will appear saying **Really delete?**, asking you to confirm that you want to delete the step as it will not be recoverable. This is shown in the following screenshot:

Figure 6.15 – A prompt to confirm whether you want to delete a step

Reordering a step

Sometimes, you might realize that your step is in the wrong place in your Zap and you want to move it. In the **Classic Editor**, clicking on the **Reorder** option in the step will open the **Outline** section, where you can drag and drop your step to another place in the Zap. This is shown in the following screenshot:

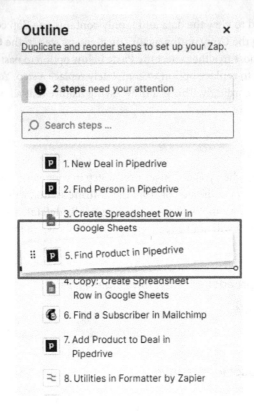

Outline   ✕

Duplicate and reorder steps to set up your Zap.

⚠ **2 steps** need your attention

○ Search steps ...

P 1. New Deal in Pipedrive

P 2. Find Person in Pipedrive

3. Create Spreadsheet Row in Google Sheets

⁞ P 5. Find Product in Pipedrive

4. Copy: Create Spreadsheet Row in Google Sheets

🐵 6. Find a Subscriber in Mailchimp

P 7. Add Product to Deal in Pipedrive

≈ 8. Utilities in Formatter by Zapier

Figure 6.16 – Overview of reordering a step in the Outline section in the Classic Editor

If the step uses data from previous steps and you move the step to before those steps that the data comes from, the data will no longer be available to use. You will be presented with a warning in the form of a popup. You can choose to cancel the action by clicking on the **Cancel** button or proceed by clicking on the **Move step** button. You must then proceed to check the step and remap the fields accordingly. This is shown in the following screenshot:

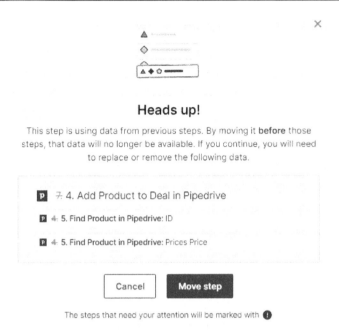

The steps that need your attention will be marked with ●

Figure 6.17 – Overview of a warning when reordering a step

Reordering of steps is easily performed in the main editor section by simply dragging and dropping the step when using the **Visual Editor**.

Reordering a step works especially well once you have duplicated a step because you can then move the copy to another part of the Zap.

> **Tip**
> Copying and pasting, duplicating, and reordering steps are new features that Zapier recently released that will save you a lot of time when you're making adjustments to your workflows. Before this feature was released, you would have to rebuild steps if you made a mistake in positioning the step or if you needed to create a copy of that step further along in the Zap. You can use this functionality to build multi-step Zaps faster.

You should now have a better understanding of how to manage your steps by renaming, deleting, duplicating, and reordering them in your Zaps. Now, let's take multi-step Zap building even further and explore all the built-in apps Zapier has created to make workflow automation all-encompassing on the Zapier platform.

Introducing apps by Zapier

The basics of creating multi-step Zaps lie in knowing how to use triggers, actions, and searches adequately. Once you have got to grips with this, you may want to take advantage of the functionality of the many built-in apps that Zapier has created to allow you to perform common tasks without having to use another app and pay additional subscription fees. Zapier has created several built-in apps to help you supercharge your workflows.

We've categorized these apps as follows:

- Apps that control run conditions and logic
- Communication apps
- Apps for extracting and compiling data
- Other useful apps
- Advanced apps
- Apps for managing your Zapier account
- Newly released apps in the alpha and beta testing phases
- The powerful Formatter by Zapier app
- Apps with AI functionality

> **Important note**
> Zapier releases new features and built-in apps regularly. In this book, we will cover the built-in apps that have been released with the triggers, actions, and search actions available at the time of publishing.

You can get access to a handy quick-reference cheatsheet to all of the Zapier built-in apps here: `https://bit.ly/zapier-book`.

Now, let's briefly review the apps in each of these categories.

Setting run conditions and using logic with apps by Zapier

You may want to customize your automations by controlling when your workflows will continue to run. You can do this by adding logic to stop a Zap from running unless the data satisfies certain criteria or by adding timed delays and scheduling your Zaps to run at specific intervals. Zapier has created the following built-in apps, all of which are commonly used for setting run conditions and using logic:

- **Filter by Zapier**: Filter by Zapier allows you to add conditional logic steps to your Zaps, allowing the automation to continue only if certain criteria have been satisfied. For example, you may want to send an email when a new row has been added to your Google Sheets spreadsheet, but only if the data in a certain column exists.

- **Delay by Zapier**: By using Delay by Zapier, you can add time delays to subsequent action steps. You can set a delay to allow the rest of the Zap to run after a set period, such as 1 hour, at a certain time such as 2 P.M., or after a delay queue if there are multiple delays in the workflow. For example, you may want to send a tweet on Twitter 1 week after an image or video has been added to Instagram.

- **Schedule by Zapier**: You can use Schedule by Zapier as a trigger step to run a workflow at set times, such as every hour, every day at a certain time, every week on a certain day, or every month on a certain day. For example, you may want to add a set of tasks to your task management app (such as Asana) at the start of every week.

- **Paths by Zapier**: Paths by Zapier allows you to add branching logic to your Zaps. This means that you can allow different paths with different actions to run based on set criteria. For example, you may want to either send an email or a text message to a customer that has filled out a contact form on your website based on the contact preferences they provide.

We will cover all of these apps by Zapier in *Chapter 7, Getting Started with Built-In Apps*.

Now, let's review the apps that Zapier has created that have communication functions.

Using apps by Zapier for communication

Zapier has created several communication-specific built-in apps that allow you to trigger workflow automations and perform actions. These are as follows:

- **SMS by Zapier**: Using SMS by Zapier, you can send a limited number of text messages to numbers that you can validate. In other words, permissions need to be granted to send messages to a number. Therefore, this is useful for sending notifications or reminders to yourself or teammates who would be able to verify the connection to Zapier but cannot be used to send messages to customers, for example.

- **Email by Zapier**: With Email by Zapier, you can enable a unique `zapiermail.com` email address to use as a trigger or action step. You can then send outbound emails, and if you've enabled read receipts, you can trigger a workflow when someone opens your sent email. You can also trigger Zaps to run when you receive forwarded emails to your `zapiermail.com` address.

- **SMTP by Zapier**: **Simple Mail Transfer Protocol** (**SMTP**) allows email client apps to send emails. If you are using a mail server other than Gmail, Zoho Mail, or Microsoft Office 365, SMTP by Zapier allows you to send emails via these mail servers.

- **IMAP by Zapier**: **Internet Message Access Protocol** (**IMAP**) allows email client apps to retrieve emails from a server. If you are using a mail server other than Gmail, Zoho Mail, or Microsoft Office 365, you can use IMAP by Zapier to retrieve emails from these mail servers.

We will cover all of these apps by Zapier in *Chapter 8, Built-In Communication Apps*.

Next, let's explore some of the apps that Zapier has created for extracting and compiling data.

Extracting and compiling data with apps by Zapier

Zapier has created a few built-in apps that allow you to extract data from emails, use RSS feeds in your automations, and create summaries of information. These are as follows:

- **Email Parser by Zapier**: Similar to Email by Zapier, you can enable a unique `@robot.zapier.com` email address to which you can forward emails and enable data extraction from the email. For example, if you receive web form submission notifications by email you can use Email Parser by Zapier to extract data to be used in subsequent action steps.

- **RSS by Zapier**: **Really Simple Syndication** (**RSS**) feeds update whenever a website publishes new content. The RSS by Zapier app allows you to use RSS feed updates as a trigger, which by then adding a notification action step such as an email, SMS, or Slack message will give you an update on new content. For example, you may want to receive updates on when your favorite business blog releases new articles. You can also create your own RSS feed with the app.

- **Digest by Zapier**: This built-in app allows you to capture data from multiple workflow trigger events and compile the data into single summaries that can be used in other action events. For example, send a weekly email with a summary of all sales invoices created over that week to your sales team. You can also search for existing digest data.

We will cover these apps by Zapier in more detail in *Chapter 9, Exploring Built-In Apps for Extracting and Compiling Data*.

Now let's take a quick look at some of the other useful apps that Zapier has created and their associated functions.

Other useful apps by Zapier

There are several other built-in apps that Zapier has created that perform a variety of useful functions. These are as follows:

- **Zapier Chrome extension**: The Zapier Chrome extension, previously called Push by Zapier, uses a Google Chrome extension to trigger one-off automations from anywhere on the web manually. For example, you may want to create a new Trello card to review content in an article that you came across while browsing the internet.

- **URL Shortener by Zapier**: If you want to make long **Uniform Resource Locator** (**URL**) strings shorter and easier on the eye, you can use URL Shortener by Zapier. This is especially useful if you have text length restrictions, for example, if you want to send an SMS or post a tweet to Twitter. This is similar to tools such as Bitly.

- **Translate by Zapier**: Translate by Zapier allows you to translate words, phrases, and web pages into over 100 languages, and it can be used to detect a language in text.

- **Lead Score by Zapier**: This app allows you to gather information from the web about a contact using their email address and can also be used to give them a qualification score. For example, if a new lead submits a web form, you may want to find out more details about the contact's company, company size, and location.

- **Weather by Zapier**: Weather by Zapier gives you access to weather conditions in your area. You can use it to get daily weather notifications and only to trigger if it will rain that day (for your local area based on your Zapier timezone settings). You can also search for current weather conditions and tomorrow's forecast for a specified location.

- **Retrograde by Zapier**: You can use Retrograde by Zapier to trigger your workflows based on Mercury retrograde astrological predictions. You can choose from trigger events of Mercury entering or leaving retrograde or trigger events once a day when Mercury is in retrograde.

We will cover all of these apps by Zapier in more detail in *Chapter 10, Other Useful Built-In Apps by Zapier*.

Now, let's take a look at the apps that Zapier has created that have more advanced functionality.

Advanced apps by Zapier

As you become more familiar with using apps by Zapier, you may want to experiment with a few more built-in apps that Zapier with slightly more advanced features. These are as follows:

- **Webhooks by Zapier**: With the Webhooks by Zapier built-in app, you can use webhooks and polling triggers with the Catch Hook or Catch Raw Hook trigger events or poll a URL for new entries. You can also use Webhooks by Zapier as an action step to make GET, POST, PUT, or custom HTTP requests.

- **Code by Zapier**: If you are familiar with **JavaScript** or **Python**, you can use Code by Zapier in your workflow automations. You can write code in JavaScript or Python to use in triggers or actions to manipulate data.

- **Storage by Zapier**: Storage by Zapier allows you to save and retrieve small data values. This allows you to store reference data each time a Zap runs and then share it with other Zaps by retrieving it. For example, let's say you want to keep a running tally of how many new subscribers have been added to your email marketing app and then use this tally so that it's displayed in a dashboard reporting tool such as **Databox**.

We will cover all of these apps by Zapier in *Chapter 11, Advanced Built-In Apps by Zapier*. We will also explore features such as the **API Requests** and **App Extension** action steps.

Now, let's take a look at the apps you can use for managing your Zapier account.

Managing your Zapier account with apps by Zapier

If you're in charge of systems administration, then you will want to know how to use these apps. They allow you to build automations that help you monitor issues with your Zapier account, such as errors and task usage. These are as follows:

- **Zapier Manager**: We introduced the Zapier Manager app in *Chapter 5, Troubleshooting and Handling Zap Errors*, where we discussed how to use it to manage error alerts such as errors with Zaps, Zaps being turned off, or tasks being halted. You can also use Zapier Manager to notify you of new public apps being added to Zapier, changes to your account such as new folders or Zaps being created, task usage limits being reached, or new Zapier invoices being released. You can search for a Zap or public app, as well as turn Zaps on or off. If you are using a Team account, you can use Zapier Manager to invite a new user to your Zapier team or notify you of new team members being added.

- **App Status by Zapier**: We introduced the App Status by Zapier app in *Chapter 5, Troubleshooting and Handling Zap Errors*, where we discussed how to use it to get notifications of new, updated, and resolved incidents with public apps.

We will cover all of these apps by Zapier in *Chapter 12, Managing Your Zapier Account with Built-In Apps*.

Next, let's explore new built-in app releases.

Newly released apps in the alpha and beta testing phases

Zapier is constantly improving functionality and releasing new features. The following apps have been released since the first edition of this book was published:

- **Looping by Zapier**: You can repeat actions in your Zaps several times through a loop for specified sets of values. This is useful when you have multiple values that need to run through a workflow individually.

- **Sub-Zap by Zapier**: You can create reusable Zap components and systems by building and calling them "Sub-Zaps." This is helpful when you want to run a workflow separate from your main Zap and connect multiple Zaps.

- **Transfer**: You can transfer data between two apps in bulk, either on-demand or by scheduling a transfer.

- **Tables**: You can store data in tables hosted on the Zapier platform without the need for using additional spreadsheet or database apps.

- **Interfaces**: You can create pages that you can connect to your Zaps, such as forms, text pages, tables, kanbans, chatbots, and link cards that are hosted on the Zapier platform.

We will cover all of these apps by Zapier in *Chapter 13, Newly Released Apps and Features*.

Now, let's provide an overview of the versatile Formatter by Zapier app.

The powerful Formatter by Zapier app

The **Formatter by Zapier** app is by far the most versatile built-in app by Zapier. Its functionality is so extensive that we will cover this app in five chapters. Using the Formatter by Zapier app allows you to format the following:

- **Dates and times**: You can convert date/time values into different formats (including time zones) and add/subtract time. We will cover date and time formatting using the Formatter by Zapier app in *Chapter 14, Formatting Date and Time*.

- **Numbers**: You can manipulate numbers, phone numbers, and currencies and use spreadsheet-type formulas and math operations. We will cover number formatting using the Formatter by Zapier app in *Chapter 15, Formatting Numbers*.

- **Text**: You can extensively format text using this function. There are so many things you can do that we will cover the functionality in two chapters. In *Chapter 16, Text Formatting Functions in Zapier – Part 1*, we will explore adjusting title case, uppercase, and lowercase, finding and replacing text, trimming whitespace, counting words and adjusting length, and pluralizing text. In *Chapter 17, Text Formatting Functions in Zapier – Part 2*, we will discuss text splitting, truncating text, extracting patterns, URLs, phone numbers, numbers, and email addresses, removing HTML tags, and creating a superhero name (a fun one). We will also provide an overview of advanced features such as how to convert Markdown into HTML and ASCII and use Default Value and URL Encode/Decode.

- **Utilities**: The Utilities function allows you to create and customize line items, convert text into line items and vice versa, use lookup tables and picklists, and import `.csv` files. We'll cover the Utilities functions in the Formatter by Zapier app in *Chapter 18, Zapier's Utilities Functions*.

Now, let's discuss the built-in apps that have **Artificial Intelligence (AI)** functionality.

Apps with AI functionality

Integrating AI functionality into their software applications has become a priority for many SaaS companies. Zapier is no different. With the release of ChatGPT to the wider market and the possibility to integrate and incorporate AI functionality, Zapier is in the process of releasing many AI-integrated features. Some of these features are **AI-powered troubleshooting**, **AI Chatbots**, **Create a Zap**, and running **AI Actions** with the Zapier Chrome extension and the **ChatGPT plugin**. We will cover all of these features and more briefly in *Chapter 19, AI and Automation*. AI features are all currently in beta. We will also explore some AI app integrations with Zapier, such as the **ChatGPT** and **OpenAI** integrations.

You should now have a better understanding of what built-in apps are available on the Zapier platform.

Summary

In this chapter, we boosted your knowledge of how to use Zapier by introducing the benefits of building multi-step Zaps. We covered how to use search functionality in action steps, how to delete, duplicate, reorder, and rename steps in Zaps, and encouraged you to test your knowledge by creating a multi-step workflow for one of your processes. Lastly, we introduced all of the built-in apps that Zapier has created to allow you to store, display, and transform data all from within the Zapier platform.

You now know how to create workflow automations with multiple action and search steps. You also now have a better understanding of all the built-in apps created by Zapier.

In the next chapter, we will introduce you to some of Zapier's built-in apps. We will cover the specific functions of using conditional logic in your workflows with Filter by Zapier and see how to add pathways with Paths by Zapier. We will also review how to use Delay by Zapier and Schedule by Zapier to apply time delays and schedule runtimes for your Zaps.

Questions

1. How many action steps can you add to a Zap?

2. When is it useful to be able to reorder steps in your Zaps?

3. Which two built-in apps can be used when you want to add conditional logic to your Zaps?

4. Which built-in app allows you to format text, dates/times, and numbers?

7
Getting Started with Built-In Apps

When you create your Zaps, you will specify what event you want your workflows to be triggered on, and the actions to take after that. You might find that there are occasions where you want to create conditions to stop your workflows from running unless they satisfy certain criteria or to run different actions depending on specific requirements. You might also want some of your actions to run only a certain amount of time after the workflow is triggered or to trigger at a certain time. Using Zapier's built-in apps, we can apply conditional logic and run conditions on our workflows to achieve this.

In this chapter, we will introduce the four built-in Zapier apps that allow you to either control run conditions or use conditional logic in workflows by filtering, delaying, scheduling, or choosing pathways. We will give descriptions of their functionality and provide practical tips on how to use them.

We will cover the following key topics in this chapter:

- Filter by Zapier – applying conditional logic to your Zaps

- Paths by Zapier – adding branching logic to your Zaps

- Delay by Zapier – adding delays to your Zaps

- Schedule by Zapier – scheduling your Zaps to run at intervals

- Exercise – creating a multi-step Zap with a scheduled trigger, search action, filter, path, and delay

Once you have worked through each of these topics, you will know how to apply conditional and branching logic and add delays or schedules to your workflows.

Technical requirements

To work through the content in this chapter, you will need access to a Zapier account. To build multi-step Zaps and use filters, you will need to subscribe to the Zapier Starter plan as a minimum. To work through the *Paths by Zapier – adding branching logic to your Zaps* section, you will need access to a Professional plan or higher to be able to use the Paths by Zapier app.

Filter by Zapier – applying conditional logic to your Zaps

Once your workflows have been triggered, you may want to control whether they continue to run and follow through with subsequent action steps. This is useful for stopping your Zaps from running unless specific criteria from your trigger or previous action steps match the conditions you specify. We can use the "if this, then that" conditional logic that has been built into the Filter by Zapier built-in app to achieve this.

Here are a couple of examples of when you can use conditional logic in your Zaps:

- You might record details of all bills and their payments on a **Smartsheet** spreadsheet. These are a combination of bills that are paid automatically by a credit card and those requiring a transfer of bank funds to settle them. You mark a column called **Paid** with **Yes** or **No** accordingly. You may want to send an email to your accounts team when a new row has been added to your Smartsheet spreadsheet to notify them, but only if the bill requires payment (if the data in the **Paid** column is **No**).

- You might want to add a copy of an email to **Evernote** only when you receive email updates from your favorite business blog. You might have created an automation to mark these emails automatically with the `My Favorite Blog` label, and only want these emails to be added to Evernote.

In these scenarios, you can use the Filter by Zapier app to set conditional logic in your Zaps.

> **Tip**
> For more inspiration and access to pre-built templates, you can review the Filter by Zapier built-in app profile page at `https://zapier.com/apps/filter/integrations`.

Using filters in your Zaps is a smart way of controlling your automations.

> **Important note**
> Filters only count toward your monthly task usage when the data passes successfully, allowing the workflow to move on to the next action step. This is very important as having this feature available allows you to have more control over your task usage and to be savvier with your allocated task quota.

Now, let's take a look at how to use Filter by Zapier.

Setting up the Filter by Zapier app

Filter by Zapier can only be used as an action event that you can customize by setting up rules to specify when your workflow should continue to the next steps. You can add the app anywhere after the trigger step and have multiple filters within a Zap.

Adding a filter step and customizing your rules

Once you have added an action step, either by selecting the **Action** step or clicking on the + icon, and chosen **Filter by Zapier** as the app and **Only continue if…** as the action event, you can edit the fields in the **Filter Setup & Testing** section, as follows:

- **Choose field…**: Use the drop-down menu to choose a field from the previous steps to enter a dynamic data value. This is the value that you want the filter to check. As the value is dynamic, it will most likely change every time the Zap runs and will be used to decide whether the Zap should pass the filter step.

- **Choose condition…**: Use the drop-down menu to choose one condition (or logic) to cross-reference the dynamic value against a reference key. We will discuss filter conditions in detail in the next section.

- **Enter text or insert data…**: This field holds the data value that will be used as the reference value to check against the dynamic data value and condition.

For example, you might only want the workflow to continue if your dynamic value from a previous step is **Value**, and the text exactly matches the reference value, 10. This is shown in the following screenshot:

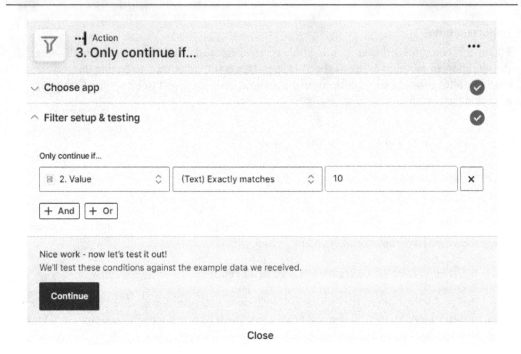

Figure 7.1 – Overview of setting up a filter with the Filter by Zapier app

Next, you can customize your filter so that it has multiple criteria using the + **And** and + **Or** buttons. Use + **And** logic if you want your filter to pass only when two or more conditions are satisfied. Alternatively, use + **Or** logic if you want your filter to pass if either of the requirements is satisfied. Then, click **Continue**.

Testing your filter

Zapier will then test your conditions against sample data in the workflow. If the conditions pass, and the Zap would have continued, this will be indicated, as shown in the following screenshot:

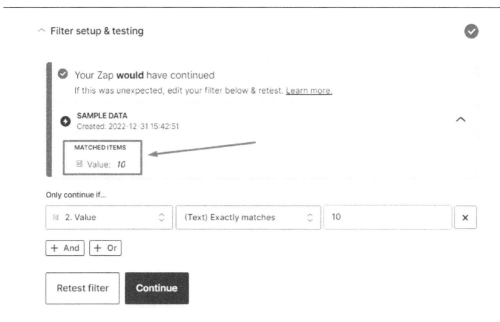

Figure 7.2 – Overview of a passed test filter in the Filter by Zapier app

If, however, the filter conditions do not pass, the Zap will be stopped. This will be indicated, as shown in the following screenshot:

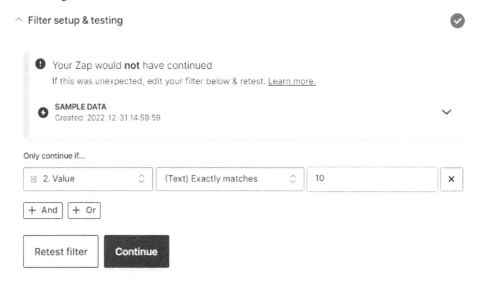

Figure 7.3 – Overview of a stopped test filter in the Filter by Zapier app

You can alter your conditions accordingly or click the **Close** button to continue, then proceed to add one or more action steps. In either case, if you click on the down arrow icon, you will be shown what item(s) matched or did not match, as indicated by the arrow in *Figure 7.2*. This will help you validate your testing of the filter.

Now, let's explore the different types of filter conditions and use cases.

Understanding filter conditions

Zapier has built multiple conditions into the app to allow you to work with various scenarios. When using the **Choose condition…** drop-down menu from the **Filter Setup & Testing** section, you will be presented with logic options involving five types of filter rules: **Text**, **Number**, **Date/time**, **Boolean**, and **Generic**. This is shown in the following screenshot:

Figure 7.4 – Overview of the choice of logic options in the Filter by Zapier app

> **Important note**
> Each condition will only work with the type of filter rule specified in parentheses unless it is generic.

Let's review each of these filter types in turn.

Text filters

There is a range of text filters to choose from, which can be case-sensitive depending on the type of rule that you use. The only case-sensitive rules are **(Text) Exactly matches** and **(Text) Does not exactly match**.

The following is a list of text filter options:

- **(Text) Contains**: This condition checks whether the dynamic data value contains the reference value

- **(Text) Does not contain**: This condition is the opposite of **(Text) Contains** and checks that the dynamic data value does not contain the reference value

- **(Text) Exactly matches**: This condition checks that the dynamic data value matches the reference value exactly, character for character

- **(Text) Does not exactly match**: This condition checks that the dynamic data value does not match the reference value exactly, character for character

- **(Text) Is in**: This condition checks that the dynamic data value is in a specified list of reference values

- **(Text) Is not in**: This condition checks that the dynamic data value is not in a specified list of reference values

- **(Text) Starts with**: This condition checks that the dynamic data value starts with the reference value

- **(Text) Does not start with**: This condition checks that the dynamic data value does not start with the reference value

- **(Text) Ends with**: This condition checks that the dynamic data value ends with the reference value

- **(Text) Does not end with**: This condition checks that the dynamic data value does not end with the reference value

Next, let's take a look at number filters.

Number filters

In *Chapter 3*, *Building Your First Automated Workflow (Zap)*, we discussed using number (integer) field types. Number filters work in the same way, and in them, you can only use numeric values, such as 9.5 or 334.

The following is a list of number filter options:

- **(Number) Greater than**: This condition checks whether the dynamic data value is greater than the reference number value

- **(Number) Less than**: This condition checks whether the dynamic data value is less than the reference number value

Now, let's review date/time filters.

Date/time filters

In *Chapter 3, Building Your First Automated Workflow (Zap)*, we discussed using date/time field types. Date/time filters work in the same way, and you can use a variety of date/time formats but cannot use text such as `today` or `tomorrow at 9 a.m.`.

The following is a list of date/time filter options:

- **(Date/time) After**: This condition checks whether the dynamic data value is after the reference date value

- **(Date/time) Before**: This condition checks whether the dynamic data value is before the reference date value

- **(Date/time) Equals**: This condition checks whether the dynamic data value is equal (identical) to the reference date value

Next, let's take a look at Boolean filters.

Boolean filters

As we discussed in *Chapter 3, Building Your First Automated Workflow (Zap)*, Boolean values are either true or false.

The following is a list of Boolean filter options:

- **(Boolean) Is true**: This condition checks whether the dynamic data value is true

- **(Boolean) Is false**: This condition checks whether the dynamic data value is false

Finally, let's review generic filters.

Generic filters

Generic filters can be used with any type of field.

The following is a list of generic filter options:

- **Exists**: Checks whether a value exists (can be used with any type of field)

- **Does not exist**: Checks that a value doesn't exist (can be used with any type of field)

You should now have a better understanding of how and when to use the Filter by Zapier app to apply conditional logic to your Zaps. Next, let's dive into using branching logic in your Zaps with the Paths by Zapier built-in app.

Paths by Zapier – adding branching logic to your Zaps

Paths by Zapier allows you to add branching logic to your Zaps. This means that you can allow different paths with different actions to run based on set criteria. This builds on what you learned about using Filter by Zapier and takes it one step further to allow you to create multi-step workflow automation pathways that run depending on what you have specified. Let's look at a few examples of how you would use Paths by Zapier:

- You might be an online retailer with an e-commerce store, and you have various products that need to be processed in a slightly different way. Product A might be a digital product that needs to be sent for printing, shipping, and fulfillment with **Printful**. Product B might require assembly before shipping, and you need to notify the warehouse team by email, add a card to Trello, and print a shipping note.

- You might have a **Gravity Forms** form on your website for customer service queries, and you allow customers to specify whether their question is related to training, technical issues, or billing. Each support query is dealt with by a different team in the business, so you might want each query to be routed to a different department by sending a Slack message to a department channel and assigning a task in **Asana** to all the members of that team.

In both of these examples, you can use Paths by Zapier to create conditions to allow each pathway to run only if those criteria were satisfied. To help you visualize what this might look like, I've created a simple workflow diagram that represents the second example previously:

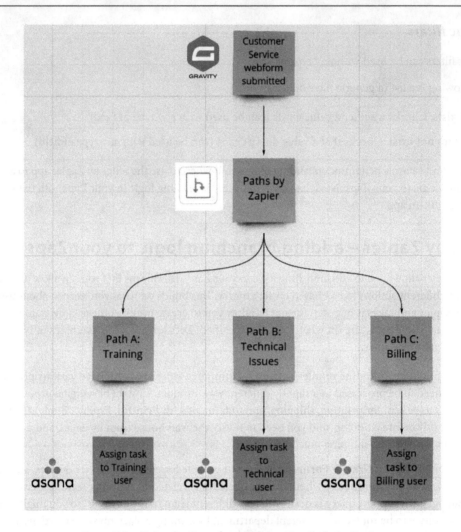

Figure 7.5 – A visualization of a workflow using Paths by Zapier

Paths by Zapier allows you to take the use of conditional logic in your Zaps to another level.

> **Tip**
>
> For more inspiration and access to pre-built templates, you can review the Paths by Zapier built-in app profile page at `https://zapier.com/apps/paths/integrations`.

Paths by Zapier is best used with simple logic; however, once you are more familiar with using it, the two main things to bear in mind are that you can only use Paths by Zapier at the end of a workflow and you are limited to creating three branches to start with. To get access to more branches, the account admin user will need to contact Zapier Support. With this being said, you can use multiple Paths by Zapier apps within each path to increase your range.

> **Important note**
>
> Zapier has a hard limit of 10 branches per path to ensure stability in the Zap editor and prevent long runtimes with potential timeouts. In addition, Zapier recommends only using three branches with three additional nested paths within each branch. The larger the Zap and the more complex it is, the greater the chance of validation problems and you may not be able to turn your Zap on. Typically, the lower the number of branches, the better the performance of the Zap. In general, the more complex your scenarios, the more risk there is for errors and data corruption. This is a reminder to keep it simple!

Creating complex pathways requires a logical assessment of what conditions are required for each, and it is recommended that you map them out. Here are a few things to consider when you're thinking about using branching logic:

- **Map out your processes visually**: Refer to *Chapter 2*, *Preparing to Automate Your Processes*, and use process mapping techniques to visualize your process and strategize the conditional logic before creating paths

- **Plan for the future**: Ask yourself whether there may be a possibility of other conditions being presented later, as this might require you to add additional paths later, bearing in mind the restriction on the number of branches you can add

This will save you time in the long run if you get it right the first time around.

> **Tip**
>
> If you are not subscribed to a Zapier plan that supports Paths by Zapier, you can use a Filter by Zapier step as a compromise. If your workflow is simple enough, you can replicate a process that would otherwise use Paths by Zapier. You can do this by creating multiple Zaps that run based on the same trigger and placing a filter directly after the trigger step. The filter in each workflow would have different filter criteria in each Zap, thus replicating those criteria specified in each branch filter of the Paths by Zapier step. Using this workaround is also appropriate if you need to add more than three unique pathways.

Now, let's review how to set up the Paths by Zapier built-in app.

Setting up the Paths by Zapier app

To get started with using Paths by Zapier, add the Paths by Zapier app to the end of your workflow, by either selecting the **Action** step or clicking the + icon. You will be presented with two pathway options, named **Path A** and **Path B**. Clicking on the **Add New Path** button will allow you to create one further path branch.

You will also see the following options within each path block:

- **Three dots icon**: Clicking on this icon will show seven options in a drop-down menu:

  - **Rename**: Selecting this option will allow you to rename the path

  - **Duplicate**: Selecting this option will allow you to duplicate the path

  - **Reorder**: Selecting this option will allow you to move the path to a different position

  - **Copy**: Selecting this option will allow you to make a copy of the path, add it to a clipboard, and then use either the **Paste below** or **Paste to replace** option

  - **Paste below**: Use this option in conjunction with the **Copy** option to paste a copy of the path below the selected path

  - **Paste to replace**: Use this option in conjunction with the **Copy** option to replace the selected path with the copy in the clipboard

  - **Delete**: Selecting this option will allow you to delete individual branch paths

This is shown in the following screenshot:

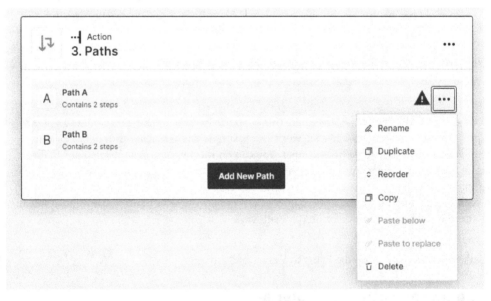

Figure 7.6 – Overview of setting up branches using the Paths by Zapier app

These functions work in the same way as described in the *Deleting, duplicating, pasting, reordering, and renaming steps in your Zaps* section of *Chapter 6, Creating Multi-Step Zaps and Using Built-In Apps.*

Next, let's review how to customize a path.

Customizing a path

Choose one path to work on first, such as **Path A**, and click on that block to customize the filter conditions for that path. You will be presented with a pop-up screen, as shown in the following screenshot:

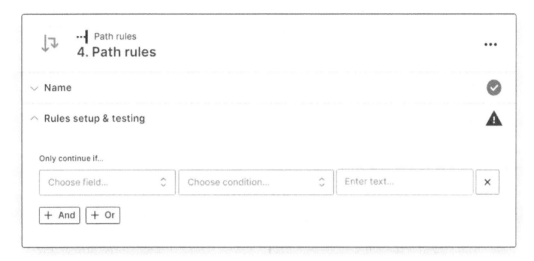

Figure 7.7 – Overview of customizing a Paths by Zapier step

The name of the path can be customized by clicking on the **Name** section if required.

Next, let's take a look at the navigational options from within a path.

Navigating within a path

You will be presented with the following navigational options in the top bar:

- **House icon**: Clicking on this icon will take you back to the main view of the Zap editor, which shows your Zap steps.

- **Path menu**: Clicking on this menu will present a drop-down menu of paths and associated nested steps. You can navigate easily between your paths using this option.

- **X icon**: Clicking on this icon closes the popup and takes you back to the main view of the Zap editor.

This is shown in the following screenshot:

Figure 7.8 – Overview of customizing a Paths by Zapier step

Now, let's review how to customize a path.

Customizing the first step in the path

The first step of the path now represents a combination of a trigger and a filter for subsequent action steps in the branch.

Work through the following steps to customize your path:

1. In the **Name** section, rename your path. This field is required for the Zap to run. It cannot be left blank.

    As we discussed in *Chapter 3, Building Your First Automated Workflow (Zap)*, naming steps in your Zaps will help you keep track of what each step of your workflow does and makes it easier to find steps and data results from those steps further down your workflow. This is equally important when you're using Paths by Zapier as naming each path properly can help you summarize your filter conditions. Then, click the **Continue** button.

2. Use the instructions we covered in the *Filter by Zapier – applying conditional logic to your Zaps* section to customize your path filter accordingly in the **Rules setup & testing** section. Then, click the **Continue** button to test the conditions against example data.

3. Alter your conditions accordingly or click the **Continue** button to continue.

You can then proceed to add one or more action steps.

> **Important note**
>
> Conditional logic should be applied carefully. Assess your logic carefully to ensure that you do not accidentally allow more than one path to run because of the way you have set your filters. You could, of course, apply this logic deliberately. For example, you could set your Path A filter to continue if X is less than 10, your Path B filter to continue if X is less than 20, and your Path C filter to continue if X is greater than 20. In this example, if X was equal to 5, then Path A and Path B would run but not Path C.

You should now have a better understanding of how and when to use the Paths by Zapier built-in app. Now, let's take a look at how to add time delays to Zaps.

Delay by Zapier – adding delays to your Zaps

The Delay by Zapier app allows you to add time delays to subsequent action steps. This can be extremely useful in both simple and more complex workflows where you may want to prevent further action steps from running for a set period or until a specific time.

> **Important note**
>
> The maximum time a delayed task can be held is 1 month – that is, 31 days.

This app can only be used as an action step and added after a trigger step or between action steps to delay the running of subsequent action steps. The following action events can be used:

- **Delay For** (action)
- **Delay Until** (action)
- **Delay After Queue** (action)

Let's look at each.

The Delay For action event

This action event waits for a set amount of time before running any further actions in the Zaps. Here are a few examples of how to use the Delay by Zapier **Delay For** action event:

- When a **Typeform** web form has been submitted, send an email with Gmail after a delay of 10 minutes
- When a new row is added to a **Microsoft Excel** spreadsheet, add new tasks to Microsoft To Do after a delay of one hour

Let's explore how to set up this action event.

Setting up the Delay For action event

Once you have added an action step, either by selecting the **Action** step or clicking on the + icon, and chosen **Delay by Zapier** as the app and **Delay For** as the action event, you can edit the fields in the **Set up action** section, as follows:

- **Time Delayed For (value)**: Enter a number with or without a decimal, as required by this decimal field type. The minimum delay you can add is one minute.

- **Time Delayed For (unit)**: Choose a unit of either minutes, hours, days, or weeks from the drop-down menu, or add dynamic data from previous steps using the **Custom** tab.

These are both required fields and must have values for the Zap to run.

An example of this is shown in the following screenshot:

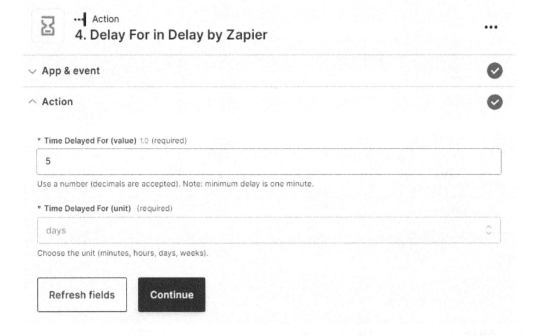

Figure 7.9 – Overview of customizing the Delay For action event

Click the **Continue** button to move to the **Test** section. You can then use the **Test** section to test this step or **Skip test**. Proceed to add one or more action steps after your delay step.

You should now be able to use the **Delay For** action event. Next, let's have a look at the **Delay Until** action event.

The Delay Until action event

This action event waits to run any further actions until a time or date you choose. Here are a few examples of how to use the Delay by Zapier **Delay Until** action event:

- When a task is completed in **Asana**, send a Slack message at 2 P.M. that day

- When an image or video has been added to **Instagram**, send a tweet on Twitter the next day at noon

Let's explore how to set up this action event.

Setting up the Delay Until action event

Once you have added an action step, either by selecting the **Action** step or clicking on the + icon, and chosen **Delay by Zapier** as the app and **Delay Until** as the action event, you can edit the fields in the **Action** section, as follows:

- **Date/Time Delayed Until**: Use the date/time field type format examples we covered in *Chapter 3, Building Your First Automated Workflow (Zap)*, to enter a relative static date/time value for this field type or a dynamic date/time value from previous steps. For example, you may want to delay until a time specified in your trigger app, such as a due date. This is a required field and must have a value for the Zap to run.

- **How Should We Handle Dates in The Past?**: This field controls how the delay will run if the **Date/Time Delayed Until** field value contains a date/time in the past. Choose an option from the drop-down menu to allow the delay task to continue if the value is either 15 minutes, 1 hour, or 1 day in the past, or to always continue regardless. The default is **Continue if it's up to one day (default)**.

An example of how to set up this action event is shown in the following screenshot:

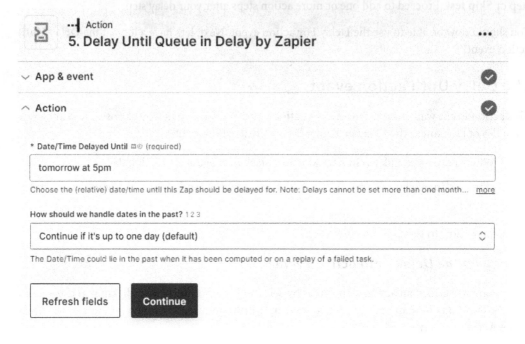

Figure 7.10 – Overview of customizing the Delay Until action event

Click on the **Continue** button to move to the **Test** section. You can then use the **Test** section to test this step or **Skip test**. Proceed to add one or more action steps after your delay step.

> **Important note**
>
> When using times by themselves, if the time has already passed, the delay task will complete immediately, and subsequent actions will run. To prevent this from happening, you could add a Filter by Zapier step after the Schedule by Zapier **Delay Until** action step, where you can specify that you do not want the Zap to continue if the time the Zap triggers is older than the time you specify in your **Delay Until** step.

You should now be able to use the **Delay Until** action event. Next, let's review the **Delay After Queue** action event.

The Delay After Queue action event

This action event waits a specified amount of time to allow Zap runs to proceed one after each other rather than all at once before running any further actions in the Zaps. This is useful if a Zap triggers multiple times over a few seconds or multiple Zaps are likely to run in parallel with each other, and you only want them to run in a series. This option is often used to deal with **race conditions** (where an attempt is made to perform two or more operations at the same time, which is considered undesirable) or **rate limiting** (where your Zap may trigger multiple times over a short period). You can read more about rate limiting here: `https://help.zapier.com/hc/en-us/articles/8496181445261-Rate-limits-and-throttling-in-Zapier#webhook-throttling-0-3`.

The Zap will be delayed at that step for a set period before releasing the next bit of trigger information through the Zap. For example, you might want to perform a series of tasks when an opportunity changes stage in Salesforce; however, your Zap will trigger if multiple opportunities change stage at the same time when you do a bulk edit. You might want your Zap to run through completely before any new data runs through the Zap. You can prevent the Zap from running multiple times at the same time by using the Delay by Zapier **Delay After Queue** action event in a step directly after the trigger step to hold trigger data for a set period, such as 5 minutes, to allow the Zap the run through completely first.

> Tip
> Estimate the time your Zap may take to run and add your queue time accordingly. For example, if your Zap is 20 steps long and each step takes 5 seconds to run, consider specifying your queue time as 5 minutes to account for the entire Zap to run.

Let's explore how to set up this action event.

Setting up the Delay After Queue action event

Once you have added an action step, either by selecting the **Action** step or clicking on the + icon, and chosen **Delay by Zapier** as the app and **Delay After Queue** as the action event, you can complete the fields in the **Action** section, as follows:

- **Queue Title**: Enter a title of up to 32 characters for the queue using static or dynamic data. This field is optional.

- **Time Delayed For (value)**: Enter a number with or without a decimal, as required by this decimal field type. The minimum delay you can add is one minute. This is a required field and must have a value for the Zap to run.

- **Time Delayed For (unit)**: Choose a unit of either minutes, hours, days, or weeks from the drop-down menu. This is a required field and must have a value for the Zap to run.

An example of this is shown in the following screenshot:

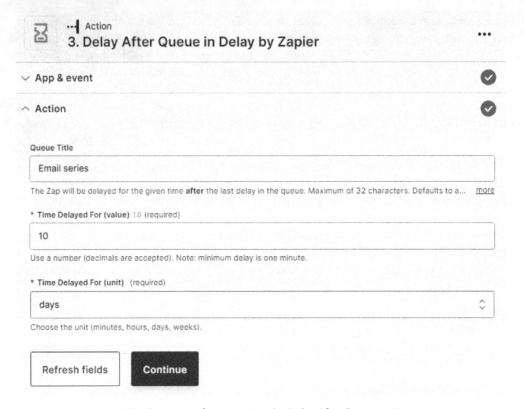

Figure 7.11 – Overview of customizing the Delay After Queue action event

Use the **Test** section to test this step and ensure your conditions will be met. Proceed to add one or more action steps after your delay step.

You should now have a better understanding of how and when to use the **Delay After Queue** action event, as well as the other Delay by Zapier built-in app action events.

> **Important note**
>
> If a Zap contains delay steps and has existing Zap runs that have not been completed because tasks are being held due to the delay, we recommend that you make edits to your Zap with caution. Publishing changes to a Zap that has active Zap runs with data held in a delay can prevent those runs from proceeding. Wait until your Zap has completed all held delay runs before making published changes.

As we have described, the Delay by Zapier built-in app is useful for adding time delays to your Zaps.

> **Tip**
> For more inspiration and access to pre-built templates, you can review the Delay by Zapier built-in app profile page at `https://zapier.com/apps/delay/integrations`.

Now, let's dive into using the Schedule by Zapier app to allow your Zaps to run at scheduled intervals.

Schedule by Zapier – scheduling your Zaps to run at intervals

The Schedule by Zapier app allows you to run a workflow at set times, such as every hour, every day at a certain time, every week on a certain day and time, or every month on a certain day and time. This is useful if you want to automate a series of repetitive tasks at specified times rather than using a traditional event in an app to trigger the workflow. This Zapier built-in app can only be used as a trigger step at the start of your workflow, replacing a traditional trigger step. When specifying times in the Schedule by Zapier app, you can use custom values in the `hh:mm aa`, `hh:mm`, or `hhmm` formats – for example, `1:30 pm`, `13:30`, or `1330`.

> **Important note**
> When specifying times, your Zaps will trigger based on your account or Zap timezone settings. If no timezone has been specified, the default runtime will be UTC (GMT +00:00). Use the instructions in *Chapter 1, Introduction to Business Process Automation with Zapier*, to change your account time zone settings and *Chapter 4, Managing Your Zaps*, for Zap settings.

You can trigger your workflows to run as follows:

- **Every Hour** (trigger)
- **Every Day** (trigger)
- **Every Week** (trigger)
- **Every Month** (trigger)

Let's look at each.

The Every Hour trigger event

This trigger event can be used to start a workflow every hour on weekdays and weekends if you choose. This event is the most basic one out of the four scheduling trigger events.

Here are a few examples of how to use the Schedule by Zapier **Every Hour** trigger event:

- Add new tasks to **Basecamp 3** every hour
- Send a Slack message reminder every hour when calendar events are due

Let's explore how to set up this trigger event.

Setting up the Every Hour trigger event

Once you have added a trigger step to the start of your workflow by selecting **1. Trigger** and chosen **Schedule by Zapier** as the app and **Every Hour** as the trigger event, you can edit the **Trigger On Weekends?** field in the **Trigger** section. This field controls whether you want your Zap to be triggered on the weekends or not. Use the Boolean field drop-down menu to choose between **yes** if you want it to trigger on Saturdays and Sundays or **no** if you only want it to trigger from Monday to Friday.

This is shown in the following screenshot:

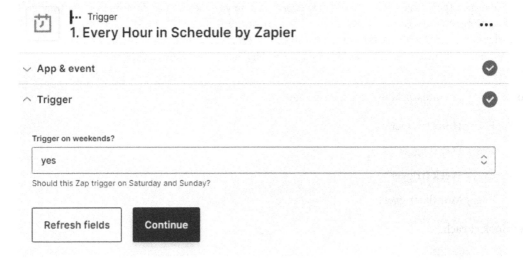

Figure 7.12 – Overview of customizing the Every Hour trigger event

You can then use the **Test** section to test the trigger and retrieve some data to use in your action steps. Proceed to add one or more action steps to your Zap using data from this trigger step.

Tip
You could use Filter by Zapier to allow your scheduled Zaps to continue if you only wanted them to run during business hours – for example, from 9 A.M. to 5 P.M.

You should now be able to use the **Every Hour** trigger event in a workflow. Next, let's review the **Every Day** trigger event.

The Every Day trigger event

This trigger event can be used to start a workflow every day at a certain time. Here are a few examples of how to use the Schedule by Zapier **Every Day** trigger event:

- Add daily notes to **Zoho Notebook** at 9 A.M. every weekday
- Post a random GIF from GIPHY to a **Microsoft Teams** channel every day at 11 A.M.

Let's explore how to set up this trigger event.

Setting up the Every Day trigger event

Once you have added a trigger step to the start of your workflow by selecting **1. Trigger** and chosen **Schedule by Zapier** as the app and **Every Day** as the trigger event, you can edit the fields in the **Trigger** section, as follows:

- **Trigger On Weekends?**: As with the **Every Hour** trigger event, this field controls whether your Zap will trigger on the weekend days or not. Use the Boolean field drop-down menu to choose between **yes** if you want it to trigger on Saturdays and Sundays or **no** if you only want it to trigger from Monday to Friday.

- **Time of Day**: Use this field to specify what time you want your Zap to run. The drop-down menu offers hourly time options from midnight to 11 P.M. You can also use the **Custom** header option to type in a custom value using the hh:mm aa, hh:mm, or hhmm formats, such as 11:45. This is a required field and must have a value for the Zap to run.

This is shown in the following screenshot:

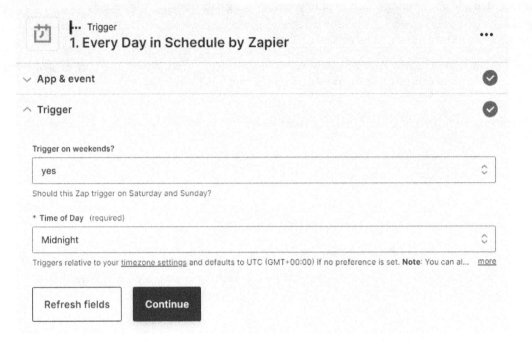

Figure 7.13 – Overview of customizing the Every Day trigger event

You can then use the **Test** section to test the trigger and retrieve some data to use in your action steps. Proceed to add one or more action steps to your Zap using data from this trigger step.

You should now be able to use the **Every Day** trigger event in a workflow. Next, let's review the **Every Week** trigger event.

The Every Week trigger event

This trigger event can be used to start a workflow every week on a day and time of your choice. Here are a few examples of how to use the Schedule by Zapier **Every Week** trigger event:

- Add new tasks to **MeisterTask** every week on a Monday at 8 A.M.

- Send an SMS reminder to yourself every week on a Wednesday at 2 P.M.

Let's explore how to set up this trigger event.

Setting up the Every Week trigger event

Once you have added a trigger step to the start of your workflow by selecting **1. Trigger** and chosen **Schedule by Zapier** as the app and **Every Week** as the trigger event, you can edit the fields in the **Trigger** section, as follows:

- **Day of the Week**: This field controls which day of the week your Zap will trigger. Use the drop-down menu to choose days from **Monday** to **Sunday**.

- **Time of Day**: As with the **Every Day** trigger event, use this field to specify what time you want your Zap to run. The drop-down menu offers hourly time options from midnight to 11 P.M. You can also use the **Custom** header option to type in a custom value using the hh:mm aa, hh:mm, or hhmm format, such as 13:30.

Both these fields are required and must have a value for the Zap to run.

This is shown in the following screenshot:

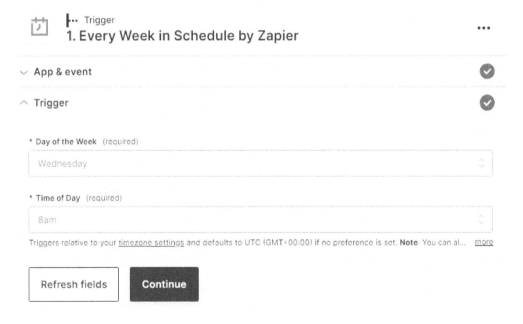

Figure 7.14 – Overview of customizing the Every Week trigger event

You can then use the **Test** section to test the trigger and retrieve some data to use in your action steps. Proceed to add one or more action steps to your Zap using data from this trigger step.

You should now be able to use the **Every Week** trigger event in a workflow. Next, let's review the *Every Month* trigger event.

The Every Month trigger event

This trigger event can be used to start a workflow every month on a date and time of your choice. Here are a few examples of how to use the Schedule by Zapier **Every Month** trigger event:

- Send a monthly recurring invoice to a customer on the 15th day of every month at 9 A.M.

- Send a reminder email to a customer and a follow-up task in **Todoist** on the first day of every month at 2 P.M.

Let's explore how to set up this trigger event.

Setting up the Every Month trigger event

Once you have added a trigger step to the start of your workflow by selecting **1. Trigger** and chosen **Schedule by Zapier** as the app and **Every Month** as the trigger event, you can edit the fields in the **Trigger** section, as follows:

- **Day of the Month**: This field controls which day of the month your Zap will trigger. Use the drop-down menu to choose dates from **1** to **31**.

- **Time of Day**: As with the **Every Day** and **Every Week** trigger events, use this field to specify what time you want your Zap to run. The drop-down menu offers hourly time options from midnight to 11 P.M. You can also use the **Custom** header option to type in a custom value using the hh:mm aa, hh:mm, or hhmm format, such as 9:15 p.m.

Both these fields are required and must have a value for the Zap to run.

This is shown in the following screenshot:

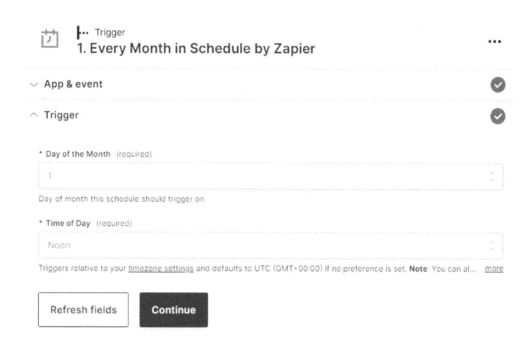

Figure 7.15 – Customizing the Every Month trigger event

You can then use the **Test** section to test the trigger and retrieve some data to use in your action steps. Proceed to add one or more action steps to your Zap using data from this trigger step.

You should now have a better understanding of how and when to use the **Every Month** trigger event, as well as the other Schedule by Zapier built-in app trigger events.

> **Tip**
> For more inspiration and access to pre-built templates, you can review the Schedule by Zapier built-in app profile page at `https://zapier.com/apps/schedule/integrations`.

Now, let's review an example of how to create a multi-step Zap with a scheduled trigger, search action, filter, path, and delay.

Exercise – creating a multi-step Zap with a scheduled trigger, search action, filter, path, and delay

You can use one of the processes that you defined in *Chapter 2, Preparing to Automate Your Processes*, to work through the content in this section, if appropriate. Try to incorporate multiple apps in your workflow.

You can perform actions with existing data in your apps at a certain time by using Schedule by Zapier as a trigger, adding a search action step to find existing data in an app, stopping your Zap from running if it doesn't meet certain conditions, delaying your workflow for a specified amount of time, and then adding branching logic if the scenarios you need to run differ. For example, you might use an Airtable base to collaborate with your **social media manager** (**SMM**) for social media posting. When the SMM adds a post to the base record, you approve it or reject it. You may want to add new posts to a Facebook group and a LinkedIn company page every weekday at 9 A.M., but only if the post has been approved. As Facebook and LinkedIn require slightly different formatting, you may also need to use different logic in your workflows. You also want to reshare the LinkedIn company post on your personal page, but only two hours later, as you know your personal page connections are more likely to engage with your posts at that time.

Here is an example of a workflow you could build to automate this process:

1. **Trigger**: Add the Schedule by Zapier **Every Day** event trigger to run on weekdays at 9 P.M.

2. **Action**: Add a **Find Record** search action to search Airtable base records for the date. Only allow the Zap to continue if a record is found.

3. **Action**: Add a filter with Filter by Zapier to only allow the Zap to continue if the **Approved** field is marked as **Yes.**.

4. **Action**: Add two branches in Paths by Zapier, where **Path A** will continue only if the **Platform** field is **Facebook** and **Path B** will continue only if the **Platform** field is **LinkedIn**.

5. **Action – Path A**: Add a **Post Message** action to **Facebook Groups**.

6. **Action – Path B**: Add a **Create Company Update** action event to **LinkedIn**.

7. **Action – Path B**: Add a Delay by Zapier **Delay For** action step where you specify the delay of 2 hours. You could also use the **Delay Until** action event to specify the runtime as 11 A.M.

8. **Action – Path B**: Add a **Create Share Update** action event to LinkedIn.

Unfortunately, Zapier does not allow you to share Zap templates with Paths by Zapier steps, so we're unable to share a Zap template with you. Try building out a similar process by repeating this exercise for any appropriate processes that you have documented and that would benefit from automation.

You should now have a better understanding of how and when to use filters, paths, schedules, and delays in your Zaps.

Summary

In this chapter, we introduced four commonly used Zapier built-in apps to help you add conditional logic and run conditions to your workflows. First, we covered how to use conditional logic in our workflows by using the Filter by Zapier app. Next, we reviewed how to use branching logic with the Paths by Zapier app. Then, we explored how to use time delays in Zaps using the Delay by Zapier app, and how to schedule our workflows to run at specific times by using the Schedule by Zapier app. Lastly, we went through an exercise to demonstrate the use of scheduled triggers, search actions, filters, paths, and delays.

You now have a better understanding of how to use filters, paths, delays, and schedules in your workflow automations.

In the next chapter, you will learn about the four communication-specific built-in Zapier apps; we will give descriptions of their functionality and provide practical tips on how to use them.

Questions

1. Do filters and paths count toward task usage?

2. Is the Paths by Zapier built-in app available with the Starter plan?

3. What is the longest time that a delayed task can be held for?

4. What built-in app can you use as a trigger in your Zap if you want to send a weather report to yourself every day at 10 A.M.?

8
Built-In Communication Apps

Communicating with your team and clients is an integral part of running any business. Using the digital communication technology that we have available to us can only help make operations smoother and more productive. Most companies that exist today use email to communicate with their teams, customers, suppliers, and, on a personal level, with friends. Some companies will take things one step further and use mobile phone text messaging for marketing purposes or sending automated reminders for meetings, for example. There are many email messaging and text messaging apps available on the market, many of which integrate with Zapier, so that you can automate email and text messaging processes, some at a cost. You may, however, want to send simple messages by email or text, at no extra cost to you and in situations where you don't need to retain history. This is where Zapier's four built-in communication apps (**SMS**, **Email**, **IMAP**, and **SMTP**) come into play.

In this chapter, we will introduce the four communication-specific built-in Zapier apps, give descriptions of their functionality, and provide practical tips on how to use them.

We will cover the following key topics in this chapter:

- SMS by Zapier – sending text messages
- Email by Zapier – sending and receiving emails
- SMTP by Zapier – sending emails through mail servers
- IMAP by Zapier – retrieving emails from mail servers

> **Tip**
> Consider using the magic of AI to assist you with writing your responses to use in your communication Zaps. We will cover examples of how to use AI in more detail in *Chapter 19, AI and Automation.*

Once you have worked through each of these topics, you will know how to send text messages and emails, as well as send and receive emails from mail servers.

Technical requirements

To work through the content in this chapter, you will need access to a Zapier account. To build multi-step Zaps, you will need to subscribe to the Zapier Starter plan as a minimum.

SMS by Zapier – sending text messages

Using the SMS by Zapier built-in app, you can send 153-character-length text messages by **Short Message Service** (**SMS**) through mobile phone cellular networks. This app allows you to send a limited number of SMS messages to specified UK or US numbers that you own or have access to.

> **Important note**
>
> To prevent misuse of the app, Zapier requires you to confirm that you have access to the numbers that you specify. Therefore, you cannot use the app for mass marketing or to send external reminders to the numbers that you have not validated.

SMS by Zapier is useful for sending internal team notifications to numbers that you have access to or reminders to yourself. Here are a few examples of how to use the SMS by Zapier app:

- Get an SMS when you make a sale in your Shopify eCommerce store
- Get an SMS reminder before a **Google Calendar** meeting event
- Get a daily SMS with the day's weather prediction using Weather by Zapier

These are just a few ways to use SMS by Zapier; however; the possibilities are endless.

You can use the SMS by Zapier app in combination with other Zapier built-in apps that we covered in *Chapter 7, Getting Started with Built-In Apps*, as follows:

- Use Filter by Zapier to specify what conditions must be present for messages to be sent, for example, if you wanted to receive an SMS only if you sold a high-value item in your **WooCommerce** e-commerce store
- Send SMS messages at a specific time using Schedule by Zapier
- Send SMS messages after a certain period using Delay by Zapier

SMS by Zapier is included in your Zapier subscription at no extra cost. However, if you want to send SMS messages to a variety of numbers, to international numbers, or in large quantities, you may want to try other apps that integrate with Zapier, such as **Twilio**, **TextMagic**, or **Voodoo SMS**.

> **Tip**
>
> For more inspiration and access to pre-built templates, you can review the SMS by Zapier built-in app profile page at `https://zapier.com/apps/sms/integrations`.

Let's explore how to set up this built-in app so that we can start sending our SMS notifications.

Setting up SMS by Zapier

Once you have added an action step and chosen **SMS by Zapier** as the app, you will be asked to sign into SMS by Zapier the first time you use it. Click on the **Sign in to SMS by Zapier** button and a popup will appear, asking you to verify a number to send messages to, as follows:

- **To Number**: Enter the full phone number with the area and country code (+44 for the UK and +1 for the US, without the + icon) – for example, 4407565901203. This is a required field to enable the app.

- **Confirm via SMS or Call?**: Choose whether to receive a PIN code by SMS or voice call. This field is optional and will default to sending the PIN code by SMS.

- **Confirm PIN**: Use the **Send PIN** button to send the PIN code. Once received, enter the PIN code into the field that appears. This is a required field to enable the app.

This is shown in the following screenshot:

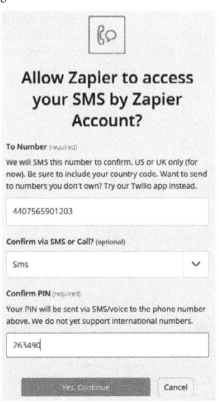

Figure 8.1 – Verifying a phone number in the SMS by Zapier app

Once you have validated your phone number, Zapier will send a confirmation message to you by SMS.

> **Tip**
>
> You can add multiple validated mobile phone numbers to the SMS by Zapier account, in the same way that you can add multiple app connections for a specific app such as Gmail (allowing you to send and receive emails for any accounts you have access to and can authenticate). This allows you to send customized messages to multiple mobile phone numbers.

Next, we can proceed to edit the **Action** section and fill in the fields, as follows:

- **From Number**: Choose from a drop-down list of fixed numbers or select **Random**. When choosing a fixed number, Zapier will attempt to send an SMS from that number; however, if it is unavailable, sending will default to a random number. It is not recommended to choose a custom value as this may cause the step to error.

- **Message**: Add static text, dynamic data from previous steps, or a combination of both in this field. Messages with over 153 characters will be truncated.

Using our working example from *Chapter 6, Creating Multi-Step Zaps and Using Built-In Apps*, we may want to send an SMS to notify us when new deals are added to Pipedrive. We illustrated how to use static text and dynamic data in the **Message** field in the following screenshot:

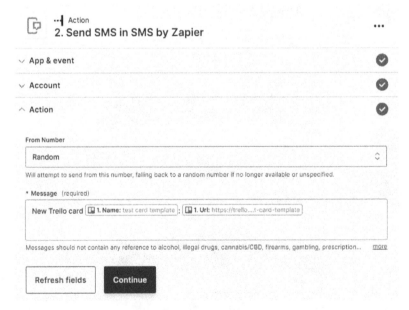

Figure 8.2 – Overview of customizing the Send SMS action event

You can then use the **Test** section to test this step or choose **Skip test**.

Proceed to add one or more action steps to your Zap.

> **Tip**
>
> For static messages, you can use the **Word Count** function in Microsoft Word or the LEN formula in Microsoft Excel to check how many characters your text message contains. When using dynamic data, to prevent messages from being truncated if they are over 153 characters, you can use the Formatter by Zapier app to transform text, dates/times, and numbers to shorten your data or display it in different ways. We will cover formatting data with the Formatter by Zapier built-in app in *Chapter 14, Formatting Date and Time*, *Chapter 15, Formatting Numbers*, *Chapter 16, Text Formatting Functions in Zapier – Part 1*, *Chapter 17, Text Formatting Functions in Zapier – Part 2*, and *Chapter 18, Zapier's Utilities Functions*.

You should now have a better understanding of how and when to use the SMS by Zapier built-in app to send SMS messages.

Now, let's take a look at how to send and receive emails using the Email by Zapier built-in app.

Email by Zapier – sending and receiving emails

Email by Zapier allows you to send and receive emails to and from a unique zapiermail.com email address to use as a trigger or action step. Therefore, you don't have to use your standard email addresses for things such as sending reminders or notifications to yourself or your team or forwarding information to any of your apps using a generic email address.

You can then send outbound emails, and if you've enabled read receipts, you can trigger a workflow when someone opens your sent email. You can also trigger Zaps to run when you receive emails that have been forwarded to the zapiermail.com address.

The following trigger and actions events are available to use:

- **New Inbound Email** (trigger)
- **Send Outbound Email** (action)
- **New Read Receipt** (trigger)

Let's look at each.

The New Inbound Email trigger event

This trigger event can be used to start a workflow when a new email has been received. This works by using a unique zapiermail.com email address, which you can use as the email recipient. This trigger event is especially handy to use with apps that allow you to create records on receipt of a new email, such as notes, tasks, and saving attachments.

Here are a few examples of how to use the Email by Zapier **New Inbound Email** trigger event:

- Send notes by email to a Slack channel

- Add new notes to Evernote by email

- Add new file attachments to **Dropbox** or **Google Drive**

Let's explore how to set up this trigger event.

Setting up the New Inbound Email trigger event

Once you have added this trigger step to the start of your workflow (to **1. Trigger**) and chosen **Email by Zapier** as the app and **New Inbound Email** as the trigger event, you can edit the **Email Address** field in the **Trigger** section. This field allows you to customize the unique email address associated with your mailbox. You can use lowercase letters and numbers only. If you want to forward notes to Evernote, you may choose to name the address notes, for example.

This is shown in the following screenshot:

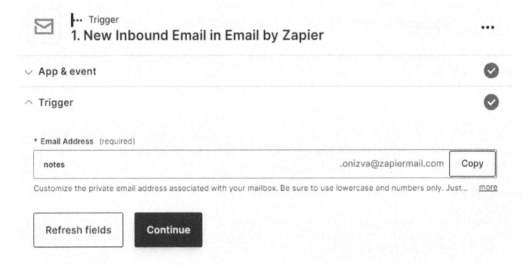

Figure 8.3 – Overview of setting up the New Inbound Email trigger event

As illustrated in *Figure 8.3*, our unique mailbox address would be notes.6fff9m@zapiermail.com.

You can then click on **Continue** to move on to the **Test** section, where you will be instructed to send an email to your unique email mailbox. Once done, use the **Test trigger** button and retrieve your test data to use in your action steps.

Proceed to add one or more action steps to your Zap using data from this trigger step.

You should now be able to receive email messages and trigger workflows using the **New Inbound Email** trigger event.

Next, let's take a look at the **Send Outbound Email** action event.

The Send Outbound Email action event

Similar to the SMS by Zapier built-in app, using the Email by Zapier **Send Outbound Email** action event is useful for sending messages, alerts, reminders, and notifications. You can send up to 10 email messages per hour. Here are a few examples of how to use this action event:

- Get an email notification for new Facebook Lead Ad leads

- Get an email notification when deals in your CRM are lost or won

- Get an email alert when your Zapier task usage has reached a certain percentage

Let's explore how to set up this action step.

Setting up the Send Outbound Email action event

Once you have added an action step and chosen **Email by Zapier** as the app and **Send Outbound Email** as the action event, you can edit the fields in the **Action** section as follows:

- **To**: Enter up to five email addresses separated with commas. Use static text or dynamic values from previous steps. This is a required field and must have at least one value for the Zap to run.

- **Subject**: Enter a subject for the email using static text or dynamic values from previous steps. This is a required field and must have at least some text for the Zap to run.

- **Body (HTML Or Plain)**: Enter the email body using customizable **Hypertext Markup Language (HTML)** or plain text. You can use static text or dynamic values from previous steps. When using plain text, Zapier will attempt to convert it into basic HTML so that it looks more pleasing to the eye; alternatively, you can use free or paid Markdown editor tools such as **Haroopad** (http://pad.haroopress.com/) or **HackMD** (https://hackmd.io/) to simply and effectively convert plain text into HTML for more customization. This is a required field and must have at least one character in it for the Zap to run.

- **Attachment**: You can attach a file object to the email and can be up to 10 MB in size. Attaching plain text content will convert the file into a .txt file.

- **From Name**: Enter a name that will be displayed when an email is received. You can use static text or dynamic values from previous steps.

- **Reply To**: Enter an email address that the recipient can reply to.

- **Cc**: Enter up to five email addresses separated with commas as secondary recipients. Use static text or dynamic values from previous steps.

- **Bcc**: Enter up to five email addresses separated with commas as blind secondary recipients. Use static text or dynamic values from previous steps.

- **Force Linebreaks?**: Use this drop-down Boolean field to select the **True** value if you want your emails to be received with line breaks or spacing. Forcing email text to use line breaks and spacing gives the email text a better appearance.

- **Enable Read Receipts?**: Use this drop-down Boolean field to select the **True** value if you want to be notified whether an email sent using this action event is read by the recipient. You must use this in combination with the **New Read Receipt** trigger event (which we will discuss in the next section) and a notification action event, such as an SMS, email, or Slack message, in a separate Zap to enable notifications to be sent.

These fields are shown in the following screenshot:

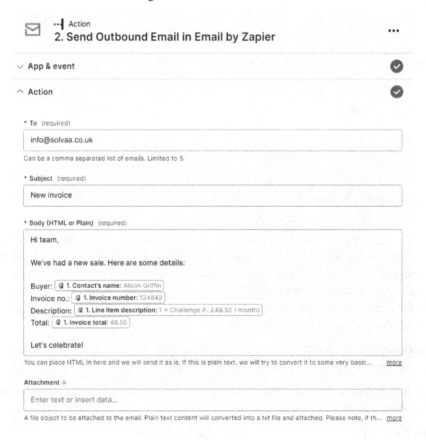

Figure 8.4 – Overview of setting up the Send Outbound Email action event in the Email by Zapier app (1)

The second part of the step customization is shown in the following screenshot:

Figure 8.5 – Overview of setting up the Send Outbound Email action event in the Email by Zapier app (2)

You can then use the **Test** section to test this step or choose **Skip test**.

> **Tip**
>
> You can use other email-sending apps such as Gmail, Microsoft Outlook, Mandrill, or SMTP by Zapier if you want to send emails to more than five recipients and if you want to send files larger than 10 MB. If you have multiple recipients being added using dynamic data from previous steps, ensure these values are separated by a comma. You can use Formatter by Zapier to alter such email values to ensure they work with the **Send Outbound Email** action event. We will cover formatting data with the Formatter by Zapier built-in app in *Chapter 14, Formatting Date and Time, Chapter 15, Formatting Numbers, Chapter 16, Text Formatting Functions in Zapier – Part 1, Chapter 17, Text Formatting Functions in Zapier – Part 2*, and *Chapter 18, Zapier's Utilities Functions*.

You should now be able to send email messages using the **Send Outbound Email** action event. Next, let's review the **New Read Receipt** trigger event.

The New Read Receipt trigger event

This trigger event can be used to start a workflow when an email sent using the **Send Outbound Email** action event is opened (if the **Enable Read Receipts** Boolean field is set to **True**). This trigger event is useful if you want to keep an eye on when emails have been opened.

Here are a few examples of how to use the Email by Zapier **New Read Receipts** trigger event:

- Send an SMS message when an email has been read
- Update an opportunity in Salesforce when an email has been read

Let's explore how to set up this trigger event.

Setting up the New Read Receipt trigger event

Let's work through the following steps to set up the **New Read Receipt** trigger event:

1. To use this trigger event, you must have a corresponding Zap set up that uses the **Send Outbound Email** action event and has the **Enable Read Receipts** Boolean field set to **True**. You can use the instructions in the *The Send Outbound Email action event* section to create this Zap.

2. Once you've done this, send a test email to your email address and view it. This will allow you to use that test data within the **Test** section of the corresponding **New Read Receipt** trigger step in *step 4*.

3. Add this trigger step to the start of your workflow (to **1. Trigger**) and choose **Email by Zapier** as the app and **New Read Receipt** as the trigger event.

4. Next, you can skip the **Trigger** section as there are no fields to customize, and then select **Continue** to use the **Test** section. You can use the **Test Trigger** button and retrieve either static test data or test data from your **Send Outbound Email** action step in the other Zap, as we did in *step 2*.

You can now proceed to add one or more action steps to your Zap based on your requirements using data from this trigger step.

You should now have a better understanding of how and when to use the **New Read Receipt** trigger event, as well as the other trigger and action events of the Email by Zapier app.

> Tip
> For more inspiration and access to pre-built templates, you can review the Email by Zapier built-in app profile page at `https://zapier.com/apps/email/integrations`.

Next, let's cover how to send emails from mail servers using the SMTP by Zapier built-in app.

SMTP by Zapier – sending emails through mail servers

Wikipedia (`https://en.wikipedia.org/wiki/Simple_Mail_Transfer_Protocol`) defines **Simple Mail Transfer Protocol** (**SMTP**) as "*a communication protocol for electronic mail transmission.*" Simply put, SMTP allows email client apps to send emails. Zapier allows you to connect to many commonly used mail client apps, such as Gmail or Zoho Mail. You may, however, have access to your own mail server and want to send emails independently. You can use SMTP by Zapier for precisely that purpose. SMTP by Zapier acts similarly to Email by Zapier; however, you can send emails without volume, recipient, and file size restrictions.

First of all, it may be useful to elaborate on what the difference is between a mail client and a mail server. The mail server is the software that runs on a computer server that processes email communications, such as Microsoft Server Exchange. You can read more about mail servers here: `https://en.wikipedia.org/wiki/Comparison_of_mail_servers`.

The mail client, on the other hand, is the software program that you use to view, write, and send incoming and outgoing emails. You can see a comparison of mail clients here: `https://en.wikipedia.org/wiki/Comparison_of_webmail_providers`.

To send and receive emails, you need both a mail client and a mail server.

The following figure shows a list of a few common SMTP settings that may be useful when you set up your SMTP by Zapier app:

Client	Server	Authentication	Port
Googlemail - Gmail	smtp.gmail.com	SSL	465
Googlemail - Gmail	smtp.gmail.com	StartTLS	587
Outlook.com	smtp-mail.outlook.com	StartTLS	587
Office365.com	smtp.office365.com	StartTLS	587
Yahoo Mail	smtp.mail.yahoo.com	SSL	465
Yahoo Mail Plus	plus.smtp.mail.yahoo.com	SSL	465
Yahoo Mail UK	smtp.mail.yahoo.co.uk	SSL	465
Yahoo Mail Deutschland	smtp.mail.yahoo.com	SSL	465
Yahoo Mail AU/NZ	smtp.mail.yahoo.au	SSL	465
AOL.com	smtp.aol.com	StartTLS	587
AT&T	smtp.att.yahoo.com	SSL	465
NTL @ntlworld.com	smtp.ntlworld.com	SSL	465
BT Connect	smtp.btconnect.com		25
O2 Deutschland	mail.o2online.de		25
T-Online Deutschland	securesmtp.t-online.de	StartTLS	587
1&1 (1and1)	smtp.1and1.com	StartTLS	587
1&1 Deutschland	smtp.1und1.de	StartTLS	587
Verizon	outgoing.verizon.net		587
Zoho Mail	smtp.zoho.com	SSL	465
Mail.com	smtp.mail.com	StartTLS	587
GMX.com	smtp.gmx.com	SSL	465
Net@ddress by USA.NET	smtp.postoffice.net	SSL	465

Figure 8.6 – Common SMTP settings (courtesy of Arclab)

You can get more details from this source: `https://www.arclab.com/en/kb/email/list-of-smtp-and-imap-servers-mailserver-list.html`.

Here are a few examples of how to use the SMTP by Zapier app:

- Send an email to customers when they purchase a product in your eCommerce store

- Send an email alert for new posts on your Facebook page timeline

As with SMS by Zapier and the **Send Outbound Email** action event of Email by Zapier, you can use SMTP by Zapier in combination with other Zapier built-in apps, such as Filter by Zapier, Schedule by Zapier, and Delay by Zapier.

> **Tip**
>
> For more inspiration and access to pre-built templates, you can review the SMTP by Zapier built-in app profile page at `https://zapier.com/apps/smtp/integrations`.

Let's explore how to set up this built-in app so that you can start sending emails.

Setting up the SMTP by Zapier app

Once you have added an action step and chosen **SMTP by Zapier** as the app, you will be asked to sign into SMTP by Zapier the first time you use it. Upon clicking the **Sign in** button, a popup will appear, asking you to provide details so that you can allow access to your SMTP by Zapier account, as follows:

- **Host**: Enter the host server that Zapier should connect to. This is a required field, and a valid value must be added for the Zap to work.

- **Email/Username**: Enter your SMTP login email address or username credentials. This is a required field, and a valid value must be added for the Zap to work.

- **Password**: Enter your SMTP password credentials. This is a required field, and a valid value must be added for the Zap to work.

- **Use TLS?**: Use this Boolean field dropdown to select **Yes** or **No** to specify whether you send encrypted emails using **Transport Layer Security** (**TLS**). Check your email client account for this information if you are unsure.

- **Port**: Choose a port number from the number (integer) field drop-down menu. If one isn't selected, 25 will be used as the default. Many SMTP servers send mail over TLS on port 25.

- **From Email**: Enter an email address to display as the email it is being sent from. Sometimes, adding this email address may fail, and you may need to define a specific **From** address.

These options are shown in the following screenshot for a Gmail account:

SMTP

Allow Zapier to access your SMTP by Zapier Account?

Host (required)

The host Zapier should connect to.

> smtp.gmail.com

Email/Username (required)

Your SMTP login credentials.

> joebloggs@companyx.com

Password (required)

> ••••••••••••

Use TLS? (optional)

> No   ∨

Port (optional) 1 2 3

We will use a default if not provided.

> 465   ∨

From Email (optional)

If adding this fails, you may need to define a specific "From" address.

>

[Yes, Continue to SMTP by Zapier]   [Cancel]

Figure 8.7 – Setting up the SMTP by Zapier app

Once you have clicked on the **Yes, Continue to SMTP by Zapier** button, we can proceed to edit the **Action** section and fill in the fields, as follows:

- **From Name**: Enter a name that will be displayed when an email is received. You can use static text or dynamic values from previous steps.

- **From Email**: Enter an email address that Zapier should attempt to send the email from. Ideally, this email address should match an email address in your SMTP settings. This is a required field and must have at least one value for the Zap to run.

- **Reply To**: Enter a specific email address that recipients can reply to other than the **from** email. Use static text or dynamic values from previous steps.

- **To**: Enter one or more email addresses separated with commas. Use static text or dynamic values from previous steps. This is a required field and must have at least one value for the Zap to run.

- **Subject**: Enter a subject for the email using static text or dynamic values from previous steps. This is a required field and must have at least some text for the Zap to run.

- **Body**: Enter the email body in plain text. You can use static text or dynamic values from the previous steps. This is a required field and must have some character in it for the Zap to run.

- **HTML Body**: Enter the email body that you used in the **Body** field duplicated in HTML. You can use static text or dynamic values from previous steps. You can use free or paid Markdown editor tools such as Haroopad or HackMD to simply and effectively convert plain text into HTML for more customization.

- **Attachment**: You can attach a file object to the email. Any plain text content attached will be converted into a `.txt` file.

Once you have selected **Continue**, you can use the **Test** section to test this step or choose **Skip test**.

> **Tip**
> Most mail clients will have help documentation, giving more information on how to activate IMAP/POP3/SMTP settings.

You should now have a better understanding of how and when to use the SMTP by Zapier app to send emails. Now, let's review how to retrieve emails from mail servers using the IMAP by Zapier built-in app.

IMAP by Zapier – retrieving emails from mail servers

Wikipedia (`https://en.wikipedia.org/wiki/Internet_Message_Access_Protocol`) defines **Internet Message Access Protocol** (**IMAP**) as "*an internet standard protocol used by email clients to retrieve email messages from a mail server over a TCP/IP connection.*" IMAP allows email client apps to retrieve emails from the server. If you are using an email server other than Gmail, Zoho Mail, or Microsoft Office 365, you can use IMAP by Zapier to retrieve emails from these mail servers. For example, these servers may include Rackspace, Zimbra, or Microsoft Exchange Server.

The following figure shows a list of a few common IMAP settings that will be useful when you set up your IMAP by Zapier app:

Client	Server	Authentication	Port
Googlemail - Gmail	imap.gmail.com	SSL	993
Outlook.com	imap-mail.outlook.com	SSL	993
Office365.com	outlook.office365.com	SSL	993
Yahoo Mail	plus.imap.mail.yahoo.com	SSL	993
Yahoo Mail Plus	plus.imap.mail.yahoo.com	SSL	993
Yahoo Mail UK	imap.mail.yahoo.co.uk	SSL	993
Yahoo Mail Deutschland	imap.mail.yahoo.com	SSL	993
Yahoo Mail AU/NZ	imap.mail.yahoo.au	SSL	993
AOL.com	imap.aol.com	SSL	993
AT&T	imap.att.yahoo.com	SSL	993
NTL @ntlworld.com	imap.ntlworld.com	SSL	993
BT Connect	imap4.btconnect.com		143
O2 Deutschland	imap.o2online.de		143
T-Online Deutschland	securimap.t-online.de	SSL	993
1&1 (1and1)	imap.1and1.com	SSL	993
1&1 Deutschland	imap.1und1.de	SSL	993
Verizon	incoming.verizon.net		143
Zoho Mail	imap.zoho.com	SSL	993
Mail.com	imap.mail.com	SSL	993
GMX.com	imap.gmx.com	SSL	993
Net@ddress by USA.NET	imap.postoffice.net	SSL	993

Figure 8.8 – Common IMAP server settings (courtesy of Arclab)

You can get more details from this source: `https://www.arclab.com/en/kb/email/list-of-smtp-and-imap-servers-mailserver-list.html`.

The IMAP by Zapier built-in app can be used as a trigger to start workflows based on the following trigger events:

- **New Email** (trigger): This triggers when a new email is received
- **New Mailbox** (trigger): This triggers when a new mailbox is created

Now, let's explore how to get started using the IMAP by Zapier app.

Setting up the IMAP by Zapier app

Once you have added an action step and chosen **IMAP by Zapier** as the app, you will be asked to sign into IMAP by Zapier the first time you use it. Click on the **Sign in** button and a popup will appear, asking you to provide details so that you can allow access to your IMAP by Zapier account, as follows:

- **Host**: Enter the host server that Zapier should connect to. This is a required field, and a valid value must be added for the Zap to work.
- **Username**: Enter your IMAP login username credentials. This is a required field, and a valid value must be added for the Zap to work.
- **Password**: Enter your IMAP password credentials. This is a required field, and a valid value must be added for the Zap to work.
- **Port**: Choose a port number of either 143 or 993 from the number (integer) field drop-down menu. Port number 143 will be used as the default.

These options are shown in the following screenshot for a Gmail account:

IMAP

Allow Zapier to access your IMAP by Zapier Account?

Host (required)

The host Zapier should connect to.

imap.gmail.com

Username (required)

Your IMAP login credentials.

joebloggs@companyx.com

Password (required)

••••••••••••

Port (optional) 1 2 3

We will use a default if not provided.

993

Yes, Continue to IMAP by Zapier   Cancel

Figure 8.9 – Setting up the IMAP by Zapier app

Then, select the **Yes, Continue to IMAP by Zapier** button to authenticate the connection.

> **Tip**
> Most mail clients will have help documentation to provide more information on how to activate IMAP/POP3/SMTP settings. Check that IMAP is allowed in your mail account settings.

The **New Email** and **New Mailbox** trigger events differ slightly in configuration. We will cover this next, starting with the **New Email** trigger event.

Customizing and using the New Email trigger event

Once we have authenticated our IMAP connection, we can proceed to edit the **Trigger** section and choose which mailbox to use, as follows:

- **Name of Mailbox**: A list of mailbox folders or labels will be brought in from your email account, and you can choose which one you want to use from a drop-down menu. Choose **Inbox** if you want to be notified of all new messages, or specify a folder or label depending on whether you want to be notified of new emails based on how you file them. This is a required field and must have at least one value for the Zap to run.

Once you have selected **Continue**, you can use the **Test** section to test this step or **Skip test**.

Here are a few examples of how you can use the IMAP by Zapier **New Email** trigger event:

- Create new Trello cards for new IMAP emails
- Send Slack channel messages for new IMAP emails

Now, let's have a look at the **New Mailbox** trigger event.

Customizing the New Mailbox trigger event

Once we have authenticated our IMAP connection, we can proceed to skip the **Trigger** section as this will be triggered when any new mailbox in that IMAP account is created. Once you have selected **Continue**, you can use the **Test** section to test this step or choose **Skip test**.

Here are a few examples of how you can use the IMAP by Zapier **New Mailbox** trigger event:

- Add new rows to a Google Sheets spreadsheet when new IMAP mailboxes are created
- Send an email when new IMAP mailboxes are created

There are many more possibilities of how you can use both the **New Email** and **New Mailbox** trigger events in your Zaps.

> **Tip**
>
> For more inspiration and access to pre-built templates, you can review the IMAP by Zapier built-in app profile page at `https://zapier.com/apps/imap/integrations`.

You should now have a better understanding of how and when to use the IMAP by Zapier app.

Summary

In this chapter, we helped you get to grips with using the four communication-specific Zapier built-in apps. We covered how to use SMS by Zapier to send text messages as notifications and reminders. Next, we discussed how to use Email by Zapier to trigger workflows on receipt of emails and when emails are read, as well as how to send emails. Lastly, we reviewed how to use IMAP by Zapier to retrieve emails from mail servers, and SMTP by Zapier to send them from mail servers.

You now know how to send text messages and emails, as well as trigger workflows on receipt of emails and read emails using built-in communication apps by Zapier.

In the next chapter, we will introduce you to a few more of Zapier's range of built-in apps. We will cover specific functions, such as how to extract data from emails (using parsing), how to use RSS feeds in automations, and how to compile data into digests.

Questions

1. Can SMS by Zapier be used to send text messages to multiple numbers?

2. Can you send text messages with more than 153 characters using SMS by Zapier?

3. Can you format the text in email messages in Email by Zapier and SMTP by Zapier with bold, embedded hyperlinks and italics?

Exploring Built-In Apps for Extracting and Compiling Data

As we discussed in *Chapter 6*, *Creating Multi-Step Zaps and Using Built-In Apps*, the power of Zapier lies in the functionality that you can take advantage of by using Zapier's built-in apps. In this chapter, we will introduce you to built-in apps that extract data from emails, use RSS feeds, and create data digests. We will describe their functionality and provide practical tips on how to use them.

In *Chapter 8*, *Built-In Communication Apps*, we covered built-in communication apps. So, in this chapter, we start with a similar theme by discussing how to extract data from emails using Email Parser by Zapier. Then, we will explore how to use RSS feed readers in automations using RSS by Zapier. After that, we will dive into how to compile data digests with Digest by Zapier. Finally, we will work through an exercise to build a Zap using RSS by Zapier and Digest by Zapier.

We will cover the following key topics in this chapter:

- Email Parser by Zapier – extracting data from emails
- RSS by Zapier – using RSS feed readers
- Digest by Zapier – compiling data in digests
- Exercise – creating a multi-step Zap with an RSS feed digest

Once you have worked through each of these topics, you will know how to parse data from email messages, use RSS feed readers, and compile data in digests.

Technical requirements

To make the most of the content and exercises in this chapter, you will need access to a Zapier account. The Zapier Starter plan will be adequate. You can get access to the Zap templates used in this chapter here: `https://bit.ly/zapier-book`. Using these templates will help you visualize how the process works.

Email Parser by Zapier – extracting data from emails

The Email Parser by Zapier built-in app allows you to extract data from emails that have been forwarded to a unique @robot.zapier.com email address. By teaching Email Parser by Zapier to understand patterns in emails that you send to it, it can consistently extract that information for you to use in other steps in your workflow.

Email Parser by Zapier can only be used as a trigger step at the start of your workflow. It is available as the following trigger events:

- **New Email**
- **New Mailbox**

Let's look at each.

The New Email trigger event

This trigger event can be used to start a workflow when a new email has been received. This works by using a unique @robot.zapier.com email address, which you would forward emails to. It is best practice that you set up multiple mailboxes to deal with separate workflows.

Here are a few examples of when to use the Email Parser by Zapier **New Email** trigger event:

- If you receive a summary of information by email after web forms are submitted, you might want to add those details to a CRM such as **Close.io** or **Airtable**
- If you receive customer payment and billing information by email after a sale is made, you might want to add those details to your accounting app, such as **QuickBooks Online** or Xero
- If you receive email inquiries in a specific mailbox, you might want to create a task for your team to deal with inquiries in a task management app, such as Trello or Asana

Let's explore how to set up this trigger event.

Setting up the New Email trigger event

Let's cover how to set up the **New Email** trigger event:

1. Once you have added this trigger step to the start of your workflow (to **1. Trigger**), and chosen **Email Parser by Zapier** as the app and **New Email** as the trigger event, you can select **Continue**.
2. In the **Choose Account** section, click on the **Sign in to Email Parser by Zapier** button to create a new Email Parser by Zapier account.

3. A new pop-up window will be displayed. To sign in using your Zapier account credentials, select the **Log in with your Zapier account** button. To use an alternative username and password, enter these details in the boxes provided and select the **Login** button. This is shown in the following screenshot:

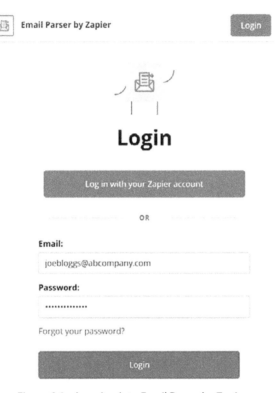

Figure 9.1 – Logging into Email Parser by Zapier

4. Allow Zapier to connect to Email Parser by Zapier by clicking on the **Authorize** button. You can also click on the **Cancel** button to cancel.

5. On the next screen, further authentication is required, so click on the **Authorize** button. Once authorized, you will be redirected back to the trigger step.

Before we can customize the trigger step, we need to create a new mailbox in our Email Parser by Zapier account. We'll take a look at how to do this next.

Setting up mailboxes in the Email Parser by Zapier account and mapping templates

We now need to create a mailbox, forward an email template, map our data, and alter the parse mapping settings. To illustrate this, we will use the example of a web form submission, where we want to extract the name, email address, service, and inquiry details. Let's get started by working through each of the following steps:

1. Navigate to `parser.zapier.com` and sign in to your Email Parser by Zapier account either by logging in with your Zapier account or adding separate login details.

2. Click on the orange **Create Mailbox** button to create a new mailbox. A new mailbox address will be provided, as shown in the following screenshot:

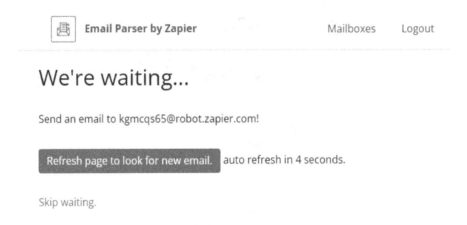

Figure 9.2 – Email Parser by Zapier mailbox creation

3. Copy the mailbox address provided and send an example of an email that you want to parse to the mailbox. You can refresh the page to look for new emails by clicking on the **Refresh page to look for new email.** button; auto-refresh will happen every 10 seconds. Alternatively, click on the **Skip waiting.** link to skip this.

4. Once a new email has been received, do the following to correctly parse information from your email:

    *   **Address**: Change your mailbox name by changing the prefix. Use a name that identifies the process but is unique and hard to guess, such as `abcompanywebform`. You can also leave the mailbox name as it was.

- **Initial Template**: This field will show the data from the email you forwarded to the mailbox. Label the data you want to consistently parse from emails forwarded to this mailbox by highlighting the text and naming it. This is shown in the following screenshot:

Email Parser by Zapier

Address:

This must be a unique word or random combination of letters. Remember, you want this hard to guess!

kgmcqs65   @robot.zapier.com

Initial Template:

Highlight the text you would like extracted and give each one a name!

New Website Form Completed

Name: {{name}}
Phone: {{phone}}
Email: {{email}}
Inquiry: Please can you contact me about a quote

inquiry

Save or cancel

Figure 9.3 – Formatting the Email Parser by Zapier mailbox's Address and Initial Template fields

- **Body Source**: Use the drop-down menu to select whether you want Email Parser by Zapier to extract content from plain text (**Always use plain text body content**), HTML (**Always use HTML body content**), or whatever the best content is (**Use the best body content available**). The latter is the default and is recommended. This is important for consistently extracting data.

- **Parser Engine**: Use the drop-down menu to choose which parser engine to use. You can choose between **Classic (v1, legacy)**, **Experimental (v2)**, and **Best Match (v1 + v2)**. The last one is the default and is recommended.

5. Select the **Save Address and Template** button to save and proceed or **Delete Mailbox** to delete the mailbox and start again.

Now, let's review how to help Zapier intelligently parse data from your emails.

Adjusting Email Parser mailbox templates for the best results

Email Parser by Zapier works best with consistent formats of information, such as data presented on the same lines with the same spacing between lines. If the parser engine extracts information incorrectly, you can teach it the correct formats by reporting inaccuracies and editing additional templates. It is recommended that you send a few example emails to the parser mailbox, check the consistency of extracted information, and edit the template or report inaccuracies. You can do this as follows:

1. From the main mailbox dashboard, click on the **View Emails** link of the appropriate mailbox.

    The emails that have been sent will be shown in list order, with the email address they were sent from and when they were sent. You can either delete the emails by checking the **Delete** box and clicking on the **Delete Selected E-mails** button or **Show** or **Hide** content using the appropriate link.

2. To review the accuracy of data for any email, click on the **Show** link.

3. Choose from the following four data view options:

    *   **extracted**: Click on the **extracted** link to show the parsed data from the email

    *   **original**: Click on the **original** link to show the original email data forwarded to the parser

    *   **template**: Click on the **template** link to show the labeled data from the original template

    *   **output**: Click on the **output** link to show parsed data output with the data labels and extracted data

    An example is shown in the following screenshot:

kgmcqs65@robot.zapier.com History

From	When
kelly@solvaa.co.uk	Mon, 02 Jan 2023 08:14:30 -0600

New Website Form Completed

Name: John Smith
Phone: 07585600801
Email: john.smith1234@gmail.com
Inquiry: Please can you contact me about a quote

extracted / original / template / output

Report inaccurate or accurate / Edit extra template

Figure 9.4 – Reviewing email history in Email Parser by Zapier

4. Notify the parser engine of whether the extracted text was incorrect by clicking on the **inaccurate** link (as shown in *Figure 9.4*) or correct by clicking on the **accurate** link.

5. Click on the **Edit extra template** link to add an additional template to the mailbox parser data.

> **Tip**
> Unless your email data is straightforward and basic, ensuring Email Parser by Zapier works consistently can be a case of trial and error that involves remapping data and changing settings to teach the parser engine to extract data correctly. If you have more complex data to extract, consider using a dedicated parser app such as **Docparser** or **Mailparser**.

Now that we have created the mailbox and tested and adjusted the settings, let's finish setting up the trigger step.

Completing the setup of the trigger step

Navigate back to your Zap in the Zap editor, and from there, complete the setup of the trigger step by editing the **Mailbox** field in the **Trigger** section. This field allows you to select which mailbox you want to use. Use the drop-down option to choose from the list of mailboxes that you have created. An example of how to set up this trigger step is shown in the following screenshot:

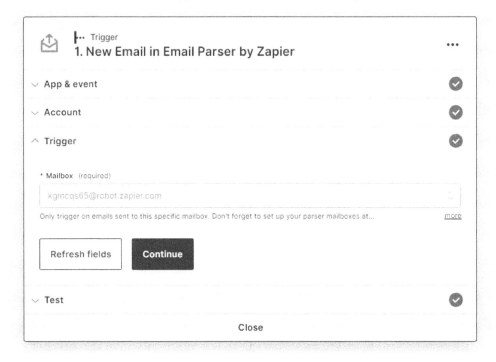

Figure 9.5 – Overview of customizing the New Email trigger event

You can then select **Continue** and, in the **Test** section, click on the **Test trigger** button to retrieve your test data so that you can use it in your action steps. If you have not yet sent a test email to your parser engine mailbox, you will be instructed to send one.

Proceed to add one or more action steps to your Zap using data from this trigger step.

> **Tip**
>
> Here is an interesting example of how you can use AI to parse data from an email using the OpenAI integration with Zapier: `https://community.zapier.com/featured-articles-65/use-openai-with-zapier-to-parse-an-email-or-other-data-22709`. We will explore the OpenAI integration in more detail in *Chapter 19, AI and Automation*.

You should now be able to use the **New Email** trigger event. Next, let's take a look at the **New Mailbox** trigger event.

The New Mailbox trigger event

This trigger event can be used to start a workflow when a new mailbox is added to your Email Parser by Zapier account. This trigger event is useful if you and your team are collaborating on Zapier, and you want to keep an eye on when mailboxes are being created.

Here are a couple of examples of how to use the Email Parser by Zapier **New Mailbox** trigger event:

- Send a message to Microsoft Teams when a new mailbox is created
- Send an email when a new mailbox is added

Let's explore how to set up this trigger event.

Setting up the New Mailbox trigger event

Once you have added this trigger step to the start of your workflow (to **1. Trigger**), choose **Email Parser by Zapier** as the app and **New Mailbox** as the trigger event. Then, select **Continue** to use the **Test** section. Use the **Test trigger** button to retrieve test data.

Proceed to add one or more action steps to your Zap using data from this trigger step.

You should now have a better understanding of how and when to use the **New Mailbox** trigger event, as well as the **New Email** trigger event of the Email by Zapier built-in app.

> **Tip**
>
> For more inspiration and access to pre-built templates, you can review the Email Parser by Zapier built-in app profile page at `https://zapier.com/apps/email-parser/integrations`.

This Zapier Community resource provides some additional insight into using the Email Parser by Zapier built-in app: `https://community.zapier.com/featured-articles-65/email-parser-common-issues-workarounds-and-tips-17539`.

> **Tip**
>
> You can also use the AI by Zapier (beta) built-in app to intelligently parse text from emails and specify conditions such as routing emails based on topics. We will cover AI by Zapier in more detail in *Chapter 19, AI and Automation*.

Next, let's cover how to use the RSS by Zapier built-in app so that you know how to use RSS feed data in your automations.

RSS by Zapier – using RSS feed readers

It can be overwhelming trying to keep on top of all the content that gets pushed our way, and we risk missing out on crucial new content. **Really Simple Syndication** (**RSS**) feeds update whenever the website publishes new content in a blog or podcast. This is useful as you can use this information to sift through what you want to see and be updated on new content. Most websites have RSS feeds in the format of `site.com/feed` or `site.com/rss`. Often, they will display in a _Feeds link in the footer bar. Private feeds often require you to use login credentials to access them. For more information on how to find the RSS feed for almost any website, check out this article: `https://zapier.com/blog/how-to-find-rss-feed-url/`.

The RSS by Zapier built-in app allows you to use RSS feed updates as a trigger, which, by then adding a notification action step such as an email, SMS, or Slack message, will give you an update on new content. You can also create your own custom RSS feed with the app.

Here are a few examples of how you can use RSS by Zapier:

- Share new blog posts from your website on your social media channels
- Add new articles from your favorite websites to a Google Sheets spreadsheet or **Knack**
- Get an email when a new blog article is published on your competitor's website

RSS by Zapier can be used as both a trigger and action step and is available as the following events:

- **New Item in Feed** (trigger)
- **New Items in Multiple Feeds** (trigger)
- **Create Item in Feed** (action)

Let's explore how to set up each of these in turn.

The New Item in Feed trigger event

The **New Item in Feed** trigger event can be used to start a workflow when new content is released from a specific website.

Let's explore how to set up this trigger event.

Setting up the New Item in Feed trigger event

Once you have added this trigger step to the start of your workflow (to **1. Trigger**), and chosen **RSS by Zapier** as the app and **New Item in Feed** as the trigger event, you can select **Continue**. You can then edit the fields in the **Trigger** section, as follows:

- **Feed URL**: This field allows you to choose the RSS feed URL that you want to be notified of when new feed items are available. Establish the correct RSS feed format to use by exploring or searching on the relevant website. The format is normally `site.com/feed` or `site.com/rss`. This is a required field and must have a value for the Zap to run.

- **Username**: If the RSS feed is private, enter username credentials to enable access. You can type in static text, map in dynamic data from previous steps, or use a combination.

- **Password**: If the RSS feed is private, type in password credentials to enable access.

- **What Triggers a New Feed Item**: This drop-down field allows you to choose what type of data triggers the event. The default option is **Different Guid/URL (recommended)**, and it is recommended that you use this. Choose **Different Content** or **Anything is Different** as advanced options if you understand the ins and outs of RSS feed functionality.

These options are shown in the following screenshot:

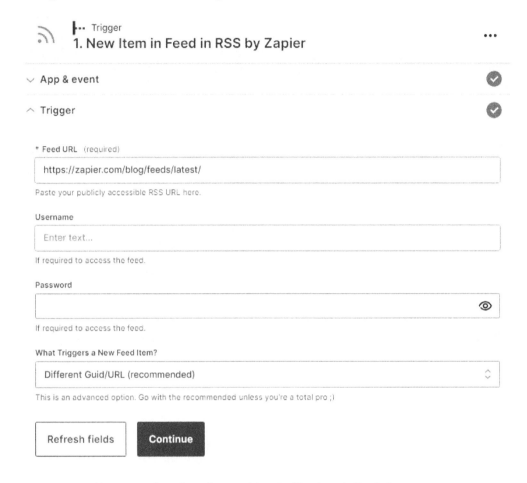

Figure 9.6 – Overview of customizing the New Item in Feed trigger event

You can then select **Continue** and, in the **Test** section, use the **Test trigger** button to retrieve your test data to use in your action steps.

Proceed to add one or more action steps to your Zap using data from this trigger step.

> **Tip**
> If you only want to see certain new items, such as posts from zoho.com, then you can add a conditional logic step with Filter by Zapier.

You should now be able to use the **New Item in Feed** trigger event. Next, let's take a look at the **New Items in Multiple Feeds** trigger event.

The New Items in Multiple Feeds trigger event

The **New Items in Multiple Feeds** trigger event can be used to start a workflow when new content is released from up to 10 websites. This saves you from having to set up multiple Zaps to trigger for each RSS feed.

Let's explore how to set up this trigger event.

Setting up the New Items in Multiple Feeds trigger event

Once you have added this trigger step to the start of your workflow (to **1. Trigger**), and chosen **RSS by Zapier** as the app and **New Items in Multiple Feeds** as the trigger event, you can select **Continue**. You can then edit the fields in the **Trigger** section, as follows:

- **Feed URLs**: These fields allow you to choose the RSS feed URLs that you want to be notified of when new feed items are available. Establish the correct RSS feed format to use by exploring or searching on the relevant website. The format is normally site.com/feed or site.com/rss. Add one URL per field; additional fields will appear once you start typing so that you can add a maximum of 10 URLs. Delete any URLs by clicking on the **x** button at the end of the field. This is a required field and must have a value for the Zap to run.

- **What Triggers a New Feed Item**: This drop-down field allows you to choose what type of data triggers the event. The default option is **Different Guide/URL (recommended)**, and it is recommended that you use this. Choose **Different Content** or **Anything is Different** as advanced options if you understand the ins and outs of RSS feed functionality.

These options are shown in the following screenshot:

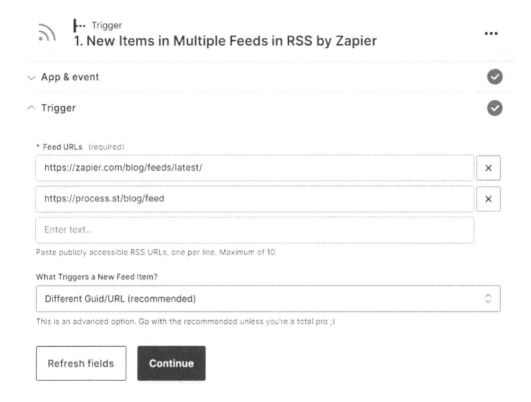

Figure 9.7 – Overview of customizing the New Items in Multiple Feeds trigger event

You can then select **Continue** and, in the **Test** section, use the **Test Trigger** button to retrieve your test data so that you can use it in your action steps.

Proceed to add one or more action steps to your Zap using data from this trigger step.

You should now be able to use the **New Items in Multiple Feeds** trigger event. Next, let's take a look at the **Create Item in Feed** action event.

The Create Item in Feed action event

The **Create Item in Feed** action event allows you to create a bespoke feed and host it on a website with a shareable link. This is best used in combination with the **New Item in Feed** or **New Items in Multiple Feeds** trigger event.

Let's explore how to set up this action event.

Setting up the Create Item in Feed action event

You can use the **Create Item in Feed** action event once you have set up your trigger step.

Once you have added an action step either by selecting the **Action** step or clicking on the + icon, and have chosen **RSS by Zapier** as the app and **Create Item in Feed** as the action event, you can edit the fields in the **Action** section, as follows:

- **Feed URL**: This field allows you to create and customize your unique and private RSS feed URL. Zapier generates the prefix, and you can customize the suffix by adding a combination of letters, numbers, and hyphens. Do not add spaces or symbols. You can also copy the URL by clicking on the **Copy** button so that you can store it somewhere for quick reference, such as in your Evernote notes. This is a required field and must have a value for the Zap to run.

- **Feed Title**: Enter the title of your new feed. You can enter static text, dynamic data mapped from previous steps, or a combination. If left blank, the title will default to **A Feed Called X**, where **X** is the prefix that you entered in the **Feed URL** field.

- **Max Records**: Enter a number for the maximum number of records you want to be returned in the feed. The maximum is 50, but adding a number in this field allows you to reduce the number. You can enter static text, dynamic data mapped from previous steps, or a combination into this integer field.

- **Item Title**: Enter a title for the item to publish. Here, you can type in static content, map dynamic content from previous steps in your Zap, or a combination. This is a required field and must have a value for the Zap to run.

- **Source URL**: Provide details of a source URL where the feed item is permanently hosted. This is a required field and must have a value for the Zap to run.

- **Content**: Provide details of the content of the feed item in either plain text or HTML format. You can type in static content, map dynamic content from previous steps in your Zap, or a combination. This is a required field and must have a value for the Zap to run.

- **Automatically Truncate Messages Over 10KB?**: Use this Boolean field to select whether you want Zapier to truncate data in your **Content** field if it is over 10 KB. Choose **Yes** to truncate the message or **No** to generate an error message if the data is too large.

- **Author Name**: Add the name of the author by typing in static content, mapping dynamic content from previous steps in your Zap, or a combination.

- **Author Email**: Add the author's email address by typing in static content, mapping dynamic content from previous steps in your Zap, or a combination.

- **Author Link**: Add a link to the author by typing in static content, mapping dynamic content from previous steps in your Zap, or a combination. This could be a link to the author's bio or website, for example.

- **Media URL**: Add a raw media URL to allow files such as podcast files, images, or videos to be downloaded. You can type in static content, map dynamic content from previous steps in your Zap, or a combination.

- **Media MIME Type**: Specify the media MIME type (a two-part identifier for file formats) of the URL you added in the **Media URL** field. If left blank, Zapier will default it to `audio/mpeg`. More details about MIME types can be found on Wikipedia: `https://en.wikipedia.org/wiki/Media_type`. You can type in static content, map dynamic content from previous steps in your Zap, or a combination.

- **Media Length In Bytes**: Some media players require a valid length. If left blank, this field defaults to `0`. You can type in static content, map dynamic content from previous steps in your Zap, or a combination.

- **Pubdate**: Provide details of the publishing date of the feed item. The most popular term to use is *now*, but you can use any compatible date/time format in this field. You can type in static content, map dynamic content from previous steps in your Zap, or a combination. Feed items are not ordered by **Pubdate**, but by the date they were inserted instead.

An example is shown in the following two screenshots, where data mapped from a **New Item in Feed** trigger event has been used:

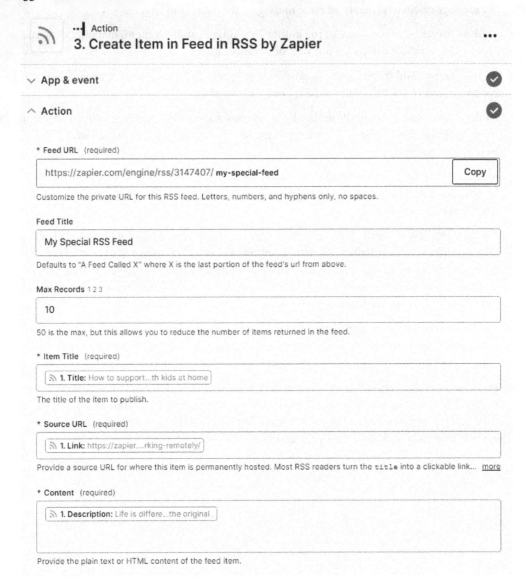

Figure 9.8 – Overview of customizing the Create Item in Feed action event (1)

The second part of the action step is shown in the following screenshot:

Automatically Truncate Messages over 10KB?

Yes

Use this field to control whether Zapier will truncate data over the 10kb limit (select Yes), or generate an error if the...   more

Author Name

1. Raw Author: wade@zapier.com (Wade Foster)

Author Email

Enter text or insert data...

Author Link

Enter text or insert data...

Media URL

Enter text or insert data...

Specify a raw download URL for your podcast file, image, or other media file.

Media MIME Type

Enter text or insert data...

What is the MIME type for your raw file? Defaults to audio/mpeg.

Media Length in Bytes

Enter text or insert data...

Some players require a valid length. Defaults to 0.

Pubdate

1. Pub Date: Fri, 04 Sep 202...13:36:00 +0000

Most people would put "now", but you can change it to something like "tomorrow" or "next week monday at 7pm" or...   more

Refresh fields   Continue

Figure 9.9 – Overview of customizing the Create Item in Feed action event (2)

Click on the **Continue** button. Once you've done this, you can use the **Test** section to test this step or click on **Skip test**.

The following screenshot shows an example of what the feed will look like:

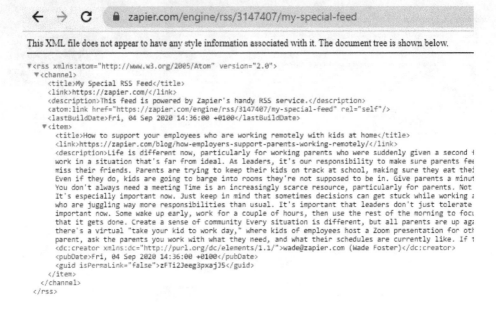

Figure 9.10 – Overview of the result of using a Create Item in Feed action event

Proceed to add one or more action steps or turn on your Zap.

You should now have a better understanding of how and when to use the RSS by Zapier built-in app and its various triggers and actions.

> **Tip**
> For more inspiration and access to pre-built templates, you can review the RSS by Zapier built-in app profile page at `https://zapier.com/apps/rss/integrations`.

Now, let's cover how to use the Digest by Zapier built-in app to compile data in digests.

Digest by Zapier – compiling data in digests

The Digest by Zapier built-in app allows you to capture data from multiple workflow trigger events and compile the data into single summaries that can be used in other action events. This is useful if you have several notifications that you want to receive a summary of at one time rather than as they happen. If you don't want to be disturbed on certain days with regular notifications, turn them off and just receive a summary at times you specify. Conversely, some of your apps may not send you notifications of certain events, and in this case, you might want reports of certain occurrences at a regular time. You can also search for existing digest data to use in your workflows.

Here are a few examples of how you can use this built-in app:

- Send a weekly email to management with a summary of all sales invoices created over that week
- Send an email with a periodic summary of all Slack notifications you have received that day at 10 A.M. and 3 P.M.
- Send a Slack message with a list of **Teamwork Projects** tasks that you have been assigned during that week
- Send a Microsoft Teams message with a weekly summary of social media mentions

There are many more possibilities of how you can use the Digest by Zapier built-in app.

> **Tip**
> For more inspiration and access to pre-built templates, you can review the Digest by Zapier built-in app profile page at `https://zapier.com/apps/digest/integrations`.

This app can only be used as an action or search action step, and the following events are available to use:

- **Append Entry and Schedule Digest** (action)
- **Release Existing Digest** (action)
- **Find Digest** (search action)

Bear in mind that once data is released from a digest using any of the action steps, the digest will be cleared and collate new digest data as events occur.

Let's look at each one.

The Append Entry and Schedule Digest action event

The **Append Entry and Schedule Digest** action event allows you to aggregate data from your trigger app, append it to the end of a list of other collected data from the trigger app, and then schedule it to run at a time that you specify.

To illustrate using Digest by Zapier, we will use the example of creating a summary of sales invoices created in Xero over a period.

Let's explore how to set up this action event.

Setting up the Append Entry and Schedule Digest action event

You can use the **Append Entry and Schedule Digest** action event once you have set up your trigger step, with the relevant trigger data you want to push to Digest by Zapier.

Once you have added an action step either by selecting the **Action** step or clicking on the + icon, and have chosen **Digest by Zapier** as the app and **Append Entry and Schedule Digest** as the action event, you can edit the fields in the **Action** section, as follows:

- **Title**: Enter a descriptive title for the digest by typing in static text, mapping dynamic values from previous steps, or using a combination of both. This will help you identify the digest when you use it in other Digest by Zapier events. For example, we could give the digest a title of New Sales Invoice Summary.

- **Entry**: In this field, you can type in static text, map dynamic data from previous steps, or use a combination of both that you want to be included in the digest. For example, we might want to include the invoice number, date, currency, and amount in the digest.

- **Frequency**: This field controls how often Zapier will deliver the digest. You can choose from **Daily, Weekly, Monthly, Threshold (when a certain number of entries is reached)**, and **Manual (pair with separate "Release Digest" Zap)**. The choice of frequency determines additional fields that are displayed.

All three fields are required and must have a value for the Zap to run.

Let's take a look at the different **Frequency** field options.

Frequency – Daily

The **Daily** option in the **Frequency** field drop-down menu is the default for this field. Once selected, the following fields will appear:

- **Time Of Day**: Use this field to specify what time you want the digest data to be released. The drop-down menu offers hourly time options, from midnight to 11 P.M. You can also use the **Custom** header option to type in a custom value using the hh:mm aa, hh:mm, or hhmm formats, such as 11:45, or map a dynamic value from a previous step. This is a required field and must have a value for the Zap to run.

- **Trigger On Weekends?**: This field controls whether your digest will be released on weekend days or not. You can use the Boolean field drop-down menu to choose between **Yes**, if you want it to trigger on Saturdays and Sundays, or **No** if you only want it to trigger from Monday to Friday.

These options are shown in the following screenshot:

Action

3. Append Entry and Schedule Digest in Digest by Zapier   ...

∨ **App & event**   ✓

∧ **Action**   ✓

* Title (required)

New Invoice Summary

The name for your digest. You can use this name to employ your digest in other Zaps. Maximum 32 characters.

* Entry (required)

Invoice: [1. Invoice Number: INV-1225]
Date: [1. Date: 2023-06-30T00:00:00]
Amount: [1. Currency Code: GBP] [1. Amount Due: 1800.00]

The content that will be appended to your digest. Read our formatting guide to learn how you can customize the style... more

* Frequency (required)

Daily

How often should we deliver this digest? Choosing "Manual" requires you to use the "Release Existing Digest" Action ... more

* Time of Day (required)

8am

Relative to the timezone: Europe/London.

Trigger on weekends?

Yes

Should this zap trigger on Saturday and Sunday?

Refresh fields   **Continue**

Figure 9.11 – Overview of customizing the Daily Frequency field option
in the Append Entry and Schedule Digest action event

Click on the **Continue** button. Now, you can use the **Test** section to test this step or click on **Skip Test**.

Proceed to add one or more action steps so that you receive your digest summaries and then turn on your Zap.

Here is a Zapier Community example that illustrates the use of the **Append Entry and Schedule Digest** action event and the **Daily** option: `https://community.zapier.com/how-do-i-3/daily-digest-of-slack-to-stay-up-to-date-19008`.

Next, we'll review the **Weekly** option.

Frequency – Weekly

When you select the **Weekly** option in the **Frequency** field dropdown, the following fields will appear:

- **Day Of The Week**: This field controls which day of the week you want the digest data to be released. Use the drop-down menu to choose days from **Monday** to **Sunday**.

- **Time Of Day**: Use this field to specify what time you want your digest to be released. The drop-down menu offers hourly time options from midnight to 11 P.M. You can also use the **Custom** header option to type in a custom value using the `hh:mm aa`, `hh:mm`, or `hhmm` formats, such as `11:45`, or map a dynamic value from a previous step.

Both of these fields are required and must have a value for the Zap to run.

These options are shown in the following screenshot:

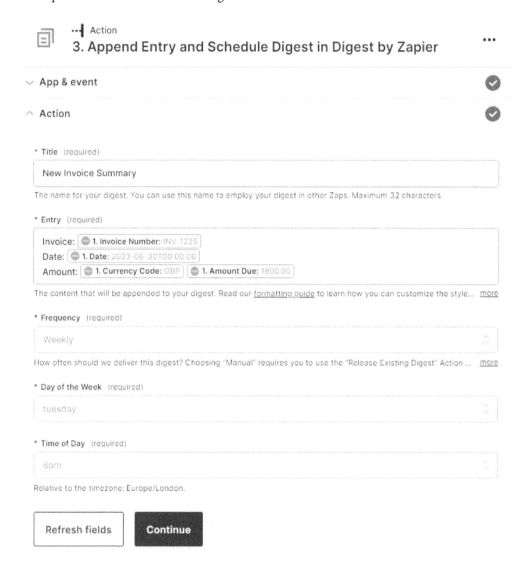

Figure 9.12 – Overview of customizing the Weekly Frequency field option
in the Append Entry and Schedule Digest action event

Click on the **Continue** button. Then, you can use the **Test** section to test this step or click **Skip test**.

Proceed to add one or more action steps so that you receive your digest summaries and then turn on your Zap.

Here is a Zapier Community example that illustrates the use of the **Append Entry and Schedule Digest** action event and the **Weekly** option: `https://community.zapier.com/featured-articles-65/send-yourself-a-weekly-digest-of-newly-added-zapier-integrations-12489`.

We'll explore the **Monthly** option next.

Frequency – Monthly

When you select the **Monthly** option in the **Frequency** field dropdown, the following fields will appear:

- **Day Of The Month**: This field controls which day of the month you want the digest data to be released. Use the drop-down menu to choose dates from **1** to **31**.

- **Time Of Day**: You can use this field to specify what time you want your digest data to be released. The drop-down menu offers hourly time options from midnight to 11 P.M. You can also use the **Custom** header option to type in a custom value using the `hh:mm aa`, `hh:mm`, or `hhmm` formats, such as `9:15 p.m.`

Both of these fields are required and must have a value for the Zap to run.

These options are shown in the following screenshot:

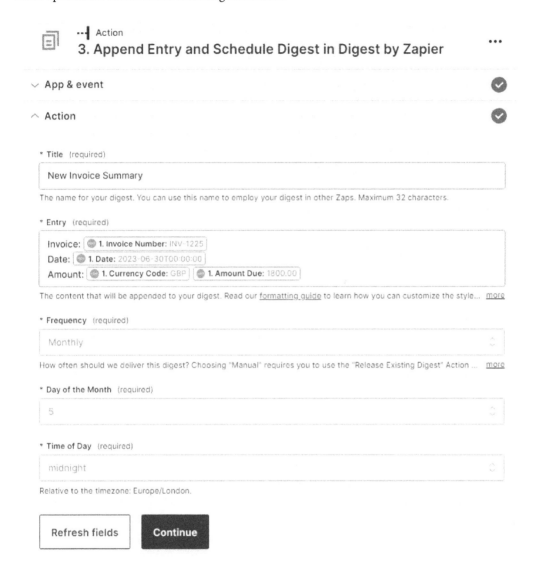

Figure 9.13 – Overview of customizing the Monthly Frequency field option
in the Append Entry and Schedule Digest action event

Click on the **Continue** button. Then, you can use the **Test** section to test this step or click on **Skip test**.

Proceed to add one or more action steps so that you receive your digest summaries and then turn on your Zap.

Here is a Zapier Community example that illustrates the use of the **Append Entry and Schedule Digest** action event and the **Monthly** option: `https://community.zapier.com/featured-articles-65/creating-a-monthly-updates-newsletter-using-digest-11917`.

We'll take a look at the **Threshold (when a certain number of entries is reached)** option next.

Frequency – Threshold (when a certain number of entries is reached)

When you select the **Threshold (when a certain number of entries is reached)** option, the **Number Of Entries** field will appear. This field controls how many entries the digest will collate before it is released. The maximum period to hold the digest is 1 month from the first entry, so if the number has not been reached in this time, the digest will automatically be released. This field is required and must have a value for the Zap to run.

This option is shown in the following screenshot:

Figure 9.14 – Overview of customizing the Threshold (when a certain number of entries is reached) Frequency field option in the Append Entry and Schedule Digest action event

Click on the **Continue** button. Then, you can use the **Test** section to test this step or click on **Skip test**.

Proceed to add one or more action steps so that you receive your digest summaries and then turn on your Zap.

We'll review the **Manual (pair with separate "Release Digest" Zap)** option next.

Frequency – Manual (pair with separate "Release Digest" Zap)

When you select the **Manual (pair with separate "Release Digest" Zap)** option in the **Frequency** field dropdown, no further fields will appear.

This option is shown in the following screenshot:

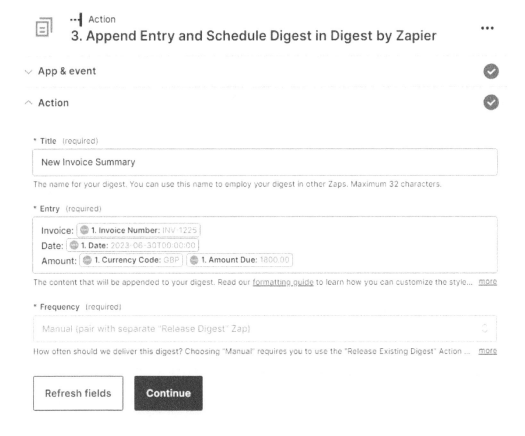

Figure 9.15 – Overview of customizing the Manual (pair with separate "Release Digest" Zap) Frequency field option in the Append Entry and Schedule Digest action event

Click on the **Continue** button. Once you've done this, you can use the **Test** section to test this step or click **Skip test**.

> **Important note**
>
> This field option works alongside the **Release Existing Digest** action event, which you must set up in your existing Zap as one of the subsequent steps or in a separate Zap for your digest to be released.

Proceed to add the **Release Existing Digest** action step or turn your Zap on.

Now, let's discuss how to set up the **Release Existing Digest** action event.

The Release Existing Digest action event

The **Release Existing Digest** action event works in conjunction with the **Manual (pair with separate "Release Digest" Zap)** option in the **Frequency** field dropdown of the **Append Entry and Schedule Digest** action event. It allows the digest that has been manually set to be released at a certain point.

This action event can be used in the same Zap as an **Append Entry and Schedule Digest** action event or in a separate Zap. Here are a couple of examples of when either situation is appropriate:

- **In the same Zap**: If you want to delay the release of your digest for a set period, such as 12 hours, you can add a Delay by Zapier **Delay For** action step, the **Release Existing Digest** action step, and a notification action step (such as the **Send Email** action event of Email by Zapier)

- **In another Zap**: If you want your digest to release after another, unrelated trigger event, such as an opportunity closing in your CRM, you can use the **Release Existing Digest** action event and a notification action step

Let's explore how to set up this action event.

Setting up the Release Existing Digest action event

You can use the **Release Existing Digest** action event once you have set an action step either in this Zap or another Zap that involves the **Append Entry and Schedule Digest** action event.

Once you have added an action step either by selecting the **Action** step or clicking on the + icon, and have chosen **Digest by Zapier** as the app and **Release Existing Digest** as the action event, you can edit the **Digest** fields in the **Action** section. This field controls which digest to use in the step. From the dropdown, you can choose from a list of digests that have been created. Alternatively, you can use the **Custom** option to enter the name of the digest by typing it in or map in a dynamic date from previous steps.

An example of how to set up this action event is shown in the following screenshot:

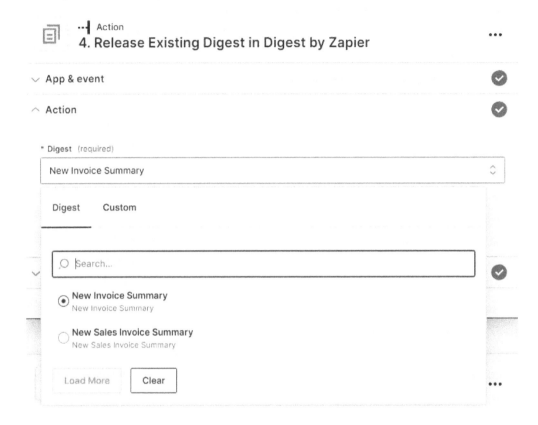

Figure 9.16 – Overview of customizing the Release Existing Digest action event

Click on the **Continue** button; then, use the **Test** section to test this step or click on **Skip test**.

The following screenshot shows an example of the released digest with two invoices:

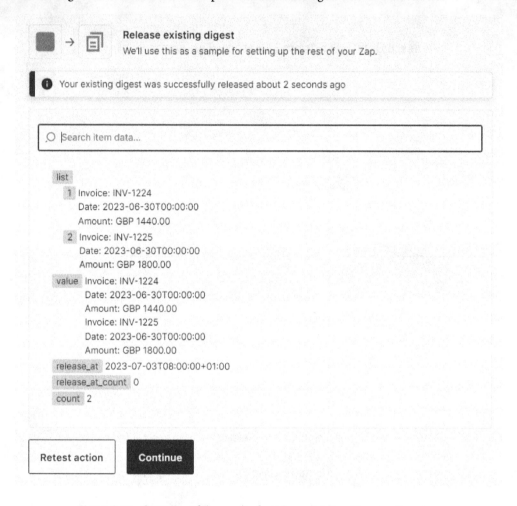

Figure 9.17 – Overview of the result of a Release Existing Digest action step

Proceed to add one or more action steps so that you receive your digest summaries and then turn on your Zap.

Here is a Zapier Community example that illustrates the use of the **Append Entry and Schedule Digest** action event with the **Manual (pair with separate "Release Digest" Zap)** option and the **Release Existing Digest** action event: `https://community.zapier.com/featured-articles-65/` `using-paths-in-loops-to-save-data-in-a-digest-and-release-it-on-` `the-last-loop-13074`.

Next, let's discuss how to set up the **Find Digest** search action event.

The Find Digest search action event

The **Find Digest** search action event is handy to use when you want to periodically retrieve all the existing data in a digest. For example, you might want to check the digest for data every day (using a Schedule by Zapier trigger) and send an email notification with the results. You could also add a subsequent step to release the data, after passing a filter with certain conditions, such as if it was the 15th day of the month.

Let's explore how to set up this action event.

Setting up the Find Digest action event

You can use the **Find Digest** search action event once you have set up a trigger step.

Once you have added an action step either by selecting the **Action** step or clicking on the + icon, and have chosen **Digest by Zapier** as the app and **Find Digest** as the action event, you can edit the fields in the **Action** section, as follows:

- **Digest**: This field controls which digest to use in the step. From the dropdown, choose from a list of digests created. Alternatively, you can use the **Custom** option to enter the name of the digest by typing it in, or map in dynamic data from previous steps.

- **Should This Step Be Considered A "success" When Nothing Is Found?**: You can use this Boolean field to select **Yes (true)** or **No (false)** from the drop-down menu, enter text, or insert data from previous steps for this step to be considered a "success" if nothing is found in the search. Refer back to the *Creating Zaps with multiple action and search steps* section in *Chapter 6*, *Creating Multi-Step Zaps and Using Built-In Apps*, for more information on how to use this feature.

These options are shown in the following screenshot:

Figure 9.18 – Overview of customizing the Find Digest search action event

Click on the **Continue** button; then, use the **Test** section to test this step or click on **Skip test**.

Proceed to add one or more action steps and then turn on your Zap.

You should now have a better understanding of how and when to use the Digest by Zapier built-in app.

Now, let's review an example of how to create a Zap that creates a digest of an RSS feed.

Exercise – creating a multi-step Zap with an RSS feed digest

You can use one of the processes that you defined in *Chapter 2, Preparing to Automate Your Processes*, to work through the content in this section, if appropriate. Try to incorporate multiple apps in your workflow.

You might want to create a monthly digest of your three favorite blogs. You want to receive the summary on the first of the month at 9 A.M. in a Slack message and add a task to MeisterTask so that you don't forget to read them. If you don't mark your task as complete after 7 days, you want to receive another reminder in Slack.

Here is an example of a simple workflow you could build to automate this process:

1. **Trigger**: Add the RSS by Zapier **New Items in Multiple Feeds** event trigger and specify the blogs that you want to receive feed updates for.

2. **Action**: Add a Digest by Zapier **Append Entry and Schedule Digest** action event and specify **Frequency** as **Monthly**, **Day Of The Month** as **1**, and **Time** as **9am**.

3. **Action**: Add a Slack **Send Direct Message** action event to yourself.

4. **Action**: Add a MeisterTask **Create Task** action event.

5. **Action**: Add a Delay by Zapier **Delay For** action step where you specify the delay for 7 days.

6. **Action**: Add a **Find Task** search action to search MeisterTask for the task you created in *Step 4*.

7. **Action**: Add a filter with Filter by Zapier to only allow the Zap to continue if the task is still open.

8. **Action**: Add a Slack **Add Reminder** action event to remind yourself that you haven't read your digest yet.

You can get access to a copy of this Zap template here: `https://bit.ly/zapier-book`.

Try building out a similar process by repeating this exercise for any appropriate processes that you have documented that would benefit from automation.

You should now have a better understanding of how and when to use email parsing, RSS feeds, and digests in your Zaps.

Summary

In this chapter, we introduced you to a few more of Zapier's range of built-in apps. We covered how to extract data from emails using Email Parser by Zapier, and then we explored how to use RSS feed readers in automations using RSS by Zapier. Then, we discussed how to compile data digests with Digest by Zapier. Lastly, we covered an exercise to create a digest of an RSS feed.

You now know how to extract or parse data from emails, use RSS feeds in your automations, and collate data into digests.

In the next chapter, you will learn about a variety of Zapier's other built-in apps. We will cover how to initiate one-off automation from any page on the internet, how to shorten URLs, and how to translate and detect text in different languages. We will also discuss how to retrieve and score a lead's company information, how to use data on weather conditions, and how to use astrological predictions in your automations.

Questions

1. Once you have mapped the variables that you want Email Parser by Zapier to parse, will it reliably extract the correct data every time?

2. Can I create my own bespoke RSS feed with RSS by Zapier?

3. What does that **Manual (pair with separate "Release Digest" Zap)** frequency option in Digest by Zapier work with?

10
Other Useful Built-In Apps by Zapier

In the previous chapter, we reviewed three Zapier built-in apps to extract and compile data. In this chapter, we will continue looking at more built-in functionality that Zapier has to offer with its range of built-in apps. We will cover descriptions of their functionality and provide practical tips on how to use them.

First, we will explore how to use the Zapier Chrome extension (previously called Push by Zapier) to initiate one-off automation from any page on the internet, and how to shorten URLs with URL Shortener by Zapier. Then, we will discuss how to translate text from different languages using Translate by Zapier, and how to score lead information using Lead Score by Zapier. Lastly, we will cover how to use data on weather conditions using Weather by Zapier, and how to use astrological predictions using Retrograde by Zapier.

We will cover the following key topics in this chapter:

- Zapier Chrome extension – triggering one-off automations from any web page
- URL Shortener by Zapier – shortening URLs in your Zaps
- Translate by Zapier – translating text
- Lead Score by Zapier – scoring and retrieving lead information
- Weather by Zapier – using weather conditions in your Zaps
- Retrograde by Zapier – using astrological predictions in your Zaps

Once you have worked through each of these topics, you will know how to initiate one-off workflows from any web page, shorten URLs, translate text, score and retrieve lead information, and use weather conditions and astrological predictions in your Zaps.

Technical requirements

To get the most out of the content and exercises in this chapter, you will need access to a Zapier account. The Zapier Starter plan will be adequate for building multi-step Zaps.

Zapier Chrome extension – triggering one-off automations from any web page

The Zapier Chrome extension built-in app, previously called **Push by Zapier**, uses a **Google Chrome extension** to manually trigger one-off automations from anywhere on the web. There are hundreds, probably thousands, of ways you can use this app to add productivity to your day. The Zapier Chrome extension built-in app can be used as a trigger step at the start of your workflow, as well as an action step, as follows:

- **New Push** (trigger)
- **Reply to Chrome** (action)

Before you can use the Zapier Chrome extension built-in app in your Zaps, you must install the Google Chrome extension in your browser. Let's review how to add the Google Chrome extension to your browser.

Setting up the Google Chrome extension on your browser

The first thing we need to do to use the Zapier Chrome extension built-in app is to install the Google Chrome extension in our browser. Follow these steps to install the extension:

1. From your Google Chrome browser window, navigate to `https://chrome.google.com/webstore/detail/zapier/ngghlnfmdgnpegcmbpgehkbhkhkbkjpj`, or search Google for `Zapier Chrome extension`.
2. Click the **Add to Chrome** button.
3. In the popup that appears, click **Add extension** to authenticate the installation.
4. Pin your Zapier Chrome extension to your browser view by clicking on the puzzle piece icon and then the pin icon next to the Zapier Chrome extension in the drop-down menu. This will ensure it is easy to trigger your workflows at any point.

The next thing you need to do is set up your workflows. Click on the **Zapier Chrome extension** icon in your browser to reveal a drop-down window with the following options:

- **Zaps**: This tab shows some instructions on how to use the extension and links to a few pre-built Zap templates to get you started. Clicking on any of these will take you to the Zap editor to use the template. Alternatively, you can click the **Create Zap** button to create a Zap from scratch in the Zap editor. You will also be shown the connected email address associated with your Zapier account. Once you have built some Zapier Chrome extension Zaps that have been turned on, they will be shown in a list, allowing you to select one to use.

- **Actions (beta)**: This tab is linked to Zapier's **Natural Language Actions** (**NLA**) AI functionality. Your NLA access to the Zapier Chrome extension can be activated by clicking on the **Log in to NLA** button. We will cover this functionality in more detail in *Chapter 19, AI and Automation*.

Now, let's explore how to set up the trigger event.

The New Push trigger event

The **New Push** trigger event allows you to retrieve details of the active browser tab's title and URL when the button is pushed for this Zap in the Zapier Chrome extension and add static data in specified custom fields that you can then use in your action steps. The time the event occurred will also be retrieved.

Here are a few examples of how you can use the Zapier Chrome extension's **New Push** trigger event with content extracted from your Google Chrome browser:

- Create a new task in Teamwork Projects to review content in an article you came across while browsing the internet

- Send a Slack message when you receive a new email

- Add data to a new row in Smartsheet when you see content you might want to share with your audience

Let's use an example to demonstrate how to set up the **New Push** trigger event, where you might want to create a Trello task for yourself to review an email you have received, which contains the sender's name, email address, and a short message.

Setting up the New Push trigger event

Once you have added a trigger step to the start of your workflow by selecting **1. Trigger** and chosen **Zapier Chrome extension** as the app and **New Push** as the trigger event, click on the **Continue** button. Then, edit the **Input Fields** form in the **Trigger** section, as follows:

1. Type a descriptive field name into each field.

2. Rearrange the field order by hovering your cursor over the six-dots icon to the left, and drag and drop to reposition.

3. Remove unnecessary fields by using the **X** icon on the right.

> **Important note**
> The **Input Fields** section is optional and you can trigger your Zap without having manual input fields.

Using the example described earlier, this is shown in the following screenshot:

Figure 10.1 – Overview of customizing the New Push trigger event

4. Click the **Continue** button to proceed.

5. In the **Trigger** section, use the **Test trigger** button to pull through some sample data to use and initiate your Zap from the Zapier Chrome extension. You can then add action steps to your Zap, and once complete, turn your Zap on.

6. Navigate to the **Zapier Chrome extension** in your browser to reveal a list of Zaps that have been created. The Zap you just started making will be displayed. If you have not named the Zap, it will be labeled Untitled Zap. Click the Zap's name to reveal the field labels and enter the relevant details. Click the **Send** button to activate the push. Once successful, the text will be highlighted in green with a green tick icon.

The details screen is shown in the following screenshot:

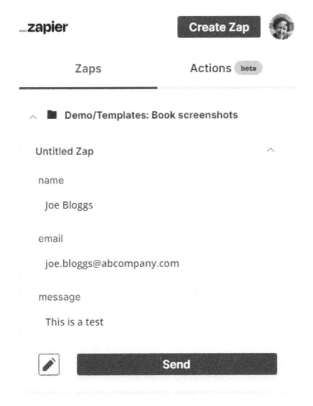

Figure 10.2 – Overview of using the Zapier Chrome extension in
the browser with the New Push trigger event

You can then adjust your Zap as required by clicking on the pencil icon.

> **Tip**
>
> You can use the timestamp data you've retrieved to add a due date to your task action steps. We will discuss using and formatting dates and times in more detail in *Chapter 14, Formatting Date and Time*, and *Chapter 24, Tips, Tricks, and Best Practices to Enhance Your Productivity*.

Now, let's discuss how to set up the action event.

The Reply to Chrome action event

The **Reply to Chrome** action event allows you to send back step results from a Zap that is triggered by a **New Push** trigger step. Here are a few examples of how you can use the Zapier Chrome extension's **Reply to Chrome** action event to send back data from your Zap to the Chrome extension:

- Get tomorrow's weather by triggering a Zap from the Zapier Chrome extension

- Search for the lead score of a prospect by triggering a Zap from the Zapier Chrome extension

- Shorten a URL from your browser by triggering a Zap from the Zapier Chrome extension

Let's use the example of getting tomorrow's weather to demonstrate how to use the **Reply to Chrome** action event.

Setting up the Reply to Chrome action event

Let's walk through the steps of how to use the **Reply to Chrome** action event:

1. Begin by setting up a Zap using the **Zapier Chrome extension** built-in app's **New Push** trigger event. If you don't need to collect any additional data from the browser, you do not need to use the **Input Fields** section.

2. Add an action step by either selecting the **Action** step or clicking on the + icon. In our example, the action step will contain the **Get Tomorrow's Forecast** action event in the **Weather by Zapier** built-in app. You can read more about how to use the Weather by Zapier built-in app in the *Weather by Zapier – using weather conditions in your Zaps* section.

3. Add another action step by either selecting the **Action** step or clicking on the + icon. By choosing **Zapier Chrome extension** as the app and **Reply to Chrome** as the action event, you can then edit the following fields in the **Action** section:

    - **Message Title**: Use this field to enter either a static URL value, a dynamic value from previous steps, or a combination of both. This is a required field and must have a value for the Zap to run.

    - **Message Details**: Use this field to enter either static URL values, dynamic values from previous steps, or a combination of both. This is a required field and must have a value for the Zap to run.

An example is shown in the following screenshot:

Action

3. Reply to Chrome in Zapier Chrome extension

⋮

∨ App & event

∧ Action

* Message Title (required)

Tomorrow's weather forecast

Specify a short title that will be displayed above the message

* Message Details (required)

Summary: 2. Summary: Rain in the mor...and afternoon.
Max temp: 2. Temperature Max: 46.16
Min temp: 2. Temperature Min: 37.92

Enter the message you would like to display in the Chrome extension after your Zap runs. It can include data from...   more

Refresh fields   Continue

Figure 10.3 – Overview of setting up the Zapier Chrome extension Reply to Chrome action event

4. Click the **Continue** button. You can then use the **Test action** button to test this step or **Skip test** to skip.

5. Click the **Publish** button to publish and turn **On** your Zap, then navigate to your Chrome browser and trigger the Zap by clicking the **Send** button.

The results of your Zap and mapped steps will be shown in your Zapier Chrome extension, as shown in the following screenshot:

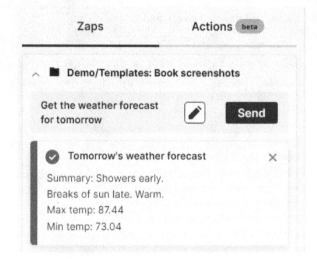

Figure 10.4 – Overview of using the Zapier Chrome extension in
the browser with the Reply to Chrome action event

You can then proceed to add more action steps if required.

> **Tip**
>
> For more inspiration and access to pre-built templates, you can review the Zapier Chrome extension built-in app profile page at `https://zapier.com/apps/zapier-chrome-extension/integrations`.

Here is a Zapier Community example that illustrates the use of the Zapier Chrome extension: `https://community.zapier.com/featured-articles-65/the-zapier-google-chrome-extension-trigger-zaps-without-leaving-your-browser-10796`.

You should now have a better understanding of how and when to use the Zapier Chrome extension built-in app.

> **Tip**
>
> You can use the magic of AI to run AI-powered actions right inside your
>
> Zapier Chrome extension with simple prompts. We will cover Zapier Chrome Extension NLA and AI Actions in more detail in *Chapter 19, AI and Automation*.

Now, let's review how to use the URL Shortener by Zapier built-in app to shorten URLs.

URL Shortener by Zapier – shortening URLs in your Zaps

If you want to make long and untidy **Uniform Resource Locator** (**URL**) strings shorter and easier on the eye, you can use the **URL Shortener by Zapier** built-in app. This is especially useful if you have text length restrictions in the app you're sending the URL to and if you want the URL to be displayed in a neater format. URLs are generated with a `zpr.io/` prefix and a unique alphanumeric suffix. This works similarly to shortened URLs generated using **Bitly**.

Here are a few examples of when you can use the URL Shortener by Zapier app:

- Sending a shortened URL in an SMS or when you post a tweet to Twitter. They both have text limit restrictions.

- Sending an email to a customer with a link to a web page with a long URL.

- Adding the shortened URLs of new blog articles to Airtable.

URL Shortener by Zapier can only be used as an action step with the **Shorten URL** action event.

Here are some examples from the Zapier blog that illustrate the use of the URL Shortener by Zapier app: `https://zapier.com/blog/automate-url-shorteners/`.

> **Tip**
> For more inspiration and access to pre-built templates, you can review the URL Shortener by Zapier built-in app profile page at `https://zapier.com/apps/url-shortener/integrations`.

Let's explore how to set up and use this action event.

Setting up the Shorten URL action event

You can use the **Shorten URL** action event once you have set up your trigger step.

Once you have added an action step, by either selecting the **Action** step or clicking on the + icon, and chosen **URL Shortener by Zapier** as the app and **Shorten URL** as the action event, you can edit the **URL** field in the **Action** section. Use this field to enter either a static URL value, a dynamic value from previous steps, or a combination of both. This is a required field and must have a value for the Zap to run.

An example of this is shown in the following screenshot:

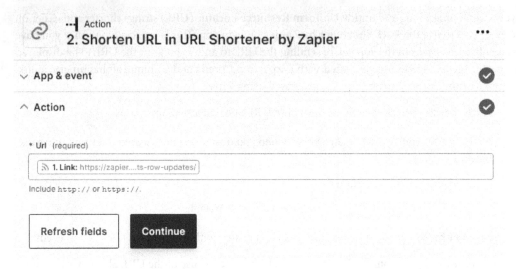

Figure 10.5 – Overview of customizing the Shorten URL action event

Click on the **Continue** button. You can then use the **Action** section to test this step to generate the shortened URL. This is shown in the following screenshot:

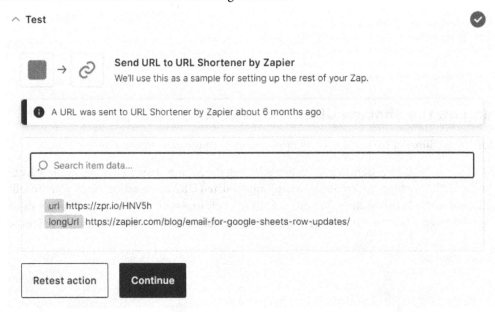

Figure 10.6 – Overview of a shortened URL result using URL Shortener by Zapier

Proceed to add one or more action steps after your **Shorten URL** step, then publish your Zap.

You should now have a better understanding of how and when to use the URL Shortener built-in app.

Now, let's discuss how to use the Translate by Zapier built-in app to translate text into different languages and detect a language in some text.

Translate by Zapier – translating text

The Translate by Zapier built-in app allows you to translate text into over 100 different languages. It can also be used to detect a language in a set of text.

Here are a few examples of how you can use this app:

- Translating a received email from German into English and adding the translated text to your **customer relationship management (CRM)** tool

- Detecting the language on a web page and raising a ticket in **Zendesk** for specific members of your multilingual team to address

The Translate by Zapier built-in app is handy to use in your Zaps if you regularly work with multiple languages.

Here is a Zapier Community example of how you can use Translate by Zapier: `https://community.zapier.com/show-tell-5/small-business-series-translate-by-zapier-22197`.

> **Tip**
> For more inspiration and access to pre-built templates, you can review the Translate by Zapier built-in app profile page at `https://zapier.com/apps/translate/integrations`.

This app can only be used as an action step. The following action events are available to use:

- **Translate Text** (action)
- **Detect Language** (action)

Let's look at each.

The Translate Text action event

The **Translate Text** action event allows you to translate words, phrases, and web pages of up to 1,000 characters into over 100 languages.

Let's explore how to set up this action event.

Setting up the Translate Text action event

You can use the **Translate Text** action event once you have set up your trigger step.

Once you have added an action step, by either selecting the **Action** step or clicking on the + icon, and chosen **Translate by Zapier** as the app and **Translate Text** as the action event, you can edit the fields in the **Action** section, as follows:

- **Source Language**: If you know the language of the source text you are using, choose a language from the drop-down list. You can also map in a dynamic field from previous steps. This is useful if you have stated the language in previous steps – for example, if you have this data on a Google Sheets spreadsheet or in a CRM. You can also leave the field blank and Zapier will detect the source language.

- **Text**: In this field, type in static text, map dynamic data from previous steps, or use a combination of both that you want to be translated. Any text over 1,000 characters will be trimmed in the result. This is a required field and must have a value for the Zap to run.

- **Target Language**: This field controls which language you want the text to be translated into. Choose a language from the drop-down list or map in a dynamic field from the previous steps. This is a required field and must have a value for the Zap to run.

For example, we may want to translate a Zapier blog post description from Latin into Swahili. This is shown in the following screenshot:

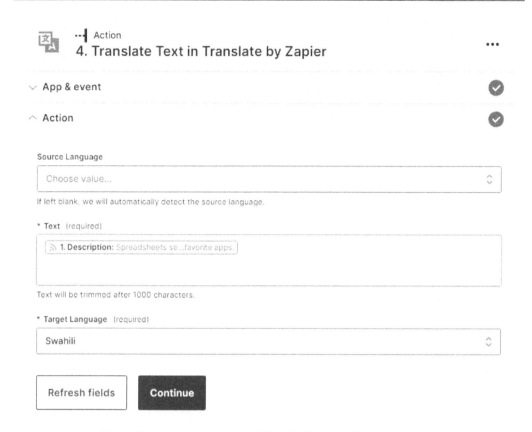

Figure 10.7 – Overview of customizing the Translate Text action event

Click the **Continue** button. Once you've done this, you can use the **Action** button to test this step or **Skip test**.

Proceed to add one or more action steps or publish your Zap.

Now, let's discuss how to detect a language in text using the **Detect Language** action event.

The Detect Language action event

The **Detect Language** action event allows you to detect one of up to 100 languages in a set of text.

Let's explore how to set up this action event.

Setting up the Detect Language action event

You can use the **Detect Language** action event once you have set up your trigger step.

Once you have added an action step, by either selecting the **Action** step or clicking on the + icon, and chosen **Translate by Zapier** as the app and **Detect Language** as the action event, you can edit the following field in the **Action** section:

- **Text**: In this field, type in static text, map dynamic data from previous steps, or use a combination of both that you want to be translated. This is a required field and must have a value for the Zap to run.

Using the same example of text in Swahili, this is shown in the following screenshot:

Figure 10.8 – Overview of customizing the Detect Language action event

Click on the **Continue** button. Once you've done this, you can use the **Test action** button to test this step or **Skip test**.

The result will display the language Zapier assumes it to be and produce a confidence score. Proceed to add one or more action steps or publish your Zap.

You should now have a better understanding of how and when to use the Translate by Zapier built-in app.

Next, let's review how to use the Lead Score by Zapier built-in app to score and retrieve information on your leads.

Lead Score by Zapier – scoring and retrieving lead information

The **Lead Score by Zapier** built-in app allows you to gather information from the web about a contact and their associated company using their email address. The search also produces a customer fit qualification score based on various data points. The app uses data from MadKudu.com, a data enrichment service, which, as a standalone service, can be quite pricey for small businesses and start-ups. With the Lead Score by Zapier app, you can perform up to 500 free searches per month using this service. However, if you're likely to need a higher number of searches, you can sign up for a paid plan at MadKudu.com and use the Zapier-**MadKudu** integration instead of Lead Score by Zapier.

The most common reasons you would want to use Lead Score by Zapier are for enriching contact data, lead prioritization, and qualification, therefore allowing you to make better decisions on which leads to follow up with first and understand your contacts better. This will allow you to create more applicable communications and better experiences for your leads and customers. Lead Score by Zapier saves you the hassle of manually searching for this data and can give you access to additional data that might not be shown in your CRM's native contact and associated company search data, such as in Salesforce or **HubSpot**.

Here are a few examples of how you can use the Lead Score by Zapier built-in app:

- If a new lead submits a web form, you may want to find out more details about the contact's company, company size, and location

- When a new contact is added to your CRM, enrich the contact data and get a customer qualification score

- When a new subscriber is added to your email marketing tool **Klaviyo**, retrieve more personal information on the contact

There are many more ways to use Lead Score by Zapier in your Zaps.

> **Tip**
>
> For more inspiration and access to pre-built templates, you can review the Lead Score by Zapier built-in app profile page at `https://zapier.com/apps/lead-information/integrations`.

Lead Score by Zapier can be used as a search action step using the **Find Person and Company Information** search action event. Let's review how to use this search action event.

The Find Person and Company Information search action event

The **Find Person and Company Information** search action event allows you to search `MadKudu.com` for data on contacts and associated companies using an email address.

Let's explore how to set up this search action event.

Setting up the Find Person and Company Information search action event

You can use the **Find Person and Company Information** search action event once you have set up your trigger step.

Once you have added an action step, by either selecting the **Action** step or clicking on the + icon, and chosen **Lead Score by Zapier** as the app and **Find Person and Company Information** as the action event, you can edit the fields in the **Action** section, as follows:

- **Email**: In this field, type in static text, map dynamic data from previous steps, or use a combination of both that you want to be translated into email format – for example, `joe@company.com`. This is a required field and must have a value for the Zap to run.

- **Should this step be considered a "success" when nothing is found?**: Use this Boolean field to select **True** or **False** from the drop-down menu, enter text, or insert data from previous steps for this step to be considered a "success" if nothing is found in the search. The default for this field is **False**, which you should choose if you want the Zap to stop running at this point if nothing is found; this is the most common use case. This means that all subsequent steps will be skipped. Use the **True** option if you want to allow the Zap to continue and subsequent steps to run. You can then add more control to your workflows by adding Filter by Zapier or Paths by Zapier conditional logic for more control and allowing those steps to pass or stop based on whether the search returned a result or not.

For example, we may want to retrieve information associated with the `joebloggs@zapier.com` email address. This is shown in the following screenshot:

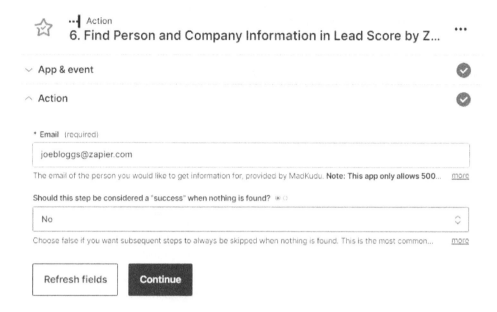

Figure 10.9 – Overview of customizing the Find Person and Company Information search action event

Click on the **Continue** button. Once you've done this, you can use the **Test** section to test this step or **Skip Test**.

The following screenshot shows an example of the data returned for joebloggs@zapier.com:

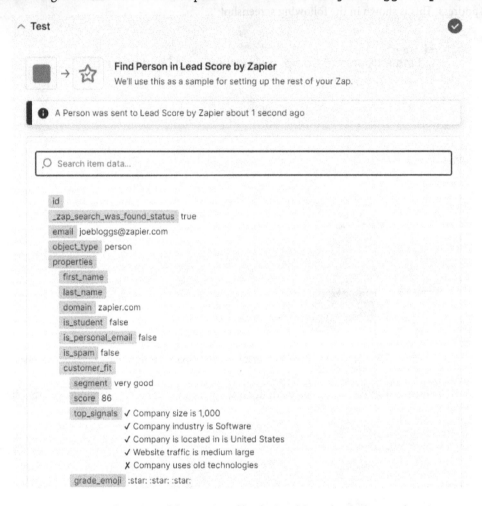

Figure 10.10 – Overview of data retrieved by the Lead Score by Zapier search action

You can proceed to add one or more action steps or publish your Zap.

The search results produce a list of properties, as follows:

- **Person properties**: first_name, last_name, domain, is_student, is_personal_email, is_spam, customer_fit, segment, score, top_signals, and grade_emoji

- **Company properties**: name, domain, location, state, state_code, country, country_code, employees, and industry

> **Tip**
> When you have limitations on API calls to your software, such as a CRM where you can only create or change a fixed number of properties in a certain period, it would be useful to turn on the **True** option for **Should this step be considered a "success" when nothing is found?** to stop your Zap running. Then, you can add filter conditions in the next step.

You should now have a better understanding of how and when to use the Lead Score by Zapier built-in app.

Now, let's cover how to use the Weather by Zapier built-in app to use weather conditions in your workflows.

Weather by Zapier – using weather conditions in your Zaps

The **Weather by Zapier** built-in app gives you access to weather conditions in a specified area, based on latitude and longitude coordinates. You can use it to get daily weather notifications and only trigger if it will rain that day (for your local area based on your Zapier timezone settings). You can also search for current weather conditions and tomorrow's forecast for a specified location. This app is handy to use personally or if you and your team work outdoors – for example, if you work in the construction, landscaping, or dog walking industry. Weather by Zapier is best used with a notification action in subsequent steps, such as sending an email or SMS.

> **Important note**
> The Weather by Zapier app uses the timezone settings specified in your account to run accurate triggers and search actions. Ensure that your timezone settings have been adjusted accordingly.

Weather by Zapier can be used as both a trigger and an action step and is available as the following events:

- **Will It Rain Today?** (trigger)
- **Today's Forecast** (trigger)
- **Get Current Weather** (search action)
- **Get Tomorrow's Forecast** (search action)

Let's explore how to set up each of these in turn.

The Will It Rain Today? trigger event

The **Will It Rain Today?** trigger event can be used to start a workflow when the weather forecast shows that it is due to rain on that day. The app checks the weather forecast for the day at around 7 A.M. (based on your timezone settings) and only triggers if rain is forecast.

Here are a few examples of how you can use the **Will It Rain Today?** trigger event:

- Send an SMS to yourself if it is going to rain today

- If your team works outdoors, send an email to them if it is going to rain today

Let's explore how to set up this trigger event.

Setting up the Will It Rain Today? trigger event

Once you have added this trigger step to the start of your workflow (to **1. Trigger**) and chosen **Weather by Zapier** as the app and **Will It Rain Today?** as the trigger event, you can select **Continue**. You can then edit the fields in the **Trigger** section, as follows:

- **Latitude**: Enter a decimal value for the latitude of the location you want to check. You can use `https://www.latlong.net/` to find the latitude if you don't know it. This is a required field and must have a value for the Zap to run.

- **Longitude**: Enter a decimal value for the longitude of the location you want to check. You can use `https://www.latlong.net/` to find the longitude if you don't know it. This is a required field and must have a value for the Zap to run.

- **Units**: This drop-down field allows you to choose to display the forecast results in **Celsius** or **Fahrenheit**. The default is **Fahrenheit**.

Using the example of Paris, France, this is shown in the following screenshot:

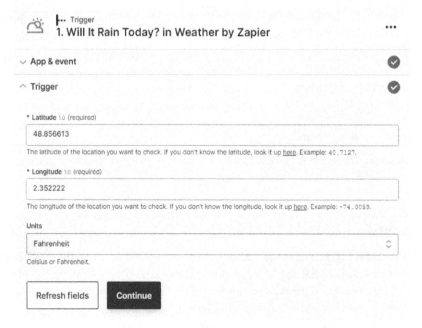

Figure 10.11 – Overview of customizing the Will It Rain Today? trigger event

You can then select **Continue** and, in the **Test** section, use the **Test Trigger** button to retrieve your test data so that you can use it in your action steps.

You can use a wide variety of data retrieved from your trigger step, such as precipitation intensity and probability, high and low temperatures, wind speed, and UV index.

Proceed to add one or more action steps to your Zap using data from this trigger step.

You should now be able to use the **Will It Rain Today?** trigger event. Next, let's take a look at the **Today's Forecast** trigger event.

The Today's Forecast trigger event

The **Today's Forecast** trigger event can be used to start a workflow with the forecast for the day. The app checks the weather forecast for the day around 7 A.M. in your local time (based on your timezone settings) and only triggers if rain is forecast.

Here are a few examples of how you can use the **Today's Forecast** trigger event:

- Send a Slack channel message with the forecast for the day
- Send a tweet on Twitter with a sun emoji when the forecast shows it will be sunny (use Filter by Zapier to specify the conditions)

Let's explore how to set up this trigger event.

Setting up the Today's Forecast trigger event

Once you have added this trigger step to the start of your workflow (to **1. Trigger**) and chosen **Weather by Zapier** as the app and **Today's Forecast** as the trigger event, you can select **Continue**. You can then edit the fields in the **Trigger** section, as follows:

- **Latitude**: Enter a decimal value for the latitude of the location you want to check. You can use `https://www.latlong.net/` to find the latitude if you don't know it. This is a required field and must have a value for the Zap to run.
- **Longitude**: Enter a decimal value for the longitude of the location you want to check. You can use `https://www.latlong.net/` to find the longitude if you don't know it. This is a required field and must have a value for the Zap to run.
- **Units**: This drop-down field allows you to choose to display the forecast results in **Celsius** or **Fahrenheit**. The default is **Fahrenheit**.

You can then select **Continue** and, in the **Test** section, use the **Test Trigger** button to retrieve your test data so that you can use it in your action steps.

You can use a wide variety of data retrieved from your trigger step, such as a summary of the forecast, humidity, precipitation intensity and probability, high and low temperatures, wind speed, and UV index.

Proceed to add one or more action steps to your Zap using data from this trigger step.

You should now be able to use the **Today's Forecast** trigger event. Next, let's take a look at the **Get Current Weather** search action event.

The Get Current Weather search action event

The **Get Current Weather** search action event is ideal to use when you need to know the weather right now or at a specific time of day.

Here are a few examples of how you can use the **Get Current Weather** search action event:

- When you're due to have a meeting, send a notification with the weather forecast
- When you want to check the weather at a point in time, rather than using a Google search, use the Zapier Chrome extension to trigger a workflow to check the weather and send you an SMS

Let's explore how to set up this search action event.

Setting up the Get Current Weather search action event

You can use the **Get Current Weather** search action event once you have set up your trigger step.

Once you have added an action step, by either selecting the **Action** step or clicking on the + icon, and chosen **Weather by Zapier** as the app and **Get Current Weather** as the action event, you can edit the fields in the **Set up action** section, as follows:

- **Latitude**: Enter a decimal value for the latitude of the location you want to check. You can use `https://www.latlong.net/` to find the latitude if you don't know it. This is a required field and must have a value for the Zap to run.

- **Longitude**: Enter a decimal value for the longitude of the location you want to check. You can use `https://www.latlong.net/` to find the longitude if you don't know it. This is a required field and must have a value for the Zap to run.

- **Units**: This drop-down field allows you to choose to display the forecast results in **Celsius** or **Fahrenheit**. The default is **Fahrenheit**.

- **Should this step be considered a "success" when nothing is found?**: Use this Boolean field to select **True** or **False** from the drop-down menu, enter text, or insert data from previous steps for this step to be considered a "success" if nothing is found in the search. The default for this field is **False**, which you should choose if you want the Zap to stop running at this point if nothing is found; this is the most common use case. This means that all subsequent steps will be skipped. Use the **True** option when you want to allow the Zap to continue and subsequent steps to run. You can then add more control to your workflows by adding Filter by Zapier or Paths by Zapier conditional logic for more control and allowing those steps to pass or stop based on whether the search returned a result or not.

Using the example of London, United Kingdom, this is shown in the following screenshot:

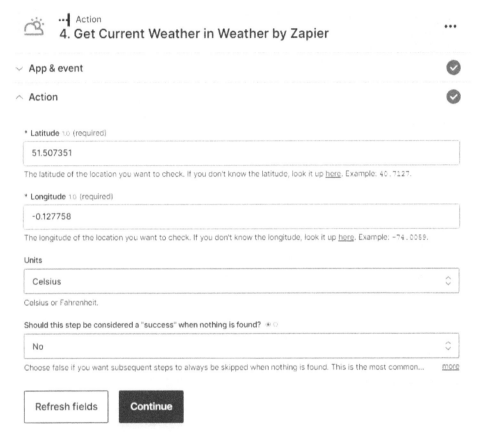

Figure 10.12 – Overview of customizing the Get Current Weather search action event

Click on the **Continue** button. Once you've done this, you can use the **Test** section to test this step or **Skip test**.

The following screenshot shows the result of some example data:

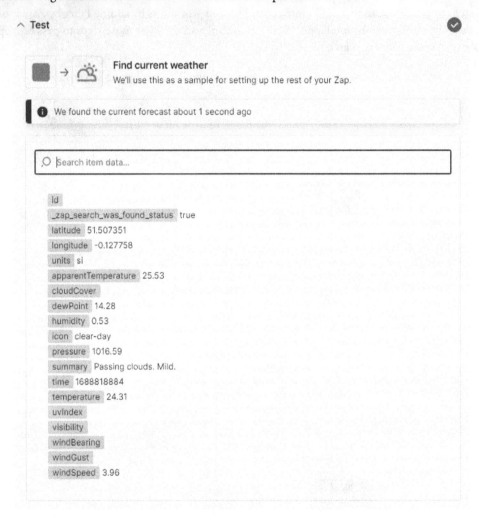

Figure 10.13 – Overview of data retrieved from a Get Current Weather search action event

You can proceed to add one or more action steps or publish your Zap.

You should now be able to use the **Get Current Weather** search action event. Next, we'll take a look at the **Tomorrow's Forecast** search action event.

The Tomorrow's Forecast search action event

The **Tomorrow's Forecast** search action event is ideal to use when you need to know the weather forecast for the next day.

Here are a few examples of how you can use the **Tomorrow's Forecast** action search event:

- Send an email with tomorrow's job list to your team, along with the weather forecast
- Use Schedule by Zapier to trigger an automation to check tomorrow's weather at 5 P.M. every day and send you an SMS

Let's explore how to set up this search action event.

Setting up the Tomorrow's Forecast search action event

You can use the **Tomorrow's Forecast** search action event once you have set up your trigger step.

Once you have added an action step, either by selecting the **Action** step or clicking on the + icon, and chosen **Weather by Zapier** as the app and **Tomorrow's Forecast** as the action event, you can edit the fields in the **Action** section, as follows:

- **Latitude**: Enter a decimal value for the latitude of the location you want to check. You can use `https://www.latlong.net/` to find the latitude if you don't know it. This is a required field and must have a value for the Zap to run.

- **Longitude**: Enter a decimal value for the longitude of the location you want to check. You can use `https://www.latlong.net/` to find the longitude if you don't know it. This is a required field and must have a value for the Zap to run.

- **Units**: This drop-down field allows you to choose to display the forecast results in **Celsius** or **Fahrenheit**. The default is **Fahrenheit**.

- **Should this step be considered a "success" when nothing is found?**: Use this Boolean field to select **True** or **False** from the drop-down menu, enter text, or insert data from previous steps for this step to be considered a "success" if nothing is found in the search. The default for this field is **False**, which you should choose if you want the Zap to stop running at this point if nothing is found; this is the most common use case. This means that all subsequent steps will be skipped. Use the **True** option when you want to allow the Zap to continue and subsequent steps to run. You can then add more control to your workflows by adding Filter by Zapier or Paths by Zapier conditional logic for more control and allowing those steps to pass or stop based on whether the search returned a result or not.

Click on the **Continue** button. Once you've done this, you can use the **Test action** button to test this step or **Skip test**.

You can proceed to add one or more action steps or publish your Zap.

You should now have a better understanding of how and when to use the Weather by Zapier app.

> **Tip**
>
> For more inspiration and access to pre-built templates, you can review the Weather by Zapier built-in app profile page at `https://zapier.com/apps/weather/integrations`. Next, let's discuss how to use the Retrograde by Zapier built-in app to use astrological predictions in your automations.

Retrograde by Zapier – using astrological predictions in your Zaps

You can use the **Retrograde by Zapier** built-in app to trigger your workflows based on Mercury retrograde astrological predictions. You can choose to trigger your workflows when Mercury enters or leaves retrograde or to trigger once a day when Mercury is in retrograde.

> **Tip**
>
> For more inspiration and access to pre-built templates, you can review the Retrograde by Zapier built-in app profile page at `https://zapier.com/apps/retrograde-by-zapier/integrations`.

The following is a list of trigger event options that Retrograde by Zapier provides:

- **Mercury enters Retrograde** (trigger): This event triggers once Mercury enters retrograde
- **Mercury in Retrograde** (trigger): This event triggers once per day when Mercury is in retrograde
- **Mercury leaves Retrograde** (trigger): This event triggers once Mercury leaves retrograde

Each of these triggers is similar in terms of setup; however, they all return slightly different data. Let's explore how to set up and use these trigger events.

Setting up a Retrograde by Zapier trigger event

Once you have added a trigger step to the start of your workflow (to **1. Trigger**) and chosen **Retrograde by Zapier** as the app and either **Mercury enters Retrograde**, **Mercury in Retrograde**, or **Mercury leaves Retrograde** as the trigger event, you can select **Continue**. As there are no fields to edit, in the **Test** section, use the **Test trigger** button to retrieve your test data so that you can use it in your action steps.

Proceed to add one or more action steps to your Zap using data from this trigger step.

Now, let's review the type of data returned by each of the trigger events.

Data retrieved for the Mercury enters Retrograde trigger event

The following screenshot shows an example of data returned by the **Mercury enters Retrograde** trigger event:

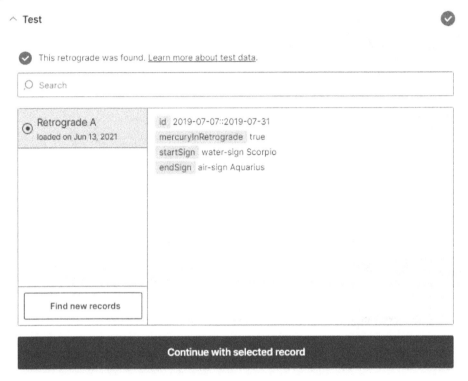

Figure 10.14 – Overview of example data returned by the Mercury enters Retrograde trigger event

Next, let's discuss the type of data returned by the **Mercury in Retrograde** trigger events.

Data returned by the Mercury in Retrograde trigger event

The following screenshot shows an example of the data returned by the **Mercury in Retrograde** trigger event:

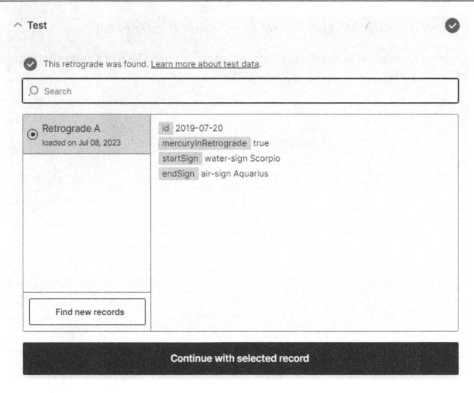

Figure 10.15 – Overview of example data returned by the Mercury in Retrograde trigger event

Next, let's discuss the type of data returned by the **Mercury leaves Retrograde** trigger event.

Data returned by the Mercury leaves Retrograde trigger event

The following screenshot shows an example of the data returned by the **Mercury leaves Retrograde** trigger event:

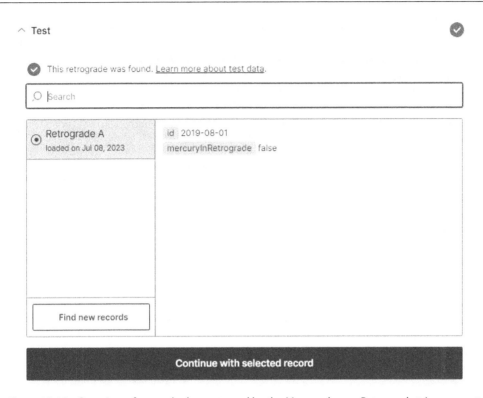

Figure 10.16 – Overview of example data returned by the Mercury leaves Retrograde trigger event

With this, you should now have a better understanding of how and when to use the Retrograde by Zapier app.

Summary

In this chapter, we learned about a few more of Zapier's built-in apps. We covered specific functions, such as how to use the Zapier Chrome extension to initiate a one-off automation from any page on the internet, how to shorten URLs with URL Shortener by Zapier, and how to translate and detect text from different languages using Translate by Zapier. We also discussed how to retrieve and score lead information using Lead Score by Zapier, how to use data on weather conditions using Weather by Zapier, and how to use astrological predictions using Retrograde by Zapier in your automations.

In the next chapter, you will learn about more advanced built-in apps. We will review how to use webhooks and polling triggers, make API calls, and use JavaScript and Python code in our Zaps, as well as how to store data.

Questions

1. Which Zapier built-in app allows you to manually trigger automations from any page on the internet?

2. How can you automate the creation of shortened URL links using Zapier?

3. If you need to perform more than 500 lead score searches each month, what paid-for alternative can you use to Lead Score by Zapier?

11
Advanced Built-In Apps by Zapier

The power of Zapier lies in using the extensive functionality made available in the built-in apps, all without using code. You can accomplish a vast array of automations using these apps. However, you will find that there will be times when you may want to achieve something with your Zaps that won't be possible using the standard, no-code, built-in app functionality or using an existing integration in Zapier. When this happens, it is time to use webhooks, code, and API requests in your Zaps, thus opening up even more possibilities to automate your manual and repetitive tasks with Zapier. You can use Webhooks by Zapier, Code by Zapier, and **API Request** action steps, respectively, to accomplish this.

It is also useful to know about one of the other built-in apps that will help when you want to store and retrieve small datasets. You can use Storage by Zapier to store reference data every time a Zap runs and then share it with other Zaps by retrieving it.

In this chapter, you will be provided with an overview of the more advanced built-in apps in Zapier, which allow you to use webhooks and polling triggers, make HTTP requests with Webhooks by Zapier, make API calls in action steps using your authenticated connection, use **App Extensions** in multiple Zaps, use JavaScript or Python code (Code by Zapier) in your Zaps, and store and retrieve data (Storage by Zapier). We will also briefly cover how to use ChatGPT to generate code for your Code by Zapier steps. These apps and built-in functions are categorized by Zapier as **Developer Tools**, and as these are advanced topics, we will only provide a brief overview of their functionality, without going into too much detail. We will, however, provide you with some use cases and further references.

This chapter will be most useful for Zapier users with a higher level of technical skill. A good understanding of concepts around the use of APIs, including reading API documentation and using programming languages such as Python and JavaScript, would be beneficial. The content that we will cover will, however, give non-technical users an introduction to what is possible with these built-in apps.

We will cover the following key topics in this chapter:

- Resources for understanding API documentation
- Webhooks by Zapier – using webhooks and HTTP requests in your Zaps
- Using API Request action steps (feature in beta)
- Using App Extensions in multiple Zaps (feature in beta)
- Code by Zapier – using JavaScript or Python code in your Zaps
- Storage by Zapier – saving and storing data

Once you have reviewed each of these topics, you will understand how to use webhooks, code, and API requests in your Zaps, as well as how to save and store data.

Technical requirements

To get the most out of the content in this chapter, you will need access to a Zapier account. The Zapier Free plan will be adequate. You will need the Zapier Starter plan to create multi-step workflows and use the Webhooks by Zapier built-in app.

Resources for understanding API documentation

In *Chapter 1, Introduction to Business Process Automation with Zapier*, we introduced how integrations work to request data from one application, producing a response in another. The information requests are usually in the form of creating new resources, retrieving existing ones, editing/updating existing resources, or deleting existing resources. In **Hypertext Transfer Protocol** (**HTTP** – the foundation for how data is passed along on the internet) terms, these requests are denoted as the following methods:

- **POST**: Used to create a new resource
- **GET**: Used to retrieve an existing resource
- **PUT**: Used to edit or update an existing resource
- **DELETE**: Used to delete an existing resource

As you already know, the API integrations that have been created between Zapier and other apps have specific trigger, action, and search events that you can use in your Zaps.

Although, in most cases, the integrations built with Zapier cover the most commonly requested events users may need, often, the app's API allows for many more events, therefore increasing flexibility. If an application has an open API, in most cases, there will be **API documentation** available on the SaaS provider's website that will provide information about how to use the API. Knowing how to read and understand API documentation is an important prerequisite for knowing how to create custom triggers and actions using the API outside of Zapier's standard integration with each app. This is a lengthy topic and is outside the scope of this book. However, here are some useful resources that will help you get to grips with reading API documentation:

- *Understanding APIs and RESTful APIs Crash Course [Video]* (`https://www.packtpub.com/product/understanding-apis-and-restful-apis-crash-course-video/9781800564121`)

- *What Is API Documentation?* (`https://blog.hubspot.com/website/api-documentation`)

If you would like to dive deeper into how to understand APIs as a whole, this Zapier resource will help: `https://zapier.com/resources/guides/apis`.

Once you have reviewed the app's API documentation to assess what other events are possible, you can then use webhooks (if they are available for use) to trigger your Zaps using the Webhooks by Zapier built-in app, make HTTP requests in action steps and polling triggers, once again using Webhooks by Zapier, use API Request action steps in certain app integrations with Zapier (a feature still in beta), and use Code by Zapier to take advantage of these options. The app's API documentation will also normally give clear instructions on how to authenticate or authorize requests and how to configure them.

> **Important**
> If you create custom HTTP requests within your Zaps, bear in mind that if an app changes its API, this may cause disruption or errors in your Zaps, stopping them from working adequately. You will need to make adjustments to your custom steps accordingly.

Next, we'll provide an overview of how to use the Webhooks by Zapier built-in app.

Webhooks by Zapier – using webhooks and HTTP requests in your Zaps

First of all, it is important to mention that perhaps the choice of name for this built-in app does not correctly describe its function, and could imply that it only works with webhooks. The **Webhooks by Zapier** built-in app allows you to use webhooks as instant triggers, create polling triggers, and also make HTTP requests to an API. Therefore, it is better to separate these uses by event type. Let's look at each.

Webhooks by Zapier trigger events

As we covered in *Chapter 1, Introduction to Business Process Automation with Zapier*, event changes in apps are identified by either using a polling method or by using webhooks, which then cause the trigger step in your Zaps to run. The polling method involves repeatedly checking for new information at scheduled intervals. However, with webhooks, you provide the app with a URL that your originating app constantly monitors for new events, thus receiving information in real time. Webhooks are an instant, and therefore a much more efficient, way of communicating event information. This means that Zaps using webhooks trigger much quicker than other Zaps where the trigger step uses the polling method.

The Webhooks by Zapier built-in app can be used with the following webhook and polling trigger events:

- **Retrieve Poll** (trigger): This trigger event polls a URL and searches for new entries. This polling trigger will search for new entries periodically based on the update time specified by your Zapier subscription plan.

- **Catch Hook** (trigger): This instant trigger event waits for a new POST, GET, or PUT notification to a URL provided by Zapier.

- **Catch Raw Hook** (trigger): This instant trigger event waits for a new POST, GET, or PUT notification to a URL provided by Zapier. This is a more detailed version of the **Catch Hook** trigger event and supplies the request body as unparsed data. It also includes headers.

Both the **Catch Hook** and **Catch Raw Hook** trigger events require you to set up webhooks in the app you are hoping to get event notifications from. These webhooks will need to point to the URL provided by Zapier for either of those trigger events. The app's API documentation will normally give clear instructions on how to configure, authenticate, or authorize new webhook connections. For example, Trello's API documentation, which covers webhooks, can be found at https://developer. atlassian.com/cloud/trello/guides/rest-api/webhooks/.

If the app you are using does not have webhooks available in the API, then you will need to use the **Retrieve Poll** trigger event using an endpoint specified in the app's API documentation.

Webhooks by Zapier action events

Now, let's have a look at how to use Webhooks by Zapier to make HTTP requests.

The Webhooks by Zapier built-in app can be used with the following HTTP request action events:

- **Custom Request** (action): This action event sends off a custom request by providing raw data

- **POST** (action): This action event sends a single request to create a new resource

- **GET** (action): This action event sends a single request to retrieve an existing resource

- **PUT** (action): This action event sends a single request to update an existing resource

Using Webhooks by Zapier is especially useful if your app or business tool does not support Zapier integration. Webhooks by Zapier allows developers who are familiar with your tools to create requests between different tools without the need to understand the new API documentation. For example, when a new user signs up to create a free trial account, you could create a POST request to create a new contact in your CRM and accounting system. If the integration with Zapier does not support a specific trigger, action, or search event that you need, it is always worth reviewing the API documentation to assess whether it is possible by using the Webhooks by Zapier built-in app.

> **Tip**
> You can use the Webhooks by Zapier built-in app to combine one or more Zaps. For example, a limitation of the Looping by Zapier built-in app is that you can only have one loop in a Zap. If you have several paths in a Zap and each path requires a loop, you can use the Webhooks by Zapier **POST** action event at the end of each path to push data to different looping Zaps. This would give each a **Catch Hook** trigger event with a custom URL that you would specify in the **POST** action events.

Zapier has created a few very useful help documents to help you get started with webhooks. You can find out more about webhooks in general at `https://zapier.com/help/doc/how-get-started-webhooks-zapier`, and how to use webhooks in Zapier at `https://zapier.com/blog/what-are-webhooks/`.

> **Important note**
> Webhooks by Zapier is a premium app and can only be used with the Zapier Starter plan or higher.

Let's explore a few examples of when you can use Webhooks by Zapier to achieve more in your automations and not be limited by existing Zapier triggers and actions.

An example of using the Catch Hook trigger event of Webhooks by Zapier

You may want to kick off a workflow in Zapier when only the contact's first name changes in an ActiveCampaign record. Although an **Updated Contact** trigger event exists in the ActiveCampaign integration with Zapier, it would be challenging to identify what the name changed from to filter out only a change in the first name. A good workaround for this is to create an automation in ActiveCampaign that contains a trigger with the right conditions, which then sends information to a webhook URL in Zapier. By using the **Catch Hook** trigger event in Zapier, you can generate a unique webhook URL that you can then copy and paste into the relevant automation step in ActiveCampaign.

The following screenshot shows an example of what this would look like in the Webhooks by Zapier **Catch Hook** trigger event:

Figure 11.1 – Overview of using the Catch Hook trigger event in Webhooks by Zapier

The following screenshot shows the ActiveCampaign automation with the Zapier webhook URL:

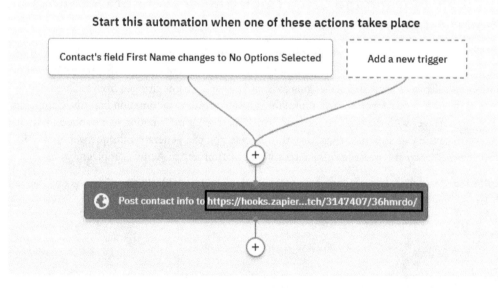

Figure 11.2 – Using a webhook step in ActiveCampaign to specify the webhook URL

Let's take a look at an example that involves an action event.

An example of using the PUT action event of Webhooks by Zapier

You may want to create a new company in **Freshdesk** when an opportunity is won in Salesforce. The Freshdesk integration with Zapier has a **Create Company** action event that only allows certain details to be added when a new company is created (**Name**, **Description**, **Notes**, and **Domain**), and there is no available action event to update the company. If you have set up custom fields in Freshdesk, you may want your new company to be updated with custom field data such as **Customer Status** or **Product Type**. The Freshdesk API allows PUT requests to update the company (`https://developers. freshdesk.com/api/#update_company`), which means you can use Webhooks by Zapier to do this using the **PUT** action event.

The following screenshot shows an example of how you can set up the Webhooks by Zapier **PUT** action event:

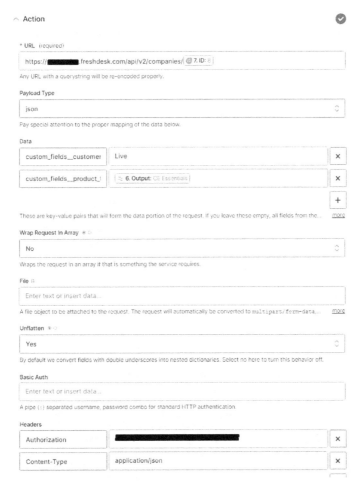

Figure 11.3 – Overview of using the PUT action event in Webhooks by Zapier

The **Authorization** field under **Headers** will contain the API key, as specified in the API documentation.

> **Tip**
>
> For more inspiration and access to pre-built templates, you can review the Webhooks by Zapier built-in app profile page at `https://zapier.com/apps/webhook/integrations`.

You should now have a better understanding of how and when to use the Webhooks by Zapier built-in app.

Next, let's review how to use the **API Request (beta)** action event.

Using the API Request action event (feature in beta)

Using Webhooks by Zapier might seem quite complicated, especially if you have to decipher API documentation. A more straightforward approach is to use a new feature that is currently in beta throughout the platform. Zapier has begun upgrading certain integrations with the **API Request (beta)** action event. Before the release of this action event feature, users would need to extensively understand API documentation and use the Webhooks by Zapier built-in app to make `PUT`, `GET`, and `POST` HTTP requests. The introduction of this new action event in many app integrations allows API requests to be made in a simpler, no-code-focused fashion. Unlike with using Webhooks by Zapier, you will have already connected the app to your Zapier account and will not need to provide any further authentication details, such as an API key. In many cases, you can make simple HTTP requests without having to understand complex API documentation jargon. You will just need to know how to find the endpoint URL required and what request parameters are essential.

When discussing how to use Webhooks by Zapier, we looked at trigger and action examples. Now, let's explore how to use the **API Request (beta)** action event to perform a search action that's not available using Zapier integration.

If you are a **ClickUp** user, you might want to retrieve the details of all lists in a specific folder. The ClickUp integration with Zapier does not have any suitable search actions. However, if you review the ClickUp API documentation (`https://clickup.com/api/clickupreference/operation/GetLists/`), you will find the endpoint (`https://api.clickup.com/api/v2/folder/{folder_id}/list`) that you need to achieve this. You can use the **API Request (beta)** action event to make a `GET` request using the API by specifying `folder_id` in the URL. `folder_id` is a required parameter for the success of the request.

The following screenshot shows the **API Request (Beta)** action event on the ClickUp integration profile page (`https://zapier.com/apps/clickup/integrations`):

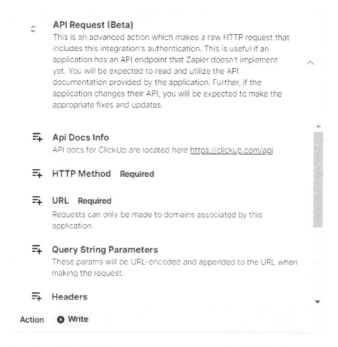

API Request (Beta)
This is an advanced action which makes a raw HTTP request that includes this integration's authentication. This is useful if an application has an API endpoint that Zapier doesn't implement yet. You will be expected to read and utilize the API documentation provided by the application. Further, if the application changes their API, you will be expected to make the appropriate fixes and updates.

Api Docs Info
API docs for ClickUp are located here https://clickup.com/api

HTTP Method   **Required**

URL   **Required**
Requests can only be made to domains associated by this application.

Query String Parameters
These params will be URL-encoded and appended to the URL when making the request.

Headers

Action   ● Write

Figure 11.4 – Overview of the API Request action event on the ClickUp integration profile page

The following screenshot shows the ClickUp API documentation, with the **Get Lists** endpoint showing the required parameters and URL:

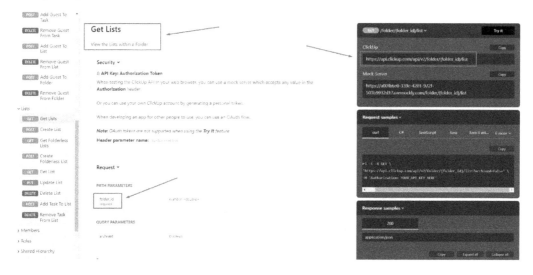

Figure 11.5 – The ClickUp API documentation showing the Get Lists endpoint

The following screenshot shows how the **API Request (Beta)** action event can be used to retrieve the details of all the lists in a ClickUp folder:

Figure 11.6 – Overview of the API Request (Beta) action event to retrieve all the lists in a ClickUp folder

You can find more detailed instructions on how to set up an API request action step using this Zapier resource: `https://help.zapier.com/hc/en-us/articles/12899607716493-Set-up-an-API-request-action-Beta`.

You should now have a better understanding of how and when to use the **API Requests (beta)** action step. Next, let's review how to create and use **App Extensions**.

Using App Extensions in multiple Zaps (feature in beta)

If you use the same **API Request (beta)** action steps in several different Zaps, you will need to replicate the information from one Zap to another normally. However, the **App Extensions** action event takes the capabilities of the **API Request (beta)** action event feature a few steps forward and allows you to create app extensions in the **App Extensions** builder, allowing you to set up API call settings that can be used in multiple Zaps. As with the **API Request (beta)** action event, the **App Extensions (beta)** action event allows you to use your already authenticated app connection information, so all you have to do is create an **App Extension template** that can be used in multiple Zaps, and shared in your team if you're using a Team or Company account. As with the **API Request (beta)** action event, the **App Extensions (beta)** action event is currently available for use with a limited number of apps. You can find the list of supported apps here: `https://help.zapier.com/hc/en-us/articles/16276574838925`. You will also need a basic understanding of how to read API documentation, send HTTP requests, and choose which API endpoint to use in the app extension.

We will use the example discussed in the *Using the API Request action event (feature in beta)* section to illustrate the differences between the **API Request (beta)** and **App Extensions (beta)** action events. Once you have built and named your app extension in the **App Extension** builder, you can use an **App Extension (beta)** action event with an app extension to make a `GET` request using the API by specifying `folder_id` in the URL. `folder_id` is a required parameter for the success of the request. The following screenshot shows how the **App Extension (beta)** action event can be used with the pre-built `Get lists in a folder in ClickUp` app extension to retrieve the details of all the lists in a ClickUp folder:

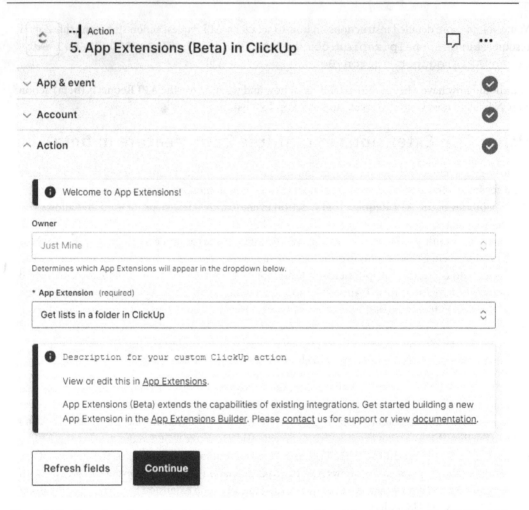

Figure 11.7 – Overview of using the App Extensions action event to retrieve all the lists in a ClickUp folder

You can find more detailed instructions on how to set up, edit, and use app extensions using these Zapier resources:

- https://help.zapier.com/hc/en-us/articles/16277139110157
- https://help.zapier.com/hc/en-us/articles/16277147937805
- https://help.zapier.com/hc/en-us/articles/16277375114637

> **Tip**
> You can use the magic of AI to draft your App Extensions for you. We will cover AI-powered App Extensions in more detail in *Chapter 19, AI and Automation.*

You should now have a better understanding of how and when to use **App Extensions**. Next, let's review how to use the Code by Zapier built-in app.

Code by Zapier – using JavaScript or Python code in your Zaps

The next step up from using webhooks and API requests in your Zaps is to use code when you can't achieve what you need to with the no-code built-in apps, Webhooks by Zapier, or API Request action steps. You can write custom code in either the JavaScript or Python programming languages and use it in your Zaps with Code by Zapier to either trigger the workflow or perform various tasks to transform and customize your data.

The Code by Zapier built-in app can be used via the following trigger and action events:

- **Run JavaScript** (trigger): This trigger event allows you to use JavaScript to start a workflow
- **Run Python** (trigger): This trigger event allows you to use Python to start a workflow
- **Run JavaScript** (action): This action event allows you to run JavaScript as an action step in your Zap
- **Run Python** (action): This action event allows you to run Python as an action step in your Zap

Let's explore an example of when you can use Code by Zapier to achieve more in your automations and not be limited by existing Zapier trigger, action, and search events.

An example of using the Run JavaScript action event of Code by Zapier

You may want to retrieve detailed information about a contact in Pipedrive, such as all the phone numbers associated with the contact, once your workflow has been triggered. You may then want to manipulate those phone numbers to extract the area code. The Pipedrive integration with Zapier has a **Find Person** search action event that only allows for one phone number to be retrieved. The Pipedrive API allows requests for information on a person (`https://developers.pipedrive.com/docs/api/v1/#!/Persons/getPerson`), so you can use Code by Zapier to do this using the **Run JavaScript** or **Run Python** action events.

Let's break this down into two steps. The following screenshot shows the first step in making an HTTP request to Pipedrive to retrieve the details of the person:

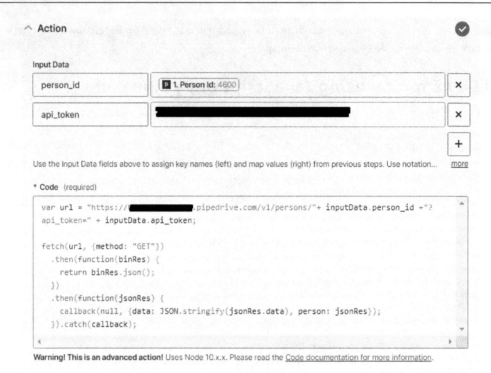

Figure 11.8 – Overview of using the Run JavaScript action event in Code
by Zapier to retrieve phone numbers for a Pipedrive contact

As per the API documentation, the API token in your Pipedrive account would be displayed in the api_token field and the URL for your Pipedrive account would be added to the code.

The next step would involve extracting only the area code from the phone number. This is shown in the following screenshot:

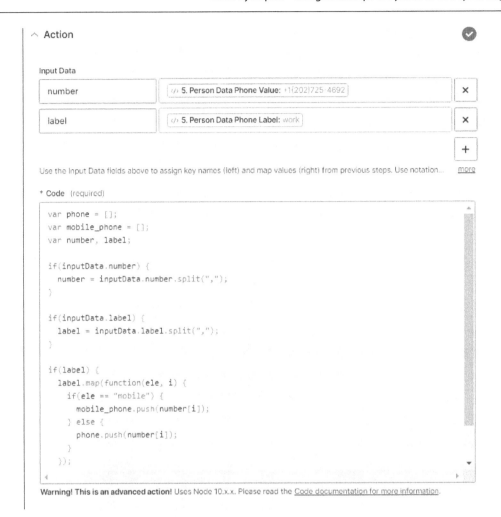

Figure 11.9 – Overview of using the Run JavaScript action event in Code
by Zapier to extract the area code from a phone number

Tip

You can use Code by Zapier steps to combine multiple actions that would normally involve several steps. This, in turn, can reduce your task usage. It is important to bear in mind that Zapier does not support code used in Code by Zapier steps, and it is the responsibility of the user to maintain the code. For example, if changes are made to the API or the data received from the API, this could "break" the code step.

Let's briefly cover how you can use AI to generate code for use in Code by Zapier code steps.

Generating JavaScript or Python code with ChatGPT

With the release of OpenAI's ChatGPT, you can now ask the AI chatbot to generate code for you to use in your Code by Zapier steps. This is extremely useful if you are not a programmer and do not know how to write any code. Using the example that we previously discussed, we gave ChatGPT the following prompt:

"I want to retrieve detailed information about a contact in Pipedrive, such as all the phone numbers associated with the contact, using Code by Zapier. I also want to manipulate those phone numbers to extract the area code from the phone number and display these results as two separate values. The Pipedrive API allows requests for information on a person, https://developers.pipedrive.com/docs/api/ v1/#!/Persons/getPerson. Can you write me some code in Python to perform this action please?"

The result is shown in the following screenshot:

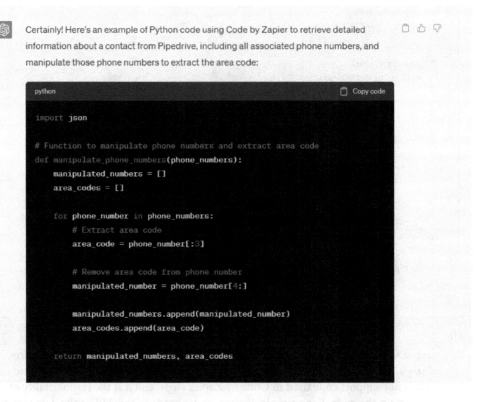

Figure 11.10 – Overview of using ChatGPT to generate code in Python to use in a Code by Zapier step

The following screenshot shows the additional instructions produced by ChatGPT:

In this code, we define a `manipulate_phone_numbers` function that takes a list of phone numbers as input, extracts the area code and removes it from the phone numbers. The function returns two separate lists: `manipulated_numbers` containing the phone numbers with the area code removed, and `area_codes` containing the extracted area codes.

The `pipedrive_contact_details` function is the main function called by Code by Zapier. It takes an `input_data` dictionary as input, which should contain the `contact_id` and `api_token`. The function retrieves the contact details using the Pipedrive API, extracts the phone numbers, and calls the `manipulate_phone_numbers` function to manipulate the phone numbers and extract the area codes. The manipulated numbers and area codes are then prepared as output data in a dictionary.

To test the function locally, you can provide sample input data in the `test_input` dictionary, including the desired `contact_id` and your Pipedrive `api_token`. The resulting output will be printed.

Please note that you will need to replace `'YOUR_API_TOKEN'` with your actual Pipedrive API token and provide the appropriate `contact_id` when using this code. Additionally, you may need to import the necessary modules and libraries depending on the environment where you are running this code.

Figure 11.11 – Instructions provided by ChatGPT on how to alter the code for use in Code by Zapier

> **Tip**
> You can use the magic of AI to write code for you from within your Code by Zapier steps. We will cover AI-powered Code by Zapier steps in more detail in *Chapter 19, AI and Automation*.

Zapier has created a few very useful help documents to help you get started with Code by Zapier:

- https://zapier.com/blog/code-by-zapier-guide/https://help.zapier.com/hc/en-us/articles/8496326417549

- https://help.zapier.com/hc/en-us/articles/8496197098253-JavaScript-code-examples-in-Zaps

- https://help.zapier.com/hc/en-us/articles/8496197130893-Python-code-examples-in-Zaps

> **Tip**
> For more inspiration and access to pre-built templates, you can review the Code by Zapier built-in app profile page at `https://zapier.com/apps/code/integrations`.

You should now have a better understanding of how and when to use the Code by Zapier built-in app.

Next, let's review how to use the Storage by Zapier built-in app.

Storage by Zapier – saving and storing data

There may be many scenarios where it would be useful to be able to store small sets of data for use in your workflows. The Storage by Zapier built-in app allows you to save and retrieve small data values. With it, you can store reference data each time a Zap runs and then share it with other Zaps by retrieving it.

Storage by Zapier does not operate with user accounts. Instead, you must specify a **secret storage key** in the format of a **Universally Unique Identifier** (**UUID4**), which acts much like a password, to identify and group storage data. You would then use this secret storage key to identify where to add data to and retrieve data from. By doing this, you can have multiple storage keys that identify your storage locations.

You can store individual values or lists of values. You can also use **child values** (nested values of data) if you want to store and retrieve several values related to a unique identifier – for example, the name and email address of a specific contact.

The Storage by Zapier built-in app can be used via the following action and search action events:

- **Set Child Value** (action): This action event allows you to set one or multiple child values that are stored at a specified key.

- **Set Value** (action): This action event allows you to set a value stored at a specified key.

- **Increment Value** (action): This action event allows you to incrementally add a value at a specified key.

- **Pop Value From List** (action): This action event allows you to remove a value from a list of values. If the list is empty, however, it will return a default value that you define.

- **Push Value Onto List** (action): This action event allows you to push a value onto an existing list of values.

- **Remove All Values** (action): This action event allows you to remove all values from a Storage by Zapier-connected account.

- **Remove Child Value** (action): This action event allows you to remove one or multiple child values stored at a specified key.

- **Remove Value** (action): This action event allows you to remove a value or a list of values stored at a specified key.

- **Set Multiple Values** (action): This action event allows you to set multiple values stored at specified keys.

- **Set Value If** (action): This action event allows you to conditionally set a value stored at a specified key if the stored value matches a previously defined value.

- **Get Child Value** (search action): This search action event allows you to retrieve a child value stored at a specified key. You can also create a new child value if none have been stored.

- **Get Value** (search action): This search action event allows you to retrieve a value stored at a specified key. You can also create a new value if none have been stored.

- **Get All Values** (search action): This search action event allows you to retrieve all values stored.

- **Get List Values** (search action): This search action event allows you to retrieve all values from a list and format the output as one value.

- **Get Multiple Values** (search action): This search action event allows you to retrieve multiple values stored at specified keys.

- **Get Secret** (search action): This search action event allows you to retrieve your secret storage key as a value so that it can be used in a Code by Zapier step.

> **Important note**
> When using the **Get Secret** search action, bear in mind that this will expose your secret key and should be used with caution.

Here are a couple of examples of how you can use Storage by Zapier:

- You may want to keep a running tally of various key performance indicators and analytics, such as how many new leads have been added to your CRM in a day or how many sales you have made in a week. You can use the **Increment Value** action event to add the values to different keys cumulatively, and then in a separate Zap use the **Remove Value** action event with a Schedule by Zapier trigger event to erase the value periodically (every day or month, for example). You can then display the values in a dashboard reporting tool such as Databox or Geckoboard.

- You may want to store the name and email address of every new user who subscribes to your email list. You can use the **Set Child Value** action event and specify the user ID as the secret storage key and the name and email address as child values. Then, you can use the **Get Child Value** search action event in a separate Zap to retrieve those values.

The following screenshot shows an example of where the **Push Value Onto List** action event has been used to add survey participants' emails to a storage list, with `automation_survey_list` as the key value for the list:

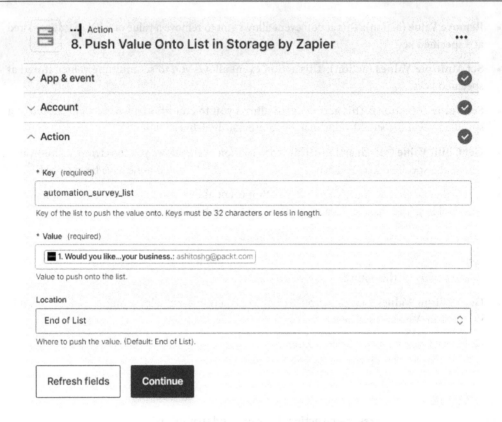

Figure 11.12 – Overview of using Storage by Zapier to add values to a list

You could then use the **Get Value**, **Get All Values**, or **Get List Values** search action events to retrieve the data, depending on how you would like it presented.

Zapier has created useful help documents to help you get started with Storage by Zapier, which you can find at `https://help.zapier.com/hc/en-us/articles/8496293271053`.

You can also access your storage data by using Code by Zapier steps in your workflows, as described in the Zapier help document at `https://help.zapier.com/hc/en-us/articles/8496062115597`.

> **Tip**
>
> For more inspiration and access to pre-built templates, you can review the Code by Zapier built-in app profile page at `https://zapier.com/apps/storage/integrations`.

You should now have a better understanding of how and when to use the Storage by Zapier built-in app.

Summary

In this chapter, we discussed three advanced built-in apps by Zapier and a new feature in beta. We began by reviewing how to use webhooks in your Zaps with Webhooks by Zapier and make HTTP requests. Then, we explored how to use the **API Request** action event feature (in beta). Next, we covered how to use JavaScript or Python code with Code by Zapier, and generate code with ChatGPT. Lastly, we explored how to use Storage by Zapier to store and retrieve data.

You now understand what the Webhooks by Zapier, Code by Zapier, and Storage by Zapier built-in apps, as well as the **API Request** action event, can be used for.

In the next chapter, you will learn about the two built-in apps that can be used for managing your Zapier account: App Status by Zapier and Zapier Manager. We will cover how to use App Status by Zapier to get notifications of integration issues and review the various trigger, action, and search action events that Zapier Manager has for managing errors and changes in your Zapier account.

Questions

1. Which three built-in apps or features in Zapier can be used to make HTTP requests?

2. If you would like to store small values secretly and securely, what Zapier built-in app can you use?

Managing Your Zapier Account with Built-In Apps

Once you have got to grips with the inner workings of Zapier and you have created several Zaps, you will want to know whether your automations are running smoothly in the background as you conduct your daily business. You will also want to know straight away when problems occur, such as when your connected apps are experiencing downtime, there are errors with your Zaps, or changes occur in your Zapier account. Thankfully, Zapier has created two built-in apps that will help you keep on top of these situations. In general, when using the trigger events from these built-in apps, you can use various action steps as alerts, such as sending an email, SMS, or Slack message, or adding a task or activity to your task management app or CRM.

In this chapter, we will discuss the two built-in apps that can be used for managing your Zapier account. We will start by covering App Status by Zapier to get notifications of integration issues. Then, we will review Zapier Manager for managing issues and changes in your Zapier account. Finally, we will cover some use cases.

This chapter will be most useful for those users who are responsible for administrating systems within the business and where there is a critical need to keep an eye on system maintenance. This is especially important when multiple users in a team are creating automations, specifically in Team and Company plan accounts, and monitoring the administrative aspect of Zapier accounts using automations is beneficial. It is worth mentioning, however, that even single-user account owners will benefit from some alert notification Zaps being created, such as those related to errors and task usage.

We will cover the following key topics in this chapter:

- App Status by Zapier – getting notifications of integration incidents
- Zapier Manager – managing errors and account changes
- Use cases

Once you have worked through each of these topics, you will know how to set up workflows to manage notifications of app integration incidents, as well as how to manage errors and changes in your Zapier account.

Technical requirements

To get the most out of the content and exercises in this chapter, you will need access to a Zapier account. The Zapier Free plan will be adequate. Some examples included in this chapter involve multi-step workflows, for which you will need a Starter plan or higher. For the *Events for Team and Company account user management* section, you will need to use a Team or Company account.

App Status by Zapier – getting notifications of integration incidents

In *Chapter 5, Troubleshooting and Handling Zap Errors*, we discussed how to manage the status alerts of your connected apps by monitoring the Zapier **Status** page and creating alert workflows. This is where we introduced the App Status by Zapier built-in app.

The App Status by Zapier built-in app can only be used as a trigger step and is available as the **New or Updated App Incident** trigger event.

This event will trigger on new, updated, and resolved app status incidents from the apps you specify.

Here are a few examples of when you could use this app:

- Send an email when there is a new, updated, or resolved incident with Mailchimp
- Add a new task to **Wrike** when there is a new incident with **Zoho Campaigns** and **Zoho CRM**

Refer to the *Setting up an app status alert workflow with the App Status by Zapier built-in app* section in *Chapter 5, Troubleshooting and Handling Zap Errors*, for a detailed explanation of how to use this built-in app to create alert notifications of new, updated, and resolved incidents with public apps that you specify. We also discussed how to create alert Zaps using pre-built Zap templates directly from the Zapier **Status** page in that chapter.

> **Tip**
> For more inspiration and access to pre-built templates, you can review the App Status by Zapier built-in app profile page at `https://zapier.com/apps/app-status/integrations`.

You should now have a better understanding of how and when to use the App Status by Zapier built-in app.

Next, let's cover how to use the Zapier Manager built-in app to manage errors and account changes in your Zapier account.

Zapier Manager – managing errors and account changes

We introduced the Zapier Manager built-in app in *Chapter 5*, *Troubleshooting and Handling Zap Errors*, where we discussed how to use it to manage error alerts such as errors with Zaps, Zaps being turned off, or tasks being halted.

You can also use Zapier Manager to notify yourself and your team about new public apps being added to Zapier, changes to your account such as new folders or Zaps being created, task usage limits being reached, or new Zapier invoices being released. You can search for a Zap or public app, as well as turn Zaps on or off. If you are using a Team account, you can use Zapier Manager to invite a new user to your Zapier team or notify you of new team members being added.

> **Tip**
> For more inspiration and access to pre-built templates, you can review the Zapier Manager by Zapier built-in app profile page at `https://zapier.com/apps/zapier-manager/integrations`.

Here is a Zapier Community article that explores using Zapier Manager for an error alert system: `https://community.zapier.com/featured-articles-65/alert-notification-system-for-business-critical-zaps-10800`.

The Zapier Manager built-in app can be used with several trigger, action, and search events, which we have categorized as follows:

1. Managing Zap errors and alerts:

   - **New Zap Error** (trigger)

   - **Zap Turned Off** (trigger)

   - **New Halted Task** (trigger)

2. Managing apps, Zaps, and folders:

   - **New Public App** (trigger)

   - **Find App** (search action)

   - **New Folder** (trigger)

   - **New Zap** (trigger)

- **Turn Zap On/Off** (action)
- **Find Zap** (search action)
- **Create Zap Report** (**Beta**) (action)

3. Zapier account administration:

- **Task Usage Limit Reached** (trigger)
- **New Invoice** (trigger)

4. Team and company account user management:

- **New Team Member** (trigger)
- **Create Team Invitation** (action)

Let's look at each of these in turn.

Events to manage Zap errors and alerts

In *Chapter 5, Troubleshooting and Handling Zap Errors*, we discussed how to use the Zapier Manager built-in app to manage error alerts using each of the three trigger events, as follows:

- **New Zap Error** (trigger)
- **Zap Turned Off** (trigger)
- **New Halted Task** (trigger)

Here are a few examples of when to use these trigger events:

- **New Zap Error**: When an error occurs in a Zap, post a message to **Twist**
- **Zap Turned Off**: When a Zap is turned off, add a task to **Podio**
- **New Halted Task**: When a task is halted, send an SMS

In *Chapter 5, Troubleshooting and Handling Zap Errors*, refer to the *Setting up an error alert workflow with the Zapier Manager built-in app* section for a detailed explanation of how to use this built-in app to create alerts for errors with Zaps, Zaps that have been turned off, or tasks that have been halted.

Now, let's review how to use the various trigger, action, and search action events to manage apps, Zaps, and folders in your Zapier account.

Events to manage apps, Zaps, and folders

In *Chapter 4, Managing Your Zaps*, we discussed managing your connected apps, and the importance of adequately naming your Zaps and sorting them into folders to maintain a clutter-free and organized Zapier account. With this in mind, you might want to know when new public apps have been connected to Zapier, and when new folders and Zaps are created if your team shares a Zapier account. You may also want to search for information on an app or a Zap, as well as turn a Zap on or off in certain scenarios.

The six Zapier Manager built-in app trigger, action, and search action events that can be used for these purposes are as follows:

- **New Public App** (trigger)
- **Find App** (search action)
- **New Folder** (trigger)
- **New Zap** (trigger)
- **Turn Zap On/Off** (action)
- **Find Zap** (search action)
- **Create Zap Report** (**Beta**) (action)

Let's look at each.

The New Public App trigger event

The **New Public App** trigger event can be used to start a workflow when Zapier announces that a new public app has been integrated with the platform. Keeping on top of these alerts is useful if you use certain apps in your business that do not currently integrate with Zapier.

Here are a few examples of how you can use this trigger event:

- Send an email when a new public app has been announced
- Send a Twitter message when a new public app has been released on the Zapier platform

Let's explore how to set up this trigger event.

Setting up the New Public App trigger event

Once you have added this trigger step to the start of your workflow (to **1. Trigger**) and chosen **Zapier Manager** as the app and **New Public App** as the trigger event, you can select **Continue**. You can then edit the **Category** field in the **Trigger** section. From the alphabetical drop-down list, choose the app category you want your trigger to fire on. You can select **All** if you want to be notified of all apps or specify the category. Categories are based on the information you can find in the app ecosystem directory: https://zapier.com/apps. Add one category per field; additional fields will appear once you have confirmed the category in each field. Delete any field lines by clicking on the **X** button at the end of the field. You can also type a static value into each field.

This is shown in the following screenshot:

Figure 12.1 – Overview of customizing the New Public App trigger event

You can then select **Continue** and, in the **Trigger** section, use the **Test trigger** button to retrieve your test data so that it can be used in your action steps.

The trigger extracts the following data, all of which can be used in your action steps:

- App ID
- App title
- Description of the app
- App site URL
- App page URL on Zapier
- Listed categories

Proceed to add one or more action steps to your Zap using data from this trigger step.

Here is a Zapier Community example of how you can use the **New Public App** action event: `https://community.zapier.com/featured-articles-65/send-yourself-a-weekly-digest-of-newly-added-zapier-integrations-12489`.

You should now be able to use the **New Public App** trigger event. Next, let's take a look at the **Find App** search action event.

The Find App search action event

The **Find App** search action event is handy to use when you want to retrieve information about a public app. For example, say you want to watch an app, such as **Cascade**, for changes to the categories it is listed in. In this case, you could set **Schedule by Zapier** as a trigger that fires every 4 weeks, then use the **Find App** search action to find the information on the Cascade app, and thereafter, add the data to a Google Sheets spreadsheet.

Let's explore how to set up this action event.

Setting up the Find App search action event

You can use the **Find App** search action event once you have set up a trigger step.

Once you have added an action step, either by selecting the **Action** step or clicking on the + icon, and have chosen **Zapier Manager** as the app and **Find App** as the action event, you can edit the fields in the **Action** section, as follows:

- **Name**: Enter the name of the app by either typing in static data, using the **Custom** tab to map in dynamic data from previous steps, or a combination of both.

- **Should this step be considered a "success" when nothing is found?**: Use this Boolean field to select **True** or **False** from the drop-down menu, enter text, or insert data from previous steps for this step to be considered a "success" if nothing is found in the search. The default for this field is **False**, which you should choose if you want the Zap to stop running at this point if nothing has been found; this is the most common use case. This means that all subsequent steps will be skipped. Use the **True** option when you want to allow the Zap to continue and subsequent steps to run. You can then add more control to your workflows by adding Filter by Zapier or Paths by Zapier conditional logic for more control and allowing those steps to pass or stop based on whether the search returned a result or not.

These are shown in the following screenshot:

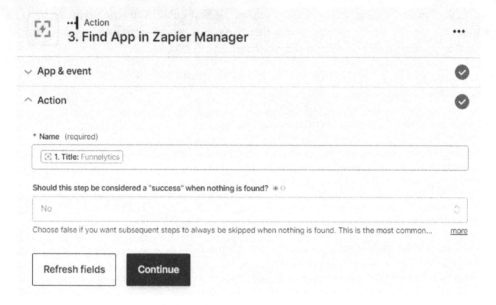

Figure 12.2 – Overview of customizing the Find App search action event

Click on the **Continue** button and, in the **Test** section, use the **Test** button to test this step or click on **Skip test**.

Proceed to add one or more action steps and then turn on your Zap.

You should now be able to use the **Find App** search action event. Next, let's take a look at the **New Folder** trigger event.

The New Folder trigger event

The **New Folder** trigger event can be used to start a workflow when a new folder is added to your Zapier account or accounts you have access to. This is especially useful if several people in your team use the same account and you want to know when new folders are being created and what Zaps they contain, or if you want to record this information somewhere.

Here are a few examples of how you can use this trigger event:

- Send a group chat message in **Chatwork** when a new folder is created
- Add a new row to a Google Sheets spreadsheet when a new folder is created

Let's explore how to set up this trigger event.

Setting up the New Folder trigger event

Once you have added this trigger step to the start of your workflow (to **1. Trigger**) and chosen **Zapier Manager** as the app and **New Folder** as the trigger event, you can select **Continue**. You can then edit the **Account** field in the **Trigger** section. If you are a member of multiple Team or Company accounts, you can use the drop-down menu to stipulate which account you want to receive alerts for. These accounts will be denoted by the name of the account – for example, Joe Bloggs' Team. If you only have access to one account, choose the relevant account (normally denoted by **Personal Account** if it's not a Team or Company account). You can also use the **Custom** tab to then type in a static value. If this field is left blank, the trigger will fire for new folders created in all the Zapier accounts you have access to.

This is shown in the following screenshot:

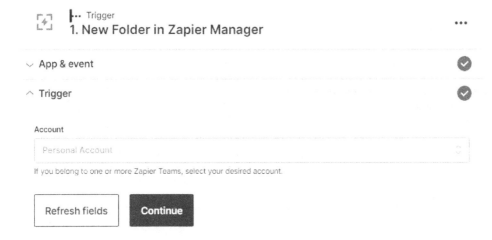

Figure 12.3 – Overview of customizing the New Folder trigger event

You can then select **Continue** and, in the **Test** section, use the **Test trigger** button to retrieve your test data so that you can use it in your action steps.

The trigger extracts the following data, all of which can be used in your action steps:

- Folder ID
- Folder title
- Whether the folder has been shared or not
- The email address of the user that created the folder

Proceed to add one or more action steps to your Zap using data from this trigger step.

You should now be able to use the **New Folder** trigger event. Next, let's take a look at the **New Zap** trigger event.

The New Zap trigger event

The **New Zap** trigger event can be used to start a workflow when a new Zap is added to your Zapier account or accounts you have access to. As with the **New Folder** trigger event, this is especially useful if several people in your team use the same account and you want to know when new Zaps are being created, or if you want to record this information somewhere.

Here are a few examples of how you can use this trigger event:

- Send an email when a new Zap is created

- Add a new record in **Airtable** when a new Zap is created

Let's explore how to set up this trigger event.

Setting up the New Zap trigger event

Once you have added this trigger step to the start of your workflow (to **1. Trigger**) and chosen **Zapier Manager** as the app and **New Zap** as the trigger event, you can select **Continue**. You can then edit the fields in the **Trigger** section, as follows:

- **Account**: If you are a member of multiple Team or Company accounts, use the drop-down menu to stipulate which account you want to receive alerts for. These accounts will be denoted by the name of the account – for example, Joe Bloggs' Team. If you only have access to one account, choose the relevant account (normally denoted by **Personal Account** if it's not a Team or Company account). You can also use the **Custom** tab to type in a static value. If this field is left blank, the trigger will fire for new Zaps created in all the Zapier accounts you have access to.

- **Folder**: Choose a folder from the drop-down list that you want the trigger to fire on. You can also use the **Custom** tab to type in a static value. As this is a number (integer) field, you should use the folder ID rather than the folder name when mapping to the **Custom** tab. If this field is left blank, the trigger will fire on all new Zaps that are created.

This is shown in the following screenshot:

Figure 12.4 – Overview of customizing the New Zap trigger event

You can then select **Continue** and, in the **Test** section, use the **Test trigger** button to retrieve your test data so that you can use it in your action steps.

The trigger extracts the following data, all of which can be used in your action steps:

- Folder root ID
- Zap title
- Zap URL
- Zap Task History URL
- Whether the Zap has been paused or not
- Whether the Zap is on or off (state)
- The email address of the last user to edit the Zap
- The date and time the Zap was last live
- The date and time the Zap was last paused

Proceed to add one or more action steps to your Zap using data from this trigger step.

You should now be able to use the **New Zap** trigger event. Next, let's take a look at the **Turn Zap On/Off** action event.

The Turn Zap On/Off action event

The **Turn Zap On/Off** action event is useful when you want to turn a Zap on or off when a specific trigger event occurs. Turning a Zap off, for example, might be useful in combination with one of the error trigger events, such as **New Zap Error**. You might want to turn the Zap off and then create a task in your project management tool to tell your team to assess the issue. Once this task has been completed, you can turn the Zap back on again.

Here are a few examples of how you can use this trigger event:

- When a Zap error occurs, turn the Zap off and add a task in **MeisterTask**
- When a task has been completed in MeisterTask, turn a Zap on

Let's explore how to set up this action event.

Setting up the Turn Zap On/Off action event

You can use the **Turn Zap On/Off** action event once you have set up a trigger step.

Once you have added an action step, either by selecting the **Action** step or clicking on the + icon, and chosen **Zapier Manager** as the app and **Turn Zap On/Off** as the action event, you can edit the fields in the **Action** section, as follows:

- **Desired Zap State**: From the drop-down list, choose a status to transition the Zap to. The options are **Turn Zap Off**, **Turn Zap On**, and **Toggle Zap State**. If you choose **Toggle Zap State**, the status of the Zap will change, depending on its current state. For example, if it is on, this action event will turn it off, and vice versa. You can also use the **Custom** tab to type in a static value, use a dynamic value from previous steps, or use a combination. Bear in mind that if you are using static or dynamic values instead of the drop-down list, the recognized values for this field are **Turn Zap Off = 0**, **Turn Zap On = 1**, and **Toggle Zap State = 2**. This is a required field and must have a value for the step to run successfully.

- **Account**: If you are a member of multiple Team or Company accounts, use the drop-down menu to stipulate which account you want to receive alerts for. These accounts will be denoted by the name of the account – for example, `Joe Bloggs' Team`. If you only have access to one account, choose the relevant account (normally denoted by **Personal Account** if it's not a Team or Company account). You can also use the **Custom** tab to type in a static value, use a dynamic value from previous steps, or use a combination.

- **Folder**: Choose a folder from the drop-down list. You can also use the **Custom** tab to type in a static value, use a dynamic value from previous steps, or a combination. As this is a number (integer) field, you should use the folder ID rather than the folder name when mapping to the **Custom** tab.

- **Zap**: Specify a Zap from the drop-down list. You can also use the **Custom** tab to type in a static value, use a dynamic value from previous steps, or a combination. As this is a number (integer) field, you should use the Zap ID rather than the Zap's name when mapping to the **Custom** tab. This is a required field and must have a value for the step to run successfully.

These fields are shown in the following screenshot:

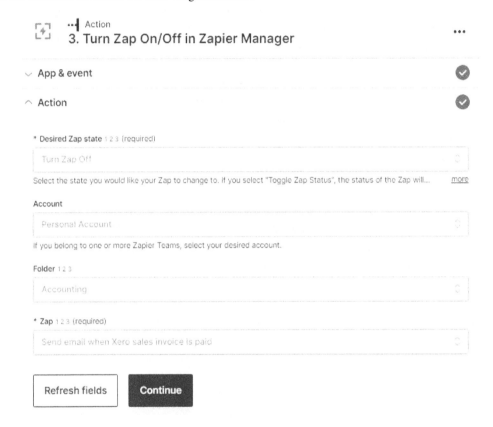

Figure 12.5 – Overview of customizing the Turn Zap On/Off action event

Click on the **Continue** button and, in the **Test** section, use the **Test** button to test this step or click on **Skip test**.

Proceed to add one or more action steps and turn your Zap on.

Here is a Zapier Community example of how you can use the **Turn Zap On/Off** action event: https://community.zapier.com/featured-articles-65/how-to-turn-a-zap-off-and-on-with-a-schedule-11673.

You should now be able to use the **Turn Zap On/Off** action event. Next, let's take a look at the **Find Zap** search action event.

The Find Zap search action event

The **Find Zap** search action event is handy to use when you want to retrieve information about a specific Zap. For example, you might want to use this to watch for when changes are made to the Zap, such as if the Zap is moved to another folder.

Here are a few examples of how you can use this search action event:

- Schedule a maintenance check on a specific Zap weekly using Schedule by Zapier, search to retrieve data on the Zap, and add it to a new record in Airtable

- When a task is halted, search for more information on the Zap and send a Slack message to your team

Let's explore how to set up this action event.

Setting up the Find Zap search action event

You can use the **Find Zap** search action event once you have set up a trigger step.

Once you have added an action step, either by selecting the **Action** step or clicking on the + icon, and chosen **Zapier Manager** as the app and **Find Zap** as the action event, you can edit the fields in the **Action** section, as follows:

- **Account**: If you are a member of multiple Team or Company accounts, use the drop-down menu to stipulate which account you want to receive alerts for. These accounts will be denoted by the name of the account – for example, `Joe Bloggs' Team`. If you only have access to one account, choose the relevant account (normally denoted by **Personal Account** if it's not a Team or Company account). You can also use the **Custom** tab to type in a static value, use a dynamic value from previous steps, or a combination.

- **Name**: Enter the name of the Zap by either typing in static data, using the **Custom** tab to map in dynamic data from previous steps, or a combination of both. This is a required field and must have a value for the step to run successfully.

- **Should this step be considered a "success" when nothing is found?**: Use this Boolean field to select **True** or **False** from the drop-down menu, enter text, or insert data from previous steps for this step to be considered a "success" if nothing is found in the search. The default for this field is **False**, which you should choose if you want the Zap to stop running at this point if nothing is found; this is the most common use case. This means that all subsequent steps will be skipped. Use the **True** option when you want to allow the Zap to continue and subsequent steps to run. You can then add more control to your workflows by adding Filter by Zapier or Paths by Zapier conditional logic for more control and allowing those steps to pass or stop based on whether the search returned a result or not.

These fields are shown in the following screenshot:

Figure 12.6 – Overview of customizing the Find Zap search action event

Click on the **Continue** button and, in the **Test** section, use the **Test** button to test this step or click on **Skip test**.

The search produces the following data, all of which can be used in further action steps:

- Zap ID
- Zap title
- Zap URL
- Zap history URL
- Whether the Zap is paused, on, or off, and configured correctly
- The email address of the user who last edited the Zap
- The timestamp of when the Zap was last live and last paused

If the search produced a true or false result, proceed to add one or more action steps and then turn on your Zap.

You should now be able to use the **Find Zap** search action event. Next, let's take a look at the **Create Zap Report (Beta)** action event.

The Create Zap Report (Beta) action event

The **Create Zap Report** action event, which is still in beta, is useful to use when you want to retrieve information about data that runs through a Zap.

Here are a few examples of how you can use this trigger event:

- When a Zap error occurs, run a Zap report and send yourself an email with the .csv file attached.
- Once a month, run a Zap report to extract all the data passing through a specific Zap with a high task volume. Trigger this Zap with a Schedule by Zapier trigger event and then create and assign a task in Asana for a team member to analyze the data.

Let's explore how to set up this action event.

Setting up the Create Zap Report action event

You can use the **Create Zap Report** action event once you have set up a trigger step.

Once you have added an action step, either by selecting the **Action** step or clicking on the + icon, and chosen **Zapier Manager** as the app and **Create Zap Report** as the action event, you can edit the fields in the **Action** section, as follows:

- **Account**: If you are a member of multiple Team or Company accounts, use the drop-down menu to stipulate which account you want to receive alerts for. These accounts will be denoted by the name of the account – for example, Joe Bloggs' Team. If you only have access to one account, choose the relevant account (normally denoted by **Personal Account** if it's not a Team or Company account). You can also use the **Custom** tab to type in a static value, use a dynamic value from previous steps, or use a combination.
- **Zap**: Specify a Zap from the drop-down list. You can also use the **Custom** tab to type in a static value, use a dynamic value from previous steps, or a combination. As this is a number (integer) field, you should use the Zap ID rather than the Zap's name when mapping to the **Custom** tab. This is a required field and must have a value for the step to run successfully.

These are shown in the following screenshot:

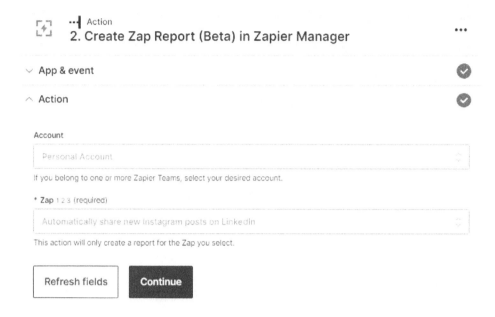

Figure 12.7 – Overview of customizing the Create Zap Report (Beta) action event

Click on the **Continue** button and, in the **Test** section, use the **Test** button to test this step or click on **Skip test**.

Proceed to add one or more action steps and then turn on your Zap.

Now, let's review how to use the various trigger events that can be used for Zapier account administration.

Events for Zapier account administration

Keeping an eye on your account from an administrative perspective is handy to identify when changes happen or urgent attention is required. You may want to know when the task limit on your current plan is soon to be reached so that you have an idea of when to upgrade your pricing plan. This ensures continuity of service with your automations as your tasks may be held back if you reach your account task limit unexpectedly. Equally, if a member of your team has upgraded your account to a higher pricing plan, you may want to be alerted when a new invoice has been generated.

The two Zapier Manager built-in app trigger events that can be used for these purposes are as follows:

- **Task Usage Limit Reached** (trigger)
- **New Invoice** (trigger)

Let's look at each.

The Task Usage Limit Reached trigger event

The **Task Usage Limit Reached** trigger event can be used to start a workflow when your Zapier account task usage has hit a specified threshold of either a percentage or the number of tasks concerning your allocated task amount denoted by your Zapier pricing plan.

Here are a few examples of how you can use this trigger event:

- Send an SMS to yourself if your task usage has reached 70% of the limit
- Send an email to your team if your task usage has hit 950 of a 1,000 task limit

Let's explore how to set up this trigger event.

Setting up the Task Usage Limit Reached trigger event

Once you have added this trigger step to the start of your workflow (to **1. Trigger**) and chosen **Zapier Manager** as the app and **Task Usage Limit Reached** as the trigger event, you can select **Continue**. You can then edit the fields in the **Trigger** section, as follows:

- **Account**: If you are a member of multiple Team or Company accounts, use the drop-down menu to stipulate which account you want to receive alerts for. These accounts will be denoted by the name of the account – for example, `Joe Bloggs' Team`. If you only have access to one account, choose the relevant account (normally denoted by **Personal Account** if it's not a Team or Company account). You can also use the **Custom** tab to type in a static value. If this field is left blank, the trigger will fire for task usage limits that have been reached in all the Zapier accounts you have access to.

- **Usage Threshold (Percent)**: Use this drop-down menu to select a percentage ranging from 10 to 90, specified in increments of 10. You can also type in static text, map dynamic data from previous steps (using the **Custom** tab), or use a combination of both. The trigger will fire when your task usage hits this percentage of included tasks in your pricing plan. The default is 80% if you do not specify a value.

- **Usage Threshold (Task)**: Use this number field to type in a numeric value less than your total number of included tasks, as per your pricing plan. The trigger will fire when your task usage hits this amount. If you have also specified a percentage in the **Usage Threshold (Percent)** field, the trigger will fire on whichever amount occurs first.

These are shown in the following screenshot:

Figure 12.8 – Overview of customizing the Task Usage Limit Reached trigger event

You can then click on **Continue** and, in the **Test** section, use the **Test trigger** button to retrieve your test data to use in your action steps.

The trigger extracts the following data, all of which can be used in your action steps:

- ID
- Task count
- Task limit
- Percent
- Time remaining before billing date (and task count renewal)

Proceed to add one or more action steps to your Zap using data from this trigger step.

You should now be able to use the **Task Usage Limit Reached** trigger event. Next, let's take a look at the **New Invoice** trigger event.

The New Invoice trigger event

The **New Invoice** trigger event can be used to start a workflow when a new invoice is generated in your Zapier account, or in one that you have access to on a Team or Company account. This is useful if you want to be notified of any new upgrades to your Zapier pricing plan, or if you want to alert your accounting team of a new invoice being created.

Here are a few examples of how you can use this trigger event:

- Send a Microsoft Teams message when a new invoice is generated, thus alerting you of a pricing plan change

- Send an email to your accounting team when a new invoice is generated

Let's explore how to set up this trigger event.

Setting up the New Invoice trigger event

Once you have added this trigger step to the start of your workflow (to **1. Trigger**) and chosen **Zapier Manager** as the app and **New Invoice** as the trigger event, you can select **Continue**. You can then edit the **Account** field in the **Trigger** section. If you are a member of multiple Team or Company accounts, use the drop-down menu to stipulate which account you want to receive alerts for. These accounts will be denoted by the name of the account – for example, `Joe Bloggs' Team`. If you only have access to one account, choose the relevant account (normally denoted by **Personal Account** if it's not a Team or Company account). You can also use the **Custom** tab to type in a static value. If this field is left blank, the trigger will fire for new invoices generated in all the Zapier accounts you have access to.

This is shown in the following screenshot:

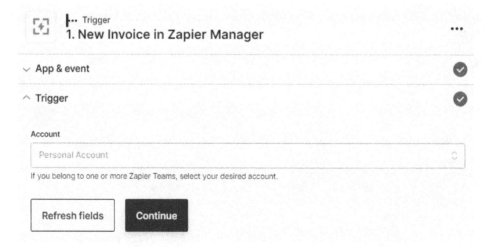

Figure 12.9 – Overview of customizing the New Invoice trigger event

You can then select **Continue** and, in the **Test** section, use the **Test trigger** button to retrieve your test data so that you can use it in your action steps.

The trigger extracts the following data, all of which can be used in your action steps:

- Invoice ID

- Date the invoice was created

- Invoice amount

- Amount due

- Invoice URL

Proceed to add one or more action steps to your Zap using data from this trigger step.

You should now be able to use the **New Invoice** trigger event. Now, let's review how to use the trigger and action events to manage Team and Company account users.

Events for Team and Company account user management

If you have a Team or Company Zapier account, you will most certainly want to make it easier for yourself to monitor new users being added and to create new user account invitations automatically. The two Zapier Manager built-in app trigger events that can be used for these purposes are as follows:

- **New Team Member** (trigger)

- **Create Team Invitation** (action)

Let's look at each.

The New Team Member trigger event

The **New Team Member** trigger event can be used to start a workflow when a new user is added to your Zapier Team account. This is especially useful if you or members of your team want to be alerted when new team members have been added as users.

Here are a few examples of how you can use this trigger event:

- Send an SMS to yourself when a new team member is added

- Send an email to your team when a new team member is added

Let's explore how to set up this trigger event.

Setting up the New Team Member trigger event

Once you have added this trigger step to the start of your workflow (to **1. Trigger**) and chosen **Zapier Manager** as the app and **New Team Member** as the trigger event, you can select **Continue**. You can then edit the **Account** field in the **Trigger** section.

If you are a member of multiple Team or Company accounts, use the drop-down menu to stipulate which account you want to receive alerts for. These accounts will be denoted by the name of the account – for example, `Joe Bloggs' Team`. If you only have access to one account, choose the relevant account (normally denoted by **Personal Account** if it's not a Team or Company account). You can also use the **Custom** tab to type in a static value. If this field is left blank, the trigger will fire for new users that have been added to all the Zapier accounts you have access to.

This is shown in the following screenshot:

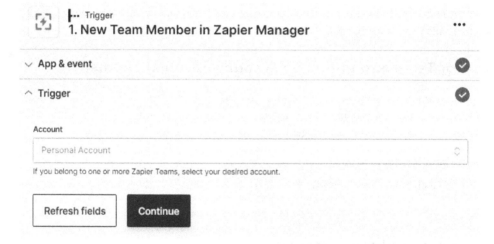

Figure 12.10 – Overview of customizing the New Team Member trigger event

You can then select **Continue** and, in the **Test** section, use the **Test trigger** button to retrieve your test data so that you can use it in your action steps.

The trigger extracts the following data, all of which can be used in your action steps:

- User ID
- User email address
- User name
- Team name

Proceed to add one or more action steps to your Zap using data from this trigger step.

You should now be able to use the **New Team Member** trigger event. Next, let's take a look at the **Create Team Invitation** action event.

The Create Team Invitation action event

The **Create Team Invitation** action event allows you to add a new user to your Team or Company Zapier account. Zapier will send an email invitation to the user, asking them to accept the invitation and access the account within 30 days.

An example of how to use this action event would be when a new employee onboarding task is completed in ClickUp; you could add a new user to Zapier and send an email to your team.

Let's explore how to set up this action event.

Setting up the Create Team Invitation action event

You can use the **Create Team Invitation** action event once you have set up your trigger step, with the relevant trigger data you want to push to Zapier Manager.

Once you have added an action step, either by selecting the **Action** step or clicking on the + icon, and chosen **Zapier Manager** as the app and **Create Team Invitation** as the action event, you can edit the fields in the **Action** section, as follows:

- **Invitee Email**: Enter an email address by either using a typed-in static value, dynamic data from previous steps (using the **Custom** tab), or a combination of both. This is a required field and must have a value for the Zap to continue.
- **Team**: If you are a member of multiple Team or Company accounts, use the drop-down menu to stipulate which account you want to receive alerts for. If you only have access to one account, choose the relevant account. You can also choose dynamic values from previous steps using the **Custom** tab.

These are shown in the following screenshot:

Figure 12.11 – Overview of customizing the Create Team Invitation action event

Click on the **Continue** button and, in the **Test** section, use the **Test action** button to test this step or click on **Skip test**.

Proceed to add one or more action steps to your Zaps, if required, and then turn on your Zap.

You should now have a better understanding of how and when to use the **Create Team Invitation** action event, as well as all the other trigger, action, and search action events of the Zapier Manager built-in app.

Next, let's look at a few scenarios where you can use App Status by Zapier and Zapier Manager to manage your Zapier account.

Use cases

As mentioned earlier in this chapter, having automations set up to manage various aspects of your Zapier account is most suited to situations when multiple users are accessing Zapier on Team and Company accounts and many processes are being automated. System administrators will want to keep a handle on what is happening in the account to monitor task usage and errors, as well as automatically take action based on certain criteria.

The most common scenarios would involve creating alerts with your favorite notification tools, such as email or Slack, that trigger on any of the trigger events in either App Status by Zapier or Zapier Manager. Zap errors, halted tasks, and Zaps being turned off, as well as app status alerts, would be the most common for maintenance purposes. However, if you're in a team, knowing when another team member creates a new folder or, more specifically, a new Zap, would be useful. You can then action other steps, such as adding information to a Google Sheets spreadsheet.

For example, it would be handy to turn high-task-usage Zaps off using the **Turn Zap On/Off** action when you reach 90% of your task limit. You would use the **Task Usage Limit Reached** trigger to start the workflow and select a specific high-usage Zap to turn off. You could then restart the workflow when your task usage refreshes the next month, being triggered by the **New Invoice** trigger.

You can get more inspiration at `https://zapier.com/blog/updates/1594/new-zapier-manager-automate-your-automations` and `https://community.zapier.com/featured-articles-65/the-zapier-manager-app-what-the-heck-is-it-and-what-can-it-be-used-for-6994`.

You should now have a better understanding of how and when to use App Status by Zapier and Zapier Manager to manage your Zapier account.

Summary

In this chapter, we discussed the two built-in apps that can be used for managing your Zapier account, both of which we introduced in *Chapter 5, Troubleshooting and Handling Zap Errors*. We began by reviewing App Status by Zapier to get notifications of integration issues; then, we covered the various trigger, action, and search action events that Zapier Manager has for managing errors and changes in your Zapier account.

You now know how to use App Status by Zapier and Zapier Manager to get alerts regarding app integration problems and manage issues and alterations in your Zapier account.

In the next chapter, you will learn how to use the newest releases of Zapier's built-in apps and modules. We will cover how to get access to early-release features and dive deeper into Looping by Zapier, Sub-Zap by Zapier, Web Parser by Zapier, Transfer, Interfaces, and Tables.

Questions

1. Which Zapier Manager built-in app trigger and action events would be best to use in a Zap if you wanted to automatically turn a Zap back on if it was turned off?

2. Which two Zapier Manager trigger events can be used for Zapier account administration workflow automations?

13

Newly Released Apps and Features

In the previous chapters, we explored a wide array of Zapier's built-in apps and their capabilities for automating tasks. In this chapter, we will dive deeper into the built-in Zapier apps that have been released since the previous edition of this book (published in 2021), offering functionality to further enhance your automation workflows. Some of these are, at the time of publication, still in the **beta** user testing phase. We will provide descriptions of their features and offer practical tips on how to make the most of them.

First, we will cover how to get early access to new Zapier features. Then, we will dive into an overview of Looping by Zapier, a built-in app designed to help you process datasets with multiple values. Next, we will explore Sub-Zap by Zapier, a game-changer for modular automation, which allows you to break down complex Zaps into multiple linked components. Then, we will dive into Web Parser by Zapier, which allows you to scrape data from web pages. Next, we will move on to Transfers by Zapier, Zapier's feature for seamless bulk data transfer between applications. We will then explore Zapier Interfaces, a dynamic module that empowers you to create custom forms, chatbots, and visual interfaces, followed by the Zapier Tables feature, Zapier's robust solution for managing and storing data.

Looping by Zapier and Sub-Zaps by Zapier are categorized by Zapier as **Developer Tools**, and as these are advanced topics, we will only provide a brief overview of their functionality, without going into too much detail. Likewise, with Zapier Interfaces and Zapier Tables, as they are still undergoing beta testing and their features are likely to change, we will only provide a brief overview of their functionality, without going into too much detail. We will, however, provide you with some use cases and further references.

We will cover the following key topics in this chapter:

- Early access to new features
- Looping by Zapier – using loops to process datasets
- Sub-Zap by Zapier (feature in beta) – building modular processes

- Web Parser by Zapier – scraping data from web pages
- Transfers by Zapier – moving bulk data between apps
- Zapier Interfaces (feature in beta) – building custom forms, chatbots, and visual interfaces
- Zapier Tables (feature in beta) – storing and structuring data in tables

By the end of this chapter, you will have acquired in-depth knowledge of the built-in Zapier apps and features that have been released since the first edition of this book was published. From looping through datasets to modularizing your Zaps, scraping data from web pages, creating interactive interfaces, and managing data in tables, you will be equipped to take your automation capabilities to new heights.

Technical requirements

To fully benefit from the content in this chapter, you will need access to a Zapier account. The Zapier Starter plan will provide you with the necessary features to effectively build and implement multi-step Zaps with the features discussed in this chapter.

Early access to new features

The Zapier team works hard to develop new features that will benefit users. These features are released in the **alpha** phase to a select number of test users, and then in the **beta** phase when enough testing has been done to release them to a larger audience in staged releases to user groups. In other words, even though a feature might be released in beta, you might not have access to it. You can, however, sign up for Zapier's **Early Access Program** to be included in the early-stage user testing groups. You can do that at `https://zapier.com/early-access`. You can also sign up for notifications about new AI feature releases at `https://zapier.com/ai`.

Next, let's dive into an overview of the **Looping by Zapier** built-in app.

Looping by Zapier – using loops to process datasets

When you have multiple items in a set of data and need to perform one or more actions for each of the individual items rather than as a bulk set, the **Looping by Zapier** built-in app becomes a handy tool in your Zap-building toolkit. This built-in app enables you to leverage looping functionality to iterate through sets of data so that you can automate bulk actions, process large datasets efficiently, and handle complex workflows with ease. The following figure illustrates how Looping by Zapier works:

Figure 13.1 – How Looping by Zapier works

Here are a few examples where leveraging loops with Looping by Zapier would be useful:

- For meetings that you have set up in your calendar, you will want to send a personalized email to each of the invitees with a Zoom link 1 hour before the meeting's start time. Instead of setting up individual email actions for each address, you can use Looping by Zapier to iterate through the list and send each attendee an email.

- You receive a bulk dataset of support ticket information and you need to assign it to different team members for resolution. You can use Looping by Zapier to iterate through the list and create cards in Trello, with assigned members and notifications sent via Slack.

The Looping by Zapier built-in app can be used to create data loops with line items, numbers, and text, and has the following action events:

- **Create Loop From Line Items**
- **Create Loop From Numbers**
- **Create Loop From Text**

Understanding how to use line items in your Zaps will help you harness the functionality of the Looping by Zapier built-in app. We will cover line items in the *Manipulating lineitems* section in *Chapter 18, Zapier's Utilities Functions*.

Let's take a look at what a Zap that uses Looping by Zapier would look like.

An example of using the Create Loop from Line Items action event of Looping by Zapier

We will use the example mentioned earlier where, for specific meetings that you have set up in your Google Calendar, you want to send a personalized email to each of the invitees with the Zoom link, 1 hour before the meeting's start time. In the Zap, there would be a Filter step to specify which meeting types we want the Zap to continue to run for, Formatter steps to extract the Zoom URL from the meeting description, a loop containing a further filter to specify which invitees should receive the email, and then finally the step to send the email. The following screenshot shows an example of what this would look like:

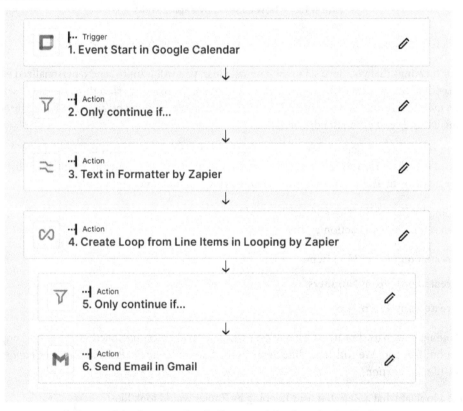

Figure 13.2 – An example of a Zap containing Looping by Zapier

In the Looping by Zapier action step, you need to add one or more fields under **Values to Loop** – in our case, these would be the `Attendees email` addresses and the `Attendee response` confirmation to use in the Send Email and Filter steps, respectively. This is shown in the following screenshot:

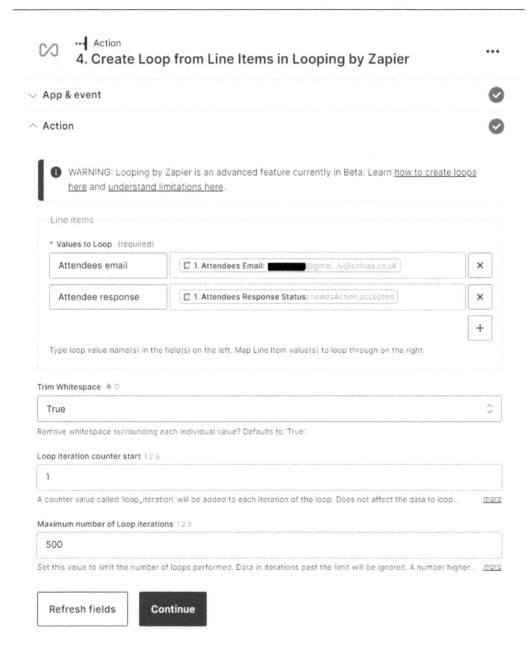

4. Create Loop from Line Items in Looping by Zapier

∨ App & event

∧ Action

ⓘ WARNING: Looping by Zapier is an advanced feature currently in Beta. Learn how to create loops here and understand limitations here.

Line items

* Values to Loop (required)

Attendees email	▯ 1. Attendees Email: ████████@gmai...ly@solvaa.co.uk
Attendee response	▯ 1. Attendees Response Status: needsAction,accepted

\+

Type loop value name(s) in the field(s) on the left. Map Line Item value(s) to loop through on the right.

Trim Whitespace ⦿ ○

True

Remove whitespace surrounding each individual value? Defaults to 'True'.

Loop iteration counter start 1 2 3

1

A counter value called 'loop_iteration' will be added to each iteration of the loop. Does not affect the data to loop...   more

Maximum number of Loop iterations 1 2 3

500

Set this value to limit the number of loops performed. Data in iterations past the limit will be ignored. A number higher...   more

Refresh fields   Continue

Figure 13.3 – Overview of how to set up a Looping by Zapier action step

You can review a more detailed overview of how to set up Looping by Zapier in your Zaps and further details on the limitations of this built-in app at `https://help.zapier.com/hc/en-us/articles/8496106701453`. You can get a very detailed dive into using Looping by Zapier that provides comprehensive examples from the following article: `https://community.zapier.com/featured-articles-65/by-zapier-learn-about-looping-11670`.

> **Tip**
>
> For more inspiration and access to pre-built templates, you can review the Looping by Zapier built-in app profile page at `https://zapier.com/apps/looping/integrations`.

You should now have a better understanding of how and when to use the Looping by Zapier built-in app.

Now, let's review how to use the **Sub-Zap by Zapier** feature to break your Zaps into reusable components.

Sub-Zap by Zapier (feature in beta) – building modular processes

With the **Sub-Zap by Zapier** built-in app, you can now break down your Zaps into reusable components called **Sub-Zaps**. This means you can connect your Zaps to Sub-Zaps to run tasks outside of your originating or parent Zap.

As Sub-Zap by Zapier is currently in beta and considered a Developer Tool, we will only provide a brief overview of the built-in app and then provide further useful resources with more details.

Here are a few examples of when you might find using Sub-Zap by Zapier useful:

- When you want to create reusable formulas using Formatter by Zapier steps across multiple Zaps with different trigger events. Instead of having multiple Zaps with the same steps, you can use Sub-Zap by Zapier to call a Sub-Zap that performs the required steps and passes the result to the parent Zap. You can read more about this example at `https://community.zapier.com/featured-articles-65/using-sub-zaps-to-create-reusable-formulas-10326`.

- When you want to retrieve API access tokens using Webhooks by Zapier or an API Request action event outside of your main Zap. You can use Sub-Zap by Zapier for this. You can read more about this example at `https://community.zapier.com/featured-articles-65/an-example-of-using-sub-zaps-by-zapier-to-retrieve-an-access-token-11001`.

The Sub-Zap by Zapier built-in app can be used with the following trigger and action events:

- **Start a Sub-Zap** (trigger)
- **Return from a Sub-Zap** (action)
- **Call a Sub-Zap** (action)

These actions and trigger events must be used together for your Sub-Zap to successfully work. The originating Zap must have a **Call a Sub-Zap** action event, and your Sub-Zap must have a **Start a Sub-Zap** trigger event and a final step with the **Return from a Sub-Zap** action event. An example of a parent Zap is illustrated in the following screenshot:

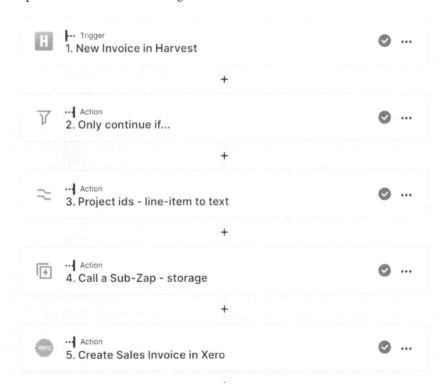

Figure 13.4 – An example of a parent Zap containing a Call a Sub-Zap action step

The related Sub-Zap is shown in the following screenshot:

Figure 13.5 – An example of a Sub-Zap showing the Start a Sub-
Zap trigger and Return From a Sub-Zap action steps

You can review a short overview of how to create a Sub-Zap and further details on the limitations of Sub-Zap by Zapier at `https://help.zapier.com/hc/en-us/articles/8496308527629-Build-reusable-Sub-Zaps`. You can get a very detailed dive into using Sub-Zaps with comprehensive examples by reading the following article: `https://community.zapier.com/featured-articles-65/by-zapier-sub-zaps-and-how-to-use-them-11497`.

> **Tip**
>
> For more inspiration and access to pre-built templates, you can review the Sub-Zap by Zapier built-in app profile page at `https://zapier.com/apps/sub-zap-by-zapier/integrations`.

You should now have a better understanding of how and when to use the Sub-Zaps by Zapier built-in app.

Now, let's review how to use the **Web Parser by Zapier** feature to scrape data from web pages.

Web Parser by Zapier – scraping data from webpages

Web parser applications offer flexibility in extracting and parsing relevant data from websites and can be valuable tools for automating data collection, research, and monitoring tasks. By using the **Web Parser by Zapier** built-in app, you can automate workflows to gather and extract product details, pricing information, job listings, news articles, and much more from multiple websites. This allows for efficient comparison, aggregation, and analysis of data, saving time and effort. It facilitates the seamless integration of web-based information into broader workflows, enabling organizations and individuals to leverage the power of web data for improved efficiency, decision-making, and productivity.

Here are a few examples where using Web Parser by Zapier would be useful:

- When performing competitor research, you can use Web Parser by Zapier to extract product information and prices from different e-commerce websites. This allows you to compare prices between different sites without manually visiting each website.

- If you're searching for job opportunities, Web Parser by Zapier can extract job titles, descriptions, locations, and application links from job listing websites. This allows you to automate the process of collecting and organizing job postings from multiple sources. This is especially useful if the job website does not have alert functionality.

- Web Parser by Zapier can scrape data from websites and extract specific information, such as product reviews, user ratings, or customer feedback. This data can then be used for market research, sentiment analysis, or other data-driven decision-making processes.

There are many more ways to use Web Parser by Zapier in your Zaps.

> **Tip**
>
> For more inspiration and access to pre-built templates, you can review the Web Parser by Zapier built-in app profile page at `https://zapier.com/apps/web-parser-by-zapier/integrations`.

The Web Parser by Zapier built-in app can only be used with the **Parse Webpage** action event. Next, let's explore how to use this built-in app and action event.

Setting up the Parse Webpage action event

You can use the **Parse Webpage** action event once you have set up your trigger step.

Once you have added an action step, by either selecting the **Action** step or clicking on the + icon, and chosen **Web Parser by Zapier** as the app and **Parse Webpage** as the action event, you can edit the fields in the **Set up action** section as follows:

- **URL to Parse**: Add the URL that you want to parse data from by adding static text or mapping in dynamic values from previous steps, or use a combination of both. This is a required field and must have a value for the Zap to run.

- **Content output format**: Choose **HTML**, **Markdown**, or **Plaintext** from the drop-down list. You can also add static text or map in a dynamic field value from previous steps using the **Custom** option.

- **Continue on failure**: Use this Boolean field to select **True** or **False** from the drop-down menu, enter text, or insert data from previous steps for this step to be considered a "success" if nothing is found in the search or the action fails. The default for this field is **False**, which you should choose if you want the Zap to stop running at this point if nothing is found; this is the most common use case. This means that all dependent steps will be skipped. Use the **True** option if you want to allow the Zap to continue and subsequent steps to run. You can then add more control to your workflows by adding Filter by Zapier or Paths by Zapier conditional logic for more control and allowing those steps to pass or stop based on whether the search returned a result or not. Filter by Zapier and Paths by Zapier were covered in *Chapter 7, Getting Started with Built-in Apps*.

Let's use the example of searching for customer service job opportunities on the job website Reed. You might want to add details of a web parse to a spreadsheet every day at 9 A.M. by using Schedule by Zapier as your trigger app, parse data from the website using Web Parser by Zapier, and then update a Google Sheet. You can start by setting up a filter and copying the URL, which in this example might be `https://www.reed.co.uk/jobs/customer-service-jobs?keywords=customer-service&parentsector=customer-service`. This is shown in the following screenshot:

--| Action
2. Parse Webpage in Web Parser by Zapier   ...

∨ **App & event**   ✓

∧ **Action**   ✓

* URL to Parse (required)

    https://www.reed.co.uk/jobs/customer-service-jobs?keywords=customer-
    service&parentsector=customer-service

The URL from which you want to extract content.

Content output format

    Plaintext

The format of the extracted content.

Continue on failure ◉ ○

    False

Should this step be considered a "success" when nothing is found?

[Refresh fields] [**Continue**]

Figure 13.6 – Customizing the Parse Webpage action event

Click on the **Continue** button. Now, you can use the **Test action** section to test this step or click **Skip test**.

The result of this parsing is shown in the following screenshot:

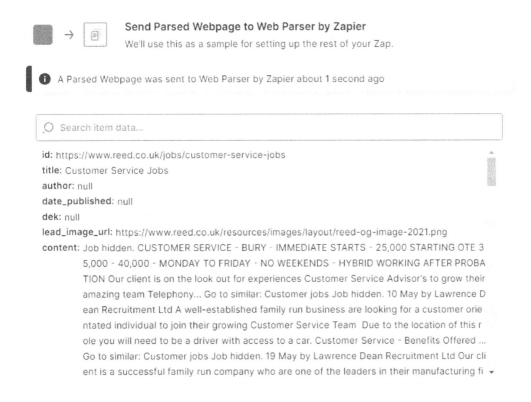

Send Parsed Webpage to Web Parser by Zapier
We'll use this as a sample for setting up the rest of your Zap.

A Parsed Webpage was sent to Web Parser by Zapier about 1 second ago

Search item data...

id: https://www.reed.co.uk/jobs/customer-service-jobs
title: Customer Service Jobs
author: null
date_published: null
dek: null
lead_image_url: https://www.reed.co.uk/resources/images/layout/reed-og-image-2021.png
content: Job hidden. CUSTOMER SERVICE - BURY - IMMEDIATE STARTS - 25,000 STARTING OTE 3
5,000 - 40,000 - MONDAY TO FRIDAY - NO WEEKENDS - HYBRID WORKING AFTER PROBA
TION Our client is on the look out for experiences Customer Service Advisor's to grow their
amazing team Telephony... Go to similar: Customer jobs Job hidden. 10 May by Lawrence D
ean Recruitment Ltd A well-established family run business are looking for a customer orie
ntated individual to join their growing Customer Service Team Due to the location of this r
ole you will need to be a driver with access to a car. Customer Service - Benefits Offered ...
Go to similar: Customer jobs Job hidden. 19 May by Lawrence Dean Recruitment Ltd Our cli
ent is a successful family run company who are one of the leaders in their manufacturing fi

Figure 13.7 – The result from the Parse Webpage action step

You can then proceed to add one or more action steps, then publish your Zap.

You should now have a better understanding of how and when to use the Web Parser by Zapier built-in app.

Now, let's review how to use the **Transfers** feature to move data in bulk between apps.

Transfers by Zapier – moving bulk data between apps

Sometimes, it is useful to move data in bulk between your apps. With the **Transfers** feature, you can do just that with certain apps. The **Transfers** feature is standalone, allowing you to move data between apps in bulk, on-demand, or at regular frequencies. In other words, this feature is not connected to your Zaps.

It might be useful to use this feature when you would like to do the following:

- Move historical data for your existing Zaps
- Create a one-off on-demand data transfer
- Move data when you begin to use one or more new apps
- Schedule regular bulk transfers

Before using the **Transfers** feature, you will need to know the following:

- **Frequency**: This specifies how many times you want your transfer to run. This could be set to **Run Once** or to run periodically based on **Schedule**.
- **Source app**: The application that you want to send data from – for example, EventBrite. Only certain apps are supported.
- **Source data**: The record type that you want to pull data from in **Source app**. For example, in EventBrite, this could be **Attendee** or **Event**.
- **Destination app**: The application that you want to send data to – for example, Google Drive.
- **Destination action**: The action event that you want to perform to push data into **Destination app** based on the existing action events for that app. For example, in Google Drive, this could be **Copy File** or **Create folder**. Certain apps, such as Shopify, QuickBooks, and Zendesk, support the **Create or update** action event in addition to the standard action events for that app.

You will also need to know what data you would like to map from **Source app** to **Destination app**.

Tip

All Zapier integrated apps can be used as destination apps. However, there are limited source apps and destination apps that support the update or create action events in the **Transfers** feature. A current list can be found at `https://help.zapier.com/hc/en-us/articles/8496260754957-Which-apps-does-Transfer-support`. If you would like to request an addition to the support app list, you can fill out this form: `https://zapier.typeform.com/to/t9z7NNlx`. A workaround, if your app does not exist as a source app, is to add your data to a Google Sheet and use that as your source. Check out the article at `https://community.zapier.com/show-tell-5/use-google-sheets-to-import-existing-data-from-your-apps-12143` for more details.

Next, let's dive into how to use this feature.

Setting up a transfer between apps

Once you have decided on the frequency of transfers, apps, records, and action events you want to use, follow these steps to set up your transfer:

1. Navigate to the **Transfers** dashboard by clicking on the **Transfers** link in the left-hand navigation menu.

2. On the next screen, click the **New Transfer** button.

3. On the next screen, select the **Run once** button for a one-off transfer or the **Schedule** button for a regularly scheduled transfer.

4. On the next screen, click the **Create a new transfer** button.

5. On the next screen, select your **Source app**, **Source data**, **Destination app**, and **Destination action** values, then click the **Next** button. An example is shown in the following screenshot:

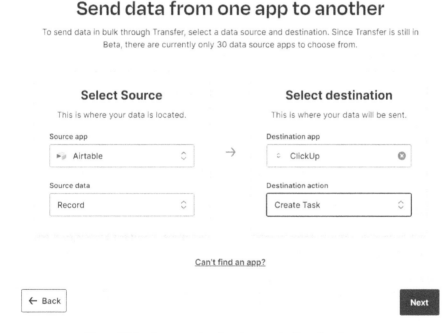

Figure 13.8 – An example of setting up the Transfers feature

6. On the next screen, select the **Source app** account you want to use, then click the **Next** button.

7. For some apps with hierarchical structures, such as databases, you might be required to specify the location of the data. For example, in Airtable, this could be **Base** and **Table**, and **Limit to View**. Upon clicking the **Next** button, Zapier will retrieve the data from your selected app.

8. On the next screen, select the **Destination app** account you want to use, then click the **Next** button.

9. On the next screen, map the relevant fields in your **Destination app** account as required.

10. On the next screen, check the preview to make sure that all your data has been mapped correctly. Click the **Edit fields** button to make changes or the **Looks good** button to continue.

11. On the next screen, if you have chosen a scheduled transfer, choose how frequently you would like the transfer to run. You can choose from **Every hour**, **Every day**, **Every week**, or **Every month**, then click the **Next** button to choose the hour and day of the week or month if relevant.

12. On the next screen, add any filters to stop your transfer from running unless the data meets certain conditions, then click **Confirm Schedule**, if it is a scheduled transfer, or **Send data**, if it is a one-off transfer.

13. Once your transfer has been confirmed, click **Go to My Transfers** to go back to the **Transfers** dashboard, where you will see a list of your transfers.

At any time while setting up your transfer, you can click the **Start over** or **Back** buttons to either start from the beginning or go back to the previous step, respectively.

Now, let's explore how to manage transfers.

Managing your transfers

From the **Transfers** dashboard, you will see each of your transfers, who owns them, when they were created, the apps involved, and whether they are **Scheduled** or **One time** transfers. You can click on the title to edit the transfer settings or click on the three dots icon to access a drop-down menu that contains the following options:

- **Edit Transfer settings**: Use this menu option to edit any part of your Transfer

- **Details**: Use this menu option to view the **Details** screen, similar to the **Zap Details** menu item in the Zap Editor

- **History**: Use this menu option to view **Transfers History**, similar to the **Zap History** menu item in the Zap Editor

- **Rename**: Use this menu option to rename your transfer

- **Delete**: Use this menu option to delete your transfer

An example is shown in the following screenshot:

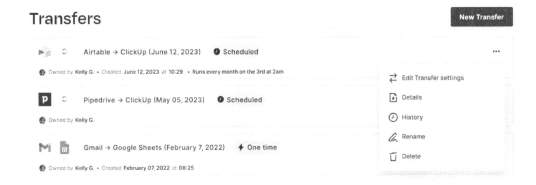

Figure 13.9 – Managing your transfers from the Transfers dashboard

> **Tip**
> For more details on possible issues and notes, check out this useful Zapier article about the **Transfers** feature at https://help.zapier.com/hc/en-us/articles/8496274335885-Bulk-import-data-into-apps-with-Transfer.

Next, let's take a look at how to transfer existing data from Zaps.

Transferring existing data from your Zaps

If an existing Zap has a trigger that is supported by the **Transfers** feature, you will be able to transfer existing data from this Zap. You will see a **Transfer existing data** option in the three dots icon in your Zap from the Zap management area. An example of this is shown in the following screenshot:

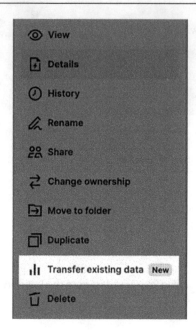

Figure 13.10 – How to transfer existing data from your Zaps

Once you've selected this option, you will be taken to the **Transfers** module, prompted to filter your data, and asked to select the records you want to transfer. Click **Next** and then **Send data**.

You should now have a better understanding of how and when to use the Transfers by Zapier feature.

Now, let's review how to use the **Interfaces** feature to build visual interfaces such as forms and chatbots.

Zapier Interfaces (feature in beta) – building custom forms, chatbots, and visual interfaces

The new **Zapier Interfaces** feature allows you to design user-friendly interfaces to collect data and trigger Zaps effortlessly. You can harness the potential of user interactions to supercharge your automation workflows by building forms and chatbots, all from within your Zapier account.

With Zapier Interfaces, you create pages and then add **components** to those pages. Components can be **Forms**, **Text**, **Tables** (using **Zapier Tables**), **Kanban**, **Link cards**, **AI prompts**, **Chatbots**, **Dividers**, and **Media**. You can read more about the different types of components at `https://help.zapier.com/hc/en-us/articles/15930394291341-Types-of-components-in-Zapier-Interfaces`.

Zapier Interfaces is available for free with all Zapier plans but with some limitations. You can get access to premium features such as tracking visitors, customizing branding, removing the Zapier logo, restricting user access, and connecting OpenAI to use other AI models with the chatbot component by upgrading to **Interfaces Premium** for an additional monthly fee. The different pricing plans are shown in the following screenshot:

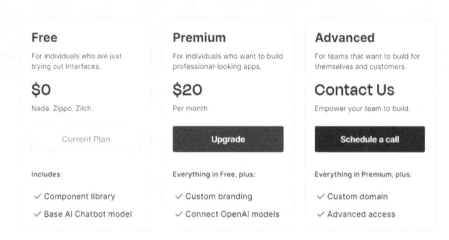

Figure 13.11 – Overview of pricing options of the Zapier Interfaces feature

You can find more details on the pricing of Zapier Interfaces and a comparison of the different prices at https://interfaces.zapier.com/pricing.

Let's take a look at how to get started with Zapier Interfaces.

Getting started with Zapier Interfaces

To give you some insight into the **Interfaces** feature, you can find the **Interfaces** dashboard by clicking on the **Interfaces (beta)** link in the left-hand navigation menu or navigating to https://interfaces.zapier.com/. Your dashboard will look similar to what is shown in the following screenshot:

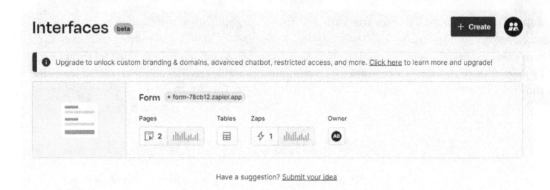

Figure 13.12 – The Zapier Interfaces dashboard

If you click the + **Create** button, you can start to create your interface. To do this, first, you must choose to build from scratch by clicking on the **Start from scratch** button, choose from one of the many templates for forms or chatbots, or choose to create your interface from an existing table. An example is shown in the following screenshot:

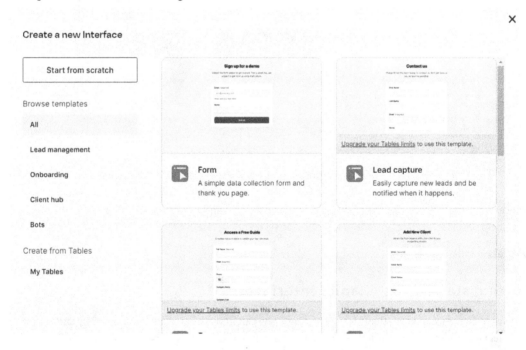

Figure 13.13 – Using Zapier Interfaces templates

As this feature is still in beta and might change, we will not cover all the details of how to create and manage your interfaces. Instead, you can stay abreast with the latest changes by reading these useful articles from Zapier that will help you understand the best practices for using Zapier Interfaces:

- **How to create pages and apps**: `https://help.zapier.com/hc/en-us/articles/14490267815949-Create-interactive-pages-and-apps-with-Zapier-Interfaces-Beta-`

- **How to customize your Zapier Interfaces project**: `https://help.zapier.com/hc/en-us/articles/15932034572685-Customize-your-Zapier-Interfaces-project`

- **How to use forms in your Zapier Interfaces**: `https://help.zapier.com/hc/en-us/articles/15927500577037-Use-forms-in-Zapier-Interfaces`

- **How to create chatbots using Zapier Interfaces**: `https://help.zapier.com/hc/en-us/articles/15931071482509-Create-chatbots-in-Zapier-Interfaces`

- **How to fix errors in your chatbots built with Zapier Interfaces**: `https://help.zapier.com/hc/en-us/articles/16451058327693-Fix-errors-in-Zapier-Interfaces-chatbots`

You should now have a better understanding of how and when to use the Zapier Interfaces feature.

Now, let's review how to use the **Zapier Tables** feature to store data in tabular records.

Zapier Tables (feature in beta) – storing and structuring data in tables

The new **Zapier Tables** feature allows you to create, edit, access, and share tabular records, all stored within Zapier, rather than using spreadsheets such as Google Sheets or databases such as Airtable to store simple data. Not having to use additional tools means that you can reduce your task history overall and have one place for storing certain data.

> **Important note**
> This feature is undergoing beta user testing and is still in active development. You should be aware that functionality could change, and it might be wise to keep a backup of your data in another app.

Zapier Tables is a perfect complement to Zapier Interfaces, whereby you can collect form submission data and tabulate it within Zapier, allowing for one easy collection point for data to be stored and transferred to your other apps.

You will be able to link your Tables to Zaps and feed them from interfaces, create filters to specify which records to display in your Tables, select which fields you want to hide or display, and share the Tables with individuals in your team and with a public link.

Your Zapier price plan determines how many **Tables**, **Fields**, **Records**, and **Views** (a feature soon to be released) you can create, as well as which features you will have access to, such as public sharing, the ability to use buttons in tables, and the number of seats you will have access to. This is shown in the following screenshot:

Tables is packaged with your Zapier plan. Upgrade to get access to power features and higher usage limits.

Free	Starter	Professional
Current plan	Learn more	Learn more
✓ 1 Table	✓ 10 Tables	✓ 20 Tables
✓ 25 Fields*	✓ 50 Fields*	✓ 100 Fields*
✓ 2k Records*	✓ 4k Records*	✓ 6k Records*
✗ Public sharing	✓ Public sharing	✓ Public sharing
✗ Buttons	✓ Buttons	✓ Buttons
✗ Views*	✓ 5 Views*	✓ 10 Views*
✗ Unlimited seats	✗ Unlimited seats	✗ Unlimited seats
* per table	* per table	* per table

Upgrade to a Teams or Company plan to get unlimited seats. Learn more.

Figure 13.14 – Pricing the Zapier Tables feature

Let's take a look at how to get started with Zapier Tables.

Getting started with Zapier Tables

To give you some insight into the **Zapier Tables** feature, you can find the **Tables** dashboard by clicking the **Tables (beta)** link in the left-hand navigation menu or navigating to https://tables.zapier.com/. Your dashboard will look similar to what is shown in the following screenshot:

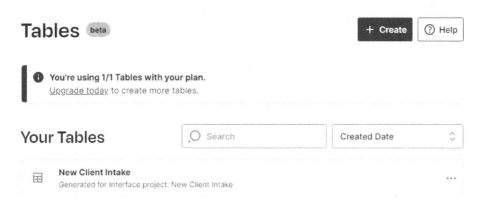

Figure 13.15 – The Zapier Tables dashboard

If you click the **+ Create** button, you can start to create your table. An example is shown in the following screenshot:

Figure 13.16 – Creating a table using Zapier Tables

As this feature is still in beta and might change, we will not cover all the details of how to create and manage your Tables. Instead, you can stay abreast with the latest changes by reading these useful articles from Zapier that will help you understand the best practices for using Zapier Tables:

- **How to create new tables and edit table settings**: `https://help.zapier.com/hc/en-us/articles/9804340895245-Store-data-with-Zapier-Tables`

- **Using different field types in your Tables**: `https://help.zapier.com/hc/en-us/articles/9775472454157-Different-field-types-in-Zapier-Tables`

- **Creating Zaps from Table records and triggering the Zap manually or automatically from records, including specific fields**: `https://help.zapier.com/hc/en-us/articles/9881673906701-Trigger-and-continue-Zaps-from-records`

- **Triggering Zaps to run or running actions such as approval steps by using button fields in your Tables**: `https://help.zapier.com/hc/en-us/articles/15720961080717-Use-button-fields-in-Zapier-Tables`

- **Sharing your Tables and managing user permissions**: `https://help.zapier.com/hc/en-us/articles/16021760381453-Manage-permissions-in-Zapier-Tables`

- **Understanding field-related, plan-related, and plan-limited limits**: `https://help.zapier.com/hc/en-us/articles/15721386410765-Zapier-Tables-usage-limits`

You should now have a better understanding of how and when you can use the **Zapier Tables** feature.

Summary

In this chapter, first, we covered how to get early access to new Zapier features and how to use the Looping by Zapier, Sub-Zap by Zapier, and Web Parser by Zapier built-in apps in our Zaps. Then, we explored how to transfer data between applications using Transfer by Zapier. After, we covered how to use the customizable **Interfaces** module to create forms, chatbots, and visual interfaces. Finally, we looked at how to use the **Tables** module to manage and store data in tables.

You should now understand how to leverage Looping by Zapier to process datasets, break down complex Zaps using Sub-Zap by Zapier, extract data from web pages with Web Parser by Zapier, seamlessly move between applications using the Transfers by Zapier module, create interfaces, and manage data effectively with tables.

In the next chapter, you will learn how to manipulate dates and times with the versatile Formatter by Zapier built-in app. We will cover how to convert and adjust date and time values into different formats, as well as how to add and subtract time.

Questions

1. What Zapier feature should you use if you want to transfer data in bulk from one app to another?

2. Which two Zapier features currently in beta work well hand-in-hand to capture data and store it in tables?

Part 3:
Using the Features of the Formatter by Zapier Built-In App

In this part, you will gain an understanding of the extensive functionality and practical uses of the Formatter by Zapier app. You will learn how to format dates, times, text, numbers, and other actions.

This part contains the following chapters:

14

Formatting Date and Time

The data that appears in your Zaps may not always be presented in the format that you need it in. You may often find that you need to change the format of that data so that it can be viewed in a certain way or it is compatible with the data formats required by your other apps. For example, say a new subscriber joins your newsletter but they have entered their name in lowercase; perhaps you may want to capitalize the first letter. Alternatively, a date might be shown in an American format but you might want to change it to an internationally recognized format instead. You may also want to strip out text that is presented in HTML format or use a spreadsheet-type formula to calculate something. All of this and more is possible to achieve without using code, by using Zapier's extremely versatile Formatter by Zapier built-in app to manipulate a huge array of values into formats you prefer or need for a specific purpose.

In this chapter, we will first introduce the Formatter by Zapier built-in app, with its range of functionality for manipulating dates and times, numbers, text, and various other values. With a primary focus on formatting dates and times, we will cover the basics of how to adjust date and time values in your Zaps. Then, we will discuss how to use the date and time your Zap runs in the rest of your action steps in the Zap. After that, we will explore how to use the Formatter by Zapier built-in app to add and subtract time and compare dates before diving into formatting date and time values using this built-in app.

We will cover the following key topics in this chapter:

- An introduction to the Formatter by Zapier built-in app
- The basics of adjusting date and time values using Zapier
- Manipulating dates and times with Formatter by Zapier

Once you have worked through each of these topics, you will have a better understanding of the different action events available for use with the Formatter by Zapier built-in app. You will also know how to adjust date and time values in your Zaps, use the date and time your Zap runs, and how to add or subtract time and manipulate date and time data using the Formatter by Zapier built-in app.

Technical requirements

To get the most out of the content and exercises in this chapter, you will need access to a Zapier account. The Zapier Starter plan will be required for you to create multi-step workflows using the Formatter by Zapier built-in app.

An introduction to the Formatter by Zapier built-in app

When creating your workflow automations, you may sometimes find that the data you retrieve from one app isn't recognized in another app, or you may want to change this data in some other way to present it differently. Having the ability to manipulate data values in this way without using code is a huge benefit. Zapier allows you to do this using a built-in app called Formatter by Zapier.

The Formatter by Zapier app is by far the most versatile and useful built-in app by Zapier. Its functionality is so extensive that we will cover this app and each of its action events in five separate chapters.

The Formatter by Zapier built-in app can only be used as an action step and has the following action events:

- **Date / Time**: This action event allows you to convert date and time values into different formats (including time zones) and add or subtract time. We will cover date and time formatting using the Formatter by Zapier built-in app in this chapter.

- **Numbers**: This action event allows you to manipulate numbers, phone numbers, and currencies, and use spreadsheet-type formulas and math operations. We will cover number formatting using the Formatter by Zapier built-in app in *Chapter 15, Formatting Numbers*.

- **Text**: You can extensively format text using this action event. You can adjust title case, uppercase, and lowercase, find and replace text, trim whitespace, count words and adjust their length, and pluralize text. We will cover these functions in *Chapter 16, Text Formatting Functions in Zapier – Part 1*. You can also create superhero names; split and truncate text; extract patterns, URLs, phone numbers, numbers, and email addresses; convert Markdown into HTML; convert text into ASCII; use **Default Value** and **URL Encode / Decode**; and remove HTML tags. We will discuss these functions in *Chapter 17, Text Formatting Functions in Zapier – Part 2*.

- **Utilities**: This action event allows you to create and customize line items, convert text into line items and vice versa, use lookup tables and picklists, and import .csv files. We will cover the **Utilities** action event in the Formatter by Zapier built-in app in *Chapter 18, Zapier's Utilities Functions*.

You should now have a better understanding of the different action events and functionalities of the Formatter by Zapier built-in app.

> **Tip**
> You can use the magic AI to ask Zapier to format data in your Zap steps, which will then create Formatter by Zapier steps with the relevant transform options. We will discuss this in *Chapter 19*, *AI and Automation*.

Next, we'll review the basics of how to adjust time and date values in your Zaps.

The basics of adjusting date and time values using Zapier

Before we dive into using the Formatter by Zapier built-in app for manipulating date and time values, it is useful to know how you can adjust date and time values in your Zaps at a basic level.

In *Chapter 3*, *Building Your First Automated Workflow (Zap)*, we introduced you to the **date/time** field type. When you are presented with this type of field in your action steps, you can use a **field modifier**, either standalone or after a static or dynamic date or time value, to adjust the date/time.

Field modifiers must consist of the following three variables:

- A plus (+) or minus (-) sign, to signify adding or subtracting time.

- A number.

- A unit of time, in either seconds (second, seconds, or s), minutes (minute, minutes, or m), hours (hour, hours, or h), days (day, days, or d), months (month or months), or years (year, years, or y). You can either use the abbreviation or the full spelling in singular or plural form.

For example, if you need to create an invoice in your accounting app and want the **Date** and **Due Date** fields to be populated with values of 1 day from the day the Zap ran and 1 month from the date a deal was due to close in your CRM, respectively, you would use modifiers, as shown in the following screenshot:

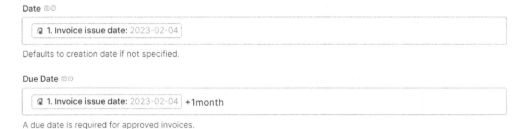

Figure 14.1 – Overview of using date/time field modifiers in your Zaps

Here are a few examples of modifiers that you can use:

- +1h: 1 hour after the date/time the Zap has run or after the date/time value in the field

- -2days: 2 days before the date/time the Zap has run or before the date/time value in the field

- +5y: 5 years after the date/time the Zap has run or after the date/time value in the field

- +30s: 30 seconds after the date/time the Zap has run or after the date/time value in the field

- -10minutes: 10 minutes before the date/time the Zap has run or before the date/time value in the field

When using modifiers after a static or dynamic value, such as in the **Due Date** field shown in *Figure 14.1*, you must ensure there is a space between the date/time value and the modifier.

You can also add multiple modifiers, either standalone or after a date/time value. In these circumstances, you must leave a space between them – for example, +1month -5days.

You should now have a better understanding of how to adjust date and time values using Zapier.

Now, let's explore how to insert the date and time your Zap runs into fields in your action steps.

Using the date and time your Zap runs in fields

There may be times that you want to insert the date and time that your Zap triggers into one or more fields in your action steps. For example, you might want to record the date and time when a new row of data was added to a Google Sheets spreadsheet. This can easily be achieved by entering {{zap_meta_human_now}} into a field. When the Zap runs, this command will output a human-readable string in the MM/DD/YY hh:mm AM/PM format; for example, 11/01/23 07:40 PM.

This command can be used in date/time field types and text fields where you can type in a static value. The command uses the time zone settings specified in your Zapier account or the Zap settings. If no time zone has been specified, the timestamp will default to **Coordinated Universal Time (UTC)**. We discussed how to adjust your account time zone settings in *Chapter 1*, *Introduction to Business Process Automation with Zapier*, and individual Zap time zone settings in *Chapter 4*, *Managing Your Zaps*.

Once you have entered the command into a field, the string will not show the timestamp data while you are creating or editing your Zap. It will be displayed in the action app that you specified only after the Zap has triggered and run. This is shown in the following screenshot:

Figure 14.2 – Overview of using the date and time your Zap runs in your action steps

You can also use the following timestamps accordingly:

- `{{zap_meta_utc_iso}}`: It is advisable to use this command if you need a string that can be read by other apps and APIs – that is, a machine-readable string as opposed to the standard, human-readable string. This command ignores your time zone settings and will produce an ISO 8601 timestamp in UTC, such as `2023-11-01T08:19:12+00:00`. ISO 8601 is an internationally recognized time standard and you can read more about it here: `https://en.wikipedia.org/wiki/ISO_8601`.

- `{{zap_meta_timestamp}}`: This command should be used when an app or API requires a timestamp format in Unix time. Unix time is widely used in computer hardware and software operating systems, as well as digital file formats, and is denoted by the number of seconds since January 1, 1970 – for example, `1591537509`. You can read more about Unix time here: `https://en.wikipedia.org/wiki/Unix_time`.

- `{{zap_meta_[timezone]_iso}}`: Substitute `[timezone]` with the three- to five-letter time zone abbreviation format you want to use. For example, `{{zap_meta_est_iso}}` is for **Eastern Standard Time (EST)**, and `{{zap_meta_gmt_iso}}` is for **Greenwich Mean Time (GMT)**. You can read more about time zone abbreviations here: `https://en.wikipedia.org/wiki/List_of_time_zone_abbreviations`.

Working with time zones in your Zaps can be tricky as it often involves trial and error to get your data correct and accepted by your various apps. You can read more about tips for handling time zone data on the Zapier website: `https://zapier.com/blog/format-datetimes/`.

> **Important note**
>
> Not all time zone abbreviations are compatible with the `{{zap_meta_[timezone]_iso}}` command. The most common American time zones as well as some European and Asia-Pacific time zones are generally compatible. It is advisable to perform some testing with the command in advance. You can read more about this in the following article: `https://help.zapier.com/hc/en-us/articles/8496275717261-Insert-the-time-your-Zap-runs-into-a-field#other-available-timestamps-0-3`.

You should now have a better understanding of how to use the date and time that your Zap runs in your action steps.

Next, let's take a look at how to use the Formatter by Zapier built-in app to manipulate dates and times.

Manipulating dates and times with Formatter by Zapier

Now that you've learned how to adjust dates and times and how to insert the date and time that your Zap ran into your action steps, we will take this a step further and explore how to manipulate dates and times more extensively with the Formatter by Zapier built-in app.

There may be many occasions where you need to transform date and time values from either your trigger or action steps by adding or subtracting time, displaying the date or time in a certain format, or comparing two dates. You can use Formatter by Zapier to accomplish this.

To manipulate dates and times, Formatter by Zapier can only be used as an action step and is available as the **Date / Time** action event.

When using this action event, you can use the following **Date / Time** transform options, which can be found within the **Set up action** section:

- **Add/Subtract Time**
- **Compare Dates**
- **Format**

Before we explore how to set up each of these transform options in turn, let's cover how to use custom date formats.

Using custom date formats

When you want to transform a date or time using the Formatter by Zapier **Date / Time** transform options, you can either select the format or style you want to use from a drop-down list or specify a custom format that is not listed. As Zapier may not always recognize the format you want to convert from, you can also use custom formats to specify the format to convert from.

The following table shows a list of date and time token formats that Zapier recognizes. These tokens can be used in any combination to produce the format you want:

Time variable	Custom token	Example output
Sub-second	SSS	000, 001, 002 … to 999
	SS	00, 01, 02 … to 99
	S	0, 1, 2 … to 9
Second	ss	00, 01, 02 … to 59
	s	0, 1, 2 … to 59
Minute	mm	00, 01, 02 … to 59
	m	0, 1, 2 … to 59
Hour	HH	00, 01, 02 … to 24
	H	0, 1, 2 … to 24
	hh	01, 02, 03 … to 12
	h	1, 2, 3 … to 12
Month	MMMM	January, February, March … to December
	MMM	Jan, Feb, Mar … to Dec
	MM	01, 02, 03 … to 12
	M	1, 2, 3 … to 12
Year	YYYY	2018, 2019, 2020, and so on
	YY	18, 19, 20, and so on
Day of the year	DDDD	001, 002, 003 … to 365
	DDD	1, 2, 3 … to 365
Day of the month	DD	01, 02, 03 … to 31
	D	1, 2, 3 … to 31
Day of the week	dddd	Monday, Tuesday, Wednesday … to Sunday
	ddd	Mon, Tue, Wed … to Sun
	d	1, 2, 3 … to 7
AM/PM	A	AM, PM
	a	am, pm
Timezone	ZZ	-07:00, -06:00 … +06:00, +07:00
	Z	-0700, -0600 … +0600, +0700
Unix timestamp	X	1347360521

Figure 14.3 – A table showing date and time custom formats accepted by Zapier

The data in *Figure 14.3* has been sourced from the Zapier help article at `https://zapier.com/help/create/format/modify-date-formats-in-zaps#customize-date-time-options`. This article should be checked for the most up-to-date information.

Using the data from *Figure 14.3*, we may want to convert the `2023-11-01T09:15:30` timestamp into `09:15 November 1 23`. For this, we can use the `HH:mm MMMM D YY` token format.

Next, we'll dive into using Formatter by Zapier to add and subtract time.

Adding or subtracting time

Adding or subtracting time to or from a timestamp value is extremely useful when you want times to be displayed differently in your consequent action steps.

Here are a couple of examples of when you can use the Formatter by Zapier **Date / Time** action event with the **Add/Subtract Time** transform option:

- When an opportunity is marked as won in Salesforce CRM, create an invoice in **QuickBooks Online** with a due date 1 month from the close date

- When a **Facebook Messenger** message is received, create a Trello card with a due time of 1 hour from the time the message was received

Let's explore how to set up the **Add/Subtract Time** transform option.

Setting up the Date/Time action event with the Add/Subtract Time transform option

You can use the **Date / Time** action event once you have set up your trigger step.

Once you have added an action step either by selecting the **Action** step or clicking on the + icon, choosing **Formatter by Zapier** as the app and **Date / Time** as the action event, you can edit the fields in the **Action** section, as follows:

- **Transform**: From the drop-down menu, select the **Add/Subtract Time** option. This is a required field and a value is needed for the step to run successfully.

- **Input**: Use this field to enter the date value you would like to manipulate. This can be either a static URL value, a dynamic value from previous steps, or a combination of both, to specify the **Input** value. For accuracy, the **Input** value must be in an accepted date/time format. Although this is not a required field, the formatter function will not return a result if there is no value.

- **Expression**: Use this field to specify the amount of time you want to add to or subtract from the value indicated in the **Input** field – for example, +1h, -3days, or +2 months. Either enter a static value, a dynamic value from previous steps, or a combination of both. For accuracy, the input must be in an accepted date/time format, as we discussed in *The basics of adjusting date and time values using Zapier* section. This is a required field and must have a value for the Zap to run.

- **To Format**: Specify the format you want the date/time output to be displayed in. Either select a date/time format from the drop-down menu or add a custom format under the **Custom** tab. You can use the custom date formats that we discussed in the *Using custom date formats* section.

- **From Format**: Zapier will attempt to read the format of the **Input** value. If Zapier gets it wrong, you can use this field to specify the exact format. Either select a date/time format from the drop-down menu or add a custom format under the **Custom** tab. You can use the custom date formats that we discussed in the *Using custom date formats* section.

These options are shown in the following screenshot:

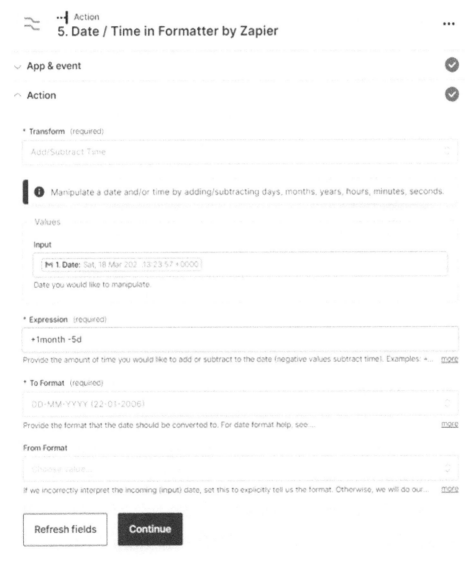

Figure 14.4 – Overview of using the Formatter by Zapier Date / Time action
event to add time and convert it into a custom date format

Click the **Continue** button. You can then use the **Test** section to test this step to generate the altered date/time format. The result from the scenario in *Figure 14.4* is shown in the following screenshot:

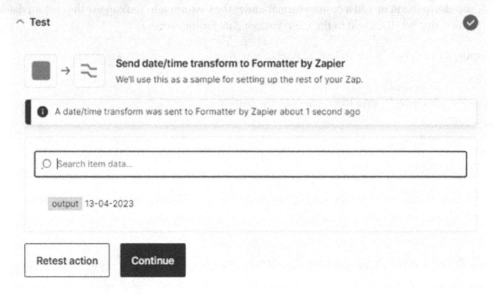

Figure 14.5 – Overview of the altered time format when using the
Date / Time action event to add or subtract time

Proceed to add one or more action steps after your **Date / Time** action step or publish your Zap.

You should now have a better understanding of how to add or subtract time from date and time values using the Formatter by Zapier built-in app.

Now, let's cover how to use the Formatter by Zapier built-in app to compare two dates.

Comparing two dates

Comparing two dates or times to either get the duration between them in seconds, minutes, hours, or days or check if they are the same can be handy in many scenarios.

Here are a couple of examples of when you can use the Formatter by Zapier **Date / Time** action event with the **Compare Dates** transform option:

- When you want to assess response times in your customer service team to ensure they address customer queries on the same day. For example, you can use the **Compare Dates** transform option to compare the time a **ClickUp** task was created to when it is closed by adding the two values to a Google Sheet. In this case, the trigger would be the task close time column changing.

- When you run a competition on a specific day and you only want to collect entries on that day. So, when a Typeform is submitted, you can use the **Compare Dates** transform option to compare the submission date to today's date and use Paths by Zapier to specify which route the workflow should follow thereafter. If the dates match, add the entry to an **Airtable** base and send a follow-up email with Gmail; otherwise, send an email with Gmail to say the competition is closed.

Now, let's explore how to set up the **Compare Dates** transform option.

Setting up the Date / Time action event with the Compare Dates transform option

You can use the **Date / Time** action event once you have set up your trigger step.

Once you have added an action step either by selecting the **Action** step or clicking on the + icon, and chosen **Formatter by Zapier** as the app and **Date / Time** as the action event, you can edit the fields in the **Action** section, as follows:

- **Transform**: From the drop-down menu, select the **Compare Dates** option. This is a required field and a value is needed for the step to run successfully.

- **Start Date**: Specify the first date that you want to compare against another date. This can be either a static URL value, a dynamic value from previous steps, or a combination of both. For accuracy, the input must be in an accepted date/time format. If this date is after the value specified in the **End Date** field, the two dates will be swapped around in the output. This is a required field and a value is needed for the step to run successfully.

- **End Date Value**: Specify the second date that you want to compare against the first value specified in the **Start Date** field. This can be either a static URL value, a dynamic value from previous steps, or a combination of both. For accuracy, the input must be in an accepted date/time format. This is a required field and a value is needed for the step to run successfully.

- **Date Format – Start Date**: Zapier will attempt to read the format of the **Start Date** value. Zapier may get this wrong; therefore, you can use this field to specify the exact format. You can also use this field if the two date values specified in the **Start Date** and **End Date** fields are in different formats. Either select a date/time format from the drop-down menu or add a custom format under the **Custom** tab. You can use the custom date formats that we discussed in the *Using custom date formats* section.

- **Date Format – End Date**: Zapier will attempt to read the format of the **End Date** value. Zapier may get this wrong; therefore, you can use this field to specify the exact format. You can also use this field if the two date values specified in the **Start Date** and **End Date** fields are in different formats. Either select a date/time format from the drop-down menu or add a custom format under the **Custom** tab. You can use the custom date formats that we discussed in the *Using custom date formats* section.

An example is shown in the following screenshot:

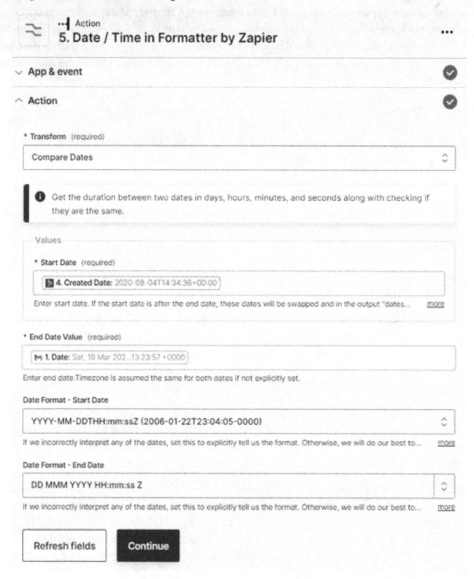

Figure 14.6 – Overview of using the Formatter by Zapier Date /
Time action event to compare two dates/times

Click the **Continue** button. You can then use the **Test** section to test this step to show the output of the date/time comparison. The result from the scenario in *Figure 14.6* is shown in the following screenshot:

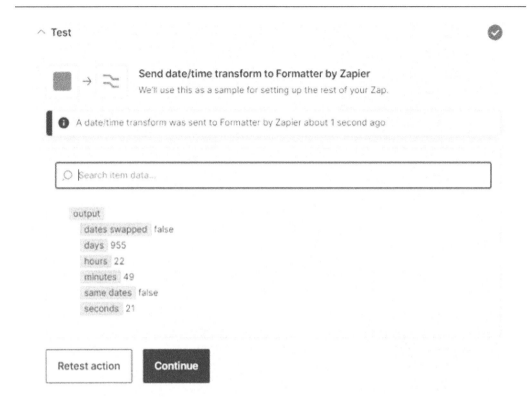

Figure 14.7 – Overview of the comparison of the two date/time values

The output shows whether the date was swapped in the output and whether the dates were the same (both denoted by `true` or `false`), as well as the difference in days, hours, minutes, and seconds.

Proceed to add one or more action steps after your **Date / Time** action step or publish your Zap.

Now, let's cover how to use the Formatter by Zapier built-in app to format date and time values.

Formatting dates and times

Formatting dates and times from your trigger or action steps may often be required when time formats between the apps you are using in your Zaps are different. You may also want to display your time formats in a more readable style, such as the date without hours, minutes, and seconds.

Here are a couple of examples of when you can use the Formatter by Zapier **Date / Time** action event with the **Format** transform option:

- When a task is marked as complete in **Asana**, convert the format of the completed date and time and create a new meeting in Google Calendar

- When a Microsoft Outlook email is received, change the display of the date received so that it's in a more readable format – for example, 29 Jan 2023

Let's explore how to set up the **Format** transform option.

Setting up the Date / Time action event with the Format transform option

You can use the **Date / Time** action event once you have set up your trigger step.

Once you have added an action step either by selecting the **Action** step or clicking on the + icon, and chosen **Formatter by Zapier** as the app and **Date / Time** as the action event, you can edit the fields in the **Action** section, as follows:

- **Transform**: From the drop-down menu, select the **Format** option. This is a required field and a value is needed for the step to run successfully.

- **Input**: Use this field to enter the date value you would like to manipulate. This can be either a static URL value, a dynamic value from previous steps, or a combination of both, to specify the **Input** value. For accuracy, the input must be in an accepted date/time format. Although this is not a required field, the formatter function will not return a result if there is no value.

- **To Format**: Specify the format you want the date/time output to be displayed in. Either select a date/time format from the drop-down menu or add a custom format under the **Custom** tab. You can use the custom date formats that we discussed in the *Using custom date formats* section. This is a required field and a value is needed for the step to run successfully.

- **To Timezone**: From the drop-down list, specify the time zone you want the date/time output that is displayed to be relevant to. You can also map in a custom value from a previous step. The default for this field is **UTC**.

- **From Format**: Zapier will attempt to read the format of the input value. If Zapier gets it wrong, you can use this field to specify the exact format. Either select a date/time format from the drop-down menu or add a custom format under the **Custom** tab. You can use the custom date formats that we discussed in the *Using custom date formats* section.

- **From Timezone**: From the drop-down list, specify the timezone related to your input value. You can also map in a custom value from a previous step. The default for this field is **UTC**.

An example is shown in the following screenshot:

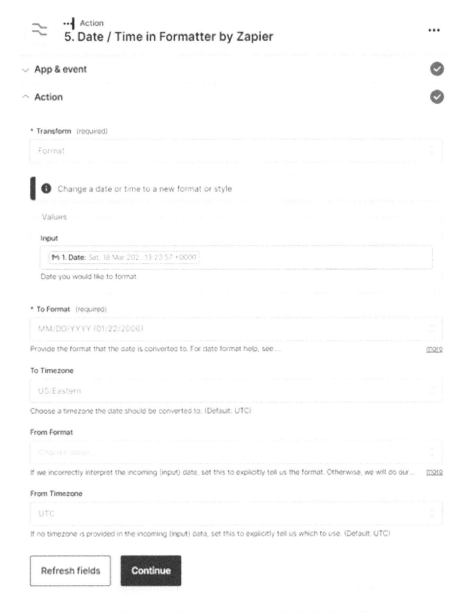

Figure 14.8 – Overview of using the Formatter by Zapier Date / Time action
event to change the format and time zone of a GMT date/time

Click on the **Continue** button. You can then use the **Test** section to test this step to generate the altered date/time format. The result from the scenario in *Figure 14.8* is shown in the following screenshot:

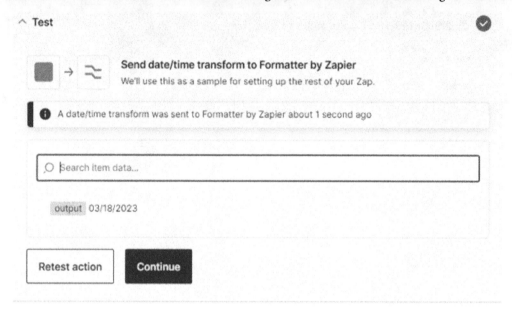

Figure 14.9 – Overview of the altered time format when using the
Date / Time action event to format dates and times

Proceed to add one or more action steps after your **Date / Time** action step or publish your Zap.

Here is a Zapier Community article that gives further context on how you can use Formatter by Zapier to manipulate dates and times: https://community.zapier.com/featured-articles-65/working-with-date-time-fields-10439.

You should now have a better understanding of how to format dates and times using the Formatter by Zapier built-in app.

Summary

In this chapter, we introduced the functionality of the Formatter by Zapier app so that you can manipulate dates and times, numbers, text, and other types of data. Thereafter, the primary focus of the content in this chapter was manipulating dates and times. We covered the basics of how to adjust date and time values in your Zaps. After that, we discussed how to use the date and time that your Zap runs in your action steps. Then, we explored how to use the Formatter by Zapier built-in app to add and subtract time and compare two dates. Lastly, we discussed how to format date and time values using the Formatter by Zapier built-in app.

You now understand what action events Formatter by Zapier offers. You also now know how to adjust dates and times in your Zaps and use the date and time your Zap runs. Lastly, you now know how to use the Formatter by Zapier built-in app to add or subtract time and convert date and time values into different formats.

In the next chapter, you will learn how to use the Formatter by Zapier built-in app to manipulate numbers, phone numbers, and currencies, and how to use spreadsheet-type formulas and math operations.

Questions

1. How can you use the date and time that your Zap runs in your Zap?

2. Can you adjust date/time values without using the Formatter by Zapier built-in app?

3. How can you manipulate dates and times using the Formatter by Zapier built-in app?

15
Formatting Numbers

Often, you might find that numerical data values do not usually appear in the way you want them to be displayed visually or in the way your other apps will accept them. There might be several scenarios where this will be the case. For example, a lead may enter a contact phone number when they submit an inquiry form, but that format may not be recognized by your SMS app. Or, if your team submits timesheets, you may need to calculate their overtime payments before sending them a summary by email. You might also want to add a space, period, or comma to a number or transform a number into a specific currency format. As you can imagine, there are many possible situations when you might need to adjust a number, and that is where the Formatter by Zapier **Numbers** action event comes in.

In this chapter, we will dive into using the Formatter by Zapier built-in app to manipulate a range of number formats. We will begin with an introduction to using Zapier to transform numerical values. Next, we will explore how to format numbers, currencies, and phone numbers. Then, we will cover how to use the Formatter by Zapier built-in app to perform basic mathematical operations and generate random numbers. Lastly, we will examine how to use spreadsheet-style formulas to perform calculations.

We will cover the following key topics in this chapter:

- Using Zapier to transform numerical values
- Formatting numbers with Formatter by Zapier
- Formatting currencies with Formatter by Zapier
- Formatting phone numbers with Formatter by Zapier
- Performing mathematical operations with Formatter by Zapier
- Generating random numbers with Formatter by Zapier
- Using spreadsheet-style formulas with Formatter by Zapier

> **Tip**
> You can use the magic AI to ask Zapier to format data in your Zap steps, which will then create Formatter by Zapier steps with the relevant transform options. We will discuss this in *Chapter 19, AI and Automation*.

Once you have worked through each of these topics, you will have a better understanding of the different number-transforming events available for use with the Formatter by Zapier built-in app. You will know how to adjust numbers, currencies, and phone numbers, as well as how to perform math operations and use spreadsheet-style formulas in your Zaps.

Technical requirements

To get the most out of the content in this chapter, you will need access to a Zapier account. The Zapier Starter plan will be required for you to create multi-step workflows using the Formatter by Zapier built-in app.

Using Zapier to transform numerical values

Formatter by Zapier can easily be used to transform numerical values from one format into another. There might be several scenarios in which you need to transform your data, such as when a value is not accepted in some of your apps, when you want to display the format differently, or if you need to make calculations.

For manipulating numbers, Formatter by Zapier can only be used as an action step and is available as the **Numbers** action event. When using this action event, you can use the following **Numbers** transform options, which can be found within the **Action** section of your action step:

- **Format Number**
- **Format Currency**
- **Format Phone Number**
- **Perform Math Operation**
- **Random Number**
- **Spreadsheet-Style Formula**

Let's get started by exploring how to transform general number formats.

Formatting numbers with Formatter by Zapier

Changing the format of a number can be very useful when you want to adjust the way decimal marks, thousands separators, and spaces are displayed. In general, these situations might arise when data from one app is presented in one format, and you want to change it to be displayed in another way. Zapier has a solution to this problem. You can use the Formatter by Zapier **Numbers** action event with the **Format Number** transform option to adjust the format of numbers.

Here are a few examples of when you can use this transform option:

- When you want to change the format of a number using a period as a decimal mark, such as 1000.00, so that it uses a comma as a decimal mark, such as 1000,00

- When you want to change the format of a number using groupings with a comma, such as 1,000,000, so that it uses spaces, such as 1 000 000

- When you want to change the format of a number where no thousands separators are present, such as 1000000, so that it has separators with commas, such as 1,000,000

Essentially, this transform option can be used to change a number so that it's in a new style. However, it does not allow you to round or pad a number.

Let's explore how to set up the **Format Number** transform option.

Setting up the Numbers action event with the Format Number transform option

You can use the **Numbers** action event once you have set up your trigger step.

Once you have added an action step either by selecting the **Action** step or clicking on the + icon and chosen **Formatter by Zapier** as the app and **Numbers** as the action event, you can edit the fields in the **Action** section, as follows:

- **Transform**: From the drop-down menu, select the **Format Number** option. This is a required field and must have a value for the Zap to run.

- **Input**: Use this field to enter the number format you want to manipulate. You can either enter a static value, a dynamic value from previous steps (using the **Custom** tab), or a combination of both, to specify the **Input** value. Although this is not a required field, the formatter function will not return a result if there is no value.

- **Input Decimal Mark**: This field is used to specify the character that denotes the decimal or fractional part of the number value in the **Input** field. You can use the drop-down options to select **Comma** or **Period**, or under the **Custom** tab, you can use a dynamic value from previous steps with the , or . character, respectively. This is a required field and must have a value for the Zap to run.

- **To Format**: Here, you can specify the format you want the number output to be displayed as. You can select a format from the drop-down menu, where you can either use the comma character, period character, or space for the thousands separator, with either a comma or period character for the decimal mark. These format options are **Comma for grouping & period for decimal**, **Period for grouping & comma for decimal**, **Space for grouping & period for decimal**, and **Space for grouping & comma for decimal**. Alternatively, you can add a dynamic value from previous steps under the **Custom** tab that matches the format code options – that is, 0, 1, 2, or 3. This is a required field and must have a value for the Zap to run.

An example is shown in the following screenshot, where we want to convert the input value containing a period as the decimal mark, and the output required has a space for the thousands separator and a comma for the decimal:

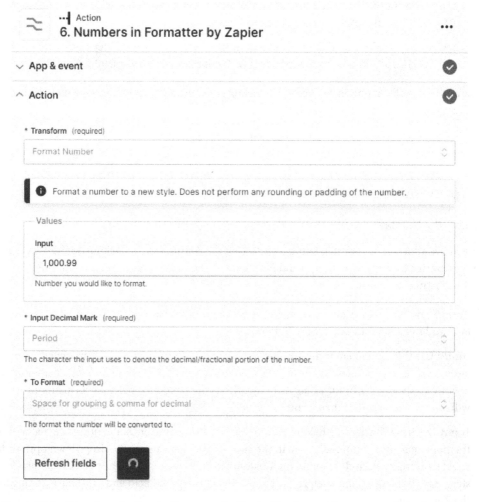

Figure 15.1 – Overview of using the Formatter by Zapier Numbers action event to format a number

Click on the **Continue** button. You can then use the **Test** section to test this step to generate the altered number format. The result from the scenario in *Figure 15.1* is shown in the following screenshot:

Figure 15.2 – Overview of the altered numerical value when using
the Numbers action event to format a number

Proceed to add one or more action steps after your **Numbers** action step or publish your Zap.

You should now have a better understanding of how to format numbers with the Formatter by Zapier built-in app.

Next, let's dive into formatting currency values.

Formatting currencies with Formatter by Zapier

Whether you work with single or multiple currencies in your business, it's likely that at some point or another, you'll need to convert numerical values into a currency format appropriate to your (or another) locale or to be displayed in a certain way. You can do this easily using the Formatter by Zapier **Numbers** action event with the **Format Currency** transform option.

Here are a couple of examples of when you can use this transform option:

- When you want to change the format of a number such as 1,000.23 to a German (Germany) locale format with the comma as the decimal mark, displayed in Euros with the currency symbol at the start, and the currency shortcode at the end, such as €1.000,23 EUR

- When you want to change the format of a number such as 1000.23 to an English (United States) locale format with the period as the decimal mark, displayed in US dollars with the currency symbol at the start, with no thousands grouping, such as $1000.23

Before we dive into setting up an action step with the **Format Currency** transform option, let's review some useful information about country locales and currency formats.

Understanding country locales and currency formatting

When working with currencies, it's useful to know that most countries have a specific format in which they display their currencies. For example, many European countries use a comma for the decimal mark, whereas the United States uses a period.

Currencies can be formatted using Zapier following **Unicode** character guidelines to display number patterns. According to Wikipedia, Unicode is defined as "*an information technology (IT) standard for the consistent encoding, representation, and handling of text expressed in most of the world's writing systems.*"

The most common Unicode characters that are used in currency pattern formatting are as follows:

- **.**: Using . in a pattern specifies where the decimal mark should be placed.
- **,**: Using , in a pattern specifies where the thousands separator should be placed.
- **0**: Using 0 in a pattern specifies that there is "zero padding." Therefore, if the input number is too short, a zero will be placed there.
- **#**: Using # in a pattern specifies that there is "no padding." Therefore, if the input number is too short, no value will be placed there.
- **¤**: Using ¤ in a pattern specifies where the currency symbol or code should be placed. If multiple symbols are used in sequence, the currency is displayed slightly differently. For example, for Euro in the English (United Kingdom) locale, ¤ equals €, ¤¤ equals EUR, and ¤¤¤ equals euros.

Therefore, you can put together a string of Unicode characters to convert currencies into the format you would like them to be displayed as.

More information on Unicode number patterns, including some example pattern formats, can be found at `http://www.unicode.org/reports/tr35/tr35-numbers.html#Number_Format_Patterns`.

Next, let's explore how to set up the **Format Currency** transform option.

Setting up the Numbers action event with the Format Currency transform option

You can use the **Numbers** action event once you have set up your trigger step.

Once you have added an action step either by selecting the **Action** step or clicking on the + icon, and chosen **Formatter by Zapier** as the app and **Numbers** as the action event, you can edit the fields in the **Action** section, as follows:

- **Transform**: From the drop-down menu, select the **Format Currency** option. This is a required field and must have a value for the Zap to run.

- **Input**: Use this field to enter the number that you want to transform into a currency format. You can either enter a static value, a dynamic value from previous steps (using the **Custom** tab), or a combination of both, to specify the **Input** value. Although this is not a required field, the formatter function will not return a result if there is no value.

- **Currency**: Here, you can specify the currency you want the number output to be displayed as. Select a format from a comprehensive list in the drop-down menu, or add the **ISO** (an international standard) 4217 three-character currency code under the **Custom** tab. Details of currency codes can be found at https://en.wikipedia.org/wiki/ISO_4217. This is a required field and must have a value for the Zap to run.

- **Currency Locale**: Here, you can specify the currency locale you want the number output to be displayed as. Select a format from a shortlist of commonly used currency locales in the drop-down menu, or add the ISO 639 language code and ISO 3166 country code in the en_US format for English (United States). Details of language codes can be found at https://en.wikipedia.org/wiki/ISO_639. Details of country codes can be found at https://en.wikipedia.org/wiki/ISO_3166. This is a required field and must have a value for the Zap to run.

- **Currency Format**: Here, you can specify the format you want the currency output to be displayed in by selecting a Unicode pattern format from the drop-down menu. Alternatively, you can add a custom format under the **Custom** tab by either entering a static value in Unicode pattern format, a dynamic value from previous steps, or a combination of both. Use the Unicode characters from the *Understanding country locales and currency formatting* section as guidance. This is a required field and must have a value for the Zap to run.

An example is shown in the following screenshot:

Figure 15.3 – Overview of using the Formatter by Zapier Numbers action event to format currencies

Click on the **Continue** button. You can then use the **Test** section to test this step to generate the altered currency format. The result from the scenario in *Figure 15.3* is shown in the following screenshot:

Send number transform to Formatter by Zapier
We'll use this as a sample for setting up the rest of your Zap.

A number transform was sent to Formatter by Zapier about 29 seconds ago

Search item data...

output: CA$1.099,00 dólares canadienses

Retest action   Publish Zap

Figure 15.4 – Overview of the altered value when using the Numbers action event to format a currency

Proceed to add one or more action steps after your **Numbers** action step or publish your Zap.

You should now have a better understanding of how to format currencies with the Formatter by Zapier built-in app.

Next, let's review the basics of how to transform phone numbers.

Formatting phone numbers with Formatter by Zapier

Telephone communication is not dead! Second to email, communicating with prospects, customers, and suppliers via telephone is an important part of any business. Being able to automate your telephone communications is a bonus. You may want to automatically send an SMS or voicemail to a prospect when they first make contact with you. However, sometimes, the telephone numbers that our contacts supply us with aren't always in a format that we can use in other apps. Therefore, having the ability to automatically adjust and manipulate telephone numbers is crucial when you use multiple apps for communicating by telephone. That is where the Formatter by Zapier **Numbers** action event with the **Format Phone Number** transform option comes in.

Here are a few examples of when you can use this option:

- When you receive a lead with a cellphone number, and you want to change it to an internationally recognized format so that you can send an automated SMS using Twilio

- When a new customer signs up to your service and provides a phone number, and you want to change it to a format that is recognized by a voicemail drop app, such as **Slybroadcast**

- When a new contact is added to your CRM, and you want to change the format of the contact phone number they provided to one that is recognized by your CRM calling module

Next, let's review how to set up the **Format Phone Number** transform option.

Setting up the Numbers action event with the Format Phone Number transform option

You can use the **Numbers** action event once you have set up your trigger step.

Once you have added an action step either by selecting the **Action** step or clicking on the + icon, and chosen **Formatter by Zapier** as the app and **Numbers** as the action event, you can edit the fields in the **Action** section, as follows:

- **Transform**: From the drop-down menu, select the **Format Phone Number** option. This is a required field and must have a value for the Zap to run.

- **Input**: You can use this field to enter the number that you want to transform into another phone number format. You can either enter a static value, a dynamic value from previous steps (using the **Custom** tab), or a combination of both, to specify the **Input** value. Although this is not a required field, the formatter function will not return a result if there is no value.

- **To Format**: Here, you can specify the format you want the number output to be displayed as. You can select a format from a list of commonly used phone number formats in the drop-down menu. Alternatively, you can add a dynamic value from previous steps under the **Custom** tab that matches the format code options – that is, 0, 1, 2, to 8. This is a required field and must have a value for the Zap to run.

- **Phone Number Country Code**: Here, you can specify the country code that you want the phone number's output to be displayed with. You can select from a list of commonly used formats in the drop-down menu, enter a static value for the 2-letter ISO country code under the **Custom** tab, or a dynamic value from previous steps. Details of ISO country codes can be found at https://countrycode.org/. For example, choosing **United States** (the US country code) will produce a phone number where the first two characters are +1. If left blank, the country code will not be displayed in the output.

- **Validate Phone Number?:** You can use this Boolean field to specify whether you want the converted phone number to be checked for validity in the country code specified in the **Phone Number Country Code** field. Use the drop-down menu to select **Yes** or **No**. Alternatively, add a custom format under the **Custom** tab by either entering a static value or a dynamic value from previous steps matching the `true` or `false` format, respectively. Set this to **No** when testing or if only formatting is required. If the number is invalid, the number specified in the **Input** field will be output unformatted. The default for this field is **Yes**.

An example is shown in the following screenshot:

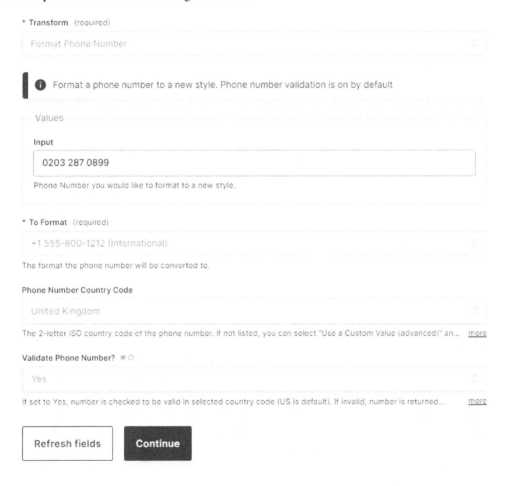

Figure 15.5 – Overview of using the Formatter by Zapier Numbers action event to format phone numbers

Click on the **Continue** button. You can then use the **Test** section to test this step to generate the altered phone number format. The result from the scenario in *Figure 15.5* is shown in the following screenshot:

Figure 15.6 – Overview of the output value when using the
Numbers action event to format a phone number

Proceed to add one or more action steps after your **Numbers** action step or publish your Zap.

You should now have a better understanding of how to format phone numbers with the Formatter by Zapier built-in app.

Next, let's take a look at how to perform basic math operations.

Performing mathematical operations with Formatter by Zapier

There will be situations where you are consistently manually performing basic mathematical functions. You might want to add two or three values together or convert a number into a percentage. Thankfully, Formatter by Zapier allows you to perform standard math operations using multiple values.

Using the **Numbers** action event and the **Perform Math Operation** transform option, Formatter by Zapier allows you to perform the following basic mathematical operations:

- **Add**
- **Subtract**
- **Multiply**
- **Divide**
- **Make Negative**

Here are a few examples of when you can use this transform option:

- When your customer fills out an order form on **Google Forms** with an order amount for red balls and an order amount for yellow balls, and you want to calculate the total order amount

- When your team members submit an expense claim form with **FastField Mobile Forms** for travel and subsistence and you want to deduct the value from their monthly allowance

- When a lead engages with you by email, and you want to add a predefined engagement point value to a lead score

Next, let's review how to set up the **Perform Math Operation** transform option.

Setting up the Numbers action event with the Perform Math Operation transform option

You can use the **Numbers** action event once you have set up your trigger step.

Once you have added an action step either by selecting the **Action** step or clicking on the + icon, and chosen **Formatter by Zapier** as the app and **Numbers** as the action event, you can edit the fields in the **Action** section, as follows:

- **Transform**: From the drop-down menu, select the **Perform Math Operation** option. This is a required field and must have a value for the Zap to run.

- **Operation**: Here, you can specify the math operation that you want to perform. Select an operation from the list in the drop-down menu, and choose from the **Add**, **Subtract**, **Multiply**, **Divide**, and **Make Negative** options. Alternatively, add a dynamic value from the previous steps under the **Custom** tab that matches the format code options of add, sub, mul, div, or neg, respectively. This is a required field and must have a value for the Zap to run.

- **Input**: You can use this field to enter the values you want to use in the calculation on multiple lines. You can either enter static values, dynamic values from previous steps, or a combination of both. Although this is not a required field, the formatter function will not return a result if there is no value.

An example is shown in the following screenshot, where we want to multiply the values 9 and 10:

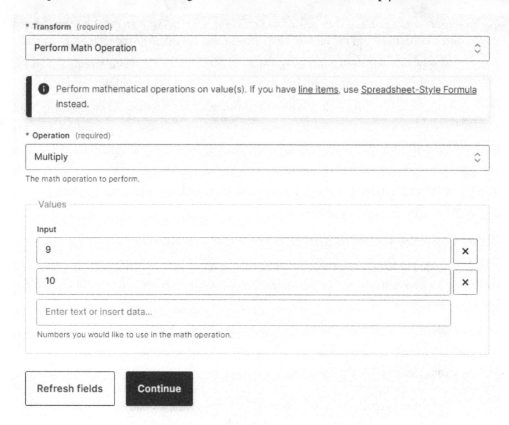

Figure 15.7 – Overview of using the Formatter by Zapier Numbers
action event to perform a math operation

Click on the **Continue** button. You can then use the **Test** section to test this step to generate the output from the math operation. The result from the scenario in *Figure 15.7* is shown in the following screenshot:

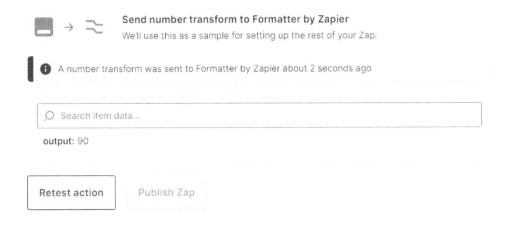

Figure 15.8 – Overview of the output value when using the
Numbers action event to perform math operations

Proceed to add one or more action steps after your **Numbers** action step or publish your Zap.

You should now have a better understanding of how to perform basic mathematical operations with the Formatter by Zapier built-in app.

Next, let's explore how to create a random number in your Zaps.

Generating random numbers with Formatter by Zapier

Another function of Formatter by Zapier is the ability to generate a random number between a lower- and upper-value range. It also allows you to specify the number of decimal points you want the output to be presented as. If you need to do more than use the five basic mathematical operations that we just discussed, you can use complex spreadsheet-style formulas in your Zaps instead. You can do this using the Formatter by Zapier **Numbers** action event's **Random Number Formula** transform option.

Here are a couple of examples of when you can use this transform option:

- When you want to randomly assign ID numbers to members of your team for your human resource records

- When you want to randomly generate a passcode for new users to access protected data that you want to send them

Next, let's review how to set up the **Random Number** transform option.

Setting up the Numbers action event with the Random Number transform option

You can use the **Numbers** action event once you have set up your trigger step.

Once you have added an action step either by selecting the **Action** step or clicking on the + icon, and chosen **Formatter by Zapier** as the app and **Numbers** as the action event, you can edit the fields in the **Action** section, as follows:

- **Transform**: From the drop-down menu, select the **Random Number** option. This is a required field and must have a value for the Zap to run.

- **Lower Range**: You can use this field to specify the lowest number for the range, which could also be a negative number. You can enter number/integer format static values, dynamic values mapped from previous steps, or a combination of both. The default value is 0. This is a required field and must have a value for the Zap to run.

- **Upper Range**: You can use this field to specify the highest number for the range, which could also be a negative number. You can enter number/integer format static values, dynamic values mapped from previous steps, or a combination of both. The default value is 100. This is a required field and must have a value for the Zap to run.

- **Decimal Points**: You can use this field to specify the number of digits to the right of the decimal point that you would like the output number to be displayed as. You can enter number/integer format static values or dynamic values mapped from previous steps, or a combination of both between 0 and 15, with the default value being 0. This field is optional.

An example is shown in the following screenshot, where we want to generate a random number between 0 and 100 with no decimal places:

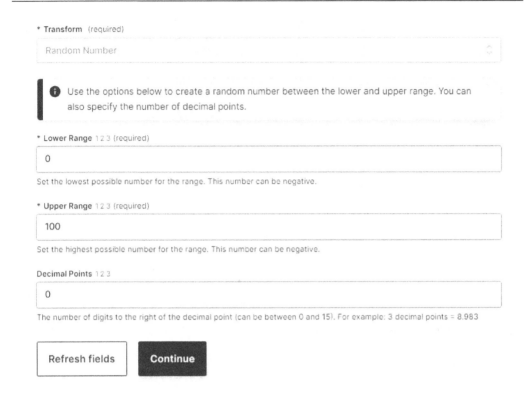

Figure 15.9 – Overview of using the Formatter by Zapier Numbers
action event to generate a random number

Click on the **Continue** button. You can then use the **Test** section to test this step to generate the output. The result from the scenario in *Figure 15.9* is shown in the following screenshot:

Figure 15.10 – Overview of the output value when using the
Numbers action event to generate a random number

Proceed to add one or more action steps after your **Numbers** action step or publish your Zap.

Next, let's explore how to use spreadsheet-type formulas in your Zaps.

Using spreadsheet-style formulas with Formatter by Zapier

If you need to do more than use the five basic mathematical operations that we just discussed, you can use complex spreadsheet-style formulas in your Zaps instead. You can do this using the Formatter by Zapier **Numbers** action event's **Spreadsheet-Style Formula** transform option.

This transform option allows you to perform complex calculations with numbers, as well as manipulate strings of text using formulas commonly used in spreadsheets instead of using code.

> **Important note**
> When using text strings with this transform option, you must use quotation marks around the string – for example, =IF("string1"="string2", "same", "different").

Here are a few examples of when you can use this transform option:

- When you want to calculate the average of several numbers, such as 8, 12, and 13 to get 11, using the AVERAGE(number, [number, ...]) formula.

- When you want to output the largest number from a list of values, such as 1, 9, and 53 to get 53, using the MAX(number, [number, ...]) formula.

- When you want to produce a random number between 0 and 1, such as `0.512453`, using the `RAND()` formula.

- When you want to perform an `if-then` statement replacement. For example, if your first value is `car` and your second value is `bicycle`, then return `orange`; otherwise, return `not relevant`. For this, you could use the `=IF(AND("string1"="red", "string2"="yellow"), "orange", "not relevant")` formula.

Here are a few Zapier Community articles that give good context for using the **Spreadsheet-Style Formula** transform option:

- *Formatter Features: using IF, AND, OR in spreadsheet-style formulas*: `https://community.zapier.com/featured-articles-65/formatter-features-using-if-and-or-in-spreadsheet-style-formulas-10367`

- *Formatter Features: MEDIAN/AVERAGE and ROUNDUP/ROUNDDOWN in spreadsheet-style formulas*: `https://community.zapier.com/featured-articles-65/formatter-features-median-average-and-roundup-rounddown-in-spreadsheet-style-formulas-10621`

- *Formatter Features: RAND/RANDBETWEEN and MIN/MAX in spreadsheet-style formulas*: `https://community.zapier.com/featured-articles-65/formatter-features-rand-randbetween-and-min-max-in-spreadsheet-style-formulas-10599`

Next, let's review how to set up the **Spreadsheet-Style Formula** transform option.

Setting up the Numbers action event with the Spreadsheet-Style Formula transform option

You can use the **Numbers** action event once you have set up your trigger step.

Once you have added an action step either by selecting the **Action** step or clicking on the + icon, and chosen **Formatter by Zapier** as the app and **Numbers** as the action event, you can edit the fields in the **Action** section, as follows:

- **Transform**: From the drop-down menu, select the **Spreadsheet-Style Formula** option. This is a required field and must have a value for the Zap to run.

- **Formula**: You can use this field to specify the formula with the values that you want to be calculated. Add static values for the formula and numeric values, or dynamic values mapped from previous steps under the **Custom** tab. This is a required field and must have a value for the Zap to run.

Zapier has created a handy reference document with various formulas that can be used with Formatter by Zapier, which you can refer to at `https://help.zapier.com/hc/en-us/articles/8496181204877`.

An example is shown in the following screenshot, where we want to divide the sum of 2 and 4 by 3:

Figure 15.11 – Overview of using the Formatter by Zapier Numbers
action event to perform a spreadsheet-style operation

Click on the **Continue** button. You can then use the **Test** section to test this step to generate the output. The result from the scenario in *Figure 15.11* is shown in the following screenshot:

Figure 15.12 – Overview of the output value when using the Numbers
action event to perform spreadsheet-style operations

Proceed to add one or more action steps after your **Numbers** action step or publish your Zap.

Here is a handy Zapier Community article with examples of how you can use Formatter by Zapier to format numbers: `https://community.zapier.com/featured-articles-65/formatter-features-currency-number-formatting-11091`.

You should now have a better understanding of how to use the **Numbers** transform option of the Formatter by Zapier built-in app.

Summary

In this chapter, we covered how to use the Formatter by Zapier built-in app to manipulate a variety of number formats. We started by introducing how to use Zapier for the general formatting of numbers. Then, we covered how to format numbers, currencies, and phone numbers in more detail. Next, we explored how to use the Formatter by Zapier built-in app to perform basic mathematical operations and generate random numbers. Lastly, we examined how to use spreadsheet-style formulas to perform calculations.

You now know how to use the Formatter by Zapier built-in app to transform numerical values such as numbers, currencies, and phone numbers, as well as how to perform basic math operations and use spreadsheet-style formulas to perform calculations.

In the next chapter, you will learn how to use some of the functionality of the Formatter by Zapier built-in app to format text. We will explore adjusting title case, uppercase, and lowercase, finding and replacing text, trimming whitespace, counting words, adjusting the length of a string of text, and pluralizing text.

Questions

1. Can you use the Formatter by Zapier built-in app to format a United Kingdom phone number so that it's in an internationally recognized format?

2. What math operations can be performed by the Formatter by Zapier built-in app?

16

Text Formatting Functions in Zapier – Part 1

So far in this book, we've covered two important functions of the versatile Formatter by Zapier built-in app. In *Chapter 14*, *Formatting Date and Time*, we discussed how to use Formatter by Zapier to manipulate dates and times. In *Chapter 15*, *Formatting Numbers*, we covered how to use it to transform numbers. As covered in those two chapters, being able to transform text into a variety of different formats is incredibly useful. For example, the name of a contact may be displayed in full (as a first name and surname), and you may want to split out the first name so that you can personalize an email rather than using the contact's full name. Or you might want to extract an email address from a block of text to be able to add that to your marketing automation software. You might also want to truncate text to a specified character length when sharing a summary of content on Twitter. There are many possibilities for when you might need to adjust text, and that is where the Formatter by Zapier **Text** action event comes in. Users familiar with Microsoft Excel will see similarities between this Zapier functionality and text transformation formula usage in Microsoft Excel spreadsheets.

In this chapter, we will continue to focus on the versatile Formatter by Zapier built-in app, and you will learn how to use some of the extensive functionality available to format text. First, we will discuss how to use Zapier to transform text values in general. Next, we will explore capitalizing text, applying title case, uppercase, and lowercase, and pluralizing words. Then, we will cover finding the position of and replacing text, counting characters and words, and removing whitespace.

We will cover the following key topics in this chapter:

- Using Zapier to transform text values
- Capitalizing the first letter of every word
- Applying title case to a string of words
- Converting all the characters in a string of text into uppercase
- Converting all the characters in a string of text into lowercase

- Pluralizing words

- Finding the first position of specified text

- Replacing characters, words, or phrases

- Counting the number of characters in a string of text

- Counting the number of words in a string of text

- Removing whitespace

Once you have worked through each of these topics, you will have a better understanding of some of the different text-transforming functions available for use with the Formatter by Zapier built-in app. You will know how to use Zapier to adjust text to various formats.

Technical requirements

To get the most out of the content in this chapter, you will need access to a Zapier account. The Zapier Starter plan will be required for you to create multi-step workflows using the Formatter by Zapier built-in app.

Using Zapier to transform text values

Formatter by Zapier can easily be used to transform text values from one format into another. There might be several scenarios in which you need to transform your data, such as when you want to display the format differently or if you need to extract a certain type of data from a block of text.

For manipulating text, Formatter by Zapier can only be used as an action step and is available as the **Text** action event.

When using this action event, you can use the following **Text** transform options. These can be found within the **Set up action** section of your action step, listed in the **Transform** drop-down menu:

- **Capitalize**

- **Convert HMTL to Markdown**

- **Convert Markdown to HTML**

- **Convert to ASCII**

- **Default Value**

- **Extract Email Address**

- **Extract Number**

- **Extract Pattern**

- **Extract Phone Number**

- **Extract URL**
- **Find**
- **Length**
- **Lowercase**
- **Pluralize**
- **Remove HTML Tags**
- **Replace**
- **Split Text**
- **Split Text into Chunks for AI Prompts (beta)**
- **Spreadsheet-Style Formula**
- **Superhero Name**
- **Titlecase**
- **Trim Whitespace**
- **Truncate**
- **Uppercase**
- **URL Decode**
- **URL Encode**
- **Word Count**

We will cover the **Convert HTML to Markdown**, **Convert Markdown to HTML**, **Convert to ASCII**, **Default Value**, **Extract Email Address**, **Extract Number**, **Extract Pattern**, **Extract Phone Number**, **Extract URL**, **Split Text**, **Spreadsheet-Style Formula**, **Superhero Name**, **Truncate**, **URL Decode**, and **URL Encode** text transform options in *Chapter 17, Text Formatting Functions in Zapier – Part 2*. We will cover the **Split Text into Chunks for AI Prompts (beta)** in *Chapter 19, AI and Automation*.

> **Tip**
> You can use the magic AI to ask Zapier to format data in your Zap steps, which will then create Formatter by Zapier steps with the relevant transform options. We will discuss this in *Chapter 19, AI and Automation*.

Let's get started by exploring how to capitalize the first letter of every word.

Capitalizing the first letter of every word

If you're a stickler for formatting text correctly, you'll most likely want to ensure that, where appropriate, words in a bunch of text display capital letters at the start of the word. This is especially important when addressing people by name or displaying business names and addresses on invoices. You can capitalize the first letter of every word in a string of text using the Formatter by Zapier **Text** action event alongside the **Capitalize** transform function. For example, if the string of text was `this is a test`, the transformed text would be `This Is A Test`. Microsoft Excel users will recognize the similarity of this Zapier functionality to the `PROPER` formula in a Microsoft Excel spreadsheet to capitalize text.

Here are a few examples of when you can use this transform option:

- When new contacts sign up for your newsletter, it is common that they may add their name in all-lowercase, such as `kelly` instead of `Kelly`. You might want to make their name look as it should when you address them in emails. So, when a new subscriber is added to Mailchimp, for example, you can transform their name into its formal setting.

- You might collect client billing addresses by asking them to complete a web form. It might be the case that they add the address in all-lowercase, such as `99 hollow avenue, washington`. Before adding the data to your accounting system, you might want to capitalize the first letter of each word in the address so that it reads `99 Hollow Avenue, Washington`.

Next, let's review how to set up an action step with the **Capitalize** transform option.

Setting up the Text action event with the Capitalize transform option

You can use the **Text** action event once you have set up your trigger step.

Once you have added an action step, by either selecting the **Action** step or clicking on the + icon, and chosen **Formatter by Zapier** as the app and **Text** as the action event, you can edit the fields in the **Action** section, as follows:

- **Transform**: From the drop-down menu, select the **Capitalize** option. This is a required field and must have a value for the Zap to run.

- **Input**: Use this field to enter the text of which you want to transform the first character of every word. You can enter either a static value, a dynamic value from previous steps, or a combination of both to specify the **Input** value. Although this is not a required field, the formatter function will not return a result if there is no value.

An example is shown in the following screenshot:

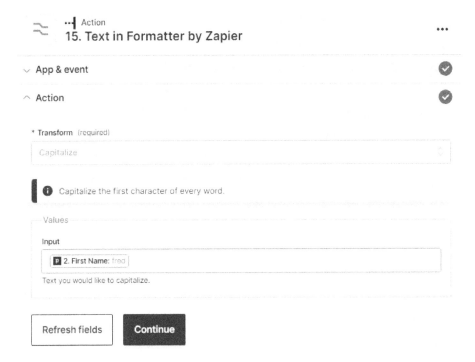

Figure 16.1 – Using the Formatter by Zapier Text action event to capitalize text

Click on the **Continue** button. You can then use the **Test** section to test this step to generate the altered capitalized text. The result from the scenario in *Figure 16.1* is shown in the following screenshot:

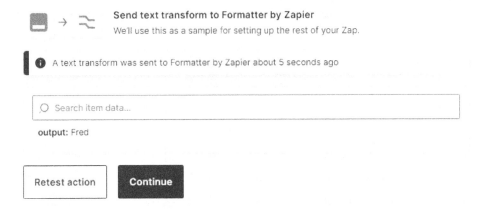

Figure 16.2 – An example of the altered value when using the Text action event to capitalize text

Proceed to add one or more action steps after your **Text** action step.

You should now have a better understanding of how to use the **Capitalize** transform function. Next, let's take a look at how to apply title case to a string of words with the **Titlecase** transform function.

Applying title case to a string of words

Following on from the **Capitalize** transform function, there may be times when you only want to capitalize the first letter of each word in a string of text if it isn't an article, conjunction, or preposition – in other words, any nouns, pronouns, verbs, adjectives, and adverbs – as well as the first word in a title or subtitle. This is known as title case, where all major words have the first letter capitalized, and all minor words have the first letter remain lowercase. It is commonly used in titles of books, songs, movies, and blog articles. In this case, you should use the Formatter by Zapier **Text** action event with the **Titlecase** transform function. For example, if the string of text were `this is an example of the best test to use`, the transformed text would be `This Is an Example of the Best Test to Use`.

Here are a few examples of when you can use this transform option:

- When your blog writers add a new draft blog post to your **WordPress** website and you want to ensure the formatting of the post title is always consistently in title case. You can use the **Titlecase** transform option to alter the formatting of the title and then update the blog post accordingly with the WordPress action event.

- You might manage your **YouTube** video publishing schedule in a Google Sheets spreadsheet or project management tool such as ClickUp. The schedule may include the title of the YouTube video, which you might want to consistently be posted in title case. You can use the **Titlecase** transform option to alter the formatting of the title and then add the corrected title when you post the new video to YouTube.

Next, let's review how to set up an action step with the **Titlecase** transform option.

Setting up the Text action event with the Titlecase transform option

You can use the **Text** action event once you have set up your trigger step.

Once you have added an action step, by either selecting the **Action** step or clicking on the + icon, and chosen **Formatter by Zapier** as the app and **Text** as the action event, you can edit the fields in the **Action** section, as follows:

- **Transform**: From the drop-down menu, select the **Titlecase** option. This is a required field and must have a value for the Zap to run.

- **Input**: Use this field to enter the text that you want to transform into title case. You can enter either a static value, a dynamic value from previous steps, or a combination of both to specify the **Input** value. Although this is not a required field, the formatter function will not return a result if there is no value.

An example is shown in the following screenshot:

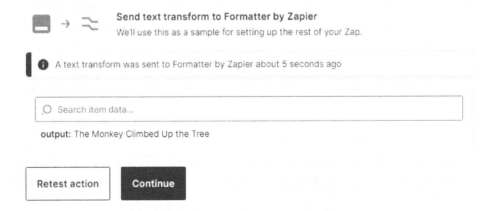

Figure 16.3 – Using the Formatter by Zapier Text action event to change the text to title case

Click on the **Continue** button. You can then use the **Test** section to test this step to generate the altered text. The result from the scenario in *Figure 16.3* is shown in the following screenshot:

Figure 16.4 – An example of the altered value when using the Text action event to change to title case

Proceed to add one or more action steps after your **Text** action step.

You should now have a better understanding of how to use the **Titlecase** transform function. Next, let's explore how to convert all the characters in a string of text into uppercase with the **Uppercase** transform function.

Converting all the characters in a string of text into uppercase

Most of us know that typing our text messages or emails in capital letters could be interpreted as raising your virtual "voice" or emphasizing a point. It's best to use this sparingly. There may, however, be other times when it's necessary to have text displayed in capital letters. The original text may be in all-lowercase or a mixture of upper and lowercase. To alter a string of text so that it is displayed in uppercase only, you can use the Formatter by Zapier **Text** action event with the **Uppercase** transform function. For example, if the string of text were `wunderlust factory`, the transformed text would be `WUNDERLUST FACTORY`. Microsoft Excel users will recognize the similarity of this Zapier functionality to the `UPPER` formula in a Microsoft Excel spreadsheet to convert text into uppercase.

Here are a few examples of when you can use this transform option:

- When leads fill out a form on your website, you might want the lead's company name to be displayed entirely in uppercase in your **Customer Relationship Management (CRM)**. You can use the **Uppercase** transform option to alter the format of the company name to uppercase and then add the lead's details to the CRM with the new company name format.

- You might want to upload a copy of a document to **Google Drive** when you receive it by email as an attachment. You might also prefer to have all your filenames in a consistent uppercase format. You can use the **Uppercase** transform option to alter the format of the title of the file to uppercase before uploading it to Google Drive.

Next, let's review how to set up an action step with the **Uppercase** transform option.

Setting up the Text action event with the Uppercase transform option

You can use the **Text** action event once you have set up your trigger step.

Once you have added an action step, by either selecting the **Action** step or clicking on the + icon, and chosen **Formatter by Zapier** as the app and **Text** as the action event, you can edit the fields in the **Action** section, as follows:

- **Transform**: From the drop-down menu, select the **Uppercase** option. This is a required field and must have a value for the Zap to run.

- **Input**: Use this field to enter the text that you want to transform into capital letters. You can enter either a static value, a dynamic value from previous steps, or a combination of both to specify the **Input** value. Although this is not a required field, the formatter function will not return a result if there is no value.

An example is shown in the following screenshot:

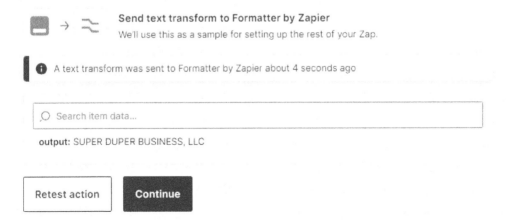

Figure 16.5 – Using the Formatter by Zapier Text action event to capitalize text

Click on the **Continue** button. You can then use the **Test** section to test this step to generate the altered text in uppercase. The result from the scenario in *Figure 16.5* is shown in the following screenshot:

Figure 16.6 – An example of the altered value when using the Text
action event to change all the text to uppercase

Proceed to add one or more action steps after your **Text** action step.

You should now have a better understanding of how to use the **Uppercase** transform function. Next, let's discuss how to convert all the characters in a string of text into lowercase with the **Lowercase** transform function.

Converting all the characters in a string of text into lowercase

Compared to the **Uppercase** transform option, there may be occasions where you want to do the opposite and change text that is purely uppercase or a combination of uppercase and lowercase to lowercase only. To do this, you can use the Formatter by Zapier **Text** action event with the **Lowercase** transform function. For example, if the string of text were The Ice-cream Parlor, the transformed text would be the ice-cream parlor. Microsoft Excel users will recognize the similarity of this Zapier functionality to the LOWER formula in a Microsoft Excel spreadsheet to convert text into lowercase.

Here are a few examples of when you can use this transform option:

- When your contacts purchase through your Shopify website, you might want to generate unique user aliases for them to use in your other apps. If you use their name in the alias, you might want to make it lowercase for consistency.

- You might be using **Google Docs** to create contracts for your prospects from a template when they book a consultation call with you through Calendly. You might want to have all Google Docs filenames in consistent lowercase formatting based on the name of the client and the date the document was created.

Next, let's review how to set up an action step with the **Lowercase** transform option.

Setting up the Text action event with the Lowercase transform option

You can use the **Text** action event once you have set up your trigger step.

Once you have added an action step, by either selecting the **Action** step or clicking on the + icon, and chosen **Formatter by Zapier** as the app and **Text** as the action event, you can edit the fields in the **Action** section, as follows:

- **Transform**: From the drop-down menu, select the **Lowercase** option. This is a required field and must have a value for the Zap to run.

- **Input**: Use this field to enter the text that you want to transform into lowercase letters. You can enter either a static value, a dynamic value from previous steps, or a combination of both to specify the **Input** value. Although this is not a required field, the formatter function will not return a result if there is no value.

An example is shown in the following screenshot:

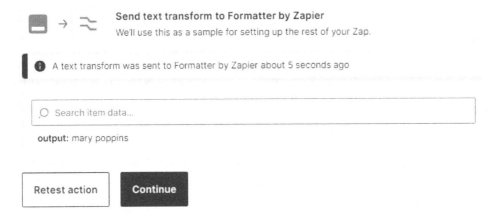

Figure 16.7 – Using the Formatter by Zapier Text action event to change the text into lowercase letters

Click on the **Continue** button. You can then use the **Test** section to test this step to generate the altered text in lowercase. The result from the scenario in *Figure 16.7* is shown in the following screenshot:

Figure 16.8 – An example of the altered value when using the
Text action event to make all the text lowercase

Proceed to add one or more action steps after your **Text** action step.

You should now have a better understanding of how to use the **Lowercase** transform function. Next, let's cover how to pluralize words using the **Pluralize** transform function.

Pluralizing words

It is sometimes handy to convert a word from a singular format into a plural format. You can change any English word so that it's plural using the Formatter by Zapier **Text** action event alongside the **Pluralize** transform function.

Here is an example of when you can use this transform option. You might have an eCommerce store that uses the WooCommerce platform. When customers buy from you, you might want to follow up purchases with an email on a more personal level, with text formatted to read better. Let's say your customer purchases six red T-shirts but your WooCommerce site lists the product as `red t-shirt`; you could use the **Pluralize** transform function to change the text to `red t-shirts` based on how many the customer ordered. Your email will then read better, with `6 red t-shirts`.

Next, let's review how to set up an action step with the **Pluralize** transform option.

Setting up the Text action event with the Pluralize transform option

You can use the **Text** action event once you have set up your trigger step.

Once you have added an action step, by either selecting the **Action** step or clicking on the + icon, and chosen **Formatter by Zapier** as the app and **Text** as the action event, you can edit the fields in the **Action** section, as follows:

- **Transform**: From the drop-down menu, select the **Pluralize** option. This is a required field and must have a value for the Zap to run.

- **Input**: Use this field to enter the text that you want to pluralize. You can enter either a static value, a dynamic value from previous steps, or a combination of both to specify the **Input** value. Although this is not a required field, the formatter function will not return a result if there is no value.

An example is shown in the following screenshot:

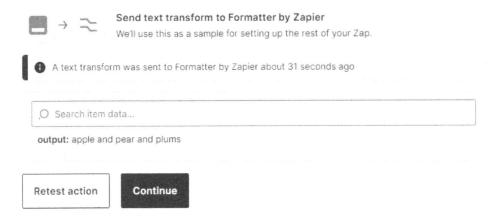

Figure 16.9 – Using the Formatter by Zapier Text action event to pluralize text

Click on the **Continue** button. You can then use the **Test** section to test this step to generate the altered pluralized text. The result from the scenario in *Figure 16.9* is shown in the following screenshot:

Figure 16.10 – An example of the altered value when using the Text action event to pluralize text

Proceed to add one or more action steps after your **Text** action step.

> **Note**
> The **Pluralize** transform function generally works best for a single word. If multiple words are presented, generally, the last word in the string will be pluralized.

You should now have a better understanding of how to use the **Pluralize** transform function. Next, let's take a look at how to find the first position of a specified text value with the **Find** transform function.

Finding the first position of specified text

On occasion, you might want to know in what numerical position a word first appears in a string of text. You can use the Formatter by Zapier **Text** action event with the **Find** transform function to find the first numerical position of a word or phrase in a string of text. A number will be returned representing the character position of the first letter of the word or phrase. For example, if you wanted to find the position of the word green in a string of text such as green is a wonderful color, the returned value would be 0. If the string of text were isn't green a wonderful color?, the returned value would be 6. If the search term does not exist in the string of text, the value that is returned would be -1. You can also skip several characters that you do not want to be included in the search. For example, if the text string is plum and apple and pear and plum, we can ignore the first position of the word plum by skipping the first four or more characters in the string during the search. This returns a result of position 28 for the start of the second occurrence of the word plum in the string.

An example of a situation where you could use this transform option would be if you have a team of blog writers that write blog posts based on a topic and **search engine optimization** (**SEO**) information that you add to a Microsoft Excel spreadsheet. When your bloggers upload the new post to WordPress, you might want to use the **Find** transform function to locate the first position of your SEO keyphrase and then be notified by email of that position.

Next, let's review how to set up an action step with the **Find** transform option.

Setting up the Text action event with the Find transform option

You can use the **Text** action event once you have set up your trigger step.

Once you have added an action step, by either selecting the **Action** step or clicking on the + icon, and chosen **Formatter by Zapier** as the app and **Text** as the action event, you can edit the fields in the **Action** section, as follows:

- **Transform**: From the drop-down menu, select the **Find** option. This is a required field and must have a value for the Zap to run.

- **Input**: Use this field to enter the text that you want to search for the numerical position of a value that you enter in the **Find** field. You can enter either a static value, a dynamic value from previous steps, or a combination of both to specify the **Input** value. Although this is not a required field, the formatter function will not return a result if there is no value.

- **Find**: Use this field to enter the word or phrase that you want to search for in the text from the **Input** field. You can enter either a static value, a dynamic value from previous steps, or a combination of both to specify this value. Although this is not a required field, the formatter function will not return a result if there is no value.

- **Skip Characters**: Use this field to enter how many characters you might want to skip when searching for the value entered in the **Find** field. You can enter either a static value, a dynamic value from previous steps, or a combination of both to specify this value. This field can be left blank. Use this field when you don't want to find the position of the first word but only subsequent words.

An example is shown in the following screenshot:

* Transform (required)

Find

ⓘ Find the first position of a value in the text, -1 if the value is not found

Values

Input

plum and apple and pear and plum

Text you would like to Search.

Find

plum

Value to find in the text

Skip Characters 1 2 3

5

Will skip the first N characters in the text.

Refresh fields   Continue

Figure 16.11 – Using the Formatter by Zapier Text action event to find the numerical position of a word

Click on the **Continue** button. You can then use the **Test** section to test this step to generate the numerical position of the word. The result from the scenario in *Figure 16.11* is shown in the following screenshot:

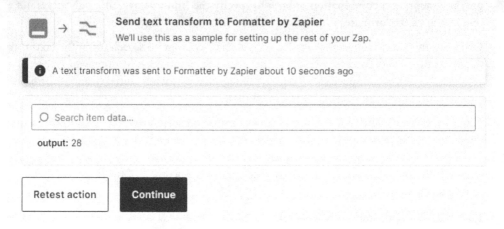

Figure 16.12 – An example of the altered value when using the Text action event to pluralize text

Proceed to add one or more action steps after your **Text** action step.

You should now have a better understanding of how to use the **Find** transform function. Next, let's explore how to replace characters, words, or phrases with the **Replace** transform function.

Replacing characters, words, or phrases

You've probably used the find and replace functionality many times before when editing a document in Microsoft Word or Google Docs, a spreadsheet in Microsoft Excel or Google Sheets, or a database such as Smartsheet or Airtable. It does what its name suggests – it finds something and then replaces it with something else. Zapier uses similar functionality, allowing you to find and replace words and phrases in text strings. You can use the Formatter by Zapier **Text** action event with the **Replace** transform function to achieve this. Microsoft Excel users will recognize the similarity of this Zapier functionality to the REPLACE or SUBSTITUTE formulas in a Microsoft Excel spreadsheet to find and replace text.

The **Replace** transform function also allows you to find special characters using special character syntax, as follows:

- **Space characters**: The [:space:] syntax is used to match space (\s) characters
- **Tab characters**: The [:tab:] syntax is used to match tab (\t) characters
- **Newline characters**: The [:newline:] syntax is used to match newline (\n) characters, which are those used to identify the end of a line of text or the start of a new line

- **Carriage-return characters**: The [:return:] syntax is used to match carriage-return (\r) characters, which are those that denote the start of the current line (at the left margin)

Let's look at an example of when you can use this transform option.

You might ask clients to submit reviews via a **Typeform** web form. After the form has been submitted, you might want to search the body of the testimonial for a certain word or phrase and replace it with another before uploading it to your WordPress website as a new post.

Next, let's review how to set up an action step with the **Replace** transform option.

Setting up the Text action event with the Replace transform option

You can use the **Text** action event once you have set up your trigger step.

Once you have added an action step, by either selecting the **Action** step or clicking on the + icon, and chosen **Formatter by Zapier** as the app and **Text** as the action event, you can edit the fields in the **Action** section, as follows:

- **Transform**: From the drop-down menu, select the **Replace** option. This is a required field and must have a value for the Zap to run.

- **Input**: Use this field to enter the text that you want to search for a word or phrase and replace it with another. You can enter either a static value, a dynamic value from previous steps, or a combination of both to specify the **Input** value. Although this is not a required field, the formatter function will not return a result if there is no value.

- **Find**: Use this field to enter the word or phrase that you want to search for in the text from the **Input** field. You can enter either a static value, a dynamic value from previous steps, or a combination of both to specify this value. This is a required field and must have a value for the Zap to run. This field supports special character syntax. For example, to find spaces, you can use the [:space:] syntax.

- **Replace**: Use this field to enter the word or phrase that you want to replace the value from the **Find** field with. You can enter either a static value, a dynamic value from previous steps, or a combination of both to specify this value. Although this is not a required field, the formatter function will not return a result if there is no value.

An example is shown in the following screenshot:

Transform (required)

Replace

ⓘ Replace all instances of any character, word or phrase in the text with another character, word or phrase.

Values

Input

plum and apple and pear and plum

Text you would like to find and replace values within.

* **Find** (required)

plum

To find a space, use [:space:]. For supported special characters, see: https://zapier.com/help/create/format/modify... more

Replace

green tomato

Leave blank to delete the found text

[Refresh fields] [Continue]

Figure 16.13 – Using the Formatter by Zapier Text action event to find and replace text

Click on the **Continue** button. You can then use the **Test** section to test this step to find and replace any text. The result from the scenario in *Figure 16.13* is shown in the following screenshot:

→ ≊ **Send text transform to Formatter by Zapier**
We'll use this as a sample for setting up the rest of your Zap.

ⓘ A text transform was sent to Formatter by Zapier about 5 seconds ago

🔍 Search item data...

output: green tomato and apple and pear and green tomato

[Retest action] [Continue]

Figure 16.14 – An example of the altered value when using the Text action event to find and replace text

Proceed to add one or more action steps after your **Text** action step.

You should now have a better understanding of how to use the **Replace** transform function. Next, let's discuss how to count the number of characters in a string of text using the **Length** transform function.

Counting the number of characters in a string of text

Having the ability to automatically count the number of characters in a string of text can be very useful in several scenarios. This is especially important if the apps involved in action steps have character limitations. One example of this would be the character limitations for tweets on Twitter. You can use the Formatter by Zapier **Text** action event with the **Length** transform function to check the character length in a string of text before passing the text to other action steps. Microsoft Excel users will recognize the similarity of this Zapier functionality to the LEN formula in a Microsoft Excel spreadsheet to count the number of characters in a string of text.

Here are a few examples of when you can use this transform option:

- You might reshare content on various social media channels; however, a piece of content might be too long to share on platforms such as Twitter. You could use the **Length** transform function to count the character length and then use Filter by Zapier to stop your workflow from continuing if the character length is over 280.

- You might want to check the number of characters in the body of a new WordPress blog post before adding the value to Airtable.

- You might want to reshare your social media posts by SMS for some clients who don't use social media, using Twilio or Voodoo SMS, for example. Most SMS platforms have character length restrictions, so you could use the **Length** transform function to count the character length before stopping the workflow with Filter by Zapier.

Next, let's review how to set up an action step with the **Length** transform option.

Setting up the Text action event with the Length transform option

You can use the **Text** action event once you have set up your trigger step.

Once you have added an action step, by either selecting the **Action** step or clicking on the + icon, and chosen **Formatter by Zapier** as the app and **Text** as the action event, you can edit the fields in the **Action** section, as follows:

- **Transform**: From the drop-down menu, select the **Length** option. This is a required field and must have a value for the Zap to run.

- **Input**: Use this field to enter the text that you want to perform a character length count on. You can enter either a static value, a dynamic value from previous steps, or a combination of both to specify the **Input** value. Although this is not a required field, the formatter function will not return a result if there is no value.

- **Ignore Whitespace**: Use this Boolean field to choose whether you want to ignore all whitespace characters, including spaces, tabs, and newlines. Select **True** to ignore whitespace and **False** to include whitespace. Although this is not a required field, the default, if neither option is selected, is to include whitespace.

An example is shown in the following screenshot:

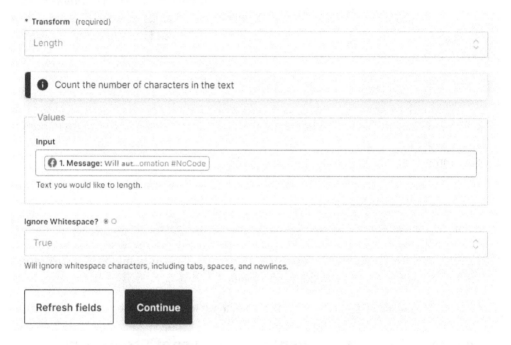

Figure 16.15 – Using the Formatter by Zapier Text action event to count the number of characters

Click on the **Continue** button. You can then use the **Action** section to test this step to count the number of characters. The result from the scenario in *Figure 16.15* is shown in the following screenshot:

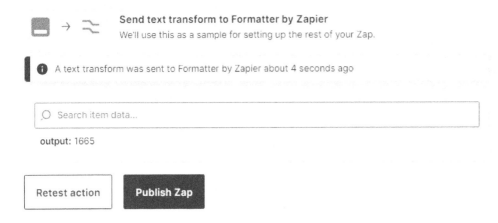

Figure 16.16 – An example of the returned value when using the
Text action event to count the number of characters

Proceed to add one or more action steps after your **Text** action step.

> **Tip**
> You can use the **Length** transform function in the same workflow as the **Truncate** transform
> function to reduce the length of strings of text if they are more than a certain character length,
> such as for tweets.

You should now have a better understanding of how to use the **Length** transform function. Next, let's
cover how to count the number of words in a string of text with the **Word Count** transform function.

Counting the number of words in a string of text

As with counting characters in a string of text, it is often handy to be able to count the number of
words. This is especially useful when dealing with documents and copywriting scenarios. You can use
the Formatter by Zapier **Text** action event with the **Word Count** transform function to achieve this.

Here are a few examples of when you can use this transform option:

- You might want to check the number of words in the body of a new WordPress blog post before
  adding the value to Knack.

- You might handle your customer service desk queries in Freshdesk and want to compare the
  number of words in each ticket update with the time between updates by adding the figures
  to a Google Sheets spreadsheet.

Next, let's review how to set up an action step with the **Word Count** transform option.

Setting up the Text action event with the Word Count transform option

You can use the **Text** action event once you have set up your trigger step.

Once you have added an action step, by either selecting the **Action** step or clicking on the + icon, and chosen **Formatter by Zapier** as the app and **Text** as the action event, you can edit the fields in the **Action** section, as follows:

- **Transform**: From the drop-down menu, select the **Word Count** option. This is a required field and must have a value for the Zap to run.

- **Input**: Use this field to enter the text in which you want to count the number of words contained. You can enter either a static value, a dynamic value from previous steps, or a combination of both to specify the **Input** value. Although this is not a required field, the formatter function will not return a result if there is no value.

An example is shown in the following screenshot:

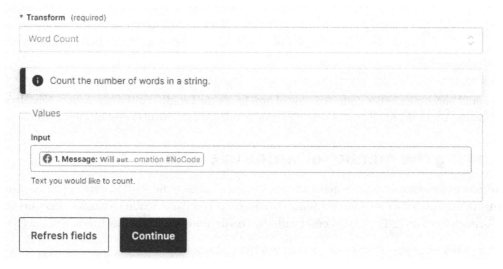

Figure 16.17 – Using the Formatter by Zapier Text action event
to count the number of words in a string of text

Click on the **Continue** button. You can then use the **Test** section to test this step to return a value that defines the number of words in the text string. The result from the scenario in *Figure 16.17* is shown in the following screenshot:

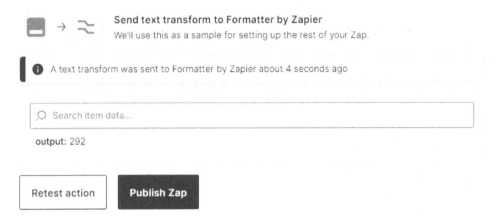

Send text transform to Formatter by Zapier
We'll use this as a sample for setting up the rest of your Zap.

ⓘ A text transform was sent to Formatter by Zapier about 4 seconds ago

🔍 Search item data...

output: 292

| Retest action | **Publish Zap** |

Figure 16.18 – An example of the value that's returned when using the Text action event to count the number of words

Proceed to add one or more action steps after your **Text** action step.

You should now have a better understanding of how to use the **Word Count** transform function. Next, let's explore how to remove whitespace using the **Trim Whitespace** transform function.

Removing whitespace

Sometimes, strings of text may not have been edited in the way we need so that they can be used in other steps in our workflows. This is often the case when certain apps present data in a certain way with blank character spacing before or after the text. In these scenarios, if you want to alter the format of the text so that no whitespace exists at the beginning or end of a string of text, you can use the Formatter by Zapier **Text** action event with the **Trim Whitespace** transform function to achieve this. Microsoft Excel users will recognize the similarity between using this Zapier functionality and the TRIM formula in a Microsoft Excel spreadsheet to remove whitespace from a string of text.

An example of a situation where you could use this transform option would be when you ask job seekers to send in applications by completing a web form. There might be formatting issues with the web form, presenting the data with large whitespace blocks before or after the body of parts of the form submission data. You can use the **Trim Whitespace** transform function to remove the whitespace before adding the application to your task management app, such as ClickUp.

Next, let's review how to set up an action step with the **Trim Whitespace** transform option.

Setting up the Text action event with the Trim Whitespace transform option

You can use the **Text** action event once you have set up your trigger step.

Once you have added an action step, by either selecting the **Action** step or clicking on the + icon, and chosen **Formatter by Zapier** as the app and **Text** as the action event, you can edit the fields in the **Action** section, as follows:

- **Transform**: From the drop-down menu, select the **Trim Whitespace** option. This is a required field and must have a value for the Zap to run.

- **Input**: Use this field to enter the text that you want to remove whitespace from. You can enter either a static value, a dynamic value from previous steps, or a combination of both to specify the **Input** value. Although this is not a required field, the formatter function will not return a result if there is no value.

An example of where the whitespace is before the word pear is shown in the following screenshot:

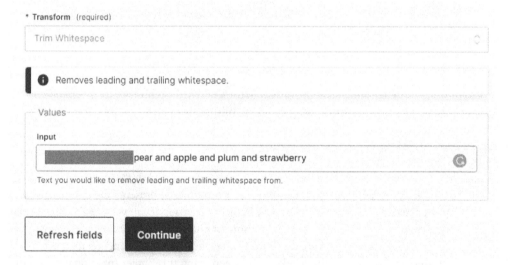

Figure 16.19 – Using the Formatter by Zapier Text action event to trim whitespace

Click on the **Continue** button. You can then use the **Test** section to test this step to return a value without leading and trailing whitespace. The result from the scenario in *Figure 16.19* is shown in the following screenshot:

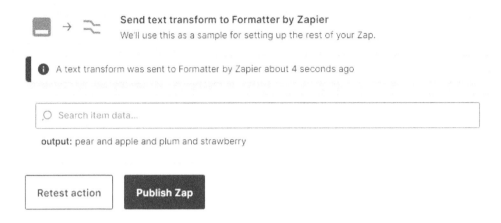

Figure 16.20 – An example of the value that's returned when
using the Text action event to trim whitespace

Proceed to add one or more action steps after your **Text** action step.

You should now have a better understanding of how to use the **Trim Whitespace** transform function.

Summary

In this chapter, we continued to focus on the versatile Formatter by Zapier built-in app and the extensive functionality available to format text. First, we covered how to use Zapier to transform text values in general. Next, we explored capitalizing text, applying title case, uppercase, and lowercase, and pluralizing words. Lastly, we explored finding the position of and replacing text, counting characters and words, truncating text, and removing whitespace.

You now know how to use the Formatter by Zapier built-in app to transform text values in several different ways, including capitalizing, applying title case, uppercase, and lowercase, pluralizing words, finding the position of and replacing text, counting characters and words, and removing whitespace.

In the next chapter, you will continue to learn how to use more functionality of the Formatter by Zapier built-in app to format text. We will explore how to create a superhero name, split text into segments, truncate text, transform text with a spreadsheet-style formula, and extract patterns, URLs, phone numbers, numbers, and email addresses. We will also briefly discuss the more advanced functions to convert HTML into Markdown and vice versa, convert text into ASCII, encode and decode URLs, use default values, and remove HTML tags.

Questions

1. What action does the **Capitalize** transform option of the **Text** action event in the Formatter by Zapier built-in app perform?

2. Which transform option of Formatter by Zapier's **Text** action event would be best to use when you need to check the number of characters in a string of text?

17

Text Formatting Functions in Zapier – Part 2

In *Chapter 16, Text Formatting Functions in Zapier – Part 1*, we introduced several of the Formatter by Zapier built-in app text transform options. In this chapter, we will continue to discuss the functionality that Zapier has available to format text.

First, we will explore how to create a superhero name, split text into segments, and truncate text. Then, we will cover how to remove HTML to leave plain text, how to assign a default value, and how to transform text with a spreadsheet-style formula. After that, we will discuss the possibilities of how to extract email addresses, numbers, URLs, and phone numbers from blocks of text. Lastly, we will briefly discuss the more advanced functions of how to extract patterns, convert HTML into Markdown and vice versa, convert text into ASCII, and finally, encode and decode URLs.

We will cover the following key topics in this chapter:

- Converting a name into the name of a superhero
- Splitting characters or words into segments
- Truncating text to a specified character length
- Removing HTML tags to leave plain text
- Assigning a default value
- Transforming text with a spreadsheet-style formula
- Extracting data from blocks of text
- Advanced text formatting features

> **Tip**
> You can use the magic AI to ask Zapier to format data in your Zap steps, which will then create Formatter by Zapier steps with the relevant transform options. We will discuss this in *Chapter 19, AI and Automation.*

Once you have worked through each of these topics, you will have a better understanding of the different text-transforming functions available for use with the Formatter by Zapier built-in app. You will know how to use Zapier to adjust text so that it's in various formats.

Technical requirements

To make the most of the content in this chapter, you will need access to a Zapier account. The Zapier Starter plan will be required for you to create multi-step workflows using the Formatter by Zapier built-in app.

Converting a name into the name of a superhero

So far in this book, we've covered plenty of useful, although quite formal, formatting functions that can be used for various business cases. Zapier is not all just about being formal. Sometimes, you might want to have a bit of fun and be playful with text formatting. Zapier can convert any name or a short string of text into a randomly chosen name of a superhero by using the Formatter by Zapier **Text** action event with the **Superhero Name** transform function. For example, if the name that you wanted to convert was `Kelly Goss`, the transformed text might be `Space Fury`. This text transform function is great to use when you want to do something fun and outside of the norm with your data.

Here are a few examples of when you can use this transform option:

- You might want new subscribers to be randomly assigned superhero names that you will address them by in your email communications. So, when `John Smith` signs up for your email newsletter in **Autopilot**, you can refer to him in the future as `Scarlet Flame`.

- You might like to have a bit of fun with your staff and decide to assign all new staff members superhero names when they are added as users to Asana. You could then send them an email to welcome them to the Asana team and let them know their new superhero name.

Next, let's review how to set up an action step with the **Superhero Name** transform option.

Setting up the Text action event with the Superhero Name transform option

Use the **Text** action event once you have set up your trigger step.

Once you have added an action step either by selecting the **Action** step or clicking on the + icon and chosen **Formatter by Zapier** as the app and **Text** as the action event, you can edit the fields in the **Action** section, as follows:

- **Transform**: From the drop-down menu, select the **Superhero Name** option. This is a required field and must have a value for the Zap to run.

- **Input**: Use this field to enter the text of the name or word string that you want to transform into a superhero name. You can either enter a static value, a dynamic value from previous steps, or a combination of both to specify the **Input** value. Although this is not a required field, the formatter function will not return a result if there is no value.

An example is shown in the following screenshot:

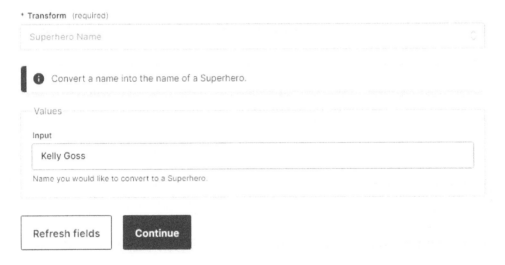

Figure 17.1 – Using the Formatter by Zapier Text action event to transform words into a superhero name

Click on the **Continue** button. You can then use the **Test** section to test this step to generate the superhero name. The result from the scenario in *Figure 17.1* is shown in the following screenshot:

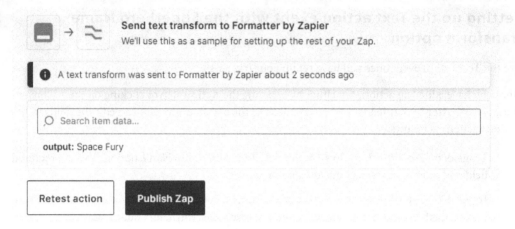

Figure 17.2 – An example of the altered value when using the Text
action event to convert words into a superhero name

Proceed to add one or more action steps after your **Text** action step.

You should now have a better understanding of how to use the **Superhero Name** transform function. Next, let's take a look at how to split characters or words into segments with the **Split Text** transform function.

Splitting characters or words into segments

Being able to manipulate text with a splitting function is possibly one of the most versatile functions of all the Formatter by Zapier text transform options. There will be many occasions where data is presented as a string of text and you will want to extract one or more words from that string to then use in other parts of your workflows. A common example of this is the need to use either the first or last name when only the full name is presented. You can use the Formatter by Zapier **Text** action event with the **Split Text** transform function to split the word string to return the two values.

You can use words or characters to split text, and the **Split Text** transform function allows you to split words or strings of words that are separated by special characters using special character syntax, as follows:

- **Space characters**: The [:space:] syntax is used to match space (\s) characters

- **Tab characters**: The [:tab:] syntax is used to match tab (\t) characters

- **Newline characters**: The [:newline:] syntax is used to match newline (\n) characters, which are those used to identify the end of a line of text or the start of a new line

- **Carriage-return characters**: The [:return:] syntax is used to match carriage-return (\r) characters, which are those that denote the start of the current line (at the left margin)

Here are a few examples of when you can use this transform option:

- When a new lead fills out a web form, you might have a field for them to enter their full name instead of separate fields for first and last name. If you wanted to use their first name only in an email or add their first and last name as individual fields to your CRM, you could use the **Split Text** transform function accordingly.

- You might use an e-sign app that does not integrate with Zapier but you receive an email confirmation once the document has been signed with the title of the document as the subject. Once that document has been signed, you might want to search for data in a row on a Google Sheets spreadsheet using the signee's company name, which you have strategically placed as the first word in the document's name. You can use the **Split Text** transform function to split out the first word in the string in the email subject.

Let's review how to set up an action step with the **Split Text** transform option.

Setting up the Text action event with the Split Text transform option

You can use the **Text** action event once you have set up your trigger step.

Once you have added an action step either by selecting the **Action** step or clicking on the + icon and chosen **Formatter by Zapier** as the app and **Text** as the action event, you can edit the fields in the **Action** section, as follows:

- **Transform**: From the drop-down menu, select the **Split Text** option. This is a required field and must have a value for the Zap to run.

- **Input**: Use this field to enter the string of text that you want to split. You can either enter a static value, a dynamic value from previous steps, or a combination of both to specify the **Input** value. Although this is not a required field, the formatter function will not return a result if there is no value.

- **Separator**: Use this field to enter the word, character, or syntax that you want to use as the splitting value from the **Input** field. You can either enter a static value, a dynamic value from previous steps, or a combination of both to specify this value. This field supports special character syntax. For example, to split text separated by spaces, you can use the [:space:] syntax. Although this is not a required field, if left blank, the default is the [:space:] syntax.

- **Segment Index**: Use this drop-down field to select which segment of split text you want to return. The options are **First**, **Second**, **Last**, **Second to Last**, **All (as Line-items)**, and **All (as Separate Fields)**. The values returned when using **All (as Line-items)** can be used in steps where line items are supported – for example, in invoicing apps. You can either enter a static value, a dynamic value from previous steps, or a combination of both to specify this value. Although this is not a required field, if left blank, the **First** index will be returned.

An example is shown in the following screenshot, where we want to extract all values as separate items that have been separated by spaces:

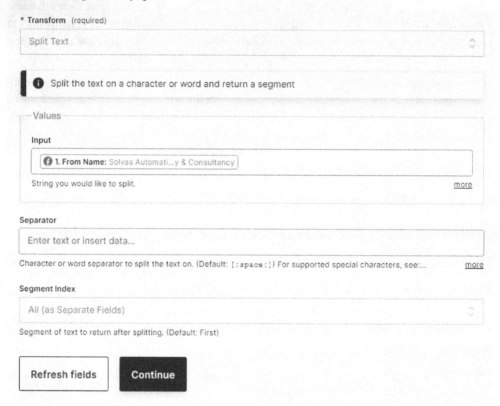

Figure 17.3 – Using the Formatter by Zapier Text action event to split text separated by spaces

Click on the **Continue** button. You can then use the **Test** section to test this step to split out text into a string of words. The result from the scenario in *Figure 17.3* is shown in the following screenshot:

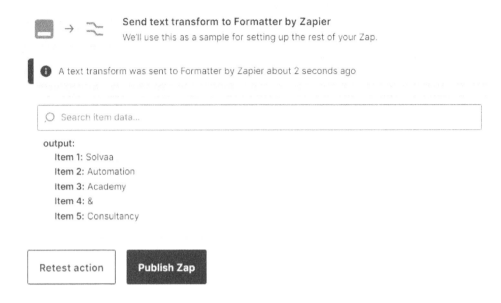

Figure 17.4 – An example of the altered value when using the Text
action event to split a string of text separated by spaces

Proceed to add one or more action steps after your **Text** action step.

You should now have a better understanding of how to use the **Split Text** transform function.

There is another similar transform function called **Split Text into Chunks for AI Prompts (beta)** that allows you to modify larger amounts of data into smaller fragments of **chunks** to use with AI apps. We will discuss this transform option in *Chapter 19, AI and Automation*.

Next, we'll discuss how to truncate text to a specified character length using the **Truncate** transform function.

Truncating text to a specified character length

There may be times when you want to reduce the character length of a block of text so that you can use it as a summary, or you might have restrictions on the number of characters. A typical example of this is when posting content on social media where you have a fixed character length, such as reposting a Facebook post (which could have over 60,000 characters) to Twitter, which has a maximum character length of 280. You can use the Formatter by Zapier **Text** action event with the **Truncate** transform function to reduce the number of characters in a block of text and optionally replace the last three characters with ....

Here are a few examples of when you can use this transform option:

- When you publish a new blog post on WordPress, you can truncate the blog post's content to produce a teaser summary suitable to use on social media

- When you post a new Facebook post, you can truncate it to a shorter character length and repost it on Twitter and LinkedIn

Let's review how to set up an action step with the **Truncate** transform option.

Setting up the Text action event with the Truncate transform option

You can use the **Text** action event once you have set up your trigger step.

Once you have added an action step either by selecting the **Action** step or clicking on the + icon and chosen **Formatter by Zapier** as the app and **Text** as the action event, you can edit the fields in the **Action** section, as follows:

- **Transform**: From the drop-down menu, select the **Truncate** option. This is a required field and must have a value for the Zap to run.

- **Input**: Use this field to enter the text that you want to truncate. You can either enter a static value, a dynamic value from previous steps, or a combination of both to specify the **Input** value. Although this is not a required field, the formatter function will not return a result if there is no value.

- **Max Length**: Use this number field to enter a number value for the maximum number of characters you want the word string to be truncated to. You can either enter a static value, a dynamic value from previous steps, or a combination of both to specify this value. This is a required field and must have a value for the Zap to run.

- **Skip Characters**: Use this number field to specify how many of the characters at the beginning of the input value you want to skip. For example, if the input began with `This is an example: Today's weather is hot and sunny.` and you wanted to truncate `This is an example:`, you would enter `19` to skip those characters. You can either enter a static value, a dynamic value from previous steps, or a combination of both to specify this value.

- **Append Ellipsis**: You can use this drop-down Boolean field to select **True** or **False** as to whether you want to shorten the text at the end by three characters and replace them with .... You can either use the dropdown or enter a static value, a dynamic value from previous steps, or a combination of both to specify this value.

An example is shown in the following screenshot, where we want to truncate a long Facebook post to 250 characters and append ellipses:

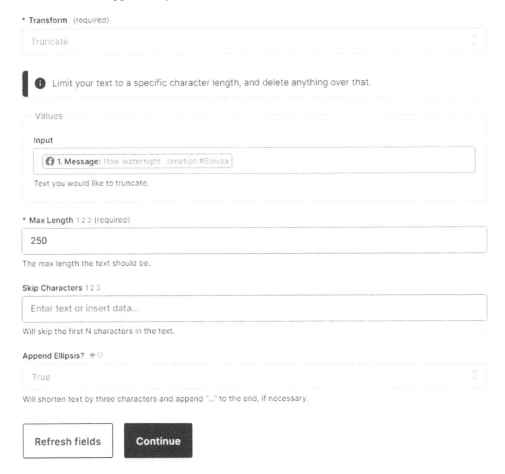

Figure 17.5 – Using the Formatter by Zapier Text action event to truncate text

Click on the **Continue** button. You can then use the **Test** section to test this step to truncate characters in a string of words. The result from the scenario in *Figure 17.5* is shown in the following screenshot:

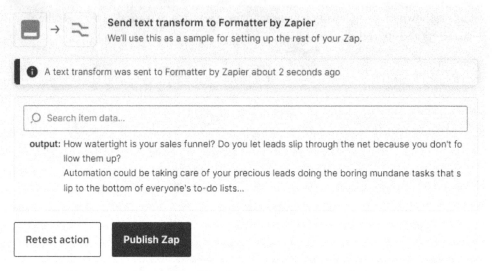

Figure 17.6 – An example of the altered value when using the Text action
event to truncate and append ellipses to a string of text

Proceed to add one or more action steps after your **Text** action step.

You should now have a better understanding of how to use the **Truncate** transform function. Next, let's cover how to remove HTML from blocks of text using the **Remove HTML Tags** transform function.

Removing HTML tags to leave plain text

As **HyperText Markup Language** (**HTML**) is used to customize the way data is displayed on the web, such as on websites, digital documents, and emails, there will be occasions when you will want to view just the plain text without any coding. You can use the Formatter by Zapier **Text** action event with the **Remove HTML Tags** transform function to achieve this by stripping out all the HTML coding to leave just the plain text behind.

Here are a few examples of when you can use this transform option:

- When you want to extract the body of an email, but the data is only presented in HTML

- When you publish a new blog post on WordPress, and you want to remove any HTML before posting a teaser summary on social media

Let's review how to set up an action step with the **Remove HTML Tags** transform option.

Setting up the Text action event with the Remove HTML Tags transform option

You can use the **Text** action event once you have set up your trigger step.

Once you have added an action step either by selecting the **Action** step or clicking on the + icon and chosen **Formatter by Zapier** as the app and **Text** as the action event, you can edit the fields in the **Action** section, as follows:

- **Transform**: From the drop-down menu, select the **Remove HTML Tags** option. This is a required field and must have a value for the Zap to run.

- **Input**: Use this field to enter the string of text that you want to remove the HTML tags from. You can either enter a static value, a dynamic value from previous steps, or a combination of both to specify the **Input** value. Although this is not a required field, the formatter function will not return a result if there is no value.

An example is shown in the following screenshot:

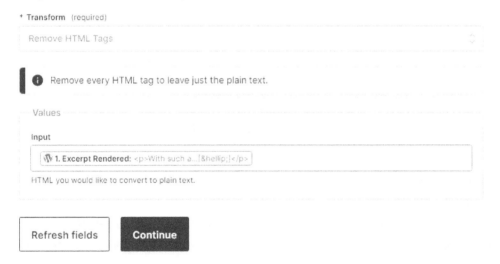

Figure 17.7 – Using the Formatter by Zapier Text action event to remove HTML from a block of text

Click on the **Continue** button. You can then use the **Test** section to test this step to remove HTML from a block of text. The result from the scenario in *Figure 17.7* is shown in the following screenshot:

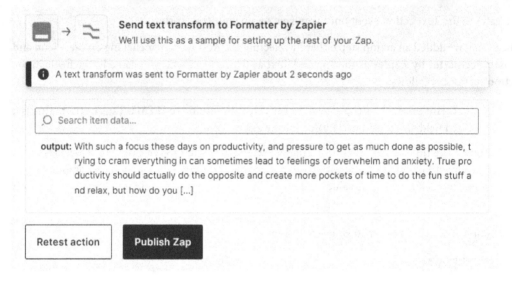

Figure 17.8 – An example of the altered value when using the Text action event to remove HTML

Proceed to add one or more action steps after your **Text** action step.

You should now have a better understanding of how to use the **Remove HTML Tags** transform function. Next, let's cover how to assign a default value.

Assigning a default value

You might encounter situations where data has not been entered for whatever reason, therefore leaving a field blank. In some cases, this lack of data may cause problems later in your workflow. To prevent such problems, you might want to conditionally assign a value that acts as the default where data might be missing from a specific field. You can use the Formatter by Zapier **Text** action event with the **Default Value** transform function to achieve this by assigning a default value when a field contains no data.

Here are a few examples of when you can use this transform option:

- When new deals are created in Zoho CRM, but an owner has not been assigned, you may want to automatically assign these deals to a specific user who can then reassign the deal to a member of the team

- When new cards are created in Trello but members have not been assigned, you may want to automatically assign these cards to a manager who then assigns the card to someone in the team

Let's review how to set up an action step with the **Default Value** transform option.

Setting up the Text action event with the Default Value transform option

Use the **Text** action event once you have set up your trigger step.

Once you have added an action step either by selecting the **Action** step or clicking on the + icon and chosen **Formatter by Zapier** as the app and **Text** as the action event, you can edit the fields in the **Action** section, as follows:

- **Transform**: From the drop-down menu, select the **Default Value** option. This is a required field and must have a value for the Zap to run.

- **Input**: Use this field to enter the text that you want to truncate. You can either enter a static value, a dynamic value from previous steps, or a combination of both to specify the **Input** value. If a line-item value is entered, a line-item field will be returned. Although this is not a required field, the formatter function will not return a result if there is no value.

- **Default Value**: Use this field to enter the default value to use if the data in the **Input** field is blank. You can either enter a static value, a dynamic value from previous steps, or a combination of both to specify **Default Value**. This field supports the `[:space:]`, `[:tab:]`, `[:newline:]`, and `[:return:]` special character syntaxes. This is a required field and must have a value for the Zap to run.

An example is shown in the following screenshot, where if a new Trello card does not have a member assigned, a senior staff member will be assigned in later steps by using their user ID in the **Default Value** field:

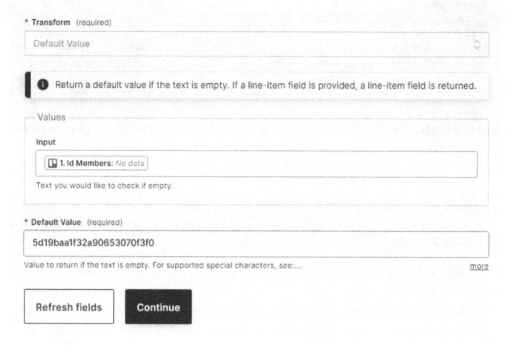

Figure 17.9 – Using the Formatter by Zapier Text action event to assign a default value

Click on the **Continue** button. You can then use the **Test** section to test this step to assign a default value if a text field is empty. The result from the scenario in *Figure 17.9* is shown in the following screenshot:

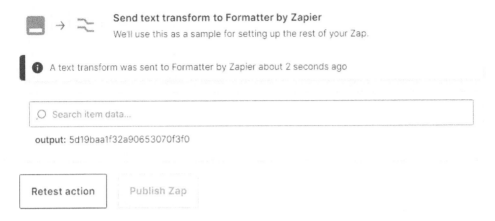

Figure 17.10 – An example of the altered value when using the Text action event to assign a default value

Proceed to add one or more action steps after your **Text** action step.

You should now have a better understanding of how to use the **Default Value** transform function. Next, let's cover how to transform text using a spreadsheet-style formula with the **Spreadsheet-Style Formula** transform function.

Transforming text with a spreadsheet-style formula

In *Chapter 15, Formatting Numbers*, we explored how to use the Formatter by Zapier **Numbers** action event and the **Spreadsheet-Style Formula** transform option to do complex calculations with numbers. You can use the Formatter by Zapier **Text** action event and the **Spreadsheet-Style Formula** transform option to do the same with text.

An example of this situation would be when you want to use complex IF, AND, or OR conditions – for example, if two text values match then output one result, otherwise output another. In this case, you could use IF("value1"="value2", "same", "different").

> **Important note**
> When using text strings with this transform option, you must use quotation marks around the string, as shown in the preceding example.

Let's review how to set up the **Spreadsheet-Style Formula** transform option.

Setting up the Text action event with the Spreadsheet-Style Formula transform option

You can use the **Text** action event once you have set up your trigger step.

Once you have added an action step either by selecting the **Action** step or clicking on the + icon, and chosen **Formatter by Zapier** as the app and **Text** as the action event, you can edit the fields in the **Action** section, as follows:

- **Transform**: From the drop-down menu, select the **Spreadsheet-Style Formula** option. This is a required field and must have a value for the Zap to run.

- **Formula**: Use this field to specify the formula with the text values that you want to use. Add static values for the formula and text values, or dynamic values mapped from previous steps under the **Custom** tab. This is a required field and must have a value for the Zap to run.

Zapier has created a handy reference document with various formulas that can be used with Formatter by Zapier, which you can refer to at `https://zapier.com/help/create/format/understand-spreadsheet-style-formula-functions`.

An example is shown in the following screenshot:

Figure 17.11 – Using the Formatter by Zapier Text action event to perform a spreadsheet-style operation

Click on the **Continue** button. You can then use the **Test** section to test this step to generate the output. The result from the scenario in *Figure 17.11* is shown in the following screenshot:

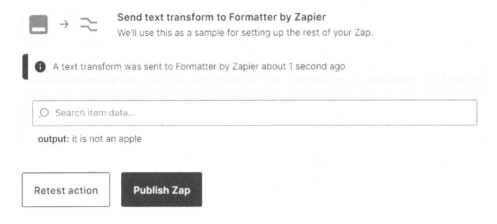

Figure 17.12 – An example of the output value when using the Text
action event to perform spreadsheet-style operations

Proceed to add one or more action steps after your **Text** action step.

You should now have a better understanding of how to use the **Spreadsheet-Style Formula** transform function. Next, let's cover how to extract email addresses, numbers, URLs, and phone numbers from blocks of text using the **Extract** transform functions.

Extracting data from blocks of text

Another brilliant feature of the Formatter by Zapier's **Text** action is its ability to extract data from blocks of text. This is especially useful if you have large strings of text and you want to return the first expressed value of an email address, number, phone number, or URL.

For example, your web form may not integrate with Zapier, but you receive a confirmation email with the submission details. The form asks the person submitting to add three email addresses, and you only want to extract the first email address entered. Alternatively, you may want to retrieve a phone number, URL, or number from this web form submission. You can use the Formatter by Zapier **Text** action event with the following transform functions to achieve this:

- **Extract Email Address**
- **Extract Number**
- **Extract URL**
- **Extract Phone Number**

To illustrate how to use each of these transform functions, we will use the trigger data highlighted in the following screenshot:

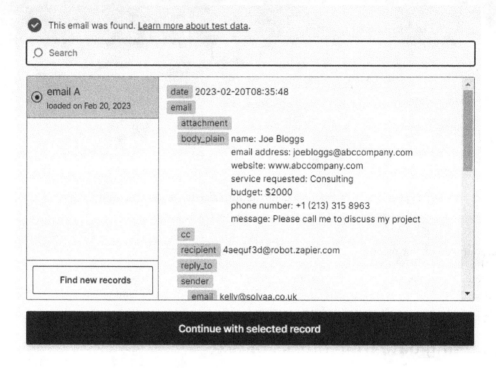

Figure 17.13 – Trigger data that will be used to illustrate extracting data from blocks of text

Now, let's dive into each of these transform functions in turn.

Extracting an email address from a block of text

When using the **Extract Email Address** transform function, the formatter will search for a string of letters, numbers, and certain symbols commonly used in email addresses, such as a plus sign, period, or dashes, that precede an @ symbol and a site domain name, such as `solvaa.co.uk` – for example, `joe-bloggs1@abccompany.com`. It will not recognize disjunct email address strings with spaces, such as `Joe Bloggs at abccompany dot com`.

Let's review how to set up an action step with the **Extract Email Address** transform option.

Extracting data from blocks of text

Setting up the Text action event with the Extract Email Address transform option

You can use the **Text** action event once you have set up your trigger step.

Once you have added an action step either by selecting the **Action** step or clicking on the + icon and chosen **Formatter by Zapier** as the app and **Text** as the action event, you can edit the fields in the **Action** section, as follows:

- **Transform**: From the drop-down menu, select the **Extract Email Address** option. This is a required field and must have a value for the Zap to run.

- **Input**: You can use this field to enter some text to extract the first email address from a block of text. You can either enter a static value, a dynamic value from previous steps, or a combination of both to specify the **Input** value. Although this is not a required field, the formatter function will not return a result if there is no value.

An example is shown in the following screenshot:

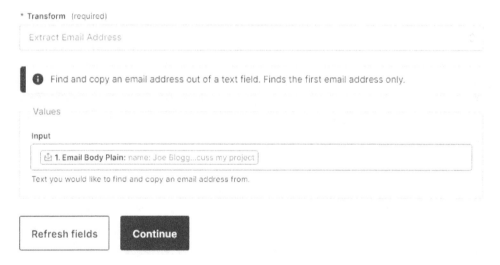

Figure 17.14 – Using the Formatter by Zapier Text action event
to extract an email address from a block of text

Click on the **Continue** button. You can then use the **Test** section to test this step to extract an email address from a block of text. The result of the scenario in *Figure 17.14* is shown in the following screenshot:

Proceed to add one or more action steps after your **Text** action step.

Next, let's discuss how to extract numbers from blocks of text using the **Extract Number** transform function.

Extracting numbers from blocks of text

When using the **Extract Number** transform function, the formatter will search for a single digit or a string of numbers in one row. The numbers in a string can be separated by a period as a decimal separator or one or more commas to indicate groupings of digits. Number strings separated by spaces and symbols such as dashes are not recognized in full; only the first number of a set of numbers in the string would be recognized. For example, if you wanted to extract the entire string of numbers, an acceptable string would be 1,758,000.82, whereas 1-758-000-82 would only extract the first number before the first dash. In other words, only 1 would be extracted. Let's review how to set up an action step with the **Extract Number** transform option.

Setting up the Text action event with the Extract Number transform option

You can use the **Text** action event once you have set up your trigger step.

Once you have added an action step either by selecting the **Action** step or clicking on the + icon and chosen **Formatter by Zapier** as the app and **Text** as the action event, you can edit the fields in the **Action** section, as follows:

- **Transform**: From the drop-down menu, select the **Extract Number** option. This is a required field and must have a value for the Zap to run.

- **Input**: Use this field to enter the block of text containing the number that you want to extract. You can either enter a static value, a dynamic value from previous steps, or a combination of both to specify the **Input** value. Although this is not a required field, the formatter function will not return a result if there is no value.

An example is shown in the following screenshot:

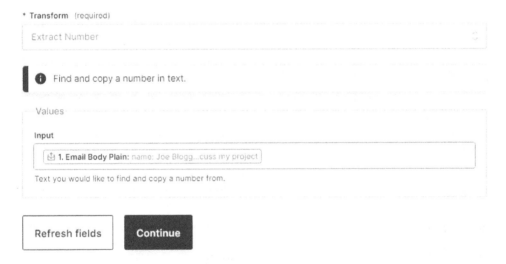

Figure 17.16 – Using the Formatter by Zapier Text action event to extract a number from a block of text

Click on the **Continue** button. You can then use the **Test** section to test this step to extract a number from a block of text. The result from the scenario in *Figure 17.16* is shown in the following screenshot:

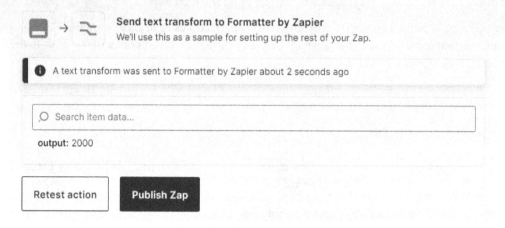

Figure 17.17 – An example of the returned value when using the Text
action event to extract a number from a block of text

Proceed to add one or more action steps after your **Text** action step.

> **Important note**
> From the trigger data shown in *Figure 17.13*, if the phone number was displayed first, the value that would be returned from the phone number would be 1.

Next, let's explore how to extract URLs from blocks of text using the **Extract URL** transform function.

Extracting URLs from blocks of text

When using the **Extract URL** transform function, the formatter will search for a string of letters, numbers, and dashes followed by a period and then a recognized **top-level domain** (**TLD**) name, such as one ending in .com, .org, .co.uk, or .com.au. You can find out more about TLDs here: https://en.wikipedia.org/wiki/Top-level_domain. The formatter also recognizes the https:// and http:// prefixes, as well as subdomains, folders, and query parameters. Therefore, an accepted string example would be https://solvaa.co.uk/?s=zapier. It will not recognize disjunct URL strings with spaces, such as solvaa dot com.

Now, let's review how to set up an action step with the **Extract URL** transform option.

Setting up the Text action event with the Extract URL transform option

You can use the **Text** action event once you have set up your trigger step.

Once you have added an action step either by selecting the **Action** step or clicking on the + icon and chosen **Formatter by Zapier** as the app and **Text** as the action event, you can edit the fields in the **Action** section, as follows:

- **Transform**: From the drop-down menu, select the **Extract URL** option. This is a required field and must have a value for the Zap to run.

- **Input**: Use this field to enter the block of text containing the URL that you want to extract. You can either enter a static value, a dynamic value from previous steps, or a combination of both to specify the **Input** value. Although this is not a required field, the formatter function will not return a result if there is no value.

An example is shown in the following screenshot:

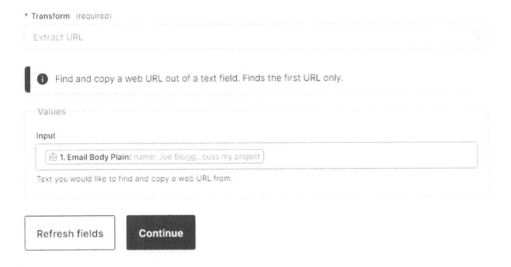

Figure 17.18 – Using the Formatter by Zapier Text action event to extract a URL from a block of text

Click on the **Continue** button. You can then use the **Action** section to test this step to extract a URL from a block of text. The result from the scenario in *Figure 17.18* is shown in the following screenshot:

Figure 17.19 – An example of the returned value when using the
Text action event to extract a URL from a block of text

Proceed to add one or more action steps after your **Text** action step.

Next, let's take a look at how to extract phone numbers from blocks of text using the **Extract Phone Number** transform function.

Extracting phone numbers from blocks of text

When using the **Extract Phone Number** transform function, the formatter will search a 10-digit phone number in groupings of 3-3-4 digits or 4-3-3 digits with or without a country code or extension number. The numbers can be separated by hyphens, periods, or spaces. Area codes in parentheses are recognized. Extension numbers are recognized when a number follows x, ext, or extension. For example, an acceptable phone number string would be +44 (758) 592-0332.

Now, let's review how to set up an action step with the **Extract Phone Number** transform option.

Setting up the Text action event with the Extract Phone Number transform option

You can use the **Text** action event once you have set up your trigger step.

Once you have added an action step either by selecting the **Action** step or clicking on the + icon and chosen **Formatter by Zapier** as the app and **Text** as the action event, you can edit the fields in the **Action** section, as follows:

- **Transform**: From the drop-down menu, select the **Extract Phone Number** option. This is a required field and must have a value for the Zap to run.

- **Input**: Use this field to enter the block of text containing the phone number that you want to extract. You can either enter a static value, a dynamic value from previous steps, or a combination of both to specify the **Input** value. Although this is not a required field, the formatter function will not return a result if there is no value.

- **Phone Number Format**: Use this drop-down field to select which phone number format you want to use for the search. The options are **North American Number Plan (NANP) e.g. (123) 456-7890, International e.g. (12) 34-56-78-90, Universal 1 (includes NANP and some International)**, and **Universal 2 (includes NANP and some International)**. The default that's used in searches is **Universal 1 (includes NANP and some International)**, which will recognize most NANP and international numbers. Choose one of the other options for more specific searches if this proves unreliable.

An example is shown in the following screenshot:

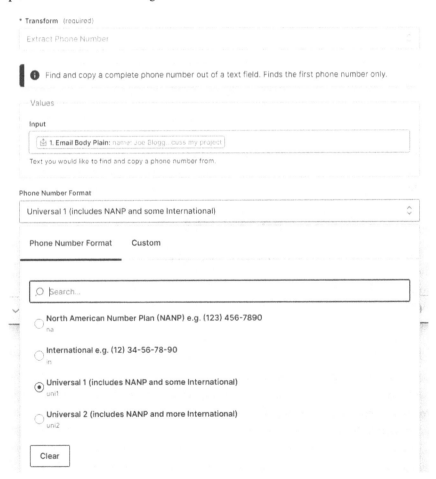

Figure 17.20 – Using the Formatter by Zapier Text action event to extract a number from a block of text

Click on the **Continue** button. You can then use the **Test** section to test this step to extract a phone number in Universal 1 format from a block of text. The result from the scenario in *Figure 17.20* is shown in the following screenshot:

Figure 17.21 – An example of the returned value when using the Text
action event to extract a number from a block of text

Proceed to add one or more action steps after your **Text** action step.

You should now have a better understanding of how to extract data from blocks of text using the **Extract Email Address**, **Extract Number**, **Extract URL**, and **Extract Phone Number** transform functions. Next, let's review the advanced text formatting features that Zapier has to offer.

Advanced text formatting features

As you have learned so far, the Formatter by Zapier built-in app allows you to manipulate text in many versatile ways without having any knowledge of coding or any technical background whatsoever. There are, however, a few transform functions that allow you to manipulate text using programming languages. As these are advanced topics, we will only provide a brief overview of their functionality, without going into too much detail.

The following transform options can be used to manipulate text with programming languages:

- **Extract Pattern**: You can use this transform option when you need to extract partial data from a field with more specificity than the other **Extract** transform options we have covered. This allows you to use Python **regular expressions (regexes)**. You can find out more about Python regexes here: https://developers.google.com/edu/python/regular-expressions.

- **Convert HTML to Markdown**: You can use this transform option when you want to convert HTML into **Markdown**, a markup language used to add formatting elements to plain text. You can find out more about Markdown here: `https://en.wikipedia.org/wiki/Markdown`.

- **Convert Markdown to HTML**: You can use this transform option to do the reverse of the preceding, converting Markdown into HTML.

- **Convert to ASCII**: You can use this transform option when you want to convert plain text into **American Standard Code for Information Interchange** (**ASCII**). You can find out more about ASCII here: `https://en.wikipedia.org/wiki/ASCII`.

- **URL Encode**: You can use this transform option when you want to encode non-approved characters such as spaces to **Uniform Resource Identifier** (**URI**) approved characters. You can find out more about **URL encoding** here: `https://en.wikipedia.org/wiki/URL_encoding`.

- **URL Decode**: You can use this transform option to do the reverse of the preceding and decode URI-approved characters to non-approved characters.

You should now have a better understanding of how to use the various advanced text formatting features of the Formatter by Zapier built-in app.

Summary

In this chapter, we continued to focus on the versatile Formatter by Zapier built-in app and the extensive functionality available to format text. First, we explored how to create a superhero name, split text into segments, truncate text, remove HTML, and use a default value. Then, we covered how to extract data from text – specifically, how to extract URLs, phone numbers, numbers, and email addresses. Lastly, we briefly discussed the more advanced functions for extracting patterns, converting Markdown into HTML and vice versa, converting text into ASCII, and encoding or decoding URLs.

In the next chapter, you will learn how to use the **Utilities** functions within the Formatter built-in app. We will cover line item creation and customization, converting text into line items and vice versa, using lookup tables and picklists, and importing CSV files.

Questions

1. Which transform option of the Formatter by Zapier built-in app could you use if you wanted to separate the full name of a person into first name and last name presented as two values?

2. When might you want to use the **Truncate** transform option of the **Text** action event of Formatter by Zapier?

18
Zapier's Utilities Functions

So far, we have discussed using the Formatter by Zapier built-in app to perform a variety of actions to transform dates and times, numbers, and text. There are a few other helpful transform functions we have not yet explored, and these are categorized under the **Utilities** action event. In this chapter, we'll conclude our exploration of the features of the Formatter by Zapier built-in app by covering the functionality of the **Utilities** action event.

First, we will provide an overview of the Formatter by Zapier **Utilities** action event and the transform functions available. Then, we will cover how to import data from CSV files and use them in our Zaps, how to use lookup tables to store and help us find related data, and how to pick data from a list of values based on its position in the list. Finally, we will introduce line items and explore the various transform functions related to using line items in your automations. This will include converting text into line items and vice versa, as well as line-item creation and customization.

We will cover the following key topics in this chapter:

- Introducing the Formatter by Zapier **Utilities** action event
- Importing data from CSV files
- Using lookup tables for related data
- Picking data from a list
- Manipulating line items

Once you have worked through each of these topics, you will have a better understanding of the different **Utilities** transform functions that you can use with the Formatter by Zapier built-in app. You will know how to use Zapier to import data from CSV files, use lookup tables, pick data from a list, and work with line items.

Technical requirements

To make the most of the content in this chapter, you will need access to a Zapier account. The Zapier Starter plan will be required for you to create multi-step workflows using the Formatter by Zapier built-in app.

Introducing the Formatter by Zapier Utilities action event

As we have discovered so far, Formatter by Zapier can easily be used to transform a wide range of values from one format into another. We have explored how to manipulate dates and times, numbers, and text into different formats. You might want to upload data from CSV files to use in your automations, find related data such as user IDs linked to a user's email address, select a value in a specific position in a list such as the first or last, or you might need to manipulate data in the form of line items, which are commonly used in invoicing and e-commerce apps. To account for these requirements, Zapier has created a grouping of these functions in the Formatter by Zapier built-in app, which is available by using the **Utilities** action event.

When using this action event, you can use the following **Utilities** transform options. These can be found within the **Action** section of your action step, listed in the **Transform** drop-down menu:

- **Import CSV File**
- **Line Itemizer (Create/Append/Prepend)**
- **Line-item to Text**
- **Lookup Table**
- **Pick from List**
- **Text to Line-Item**

We will review each of these functions in turn.

> **Tip**
> You can use the magic AI to ask Zapier to format data in your Zap steps, which will then create Formatter by Zapier steps with the relevant transform options. We will discuss this is *Chapter 19, AI and Automation*.

Let's start by exploring how to import CSV files using the **Import CSV File** transform option.

Importing data from CSV files

Wouldn't it be handy to be able to automatically extract data from spreadsheet files so that you could use it in your Zaps? Well, Zapier allows you to do this. For example, you might receive a summary of the day's transactions in a CSV file by email, and you want to pull this data straight into your accounting software. Zapier can help you extract data from a CSV file and present it in a string of text and as line items by using the Formatter by Zapier **Utilities** action event with the **Import CSV File** transform function.

Here are a few examples of when you can use this transform option:

- You might use an Excel spreadsheet to record details of sales and associated lead-to-sales conversion times. A CSV copy of this is forwarded to you by email every day at 5 P.M. from your CRM; normally, you would have to extract the data you want and manually share it with your team. You could extract that data from that CSV using the **Import CSV File** transform function and forward the most important parts of the day's data to your Slack channel for your sales team to see.

- You might have access to a report file (via a publicly accessible URL) that allows you to download the data in the form of a CSV. The report file provides you with information about your daily sales transactions from your till system. The file clears all data and refreshes at midnight. Using the **Import CSV File** transform function, you could extract the data in the CSV and automatically create invoices in your accounting system daily (with a Schedule by Zapier trigger).

In *Chapter 3, Building Your First Automated Workflow (Zap)*, we introduced and discussed file field types. The principles aligned with these field types and what is accepted by them apply to the **Import CSV File** transform option's input. Essentially, the Formatter by Zapier built-in app can only import a CSV file object from an app, such as when it is an attachment in a Gmail email, or from a publicly accessible URL that points to a CSV file such as a Microsoft Excel or Smartsheet sheet. The **File** field also accepts text that would be converted into a `.txt` file.

Next, let's review how to set up an action step with the **Import CSV File** transform option.

Setting up the Utilities action event with the Import CSV File transform option

To illustrate how to use each of the **Import CSV File** transform functions, we will use the example of receiving a CSV file by email with sales for the day. The following screenshot shows an example of a CSV file that contains data:

◢	A	B	C
1	**Fruit**	**Quantity**	**Cost**
2	Apples	1	0.5
3	Bananas	4	0.7
4	Pears	12	0.6

Figure 18.1 – Data in a CSV file that will be used to illustrate using the Import CSV File transform function

You can use the **Utilities** action event once you have set up your trigger step.

Once you have added an action step, either by selecting the **Action** step or clicking on the + icon, and have chosen **Formatter by Zapier** as the app and **Utilities** as the action event, you can edit the fields in the **Action** section, as follows:

- **Transform**: From the drop-down menu, select the **Import CSV File** option. This is a required field and must have a value for the Zap to run.

- **CSV File**: You can use this field to map the CSV file you want to extract data from. This is a **File** field type and will require a URL or an actual file object from a previous step to be mapped to this field. You can enter a dynamic value from previous steps to specify the file to use. In our example, we will use the attachment value from our email trigger step. This is a required field and must have a value for the Zap to run.

- **Force First Row As Header Row**: You can use this drop-down Boolean field to select either **Yes** or **No** as to whether you want to force the formatter to recognize the first row as a header row. By default, it will try to determine whether a header row exists. When testing, if it has not detected the header row, you can force it by selecting the **Yes** option.

- **Type Of CSV File**: You can use this drop-down field to select the type of CSV file. The options are **Detect Automatically**, **Comma Delimited**, **Semicolon Delimited**, **Excel Comma Delimited**, **Excel Tab Delimited**, **One Column**, and **Text File (no csv parsing)**. By default, the Formatter will attempt to detect the type of file. When testing, if it has not detected the file type, you can force it to by selecting the appropriate file option. You can also map this field with dynamic data from a previous step where the type is file is known.

- **Encoding of CSV file**: You can use this drop-down field to select the type of encoding. The options are **UTF-8**, **Latin-1**, and **UTF-16**. By default, the Formatter will assume that the file is UTF-8 encoded. If you find that you get an error when testing the action step, you can specify the encoding type by selecting the relevant option. You can use the **Custom** option to add other encoding options. Supported options can be found using this reference: `https://docs.python.org/3/library/codecs.html#standard-encodings`.

Data imports are limited to around 150 KB, which is the equivalent of approximately 1,000 rows, which might cause some limitations for some users.

An example is shown in the following screenshot:

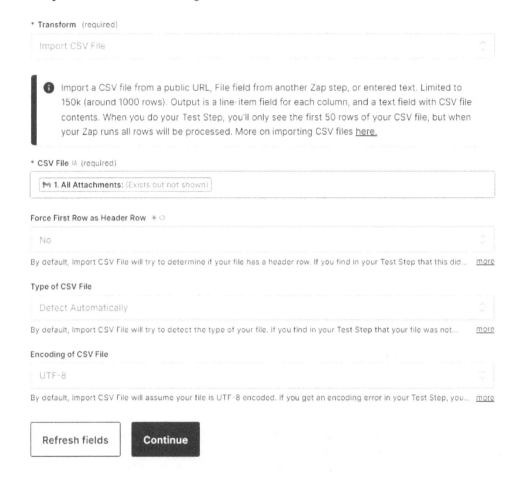

Figure 18.2 – Overview of using the Formatter by Zapier Utilities
action event to import data from a CSV file

Click on the **Continue** button. You can then use the **Test** section to test this step to extract the data from the CSV file. The result from the scenario in *Figure 18.2* is shown in the following screenshot:

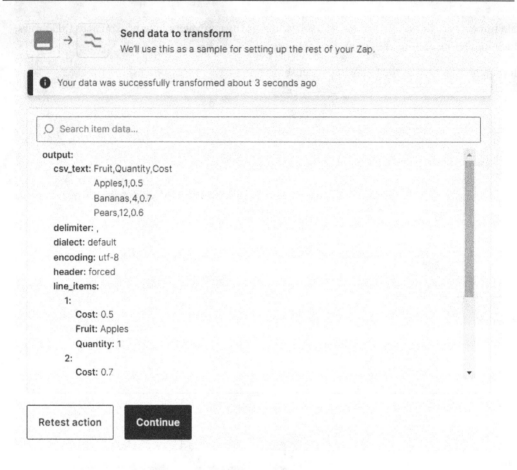

Figure 18.3 – Overview of the extracted data when using the Utilities action event to import a CSV file

Proceed to add one or more action steps after your **Utilities** action step. You can either use the text field presented in the csv_text output or the line items presented in the line_items output (specifically for apps that support line items) or both. We will discuss line items in more detail in the *Manipulating line items* section.

> **Important note**
>
> When testing your action step, bear in mind that you will only see a limited number of rows (normally 50) of your CSV file. However, when your Zap runs in real time, all the data in the file will be processed.

You should now have a better understanding of how to import CSV files using the **Import CSV File** transform function.

Next, let's explore how to use lookup tables to store and help us find related data using the **Lookup Table** transform function.

Using lookup tables for related data

The more you work with Zapier to connect your apps and automate your processes, the more you will find that commonly used key values in your various apps are represented differently. For example, if you sell online courses, passing data between your shopping cart, **ThriveCart**, and your course platform, **Kajabi**, could be a challenge as products are recorded with different IDs in each of the systems. This is where the Formatter by Zapier **Utilities** action event and the **Lookup Table** transform function are useful. You can use this transform function to store related search keys and matching result data, such as product names and their respective IDs, so that you can use them in other steps in your workflows. Microsoft Excel users are likely to be quite familiar with this type of functionality, which is comparable to the VLOOKUP function. Bear in mind that the main difference to consider is that in Microsoft Excel, this function is case-insensitive, whereas in Zapier, it is case-sensitive.

Here are a couple of examples of when you can use this transform option:

- Let's say that when a deal or opportunity hits a certain stage in your pipeline in your CRM, you want to assign a card to the deal owner in your task management app. In this case, your users have different identifiers in your CRM to your task management app. For example, your sales manager, John, might be identified by name as John Smith in Pipedrive and J A Smith in Trello. Users are also identified by unique IDs in most systems, so in this case, John has a user ID of 125869 in Pipedrive and a user ID of 51f8a8cd179ff019a67e95312 in Trello. We can assign John as the member to the card using his Trello user ID. Therefore, we can use a lookup table in the Formatter by Zapier **Utilities** action event to list all the Pipedrive usernames and the Trello user IDs of the users for who we might need this data. We would then use the username in Pipedrive as the search key to return the user ID for Trello.

- You might use a scheduling and appointment booking app such as **Acuity Scheduling** and need to pass your sales data to your accounting app, QuickBooks Online. As the names and IDs of the products are different in the two systems, you can use a lookup table in the Formatter by Zapier **Utilities** action event to record the search data you need. You can record the **Acuity Scheduling** product name as the search key and the QuickBooks Online product ID as a value to be returned.

Next, let's review how to set up an action step with the **Lookup Table** transform option.

Setting up the Utilities action event with the Lookup Table transform option

You can use the **Utilities** action event once you have set up your trigger step.

Once you have added an action step, either by selecting the **Action** step or clicking on the + icon, and have chosen **Formatter by Zapier** as the app and **Utilities** as the action event, you can edit the fields in the **Action** section, as follows:

- **Transform**: From the drop-down menu, select the **Lookup Table** option. This is a required field and must have a value for the Zap to run.

- **Lookup Key**: You can use this field to map the search key value of the data you want to search for in the lookup table. You can either enter a static value, a dynamic value from previous steps, or a combination of both to specify this value. This field supports line items, which means that if dynamic data from a previous step is mapped to this field and the data is in the form of line-item arrays, the result of the lookup will produce multiple values, one for each of the line-item array keys. Although this is not a required field, the formatter function will not return a result if there is no value.

- **Lookup Table**: This table is comprised of two columns. In the left column, you can enter the data you want to use as the search reference. This is the data that Zapier will use to match against the search value in **Lookup Key** – for example, the username. This column only accepts static text being entered. It is also case-sensitive and will only return an exact match with the **Lookup Key** value. In the right column, you can enter the data that you want to be returned from the search – for example, the corresponding user ID. You can either enter a static value, a dynamic value from previous steps, or a combination of both to specify the value in this column.

- **Fallback Value**: Here, you can enter a default value to use if the **Lookup Key** value does not match any of the search reference data in the left column. This is especially useful if the **Lookup Key** value is empty.

An example is shown in the following screenshot:

Figure 18.4 – Overview of using the Formatter by Zapier Utilities
action event to find related data in a lookup table

Click on the **Continue** button. You can then use the **Test** section to find reference data in a lookup table. The result from the scenario in *Figure 18.4* is shown in the following screenshot:

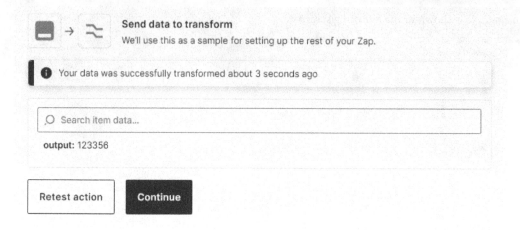

Figure 18.5 – Overview of the matching data retrieved from the
lookup table when using the Utilities action event

Proceed to add one or more action steps after your **Utilities** action step.

> **Tip**
> Although there is only one field for **Lookup Key**, you can retrieve and find multiple values
> from **Lookup Table** if your search key is in line-item format. You can also have multiple steps
> using this function in one Zap. This is ideal if you need to use various search criteria to find
> related data.

You should now have a better understanding of how and when to use lookup tables using the **Lookup
Table** transform function.

Next, let's discuss how to pick data from a list of values using the **Pick from List** transform function.

Picking data from a list

Have you ever wanted to run a quiz or assign a random result to your participants? Or perhaps you
need to assign a support query to a member of your team based on a priority rating. You can easily
do this by using the Formatter by Zapier **Utilities** action event with the **Pick from List** transform
function to choose a value from a list based on its position.

Here are a couple of examples of when you can use this transform option:

- You might create a single-question, fun Q&A that you push out on social media to engage your audience and drive traffic to your website. You ask them to complete one question in Google Forms, such as "What is your birth month?" and then randomly assign them an "inner mythical beast" based on their answer. You can pick a random result from a list of "inner mythical beast" values, such as `Unicorn`, `Dragon`, `Pheonix`, `Kraken`, and `Pegasus`, then display the result on a page on your website.

- You might have a list of team members that you assign help desk requests to. The team could be assigned the requests by you randomly picking their names from a list. Alternatively, you might want to assign the requests to specific users based on a priority rating. For example, Jim (the customer service assistant) is assigned level 0 requests, Jenny (the supervisor) is assigned level 1 requests, and June (the manager) is assigned all level 2 ratings. You can create a list with Jim, Jenny, and June, in that order to pick which person to route a request to.

Let's review how to set up an action step with the **Pick from List** transform option.

Setting up the Utilities action event with the Pick from List transform option

You can use the **Utilities** action event once you have set up your trigger step.

Once you have added an action step, either by selecting the **Action** step or clicking on the + icon, and have chosen **Formatter by Zapier** as the app and **Utilities** as the action event, you can edit the fields in the **Action** section, as follows:

- **Transform**: From the drop-down menu, select the **Pick from List** option. This is a required field and must have a value for the Zap to run.

- **Operation**: You can use this drop-down field to specify the position of the value you want to find in the **Input** fields. The options are **Choose First**, **Choose Last**, and **Choose Random**. These will choose the first or last positions, or a randomly selected position, respectively, in the list of **Input** fields. You can also enter a static value, a dynamic value from previous steps, or a combination of both, to specify the nth position in the list, if you select the **Custom** option. Bear in mind that the first position will be 0, the second will be 1, the third will be 2, and so on. You can also use negative numbers to select from the end of the list, such as -1 for the last, -2 for the second last, and so on. This is a required field and must have a value for the Zap to run.

- **Input**: You can use this field to map in the values of the data that you want to return. As you enter a value in one field line, another will appear just below. Add the values in the order you want to set them. You can remove lines by clicking on the **X** button at the end of the line. You can either enter a static value, a dynamic value from previous steps, or a combination of both to specify this value. Although this is not a required field, the formatter function will not return a result if there is no value.

- **Default**: Here, you can enter a default value to use if the **Operation** value does not match any position in the **Input** section.

An example is shown in the following screenshot:

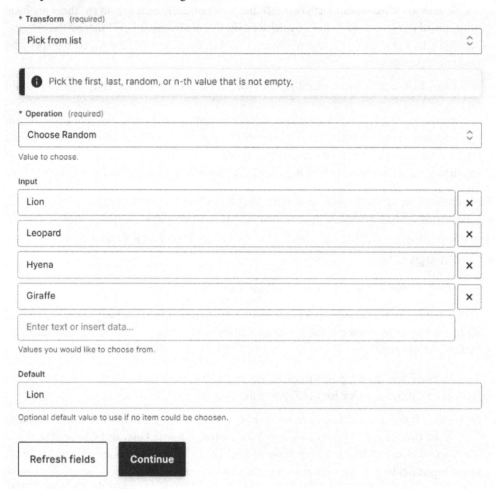

Figure 18.6 – Overview of using the Formatter by Zapier Utilities action event to pick a value from a list

Click on the **Continue** button. You can then use the **Test** section to pick a value from a list. The result from the scenario in *Figure 18.6* is shown in the following screenshot:

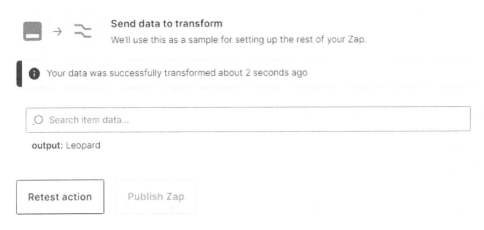

Send data to transform
We'll use this as a sample for setting up the rest of your Zap.

Your data was successfully transformed about 2 seconds ago

Search item data...

output: Leopard

Retest action   Publish Zap

Figure 18.7 – Overview of the data returned when picking from a list

Proceed to add one or more action steps after your **Utilities** action step.

You should now have a better understanding of how and when to use the **Pick from List** transform function.

Next, let's cover how to manipulate data in or convert data to line-item format.

Manipulating line items

Line items are blocks of data that have multiple items associated with them and are used in a special field within Zapier. They are essentially objects containing what is commonly known as an **array** of objects. The use of line-item data is very common in e-commerce, payment processing, and accounting apps, such as Shopify, PayPal, and Xero, where you often have multiple lines of data in an order or invoice, such as itemized lines on a paper receipt. For example, in one order, a customer might purchase an initial product, such as two medium T-shirts priced at $9.99 each, and a second product, such as one large T-shirt priced at $10.99. They may also have paid for shipping at $7.50, and a coupon of $5.00 off was applied to the entire order. The details for each individualized item consist of the product name, description, quantity, and price, and these details are normally shown as one line on an invoice. You can also think of each line as a row in a spreadsheet where the details are displayed in columns. Therefore, one invoice can consist of multiple lines with specific details related to that line.

The content in this section might be most useful for users in bookkeeping or accounting roles that deal with financial transactions, as well as those in operations roles concerning shipping and logistics.

Understanding line items

When you map data into your fields in your action steps in your Zaps, you usually have one piece of text data, represented individually or as a string of text. Line items are complex in the sense that they often contain several bits of data clumped together, and having more than one line item complicates things further. As you can imagine, when data bunched into line items or multiple line items exists in one app that you want to transfer to another app, being able to use line-item automation is a huge time-saver so that you don't need to enter all those details manually.

You can quickly identify data that is presented as line items as an item with rows of data, as shown in the following screenshot:

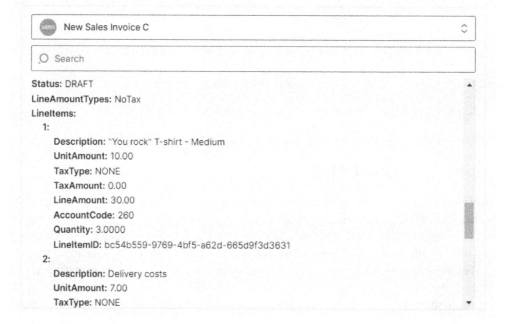

Figure 18.8 – Overview of how line-item data is displayed in rows

The data is also labeled with **Line Items**, as shown in the following screenshot:

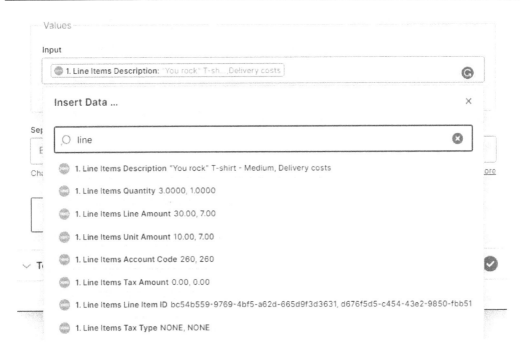

Figure 18.9 – Overview of how line-item data is labeled

There are a few apps that integrate with Zapier that offer **line-item support**. Here are a few examples:

- **Accounting apps**: QuickBooks Online, Xero
- **CRM apps**: Keap
- **E-commerce apps**: ShipStation, Shopify, WooCommerce
- **Invoicing apps**: Harvest, Wave, Zoho Invoice
- **Payment processing apps**: Chargify, PayPal
- **Other apps**: Google Sheets
- **Zapier built-in apps**: Formatter by Zapier

Many of Zapier's Formatter action events and transform functions support the use of line items so that you can manipulate multiple rows of text, numbers, dates, and times with line-item data in one action.

It is, of course, much simpler if the apps you are transferring data between all support line items, but as only a few apps do, there is often the need to manipulate data to either create line items or change line items back into text field data. Therefore, to use line items, both your trigger app and action app(s) must support their use. If one or the other doesn't, you can use Formatter by Zapier with the **Utilities** action event to transform line-item data so that it's compatible and can be used with apps that either require data in line-item format or support it. We can use the following transform functions:

- **Text to Line-item**
- **Line-item to Text**
- **Line Itemizer (Create/Append/Prepend)**

Let's review how to convert text into line items using the **Text to Line-item** transform function.

Converting text into line items

By using the Formatter by Zapier built-in app with the **Utilities** action event and the **Text to Line-item** transform option, you can easily convert a grouping of different **comma-delimited text** variables into line items. Comma-delimited text is also known as **comma-separated text**. These are values that are normally separated by a comma, such as `Apple, Pear, Kiwi` or `Apple, Pear, Kiwi`.

You might want to perform this action when you have data in text format and want to create line items to use in other apps that support line-item usage. In the preceding example, the text would be transformed into `["Apple","Pear","Kiwi"]`.

Here are a few examples of when you can use this transform option:

- Your CRM might have multiple product listings, quantities, and prices associated with your deals, and when a deal hits a certain stage in the pipeline, you might want to create an invoice in your accounting system. Your CRM doesn't support line items, so the product information in the deal is presented as text. You can use the **Text to Line-item** transform function to change the text into line items so that you can generate invoices in your accounting system, QuickBooks Online.

- You might take orders for special products using a web form embedded in your website. Once an order comes through, you want to convert each part of the order into line items so that you can create separate lines in a Google spreadsheet. You can use the **Text to Line-item** transform function to do that.

Let's discuss how to set up an action step with the **Text to Line-item** transform option.

Setting up the Utilities action event with the Text to Line-item transform option

You can use the **Utilities** action event once you have set up your trigger step.

Once you have added an action step, either by selecting the **Action** step or clicking on the + icon, and have chosen **Formatter by Zapier** as the app and **Utilities** as the action event, you can edit the fields in the **Action** section, as follows:

- **Transform**: From the drop-down menu, select the **Text to Line-item** option. This is a required field and must have a value for the Zap to run.

- **Input**: You can use this field to map in the comma-separated text values that you want to convert into line items. You can either enter a static value, a dynamic value from previous steps, or a combination of both, to specify this value. Although this is not a required field, the formatter function will not return a result if there is no value.

An example is shown in the following screenshot:

Figure 18.10 – Overview of using the Formatter by Zapier Utilities
action event to change text into line items

Click on the **Continue** button. You can then use the **Test** section to transform comma-separated text into line-item arrays. The result from the scenario in *Figure 18.10* is shown in the following screenshot:

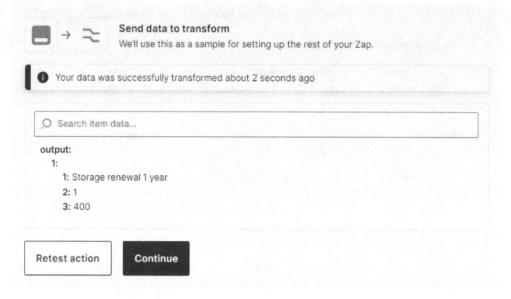

Figure 18.11 – Overview of the data returned when transforming text into line items

The output shown in *Figure 18.11* is displayed as one line item with three rows of data.

Proceed to add one or more action steps after your **Utilities** action step.

You should now have a better understanding of how and when to use the **Text to Line-item** transform function.

Next, let's cover how to reverse this action and convert line items into text using the **Line-item to Text** transform function.

Converting line items into text

We've just discussed how to convert comma-delimited text into line items. There will be scenarios where you want to do the opposite, in that you will want to change line-item data into comma-delimited text. We can use the Formatter by Zapier built-in app with the **Utilities** action event and the **Line-item to Text** transform option to do just that.

In the same action step, we can also split the resulting text into separate fields in the same way the **Split Text** transform function works, as discussed in *Chapter 17, Text Formatting Functions in Zapier – Part 2*.

For example, you might raise invoices in your accounting app, Xero, for products that you sell. You also include delivery charges on the invoice as a separate invoice line. Once the invoice has been created, you want to send a message in Slack to your team with the details of the product that's been sold, not the delivery charge.

Let's use this example to illustrate how to use and set up an action step with the **Line-item to Text** transform option.

Setting up the Utilities action event with the Line-item to Text transform option

You can use the **Utilities** action event once you have set up your trigger step.

Once you have added an action step, either by selecting the **Action** step or clicking on the + icon, and have chosen **Formatter by Zapier** as the app and **Utilities** as the action event, you can edit the fields in the **Action** section, as follows:

- **Transform**: From the drop-down menu, select the **Line-item to Text** option. This is a required field and must have a value for the Zap to run.

- **Input**: You can use this field to map the values of the data that you want to convert into line items. You can either enter a static value, a dynamic value from previous steps, or a combination of both, to specify this value. Although this is not a required field, the formatter function will not return a result if there is no value.

- **Separator**: You can use this field to enter the word, character, or syntax that you want to use as the splitting value from the **Input** field. You can either enter a static value, a dynamic value from previous steps, or a combination of both, to specify this value. This field supports special character syntax. For example, to split text separated by spaces, you can use the `[:space:]` syntax. Although this is not a required field, if left blank, the default will be the `,` character.

An example is shown in the following screenshot:

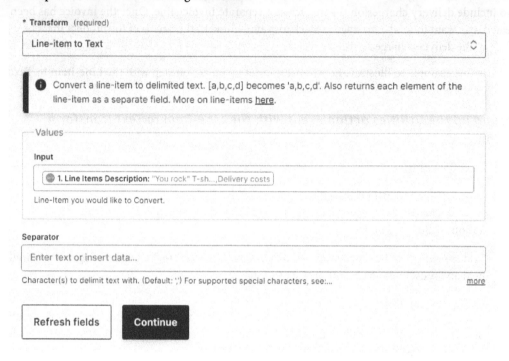

Figure 18.12 – Overview of using the Formatter by Zapier Utilities action event
to change line items into text and split them into separate fields

Click on the **Continue** button. You can then use the **Test** section to transform line items into comma-delimited text split into separate fields. The result from the scenario in *Figure 18.12* is shown in the following screenshot:

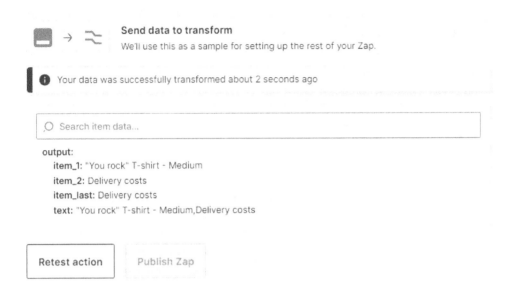

Figure 18.13 – Overview of the data returned when transforming line items into text split into fields

The output shown in *Figure 18.13* is separate field items (item_1, item_2, and item_last), as well as the fully converted comma-separated text.

Proceed to add one or more action steps after your **Utilities** action step.

You should now have a better understanding of how and when to use the **Line-item to Text** transform function.

Next, let's explore creating, appending, and prepending line items using the **Line Itemizer (Create/Append/Prepend)** transform function.

Using a line itemizer to create, append, or prepend line items

Being able to create line items, attach additional items to the end of a line-item grouping, or insert additional items at the start of a line-item grouping – and all in one action step – is very useful. This will be most commonly needed if you have variables in your data from your trigger app that you need to push into another app where there needs to be consistency. Alternatively, you might need to collate data from several different action steps and combine the data to form line items. For example, you might sell your products through a shopping cart app such as ThriveCart and need to add the transaction information to QuickBooks Online. You might find that you need to use product searches to retrieve product IDs and combine order information from an upsell. You might also need to add a quantity of 1 for a coupon and delivery costs, which may not be represented in the data from the shopping cart. You can do all of this using the Formatter by Zapier built-in app with the **Utilities** action event and the **Line Itemizer (Create/Append/Prepend)** transform option. It allows you to convert comma-delimited text into line items, as well as append or prepend to a group of existing line items by adding them to the same field as comma-delimited text or as single values. You can also generate subtotals with a specified number of decimal places if you include properties such as `Price` and `Quantity`.

Let's use this example to illustrate how to use and set up an action step with the **Line Itemizer (Create/Append/Prepend)** transform option.

Setting up the Utilities action event with the Line Itemizer (Create/Append/Prepend) transform option

You can use the **Utilities** action event once you have set up your trigger step.

Once you have added an action step, either by selecting the **Action** step or clicking on the + icon, and have chosen **Formatter by Zapier** as the app and **Utilities** as the action event, you can edit the fields in the **Action** section, as follows:

- **Transform**: From the drop-down menu, select the **Line Itemizer (Create/Append/Prepend)** option. This is a required field and must have a value for the Zap to run.

- **Line-item(s) Group Name**: You can use this field to add an identifier for the group of line items that you want to produce. For example, you could use `Invoices`, `Orders`, or `Line-items for Invoice`. You can either enter a static value, a dynamic value from previous steps, or a combination of both, to specify this value. The default is **Line-Item(s)**.

- **Line-item Properties**: This table is comprised of two columns. In the left column, enter the line-item property's name, such as `Product code`, `Description`, `Price`, `Qty`, and so on. The left column only accepts static text. In the right column, enter the comma-separated text or single values when creating line items. When appending or prepending, you can combine line items with comma-separated text or single values. You can either enter a static value, a dynamic value from previous steps, or a combination of both, to specify the values in the right column. You can add additional rows by clicking on the + button, and remove rows by clicking on the **X** button at the end of the row. Although this is not a required field, the formatter function will not return a result if there is no value.

- **Create Subtotal Property?**: You can use this drop-down Boolean field to select **Yes** or **No** to create a subtotal property. If you label your **Line-item Properties** `Price` or `Quantity` (`Qty`), these values can be multiplied together to create a `Subtotal` property. This is useful if the app you're sending data to requires `Total` values, which saves you from having to add another Formatter action step to create these values. You can either enter a static value, a dynamic value from previous steps, or a combination of both, to specify this value. The default is **No**.

- **Decimal Places For Subtotal Values**: If you select **Yes** for the **Create Subtotal Property?** field, you can enter a numerical value for how many decimal places you want the subtotal to be displayed as. You can either enter a static value, a dynamic value from previous steps, or a combination of both, to specify this value.

An example is shown in the following screenshot, where an additional item, such as a standard delivery charge, has been added to a collection of line items:

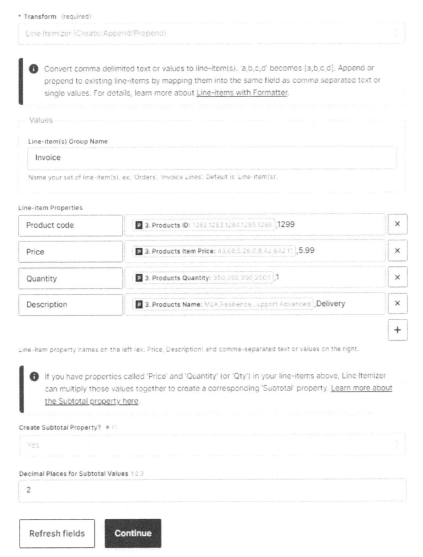

Figure 18.14 – Overview of using the Formatter by Zapier Utilities
action event to create, append, or prepend line-item data

Click on the **Continue** button. You can then use the **Test** section to create, append, and prepend line items. The result from the scenario in *Figure 18.14* is shown in the following screenshot:

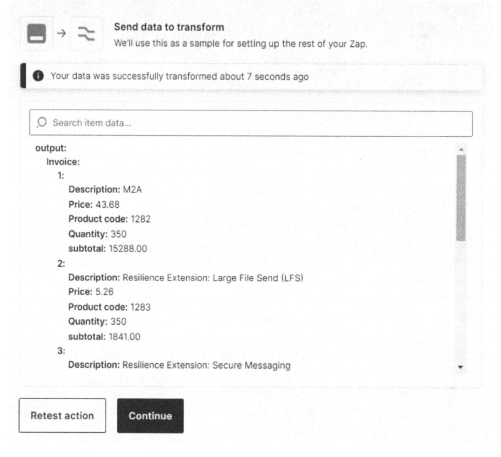

Figure 18.15 – Overview of the data returned when creating, appending, and prepending line-item data

The output shown in *Figure 18.15* is separate line items for Description, Price, Product code, Quantity, and subtotal.

Proceed to add one or more action steps after your **Utilities** action step.

The following are a few useful resources that have been created by Zapier that will help you further when using line items with Formatter by Zapier:

- https://zapier.com/blog/formatter-line-item-automation/
- https://help.zapier.com/hc/en-us/articles/8496277737997-Use-line-items-in-Zaps#1-identify-your-trigger-s-line-item-fields-0-0

- `https://community.zapier.com/featured-articles-65/formatter-features-line-itemizer-overview-11844`

- `https://community.zapier.com/featured-articles-65/an-example-of-how-to-use-the-line-itemizer-feature-of-our-formatter-app-7272`

You should now have a better understanding of how and when to use the **Text to Line-item**, **Line-item to Text**, and **Line Itemizer (Create/Append/Prepend)** transform functions to manipulate line items.

Summary

In this chapter, we completed our exploration of the features of the Formatter by Zapier built-in app by covering the functionality of the **Utilities** action event. First, we introduced the Formatter by Zapier **Utilities** action event. Then, we discussed how to import CSV files, how to use lookup tables to store and help you find related data, and how to pick data from a list of values. Finally, we covered the various transform functions related to using line items in your automations.

You now know how to use the Formatter by Zapier built-in app to transform several different functions, including importing CSV files, using lookup tables, picking data from lists, converting text into line items, and vice versa, as well as line-item creation and customization.

In the next chapter, you will learn how to boost your productivity by combining **Artificial Intelligence (AI)** and automation. We will explore some of the Zapier's built-in AI functionality such as the ChatGPT plugin and the Build A Zap AI feature, as well as dive into the OpenAI and ChatGPT integrations with Zapier.

Questions

1. If you were running a customer support desk and wanted to randomly assign tickets to your support agents, which Formatter by Zapier **Utilities** transform option could you use?

2. What type of apps commonly express data as line items?

Part 4:
Getting the Most Out of Zapier

In this part, you will learn more about how Generative AI used with Zapier can help you to boost your productivity further. You will also gain an understanding of the different types of business processes that can be automated using Zapier, and we will explore practical examples of how to automate marketing, sales, operations, finance, and reporting processes with commonly used digital tools integrated with Zapier. You will also learn best practices for using Zapier to enhance your productivity, and be able to test your knowledge with planned exercises.

This part contains the following chapters:

- *Chapter 19, AI and Automation*
- *Chapter 20, Automating Your Marketing Processes*
- *Chapter 21, Automating Your Sales Processes*
- *Chapter 22, Automating Your Operations Processes*
- *Chapter 23, Automating Your Finance and Reporting Processes*
- *Chapter 24, Tips, Tricks, and Best Practices to Enhance Your Productivity*
- *Chapter 25, Challenge Your Problem-Solving and Zap-Building Skills*

19
AI and Automation

As many software users are embracing better ways of making their days more productive by using **Generative Artificial Intelligence** (**AI**), integrating **AI** functionality into their software applications has become a priority for many SaaS companies. Zapier is no different. With the release of ChatGPT to the wider market and the possibility of integrating and incorporating AI functionality, Zapier is also in the process of releasing many AI-integrated features and has specified this as a key business objective for the near future. Several AI SaaS companies are also using the opportunity to integrate their apps with Zapier, making the combination of AI and automation a productivity booster.

In this chapter, we will discover how you can increase efficiency by merging AI and automation. We will explore some of Zapier's built-in AI functionality as well as AI app integrations with Zapier. First, we will cover how to get early access to new Zapier features that have incorporated AI functionality, then we will dive into an overview of the **Create a Zap** feature as used in the dashboard and the Zap editor. Then, we will explore NLA and AI actions functionality in the **Zapier Chrome extension** and **ChatGPT plugin**. After that, we will cover how to create **AI chatbots** with **Zapier Interfaces**. We will then cover a few new built-in apps and features such as **AI-powered Formatter by Zapier steps**, **AI-powered Code by Zapier steps**, **AI-powered troubleshooting**, **AI by Zapier built-in app**, and more. Finally, we will explore the **ChatGPT** and **OpenAI** integrations with Zapier, and the basics of GPT AI prompting.

> **Note**
> As all of these features are still undergoing beta testing and their features may change, we will only provide a brief overview of their functionality, without going into too much detail. We will, however, provide you with some use cases and further references.

We will cover the following key topics in this chapter:

- Early access to new AI features
- Create a Zap (beta) – drafting your Zaps using AI
- Running Zap AI actions (beta) using the Zapier Chrome extension and the ChatGPT plugin (beta)

- Building AI chatbots (beta) using Zapier Interfaces (beta)
- Other AI-powered built-in apps and features in beta
- The OpenAI and ChatGPT integrations with Zapier
- GPT AI prompting guidelines

By the end of this chapter, you will have acquired knowledge of the AI features that have been released by Zapier since the first edition of this book was published.

Technical requirements

To fully benefit from the content in this chapter, you will need access to a Zapier account. The Zapier Starter plan will provide you with the necessary features to effectively build and implement multi-step Zaps with the features discussed in this chapter. You must join Zapier's Early Access Program to get access to features in beta. To use the Zapier ChatGPT plugin, you must subscribe to a ChatGPT Plus account, and to use the OpenAI integration with Zapier, you must subscribe to a paid account.

Early access to new AI features

The Zapier team is hard at work developing new AI features that will benefit users. These features are released in the **alpha** phase to a select number of test users, and then in the **beta** phase when enough testing has been done to release it to a larger audience in a staged release to user groups. In other words, even though a feature might be released in beta, you might not have access to the feature. You can, however, sign up for Zapier's **Early Access Program** to be included in the early-stage user testing groups. You can do that at `https://zapier.com/early-access`. You can also sign up for notifications specifically about new AI features due for release at `https://zapier.com/ai`.

You can read about some of the AI features in development in this article from Wade Foster, Zapier's CEO: `https://zapier.com/blog/ai-open-letter/`, some of which we will cover in this chapter.

> **Important note**
> You must agree to Zapier's AI Supplementary Terms to use many (but not all) Zapier built-in AI features. You can find these terms here: `https://zapier.com/legal/ai-supplementary-terms`.

You can read an overview of what generative AI actually is in this McKinsey article: `https://www.mckinsey.com/featured-insights/mckinsey-explainers/what-is-generative-ai`.

For some inspiration on how to use automation and AI, watch Zapier's webinar *Zapathon: How to put AI to work*: `https://zapier.com/resources/webinar/zapathon-put-ai-to-work`.

Next, let's dive into an overview of the **Create a Zap (beta)** feature.

Create a Zap (beta) – drafting your Zaps using AI

We briefly touched on the **Create a Zap (beta)** feature in *Chapter 3, Building Your First Automated Workflow (Zap)*. This feature is available in the dashboard and in the Zap editor, and as it is still in beta, only some users will have access to it. Thinking about what your Zap should look like and how to start creating in the Zap editor can be a bit daunting when you first start using Zapier. It can also be very time-consuming when creating long multi-step Zaps. Using the Create a Zap (beta) feature allows you to use plain language to write a prompt that will generate a draft version of a Zap that you can start using and customizing immediately, saving you brain power and time. You do not need to use technical language but, for best results, explain which apps you are using, the trigger point, and what actions you want to occur. Just type your prompt into the box, click on **Generate**, and watch this AI tool do its magic to create a draft Zap ready for your use. For example, your prompt could be `When I receive an email in Email, create a task in ClickUp assigned to me, draft a response using ChatGPT, and send this response in reply with Gmail`. The response is shown in the following screenshot:

Figure 19.1 – An example of a Create a Zap (beta) prompt and response

You can click on **Show more examples** to expand the **Examples** section, share the Zap using the **Share** button, start customizing it in the Zap editor using the **Try it** button, or specify whether it was helpful or not by clicking on the **Yes** or **No** buttons. Giving feedback is important to train the AI to work better for you.

The following Zapier resource provides some additional context and prompt examples on how to best use prompts with this feature: `https://help.zapier.com/hc/en-us/articles/15703650952077/`.

You should now have a better understanding of how and when to use the Create a Zap (beta) feature.

Now, let's explore how to run Zap actions using AI.

Running Zap AI Actions (beta) using the Zapier Chrome extension and the ChatGPT plugin (beta)

Zapier has integrated AI-powered or AI-related features into a few Zapier built-in apps, and more developments are underway. For example, the Zapier Chrome extension built-in app now has **Natural Language Action** (**NLA**) and **AI Actions (beta)** features, and the Formatter by Zapier built-in app now has a transform function available named **Split Text into Chunks for AI Prompt**. Many of these features are currently in beta and may change. Before we explore these features, let's cover NLA and AI Actions in more detail.

NLA and AI Actions

With the **NLA API** from Zapier, you can use the Zapier platform to power your own products, and it is optimized for products that use natural languages, such as chatbots, for example. You can read more about the NLA API and use cases in the article at `https://zapier.com/l/natural-language-actions`. The NLA API allows you to create **AI Actions** to use with Zapier's 6,000+ app integrations and 30,000+ action events. You can read more about AI actions in the article at `https://help.zapier.com/hc/en-us/articles/17013994198925-Zapier-AI-actions-in-other-apps`.

The Zapier Chrome extension and Zapier ChatGPT plugin (beta) are two examples where NLA features and AI Actions have been introduced. We will cover these features in the next two sections.

The following Zapier help articles provide more details on creating, using, and managing AI actions:

- *Create AI actions within an AI app*: `https://help.zapier.com/hc/en-us/articles/17014153949709`

- *Use AI actions within an AI app*: `https://help.zapier.com/hc/en-us/articles/17014427470477`

- *Manage your AI actions*: `https://help.zapier.com/hc/en-us/articles/17014677921037`

- *Decide if AI should guess the value of specific fields in AI actions*: `https://help.zapier.com/hc/en-us/articles/17014876778381`

Let's start with the Zapier Chrome extension NLA actions (beta).

Zapier Chrome extension NLA actions (beta)

The NLA API and the use of AI Actions are the basis for the new functionality in the Zapier Chrome extension, thus allowing you to run AI-powered actions right inside your Zapier Chrome extension with simple prompts. For example, you could use this functionality to draft a reply to an email.

Using AI actions with the Zapier Chrome extension

To get started, follow the instructions in *Chapter 10, Other Useful Built-In Apps by Zapier*, to set up the Zapier Chrome extension built-in app ahead of using the NLA functionality. Let's explore the next steps once this is set up:

1. Select the **Zapier Chrome extension** icon in your browser, then click on the **Actions (beta)** tab, and then click on the **Set up actions** button.

2. In the popup that appears, click on the **Allow** button to give Zapier access to AI Actions in your account.

3. In the new browser window that appears, click on **Add a new action**. You can also manage NLA access to your Zapier apps by clicking on the **Manage access** link.

4. Set up your Zapier Chrome extension action by mapping the fields. For example, we might want to send a direct message to ourselves in Slack with a random motivational quote. The setup of the action for this example is shown in the following screenshot:

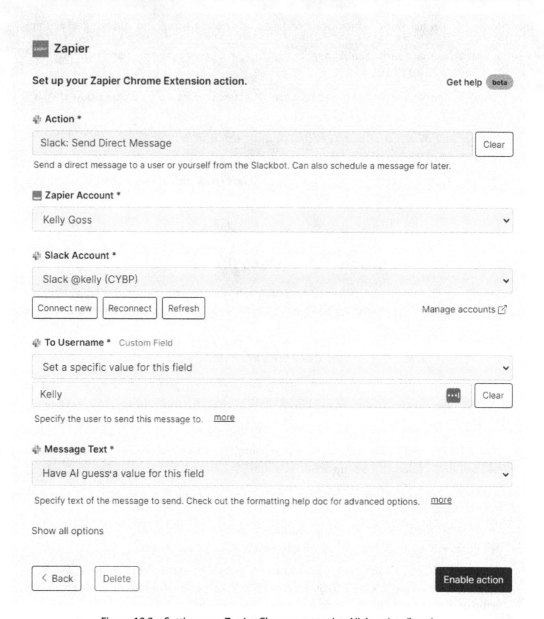

Figure 19.2 – Setting up a Zapier Chrome extension NLA action (beta)

5.   Turn on your action by clicking on the **Enable action** button.

6.   Navigate to your browser window and click on the **Zapier Chrome extension** icon, select your action from the dropdown, add your instructions in the **Instructions** field, and select the **Preview** button to show a preview or **Run** to run the action. This is shown in the following screenshot:

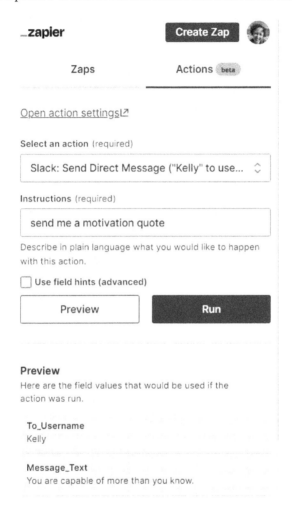

Figure 19.3 – Creating a Zapier Chrome extension NLA run

You can also activate field hints by selecting the **Use field hints (advanced)** checkbox.

The result in Slack is shown in the following screenshot:

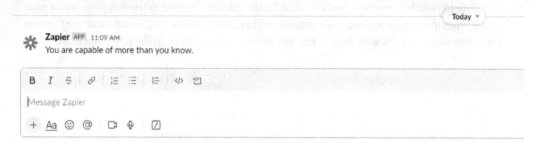

Figure 19.4 – The result of the NLA prompt using a Zapier Chrome extension run action

Now, let's review how to use the ChatGPT plugin (beta) feature to connect and run Zapier actions straight from your ChatGPT chatbot interface.

The Zapier ChatGPT plugin (beta) – running Zap actions from ChatGPT

The development and release of the **OpenAI ChatGPT chatbot** have encouraged users to take advantage of AI to perform a multitude of tasks that normally would have taken hours and might require specific skills, such as copywriting. Some examples of the tasks that ChatGPT is helping users to perform are as follows:

- Writing cold outreach emails
- Drafting responses to emails
- Writing blog articles and newsletters
- Researching topics and creating presentations

You can now supercharge your newly found AI-enhanced productivity by connecting Zapier to ChatGPT with the Zapier ChatGPT plugin (beta) to run AI actions to perform a variety of tasks without copying and pasting text from the ChatGPT chatbot interface. For example, you could ask ChatGPT to perform the following tasks and then perform the relevant Zapier AI action:

- Write a response to an email sent by a specific person and create a draft email response in Gmail

- Write a blog article and create a new post in WordPress

- Draft a presentation and create a Google Slides presentation from a template

The article at `https://zapier.com/blog/announcing-zapier-chatgpt-plugin/` presents several more use cases of the Zapier ChatGPT plugin (beta).

> **Important note**
> You must be subscribed to a ChatGPT Plus account in order to use plugins.

Using the Zapier ChatGPT plugin (beta)

Before you can use the Zapier ChatGPT plugin (beta), you must connect your ChatGPT account to your Zapier account by installing the Zapier plugin in ChatGPT, and then set up your ChatGPT AI Actions. Comprehensive instructions can be found at `https://zapier.com/blog/use-the-zapier-chatgpt-plugin/` and `https://help.zapier.com/hc/en-us/articles/14058263394573`.

To illustrate how the Zapier ChatGPT plugin (beta) works, we will use the example of prompting ChatGPT to write a response to an email sent by a specific person and then an associated Zapier ChatGPT plugin (beta) AI action to create a draft email response in Gmail.

You can set up your ChatGPT plugin AI actions by navigating to `https://nla.zapier.com/openai/actions/`, similar to as described in the *Zapier Chrome extension NLA actions (beta)* section. The following screenshot shows how the ChatGPT action would be set up:

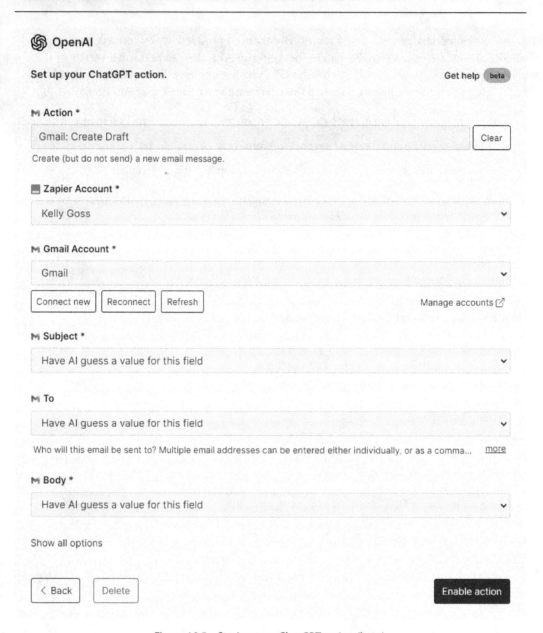

Figure 19.5 – Setting up a ChatGPT action (beta)

The following screenshot shows the `Please draft an email for Joe Bloggs (joe@sabcompany.com) and let them know the report that was due Friday is ready for review today.` prompt and result in ChatGPT:

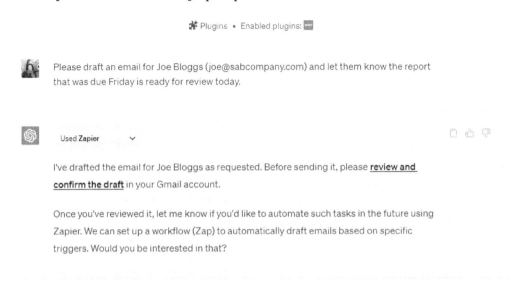

Figure 19.6 – Using the Zapier ChatGPT plugin (beta)

Clicking on the **review and confirm the draft** link opens another browser window for you to choose to alter the AI action by clicking on the **Edit** button or process the run request by clicking on the **Run** button. This is shown in the following screenshot:

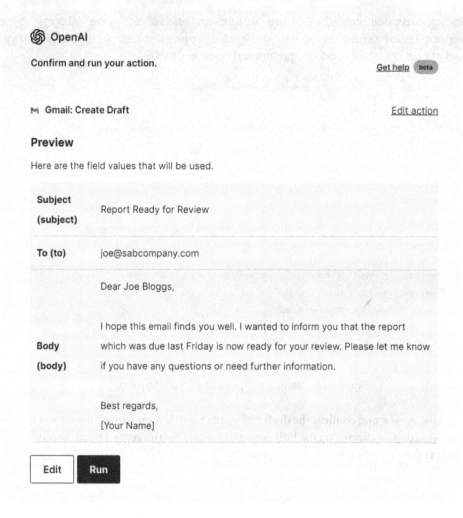

Figure 19.7 – Reviewing the ChatGPT plugin (beta) action result

The result of running the action is shown in the following screenshot:

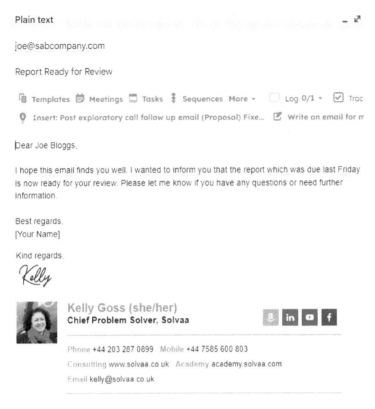

Figure 19.8 – The result of the ChatGPT plugin (beta) AI action run in Gmail

You should now have a better understanding of how and when to use the Zapier ChatGPT plugin (beta).

Now, let's review how to build AI chatbots with Zapier Interfaces.

Building AI chatbots (beta) using Zapier Interfaces (beta)

In *Chapter 13*, *Newly Released Apps and Features*, we explored the exciting capabilities of the Zapier Interfaces tool, allowing you to build custom pages with visual interfaces such as forms and kanban boards, which can then also be linked to data collection tables with Zapier Tables. Now, with the magic of AI, you can create **AI-powered chatbots** using Zapier Interfaces. You can also create landing pages that display multiple chatbots and even embed your chatbots on your website if you use a paid Interfaces plan. You can read more about Zapier's AI chatbots (beta) feature at `https://zapier.com/ai/chatbot`.

Here are some examples of chatbots you could create:

- **PR**: You could create a chatbot that helps you generate press releases. See a Zapier-built example at `https://external-communications.zapier.app/press-release`.

- **Marketing**: You could create a chatbot that helps users translate corporate jargon into plain English.

- **Feedback**: You could create a chatbot that helps you to formulate positive feedback that can be used in appraisals.

Let's explore how to get started with building AI chatbots.

Creating an AI chatbot (beta)

All you have to do to get started is create a Zapier Interfaces web page with a chatbot component that uses OpenAI's GPT. Review the *Zapier Interfaces (feature in beta) – building custom forms, chatbots, and visual interfaces* section in *Chapter 13, Newly Released Apps and Features*, to kick off your Zapier Interfaces journey. For detailed instructions on how to create your AI-powered chatbot, refer to this Zapier article: `https://zapier.com/blog/create-custom-ai-chatbots-with-interfaces/`.

Let's look at an example whereby you have created a chatbot that assesses brand risk, such as in the example created by Zapier at `https://external-communications.zapier.app/brand-risk-assessment`. Using a prompt such as `An employee has made damaging remarks about a customer publicly` produces a response as shown in the following screenshot:

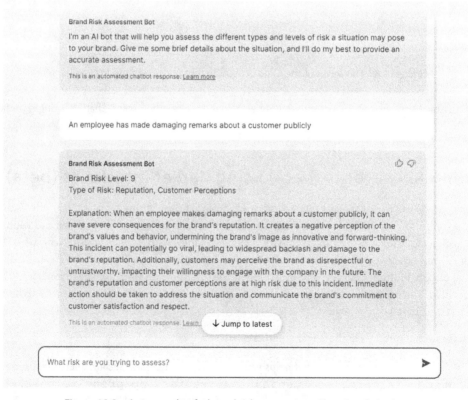

Figure 19.9 – An example of a brand risk assessment AI-assisted chatbot

You could then even ask the chatbot what you could do to rectify the situation, where the response is shown in the screenshot:

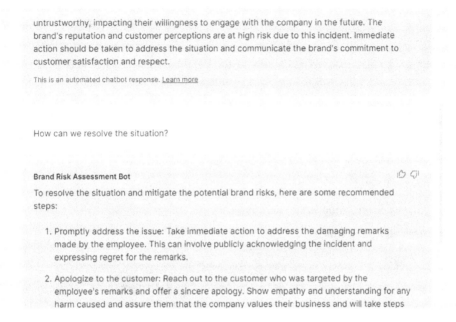

untrustworthy, impacting their willingness to engage with the company in the future. The brand's reputation and customer perceptions are at high risk due to this incident. Immediate action should be taken to address the situation and communicate the brand's commitment to customer satisfaction and respect.

This is an automated chatbot response. Learn more

How can we resolve the situation?

Brand Risk Assessment Bot

To resolve the situation and mitigate the potential brand risks, here are some recommended steps:

1. Promptly address the issue: Take immediate action to address the damaging remarks made by the employee. This can involve publicly acknowledging the incident and expressing regret for the remarks.

2. Apologize to the customer: Reach out to the customer who was targeted by the employee's remarks and offer a sincere apology. Show empathy and understanding for any harm caused and assure them that the company values their business and will take steps

Figure 19.10 – An example follow-up response in a brand risk assessment AI-assisted chatbot

Bear in mind that how you train the chatbot is crucial to the responses it produces. You can read more about how to customize the user interaction experience at `https://help.zapier.com/hc/en-us/articles/15931071482509-Create-chatbots-in-Zapier-Interfaces`, and how to train your chatbot at `https://help.zapier.com/hc/en-us/articles/17211863510541-Use-a-data-source-with-your-Interfaces-AI-Chatbot`.

> **Important note**
>
> The chatbot component of Zapier Interfaces uses GPT-3.5-turbo by default. You can use GPT-4 and other models by adding your own API key from your OpenAI account. Using the default setting is free; however, bear in mind that to use the OpenAI API, you will need to be subscribed to a paid service and will be charged for usage of the chatbot accordingly.

You should now have a better understanding of how and when to use Zapier Interfaces for building AI chatbots.

Now, let's explore AI functionality that has been built into some other Zapier built-in apps and features.

Other AI-powered Zapier built-in apps and features

So far in this chapter, we have covered several AI-powered features in Zapier, yet there are many more that have been released in beta and several in development. Many of these features have been incorporated into existing Zapier built-in apps and modules.

In this section, we will explore some of these features and provide use cases and further references where appropriate. We will cover the following features:

- Formatter by Zapier – Split Text into Chunks for AI Prompt
- AI-powered Formatter by Zapier steps
- AI-powered Code by Zapier steps
- AI-powered Notes
- AI-powered troubleshooting
- AI-powered App Extensions
- AI by Zapier

First, let's take a look at the Formatter by Zapier built-in app **Split Text into Chunks for AI Prompt (beta)** transform option, which is not an AI-powered feature but rather an AI helper.

Formatter by Zapier – Split Text into Chunks for AI Prompt (beta) transform option

When using AI apps with Zapier, a common problem that can arise is hitting token limits because the number of characters is too high. This is common when using large datasets in **Large Language Models** (**LLMs**) – for example, scraping data from web pages that you want to use in AI-related Zaps. With OpenAI, for example, one token could be four characters in an English word. More details on how OpenAI counts tokens can be found at `https://help.openai.com/en/articles/4936856-what-are-tokens-and-how-to-count-them`. With the Formatter by Zapier Split Text into Chunks for AI Prompt (beta) transform option, you can take large bodies of text and modify the data to produce smaller bits to use in your AI prompts, therefore reducing the chance of experiencing errors with token limits being hit.

> **Important note**
> The Formatter by Zapier Split Text into Chunks for AI Prompt transform option only supports English text.

You can read more about how to set up the Formatter by Zapier Text action event in *Chapter 17, Text Formatting Functions in Zapier – Part 2*. A good place to start would be to review the **Split** transform option.

When setting up the action step, map your large dataset in the **Input** field, and add your expected prompt text in the **Prompt** field to help Zapier calculate the chunk size. You should also specify in the **Output Style** field whether the result should be produced as line items or separate fields, as with the **Split** transform option.

Bear in mind that you should specify the recommended **Response Size** and **Chunk Size** based on the token limits of the AI model you plan to use in the rest of your Zap. For example, if you were using the OpenAI integration in your Zap, the OpenAI recommended response size is 256 and the chunk size is 4096 tokens if using the GPT-3.5/ChatGPT model, both of which are the default values for these respective fields. An example is shown in the following screenshot:

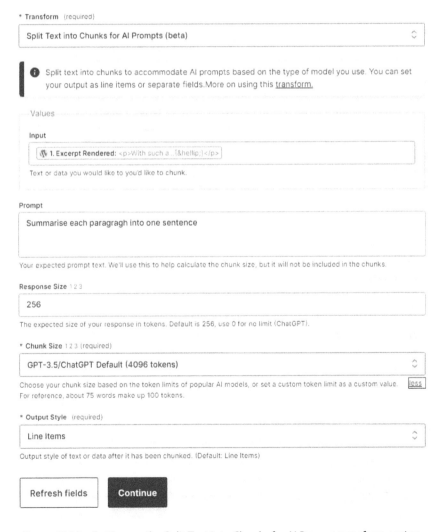

Figure 19.11 – Setting up the Split Text into Chunks for AI Prompt transform option

There is a useful help article that explains how to use this transform option in more detail and provides an example with a Zap template to illustrate it here: `https://help.zapier.com/hc/en-us/articles/15406374106765-Modify-large-data-for-your-AI-prompts`. It is recommended that you use Looping by Zapier action events in combination with the Formatter by Zapier Split Text into Chunks for AI Prompt transform option to run your chunks through multiple iterations. You can read more about Looping by Zapier in *Chapter 13*, *Newly Released Apps and Features*.

Next, let's cover AI-powered Formatter by Zapier steps.

AI-powered Formatter by Zapier steps (feature in beta)

We extensively discussed the power of the Formatter by Zapier built-in app in *Chapters 14* to *18*. Now, the magic of AI-powered functionality allows you to use plain language prompts to ask Zapier to format data in your Zap steps, which will then create Formatter by Zapier steps with the relevant transform options. As you then do not have to create the step yourself manually, this saves time during the Zap building process.

To use the **AI-powered Formatter** functionality from within an action step, simply hover your cursor on the right side of the field to expose a **Format data** button. This is shown in the following screenshot:

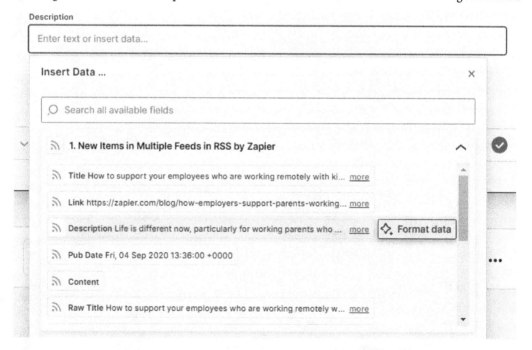

Figure 19.12 – The Format data button exposed in an action step

Once you have clicked on the **Format data** button, in the **Format data (Beta)** popup that appears, use the **Describe how to edit the format of this data** field to add a descriptive prompt specifying what formatting action you would like performed, and then click on the **Create step** button. This is shown in the following screenshot:

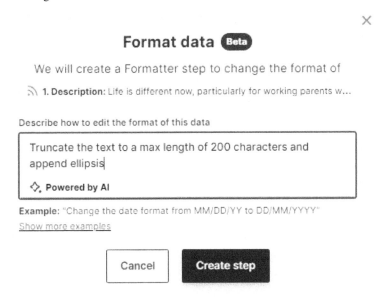

Figure 19.13 – Overview of using Format data (beta) with a prompt

A customized Formatter by Zapier step will be created before the originating action step, and the Output value will be mapped to the field in the originating action step. The result is shown in the following screenshot:

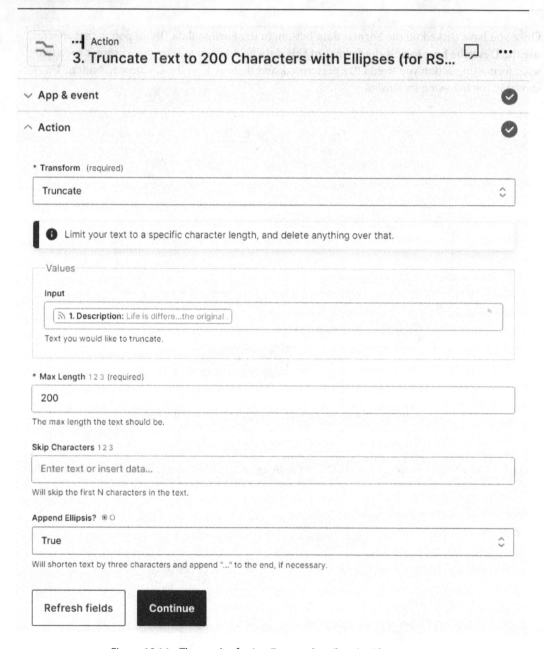

Figure 19.14 – The result of using Format data (beta) with a prompt

> **Tip**
>
> The more accurate the prompt is in Zapier terminology, the more relevant the resulting Formatter by Zapier step will be. For example, using the prompt `Shorten this text to 200 characters with ellipsis` may produce a Formatter by Zapier step that does not fill the **Max Length** and **Append Ellipsis** fields correctly, whereas using the prompt `Truncate the text to a max length of 200 characters and append ellipsis` will.

The following Zapier help articles provide further context on how to use this feature:

* `https://help.zapier.com/hc/en-us/articles/16727828367885-Easily-format-your-data-using-AI-Beta-`

* `https://help.zapier.com/hc/en-us/articles/16720031282189-Use-Formatter-with-AI-to-automatically-format-data`

Next, let's explore AI-powered Code by Zapier steps.

AI-powered Code by Zapier steps (feature in beta)

In the *Code by Zapier – using JavaScript or Python code in your Zaps* section in *Chapter 11, Advanced Built-In Apps by Zapier*, we explored how to use Code by Zapier. As not everyone understands how to write code with JavaScript or Python, in the *Generating JavaScript or Python code with ChatGPT* section, we covered some useful tips on using ChatGPT to generate code to use in your Code by Zapier steps. Now, with AI-powered functionality, you can use plain language prompts within Code by Zapier steps to write code for you. Once again, this is a time-saver to help you in the Zap building process.

To use the **AI-powered code-generating** functionality from within a Code by Zapier action step, simply click on the **Generate with AI** button. This is shown in the following screenshot:

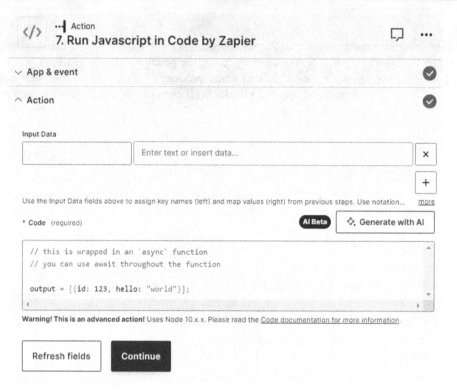

Figure 19.15 – Overview of the Generate with AI button in a Code by Zapier step

In the **Generate code with AI (AI Beta)** popup that appears, use the **Prompt** field to add a descriptive prompt specifying the details of the code you require, with a maximum of 500 characters, and then click on the **Generate Code** button. To illustrate this functionality, we will use the following prompt example: I want to retrieve detailed information about a contact in Pipedrive, such as all the phone numbers associated with the contact. I also want to manipulate those phone numbers to extract the area code from the phone number and display these results as two separate values. The Pipedrive API allows requests for information on a person https://developers.pipedrive.com/docs/api/v1/#!/Persons/getPerson. Please generate the code in JavaScript to perform this act. This is shown in the following screenshot:

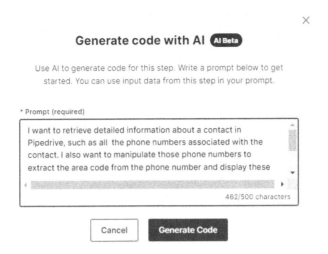

Figure 19.16 – The Generate code with AI (AI Beta) popup with prompt

The code will be generated in the popup, which you can review, and then click on the **Add Code** button to add the code to the **Code** field in the action step. The code will be added, and the **Input Data** fields will be drafted and mapped if you have specified enough information in your prompt. This is shown in the following screenshot:

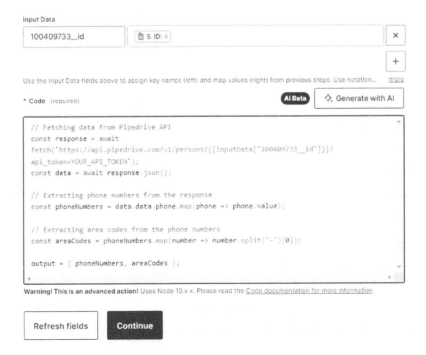

Figure 19.17 – Overview of result from using the Generate code with AI feature with a prompt

You can read more about using this feature in the Zapier help article at `https://help.zapier.com/hc/en-us/articles/15666688064013-Generate-a-Code-step-using-AI-Beta-`.

Next, let's explore AI-powered notes.

AI-powered Notes (feature in beta)

In the *Creating your first Zap in the Zap editor* section in *Chapter 3, Building Your First Automated Workflow (Zap)*, we briefly covered using the **Notes** feature to add comments to Zap steps and creating an overall Zap description. Now, you can use AI-powered functionality to save you time when creating Zap notes by generating your Zap notes based on the steps in the Zap.

To use the **AI-powered Notes functionality**, from within any step, simply click on the *comment box* icon to **Add a note**. You can also click on the **Notes** menu option in the right-side panel menu in the Classic Editor or the left-side panel in the Visual Editor. This will expand to show the **Zap notes (Beta)** section. Clicking on the **Generate with AI** button will create a draft description for your Zap, which you can edit manually, or use the **Regenerate with AI** button to try another version. This is shown in the following screenshot:

Figure 19.18 – Creating Zap notes with the Generate with AI feature

> **Important note**
>
> The AI-powered notes feature only currently works with the overall Zap description, and not with step notes. These need to be added manually.

The following Zapier help article provides further context on how to use this feature: `https://help.zapier.com/hc/en-us/articles/16791272000525`.

Next, let's explore AI-powered troubleshooting.

AI-powered troubleshooting (feature in beta)

In *Chapter 5, Troubleshooting and Handling Zap Errors*, we explored the **Zap History** module and how to go about solving problems when errors occur in your Zap runs. When a **Stopped Errored** status occurs in one of your Zap steps in a run, the new AI-powered **Troubleshoot (beta)** feature uses AI to suggest possible reasons for the error and describes a solution. The functionality uses the Zapier Help Center to search for information that might be relevant to the error. This is extremely useful when you are getting used to how Zapier works, and you are learning how to navigate Zapier troubleshooting; however, bear in mind that the feature is still in beta and might be inaccurate.

To use the feature when a Stopped Errored status occurs in a Zap run, find the step with the relevant status in the Zap History and click on the **Troubleshoot (beta)** tab. A suggested result will be produced. An example is shown in the following screenshot:

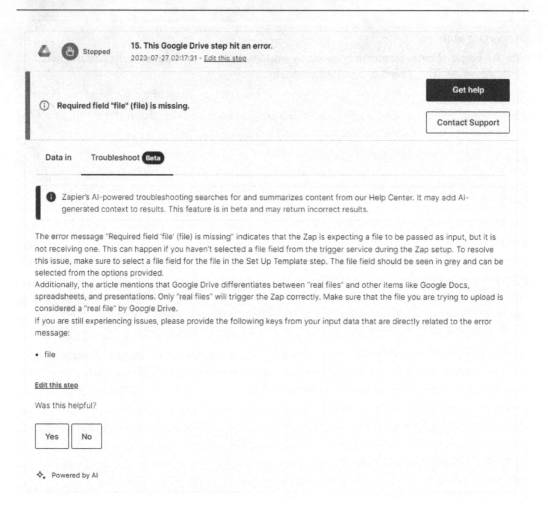

Figure 19.19 – An example result of using the Troubleshoot (beta) AI feature

More details about this feature can be found in this Zapier help article: `https://help.zapier.com/hc/en-us/articles/16977917727757`.

Next, let's explore AI-powered App Extensions.

AI-powered App Extensions (feature in beta)

In the *Using App Extensions in multiple Zaps (feature in beta)* section in *Chapter 11, Advanced Built-In Apps by Zapier*, we briefly covered how to use the App Extensions (beta) feature, which allows you to set up API call settings that can be used in multiple Zaps. Using this feature does require more advanced technical knowledge about using APIs; however, the **AI-powered App Extensions functionality** can save you time if you use the same API calls settings across multiple Zaps as you will not need to rebuild the step in each Zap.

To use this functionality when creating your App Extension, add a descriptive prompt to the **Get started building an App Extension with an AI assistant** block and click on the **Generate** button. Using the same example from *Chapter 11, Advanced Built-In Apps by Zapier*, we could use the prompt `Retrieve all lists in a specific folder in ClickUp where the folder id is specified`. The AI will produce possible options to use, which you can preview by clicking on the **Preview** button, or use to create the App Extension by clicking on the **Use** button. This is shown in the following screenshot:

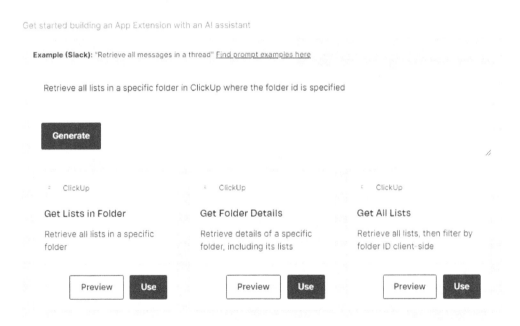

Figure 19.20 – Using the AI-powered App Extensions functionality with a prompt

In our example, we would click on the **Use** button to choose the **Get Lists in Folder** option, which would prefill the App Extension with all the relevant information we need. The prefilled details in the **API Request** tab are shown in the following screenshot:

Get Lists in Folder ✏ ⟳ ClickUp

Not yet saved

API Request   Input Fields   About

Configure API Request

> **API docs for ClickUp are located here:** https://clickup.com/api
> Use curly braces when referencing the Key from the defined input fields, for example {{some_input_key}}

* Method (required)   *** URL** (required)

| GET   ⌄ | | https://api.clickup.com/api/v2/folder/{{folder_id}}/list |

Requests can only be made to domains associated by this application.

Query Parameters

| Key | Value | + |

Zapier will encode these optional keys and values into params and append them to the URL.

Additional Headers

> Authentication headers are included automatically.

| Key | Value | + |

Zapier will apply these optional headers and values to the request in addition to any headers created as part of the authentication...   more

Figure 19.21 – An example of an App Extension API Request tab prefilled using AI functionality

The prefilled details in the **Input Fields** tab are shown in the following screenshot:

Get Lists in Folder ✎   ⌀   ClickUp

Not yet saved

API Request   Input Fields   About

Define Input Fields

These fields are displayed in the Zap Editor, when setting up a Zap with this App Extension. This documentation provides more info about how these settings interact within the Zap Editor.

Label	Key	Required	
Folder ID	folder_id	True	•••

+ Add Inp...

Save

Figure 19.22 – Overview of an App Extension Input Fields tab prefilled using AI functionality

Further information about using the App Extensions AI-powered feature can be found in this Zapier help article: `https://help.zapier.com/hc/en-us/articles/17569084310925/`.

Next, let's explore the AI by Zapier built-in app.

AI by Zapier (feature in beta)

The AI by Zapier built-in app can help you to perform a number of different actions, such as answering questions based on text inputs such as emails or Google documents, or based on web page data such as blogs and knowledge bases. This built-in app can also help you to analyze and parse text – for example, to route emails to the correct team and identify spam content.

AI by Zapier has five action events, and these are shown in the following screenshot:

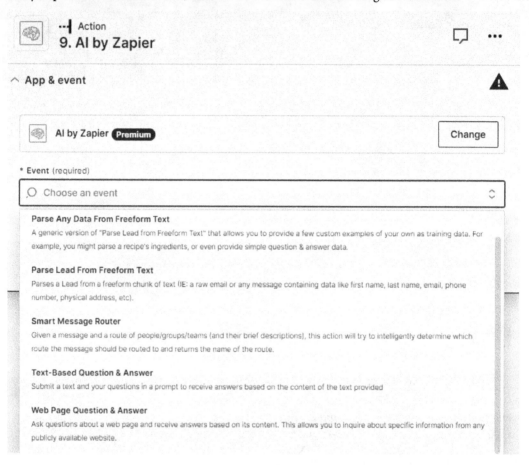

Figure 19.23 – Overview of the AI by Zapier built-in app action events

This Zapier help article provides more information on use cases and how to set up the app: `https://community.zapier.com/product-updates/announcing-ai-by-zapier-beta-launch-7354`.

Let's use this blog article as an example: `https://zapier.com/blog/how-employers-support-parents-working-remotely/`. The following screenshot illustrates how to use this built-in app to understand how many topics are covered in the article and what they are:

Figure 19.24 – Overview of the Web Page Question & Answer action event with question prompts

The result from the AI prompt is shown in the following screenshot:

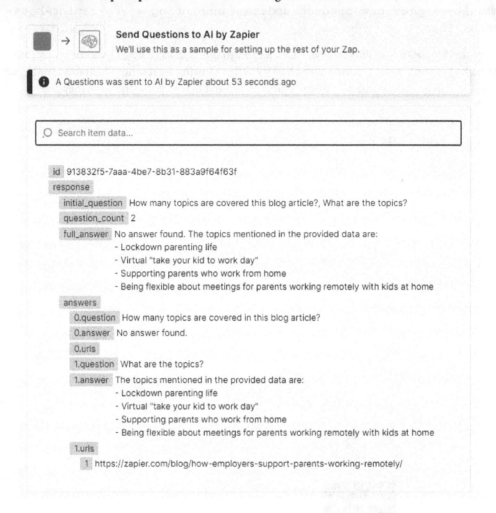

Figure 19.25 – A result from testing the AI questions prompt in AI by Zapier

The following Zapier help articles provide more information on use cases:

- *Answer questions from text documents*: `https://help.zapier.com/hc/en-us/articles/16287563950349-Answer-questions-from-text-documents-using-AI-by-Zapier`

- *Answer questions from web pages documents*: `https://help.zapier.com/hc/en-us/articles/16287096270221-Answer-questions-from-web-pages-using-AI-by-Zapier`

- *Analyze and parse data*: `https://help.zapier.com/hc/en-us/articles/8496342944013-Use-AI-in-Zaps-to-analyze-and-parse-your-text`

You should now have a better understanding of how and when to use some of the AI functionality that has been built into Zapier's built-in apps and features.

Next, let's dive into using AI in your Zaps with AI-integrated apps and, specifically, the OpenAI and ChatGPT integrations.

The OpenAI and ChatGPT integrations with Zapier

Zapier currently has 60+ integrations with AI applications, allowing you to do more with AI and automation. For example, the **Synthesia** app allows you to turn text into videos using AI avatars. With the Zapier-Synthesia integration, you can trigger Zaps when new videos are ready and create new videos, for example, when you receive a service information request from a lead. More information can be found at `https://www.synthesia.io/` and `https://zapier.com/apps/synthesia/integrations`.

You can explore all the integrations at `https://zapier.com/apps/categories/artificial-intelligence`.

Two of the most popular integrations are the **OpenAI** and **ChatGPT** integrations. Let's look at each of these in turn.

The Zapier-OpenAI integration

OpenAI is the maker of the **GPT**, **DALL-E**, and **Whisper** models, and is known by most users for the ChatGPT chatbot. With the GPT models, OpenAI uses natural language prompts to solve problems. With the DALL-E 2 model, OpenAI uses natural language descriptions to create realistic art and images. With the Whisper model, OpenAI can transcribe, identify, and translate text and languages. You can read more about the OpenAI products at `https://openai.com/product`.

With the OpenAI integration, you can check the moderation of text, send prompts, and search text using query strings with GPT, create transcriptions and translations with Whisper, and generate images with DALL-E. You can also use the **App Extensions (beta)** and **API Request (beta)** action events with the OpenAI API: `https://platform.openai.com/docs/api-reference`.

The following screenshot shows the supported triggers and actions of the OpenAI integration:

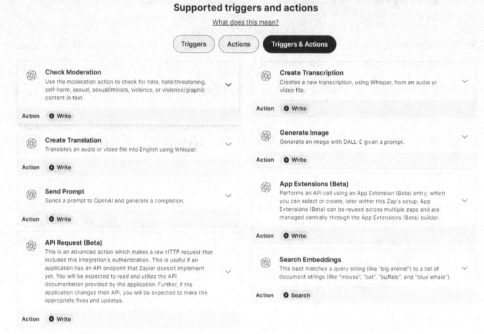

Figure 19.26 – Overview of supported triggers and actions of the Zapier-OpenAI integration

Further details of the Zapier-OpenAI integration can be found at `https://zapier.com/apps/openai/integrations`.

> **Important note**
>
> You must be subscribed to an OpenAI paid account in order to use the OpenAI integration and API.

The following are some useful articles demonstrating use cases of OpenAI with Zapier:

- *How to analyze and score leads with OpenAI's GPT and Zapier*: `https://zapier.com/blog/analyze-leads-with-gpt-3/`

- *How to enrich lead info from sales forms with OpenAI*: `https://zapier.com/blog/enrich-leads-with-openai`

- *How to write sales emails with OpenAI and Zapier*: `https://zapier.com/blog/write-sales-emails-with-openai`

Using the OpenAI integration with Zapier

We will use the **Generate Image** action event to demonstrate how to use the OpenAI integration for DALL-E to generate an image as follows:

1. Add a detailed prompt description in the **Prompt** field. For example, the prompt could be A watercolor painting of a bulldog with wings sitting on a fence.

2. Add the number of image variations between 1 and 10 in the **n** field.

3. Use the **Size** drop-down menu to select the size of the image.

This is shown in the following screenshot:

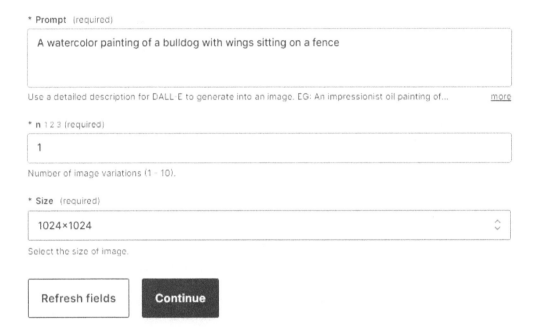

Figure 19.27 – Overview of customizing the Generate Image action
event in the OpenAI integration using the DALL-E model

The test produces a result with the URL, which is shown in the following screenshot:

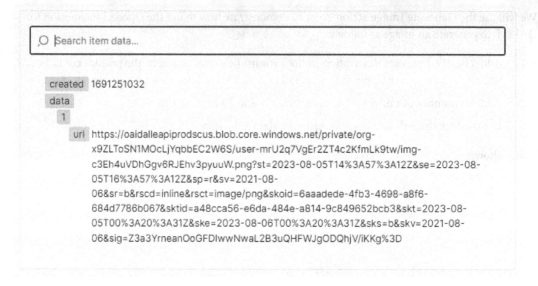

Search item data...

created   1691251032
data
  1
    url https://oaidalleapiprodscus.blob.core.windows.net/private/org-
         x9ZLToSN1MOcLjYqbbEC2W6S/user-mrU2q7VgEr2ZT4c2KfmLk9tw/img-
         c3Eh4uVDhGgv6RJEhv3pyuuW.png?st=2023-08-05T14%3A57%3A12Z&se=2023-08-
         05T16%3A57%3A12Z&sp=r&sv=2021-08-
         06&sr=b&rscd=inline&rsct=image/png&skoid=6aaadede-4fb3-4698-a8f6-
         684d7786b067&sktid=a48cca56-e6da-484e-a814-9c849652bcb3&skt=2023-08-
         05T00%3A20%3A31Z&ske=2023-08-06T00%3A20%3A31Z&sks=b&skv=2021-08-
         06&sig=Z3a3YrneanOoGFDIwwNwaL2B3uQHFWJgODQhjV/iKKg%3D

Figure 19.28 – An example of the result of the Generate Image action event

The actual image result is shown in the following screenshot:

Figure 19.29 – An example of an image produced when using the
Generate Image action event in the OpenAI integration

Next, let's cover the ChatGPT integration with Zapier.

Zapier-ChatGPT integration

The GPT chatbot ChatGPT has taken the world by storm, allowing significant productivity increases using AI, as described in the *The Zapier ChatGPT plugin (beta) – running Zap actions from ChatGPT* section. You can find out more about ChatGPT at `https://openai.com/chatgpt`. With the ChatGPT integration, you can send prompts and save conversations that can later be recalled in other steps or Zaps, as well as use OpenAI's **Function Calling** capability. Further details on Function Calling can be found at `https://openai.com/blog/function-calling-and-other-api-updates`. Most importantly, the Zapier integration with ChatGPT allows some **ChatGPT Plus** account users to use OpenAI's most advanced model, **GPT-4**, in Zaps, which is currently not available with the OpenAI integration.

The following screenshot shows the supported triggers and actions of the ChatGPT integration:

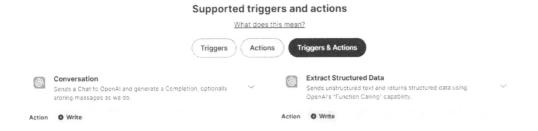

Figure 19.30 – Overview of supported triggers and actions of the Zapier – ChatGPT integration

Further details of the Zapier-ChatGPT integration can be found at `https://zapier.com/apps/chatgpt/integrations`.

Using the ChatGPT integration with Zapier

To illustrate how to use the ChatGPT integration, we shall use the example of using ChatGPT to create a list of social media ideas and quotes once a month and add each individual idea and quote as a separate task in ClickUp. The steps are as follows:

1. **Trigger**: **Every Month in Schedule by Zapier** to trigger the Zap on the first day of each month
2. **Action**: **Conversation in ChatGPT** to prompt ChatGPT for a response
3. **Action**: **Text** action event with **Split** transform option in Formatter with Zapier to split the text in to separate line items
4. **Action**: **Create Loop From Line Items in Looping by Zapier** to loop the line items
5. **Looping Action**: **Create Task in ClickUp** to create each line item as a task in ClickUp

This is shown in the following screenshot:

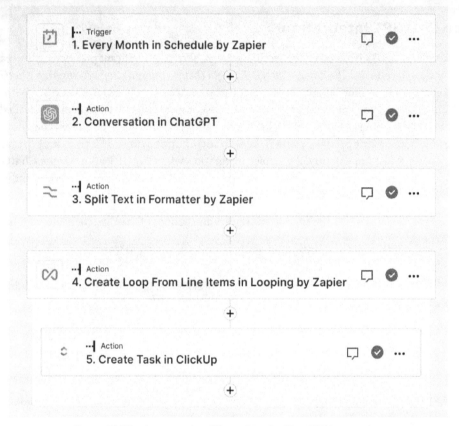

Figure 19.31 – An example of Zap using the ChatGPT integration

In the **Conversation in ChatGPT** step, enter a descriptive prompt in the **User Message** field, a name in the **User Name** field, a name for the assistant in the **Assistant Name** field, and instructions to use in the **Assistant Instructions** field. Then select the model from the **Model** drop-down list, a unique **Memory Key** that can be used in other steps or Zaps to find the record of the conversation, and the maximum number of tokens in the **Max Tokens** field. GPT models are explained in the documentation at `https://platform.openai.com/docs/guides/gpt/chat-completions-api`. Refer back to the *Formatter by Zapier – Split Text into Chunks for AI Prompt (beta) transform option* section earlier in this chapter for more information on tokens.

The **Temperature** and **Top P** fields are both defaulted to the **1.0** value. Both can be adjusted to produce a more accurate or random output; however, it is recommended that only one is adjusted and not both. Instructions on how to adjust the field values and relevance are stated in the action step.

Our example is shown in the following screenshot:

* User Message (required)

> Provide 10 social media content ideas and 3 quotes about business process automation and productivity. The list should not include any other sentences, and each point should start with the text "Idea:" for social media ideas and "Quote:" for quotes.

The most recent message the assistant (ChatGPT) responds to.

User Name

> user

The name of the user sending a message to the assistant. *Feel free to experiment with this!*

Assistant Name

> assistant

The name of the assistant receiving the message. *Feel free to experiment with this!*

Assistant Instructions

> You are an experienced social media expert who writes high converting social media posts

Instructions to the assistant. *Feel free to experiment with this!*

Model

> gpt-3.5-turbo

GPT-4 not available? **Join OpenAI's waitlist** for access.

Memory Key

> 📅 **1. Pretty Date:** Mar 4, 2023

If provided, this unique value will allow the assistant to continue a conversation from previous messages. Use...   more

Max Tokens 1.0

> 250

The maximum number of tokens to generate in the output. We will do our best to trim old messages to provide this...   more

Temperature 1.0

> 1.0

A number between 0 and 2. Higher values like 0.8 will make the output more random, while lower values like 0.2 will...   more

Top P 1.0

> 1.0

Nucleus sampling, where the model considers the results of the tokens with top_p probability mass. So 0.1 means onl...   more

Figure 19.32 – Overview of customizing the Conversation in ChatGPT action event

The result is shown in the following screenshot:

 → **Send Conversation to ChatGPT**
We'll use this as a sample for setting up the rest of your Zap.

> ℹ️ A Conversation was sent to ChatGPT about 8 minutes ago

🔍 Search item data...

`id` chatcmpl-6r3f3bNSYrMd0ASmIMc5L93Hv63y2
`response`
  `role` assistant
  `content` Idea:
      1. Highlight different automation tools and explain how they can help businesses save time and money.
      2. Share real-life examples of how automation has helped your business or your clients' businesses become more efficient and productive.
      3. Create infographics that compare the productivity levels of manual workflows versus automated workflows.
      4. Curate and share industry news and studies about automation's impact on the future of work.
      5. Host a live webinar with a guest speaker who can offer insights into the benefits of business process automation.
      6. Provide tips and tricks for businesses to get started with automation, including how to choose the right tools and software.
      7. Interview industry leaders who have implemented automation and have seen significant productivity gains.
      8. Share case studies of companies that utilized automation to overcome hurdles and achieve their business goals.
      9. Offer a checklist of critical factors to consider before implementing automation in your workflow.
      10. Create memes or humorous graphics about automation to engage your social media audience.

      Quote:
      1. "Automation is not just a mechanism, but it is a mindset." - Dinesh Paliwal
      2. "Automation is good, so long as you know exactly where to put the machine." - Eliyahu Goldratt
      3. "The only way for companies to stay ahead of the competitive curve and to compete with the best in the business is to embrace the digital revolution and go for automation." -David Cummings

Figure 19.33 – The result of the Conversation in ChatGPT action event test

You should now have a better understanding of AI-integrated apps with Zapier.

Next, let's briefly explore some guidelines on **GPT AI prompting**.

GPT AI prompting guidelines

Writing prompts well enough to get high-quality responses from the AI-powered tools that you are using can be a matter of trial and error and can take some practice. Learning to write prompts to get the best results could be an entire chapter on its own and, ultimately, you must train the AI to give you better results. Here are some tips on prompt writing:

- Use descriptive inputs to frame the scenario, and explain the purpose of the prompt and what you are trying to achieve

- Outline clear, specific expectations and guidelines

- Specify what character or profession the AI should mimic, what tone of voice to use, and who the audience is

- Give your own examples of what the result could look like

- Provide references with URLs sourced from the internet for further examples

We have collated some useful Zapier resources that will help you in your journey to becoming an AI-prompting expert:

- `https://zapier.com/blog/gpt-prompt/`

- `https://community.zapier.com/featured-articles-65/prompting-basics-get-quality-responses-when-interacting-with-ai-24314`

- `https://community.zapier.com/how-do-i-3/ai-voice-tone-when-creating-content-23182`

The OpenAI API documentation also provides very useful information on best practices here: `https://platform.openai.com/docs/guides/gpt-best-practices`.

You should now have a better understanding of the best practices for GPT AI prompting.

Summary

In this chapter, we covered how you can boost your productivity by combining AI and automation. We explored some of Zapier's built-in AI functionality as well as AI app integrations with Zapier.

First, we explored how to get early access to new Zapier features that have incorporated AI functionality, then we covered an overview of the Create a Zap feature. Next, we looked at the NLA and AI Actions functionality in the Zapier Chrome extension and ChatGPT plugin. Then, we explored how to create AI chatbots with Zapier Interfaces. Next, we covered a few new built-in apps and features such as

AI-powered Formatter by Zapier steps, AI-powered Code by Zapier steps, AI-powered troubleshooting, and the AI by Zapier built-in app. Finally, we explored the ChatGPT and OpenAI integrations with Zapier and the basics of GPT AI prompting.

In the next chapter, you will learn how to automate your marketing workflows. We will discuss the different types of marketing processes and give working examples of how these processes can be automated using Zapier. We will also provide practical tips on how to solve problems relating to marketing workflows.

Questions

1. Name three built-in Zapier apps and features that are powered by AI.

2. What models and functions has OpenAI created?

3. How many AI apps does Zapier integrate with currently?

Answers

1. There are multiple AI-powered Zapier built-in apps and features. A few examples are AI-powered Formatter by Zapier steps, AI-powered Code by Zapier steps, and AI-powered troubleshooting.

2. OpenAI is the maker of the GPT, DALL-E, and Whisper models, and is known by most users for the ChatGPT chatbot.

3. Zapier currently integrates with over 60 AI-based apps, including ChatGPT and OpenAI.

20

Automating Your Marketing Processes

So far in this book, we've reviewed how to get started with building workflow automations with Zapier and how to use the various built-in apps, including Formatter by Zapier, to boost your automations. Now that we've covered those topics, it will be useful to go into more detail regarding the different types of business processes that can be automated by using Zapier as a connector tool between thousands of business applications. In the following few chapters, we will cover how to automate processes in five of the central business functions, namely marketing, sales, operations, finance, and analytics, and explore examples relating to some commonly used digital tools that integrate with Zapier. We will also go into more detail about how to use one specific integration related to each function.

To start off, marketing is generally the first part of the business cycle, and an important one at that. All businesses need marketing processes to varying degrees to ensure they have a way of attracting potential customers. In this chapter, we will discuss the different types of marketing processes that can be automated with Zapier, and we will provide examples of workflows used with some common marketing applications. First, we will take an overview of the types of marketing processes that can be automated with Zapier. Then, we will explore where to start with automating marketing processes with Zapier. Finally, we will dive into how to automate social media marketing with the Facebook Pages integration.

We will cover the following key topics in this chapter:

- An introduction to automating your marketing processes with Zapier
- Where to start with automating your marketing processes with Zapier
- Automating social media marketing processes, illustrated with the Facebook Pages integration

Once you have worked through each of these topics, you will have a better understanding of the different marketing processes that can be automated with Zapier. You will know how to use Zapier to automate marketing processes with some of the most common marketing applications.

Technical requirements

To make the most of the content in this chapter, you will need access to a Zapier account. The Zapier Free plan will be required for you to create single-step workflows and use Zapier's pre-built templates. The Zapier Starter plan will be required for you to use Premium apps and to create multi-step workflows.

You can get access to the Zap template used in this chapter at `https://bit.ly/zapier-book`. Using the template will help you to visualize how the process works.

An introduction to automating your marketing processes with Zapier

Every business needs some form of marketing to make sure they get the customers physically through the door or purchasing their products and services online. What every business strives for is lead generation by means of word of mouth or recommendation; in other words, getting your valued and happy customers to do the marketing work for you. However, when you're first starting out, the onus is on the business to get its name out there in one way or another. In the past, some of the most popular forms of marketing were newspaper and magazine ads, leaflet drops, radio ads, and, for those who could afford it, television ads, where customers were often limited to specific geographical areas. In this digital age, where we have the far reaches of the internet to attract everyone, businesses have more tools and services available for cost-effective marketing. However, with more options come more things that we need to do to stay ahead of the competition.

First of all, most businesses need some form of digital presence so that prospective buyers can find them, and that might be a website or a **Google My Business** page. Your website might have a blog so that you can improve your searchability on search engines such as Google. You might need to share your blog articles on your various social media channels, while engaging your followers with useful content, memes, and motivational posts, or strategic social media campaigns to drive traffic back to your website. You might embed forms into your website to allow people to subscribe to your newsletter. You might have landing pages to help you collect email addresses or prospects to add to your marketing campaigns. You might also use digital ads to increase traffic to these dedicated landing pages. All this effort, and all these tools being used, are purely for the purpose of getting an audience into your sales cycle and buying your product or service.

Understanding what marketing processes can be automated with Zapier

Zapier has several integrations with a range of marketing tools spanning numerous functions allowing you to automate your **marketing processes**. You can connect these apps with thousands of other apps, such as Slack, Google Drive, Airtable, and SMS by Zapier, to automate your social media marketing processes.

Here are a few examples of marketing processes that can be automated with Zapier:

- Online presence processes

- Social media marketing processes

- Social media scheduling processes

- Ad processes

- Email marketing and marketing automation processes

Let's explore each one of these and give some examples of marketing apps that can be used with Zapier to automate the processes that involve them.

Automating processes involving apps for online presence

Most businesses these days have some form of digital presence, and in most cases, that starts with a website. To help improve search engine optimization, it is generally recommended that you have a blog where you publish new and relevant content regularly. You might use **Tumblr**, **WordPress**, **Drupal**, or **Webflow** to manage your website and blog content.

Managing a blog can be a time-consuming activity, so you might find it useful to automate some of the related processes. One popular website builder and blog that integrates with Zapier is WordPress. You can use Zapier to automate your WordPress blog processes, such as creating, updating, and sharing new content, as well as managing comments and users. You can trigger workflows when you receive new comments, when a new user is added, when posts are added or updated, and when new media is added. Combine these trigger events with action events in notification apps such as Email by Zapier to get an email, social media apps such as Twitter or Medium to share new posts, or a Google Sheets spreadsheet to add new users to a list. You can also create new posts, update existing posts, upload media, create new users, and search for posts when, for example, new images are added to Google Drive or new users are added to your CRM, **Dubsado**, or task management app, Asana.

Many businesses that have a physical, bricks-and-mortar location, such as retail shops, dentists, or legal firms, may advertise their business on services such as Google My Business. With this type of service, you can advertise your opening hours and contact details, and collect customer reviews. Using Google My Business also increases your searchability on Google. As Google My Business integrates with Zapier, you can use Zapier to connect to other apps in your processes and automate your online presence. For example, you can trigger workflows when you receive a new review and get notifications such as a Slack message or SMS. You can respond to specific reviews, as soon as you receive a new review, or update a reply when a record appears in a view in Airtable.

There are many website builder apps that integrate with Zapier, which you can check out at `https://zapier.com/apps/categories/website-app-building`.

Next, let's discuss how to automate social media marketing processes with Zapier.

Automating social media marketing processes

Most businesses use some form of social media to engage their prospects and existing customers. You might only use one or perhaps several social media platforms, depending on the needs of your business. To name a few, these could be Facebook Groups, Twitter, Instagram for Business, or **Pinterest**, for example. Whatever your social media marketing processes are, there will be ways to connect your tools and automate those processes with Zapier.

With the Instagram for Business integration, you can trigger workflows when new videos or photos are posted to your account or when your account is tagged in a photo or video. You could combine these triggers with action events to share on your Facebook Page or on LinkedIn, or save the file in Google Drive. You can also publish a new photo to your feed when, for example, you publish new Shopify or WooCommerce products.

With the Pinterest integration, you can trigger workflows when new pins are added, a new board is created, or you get a new follower. Combine these with action events to post something to Facebook Pages or notify your team in Slack. You can also create a new pin when, for example, you publish a new post on WordPress.

There are many social media marketing apps that integrate with Zapier, which you can check out here: `https://zapier.com/apps/categories/social`.

Next, let's explore how to automate social media scheduling processes with Zapier.

Automating social media scheduling processes

Posting content on social media is another time-consuming marketing activity. Writing the content, designing graphics, planning when to post it, and then actually doing the posting can take some time and be a very manual process. Using social media scheduling tools such as **Buffer**, **Meet Edgar**, and **Hootsuite** can make lighter work of part of that process by helping you post to multiple social media platforms at once on days and at times of your choosing. Being able to then automate processes involving these scheduling apps makes things even easier. You can, therefore, use Zapier to automate many social media scheduling workflows.

With the Meet Edgar integration, you can add new content to your library when new pins are added on Pinterest or when you release new videos on YouTube.

With the Buffer integration, you can trigger workflows when new items are added, and then share the new item on WordPress as a new post, create Trello cards, or create Google Calendar events. You could also add new rows to a Google Sheets spreadsheet when a new profile is added. You might also want to add an item to your schedule for posting at a later date or send an immediate update when, for example, a new Instagram photo is posted, or a new Evernote note is created.

There are many social media scheduling apps that integrate with Zapier, which you can check out at `https://zapier.com/apps/categories/social-marketing`.

Next, let's cover how to automate online advertising processes with Zapier.

Automating ad processes

Online paid advertising is a popular way of driving traffic to your website or specific landing pages to promote your products and services. Facebook Lead Ads, Google Ads, and Instagram Lead Ads are popular apps used for online paid advertising, and you can use Zapier to automate ad workflows involving these three apps.

With the Facebook Lead Ads integration, for example, you can trigger workflows when a new lead is created, add new rows to a Google Sheets spreadsheet, or add the lead to your CRM.

With the **Google Ads** integration, you can trigger workflows when a new campaign is created or a lead form is created, and add new posts to LinkedIn or create events in Google Calendar. You can also create a customer list, add or remove contacts to and from a list, or set a status and send offline conversion information from your other apps. You can search for customer lists and campaigns and create a customer list if one does not exist.

There are several online advertising apps that integrate with Zapier, which you can check out at `https://zapier.com/apps/categories/ads-conversion`.

Next, let's explore how to automate email marketing and marketing automation processes with Zapier.

Automating email marketing and marketing automation

Another popular way to nurture your leads and get your customer buying more from you is to use email marketing or marketing automation. In order to use these methods, once you've pushed new prospects to your website or specific landing pages using social media or ads, you first of all need to collect the email addresses of your contacts so that you can send them new free but valuable content, let them know of special offers, or introduce them to your team and services. You might do this by embedding forms into your website to allow people to subscribe to your newsletter, or setting up landing pages with free downloads such as cheat sheets, e-books, or fun quizzes to help you collect email addresses so that you can add them to your marketing campaigns.

Email marketing processes

Email marketing apps such as **Constant Contact**, Mailchimp, and **Campaign Monitor** generally allow you to send one-off newsletter-style emails with some simple automations.

With the Constant Contact integration, you can trigger workflows when new contacts or lists are added and when an email is opened. You can combine these triggers with action events such as adding new contacts to Salesforce CRM and labeling them when they have opened an email. You can also create or update contacts in your account, find a contact or create one if it doesn't exist when, for example, new Gravity Forms or Typeform form submissions are made, or when you receive a new Facebook Lead Ad lead.

There are several email marketing apps that integrate with Zapier, which you can check out at `https://zapier.com/apps/categories/email-newsletters`.

Marketing automation processes

Marketing automation apps such as ActiveCampaign, **Click Funnels**, and Keap allow you to set up automation sequences with conditional logic where you can remove and add contacts to different lists, segments, and automations based on their activity and behavior. They can often have additional functionality such as working as CRMs as well.

The ActiveCampaign integration has a long list of 15 trigger events, 12 action events, and 4 search action events. As ActiveCampaign also has CRM functionality such as contact management, deals, tasks, and notes, there are several CRM-specific events you can use, which we won't discuss here. However, for the marketing functionality, you can trigger workflows when a campaign starts sending emails, a campaign bounces, links in a campaign have been clicked, a contact unsubscribes from a campaign, or a campaign email is opened. You can combine these triggers with action events such as getting notifications in Slack or by email using Email by Zapier or posting new campaigns to your Facebook Page. You can also find a contact, create contacts, add them to automations, create and send a new campaign, or add a tracked event when, for example, you have new Thinkific orders, get new form entries from Google Forms or **JotForm**, close a **ManyChat** chat, or receive a PayPal sale.

There are several marketing automation apps that integrate with Zapier, which you can check out at `https://zapier.com/apps/categories/marketing-automation`.

> **Tip**
>
> If you're a business that serves the B2B market, then you can take advantage of the data extracted with the built-in Lead Score by Zapier app, which can then be used in lead qualification and scoring. This is especially useful for small companies and start-ups who don't have a large lead volume yet and may not be able to afford the fees associated with data insights platforms. The additional data you can retrieve about your prospects as they come in to your systems is invaluable, and at no extra cost for low volumes. You can explore the built-in Lead Score by Zapier app in more detail in *Chapter 10, Other Useful Built-In Apps by Zapier*.

You now understand what kind of marketing processes can be automated with Zapier.

Let's now take a look at the essential first steps to take to start automating your marketing processes.

Where to start with automating your marketing processes with Zapier

It is always good to do some pre-work before your start automating your processes. In *Chapter 2, Preparing to Automate Your Processes*, and *Chapter 3, Building Your First Automated Workflow (Zap)*, we covered a few important points that will help you when you are strategizing your marketing workflows, and they are as follows:

- **Map out your marketing processes**: You probably already have a marketing strategy in place and you have a clear idea of how your marketing processes work with all your tools. If you don't, however, follow the steps in the *Simplifying your processes and assessing what can be automated* section in *Chapter 2, Preparing to Automate Your Processes*, to visually map out your processes so that you have a high-level overview of how your tasks work with your existing software.

- **List your marketing tools**: Make a list of all the marketing tools and services that you use in your business to achieve your goals. Then, assess how these tools fit within your mapped-out processes. You will then be able to simplify those processes and decide on what can be automated. Once you have this overview of your processes and tools, you will be better placed to understand where the holes are, and how Zapier can help you to close the gaps and automate your processes.

- **Review your app profile pages**: In *Chapter 2, Preparing to Automate Your Processes*, we also discussed reviewing your individual app profile pages as the best way to establish how your business apps integrate with Zapier. This will give you insights into the triggers, actions, and searches available to use in your workflows. Make a list of these for quick reference.

- **Use Zapier's pre-built guided workflow templates**: This is the easiest way to get started with automating your marketing processes. These templates are built from workflows that are commonly used by other users. They are perfect for inspiration, quick to set up, and will save you time immediately.

- **Customize your marketing workflows**: Get creative and start building multi-step workflows to achieve more in your automations. Use Zapier's built-in apps to help you do more and connect your marketing workflows to other parts of your business processes, such as your sales process.

- **Combine AI and automation**: Use the magic of AI-powered Zapier features and integrated AI apps to supercharge your marketing workflows. Find out more in *Chapter 19, AI and Automation*.

With all of this, you'll be well on your way to creating marketing automations for your business.

> **Tip**
>
> If you're looking for ideas of other marketing apps to use in your business, you can review the **Marketing** category in the app ecosystem directory to give you a list of public apps that integrate with Zapier at `https://zapier.com/apps/categories/marketing`. Review the *A brief guide to choosing new apps for your business* section in *Chapter 2, Preparing to Automate Your Processes*, for guidance on choosing new apps.

You now know how to get started with automating your social media processes with Zapier.

Let's get more specific and discuss how social media marketing processes can be automated using Zapier's Facebook Pages integration.

Automating social media marketing processes, illustrated with the Facebook Pages integration

Facebook is one of the most commonly used social media platforms, and it has two popular social media apps that integrate with Zapier, namely Facebook Pages and Facebook Groups. To give you some insight into how you can automate your social media marketing processes, we'll focus on the Facebook Pages integration with Zapier.

Most businesses don't use personal Facebook accounts for their social media marketing but will set up Facebook Pages. Facebook Pages are perfect for giving a business better online visibility, showcasing its products and services, opening hours, and customer recommendations, as well as sharing content, special offers, and news to engage prospects and customers.

You can use Zapier to automate your marketing processes if you use Facebook Pages in your business, and the Facebook Pages integration supports numerous trigger and action events. A full list can be found on the Facebook Pages app profile page at `https://zapier.com/apps/facebook-pages/integrations`.

Facebook Pages trigger events and use cases

The following is a list of some of the supported trigger events that you can use with Facebook Pages with examples of when to use them:

- **New Post to Your Timeline**: This event triggers when a new post is added by you or someone else to the timeline of your Facebook Pages account. Among other things, you can use this trigger event in your automations when you want to be notified of a new post on your timeline. For example, combine this trigger event with a notification action event such as **Send SMS** with SMS by Zapier to send you an SMS, or the **Send Channel Message** action event with Slack to send a message to your team on a specified channel.

- **New Recommendation**: This event triggers when your Facebook Page receives a new recommendation. Among other things, you can use this trigger event in your automations when you want to assign a task to your team to review the recommendation. For example, combine this trigger event with the **Create Card** action event with Trello to add a new card to Trello and assign a member to it, or add a task to Clickup with the **Create Task** action event. You could also use it when you want to share the recommendation on other social media platforms.

- **New Post by You**: This event triggers when you post an update to the timeline of your Facebook Page. Among other things, you can use this trigger event in your automations when you want to reshare your post on other social media platforms. For example, combine this trigger event with an action event such as **Create Tweet** to post a tweet on Twitter. If you needed to make sure that your message is not over the maximum character length of 280 for a tweet, in a step prior to the action step, add the Formatter by Zapier **Text** action event with the **Truncate** transform option to truncate the character length.

Next, let's have a look at some of the Facebook Pages action events and use cases.

Facebook Pages action events and use cases

The following is a list of some of the supported action events that you can use with Facebook Pages with examples of when to use them:

- **Create Page Photo**: You can use this action event to upload a photo to your Facebook Page, which then is posted on your Facebook Page stream. You could use this action event in combination with a trigger event such as **New File in Folder** in Google Drive to post new photos to your Facebook Page. Use the `File` field from your trigger to map in the file object. Photos should be smaller than 4 MB and saved as either `.jpg`, `.png`, `.gif`, `.tiff`, HEIF, or WebP files.

- **Create Page Post**: You can use this action event to create and post a new stream item to your Facebook Page. You could use this action event in combination with a trigger event such as **New Item in Feed** in RSS by Zapier to post new feed items from your favorite blog and share them with your Facebook audience, or **New Post** in WordPress to share new posts from your blog.

- **Create Page Video**: You can use this action to upload a video to your Facebook Page, which then is posted on your Facebook Page stream. You could use this action event in combination with a trigger event such as **New Video in Channel** in YouTube to post your latest videos to your Facebook Page. Use the `play_url` field from your trigger to map in the publicly accessible YouTube URL.

- **Change Page Profile Photo**: You can use this action event to change the profile picture on your Facebook Page. You could use this action event in combination with a trigger event such as **New Record** in Airtable to post new photos to your Facebook Page when a new record is created in Airtable with an image associated. Use the `File` field from your trigger to map in the file object.

Next, let's explore how to set up an example of a multi-step Zap using the Facebook Pages integration.

Setting up a multi-step Zap with the Facebook Pages integration

To illustrate this, we will use the example of creating a new page post on Facebook Pages when an RSS feed item is added to one of our favorite blogs, `https://zapier.com/blog/feeds/latest/`. We will truncate the blog description so that our message is more readable.

The Zap will involve the following three steps:

1. **Trigger**: The **RSS by Zapier** app with the **New Item in Feed** trigger event.
2. **Action**: The **Formatter by Zapier** app with the **Text** action event and the **Truncate** transform option.
3. **Action**: The **Facebook Pages** app with the **New Page Post** action event.

The following screenshot shows how your Zap should look once built, with some custom labeling:

Figure 20.1 – A multi-step Zap using Facebook Pages as an action step

Let's walk through this step by step, starting with the trigger step.

Setting up the trigger step

We will use the RSS by Zapier built-in app with the **New Item in Feed** trigger event as the trigger step. Follow the instructions in the *RSS by Zapier – using RSS feed readers* section in *Chapter 9, Exploring Built-In Apps for Extracting and Compiling Data*, to add `https://zapier.com/blog/feeds/latest/` to the **Feed URL** field.

The following screenshot shows how this step should look:

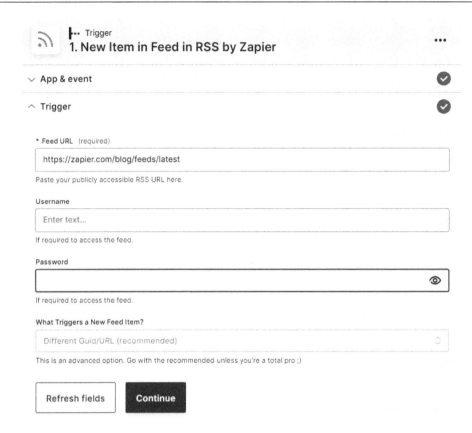

Figure 20.2 – Overview of using RSS by Zapier to trigger a workflow when there is a new item in a feed

Next, let's set up the second step in the Zap – the first action step.

Setting up the second step in the Zap

We will use the Formatter by Zapier app with the **Text** action event and the **Truncate** transform option. Follow the instructions in the *Truncating text to a specified character length* section in *Chapter 17, Text Formatting Functions in Zapier – Part 2*, to customize this action step so that we truncate the dynamic Description data from the trigger step by mapping it to the **Input** field, setting **Maximum Length** to 100 characters without skipping characters, and adding ... to the end by selecting **True** in the **Append Ellipsis?** field.

The following screenshot shows how this step should look:

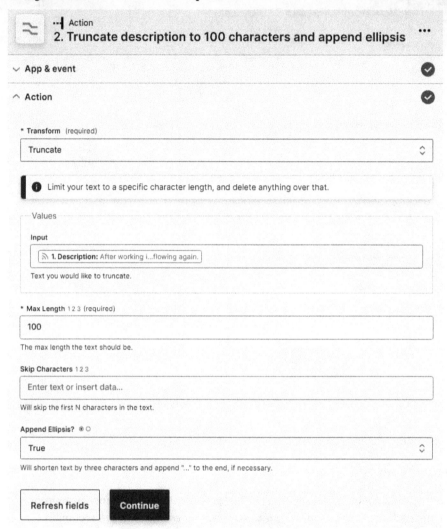

Figure 20.3 – Overview of using the Formatter by Zapier Text action event to truncate the Description data

Click on the **Continue** button. You can then use the **Test** section to truncate the text.

Next, let's set up the final action step.

Setting up the third step in the Zap

We will use the Facebook Pages app with the **New Page Post** action event, and we will customize this action step by completing the fields as follows:

- **Page**: We will use this drop-down field to select a Facebook Page account that we have admin access to. In this case, we choose the **Solvaa – Zapier Experts** option.

- **Message**: We will add static text reading `Here's the latest from the Zapier blog:`, the dynamic blog **Title** data from the trigger step, and the formatted `Description` output from *step 2*.

- **Link Url**: We will map in the dynamic **Link** data from the *step 1* trigger so that the reader can click on a link to take them to the actual blog post.

The following screenshot shows how this step should look:

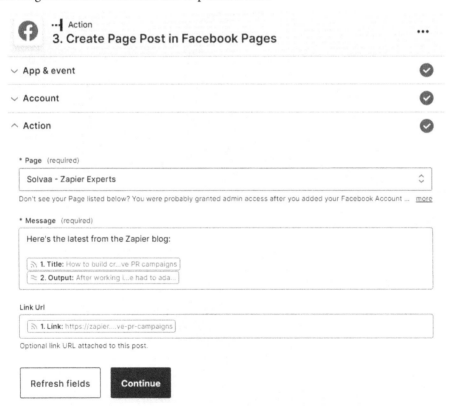

Figure 20.4 – Overview of using the Facebook Pages integration to create a new page post

Click on the **Continue** button. You can then use the **Test** section to create the post on Facebook Pages. The result of our scenario is shown in the following screenshot:

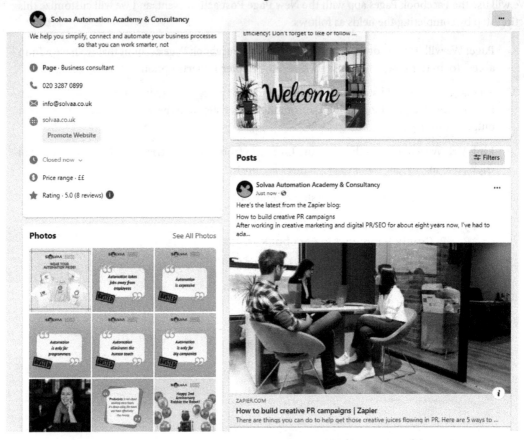

Figure 20.5 – Overview of the new page post created by Zapier in Facebook Pages

You can get access to a copy of this Zap template here: `https://bit.ly/zapier-book`.

You should now have a better understanding of how to automate social media marketing processes with the Facebook Pages integration.

Summary

In this chapter, we discussed the different types of marketing processes that can be automated with Zapier, and we explored some examples of workflows used with some common marketing applications. First, we got an overview of the types of marketing processes that can be automated with Zapier. Then, we covered where to start with automating marketing processes with Zapier. Finally, we discussed how to automate social media marketing with the Facebook Pages integration.

You now know how to automate your marketing processes with Zapier and specifically with the Facebook Pages integration.

In the next chapter, you will learn how to automate your sales workflows. We will discuss the different types of sales processes and give working examples of how these processes can be automated using Zapier. We will also provide practical tips on how to solve problems related to sales workflows.

Questions

1.   What types of marketing processes can be automated using Zapier?

2.   Which file types can be uploaded as a new Facebook Pages photo?

21
Automating Your Sales Processes

Now that we've covered how to automate marketing processes with Zapier, the next important business function to explore is the sales cycle and how to automate its processes. Sales, of course, is one of the most important business functions. Once your marketing processes are working on autopilot to push new leads your way, you will need an efficient way of converting them into sales. No sales means no revenue, and a business without revenue will not survive long at all. Therefore, having a streamlined and automated sales process will most definitely help ensure business success.

In this chapter, we will discuss the different types of sales processes that can be automated with Zapier, and we will provide examples of workflows used with some common sales applications. First, we will give an overview of the types of sales processes that can be automated with Zapier, such as data collection, appointment scheduling, lead capture and management, getting digital signatures, and handling online sales transactions. Then, we will explore where to start with automating sales processes with Zapier. Finally, there are several different sales tools that integrate with Zapier, allowing you to automate your sales processes. To illustrate this, we will dive into how to automate lead management processes with the Pipedrive CRM integration.

We will cover the following key topics in this chapter:

- An introduction to automating your sales processes with Zapier
- Where to start with automating your sales processes with Zapier
- Automating lead management processes with CRM integrations, illustrated with the Pipedrive integration

Once you have worked through each of these topics, you will have a better understanding of the different sales processes that can be automated with Zapier. You will know how to use Zapier to automate sales processes with some of the most common sales applications.

Technical requirements

To make the most of the content in this chapter, you will need access to a Zapier account. The Zapier Free plan will be required for you to create single-step workflows and use Zapier's pre-built templates. The Zapier Starter plan will be required for you to use Premium apps and to create multi-step workflows.

You can get access to the Zap template used in this chapter at `https://bit.ly/zapier-book`. Using the template will help you to visualize how the process works.

An introduction to automating your sales processes with Zapier

In days gone by, many businesses owned cash registers that made a "cha-ching" chime every time they received money from a sale. These days, it's not likely that many businesses have these antique cash registers, but many business owners might imagine that "cha-ching" sound when they make a sale and secretly do a little jig. Sales are what keep the business going and pay the employees, suppliers, and business owners.

Before the internet came along, companies often needed to have premises to trade from and made sales of their products or services when customers walked through the door. Some customers knew what they wanted, and others needed more information or a bit of convincing. The sales personnel worked the room and attended to potential buyers while having to answer the telephone, deal with inquiries, and book appointments. Customer details might have been recorded on a paper registration form, in a book or a spreadsheet, or not at all. Contracts were written out by hand or typed out, requiring a signature in person.

Things have moved on since then with the digital age, and companies now have many tools available to them to be able to run their sales cycle more efficiently and effectively. Salespeople now have better processes at their fingertips for building stronger relationships with their prospective customers so that they buy and keep coming back for more without losing the personal touch.

An example of how a sales process can be improved significantly by using connector tools such as Zapier to automate various tasks can be found at `https://solvaa.co.uk/automate-dental-practice/`.

Understanding what sales processes can be automated with Zapier

Zapier has many integrations with a range of sales tools spanning numerous functions allowing you to automate your **sales processes**. You can connect these apps with thousands of other apps such as Microsoft Outlook, Asana, Dropbox, and Xero to automate your sales processes.

Here are a few examples of sales processes that can be automated with Zapier:

- Data collection processes with forms
- Appointment booking and scheduling processes
- Lead management processes
- Contract, proposal, and digital signature collection processes
- E-commerce processes

Let's explore each one and give some examples of sales apps that can be used with Zapier to automate processes that involve them.

Automating processes involving data collection

Many businesses use form builders to collect information from prospective customers. You might use Gravity Forms, Google Forms, JotForm, Typeform, or another form builder. These forms might be for the purpose of sending through an inquiry about the company's services and products when embedded into the company website or for marketing purposes so that people can sign up for the company's newsletter or fill out a survey.

It's common that you might receive an email notification when a form entry is made, but then it can be time-consuming and repetitive to process that data and add it to other systems. By automating the process, you can then add that form data to multiple tools in your app stack and kick off workflows accordingly. For example, when a new form entry has been made, you could notify your team with a Slack message, send an SMS to yourself, add the entry to Google Drive or Dropbox as a text tile, create a new issue in **Jira**, create a new contact and opportunity in **Close.io**, and more.

Gravity Forms is a popular WordPress plugin that allows you to create a custom form that you can embed into web pages so that you can collect data. With the Gravity Forms integration, you can trigger workflows when a form is submitted. You can combine this trigger with action events to add the form data to your CRM, add a new task to your project management app, or send an automated email with Gmail, for example. You can also create a form entry and, additionally, trigger rules associated with the form submission, such as notifications and feed add-ons.

When using Google Forms, you can create forms and then use them as standalone URLs or embed them into web pages. Form entries are also recorded on a Google Sheets spreadsheet. With the Google Forms integration, you can trigger workflows when a new form response is added to the bottom of the associated Google Sheets and, additionally, when a form response is modified. You can combine these triggers with action events to add or update data in your email marketing tool, such as **ConvertKit**, add events to Google Calendar, or send out an automated voicemail with Slybroadcast, for example. You can also create a new form response and row entry, find and create a new response, and look up a response row by column and value, returning the data in that row.

There are many form and survey apps that integrate with Zapier, which you can check out at `https://zapier.com/apps/categories/forms`.

Next, let's discuss how to automate appointment booking and scheduling processes with Zapier.

Automating appointment booking and scheduling processes

If you're a service business, getting appointments booked is a surefire way to get that revenue streaming in. Those appointments might be for free discovery or informative calls, charged consulting sessions, or other in-person services such as massages or therapy. The first step in improving your appointment booking and scheduling processes is to use either built-in booking functionality in your existing apps, such as with some CRMs such as Pipedrive, Dubsado, or HubSpot, or to use a dedicated scheduling app, such as Acuity Scheduling or Calendly. These apps allow you to create custom time slots that can be displayed on your website or shared using a URL. They integrate with your calendar so that your availability is displayed and events are automatically created in the calendar once a booking has been made. Some apps also allow you to take payments in advance. Once you're using this functionality, you can then automate processes accordingly by creating workflows that include these apps.

With the Acuity Scheduling integration, you can trigger workflows when new appointments are scheduled, canceled, or rescheduled, when appointments start, or when a new product order is completed. You can combine these triggers with action events to create new subscribers and deals in ActiveCampaign, create new Asana tasks, and add or update rows in a Google Sheet, for example. You can also add coupon and package codes, block off time in your Acuity schedule, and find existing appointments by client info or ID.

With the Calendly integration, you can trigger workflows when an invitee schedules an event or when an invitee cancels a scheduled event. Combine these triggers with action events to create meetings in **Zoom**, send Slack messages, and create or update contacts in your CRM, for example.

There are many scheduling apps that integrate with Zapier, which you can check out at `https://zapier.com/apps/categories/scheduling`.

Next, let's explore how to automate lead management processes with Zapier.

Automating lead management processes

Many businesses use either a contact database or a CRM app to centralize data so that they can manage their leads and customers. These tools quite often are the single source of truth about the contact and, therefore, hold all the information about the contact and communications with that contact. Most CRM apps allow you to classify contacts by the stage they are at in the buyer process, such as a lead, opportunity, or customer, and how warm a prospect they are based on their activities. You can create deals or opportunities to track your prospect's progress through your sales cycle and create activities or tasks to help manage your touchpoints with the prospect. In some cases, you can connect your email account, then send and record email communications, connect your calendar, and schedule appointments directly from the CRM. Some CRMs have product modules enabling you to add products and pricing to your deals, and some allow you to manage support tickets and perform email marketing functions.

There are hundreds of CRMs on the market, including popular apps such as HubSpot, Salesforce, Zoho CRM, Microsoft Dynamics 365 CRM, Capsule CRM, Dubsado, ActiveCampaign, and Pipedrive. Many of these integrate with Zapier, allowing you to take your lead and contact management processes to the next level with automation. Most of the integrations have many triggers, actions, and searches available to use, allowing you to supercharge your lead management processes.

With the Salesforce integration, you can trigger workflows when new records such as **Contact**, **Lead**, and **Opportunity** records are added or updated, when a field within a record such as email address or status is updated, or when a new outbound message is received. Combine these triggers with action events such as creating new contacts and invoices in QuickBooks Online when an opportunity hits a certain stage, adding leads to Mailchimp or MailerLite, or adding new cards to Trello. You can also create new and update existing records, add contacts or leads to a campaign, create new attachments, find one or more records, and find or create a record if one does not exist (when, for example, you receive new Typeform entries, new Facebook Lead Ads leads, or new **Unbounce** leads).

Instead of using a CRM, you could use a customizable data table such as Airtable to manage your sales process, as well as other parts of your business such as social media planning, inventory management, staff vacation planning, and more. Airtable works similarly to a spreadsheet; however, you have the additional benefits of using forms and displaying data in specific views as well, such as Kanban. With the Airtable integration, you can trigger workflows when new records are available, new records are available in a view, and records are created or updated.

Combine these triggers with action events such as sending an email with Gmail or Microsoft Outlook and creating Google Calendar events or ClickUp tasks. You can also create or update records, find records, and find or create records when, for example, you receive a new Google Forms submission or new contacts have been added to **Google Contacts**.

There are several lead management and CRM apps that integrate with Zapier, which you can check out at https://zapier.com/apps/categories/crm.

Next, let's explore how to automate contract, proposal, and digital signature collection processes with Zapier.

Automating contract, proposal, and digital signature collection processes

Some businesses need to send client-facing documents such as proposals, quotes, or contracts. In some situations, these documents might need to be digitally signed by the client. Many businesses use a collection of tools to accomplish this, often involving manual processes of copying and pasting information into Microsoft Word or **PowerPoint** documents, or perhaps Google Docs or **Google Slides** documents. The documents are manually sent by email, and then, when a signature is required, customers often need to print, sign, and scan to sign the document or download software to use. We can make the whole process easier for ourselves and our clients by using digital proposal, quoting, and eSign tools, such as PandaDoc, **Proposify**, **HelloSign**, **DocuSign**, and **ZohoSign**, to streamline sales workflows. Users can create beautiful, branded templates, and as these tools quite often integrate with numerous CRM systems, they allow the user to create mail merge fields that pull required information into the new document, such as names, email addresses, addresses, and products, for example. Some apps also allow you to take payments. Once you're using these tools, you can use Zapier to automate other processes.

With the PandaDoc integration, you can trigger workflows when a document has been sent, is completed, is paid, or when a status has changed to something such as `draft`, `sent`, `viewed`, `completed`, or `paid`. You can combine these triggers with action events such as uploading the completed PDF documents to Google Drive or Dropbox, creating contacts and invoices in Xero or FreshBooks, updating deal stages in ActiveCampaign or HubSpot, or sending notifications by email, SMS, or Slack message. You can also create a new contact and a document from a template when, for example, new form submissions are made in **Ninja Forms**, opportunities move to a certain stage in Salesforce, or tasks are marked as complete in Google Tasks.

With the DocuSign integration, you can trigger workflows when a new folder is created and when an envelope is sent or completed. You can combine these triggers with action events such as uploading completed envelopes to Dropbox, creating tasks in Todoist, and adding new subscribers to Autopilot. You can also create a signature request when, for example, a Smartsheet row is updated or a new row is added to a Google Sheet.

There are several contract, proposal, and digital signature collection apps that integrate with Zapier, which you can check out at `https://zapier.com/apps/categories/signatures`.

Next, let's explore how to automate e-commerce processes with Zapier.

Automating e-commerce processes

So far, we have mainly focused on sales processes that involve an element of human interaction and various touchpoints prior to a sale being made. Many businesses, however, already run their sales processes on autopilot by listing their physical or digital products, including online courses and subscriptions, on the internet using shopping carts such as ThriveCart or **SamCart**, e-commerce stores such as Shopify or WooCommerce, sales directories such as **eBay** or **Gumroad**, and online course platforms such as Kajabi or **Thinkific**. Many of these platforms integrate with Zapier, thereby allowing you to automate your processes further.

With the eBay integration, you can trigger workflows when a new order is made and then combine this with action events to create new Google Sheets rows, create new sales invoices in Xero, create new Airtable records, or create new Printful orders, for example. You can also create a shipping fulfillment to a line item and search for an order when you receive a new Shopify order or for new ShipStation orders.

With the SamCart integration, you can trigger workflows when new orders are made, new prospect entries are created, recurring subscriptions are charged, new refunds are made, and new subscriptions are canceled. You can combine these triggers with action events such as granting or removing access to Kajabi offers, tagging Intercom users with their specific orders, adding new orders to ShipStation, or unenrolling Thinkific users from courses when payments are refunded.

There are many e-commerce apps that integrate with Zapier, which you can check out at `https://zapier.com/apps/categories/ecommerce`.

You now understand what kind of sales processes can be automated with Zapier.

Let's now take a look at the essential first steps to take to start automating your sales processes.

Where to start with automating your sales processes with Zapier

It is always good to do some pre-work before you start automating your processes. In *Chapter 2, Preparing to Automate Your Processes*, and *Chapter 3, Building Your First Automated Workflow (Zap)*, we covered a few important points that will help you when you are strategizing your sales workflows, and these are as follows:

- **Map out your sales processes**: If you don't have a clear idea of how your sales processes work with all your tools, follow the steps in the *Simplifying your processes and assessing what can be automated* section in *Chapter 2, Preparing to Automate Your Processes*, to visually map out your processes so that you have a high-level overview of how your tasks work with your existing software.

- **List your sales tools**: Make a list of all the sales tools and services that you use in your business to achieve your goals. Then, assess how these tools fit within your mapped-out processes. You will then be able to simplify those processes and decide on what can be automated. Once you have this overview of your processes and tools, you will be better placed to understand where the holes are and how Zapier can help you to close the gaps and automate your processes.

- **Review your app profile pages**: In *Chapter 2, Preparing to Automate Your Processes*, we also discussed reviewing your individual app profile pages as the best way to establish how your business apps integrate with Zapier. This will give you insight into the triggers, actions, and searches available to use in your workflows. Make a list of these for quick reference.

- **Use Zapier's pre-built guided workflow templates**: This is the easiest way to get started with automating your sales processes. These templates are built from workflows that are commonly used by other users. They are perfect for inspiration, quick to set up, and will save you time immediately.

- **Customize your sales workflows**: Get creative and start building multi-step workflows to achieve more from your automation. Use Zapier's built-in apps to help you do more and connect your sales workflows to other parts of your business processes, such as your operations process.

- **Combine AI and automation**: Use the magic of AI-powered Zapier features and integrated AI apps to supercharge your sales workflows. Find out more in *Chapter 19, AI and Automation*.

You'll be well on your way to creating sales automation for your business.

> **Tip**
>
> If you're looking for ideas of other sales apps to use in your business, you can review the **Sales & CRM** category in the app ecosystem directory to give you a list of public apps that integrate with Zapier at `https://zapier.com/apps/categories/sales-crm`. Review the *A brief guide to choosing new apps for your business* section in *Chapter 2, Preparing to Automate Your Processes*, for guidance on choosing new apps.

You now know how to get started with automating your sales processes with Zapier.

Let's get more specific and discuss how lead management processes can be automated using Zapier's integrations with CRMs, illustrated with Pipedrive.

Automating lead management processes with CRM integrations, illustrated with the Pipedrive integration

As we've seen so far in this chapter, there are so many different sales tools that connect with Zapier and allow you to automate your sales processes. We specifically covered automating lead management processes and noted that there is a range of CRMs that integrate with Zapier. To further illustrate what the possibilities are, we're now going to focus on one of Zapier's most popular sales app integrations, which is Pipedrive.

This section will mostly help Pipedrive users who are considering automating their processes with Zapier to understand the options available to them. However, if you're not a Pipedrive user, this section will still be helpful for you as many similarities exist in the Zapier integrations with other well-known CRM tools such as Salesforce and HubSpot, where the integrations are just as comprehensive and, in some cases, more extensive. This section may also be loosely useful for those users who are trying to assess whether a CRM might be appropriate for their business and how this fits with automating their sales processes.

Pipedrive is a popular CRM used by businesses that want to simply and effectively manage their sales process from lead capture through sales cycle stages in pipelines to integrating with other tools to connect other business functions, such as calling and invoicing. Pipedrive is primarily built for B2B interactions but can be adapted to a B2C process. Pipedrive allows you to build forms to use standalone or to embed into your website so that you can automatically add new leads to the CRM. You can create and manage contacts in the form of people and associated organizations, and you can create leads and then convert qualified leads into deals to move them through your sales cycle in one or more pipelines. You can create activities or tasks set to certain dates and times to ensure that you and your sales team remember to work through various touchpoints to engage your prospects. You can connect your email account so that you can send and receive emails straight from within the platform and emails are logged against the contact and associated deals. You can also connect your calendar and schedule meetings. Pipedrive also has a products module, allowing you to create and manage line items with quantities and pricing that can be added to deals.

For reporting purposes, Pipedrive has dashboard reporting, and you can create custom filters for activities, persons, organizations, leads, and deals, which can be used in Zapier automations. Pipedrive does allow you to create automation rules within the app, and it has several robust native integrations with other apps, such as calling apps, proposal and eSign tools, marketing apps, and invoicing apps. You can, however, use the Zapier integration to add power to your processes by connecting Pipedrive to thousands of other apps so that you can automate many parts of your sales processes. The Pipedrive integration is very comprehensive and currently supports multiple trigger, action, and search events. A full list can be found on the Pipedrive app profile page at `https://zapier.com/apps/pipedrive/integrations`.

Let's take a look at the Pipedrive trigger events and some possible use cases.

Pipedrive trigger events and use cases

The following is a list of some of the supported trigger events that you can use with Pipedrive with examples of when to use them:

- **New Person**: This event triggers when a new person is added to Pipedrive. Among other things, you can use this trigger event in your automations when you want to add new contacts to other apps such as your email marketing app or invoicing platform as soon as they have been added to Pipedrive. For example, combine this trigger event with an action event such as **Create Contact** with Constant Contact or **Create Client** with FreshBooks Classic.

- **Updated Person**: This event triggers when an existing person is updated in Pipedrive. You can use this trigger event in your automations when you want to update existing contacts in your other apps as soon as they have been added to Pipedrive. For example, combine this trigger event with action events to update a row in Google Sheets such as **Lookup Spreadsheet Row** first to find the ID for the row you want to update using a unique identifier such as the email address, and then use **Update Spreadsheet Row** to update the row.

- **Person Matching Filter**: This event triggers when a person matches a filter. For this trigger to work, you must create an appropriate filter within Pipedrive. For example, you could create a filter that includes a person when a `Warm` label is applied. When setting up this trigger event, select your filter from the **Filter** drop-down menu. Among other things, you can use this trigger event in your automations when you want to trigger workflows only when a person matches a certain condition, without using Filter by Zapier, and then create a contact and add them to an automation in marketing automation apps. For example, combine this trigger event with an action event such as **Add Contact to Automation** in ActiveCampaign to add the contact to a nurturing sequence.

- **New Organization**: This event triggers when a new organization is added to Pipedrive. You can use this trigger event in your automations when you want to add new company details to other records such as spreadsheets or databases. For example, combine this trigger event with an action event such as **Add Row to Sheet** with Smartsheet or **Create Record** with Airtable.

- **Updated Organization**: This event triggers when an existing organization is updated in Pipedrive. Use this trigger event in your automations similarly to the **Updated Person** trigger.

- **Organization Matching Filter**: This event triggers when an organization matches a filter. For this trigger to work, you must create an appropriate filter within Pipedrive. For example, you could create a filter that includes an organization when a Customer label is applied. When setting up this trigger event, select your filter from the **Filter** drop-down menu. You can use this trigger event in your automations when you want to trigger workflows only when an organization matches a certain condition, without using Filter by Zapier, and then add these details in other apps. For example, combine this trigger event with an action event such as **Create Task List** in Google Tasks to perform customer onboarding tasks.

- **New Lead**: This event triggers when a new lead is added to Pipedrive. Among other things, you can use this trigger event in your automations when you want to create new deals in Pipedrive when new leads are added. For example, combine this trigger event with an action event such as **Create Deal** with Pipedrive.

- **New Deal**: This is an instant trigger event that triggers when a new deal is added to Pipedrive. You can use this trigger event in your automations when you want to send out notifications to your team or send an email or SMS to your prospect. For example, combine this trigger event with an action event such as **Send Email** with Gmail or **Send SMS** with Twilio.

- **Updated Deal**: This is an instant trigger event that triggers when deal components such as fields, followers, and notes are updated in Pipedrive. As you cannot specify under which conditions this event will trigger, it is best used with a Filter by Zapier action step immediately following it. You can, for example, use this trigger event in your automations when you want to update existing elements in another app, such as updating a task in your task management app. Combine this trigger event and filter with an action event such as **Add Label to Card** with Trello or **Create Update** with monday.com.

- **Updated Deal Stage**: This is an instant trigger event that triggers when a deal moves to a specified stage in a pipeline. Among other ways, you can use this trigger event in your automations when you want to create deal stage-specific activities in Pipedrive or your other apps. For example, combine this trigger event with an action event such as **Create Checklist** with Process Street to create a detailed screening checklist when a deal hits the "Screening" stage, or create a proposal in Proposify using **Create Proposal** when a deal hits the "Proposal" stage.

- **Deal Matching Filter**: This event triggers when a deal matches a filter. For this trigger to work, you must create an appropriate filter within Pipedrive. For example, you could create a filter that includes a deal when the deal moves to a certain stage, such as "Needs Defined," and the email count is more than 10. When setting up this trigger event, select your filter from the **Filter** drop-down menu. You can use this trigger event in your automations when you want to trigger workflows only when a deal matches a certain condition, without using Filter by Zapier, and then add these details in other apps. For example, combine this trigger event with an action event such as **Find Person and Company Information** in Lead Score by Zapier to get lead scoring information for the person and organization.

- **New Activity**: This event triggers when a new activity is added in Pipedrive to a person, organization, or deal record. You can use this trigger event in your automations when you want to send out notifications to your team for new activities or assign tasks to your team to match the activities if not all of your team use Pipedrive. For example, combine this trigger event with an action event such as **Send Channel Message** with Slack or **Create Task** with Teamwork projects.

- **Activity Matching Filter**: This event triggers when an activity matches a filter. For this trigger to work, you must create an appropriate filter within Pipedrive. For example, you could create a filter that includes an activity with a due date of the next day, assigned to a specific user, and an "In-Person" meeting type. When setting up this trigger event, select your filter from the **Filter** drop-down menu. You can use this trigger event in your automations when you want to trigger workflows only when an activity matches a certain condition, without using Filter by Zapier, and then add these details in other apps. For example, combine this trigger event with an action event such as **Get Tomorrow's Forecast** with Weather by Zapier to get the weather forecast for the next day and then send an email to the owner of the activity using **Send Outbound Email** with Email by Zapier.

- **New Note**: This event triggers when a new note is added in Pipedrive to a person, organization, or deal record. Among other ways, you can use this trigger event in your automations when you want to add a follower to a deal if a note contains a certain word or phrase. For example, combine this trigger event with an **Only continue if...** action event with Filter by Zapier where the Content field is mapped, the condition is Text (Contains), and the value is the word or phrase you specify, and then another action event such as **Add Follower** with Pipedrive.

In comparison, the HubSpot integration has a similar trigger structure with contacts, company tasks, and deal creation and updates; however, it has a much more comprehensive range of trigger events covering other module components such as form submissions, products, tickets, line items, and email engagements, for example. Conversely, the Salesforce integration may have fewer triggers, but these are generally based on records being grouped together to allow the record type to be selected from a drop-down menu, such as **New Record**, **Updated Record**, and **Updated Field on Record**, allowing for significant flexibility covering most Salesforce module properties.

Next, let's have a look at some Pipedrive action events and use cases.

Pipedrive action events and use cases

The following is a list of some of the supported action events that you can use with Pipedrive with examples of when to use them:

- **Create Person**: You can use this action event when you want to create a new person record in Pipedrive. You could use this action event in combination with a trigger event such as **New Subscriber** with **AWeber** to add new email newsletter subscribers to Pipedrive and label them accordingly.

- **Update Person**: You can use this action event when you want to update an existing person record in Pipedrive. You could use this action event and the search action event in combination with a trigger event such as **Appointment Start** with Acuity Scheduling to update custom fields in a person's record when a customer attends an appointment.

- **Create Organization**: You can use this action event when you want to create a new organization record in Pipedrive. You could use this action event in combination with a trigger event such as **New Entry** with Typeform to add company details from new form entries to Pipedrive as organizations.

- **Update Organization**: You can use this action event when you want to update an existing organization record in Pipedrive. You could use this action event and the search action event in combination with a trigger event such as **New or Updated Spreadsheet Row** with Google Sheets to update custom fields in an organization record when new details are added to company details in a spreadsheet row.

- **Create Lead**: You can use this action event when you want to create a new lead record in Pipedrive. You could use this action event in combination with a trigger event such as **New Form Response** with **LinkedIn Lead Gen Forms** to add new form submission contact details as a lead. Prior to this step, you can use either the **New Person** or **New Organization** action events to create a record of an associated person or organization and then map the relevant ID values to the **Create Lead** action event accordingly.

- **Create Deal**: You can use this action event when you want to create a new deal record in Pipedrive. You could use this action event in combination with a trigger event such as **New Email** with Email Parser by Zapier to add new parsed email details to Pipedrive as new deals.

- **Update Deal**: You can use this action event when you want to update an existing deal record in Pipedrive. You could use this action event and the search action event in combination with a trigger event such as **New Payment** with QuickBooks Online to change the deal status to Won when a new payment has been received for a sales invoice.

- **Create Note**: You can use this action event when you want to create a new note in Pipedrive in a person, organization, or deal record. You could use this action event in combination with a trigger event such as **Subscription Paused** or **Subscription Resumed** with ThriveCart to add notes when changes are made to a customer's subscription.

- **Create Product**: You can use this action event when you want to create a new product record in Pipedrive. You could use this action event in combination with a trigger event such as **New Product** with Shopify to add new products to Pipedrive when products are added to your Shopify e-commerce store.

- **Add Product to Deal**: You can use this action event when you want to add a product to an existing deal record in Pipedrive. You could use this action event and the search action events in combination with a trigger event such as **New Submission** with JotForm to add new products to a deal when a prospect fills out a survey form and selects a product.

- **Create Activity**: You can use this action event when you want to create a new activity in Pipedrive in a person, organization, or deal record. You could use this action event in combination with a trigger event such as **Updated Deal Stage** with Pipedrive to add activities to a deal when it changes to a specific stage. In this case, there is no need to use search actions to find the record IDs; they can be mapped from the trigger step.

- **Update Activity**: You can use this action event when you want to update an existing activity record in Pipedrive. You could use this action event and the search action event in combination with a trigger event such as **Completed Task** with Asana to mark an activity status as `Done` when an Asana task is completed.

- **Attach File**: You can use this action event when you want to upload a file and attach it to a person, organization, deal, activity, product, or note record in Pipedrive. You could use this action event in combination with a trigger event such as **Document Completed** with PandaDoc to add completed PDF files to Pipedrive deals.

- **Add Follower**: You can use this action event when you want to add a follower file and attach it to a person, organization, deal, or product record in Pipedrive. You could use this action event in combination with a trigger event such as **Deal Matching Filter** with Pipedrive to add yourself as a follower when a deal matches certain conditions.

Once again, in comparison, the HubSpot integration has a similar action event structure with contacts, companies, tasks, and deal creation and updates; however, it has a much more comprehensive range of action events covering other module components, allowing for more flexibility in your automations. The Salesforce integration may have fewer actions; however, these generally are based on records being grouped together to allow the record type to be selected from a drop-down menu, allowing for significant flexibility covering most Salesforce module properties.

Next, let's have a look at Pipedrive search action events.

Pipedrive search action events

Refer to the *Pipedrive action events and use cases* section for examples of how to use the various search action events followed by Pipedrive action steps.

As with trigger and action events, in relation to search action events, the HubSpot integration has a much more comprehensive range of action events covering other module components. The Salesforce integration may have fewer search actions available, but they are based on records being grouped together to allow the record type to be selected from a drop-down menu.

> **Tip**
>
> One of the most useful values that is used within searches, particularly in CRM integrations, is the record ID. For example, when searching for a contact, an email address is likely to be a unique value; however, there might be a slight possibility of duplicate contacts within a system. The most reliable value for retrieving a record is the unique ID associated with that record. When assessing what CRM might be appropriate for use in your business, one thing to consider is how robust the API is. A good reference point is whether the integration allows you to retrieve information based on record ID and what range of information you can retrieve.

Next, let's review a few tips for the best use of the Pipedrive integration.

Tips for using the Pipedrive integration

Here are a few tips for the successful use of the Pipedrive integration:

- Always check what type of field you are entering or mapping data to, and ensure your data is formatted accordingly. This will ensure data accuracy. You can review the *Understanding field data types* section in *Chapter 3, Building Your First Automated Workflow (Zap)*, for more information on field types.

- When using the **Custom** tab to type in or map data from previous steps to fields that display Pipedrive field options in drop-down menus, such as with **Field To Search By**, use the field label rather than the field name – for example, the field name is Name, field label is 0. An example is shown in the following screenshot:

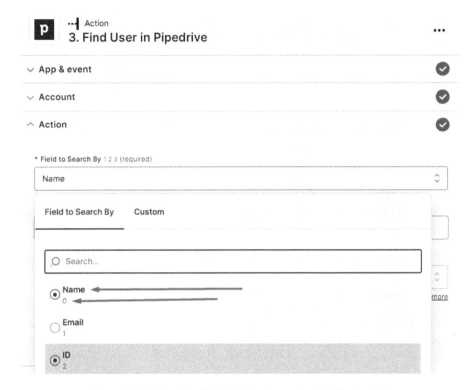

Figure 21.1 – Mapping field labels when using the Custom tab

- If you are using a combination of Pipedrive trigger and action events in your workflows, bear in mind that if you are mapping ID values, the name may vary between the steps. For example, in a trigger step of **New Note**, id is the note ID, deal_id is the ID of the associated deal, and org_id is the ID of the associated organization. If you then use an action step such as **Create Deal**, the resulting ID would be the deal ID.

- The Pipedrive integration does not have a specific trigger event that allows you to trigger a workflow when a field is updated, unlike the Salesforce **Updated Field on Record** trigger. A workaround for this involves using workflow automations in Pipedrive, which are only available on Advanced plans and higher, and filtered lists. You can create a workflow automation in Pipedrive that triggers a deal being updated, with a filter on one or more fields being changed, and an action to create an activity marked as complete that is used in a filtered list. In the list filter, the specific activity would be already done but due on that day. You can then combine this with the Zapier-Pipedrive **Activity Matching Filter** trigger event to trigger a workflow as appropriate.

- To avoid using search action steps, display values for IDs for Pipedrive records in your other apps that you have connected in workflows, and vice versa. For example, if your Zap involves Pipedrive and Google Sheets, add Pipedrive record IDs to columns in your Google Sheet and Google Sheet row IDs to custom fields in Pipedrive. This allows for more reliability than using search actions.

- Review the Pipedrive API at `https://developers.pipedrive.com/docs/api/v1/#/` for information on other triggers and actions you can perform using Webhooks by Zapier and Code by Zapier. You can hire a Zapier Expert to help you with custom integration work at `https://experts.zapier.com/`.

You can view common problems with the Pipedrive integration by navigating to the **Help** tab of the app profile or following this link: `https://help.zapier.com/hc/en-us/articles/8495937445773`.

Next, let's explore how to set up an example of a multi-step Zap using the Pipedrive integration.

Setting up a multi-step Zap with the Pipedrive integration

To illustrate this, we will use the example of retrieving tomorrow's weather forecast, sending a reminder email to the deal owner, and adding a note to Pipedrive when an activity for an in-person meeting is due the next day.

The Zap will involve five steps as follows:

1. **Trigger**: The Pipedrive app with the **Activity Matching Filter** trigger event.
2. **Action**: The Weather by Zapier app with the **Get Tomorrow's Forecast** action event.
3. **Search action**: The Pipedrive app with the **Find User** search action event.
4. **Action**: The Email by Zapier app with the **Send Outbound Email** action event.
5. **Action**: The Pipedrive app with the **Create Note** action event.

The following screenshot shows how your Zap should look once built:

Figure 21.2 – A multi-step Zap using Pipedrive trigger and action events

The Pipedrive filter for this scenario is set up as shown in the following screenshot:

Figure 21.3 – A Pipedrive filter for in-person meetings due the next day (courtesy of Pipedrive)

Let's walk through setting up the Zap step by step, starting with the trigger step.

Setting up the trigger step in the Zap

We will use the Pipedrive app with the **Activity Matching Filter** trigger event as the trigger step. Select the relevant filter from the **Filter ID** drop-down menu.

The following screenshot shows how this step should look:

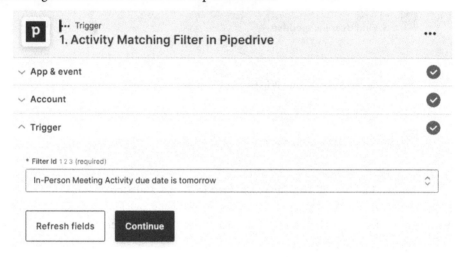

Figure 21.4 – Using Activity Matching Filter in Pipedrive to trigger a workflow

Click on the **Continue** button, then click on the **Test trigger** button to pull through some sample data.

Next, let's set up the second step in the Zap – the first action step.

Setting up the second step in the Zap

We will use the Weather by Zapier app with the **Get Tomorrow's Forecast** action event. Follow the instructions in the *Weather by Zapier – using weather conditions in your Zaps* section in *Chapter 10, Other Useful Built-In Apps by Zapier*, to customize this action step to add **Latitude** and **Longitude** details for New York, set **Units** as **Fahrenheit**, and leave **Should this step be considered a "success" when nothing is found?** as **False**.

The following screenshot shows how this step should look:

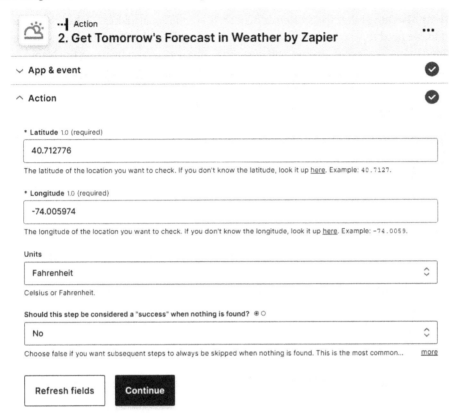

Figure 21.5 – Overview of using the Get Tomorrow's Forecast in Weather by
Zapier action event to retrieve the weather forecast for the next day

Click on the **Continue** button. You can then use the **Test** section to get the forecast.

Next, let's set up the next action step.

Setting up the third step in the Zap

As the **Activity Matching Filter** trigger step does not retrieve the email address of the user the activity is assigned to, we need to search for the user by name. We will use the Pipedrive app with the **Find User in Pipedrive** action event, and we will customize this action step by using the **Name** field in **Field to Search By** and mapping Owner Name from the trigger step to the **Term** (or **Name**) field. Leave **Should this step be considered a "success" when nothing is found?** as **False**.

This is shown in the following screenshot:

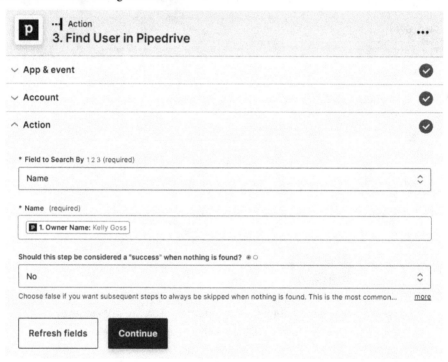

Figure 21.6 – Overview of using the Find User in Pipedrive search action event

Click on the **Continue** button. You can then use the **Test** section to retrieve the user data. The result from the scenario is shown in the following screenshot:

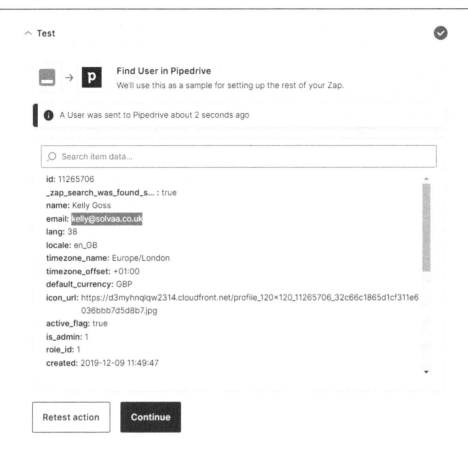

Figure 21.7 – Details of a user found using the Find User in Pipedrive search action event

Next, let's set up the next action step.

Setting up the fourth step in the Zap

We will use the Email by Zapier app with the **Send Outbound Email** action event, and we will customize this action step by completing the **To** field with the user's Email address from the search action in the second step of your Zap, and customize the **Subject** and **Body (HTML Or Plain)** fields with the relevant text and mapped dynamic data from previous steps, as shown in the following screenshot:

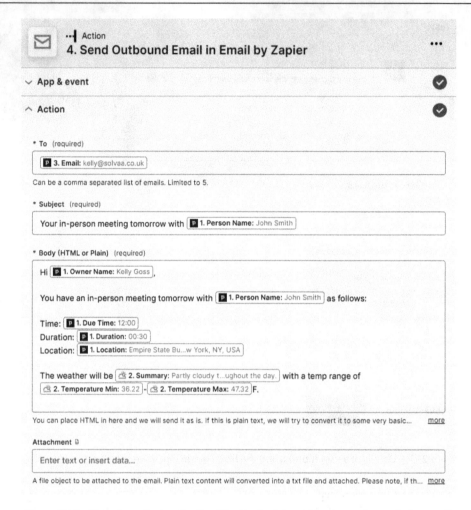

Figure 21.8 – Overview of using the Email by Zapier integration to send a reminder email

Click on the **Continue** button. You can then use the **Test** section to send the email.

Next, let's set up the final action step.

Setting up the fifth step in the Zap

Finally, we will add a note to Pipedrive to the associated deal, person, and organization to which the activity is linked. We will use the Pipedrive app with **Create Note** with text and `{{zap_meta_human_now}}` to produce the time the Zap runs and add it to the note. Map `Deal ID` to the **Deal** field, `Person ID` to the **Person** field, and `Organization ID` to the **Organization** field from *step 1*. This is shown in the following screenshot:

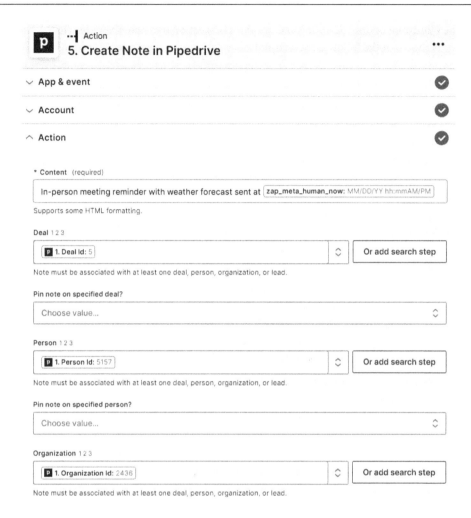

Figure 21.9 – Overview of using the Create Note in Pipedrive action event

We cover how to use **Zap Meta Human Now** and the other timestamp variations in more detail in *Using the date and time your Zap runs in fields* in *Chapter 14, Formatting Date and Time.*

Click on the **Continue** button. You can then use the **Test** section to create the note. The result from the scenario is shown in the following screenshot:

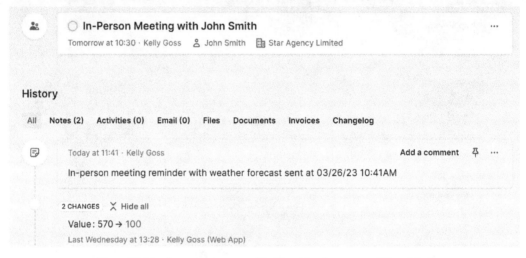

Figure 21.10 – A new note created in Pipedrive (courtesy of Pipedrive)

You can get access to a copy of this Zap template at `https://bit.ly/zapier-book`.

You should now have a better understanding of how to automate lead management processes with the Pipedrive integration.

Summary

In this chapter, we discussed the different types of sales processes that can be automated with Zapier, and we explored some examples of workflows used with some common sales applications. First, we got an overview of the types of sales processes that can be automated with Zapier. Then, we covered where to start with automating sales processes with Zapier. Finally, we discussed how to automate contact management with the Pipedrive CRM integration.

You now know how to automate your sales processes with Zapier and specifically, with the Pipedrive CRM integration.

In the next chapter, you will learn how to automate your operations workflows. We will discuss some of the different types of operations processes and give working examples of how these processes can be automated using Zapier. We will also provide practical tips on how to solve problems related to operations workflows.

Questions

1. What type of sales processes can be automated using Zapier?

2. Where can you find information about what types of scheduling applications integrate with Zapier?

22

Automating Your Operations Processes

Once you've got the money rolling in with efficient marketing and sales processes, the next important topic to explore is how to automate various business operations processes. Having efficient operations processes will certainly help you and your team to keep things ticking along in the background on autopilot, giving you more time to focus on keeping your customers happy with better customer service and targeted retention activities.

In this chapter, we will discuss some of the different types of operations processes that can be automated with Zapier, and we will provide examples of workflows used with some common operations-focused applications. First, we will give an overview of the types of operations processes that can be automated with Zapier, such as task and project management, storage and organization, communication, and data handling with spreadsheets and databases. Then, we will explore where to start with automating operations processes with Zapier. Finally, we will dive into how to automate online Word document processes with the Google Docs integration to illustrate how operations processes can be automated.

We will cover the following key topics in this chapter:

- An introduction to automating your operations processes with Zapier
- Where to start with automating your operations processes with Zapier
- Automating online Word processing processes with the Google Docs integration

Once you have worked through each of these topics, you will have a better understanding of the different operations processes that can be automated with Zapier. You will know how to use Zapier to automate operations processes with some of the most common operations-focused applications.

Technical requirements

To make the most of the content in this chapter, you will need access to a Zapier account. The Zapier Free plan will be required for you to create single-step workflows and use Zapier's pre-built templates. The Zapier Starter plan will be required for you to use Premium apps and to create multi-step workflows.

You can get access to the Zap template used in this chapter at `https://bit.ly/zapier-book`. Using the template will help you visualize how the process works.

An introduction to automating your operations processes with Zapier

Once you've made those ever-important sales, you need to provide your customers with the product or service that their well-earned money is paying for. Of course, in order for your business to succeed and be competitive, your product or service needs to fulfill a need or solve a problem, and it should be of exceptional quality to ensure your customers come back to buy more. While you can have the best processes in place to market and sell your products and services, and have exceptional offerings with good value for money, if the processes behind production and delivery are extremely manual, repetitive, and error-prone, delivery will be poor, and the customers you worked so hard to find will run a mile. Inefficient operations processes could cause you to have significant delays in responding to customer service queries, or you might forget to respond altogether. It could also mean that you experience order processing delays in stages such as manufacturing or shipping because someone forgot to order a crucial component. Having inefficient and poorly organized operations processes generally creates stress for the team, and ultimately results in more time and expense being spent recruiting new employees because staff leave when their jobs are too difficult.

Once you have the right cloud-based apps in place to help you stay organized and run your business better, being able to automate anything mundane and repetitive will increase productivity among members of the team. You will be able to automate task creation, project updates, document creation, communications (internally and with customers or suppliers), document storage, and more with Zapier.

An example of how operations processes can be improved significantly by using connector tools such as Zapier to automate various tasks can be found at `https://solvaa.co.uk/how-iq-glass-saves-45-hours-per-week-with-zapier/`.

Understanding what operations processes can be automated with Zapier

Zapier has integrations with a range of different operations-focused tools spanning numerous functions, allowing you to automate your **business operations processes**. You can connect these apps with thousands of other apps, such as Google Drive, Microsoft 365, Asana, and Wrike, to automate your operations processes.

Operations can span many facets of the business, including human resource functions such as recruitment and onboarding, as well as customer support. Although Zapier allows you to automate many operations processes, and we could go further to expand on this topic, we will only skim the surface with a few examples of ones that can be automated with Zapier:

- Task and project management processes
- Document storage processes
- Communication processes
- Word document and spreadsheet processes

Let's explore each one and give some examples of operations-focused apps that can be used with Zapier to automate processes that involve them.

Automating task and project management processes

Whether you're a service business or one that sells physical or digital products, at some point, someone in the business will be making a to-do list of some description. Most of us make lists of the things we need to accomplish, whether this is for personal use or for work. You might still like to record these items on paper or in your Notes app on your smartphone, or in a dedicated task management app. You might use Google Tasks, Todoist, or Microsoft To Do for your task recording and management. Many of these apps can help you with productivity by allowing you to create subtasks, set due dates and times, integrate with your calendar, and send yourself alerts. Once you have these apps set up, you can use Zapier to automate various other tasks based on triggers and actions.

With the Microsoft To Do integration, you can trigger workflows when new tasks or lists are created, a task is updated, or a task is completed. You can combine these triggers with action events to send an automated email with Microsoft Outlook, send an SMS with ClickSend SMS, or create tasks in Teamwork.com Projects, for example. You can also create a task or list, mark a task as complete, and find a task, and if one is not found, you can optionally create a task. Combine these actions with triggers to add new Facebook lead ads as tasks, add tasks when new messages are saved in Slack, or when new notes are added to OneNote.

Task management apps help you maintain individual productivity. However, when you need to manage simple or more complex projects with multiple tasks and categories, and if you need to assign tasks to different members of the team, customers, or contractors, it's better to use a dedicated project management app. Although many businesses handle their project management processes on spreadsheets, using a dedicated project management app can, in many scenarios, allow you to visualize your tasks and projects in lists or Kanban views, as well as Gantt charts. These apps also help you display team schedules and availability, manage timelines, and allow notifications, comments, and communications. Trello, Asana, monday.com, Teamwork.com Projects, Zoho Projects, Wrike, and ClickUp are a few examples of project management apps that integrate with Zapier.

With the ClickUp integration, you can trigger workflows when new tasks, folders, or lists are created or when a task changes. You can combine these triggers with action events to create and send an invoice in Xero or create and assign a new task within ClickUp itself. You can also create a task, subtask, folder, or list; add a new checklist to a task; post a comment or attachment to a task; and add time tracking to a task. Combine these actions with triggers such as new starred Gmail emails, new Google Form responses, or new GitHub issues.

There are several task and project management apps that integrate with Zapier, which you can check out at `https://zapier.com/apps/categories/todo-lists` and `https://zapier.com/apps/categories/project-management`.

Next, let's discuss how to automate document storage processes with Zapier.

Automating document storage processes

Every business will have either paper or online documents that they deal with from customers or suppliers, and potentially, internally from employees. Organizing your documents in a dedicated storage location means that you will be able to locate documents easily once you have stored them. In days gone by, many businesses used folders and filing cabinet systems to store paper documents, and some businesses may still do this. Nowadays, in the digital age, it's common to store scanned versions of these paper documents or digital documents on a desktop computer or, preferably, in the cloud in a document storage app where those documents can be accessed from any location. Apps such as Google Drive, Dropbox, OneDrive, and Box are popular online storage solutions, which, once implemented, can be integrated with Zapier so that you can automate document storage. For example, you might receive documents by email that you need to then file in your online document storage app, you might need to store a PDF copy of a contract in a specific location once it has been signed, or you might want to save an image once it has been posted to Facebook Pages.

With OneDrive integration, you can trigger workflows when a new file is added to a folder or when a folder is added. You can combine these triggers with action events to copy new files to another storage app, such as Google Drive or Dropbox, or add new notes to Evernote with attachments, for example. You can also upload a file, create a folder or new text file, and search for a file or folder, and if they are not found, you can optionally create a file or folder. Combine these actions with triggers to upload new Google Docs files, Gmail attachments, or YouTube videos.

With Google Drive integration, you can trigger workflows when a new file is added to any folder, a new file is added to a specific folder, a folder is added, or when a file is updated. You can combine this trigger with action events to send team notifications with Slack or create new Asana tasks, for example. You can also upload a file; create a folder; create a file from text; copy, move, or replace a file; or add file-sharing preferences. You can also search for a file or folder, and if it is not found, you can optionally create a file or folder. Combine these actions with triggers to add new Instagram images, create folders when deals are marked as won in your CRM, or when new Google Calendar events are created in order to back them up.

There are several document storage apps that integrate with Zapier, which you can check out at `https://zapier.com/apps/categories/files`.

Next, let's discuss how to automate communication processes with Zapier.

Automating communication processes

Communication is an essential part of any business. We need to be able to communicate with each other internally, with prospective and existing customers, and with suppliers. Communication methods have changed significantly for businesses over the years, where perhaps some time ago, the only methods were face-to-face verbal conversations, or by telegraph, telephone, or fax. Now, many companies rely on other forms of communication such as email, SMS, telephone calls and voicemail drops, video conferencing, and online messaging tools. You might be using Gmail or Microsoft Outlook for your emails; Slack, Google Hangouts Chat, or Microsoft Teams for team collaboration; Zoom or GoToMeeting for video conferencing; RingCentral for voice calls, sending fax, and SMS; VoodooSMS for sending SMS; and Slybroadcast for voice drops. There is such a broad range of communication apps that integrate with Zapier, enabling you to automate many, if not all, of your communication processes.

Zoom is a video conferencing tool that has become extremely popular as businesses and teams embrace remote working and collaboration. The platform supports video and voice meetings, as well as webinars. With Zoom integration, you can trigger workflows when a new meeting or webinar is created, a new registrant is added to a webinar, or a new recording is completed for a meeting or webinar. You can combine these triggers with action events to add new registrants to ClickFunnels, create new Google Calendar events, or send a notification in Slack. You can also create a new meeting or webinar registrant. You can combine these action events with triggers such as when new Eventbrite orders are created, successful PayPal sales are made, or new Calendly events are created.

Slybroadcast allows you to send voice messages straight to voice mailboxes. This is perfect for sending appointment reminders or verbal company introductions to leads. With Slybroadcast integration, you can send a voicemail message to a person or group of people using an audio file uploaded to your Slybroadcast account or using an audio file URL. You can combine these action events with triggers such as when new contacts are added to Agile CRM, new orders are placed in WooCommerce, or when you enroll a new user on a Teachable course.

There are several communication apps that integrate with Zapier, which you can check out at `https://zapier.com/apps/categories/communication`.

Next, let's discuss how to automate Word document and spreadsheet processes with Zapier.

Automating Word document and spreadsheet processes

For most businesses, gone are the days of handwriting letters and using a typewriter or manual word processor to create documents that need to be faxed or posted. These days, companies generally use desktop word processing and presentation packages such as Microsoft Word and Microsoft PowerPoint. A lot more can be achieved by using cloud-based alternatives such as Google Docs or Zoho Writer, for example, as well as Google Slides. Zapier integrates with these cloud-based apps and many more, allowing you to automate your text and presentation document processes.

With Google Slides integration, you can trigger workflows when a new presentation is created. You can combine this trigger with action events such as posting presentations to a Slack channel or tweeting the presentation on Twitter. You can also search for an existing presentation, create a presentation from a template using mail merge placeholder variables, or refresh data for all charts in a presentation linked to a Google Sheets spreadsheet. You can combine these action events with triggers such as when data is parsed from PDFs in Docparser, when deals reach a certain stage in Zoho CRM, or when forms are submitted in Gravity Forms.

As with documents, many businesses have moved away from desktop versions of spreadsheets and databases, allowing them to access the data from anywhere if they are using a cloud-based app such as Google Sheets, Smartsheet, Airtable, Knack, or Microsoft Excel. Using Zapier with these apps allows you to automate processes involving recording, amending, sharing, and reporting on data in these online tools.

With Microsoft Excel integration, you can trigger workflows when a new row is added to a worksheet or table in a spreadsheet, when a row is added or updated, or when a new worksheet is added to a spreadsheet. You can combine these triggers with action events such as creating a new deal in your CRM, adding new rows to a Google spreadsheet, or adding new subscribers to ConvertKit. You can also add a new row to the end of a specific worksheet or table, update a row in a specific worksheet, create a new spreadsheet, search for an existing row by column or value, and optionally, create a new row if one is not found. You can combine these action events with triggers such as when new **SurveyMonkey** responses are created, with new **Formstack** submissions, or when **Toggl** time entries are made.

> **Important note**
>
> One thing to bear in mind when using Microsoft Excel integration is that Zapier only works with the cloud-based Business Edition of Microsoft Excel Online. You can get more information at `https://zapier.com/help/doc/how-get-started-microsoft-excel`.

There are many different text document and spreadsheet apps that integrate with Zapier, which you can check out at `https://zapier.com/apps/categories/documents` and `https://zapier.com/apps/categories/spreadsheets`.

You now understand what kind of operations processes can be automated with Zapier.

Let's now take a look at the essential first steps to take to start automating your operations processes.

Where to start with automating your operations processes with Zapier

It is always good to do some pre-work before you start automating your processes. In *Chapter 2, Preparing to Automate Your Processes*, and *Chapter 3, Building Your First Automated Workflow (Zap)*, we covered a few important points that will help you when you are strategizing your operations workflows, and they are as follows:

1. **Map out your operations processes**: If you don't have a clear idea of how your operations processes work with all your tools, follow the steps in the *Simplifying your processes and assessing what can be automated* section in *Chapter 2, Preparing to Automate Your Processes*, to visually map out your processes so that you have a high-level overview of how your tasks work with your existing software.

2. **List your operations tools**: Make a list of all the operations tools and services that you use in your business to achieve your goals. Then, assess how these tools fit within your mapped-out processes. You will then be able to simplify those processes and decide on what can be automated. Once you have this overview of your processes and tools, you will be better placed to understand where the holes are and how Zapier can help you to close the gaps and automate your processes.

3. **Review your app profile pages**: In *Chapter 2, Preparing to Automate Your Processes*, we also discussed reviewing your individual app profile pages as the best way to establish how your business apps integrate with Zapier. This will give you an insight into the triggers, actions, and searches available to use in your workflows. Make a list of these for quick reference.

4. **Use Zapier's pre-built guided workflow templates**: This is the easiest way to get started with automating your operations processes. These templates are built from workflows that are commonly used by other users. They are perfect for inspiration, quick to set up, and will save you time immediately.

5. **Customize your operations workflows**: Get creative and start building multi-step workflows to achieve more in your automations. Use Zapier's built-in apps to help you do more and connect your operations workflows to other parts of your business processes, such as your invoicing process.

6. **Combine AI and automation**: Use the magic of AI-powered Zapier features and integrated AI apps to supercharge your operations workflows. Find out more in *Chapter 19, AI and Automation*.

You'll be well on your way to creating operations automations for your business.

> **Tip**
>
> If you're looking for ideas of other operations-focused apps to use in your business, you can review the various categories in the app ecosystem library to give you a list of public apps that integrate with Zapier at https://zapier.com/apps/. Review the *A brief guide to choosing new apps for your business* section in *Chapter 2, Preparing to Automate Your Processes,* for guidance on choosing new apps.

You now know how to get started with automating your operations processes with Zapier.

Let's get more specific and discuss how online Word document processes can be automated using Zapier's Google Docs integration.

Automating online Word document processes with the Google Docs integration

Zapier currently integrates with 20 apps in the Google suite of tools, including Google Sheets, Gmail, Google Drive, Google Docs, Google Analytics, and Google Ads. Google Docs is a popular online word processor app that allows you to create and edit text documents as well as to invite and collaborate with other people. Collaborators can make changes and add comments in real time. You can also upload a Word document and convert it into a Google Docs format, view your document's revision history, and translate the document into different languages. You can download documents in other file formats, such as Word, RTF, PDF, HTML, OpenOffice, or as a .zip file, or email documents as attachments. If you're a die-hard fan of Microsoft Word but want a cloud-based word processor with similar features and functions with the added bonus of being able to collaborate in real time and integrate it with connector tools such as Zapier, you won't go wrong with Google Docs.

You can use Zapier's Google Docs integration to add power to your online Word document processes by connecting Google Docs to thousands of other apps so that you can automate many parts of your business processes. The Google Docs integration supports many trigger events, action events, and search action events. A full list can be found on the Google Docs app profile page at https://zapier.com/apps/google-docs/integrations.

Let's take a look at the Google Docs trigger events and some possible use cases.

Google Docs trigger events and use cases

The following is a list of some of the trigger events that you can use with Google Docs with examples of when to use them:

- **New Document**: This event triggers when a new document is added to any folder. You can use this trigger event in your automations when you want to forward a copy of the document or extract the content of the document and add it to another app. For example, combine this trigger event with an action event such as **Send Email** with Gmail to send an email with a PDF of the document attached, or the **Update Record** event with Salesforce to update a field in an opportunity with the direct URL for the document.

- **New Document in Folder**: This event triggers when a new document is added to a specified folder. You can use this trigger event in your automations similarly to the **New Document** trigger but when you want to be specific about the document location. For example, combine this trigger event with an action event such as **Create Expense** with FreshBooks Classic when a new supplier bill is added to your `Expenses` folder.

Next, let's have a look at some of the Google Docs action events and use cases.

Google Docs action events and use cases

The following is a list of some of the action events that you can use with Google Docs with examples of when to use them:

- **Create Document from Text**: You can use this action event to create a new document from text or limited HTML. You could use this action event in combination with a trigger event such as **New Email** with Microsoft Outlook to back up your emails by creating a Google Docs file, or **Meeting Stop** with **Solid** to add meeting notes to new Google Docs documents.

- **Upload Document**: You can use this action event to copy an existing file from another app and add it as a Google Docs file. You could use this action event in combination with a trigger event such as **New File in Folder** with Dropbox to copy new documents to Google Docs or **New Note** with Evernote to copy new note files to Google Docs.

- **Append Text to Document**: You can use this action event when you want to append text to the end of an existing Google Docs document. You could use this action event in combination with a trigger event such as **New Comment** with WordPress to add new comments to the end of a specified Google Docs document, or **New Entry** with **Cognito Forms** to back up form entries to a specified Google Docs document.

- **Create Document from Template**: You can use this action event when you want to create a new document from an existing template document with custom variables that can be filled with alphanumeric values. You could use this action event in combination with a trigger event such as **Updated Deal Stage** with Pipedrive to create proposals, quotes, or invoices from templates when a deal reaches a certain stage, or **New Row** with Smartsheet to add details to a new document from a template.

Next, let's have a look at the Google Docs search action events and use cases.

Google Docs search action events

Google Docs only has one supported search action event, which is **Find Document**. You can use this search action event when you want to find a Google Docs document to use in other steps.

It can be combined with Google Docs actions to make document specification more accurate as you can retrieve the document ID.

> **Tip**
>
> In Google Docs action steps, always use the ID of the file or folder when mapping dynamic data from previous steps or entering text into the **Document Name** or **Folder** fields, respectively, rather than the name.

You can view common problems with the Google Docs integration by navigating to the **Help** tab of the app profile or at `https://help.zapier.com/hc/en-us/articles/8495982583053`.

Next, let's explore how to set up an example of a multi-step Zap using the Google Docs integration.

Setting up a multi-step Zap with the Google Docs integration

To illustrate this, we will use the example of creating a new onboarding document in Google Docs from a template when a row containing contact details is updated in a Google spreadsheet with the date the contact became a customer. Once the template has been created, an email with the document link and a PDF copy will be sent to the contact.

The Zap will involve five steps, as follows:

1. **Trigger**: The Google Sheets app with the **New or Updated Spreadsheet Row** filter trigger event.
2. **Action**: The *Formatter by Zapier* app with the **Text** action event and **Split Text** transform option.
3. **Action**: The Google Docs app with the **Create Document from Template** action event.
4. **Search Action**: The *URL Shortener by Zapier* app with the **Shorten URL** action event.
5. **Action**: The Gmail app with the **Send Email** action event.

The following screenshot shows how your Zap should look once built with some step title editing:

Figure 22.1 – A multi-step Zap using a Google Docs action event

Let's walk through setting up the Zap step by step, starting with the trigger step.

Setting up the trigger step

The Google Sheet spreadsheet we are using as part of the trigger step looks as follows:

Figure 22.2 – Using a Google spreadsheet to trigger when a field is updated

Once the `Date signed` column is updated with the date, the Zap will trigger. We will use the Google Sheets app with the **New or Updated Spreadsheet Row** trigger event as the trigger step. Select the relevant document and specify the worksheet in the **Spreadsheet** and **Worksheet** fields. We want the Zap to trigger only when the `Date signed` column is updated in the sheet and, therefore, we will select that column from the drop-down menu of the **Trigger Column** field.

The following screenshot shows how this step should look:

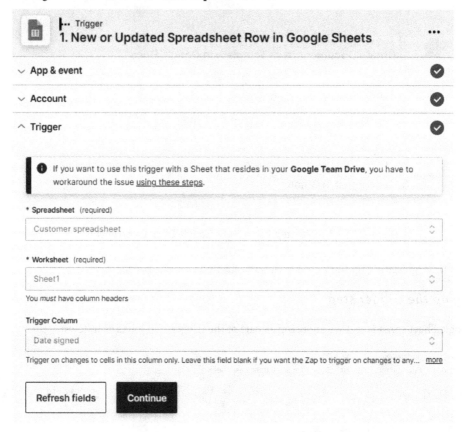

Figure 22.3 – Overview of using the New or Updated Spreadsheet in Google Sheets trigger event

Click on the **Continue** button, then click on the **Test trigger** button to pull through some test data.

Next, let's set up the second step in the Zap – the first action step.

Setting up the second step in the Zap

We want to extract the first name of the contact from the full name so that we can personalize the document and email with a less formal salutation. We will, therefore, use the *Formatter by Zapier* app with the **Text** action event and **Split Text** transform option to accomplish this. Follow the instructions in the *Splitting characters or words into segments* section in *Chapter 17, Text Formatting Functions in Zapier – Part 2*, to customize this action step to map the Name dynamic data from the trigger step to the **Input** field and select **First** for **Segment Index**.

The following screenshot shows how this step should look:

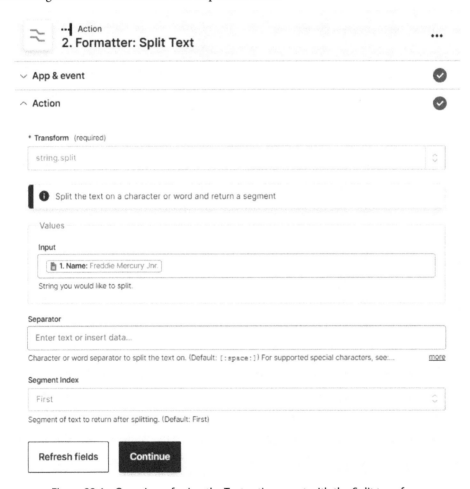

Figure 22.4 – Overview of using the Text action event with the Split transform option of Formatter by Zapier to split off the first name

Click on the **Continue** button. You can then use the **Test** section to split out the first name.

Next, let's set up the next action step.

Setting up the third step in the Zap

Firstly, we need to create and name the Google Docs template and store it in a specific folder location, which, in this example, we will name `Templates`. Next, create custom mail merge fields as appropriate for the fields you want to add to the template. In this example, we will use `{{name}}`, `{{company}}`, `{{date}}`, and `{{products}}`; however, you can name them as you please. Our Google Docs template for this scenario is set up as shown in the following screenshot:

Figure 22.5 – A Google Docs template created with mail merge fields

Next, follow these steps to customize the action step:

1. Select the `Templates` folder from the drop-down menu in the **Folder for new Document** field so that we can locate the template we want to use. You can change this to a new location once your template document is retrieved if you want to store the new documents in another folder.

2. In the **Template Document** field, use the drop-down menu to select the template, in this case, `My Onboarding Template`.

3. Then map in the `Company Name` data from the trigger step and type the text `onboarding plan` into the **New Document Name** field.

4. Select the **Anyone with link can view** option from the drop-down menu of the **Sharing Preference** field so that the contact can view the document.

5. Select the **keep** option in the **Unused Fields Preference** field as the data will always be available.

6. Complete the custom mail merge fields by mapping dynamic data from the trigger step and the formatted text output from the second step in the Zap accordingly, as shown in the following two screenshots:

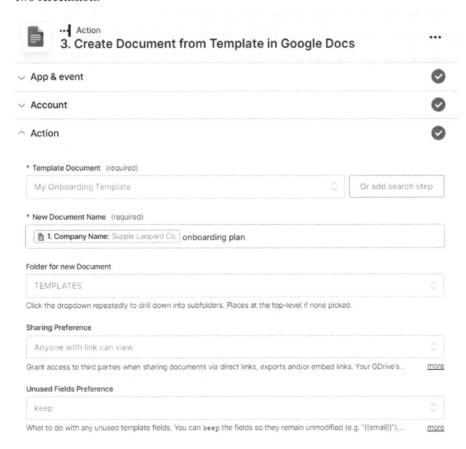

Figure 22.6 – Overview of using the Create Document from Template
action event in the Google Docs integration (1)

The second part of the action step is shown in the following screenshot:

name

> 📄 **1. Name:** Freddie Mercury Jnr.

This is a custom/template field that was discovered within the document's contents.

company

> 📄 **1. Company Name:** Supple Leopard Co.

This is a custom/template field that was discovered within the document's contents.

date

> 📄 **1. Date signed:** 04/25/2023

This is a custom/template field that was discovered within the document's contents.

first_name

> 🔀 **2. Output:** Freddie

This is a custom/template field that was discovered within the document's contents.

products

> 📄 **1. Products:** Automation cons...rkflow building

This is a custom/template field that was discovered within the document's contents.

Figure 22.7 – Using the Create Document from Template action event in the Google Docs integration (2)

7. Click on the **Continue** button. You can then use the **Test** section to create the document. The result from the scenario is shown in the following screenshot:

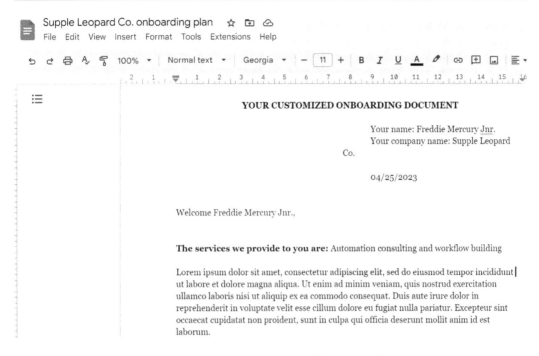

Figure 22.8 – A Google Doc created from a template

Next, let's set up the third action step.

Setting up the fourth step in the Zap

We want to be able to share the document link with the customer; however, we want to make it shorter and more visually pleasing. We will, therefore, use the *URL Shortener by Zapier* app with the **Shorten URL** action event to accomplish this. Follow the instructions mentioned in the *URL Shortener by Zapier – shortening URLs in your Zaps* section in *Chapter 10, Other Useful Built-In Apps by Zapier*, to customize this action step to map the `Alternate Link` data from the action in the third step in the Zap, which is a sharable link.

The following screenshot shows how this step should look:

Figure 22.9 – Overview of using the URL Shortener by Zapier integration to shorten a URL

Click on the **Continue** button. You can then use the **Test** section to create the shortened URL.

Next, let's set up the final action step.

Setting up the fifth step in the Zap

Finally, we want to send an email with the document URL and a PDF attachment to the contact. We will use the Gmail app with the **Send Email** action event, and we will customize this action step as follows:

1. Complete the **To** field by mapping the Email address dynamic data from the trigger step of your Zap.

2. Use the **From** and **Signature** drop-down fields to select the email address and signature to use from your Gmail account.

3. Customize the **Subject** and **Body (HTML or Plain)** fields with relevant text and mapped dynamic data for the first name from the second step of the Zap and the shortened URL from the fourth step of the Zap.

4. Map the Export Links Application/pdf dynamic data from the third step of the Zap to the **Attachments** field.

This is shown in the following three screenshots:

Figure 22.10 – Overview of using Gmail integration to send an email with links and attachments (1)

The second part of the action step is shown in the following screenshot:

From

```
kelly@solvaa.co.uk                                                         ⌄
```

Select an email address or alias from your Gmail Account. Defaults to the primary email address.

From Name

```
Kelly Goss @ Solvaa
```

Reply To

```
Enter text or insert data...
```

Specify a single reply address other than your own.

* Subject (required)

```
Your personal onboarding plan
```

Body Type

```
plain                                                                      ⌄
```

If using the HTML option, you must add any and all formatting (paragraphs, lists, etc) directly using HTML. Learn more.

* Body (required)

```
Dear [ ⇌ 2. Output: Freddie ],

Welcome onboard. Here's a link to your personal onboarding plan: [ 🔗 4. URL: https://zpr.io/nyPWX ]
I've also attached a downloadable PDF.
```

Figure 22.11 – Using Gmail integration to send an email with links and attachments (2)

The third part of the action step is shown in the following screenshot:

Signature

kelly@solvaa.co.uk	⌄

Include a default signature with the email? Will be placed at end of the message after a line break and another "--" lin... <u>more</u>

Label/Mailbox

Choose value...	⌄

Attachments 🗋

📄 **3. Export Links Application Pdf:** https://docs.go...xportFormat=pdf	✕

Enter text or insert data...

A file to be attached. Can be an actual file or a public URL which will be downloaded and attached.

Refresh fields	**Continue**

Figure 22.12 – Using Gmail integration to send an email with links and attachments (3)

5. Click on the **Continue** button. You can then use the **Test** section to send the email.

The following are two screenshots of the resulting email:

Your personal onboarding plan   Inbox ×

Kelly Goss @ Solvaa <kelly@solvaa.co.uk>
to freddie ▾

Dear Freddie,

Welcome onboard. Here's a link to your personal onboarding plan: https://zpr.io/Rh9LK
I've also attached a downloadable PDF.

--

Kind regards,

Kelly

Figure 22.13 – The email sent to the contact showing the link (1)

The second part of the email with the attachment is shown in the following screenshot:

Please respect that the information transmitted is intended only for the person or entity to which it is addressed and may contain confidential information by persons or entities other than the intended recipient is prohibited. If you received this in error, please contact the sender at Cl unsubscribe from these communications at any time. For information on how to unsubscribe, as well as our privacy practices and commitme England & Wales No. 10856404 | Registered Office: Amelia House, Crescent Road, Worthing, BN11 1QR

"If we did all the things we are capable of, we would literally astound ourselves." Thomas A. Edison

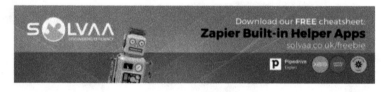

One attachment • Scanned by Gmail ⓘ

Figure 22.14 – Overview of the email sent to the contact showing the attachment (2)

If you are unable to view the file as a PDF, check and adjust your Google Drive sharing preferences. You can get access to a copy of this Zap template at `https://bit.ly/zapier-book`.

You should now have a better understanding of how to automate online Word document processes with the Google Docs integration.

Summary

In this chapter, we discussed the different types of operations processes that can be automated with Zapier, and we covered some examples of workflows used with some common operations-focused applications. First, we got an overview of some of the types of operations processes that can be automated with Zapier. Then, we explored where to start with automating operations processes with Zapier. Finally, we discussed how to automate online Word document processes with Google Docs integration.

You now know how to automate your operations processes with Zapier – specifically, with the Google Docs integration.

In the next chapter, you will learn how to automate your finance and reporting workflows. We will discuss some of the different types of finance and reporting processes and give working examples of how these processes can be automated using Zapier. We will also provide practical tips on how to solve problems relating to finance and reporting workflows.

Questions

1. What type of operations processes can be automated using Zapier?

2. When using the Google Docs integration, should you use the name or ID of a file for mapping in your action steps?

23
Automating Your Finance and Reporting Processes

So far, we've covered how to automate three essential business functions, namely, marketing, sales, and operations. Having efficient processes in those three areas directly impacts your finance processes as more leads are converted into sales, which are then smoothly served, which means that there are more accounting transactions to handle. Automating your finance processes, therefore, means that as you scale, you can handle larger volumes of transactions quicker and more accurately, thereby giving you access to real-time financial performance data.

Once you've got a better handle on your accounting processes, you can focus on getting better visibility of the higher-quality data coming from all aspects of your business by automating reporting processes. Having access to this up-to-date and accurate data allows you to proactively gain insights into business performance when you need to, without much manual intervention. You can easily produce management reports for key stakeholders and analyze the business for weaknesses and opportunities for improvement.

In this chapter, we will discuss the different types of finance and reporting processes that can be automated with Zapier, and we will provide examples of workflows used for some common applications. First, we will give an overview of the types of finance processes that can be automated with Zapier, such as handling sales and purchase invoices and managing online payment transactions. Then, we will give an overview of the types of reporting processes that can be automated with Zapier, such as creating datasets for reporting on and visualizing business performance data. After that, we will look at where to start with automating finance and reporting processes with Zapier. Finally, we will dive into how to automate accounting processes with the Xero integration.

We will cover the following key topics in this chapter:

- An introduction to automating your finance processes with Zapier
- An introduction to automating your reporting processes with Zapier

- Where to start with automating your finance and reporting processes with Zapier

- Automating accounting processes with the Xero integration

Once you have worked through each of these topics, you will have a better understanding of the different finance and reporting processes that can be automated with Zapier. You will know how to use Zapier to automate finance and reporting processes for some of the most common applications.

Technical requirements

To make the most of the content in this chapter, you will need access to a Zapier account. The Zapier Free plan will be required for you to create single-step workflows and use Zapier's pre-built templates. The Zapier Starter plan will be required for you to use Premium apps and to create multi-step workflows.

You can get access to the Zap templates used in this chapter at `https://bit.ly/zapier-book`. Using the templates will help you to visualize how the process works.

An introduction to automating your finance processes with Zapier

Many businesses struggle with the drudgery of keeping their financial records up to date. In fact, bookkeeping is one of the tasks that many business owners leave to the last minute if they don't have a dedicated bookkeeper or accounting team. We would like to think that most businesses are now completely paperless in their approach to keeping their finances under control; however, sometimes, you can't avoid having paper copies of purchases and expenses. And even when a business can move to a completely digital accounting management system by receiving all purchase invoices from suppliers by email, using expense management tools that allow you to take photographs of your expenses and purchases, and creating digital sales invoices and sending them to customers by email, the process of recording all of this data in one place can still be a manual, repetitive, time-consuming, and extremely error-prone process.

With advances in using native integrations between apps and using connector tools such as Zapier to connect other parts of your business processes to finance-specific tools, businesses are now able to quickly and accurately create purchase invoices and receipts, create and send sales invoices, and allocate payments to existing invoices – all this alongside attaching copies of the original transaction, if required. Improving these processes ultimately increases the efficiency and accuracy of real-time financial reporting.

An example of how finance processes can be improved significantly by using native integrations and connector tools such as Zapier to automate various tasks can be found at `https://solvaa.co.uk/optimising-xero-to-deliver-cost-and-time-savings/`.

Understanding what finance processes can be automated with Zapier

Zapier has many integrations with a range of finance tools that allow you to automate your **finance processes** with ease and accuracy. You can connect these finance apps to thousands of other apps, such as Salesforce, Shopify, Google Drive, and Microsoft Excel, to automate all parts of your business processes, including your finance processes.

Here are a couple of examples of finance processes that can be automated with Zapier:

- Invoice management and accounting workflows
- Payment processing workflows

Let's explore each one and give some examples of finance apps that can be used with Zapier to automate the processes involved.

Automating invoice management and accounting processes

As a typical business, you will most likely need to deal with bills from suppliers and expense transactions, such as when you buy lunch at a restaurant for your clients or when your sales teams travel and incur hotel and subsistence costs and collect receipts. You can automate the creation of these purchase invoices and expenses in your accounting app by automatically forwarding emails with attachments to **Optical Character Recognition** (**OCR**) apps such as **Dext** (previously called **ReceiptBank**) and **Hubdoc**. These OCR apps transcribe the details on the invoices and push the data straight into accounting apps such as Xero and QuickBooks Online.

Dext has an integration with Zapier, allowing you to trigger workflows when processed receipt data is available, receipt data is ready for export, and processed receipt notifications occur. You can combine these triggers with action events to create new invoices or bills in your accounting software or add the information to a Google Sheets spreadsheet. You can also submit receipts or sales invoices, check the number of process receipts, and create a new client account if you're using a partner account. You can combine these actions with triggers such as new files being added to Google Drive or Box or new emails with attachments being received. Alternatively, if you are using an OCR app such as Hubdoc that doesn't have a Zapier integration, you can use the Gmail or Microsoft Outlook Zapier integrations with the **New Labeled Email** or **New Email** trigger events, respectively, to forward emails with an attachment to an email address linked to the OCR app.

If you're using expense management apps such as **Expensify**, you can automate expense-handling processes with Zapier by organizing receipts, creating reports, and exporting data to your accounting app. With the Expensify integration, you can trigger workflows when a new report is created. You can combine this trigger with action events to add or create purchase invoices for contractors in Xero or Quickbooks Online, or email copies of expense reports to a manager. You can also create a single expense item, create an expense report, export a report to PDF, and find a report. Combine these actions with triggers to create expense items from new Dropbox files or Google Sheets spreadsheet rows.

Dedicated invoice apps such as Zoho Invoice, **Invoice Ninja**, and **InvoiceBerry** allow you to create invoices on the fly and send them to customers. They also allow you to keep track of your accounts receivable processes with useful dashboards and analytics, often to take payments and send reminders. These apps integrate with Zapier, thereby allowing you to automate invoice creation and a number of other functions.

With Zoho Invoice integration, you can trigger workflows when a new contact, point of contact, estimate, item, invoice, or project is created. You can combine these triggers with action events to add invoice or estimate details to Smartsheet or send an invoice to a contact with Email by Zapier. You can also create a new contact, point of contact, estimate, item, or invoice, as well as search for an invoice. Combine these with trigger events to create contacts when a deal is won in ActiveCampaign or add invoices when new appointments are booked in Acuity Scheduling or Calendly.

If, on the other hand, you're using a dedicated accounting app such as Xero, Quickbooks Online, Freshbooks Classic, or Zoho Books to manage all of your accounts payable and receivable processes in one place, you can use Zapier to automate a large number of finance processes and then streamline other business processes that involve them. Each of these apps integrates with Zapier and offers many trigger, action, and search action events. The Zapier integrations with accounting apps generally have line-item support, allowing you to create multiple rows of data in sales invoices, bills, and expenses.

With the Quickbooks Online integration, you can use several trigger, action, and search action events. There are so many that we will only give a few examples of what you can do with this integration. You can trigger workflows when a new account, customer, estimate, invoice, sales receipt, payment, vendor, bill, or purchase order is added, a new payment is received, or when a customer record is updated. You can combine these triggers with action events to add new rows to a Microsoft Excel sheet, create new orders in ShipStation, or update a deal or opportunity in your CRM, for example. You can also create a new customer, estimate, invoice, sales receipt, refund receipt, credit memo, product or service, payment, vendor, bill, time activity, or purchase order, send an invoice or sales receipt, and update a customer or invoice. Combine these actions with triggers to create invoices and payments when new payments are confirmed in Stripe or Paypal, or to create new customers when form entries are submitted in Gravity Forms or **Wufoo**. You can also search for or create a customer or vendor, and you can find an account, invoice, product, or group of products.

The power of using automations in your finance processes is really highlighted if your business has a large volume of sales transactions – for example, if the business sells popular digital products and services such as courses and memberships through an e-commerce platform such as Shopify, Woocommerce, Kajabi, or Thinkific. Being able to automate the creation of sales invoices in your accounting app is literally a game-changer for many businesses, reducing bookkeeping time significantly. You can refer to the *Automating e-commerce processes* section in *Chapter 21, Automating Your Sales Processes*, for more information.

There are a few accounting and invoicing apps that integrate with Zapier, which you can check out at `https://zapier.com/apps/categories/accounting` and `https://zapier.com/apps/categories/invoices`.

Next, let's discuss how to automate payment processing processes with Zapier.

Automating payment processing processes

We've just touched on how you can use Zapier to automate the creation of sales invoices in your invoicing or accounting apps. Having accurate records of your sales is extremely important to any business, but what might be even more important is making sure that you're being paid as quickly as possible for your sales. Using online payment solutions to automatically take payments for invoices or allow customers to pay those invoices without having to do a bank transfer improves invoice payment times and cash flow in the business. Stripe and Paypal are two of the most popular online payment solutions that integrate with many invoicing and e-commerce apps.

With the Paypal integration, you can trigger workflows when a successful sale has been made, a sale is refunded, or any merchant transaction occurs. You can combine these triggers with action events to create new contacts in ActiveCampaign and add them to an automation, send post-sale or refund emails with Gmail, add new invoices or credit notes to Xero, or add records of sales to a Google Sheets spreadsheet.

Many businesses have embraced the opportunities for recurring revenue based on providing memberships, clubs, and product subscriptions. This might involve paying a monthly subscription for your favorite chocolate bar or health food products, or an annual subscription linked to an online course-support community. There are several subscription management tools, such as **Chargebee**, **Recurly**, and **Chargify**, that help you to manage recurring payments.

With the Chargify integration, you can trigger workflows when a new subscription or invoice is created, a new customer is added, and when a subscription changes state or is updated. Combine these triggers with action events to get notifications in Slack or in Microsoft Outlook, update contacts in Mailchimp, or add tasks to Asana. You can also create a customer, coupon, and product price point and create or update a subscription. You can combine these actions with triggers so that you can create new subscriptions when a row is updated in Smartsheet or new contacts are added to Salesforce. You can add search actions to find a product, product family, or component, and, optionally, create a subscription or customer if one doesn't exist.

Using digital banking solutions such as **Revolut Business** can also improve efficiency by allowing you to automate many finance-related processes. With the Revolut Business integration, you can trigger workflows when you exchange, send, or receive money. Combine this trigger with action steps such as sending notifications using Email by Zapier when you receive money. You can also search for an account, allowing you to retrieve information when, for example, you send money in Revolut Business and then add the details to a Google Sheets spreadsheet.

Once again, being able to automate payment notifications in your accounting app, especially where high volumes of transactions are concerned, increases productivity in bookkeeping processes significantly.

There are many payment processing apps that integrate with Zapier, which you can check out at `https://zapier.com/apps/categories/payment-processing`.

You now understand what kind of finance processes can be automated with Zapier. Let's now take a look at automating reporting processes with Zapier.

An introduction to automating your reporting processes with Zapier

Now that you have taken the time to simplify and automate your marketing, sales, operations, and finance processes, it's crucial to understand how all of these key areas perform against key performance indicators (KPIs) and metrics. Businesses can only make good decisions if they have up-to-date and accurate reporting information to hand. If this information is available instantly, you won't have to spend hours downloading and manipulating data to present it to key decision-makers; they will have top-level critical data on demand.

With advances in technology, businesses no longer have to rely on hand-produced bar graphs and charts to visualize business performance data. Spreadsheet tools have become advanced reporting tools in themselves, allowing complex calculations and data manipulation. Many of the apps that we use for various business functions have their own reporting modules. which enable businesses to extract useful reports and visualize reporting data internally. The issue businesses then have is that their reporting exists in multiple systems and tools and still needs to be collated and condensed so that you have fewer places to log in to and view your important reporting data. Automation using tools such as Zapier can help you to get your key data into the right places for enhancing your reporting and metric visualization processes.

Understanding what reporting processes can be automated with Zapier

Zapier has integrations with a few reporting tools, allowing you to automate your **reporting processes**. You can connect these apps with thousands of other apps, such as Paypal, AgileCRM, **Quaderno**, and Google Sheets, to automate reporting from other business functions.

Here are a few examples of reporting processes that can be automated with Zapier:

- Spreadsheet reporting workflows
- Website analytics workflows
- Business intelligence and dashboard workflows

Let's explore each one and give some examples of reporting apps that can be used with Zapier to automate processes that involve them.

Automating spreadsheet reporting processes

In the *Understanding what operations processes can be automated with Zapier* section of *Chapter 22, Automating Your Operations Processes*, we covered using spreadsheet tools such as Microsoft Excel, Google Sheets, and Smartsheet in your various operations processes. These tools are widely used for recording and manipulating numerical data with simple or complex formulas, which can then be used for visual reporting in graphs and tables. You can also use add-ons with Google Sheets to extract data from other sources such as Google Analytics or integrate Google Sheets with dashboard tools such as Infogram to display custom data in one place. By using Zapier, you can push key reporting data into your spreadsheet, which can be significantly manipulated and transformed to automatically display your data visually.

Next, let's discuss how to automate website analytics processes with Zapier.

Automating website analytics processes

Many businesses invest a vast amount of time and money in their online presence in creating a website and promoting their products, services, and reputation by pushing traffic from various sources to their website. As we discussed in *Chapter 20, Automating Your Marketing Processes*, businesses can use several methods to push traffic to their website, which could include paid ads, guest blog posting, and social media marketing. They also try to improve their online visibility in searches with **Search Engine Optimization** (**SEO**). With all this happening, a business needs to have a way to see the results of its marketing efforts at a glance, and both Google Analytics, an industry-standard tool for analyzing and visualizing website traffic, and **Hotjar**, an app that allows you to analyze your website traffic data, are examples of apps that enable you to do so. By using tools such as these, you will have better insights into your website visitors, such as their sources and geographical locations, and understand behaviors such as how long they spend on your website and on which pages. Then, by using automation tools such as Zapier, you can boost your productivity by automating your reporting processes, such as scheduling reports to run at a specific time each week and delivering the report by email, and tracking offline conversions for completed calls from your calling app, Twilio.

When using Google Analytics, you can create goals and measurements against those goals to track data from various sources. With the Google Analytics integration, you can trigger workflows when new goals are added, and then combine this with an action to send notifications by SMS. You can also create a measurement, update a goal, and run a report, as well as search for a goal. You can combine these actions with triggers to create new measurements from Typeform responses or Calendly bookings or schedule a report to run every week on a Friday at 9 A.M. using Schedule by Zapier.

There are several analytics apps that integrate with Zapier, which you can check out at `https://zapier.com/apps/categories/analytics`.

Next, let's discuss how to automate business intelligence and dashboard processes with Zapier.

Automating business intelligence and dashboard processes

Aside from website analytics, most of the tools in your tech stack probably have some kind of reporting functionality. However, when you have multiple tools, that means you have many places that you need to extract reporting data from. Wouldn't it be fantastic if we could collate all of the key reporting from our various apps on one dashboard or on a few key dashboards, but all in one place where the data is refreshed automatically? That's where business intelligence and dashboard tools come in. These apps allow you to collate all your important reporting data in one place, create KPIs to measure your collected data against, and represent this data in graphical forms that suit your needs. Many of these tools have integrations with popular apps such as Facebook and Salesforce, but often, integrations don't exist. Automation tools such as Zapier increase the efficiency of your reporting processes by extracting key segments of data and pushing the exact data you want to change metrics in these dashboard tools. This is especially handy if integrations don't exist between your apps and the chosen dashboard tool. **Databox**, **Geckoboard**, **Klipfolio**, **Dasheroo**, and **Zoho Analytics** are examples of business intelligence and dashboard reporting tools that integrate with Zapier.

With the Klipfolio integration, for example, you can add data to a source, update data in a data source, and refresh a data source. You can combine these action events with triggers involving other apps, allowing you to update insights without you having to manually import data. You could track the growth of a specific segment of your subscriber list in Klaviyo or Autopilot, or track unsubscribes and campaign clicks in ActiveCampaign. You could also monitor Twitter follower numbers, SurveyMonkey responses, Toky calls, or closed Asana tasks.

There are several business intelligence and dashboard apps that integrate with Zapier, which you can check out at `https://zapier.com/apps/categories/dashboards`.

> **Tip**
> You can use business intelligence and dashboard processes to link in with other key areas such as marketing analytics from Google Analytics and YouTube, for example, to get better visibility of how your business is performing in all of your business functions.

You have now learned what kind of reporting processes can be automated with Zapier. Let's take a look at the essential first steps to take to start automating your finance and reporting processes.

Where to start with automating your finance and reporting processes with Zapier

It is always good to do some pre-work before your start automating your processes. In *Chapter 2, Preparing to Automate Your Processes*, and *Chapter 3, Building Your First Automated Workflow (Zap)*, we covered a few important points that will help you when you are strategizing your finance and reporting workflows; they are as follows:

1. **Map out your finance and reporting processes**: If you don't have a clear idea of how your finance and reporting processes work with all your tools, follow the steps in the *Simplifying your processes and assessing what can be automated* section in *Chapter 2, Preparing to Automate Your Processes*, to visually map out your processes so that you have a high-level overview of how your tasks work with your existing software.

2. **List your finance and reporting tools**: Make a list of all the finance and reporting tools and services that you use in your business to achieve your goals. Then, assess how these tools fit within your mapped-out processes. You will then be able to simplify those processes and decide on what can be automated. Once you have this overview of your processes and tools, you will be better placed to understand where the holes are and how Zapier can help you to close the gaps and automate your processes.

3. **List your finance and reporting tools**: Follow the steps in *Chapter 2, Preparing to Automate Your Processes*, to simplify your processes and make a list of all the tools that you use in your business to achieve your goals, so that you can assess what can be automated.

4. **Review your app profile pages**: In *Chapter 2, Preparing to Automate Your Processes*, we also discussed reviewing your individual app profile pages as the best way to establish how your business apps integrate with Zapier. This will give you an insight into the triggers, actions, and searches available to use in your workflows. Make a list of these for quick reference.

5. **Use Zapier's pre-built guided workflow templates**: This is the easiest way to get started with automating your finance and reporting processes. These templates are built from workflows that are commonly used by other users. They are perfect for inspiration, quick to set up, and will save you time immediately.

6. **Customize your finance and reporting workflows**: Get creative and start building multi-step workflows to achieve more in your automations. Use Zapier's built-in apps to help you do more and connect your finance and reporting workflows to other parts of your business processes, such as your operations process.

7. **Combine AI and automation**: Use the magic of AI-powered Zapier features and integrated AI apps to supercharge your finance and reporting workflows. Find out more in *Chapter 19, AI and Automation.*

You'll be well on your way to creating finance and reporting automations for your business.

> **Tip**
>
> If you're looking for ideas of other finance and reporting apps to use in your business, you can review the **Commerce** and **Business Intelligence** categories in the app ecosystem directory to give you a list of public apps that integrate with Zapier at `https://zapier.com/apps/categories/commerce` and `https://zapier.com/apps/categories/business-intelligence`. Review the *A brief guide to choosing new apps for your business* section in *Chapter 2, Preparing to Automate Your Processes*, for guidance on choosing new apps.

You now know how to get started with automating your finance and reporting processes with Zapier. Let's get more specific and discuss how accounting processes can be automated using Zapier's Xero integration.

Automating accounting processes with the Xero integration

Xero is a popular cloud-based accounting package used by small- and medium-sized businesses. With Xero, you can manage your accounts payable and accounts receivable processes, as well as manage expense claims and payroll and track inventory projects. You can create and send quotes, sales invoices, and purchase orders, and you can comprehensively report on your financials. You can also connect payment processing solutions such as PayPal, **GoCardless**, and **Stripe** to help you get paid faster by your customers. The ability to connect bank feeds to Xero automates part of the transaction reconciliation process, removing the need to manually import bank statements and transaction line entries. Depending on your location, you can submit tax returns and pay bills straight from Xero. Xero also allows you to handle multiple currencies.

Xero natively integrates with hundreds of other apps to allow you to connect other parts of your business to your finance system. You can, however, use the Zapier integration to add power to your processes by connecting Xero to thousands of other apps so that you can automate many parts of your accounting processes. The Xero integration is very comprehensive and currently supports several trigger, action, and search events. A full list can be found on the Xero app profile page at `https://zapier.com/apps/xero/integrations`.

Let's take a look at some of the Xero trigger events and some possible use cases.

Xero trigger events and use cases

The following is a list of supported trigger events that you can use with Xero with examples of when to use them:

- **New Contact**: This event triggers when a new contact is added to Xero. Among other things, you can use this trigger event in your automations when you want to add new contacts to other apps such as your email marketing app or inventory management app as soon as they have been added to Xero. For example, combine this trigger event with an action event such as **Create Subscriber** with Klaviyo, or combine **Create Customer** with Dear Inventory.

- **New Quote**: This event triggers when a new quote is created in Xero. Among other things, you can use this trigger event in your automations when you want to set a reminder in your CRM to follow up with the recipient when a quote has been sent or if you want to send a notification to your team if a quote is accepted. For example, combine this trigger event with an action event such as **Create Task** with AgileCRM, or combine **Create Post** with **Ryver**.

- **New Sales Invoice**: This event triggers when a new sales invoice (accounts receivable) is created in Xero. You can use this trigger event in your automations when you want to add details of newly submitted sales invoices to a spreadsheet or send a fax to your client for all authorized sales invoices. For example, combine this trigger event with an action event such as **Add Row** with Microsoft Excel, or combine **Send Fax** with ClickSend SMS.

- **New Purchase Order**: This event triggers when a new purchase order is added to Xero. Among other things, you can use this trigger event in your automations when you want to add details of new purchase orders to a database or notify your team depending on the status of the purchase order. For example, combine this trigger event with an action event such as **Create Record** with Knack or combine **Send Channel Message** with Microsoft Teams.

- **New Bill**: This event triggers when a new bill (accounts payable) is created in Xero. You can use this trigger event in your automations when you want to add a new calendar event on the bill due date or add a task to your task management app to pay the bill on the due date. For example, combine this trigger event with an action event such as **Create Event** with Microsoft Outlook or combine **Create Task** with **Any.Do**.

- **New Expense Claim Receipt**: This event triggers when a new draft expense claim receipt is created in Xero. Among other things, you can use this trigger event in your automations when you want to notify an approver that a new expense claim is ready to be reviewed or add a task to your to-do list. For example, combine this trigger event with an action event such as **Send Outbound Email** with Email by Zapier or combine **Create Task** with Teamwork Projects.

- **New Bank Transaction**: This event triggers when a new bank transaction is made in Xero. Among other ways, you can use this trigger event in your automations when you want to keep track of what transactions are being processed by adding them to a spreadsheet. For example, combine this trigger event with an action event such as **Create Spreadsheet Row** with Google Sheets.

- **New Payment**: This event triggers when a new payment is made in Xero. You can use this trigger event in your automations when you want to send a thank you email to your customer for paying your invoices or send a summary to your team of all paid invoices that day. For example, combine this trigger event with an action event such as **Send Email** with Gmail or **Append Entry and Schedule Digest** with Digest by Zapier and **Send Channel Message** with Slack. You can download the Zap template from `https://bit.ly/zapier-book`.

Next, let's have a look at some of the Xero action events and use cases.

Xero action events and use cases

The following is a list of supported action events that you can use with Xero with examples of when to use them:

- **Create/Update Contact**: You can use this action event when you want to create a new contact or update an existing contact in Xero. You could use this action event in combination with a trigger event such as **Updated Deal Stage** with Pipedrive to add contacts to Xero when a deal reaches a certain stage in your CRM or in combination with **Link Clicked** in Mailchimp to update contacts in Xero when a link is clicked in a campaign email.

- **Create New Quote Draft**: You can use this action event when you want to create a new draft quote in Xero. You could use this action event in combination with a trigger event such as **New Form Submission** with HubSpot to create new draft quotes when a contact requests a quote via a HubSpot form, or combine **New Contact** with Xero to create a draft quote when new contacts are added to Xero.

- **Create Sales Invoice**: You can use this action event when you want to create a new sales invoice (account receivable) in Xero. You could use this action event in combination with a trigger event when, for example, a deal moves to the **Invoicing** stage in your CRM and you only want to add a detailed contact to Xero if that contact does not exist and then create a sales invoice in Xero associated with that contact. You can use the **New Deal in Stage** trigger event in HubSpot with the **Find Contact** search action with Xero, and the **Create Sales Invoice** action event with Xero. You can watch a video about a working example using a Pipedrive CRM trigger event and download the Zap template from `https://bit.ly/zapier-book`.

- **Add Items to Existing Sales Invoice**: You can use this action event when you want to update an existing sales invoice in Xero with new items. You could use this action event in combination with a trigger event such as **Updated Order** with Shopify to add additional items to an existing invoice in Xero, and you could use the Xero **Find Invoice** search action to find the invoice when the invoice number or reference has been filled out with an appropriate reference from Shopify.

- **Send Sales Invoice by Email**: You can use this action event when you want to send an existing sales invoice in Xero. You could use this action event in combination with a Xero **Create Invoice** action event when you want to create a new invoice and then send it to the contact from Xero.

- **Create Purchase Order**: You can use this action event when you want to create a new purchase order in Xero. You could use this action event in combination with a trigger event with **New or Updated Record** with Airtable to create a purchase order when a field is filled in Airtable.

- **Create Bill**: You can use this action event when you want to create a new bill (account payable) in Xero. You could use this action event in combination with a trigger event such as **Parsed Document Data Available** with Docparser when you want to parse bill details using Docparser and then create the corresponding bill in Xero.

- **Create Credit Note**: You can use this action event when you want to create a new accounts payable or accounts receivable credit note associated with a contact in Xero. You could use this action event in combination with a trigger event such as **New Sales Order Credit Memo** with Magento and **Find Invoice** with Xero to create credit notes in Xero against the associated invoice when a credit memo is raised in Magento.

- **Create Bank Transaction**: You can use this action event when you want to create a new send or receive money transaction in Xero. You could use this action event in combination with a trigger event such as **New Charge** or **New Refund** in Stripe to create, receive, or send money direct payments when new payments or refunds are made with Stripe.

- **Create Bank Transfer**: You can use this action event when you want to transfer money between your different bank accounts in a specified Xero organization. You could use this action event in combination with a trigger event such as **Successful Sale** in PayPal when you routinely transfer funds from your PayPal bank account to your current bank account in Xero whenever a sale is made.

- **Create Payment**: You can use this action event when you want to create a new payment against an invoice, credit note, prepayment, or overpayment in Xero. You could use this action event in combination with a trigger event such as **New Transaction** with Square and **Find Invoice** with Xero to create payments against Xero invoices when transactions are completed in Square.

Next, let's have a look at some of the Xero search action events and use cases.

Xero search action events and use cases

Now let's cover the two supported search action events that you can use with Xero:

- **Find Contact**: You can use this search action event when you want to find a contact in Xero. You can use this search action in combination with other Xero trigger or action events in your automations. Refer to the *Xero action events* and use cases section for an example of how to use this search action event followed by the Xero **Create Sales Invoice** action steps.

- **Find Invoice**: You can use this search action event when you want to find an invoice in Xero. You can use this search action in combination with other Xero trigger or action events in your automations. For example, when you want to send a thank you email to your customer for paying your invoices and you want to attach a PDF copy of the invoice, you can use the **New Payment** trigger event with the **Find Invoice** search action and **Send Email** with the Gmail action event. You can download the Zap template at `https://bit.ly/zapier-book`.

Next, let's review a few tips for the best use of the Xero integration.

Tips for using the Xero integration

Here are a few tips for the successful use of the Xero integration:

- **Read Only**, **Invoice Only**, and **Cashbook Client** users will not be able to use the integration. You must have *Standard* or *Advisor* access, and the triggers and actions you will be able to use will depend on your access rights to certain modules.

- Only connect your Xero account to one Zapier account. This will prevent disconnection issues.

- Always check what type of field you are entering or mapping data to, and ensure your data is formatted accordingly. This will ensure data accuracy. You can review the *Understanding field data types* section in *Chapter 3, Building Your First Automated Workflow (Zap)*, for more information on field types.

- When using the **Custom** tab to type in or map data from previous steps to fields that display Xero field options in drop-down menus, such as with **Status**, use the field label rather than the field name – for example, field name = **Awaiting Payment**, field label = authorized.

- The Xero integration supports the use of line items. To optimize using this integration in your workflows, you can review the *Manipulating lineitems* section in *Chapter 18, Zapier's Utilities Functions*, for more information on transforming line-item data. If your trigger and action steps both support line items, you will not need to transform the data.

- You can create connections between your different apps by displaying clickable URL links to Xero records by using the Xero record ID plus the view URL. For example, when you create a sales invoice in Xero, update a custom field in the deal or opportunity record in your CRM with the invoice URL so other Xero users in the organization can view the invoice. The URL plus ID combination, in this case, would be https://go.xero.com/AccountsReceivable/View.aspx?InvoiceID=b2f9e6df-73ab-4ccd-9978-258f22ef4665, where b2f9e6df-73ab-4ccd-9978-258f22ef4665 is the sales invoice ID.

- Review the Xero API at https://developer.xero.com/documentation/ for information on other triggers and actions you can perform using Webhooks by Zapier and Code by Zapier. You can hire a Zapier expert to help you with custom integration work from https://experts.zapier.com/.

- You can view common problems with the Xero integration by navigating to the **Help** tab of the app profile or following this link: https://help.zapier.com/hc/en-us/articles/8495985208589.

Next, let's explore how to set up an example of a multi-step Zap using the Xero integration.

Setting up a multi-step Zap with the Xero integration

To illustrate this, we will use the example of creating a sales invoice and bill for associated Stripe transaction fees in Xero when a new charge is made in Stripe. We also want to correctly allocate the Xero tax code based on the buyer's country location.

The Zap will involve four steps, as follows:

1. **Trigger**: The Stripe app with the **New Charge** trigger event.

2. **Action**: The Formatter by Zapier app with the **Utilities** action event with the **Lookup Table** transform function.

3. **Action**: The Xero app with the **Create Sales Invoice** action event.

4. **Action**: The Xero app with the **Create Bill** action event.

The following screenshot shows how your Zap should look once built with some step name customization:

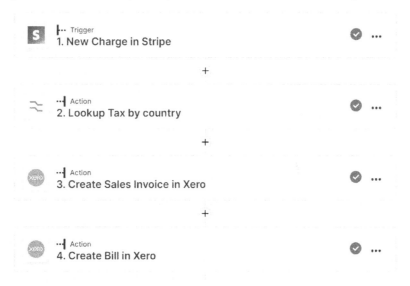

Figure 23.1 – A multi-step Zap using Xero action events

Let's walk through setting up the Zap step by step, starting with the trigger step.

Setting up the trigger step

We will use the Stripe app with the **New Charge** trigger event as the trigger step. In the **Include Failed Charges?** field, choose **False** as we do not want the Zap to trigger on failed charges.

The following screenshot shows how this step should look:

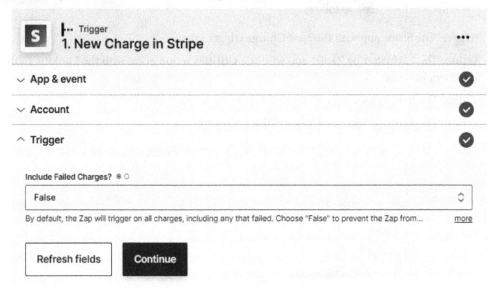

Figure 23.2 – Overview of customizing the New Charge in Stripe trigger event to trigger a workflow

Click on the **Continue** button and then use the **Test trigger** button to pull through some test data.

Next, let's set up the second step in the Zap – the first action step.

Setting up the second step in the Zap

We want to customize the sales invoice tax to match the country that the customer's card is linked to. In this scenario, we want all European customer locations to have **20% VAT (on Income)** (OUTPUT2) and all other countries to have **No VAT** (NONE). Your tax settings differ based on your Xero region. We will use the Formatter by Zapier app with the **Utilities** action event and the **Lookup Table** transform option. Follow the instructions in the *Using lookup tables for related data* section in *Chapter 18, Zapier's Utilities Functions*, to customize this action step to add the **Lookup Key** value as Payment Method Details Card Country, and the **Lookup Table** fields will contain the Stripe European country codes on the left and Xero tax code (OUTPUT2) on the right. We will set **Fallback Value** as NONE for all other countries.

The following screenshot shows how this step should look:

Figure 23.3 – Overview of using the Utilities action event with the Lookup Table
transform option in a Formatter by Zapier action event to look up a tax code

Click on the **Continue** button. You can then use the **Test** section to get the tax code. In this case, the step output will be OUTPUT2 for the CZ country code.

Next, let's set up the next action step.

Setting up the third step in the Zap

We will use the Xero app with the **Create Sales Invoice** action event, and we will customize this action step by completing the **Organization**, **Contact Name**, **Email Address**, **Status**, **Date**, **Due Date**, **Currency**, **Branding Theme**, **Reference**, **Description**, **Quantity**, **Unit Price**, **Account**, and **Tax Rate** fields by using the drop-down menu options or mapping dynamic data from previous steps. Importantly, we can enter the contact's name and email address and create a new contact straight from this step, and then map the **Tax Rate** field with the output from the second step in the Zap. Use the following three screenshots to complete the step. Here is the first part:

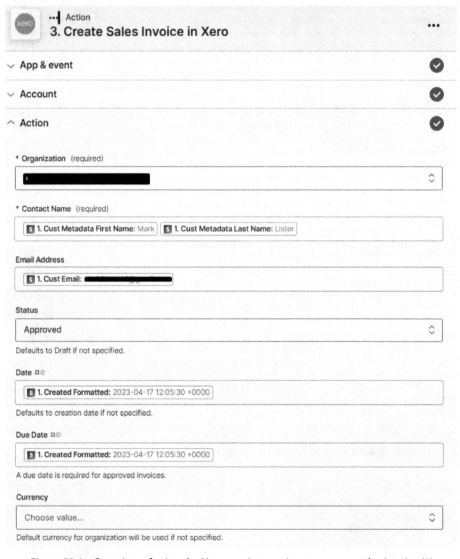

Figure 23.4 – Overview of using the Xero app integration to create a sales invoice (1)

The second part of the action step is shown in the following screenshot:

Url

Enter text or insert data...

URL link to a source document.

Attachment ▣

Enter text or insert data...

Branding Theme

Choose value...   ⌄

The branding theme to use for this invoice.

Number

Enter text or insert data...

Unique alpha numeric code identifying invoice - leave blank for auto-generated value.

Reference

$ 1. ID: ch_3MxqhGCi0RYOmpoS0IHIh2XD   **$ 1. Payment Method...Is Card Country:** GB

An additional reference number

Sent To Contact ◉ ○

Choose value...   ⌄

Mark invoice as "sent" (note: does not actually send an email). This can be set only on invoices that have a status of...   more

Figure 23.5 – Using the Xero app integration to create a sales invoice (2)

The third part of the action step is shown in the following screenshot:

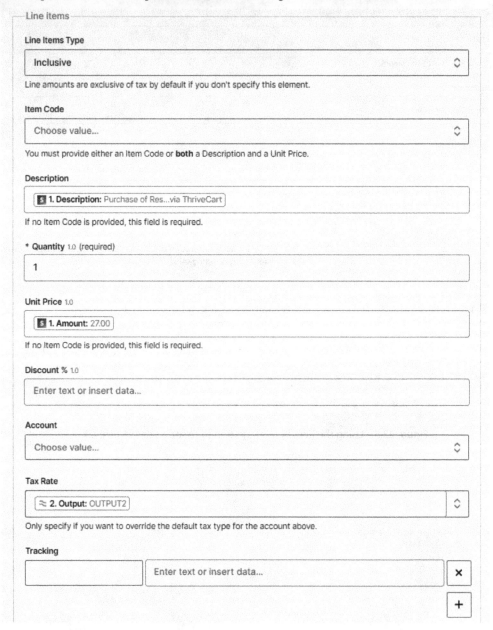

Figure 23.6 – Overview of using the Xero app integration to create a sales invoice (3)

Click on the **Continue** button. You can then use the **Test** section to send the email.

Next, let's set up the final action step.

Setting up the final step in the Zap

We will use the Xero app with the **Create Bill** action event, and we will customize this action step by completing the **Organization**, **Contact Name**, **Status**, **Date**, **Due Date**, **Reference**, **Line Items Type**, **Description**, **Quantity**, **Unit Price**, **Account**, and **Tax Rate** fields by using the drop-down menu options, entering text, or mapping dynamic data from previous steps. Use the following two screenshots to complete the step:

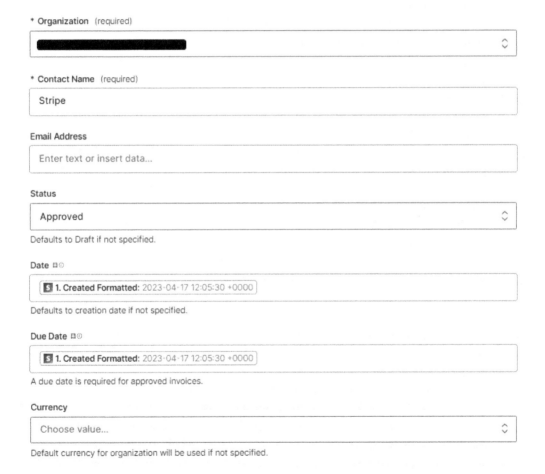

Figure 23.7 – Overview of using the Xero app integration to create a sales invoice (1)

The second part of the action step is shown in the following screenshot:

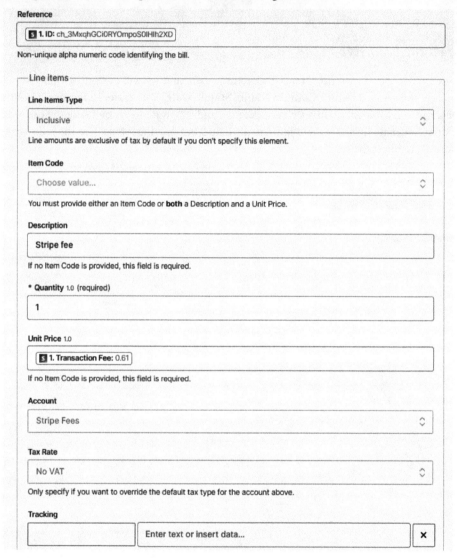

Figure 23.8 – Overview of using the Xero app integration to create a sales invoice (2)

Click on the **Continue** button. You can then use the **Test** section to create the note.

You can get access to a copy of this Zap template at `https://bit.ly/zapier-book`.

You should now have a better understanding of how to automate finance processes with the Xero integration.

Summary

In this chapter, we discussed the different types of finance and reporting processes that can be automated with Zapier and we explored some examples of workflows used with some common applications. First, we got an overview of the types of finance processes that can be automated with Zapier. Then, we covered the types of reporting processes that can be automated with Zapier. After that, we explored where to start with automating finance and reporting processes with Zapier. Finally, we discussed how to automate accounting processes with the Xero integration.

You now know how to automate your finance and reporting processes with Zapier and, specifically, finance processes involving the Xero integration.

In the next chapter, you will learn some practical tips, tricks, and best practices for enhancing your success when using Zapier in your business.

Questions

1. What type of finance processes can be automated using Zapier?
2. What type of reporting processes can be automated using Zapier?

24

Tips, Tricks, and Best Practices to Enhance Your Productivity

We'll soon be coming to the end of our Zapier coaching journey. We have covered many topics that will help you to create effective workflow automations in your business or for your clients using Zapier. In this chapter, we will discuss the best practices for utilizing Zapier effectively and build on the tips and tricks we learned in each chapter. First, we will recap the steps covered throughout this book to help you with your Zap building. We will also explore a range of tips and tricks that you can use to effectively create workflows in Zapier for top performance.

We will cover the following key topics in this chapter:

- Best practices for using Zapier effectively
- Tips and tricks to enhance your use of Zapier

Once you have worked through each of these topics, you will have a better understanding of the best practices to use when building workflow automations in Zapier.

Technical requirements

To get the most out of the content in this chapter, you will need access to a Zapier account. The Zapier Free plan will be adequate for you to create single-step workflows and use Zapier's pre-built templates. The Zapier Starter plan will be required for you to use Premium apps and to create multi-step workflows.

Best practices for using Zapier effectively

The best way to understand how to optimize using Zapier in your business is to review the content we explored in each chapter of this book so that you have a point for quick reference. Let's briefly explore the content we covered in this book as an overview of the best practices to use when building workflows in Zapier.

Starting with the basics

Getting the groundwork done at the beginning will prepare you for success. Once you've chosen the best Zapier plan for you and created a Zapier account, the next step is to familiarize yourself with navigation on the Zapier platform and then edit your settings and preferences to suit. Make sure you've also grasped the terminology used on the Zapier platform as this will help you when troubleshooting. We covered these topics in *Chapter 1, Introduction to Business Process Automation with Zapier*.

Preparing before you automate

Preparation is the key to success and will save you a lot of time from the start. A large part of implementing effective automations is ensuring you have identified your manual and repetitive processes, documented them, and simplified them first. Once you've done that, you should establish how your business apps fit into those processes and how those apps integrate with Zapier. Make the most of the information provided in the Zapier app ecosystem directory to help you do this. We covered these topics in *Chapter 2, Preparing to Automate Your Processes*.

When you're ready to start building your Zaps, strategize the best flow structure first. As you can't drag and drop your steps around in the Zap editor, planning out the steps in advance of building your Zaps will save you time. We covered this topic in *Chapter 3, Building Your First Automated Workflow (Zap)*.

Getting to grips with steps, fields, and data mapping

A crucial first step in your Zap building is understanding how trigger, action, and search action steps work together. It's also important to have a firm grasp on how to enter data into fields in your action steps by using dropdowns, data mapping from the previous steps of your Zap, and entering text. You will also need to know about the different field types used in action steps and what kind of data is accepted in these fields. We covered these topics in *Chapter 3, Building Your First Automated Workflow (Zap)*.

Managing your Zaps effectively

Having a well-organized Zapier account will help you maintain structure the more Zaps you build and the more you automate in your business. Keeping your Zaps organized with appropriate naming and storage in specific folders helps maintain a tidy account. It's also useful to know how to individually manage your Zaps and connected apps, as well as understand statuses, to save you time with troubleshooting.

You might also want to share Zaps with other Zapier users, and Zaps, app connections, and folders with team members. We covered these topics in *Chapter 4, Managing Your Zaps*.

Staying on top of your task usage

While you're getting to grips with Zapier, you will want to keep an eye on your task usage. It may not seem obvious from the start; however, it is easy to make a mistake in your Zaps that can cause your Zaps to trigger excessively, resulting in high task usage. This is even more important when you're using lower-priced plans with less task allocation. The solution is often adding a Filter by Zapier step soon after the trigger step to allow your Zap to run only if the trigger data satisfies certain conditions. Now, to ensure you are able to monitor your task usage, you can set up a Zap using the Zapier Manager built-in app and turn off a specific Zap if required. We covered this topic in *Chapter 12, Managing Your Zapier Account with Built-In Apps*.

Setting up alerts and understand how to troubleshoot

At some point, you will experience errors and issues with your Zaps. A key tip for success is to have a well-monitored Zapier account so that you can address these problems swiftly. Make sure that you have adjusted your account settings accordingly and have created Zap error and app status alerts to notify you of problems with your Zaps and your Zapier account. Once you've done that, knowing how to troubleshoot when you see errors or when things don't go according to plan with workflows is critical to success with Zapier. When you can't solve the problem yourself, you'll also need to know where to go to find assistance. We covered these topics in *Chapter 5, Troubleshooting and Handling Zap Errors*, and *Chapter 12, Managing Your Zapier Account with Built-In Apps*.

Understanding the different built-in Zapier apps and features

You don't need to know how to use all of the built-in apps by Zapier at once, but having a good understanding of what they all do and how they can help you when you're building your Zaps is extremely useful.

We started with a handy overview of all the approved built-in apps (those not in the beta phase) in *Chapter 6, Creating Multi-Step Zaps and Using Built-In Apps*, then discussed each one in detail from *Chapter 7, Getting Started with Built-In Apps*, onward.

The most useful built-in apps to start with are Filter by Zapier, which we covered in *Chapter 7, Getting Started with Built-In Apps*, and the versatile Formatter by Zapier built-in app, which we covered from *Chapter 14, Formatting Date and Time*, to *Chapter 18, Zapier's Utilities Functions*.

You can also explore how to supercharge your automations with AI. We discussed using AI with Zapier in *Chapter 19, AI and Automation*.

You can get access to a comprehensive cheat sheet for all the Zapier built-in apps at `https://bit.ly/zapier-book`.

Getting inspired

Having a good idea of what you can automate in your business is an important starting point in your Zap-building process. If you need some inspiration and examples of ways in which you can automate your different business function processes with Zapier, you can check out the content from *Chapter 20, Automating Your Marketing Processes*, to *Chapter 23, Automating Your Finance and Reporting Processes*.

Reviewing your processes and automations regularly

Continuous improvement is another key factor in maintaining successful automated processes. Once you have built your first few Zaps, make sure that you review them regularly and adjust them accordingly based on errors and changes in your processes. Reviewing your Zaps regularly and ensuring they have the minimum number of required steps will also help reduce task usage and prevent you from paying more than you need to. We covered this topic in *Chapter 3, Building Your First Automated Workflow (Zap)*.

You should now have a better understanding of the best practices for using Zapier effectively. Next, let's review a few tips and tricks that will further optimize your Zapier usage.

Tips and tricks to enhance your use of Zapier

Now that you've learned how to build your first few Zaps and you're on your way to supercharging your business and running it on autopilot, there might be times that you come across pain points that can be solved relatively easily if you know what to do next. Let's go over a few tips and tricks that will help you.

Trigger data not pulling through

Some app integrations may have issues pulling through real trigger data for you to use when building your Zap and you try to test your trigger. In many cases, if no trigger data can be found, Zapier will pull through dummy data that you can use in your action step mapping. Sometimes, Zapier doesn't produce any dummy data, and if you click on the **Skip Test** button, you should be able to use placeholders in your action steps that will fill with data once the Zap is turned on and running. Rest assured that your Zap will run with the correct mappings once you have turned it on.

You can also manually map data using the code for the node ID for the step containing the data and the field name, which might, for example, look like this: `{{122484559__First Name}}`. You can read more about how to handle this in the Zapier Community article at `https://community.zapier.com/featured-articles-65/how-to-manually-map-fields-that-do-not-appear-in-the-sample-data-aka-custom-pill-mapping-9738`.

Timezone settings

Ensure that you have specified your timezone settings in **Account Settings**, and if applicable, in specific Zaps. While many apps use your computer or location settings to set timezones, there might be differences between how your apps handle this information. This can cause problems in your Zaps by causing time or date discrepancies in your Zap run results. Timezones can be tricky to work with, so you should reach out to Zapier Support if you need some extra help assessing issues with timezones. You can read more about handling time and dates in *Chapter 14, Formatting Date and Time*.

Extra Fields alerts

You might find that, once you have built your steps, when you change the app or folder within an action step, you will be presented with an **Extra Fields** warning. This means that fields that you had previously filled in no longer exist. This is shown in the following screenshot:

Figure 24.1 – Overview of an Extra Fields warning message

It is best to ensure that you always clear unused field data or this can cause errors when your Zaps run. Just click on the **Remove these extra fields** button to do so.

Refreshing fields when you make adjustments in your app

When you add new custom fields to your apps, make sure that you refresh the fields in any steps involving this change. This is important as, often, data in old fields may remap against newer fields, causing inaccuracies when your Zap is turned on. This is shown in the following screenshot:

Groups

Choose value...	⇅

Language Code

Enter text or insert data...

This should be a two letter language code (ISO639-1) See here for the list of language codes.

Tag(s)

Choose value...	⇅

The tag(s) to which the subscriber will be added. Tags will be added to any existing tags on existing subscribers.

Refresh fields	To continue, finish required fields

Figure 24.2 – Overview of using the Refresh fields button to bring through new field information

This is quite common, for example, if you add additional columns to a Google Sheets spreadsheet, particularly between existing columns, or new merge fields in a Google Docs template. Click on the **Refresh fields** button to bring in new field information.

Doing more than what Zapier integration with an app allows

You might find that the Zapier integration with one or more apps that you use in your business is tailored to common use cases. However, you might want to achieve more with the integration, with different triggers, actions, or searches, or you might want certain fields to be added and data to be restructured in a more usable way. Often, you can achieve more by becoming familiar with reading API documentation and then making HTTP requests with the Webhooks by Zapier built-in app, via the **API Request** action available in some apps in beta, or by using code with the Code by Zapier built-in app. You can also approach Zapier Support to find out who built the integration, be it a **Software-as-a-Service** (**SaaS**) app vendor or Zapier, and discuss whether improvements can be made to the integration. When app integrations are in the beta phase, this is usually a good opportunity to give feedback and suggest improvements.

Thinking outside the box

When you're creating your workflows, be creative. If you can't achieve something with the Zapier integration with your app and you've explored all avenues, think about using a free tool as a stepping stone. You don't have to stick to conventional uses of the app. For example, you can use the Formatter by Zapier **Utilities** action event with the **Lookup Table** transform function to look up one value matching a key. If, however, you want to search for numerous values related to one key, you could use a Google Sheets spreadsheet as the lookup table instead.

Using the Zapier community as a resource

If you run into a problem, chances are that other Zapier users will have experienced it too. The Zapier Community forum, which can be found at `https://community.zapier.com/`, holds a log of searchable questions and answers to problems experienced by other users. The forum is also frequented by the Zapier Support team, several Zapier Experts, and other advanced users who will happily help with your issue if you find it hasn't been addressed previously.

You should now have a better understanding of the tips and tricks for enhancing your use of Zapier.

Summary

In this chapter, we discussed the best practices to adopt to enhance your success with using Zapier in your business. First, we did a recap of the topics that were covered in this book, which will help you use Zapier effectively. Then, we explored some practical tips and tricks for optimum Zap building.

You now know the best practices to follow to enhance your success with Zapier while implementing and using it in your business.

In the next chapter, we'll look at various scenarios that will help you assess your problem-solving and Zapier workflow-building skills. We will look into a specific problem that can be solved using Zapier and work through each example practically, with tips given along the way. The scenarios are classified by skill level, and you will have the opportunity to put your knowledge to the test and adapt your problem-solving and Zap-building skills.

Questions

1. What are the two first best practices to follow to ensure success in automating your processes?

2. Is it possible to do more than what is presented to you with the triggers, actions, and searches in a Zapier integration?

25

Challenging Your Problem-Solving and Zap-Building Skills

In this chapter, we will take a look at three scenarios that will help you assess your problem-solving and Zapier workflow-building skills. First, we will describe a specific problem that can be solved using Zapier and work through each example with a suggested solution, with tips provided along the way. The scenarios are classified by skill level, and you will have the opportunity to put your knowledge to the test and adapt your problem-solving and Zap-building skills.

We will cover the following key topics in this chapter:

- Introduction and guidance

- Three scenarios (novice, intermediate, and advanced)

- Guidance on suggested solutions for each scenario

Once you have worked through each of these topics, you will be able to build complex Zaps from scratch.

Technical requirements

To get the most out of this chapter, you will need access to a Zapier account. The Zapier Starter plan will be required for you to use Premium apps and to create multi-step workflows. The Professional plan will be required for you to create Zaps with Paths by Zapier.

Introduction and guidance

We have provided three different scenarios that increase in difficulty to test your problem-solving and workflow-building skills. When formulating your solutions, try to use the built-in apps by Zapier in your problem-solving where possible. This will optimize your Zap building without you having to use other apps. Also, try to use as few steps as possible to reduce your task usage.

Remember, there are many ways that you can create a workflow. Just like the apps that you're using in your business are likely to be different from someone else's, the logic that you use for your Zaps is also likely to be different from someone else's. The aim is to create Zapier workflows for repeatable processes with as few steps as possible and no errors. There are no wrong answers if the Zap achieves the objective. You can do this by designing a process that makes the most of the available features and integrations in the apps that are being used, and then balancing this with Zapier workflows to achieve the ultimate automation goal.

Remember, be creative and think outside the box.

Once you have read through the scenarios, go ahead and try to build out the Zap. If you need some inspiration, you can review a suggested solution in the *Guidance on suggested solutions for each scenario* section.

Now that you have a better understanding of how to tackle the three scenarios and get the best results from these challenges, let's dive into the scenarios.

Three scenarios (novice, intermediate, and advanced)

In this section, you have the opportunity to work through three scenarios of increasing difficulty. Once you have read through the scenarios, go ahead and try to build out your Zaps to solve the problems presented.

Let's explore the first one.

Scenario 1 – novice

Dave runs an online business selling courses and membership programs. He uses Kajabi, a popular course platform, to host multiple courses and memberships. However, he wants to implement a highly converted standalone sales page app with a payment solution that gives him more flexibility with offers, discounts, and upsells. Kajabi does not integrate with many third-party apps, so whatever solution Dave chooses might not integrate with the course platform. Dave wants to streamline and automate his processes to reduce the time he spends manually granting access to the relevant course or membership program once the person has purchased the product through the sales page app. The problem Dave is likely to have when creating his workflow is that the product IDs in the two apps may not match. As the Kajabi integration with Zapier does not have any search actions, he is not able to use the product name to find the course product. Dave would also like to incorporate upsells and downsells, as well as account for access being removed after a refund is processed.

Can you suggest a better process for Dave by introducing a sales page app to his business and connecting this to Kajabi with Zapier?

You should now be able to solve a problem that requires novice Zap-building skills. Now, let's have a look at a more complex scenario.

Scenario 2 – intermediate

Winnie runs a small gardening and landscaping service with a team member, Eugene. Winnie receives inquiries for quotations via a contact form on her website. These inquiries include the lead's name, email address, contact number, job location address, budget, preferred project date, and inquiry notes. She creates a quotation by email; once a customer has accepted a quotation for a job with a response, Winnie adds the new customer details to her Rolodex and writes the agreed project dates in her diary. She then emails her colleague, Eugene, with the date, start time, number of hours, and location of the project. She does not book more than one project in a day to allow for travel time; all projects start at 9 A.M. and they never leave for the job before 7 A.M. On the day the project starts, both she and Eugene check the weather separately to decide whether they need to take waterproof clothing just in case it rains. They both also have to double-check the start time and location in the diary or the email Winnie sent. Once the job is complete, Winnie writes out an invoice for the number of hours Eugene and she has worked on the job and posts it through the customer's letterbox with payment instructions.

With this current process, Winnie spends a lot of time manually writing out details for her quotation in her Rolodex, diary, and invoice book, as well as typing out emails to Eugene and checking the weather. This process is not scalable, and as Winnie would like to grow the business, she would like to migrate to a digital process by using appropriate apps and automations that will make her job much more efficient. Both Winnie and Eugene use Gmail for their emails, all their jobs are localized to San Diego, and the customer's invoice address is always the same as the project's location.

Can you suggest a better process for Winnie by introducing other apps to her business that are more fit for purpose and connect her processes with Zapier? For this challenge, you must stick to a monthly app subscription budget of $50 per month for any additional apps and limit the additional apps you introduce to three new paid apps (including Zapier). There is no limit to the number of built-in apps by Zapier that you can use in your workflows.

You should now be able to solve problems that require intermediate Zap-building skills. Next, we'll have a look at the last scenario, which will test your advanced problem-solving skills.

Scenario 3 – advanced

Liv is a career coach who runs a small firm with two other team members. The firm offers three types of coaching services with different prices and each team member is responsible for one of them. She currently receives inquiries via contact form submissions on her website. The contact form collects the lead's name, email address, mobile number, the requested service, and additional inquiry notes. She responds to the inquiry by pasting a response template into an email from a document and customizing it to the inquiry, asking the contact the best time for them to have a Zoom call. Once she has responded, she manually adds the leads to a spreadsheet to track their progress through her sales cycle. The sheet has columns for each touchpoint in the sales cycle and Liv fills in each column once it is complete.

If the lead does not respond to the email, Liv manually follows this up with two further emails and a text message from her mobile over 3 days. If the lead does not respond after 5 days, she updates the spreadsheet to mark the lead as Dead.

If the lead responds to the emails or text messages, after some back-and-forth communication to arrange a meeting time, Liv meets with the lead on a Zoom call to discuss the inquiry. Once she has met with the lead, and if the project is not appropriate, Liv updates the spreadsheet to mark the lead as Lost.

If the project is appropriate, depending on the service the lead has requested, Liv chooses from three templates based on the service that has been selected, then manually creates a proposal in a document and sends the lead a PDF of the proposal by email. She then manually follows up the proposal with two emails spread over 4 days if the lead has not responded by email to accept the proposal. If she is unable to contact the lead or the lead does not respond, she updates the spreadsheet to mark the lead as Dead. If the lead accepts the terms and conditions in her proposal with a response to the email, she assigns the project to the relevant service owner in the team for them to start the onboarding process using another spreadsheet. The first step in the process is for the team member to send an email to the customer to book the coaching session with them.

With this current process, Liv spends a lot of time manually pasting templates into emails, following up on email responses, and updating the spreadsheet. Sometimes, she forgets to perform part of the process, doesn't respond to leads, and forgets to record the progress on the spreadsheet, which results in her precious leads falling through the cracks. She uses Microsoft Outlook for her emails, WordPress for her website, a Microsoft Excel spreadsheet to record her leads, and a Microsoft Word document to record her email and proposal templates.

Can you suggest a better process for Liv by introducing other apps to her business that are more fit for purpose and connect her processes with Zapier? For this challenge, you must stick to a monthly app subscription budget of $150 per month for any additional apps and limit the additional apps you introduce to five new apps (including Zapier). There is no limit to the number of built-in apps by Zapier that you can use in your workflows.

You should now be able to solve a problem that requires advanced problem-solving and Zap-building skills. Now, let's explore some suggested solutions for the three scenarios we have just presented.

Guidance on suggested solutions for each scenario

Now that you've given it a go and tried to build out your Zaps to solve the problems in each of the three scenarios, let's go over a few suggested solutions to solve each of the problems. Remember, there are many ways to solve these problems, and the suggested solutions may allow you to broaden your thought process.

Scenario 1

There may be several ways to solve the problem that Dave has. To give you a hint at how you can potentially solve this problem, we will suggest that Dave uses ThriveCart as the sales page. You could suggest to Dave that he change from Kajabi to another course platform with more native integrations; however, in this case, it's more practical to use Zapier to join the dots. To address the problem of product IDs not matching, the most important thing to include is a lookup table, using the ThriveCart product ID as the key and the Kajabi offer ID as the lookup value.

If you haven't done so already, go ahead and try to build out the Zap.

You can then proceed to create other Zaps that perform similar actions for upsells and downsells, as well as accounting for access being removed after a refund.

> **Tip**
> If you have multiple apps that you need to add as action steps and you consistently need to find data IDs to perform actions in the other apps, it is better to use a spreadsheet or database that can return multiple field values for one lookup key as opposed to adding multiple Formatter by Zapier Utilities Lookup Table steps.

Next, we'll have a look at a possible solution to the second scenario.

Scenario 2

There are many ways to make Winnie's processes more efficient. To give you a hint at how you can potentially solve this problem, I would suggest that, first of all, Winnie implements a quoting and invoicing tool that can hold her customer details. It might be useful if this is an accounting app, such as Xero, that allows her to keep track of her payments and expenses too.

When Winnie receives a contact form submission, she will use Email Parser by Zapier to extract the inquiry information. This will trigger a workflow in Zapier to create a new contact with their name, email address, phone number, and address in Xero, and create a quote with a standard description of Gardening services, noting the budget. In the quote, Winnie could specify the preferred project date in the **Reference** field; if she has no other place to add it, then she could put it as the last variable in the string of text in the line item in the quote. She will also use the **Quantity** field for the number of hours that they will work on the project.

When the quote is accepted digitally, it will trigger a workflow in Zapier to split the project date from the quote line item (if she is not using the **Reference** field) using Formatter by Zapier and create a new event in her and Eugene's Google Calendars. The new event will be created with a start time of 9 A.M.; the number of hours from the quote will be used for the duration and the customer's address will be used for the location. As Winnie and Eugene use their calendars for other events, the new event will be created with the description set to **Job** to identify it.

At 5 P.M., the day before the Google Calendar event starts (16 hours prior), a workflow will be triggered in Zapier that will use Filter by Zapier to continue only if the event description is **Job**. At this point, Zapier will check the weather forecast in San Diego for the next day with Weather by Zapier, and send an email using Email by Zapier to Winnie and Eugene with the weather forecast and job location. As Winnie forgets to check her emails regularly, she also needs an SMS to be sent to her using SMS by Zapier.

When the job is complete, Winnie converts the quote into an invoice and emails it to the customer from Xero, giving them the option to pay online using Stripe.

Winnie's additional app costs are $20 per month for the Xero Starter Plan and $29.99 per month for the Zapier Starter Plan. Google Calendar is included in Winnie and Eugene's Google Workspace subscriptions. That's a total of two new apps at $49.99 per month.

If you haven't done so already, go ahead and try to build out the Zaps involved in these improvements.

Next, let's have a look at a possible solution to the final scenario.

Scenario 3

There are many ways to make Liv's processes more efficient. To give you a hint at how you can potentially solve this problem, I suggest that, first of all, Liv consolidates her lead management processes by introducing an app such as a CRM. A CRM such as HubSpot will help Liv visualize her sales cycle in a pipeline with different stages that will mirror her touchpoints. It will also allow her to use email templates, use embeddable forms, and send emails straight from the CRM, among other features.

In HubSpot, Liv could set up her sales pipeline to have five stages called New lead, Call booked, Proposal Sent, Closed lost, and Closed won. She will also create a contact form that she can embed into her WordPress website. Now, Liv won't need the spreadsheet.

We also suggest that Liv sets up a Calendly account with three users so that customers can book and pay for their coaching sessions via Stripe and integrate them with their Outlook calendars. For each team member, Liv could create coaching session events for each of the services.

When a contact form is submitted, the workflow will be triggered in Zapier to use Formatter by Zapier, which will look up the project price of the service from a **Lookup Table** action step. Then, Zapier will create a new deal in the New lead stage with the contact association that was created when the form was submitted; the project price will be the deal value, and the requested service and inquiry notes will be in custom fields within the deal. We will use Delay by Zapier to wait for 10 minutes before sending out an email using Microsoft Outlook. The email will be customized from a template that includes Liv's Calendly meeting booking link and personalized with the contact's first name and inquiry notes. The next steps in the Zap will involve a sequence that includes delays, checkpoints to establish which stage the deal is in, filters, and follow-up emails or SMS messages. For example, once the email has been sent, we will use Delay by Zapier to delay the workflow for 1 day, then after the delay, search for the deal details in HubSpot. Using Filter by Zapier, if the deal is still in the New lead stage, then

Zapier will send the first follow-up email using Microsoft Outlook. This can be repeated for the next follow-up email and the follow-up SMS message, which could be sent by a service such as Voodoo SMS. After the SMS has been sent, we can delay the workflow for another 2 days, search for the deal, and if the deal is still in the `New lead` stage, update the deal to `Closed lost`.

If during this time the lead books a Zoom meeting through Calendly, this will trigger a workflow in Zapier to update the deal to the `Call booked` stage. The Calendly integration with Liv's calendar and Zoom will create the relevant events.

Once Liv has had the call, if the project is not appropriate, Liv can update the deal to `Closed lost`. If it is appropriate, Liv can update the deal to `Proposal sent`. We could suggest that Liv uses a proposal or e-signature tool but as Liv does not require a signature for her service to be accepted, to keep the costs of additional apps down, we suggest Liv creates a free Google account and uses Google Slides to create customizable branded templates. She will have one template for each of her services with `{{proposal date}}`, `{{name}}`, and `{{price}}` placeholder variables to prefill the lead's inquiry details.

The deal being moved to `Proposal sent` will trigger a new Zapier workflow that will involve a Formatter by Zapier step to format the date when the proposal is created (when the Zap runs) from `{{zap_meta_human_now}}` or `today` to a prettier format. We will use Paths by Zapier to create a path for each service, where the filter will only allow the path to continue if `Service` from the HubSpot custom field matches the text of the relevant service name. Then, we will create the Google Slides document from the template and send the PDF attached to a personalized email using Microsoft Outlook. Liv would also add the relevant team member's Calendly links to each of the proposals to indicate that if they book a coaching call, they are agreeing to their terms and conditions and accepting the proposal. The next steps in the Zap will involve a sequence of steps that includes delays, checkpoints to establish which stage the deal is in, filters, and follow-up emails over 4 days.

To manage the rest of the onboarding process, we could suggest that Liv creates a free Trello account and invites her team members to a "Coaching Onboarding" board. Once the lead books and pays for the call through Calendly, a workflow will be triggered in Zapier to search for a deal associated with the contact, update the deal to `Closed won`, and create a new card in Trello. The rest of the onboarding process can then be followed.

Liv's additional app costs are $0 per month for HubSpot's free CRM, $0 for Google Slides, $15 per month for the Calendly Pro plan, plus $8 per month per additional user, $0 per month for the Trello Free plan, and $73.50 per month for the Zapier Professional plan. That's a total of five new apps at $104.50 per month.

If you haven't done so already, go ahead and try to build out the Zaps involved in these improvements.

You should now be able to solve a variety of problems that require different levels of problem-solving and Zap-building skills.

Summary

In this chapter, you worked through three scenarios, ranging from novice to intermediate to advanced skill levels, to allow you to put your knowledge to the test and adapt your problem-solving and Zap-building skills. We described specific problems classified by skill level that can be solved using Zapier in combination with introducing new apps to a business to make the process more efficient. We also worked through each example to demonstrate how it could be solved.

You now know how to use Zapier to build complex workflow automations that will help you to make your business, or your clients' businesses, more efficient.

Congratulations! You've completed this book and you're now well on your way to becoming a Zapier pro. You can get access to all the resources that were used in this book at `https://bit.ly/zapier-book`.

Assessments

Chapter 1 – Introduction to Business Process Automation with Zapier

1. Reduced operational costs and more time for growing sales.

2. Through API integrations.

3. None. You must be subscribed to a paid plan to connect premium apps.

4. Zapier will be able to customize your user recommendations and provide you with tailored workflow recommendations.

Chapter 2 – Preparing to Automate Your Processes

1. Where, When, What, Who, Why, and How.

2. The three questions are as follows:

   * Is it repeatable?

   * Can it be done with minimal logical thinking and human intervention?

   * Is it prone to error when done manually?

3. On each app's integration page in the Zapier app ecosystem directory.

Chapter 3 – Building Your First Automated Workflow (Zap)

1. By authenticating the connection with your Google credentials, username, and password, or by adding an app domain or subdomain URL with an API key and token.

2. Choosing from a set of values from a drop-down list, adding static text, or inserting dynamic data values from previous steps.

3. Date/time, number (integer), Boolean (true/false), file, and decimal.

Chapter 4 – Managing Your Zaps

1. Two ways that you can keep your Zapier account organized are presented here:

    • Labeling your Zaps adequately with trigger and action descriptions, unique identifiers, and preceding with numbers, letters, and Roman numerals

    • Organizing your Zaps into folders and sub-folders

2. You can add more details about a Zap or any important notes in the **Description** section in the Zap **Settings** area.

3. Zaps that contain **Paths by Zapier** or **Looping by Zapier** built-in apps cannot be shared with external accounts.

Chapter 5 – Troubleshooting and Handling Zap Errors

1. Zapier Manager and App Status by Zapier are two Zapier built-in apps that can help you to manage error and maintenance alerts in your Zapier account.

2. Email notification alerts, the Zap history module, and the **Zapier Status** page are three native features that will help you to troubleshoot errors.

3.   You can get help while troubleshooting by checking the app-specific help in app profiles, utilizing the Zapier help center, asking for help in the Zapier community, reaching out to Zapier customer support, hiring a Zapier Certified Expert, and getting help through workshops and privately hosted communities such as those provided by Solvaa Automation Academy.

Chapter 6 – Creating Multi-Step Zaps and Using Built-In Apps

1. You can add up to 99 action steps to a Zap.

2. It is useful to be able to reorder steps in your Zaps when you have made a mistake with the positioning of a step and you want to move it to another location.

3. Filter by Zapier and Paths by Zapier allow you to use conditional logic in your Zaps. Use Paths by Zapier if you want to use conditional branching logic for your Zaps.

4. The Formatter by Zapier built-in app allows you to manipulate text, dates/times, and numbers, as well as customize line items, use lookup tables and picklists, and import `.csv` files.

Chapter 7 – Getting Started with Built-In Apps

1. Filters and paths only count toward your monthly task usage when the data passes successfully, thus allowing the workflow to move on to the next action step in the Zap.

2. You must be subscribed to a Professional plan or higher to use Paths by Zapier.

3. A delayed task can be held for a maximum of 31 days.

4. You can use Schedule by Zapier with the **Every Day** action event to schedule a Zap to run every day at 10 A.M.

Chapter 8 – Built-In Communication Apps

1. You can set up multiple SMS by Zapier accounts to send text messages to a single number each. You must have access to this number to validate it for use. You would not be able to send text messages to a group of numbers that you are not able to validate.

2. Yes, you can send text messages with more than 153 characters using SMS by Zapier. However, they will be truncated.

3. Yes, both email built-in apps recognize HTML, which allows you to customize text in the email body.

Chapter 9 – Exploring Built-In Apps for Extracting and Compiling Data

1. Email Parser by Zapier requires some degree of teaching to help it understand what data you require extracted. This is especially the case if the data is not always presented in the same format. It is recommended that you indicate whether the extracted data is correct or incorrect, and remap accordingly.

2. Yes, you can create your own RSS feed using the **Create Item in Feed** action event.

3. You must create a Zap with the Digest by Zapier **Release Digest** action event for a step with the **Manual (pair with separate "Release Digest" Zap)** frequency option to work.

Chapter 10 – Other Useful Built-In Apps by Zapier

1. The Zapier Chrome extension built-in app allows you to initiate your Zaps so that they trigger from any page on the internet when using a Google Chrome browser with the Zapier Google Chrome extension.

2. You can use URL Shortener by Zapier to create shortened URL links that you can use in your automated workflows.

3. You can sign up to MadKudu.com and use the MadKudu-Zapier integration to perform a higher amount of searches than offered with the free Lead Score by Zapier built-in app.

Chapter 11 – Advanced Built-In Apps by Zapier

1. The Webhooks by Zapier and Code by Zapier built-in apps, as well as the API **Request** action event, can be used to make HTTP requests.

2. You can use Storage by Zapier to store small values and lists of data.

Chapter 12 – Managing Your Zapier Account with Built-In Apps

1. The Zapier Manager built-in app's **Zap Turned Off** trigger event and the **Turn Zap On/Off** action event would be best to use in this scenario. You could also add an additional step so that you're alerted with a Slack direct message, SMS, or email.

2. If you want to monitor your Zapier account, you can use two Zapier Manager trigger events to kick off your Zaps – **Task Usage Limit Reached** and **New Invoice**.

Chapter 13 – Newly Released Apps and Features

1. You can use Transfers by Zapier to transfer data in bulk between apps, so long as those apps are supported by this feature.

2. Zapier Interfaces and Zapier Tables are a supercharged combo that helps you collect data from forms and chatbots while storing and managing that data in tables.

Chapter 14 – Formatting Date and Time

1. You can use the `{{zap_meta_human_now}}` script in fields in your Zap to create a timestamp based on the date and time that your Zap triggered.

2. Yes – in date/time fields, you can use field modifiers to adjust the dates and times in your Zaps. For example, you can use +1d to add 1 day.

3. You can add or subtract time, compare two date/time values, and change the format of a date/time value using the Formatter by Zapier built-in app.

Chapter 15 – Formatting Numbers

1. Yes, the Formatter by Zapier built-in app allows you to convert phone numbers from a range of countries using the country ISO codes into several different formats

2. Using the Formatter by Zapier built-in app, the **Numbers** action event, and the **Perform Math Operation** transform option, you can add, subtract, multiply, and divide multiple numbers or make one number negative.

Chapter 16 – Text Formatting Functions in Zapier – Part 1

1. The **Capitalize** transform option of the **Text** action event in the Formatter by Zapier built-in app allows you to automate changing the first letter of every word in a string of text into a capital letter.

2. The **Length** transform option of the Formatter by Zapier **Text** action event would be the best function to use to count the number of characters in a string of text.

Chapter 17 – Text Formatting Functions in Zapier – Part 2

1. You could use the **Split** transform option in the **Text** action event of Formatter by Zapier to separate a string of text so that each word is presented as an individual value.

2. The **Truncate** transform option can be used to reduce the character length of a block of text. This might be useful if you want to use it as a summary with ellipses appended or if you want to shorten the length because you have restrictions on the number of characters.

Chapter 18 – Zapier's Utilities Functions

1. You could use the **Pick from List** transform option of the **Utilities** action event in the Formatter by Zapier built-in app to randomly assign tickets to support agents.

2. Accounting and payment processing apps often express data as line items.

Chapter 19 – AI and Automation

1. There are multiple AI-powered Zapier built-in apps and features. A few examples are AI-powered Formatter by Zapier steps, AI-powered Code by Zapier steps, and AI-powered troubleshooting.

2. OpenAI is the maker of the GPT, DALL-E, and Whisper models, and is known by most users for the ChatGPT chatbot.

3. Zapier currently integrates with over 60 AI-based apps, including ChatGPT and OpenAI.

Chapter 20 – Automating Your Marketing Processes

1. There are many different marketing processes that can be automated with Zapier. If you use one or more cloud-based marketing applications that integrate with Zapier, you will be able to automate processes that involve these applications. A few examples are as follows:

   - Online presence processes

   - Social media marketing processes

   - Social media scheduling processes

   - Ad processes

   - Email marketing and marketing automation processes

2. New Facebook Pages photo uploads should be smaller than 4 MB and saved as either `.jpg`, `.png`, `.gif`, `.tiff`, HEIF, or WebP files.

Chapter 21 – Automating Your Sales Processes

1. There are many different sales processes that can be automated with Zapier. If you use one or more cloud-based sales applications that integrate with Zapier, you will be able to automate processes that involve these applications. A few examples are as follows:

   - Data collection processes with forms

   - Appointment booking and scheduling processes

   - Lead management processes

   - Contract, proposal, and digital signature collection processes

   - E-commerce processes

2. There are many scheduling apps that integrate with Zapier, which you can find details of at `https://zapier.com/apps/categories/scheduling`. Using scheduling apps that integrate with Zapier will allow you to automate this part of your sales process.

Chapter 22 – Automating Your Operations Processes

1. There are many different operations processes that can be automated with Zapier. If you use one or more cloud-based sales applications that integrate with Zapier, you will be able to automate processes that involve these applications. A few examples are as follows:

   - Task and project management processes

   - Document storage processes

   - Communication processes

   - Word document and spreadsheet processes

2. In Google Docs action steps, always use the ID of the file or folder when mapping dynamic data from previous steps or entering text into the **Document Name** or **Folder** fields, respectively, rather than the name.

Chapter 23 – Automating Your Finance and Reporting Processes

1. There are many different finance processes that can be automated with Zapier. If you use one or more cloud-based sales applications that integrate with Zapier, you will be able to automate processes that involve these applications. Two examples are as follows:

   - Invoice management and accounting workflows

   - Payment processing workflows

2. There are many different reporting processes that can be automated with Zapier. If you use one or more cloud-based sales applications that integrate with Zapier, you will be able to automate processes that involve these applications. A few examples are as follows:

   - Spreadsheet reporting workflows

   - Website analytics workflows

   - Business intelligence and dashboard workflows

Chapter 24 – Tips, Tricks, and Best Practices to Enhance Your Productivity

1. Begin by learning the basics with Zapier and then documenting and simplifying processes, as well as establishing whether you are using the right applications for your business. Starting with these two best practices will set you up for success.

2. If you feel the triggers, actions, and searches presented by the standard Zapier integration with the app you are using are limited, you can explore the API documentation and use Webhooks, as well as make HTTP requests using Webhooks by Zapier or Code by Zapier if possible. You can also ask Zapier Support or the SaaS provider to further develop the Zapier integration.

Index

www.packtpub.com

Subscribe to our online digital library for full access to over 7,000 books and videos, as well as industry leading tools to help you plan your personal development and advance your career. For more information, please visit our website.

Why subscribe?

- Spend less time learning and more time coding with practical eBooks and Videos from over 4,000 industry professionals

- Improve your learning with Skill Plans built especially for you

- Get a free eBook or video every month

- Fully searchable for easy access to vital information

- Copy and paste, print, and bookmark content

Did you know that Packt offers eBook versions of every book published, with PDF and ePub files available? You can upgrade to the eBook version at packtpub.com and as a print book customer, you are entitled to a discount on the eBook copy. Get in touch with us at customercare@packtpub.com for more details.

At www.packtpub.com, you can also read a collection of free technical articles, sign up for a range of free newsletters, and receive exclusive discounts and offers on Packt books and eBooks.

Other Books You May Enjoy

If you enjoyed this book, you may be interested in these other books by Packt:

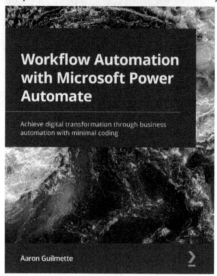

Workflow Automation with Microsoft Power Automate

Aaron Guilmette

ISBN: 978-1-83921-379-3

- Learn the basic building blocks of Power Automate capabilities
- Explore connectors in Power Automate to automate email workflows
- Discover how to make a flow for copying files between cloud services
- Configure Power Automate Desktop flows for your business needs
- Build on examples to create complex database and approval flows
- Connect common business applications like Outlook, Forms, and Teams
- Learn the introductory concepts for robotic process automation
- Discover how to use AI sentiment analysis

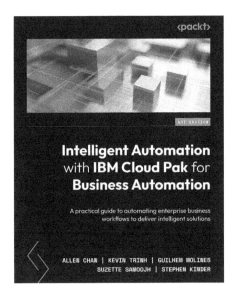

Intelligent Automation with IBM Cloud Pak for Business Automation

Allen Chan, Kevin Trinh, Guilhem Molines, Suzette Samoojh, Stephen Kinder

ISBN: 978-1-80181-477-5

- Understand key IBM automation technologies and learn how to apply them
- Cover the end-to-end journey of creating an automation solution from concept to deployment
- Understand the features and capabilities of workflow, decisions, RPA, business applications, and document processing with AI
- Analyze your business processes and discover automation opportunities with process mining
- Set up content management solutions that meet business, regulatory, and compliance needs
- Understand deployment environments supported by IBM Cloud Pak for Business Automation

Packt is searching for authors like you

If you're interested in becoming an author for Packt, please visit authors.packtpub.com and apply today. We have worked with thousands of developers and tech professionals, just like you, to help them share their insight with the global tech community. You can make a general application, apply for a specific hot topic that we are recruiting an author for, or submit your own idea.

Share Your Thoughts

Now you've finished *Automate It with Zapier and Generative AI – Second Edition*, we'd love to hear your thoughts! Scan the QR code below to go straight to the Amazon review page for this book and share your feedback or leave a review on the site that you purchased it from.

https://packt.link/r/1-803-23984-0

Your review is important to us and the tech community and will help us make sure we're delivering excellent quality content.

Download a free PDF copy of this book

Thanks for purchasing this book!

Do you like to read on the go but are unable to carry your print books everywhere?

Is your eBook purchase not compatible with the device of your choice?

Don't worry, now with every Packt book you get a DRM-free PDF version of that book at no cost.

Read anywhere, any place, on any device. Search, copy, and paste code from your favorite technical books directly into your application.

The perks don't stop there, you can get exclusive access to discounts, newsletters, and great free content in your inbox daily

Follow these simple steps to get the benefits:

1. Scan the QR code or visit the link below

https://packt.link/free-ebook/9781803239842

2. Submit your proof of purchase
3. That's it! We'll send your free PDF and other benefits to your email directly

www.ingramcontent.com/pod-product-compliance
Lightning Source LLC
Chambersburg PA
CBHW060633060326
40690CB00020B/4386